The Practice of Public Relations

Seventh Edition

Fraser P. Seitel

Managing Partner, Emerald Partners
Senior Counselor, Burson-Marsteller

Prentice Hall, Upper Saddle River, New Jersey 07458

To Uncle Howard, The Godfather

Acquisitions Editor: Don Hull / Gabrielle Dudnyk
Associate Editor: John Larkin
Editorial Assistant: Jim Campbell / Rachel Falk
Editor-in-Chief: Natalie Anderson
Marketing Manager: John Chillingworth
Production Editor: Michelle Rich
Production Coordinator: Carol Samet
Permissions Coordinator: Jennifer Rella
Permissions Researcher: Melinda Alexander
Managing Editor: Dee Josephson
Associate Managing Editor: Linda DeLorenzo
Manufacturing Supervisor: Arnold Vila
Manufacturing Manager: Vincent Scelta
Design Director: Patricia Smythe
Interior Design: A Good Thing Incorporated
Cover Design: A Good Thing Incorporated
Illustrator (Interior): University Graphics, Inc.
Composition: University Graphics, Inc.
Cover Art/Photo: Courtesy of the White House

Credits and acknowledgments for materials borrowed from other sources and reproduced, with permission, in this textbook appear on page 549.

Copyright © 1998, 1995 by Prentice-Hall, Inc.
Upper Saddle River, New Jersey 07458

Library of Congress Cataloging-in-Publication Data

Seitel, Fraser P.
    The practice of public relations / Fraser P. Seitel. — 7th ed.
        p.   cm.
    Includes bibliographical references and index.
    ISBN 0-13-613811-X
    1. Public relations—United States.   I. Title.
    HM263.S42   1997
    659.2—dc21   97-29845
                                                 CIP

Prentice-Hall International (UK) Limited, London
Prentice-Hall of Australia Pty. Limited, Sydney
Prentice-Hall Canada Inc., Toronto
Prentice-Hall Hispanoamericana, S.A., Mexico
Prentice-Hall of India Private Limited, New Delhi
Prentice-Hall of Japan, Inc., Tokyo
Pearson Education Asia Pte. Ltd., Singapore
Editora Prentice-Hall do Brasil, Ltda., Rio de Janeiro

Printed in the United States of America

10 9 8 7 6

Contents

Foreword

THERE WAS A TIME WHEN PUBLIC RELATIONS WAS LOOKED UPON by many organizations as a relatively innocuous way of keeping employees informed about what was going on, and getting the boss's picture in the paper on suitably celebratory occasions.

But in our current complex social, economic, and political environment, where reputations are at stake every day, public relations is increasingly being recognized as a management function fully as important in its way as finance or production or marketing in carrying out an organization's basic strategy.

In this seventh edition of his widely used textbook, *The Practice of Public Relations*, Fraser Seitel shows how public relations can play a vital role in any organization, whether business, government, education, health care or whatever. He does this not only through easy-to-follow instructional chapters but also through dramatic case studies of recent headline events, ranging from the tragic ValuJet crash to Texaco's racial problems, and from the military's sexual harassment flap to the Swiss banks' controversy over the assets of Holocaust victims. In keeping with the growing impact of new technology, this latest edition contains an illuminating chapter on "Public Relations and the Net."

As a practitioner, I worked with Seitel for several years and came to appreciate his penetrating intelligence, impressive mastery of the tools of communications and persuasion, and remarkable skill in applying these to the management of difficult situations.

As a professor, I used the Seitel text in my own university classes and saw firsthand how students were challenged by the material to think through tough problems and develop effective action plans for dealing with them.

For students preparing for a career in public relations as well as for others who want to gain a more practical knowledge of the intricacies of this exciting field, I know of no better guide than Seitel's seventh edition of *The Practice of Public Relations*.

Joseph T. Nolan,
Ph.D., APR, Fellow
Former Gannett Distinguished Visiting Professor, University of Florida,
and former faculty member at University of South Carolina, University of North Florida,
and Flagler College
Former Vice President, Public Relations, Chase Manhattan
Bank and Monsanto Company

Preface

THE PRACTICE OF PUBLIC RELATIONS will never be replaced by a computer.

It's too personal, too nuancy, too relationship-oriented. Building relationships, in fact—with the media, the government, employees, neighbors, consumers and myriad other publics—lies at the essence of public relations work. At base, public relations is an intensely personal, brutally practical, entirely human profession. The successful practitioner of public relations must combine three essential characteristics—knowledge, experience, and judgment. Every day, the public relations professional must deal with different situations, demanding diferent solutions.

This book has two purposes: (1) to introduce readers to effective public relations and (2) to prepare students and professionals to deal with the situations and arrive at the solutions that distinguish the practice.

At the heart of public relations practice are real-life experiences—cases—that alter the communications landscape and redefine how we assess and handle communications challenges. The contemporary cases that dominate public relations discussion are the same ones that dominate the news of the day.

Texaco. Whitewater. Denny's. ValuJet. TWA. The tobacco industry and its war with the government. Pepsi-Cola and its syringe scare. General Motors and NBC's exploding trucks. Kathie Lee Gifford. O. J. Simpson. Susan Smith. JonBenet Ramsey. Dick Morris. Notorious B.I.G. Marv Albert. Beavis and Butt-Head. All play a part in public relations lore and learning.

That's what this book is all about. The *Practice of Public Relations*, 7th edition, is different from other introductory texts in the field. Its premise is that public relations is a thoroughly engaging, constantly changing, thoroughly fascinating field. Although other texts may steer clear of the cases, the "how to" counsel, and the public relations conundrums that force students to think, this book confronts them all. It is, if you'll forgive the vernacular, an "in-your-face" textbook for an "in-your-face" profession.

Part One deals with the philosophical underpinnings of public relations practice, including the importance of management and planning, ethics and research, communications and public opinion. Part Two explores the practical communications applications of the field, including the emergence of the Internet, electronic communications and the integration of public relations, marketing, and advertising into the discipline of integrated marketing communications. Part Three discusses the primary constituents with which the field deals, including multicultural communities. Part Four dissects important, emerging trends, including crisis management and the law.

The 40 case studies included here confront the reader with the most prominent and perplexing public relations problems—Intel and its pentium chip snafu, Exxon and the Gulf of Valdez, Dow Corning and silicone breast implants, Jack-in-the-Box and contaminated burgers, AOL and its customer rebate policy and many more.

Beyond this, a number of unique elements set this book apart:

- An entire chapter is devoted to public relations and the Net, including discussions about the World Wide Web, Internet, Intranet, and the other relevant elements of cyberspace.
- The prominence of ethics in the practice of public relations is highlighted with "A Question of Ethics" mini case in every chapter.
- "The Rest of the Story" features complement the text with provocative examples of what's right and what's wrong about public relations practice.
- Chapter Summaries and Discussion Starter Questions highlight the key messages delivered in each chapter.
- Updated Suggested Readings, nourishing Appendices, and "Top-of-the-Shelf" book reviews supplement the text with the field's most current literature.
- "Voice of Experience" interviews air the views of the field's most prominent professionals—from President Clinton's White House press secretary to First Lady Hillary Clinton's communications director to the founder of the field's most technologically sophisticated agency to the architect of General Motors' NBC defense to the field's most notorious critic to the public relations spokesman for the Pope.

Finally, fittingly, *The Practice of Public Relations*, 7th edition, is produced in a full-color format to underscore the liveliness, vitality, and relevance of a field that is built on the important personal relationships that will dominate the twenty-first century.

Fraser P. Seitel

Acknowledgments

The 7th edition of *The Practice of Public Relations* has a brand new cast of characters—Dennis Rodman, Kathie Lee Gifford, Don Imus, Rush Limbaugh, Dick Morris, the CEOs of Exxon, ValuJet, Dow Corning, Texaco, Pepsi-Cola et al.

But those are only the supporting actors.

The real "stars" in this production are the ones responsible for producing the new interviews, cases, and chapter material that make up this new book.

First, of course, is the Prentice Hall brain trust. Don Hull, the man who literally holds Simon together with Schuster, shepherded this project with great leadership and understanding for the author's multitudinous procrastinations. He was complemented in that effect by the dutiful Gabrielle Dudnyk. They were ably supported by the exceedingly able Jim Campbell and the multitalented Michelle Rich, a production editor extraordinaire. I am most grateful to all four.

I was also assisted in this effort by a crew of valiant citizens. Kathleen Huchel was a marvelous researcher, and Melanie Eisenberg continued to provide magnificent support. Joe Nolan, the single best public relations professional I've ever known, was, as always, most kind and insightful in assisting with this work and authoring the "Foreword." I am indebted as well to the other willing and well-known experts in the field who provided "Voice of Experience" interviews—Presidential Press Secretary Mike McCurry, First Lady Communications Director Marsha Berry, Archbishop John Foley, GM's Harry Pearce, Internet visionary Larry Weber, public relations leaders Harold Burson, Bill Adams, Terrie Williams, Debbie Miller, and all the others. I appreciate their participation very much.

I am also most grateful to Jack O'Dwyer, one of the field's most fearsome critics (but actually a pussycat), who contributed the "The Last Word" feature in Chapter 20. In addition, the public relations managers at Pepsi-Cola, General Motors, Taco Bell, Southwest Airlines, and others were most kind to allow me to use both written materials and videotapes surrounding the significant public relations issues with which they were directly involved.

I also thank the public relations teachers whose insightful suggestions aided this 7th edition: Nickieann Fleener, Department of Communication, University of Utah; Mort Kaplan, Department of Marketing Communication, Columbia College (Chicago);

Jack Mauch, Department of Communication, University of Idaho; Donnalyn Pompper, Department of Communication, Cabrini College; Cornelius B. Pratt, Department of Communications, Michigan State University; J. D. Rayburn II, Department of Communication, Florida State University; and Nancy Roth, Department of Communication, Rutgers—The State University (New Jersey). I thank as well the other professors who have reviewed past editions of this work, including William C. Adams, School of Journalism and Mass Communications, Florida International University; John Q. Butler; Rachel L. Holloway, Department of Communications Studies, Virginia Polytechnic Institute and State University; Diana Harney, Department of Communication and Theater, Pacific Lutheran University; Cornelius Pratt, Department of Advertising, Communications, and Public Relations, Michigan State University; Robert Cole, Pace University; Janice Sherline Jenny, College of Business, Herkimer County Community College, and Craig Kelly, School of Business, California State University, Sacramento.

Lyle J. Barker, Ohio State University; William G. Briggs, San Jose State University; E. Brody, Memphis State University; John S. Detweiler, University of Florida; Jim Eiseman, University of Louisville; Sandy Grossbart, University of Nebraska; Marjorie Nadler, Miami University; Sharon Smith, Middle Tennessee State University; Robert Wilson, Franklin University; Paul Brennan, Nassau Community College; Carol L. Hills, Boston University; George Laposky, Miami-Dade Community College; Mack Palmer, University of Oklahoma; Judy VanSlyke Turk, Louisiana State University; Roger B. Wadsworth, Miami-Dade Community College; James E. Grunig, University of Maryland; Robert T. Reilly, University of Nebraska at Omaha; Kenneth Rowe, Arizona State University; Dennis L. Wilcox, San Jose State University; Albert Walker, Northern Illinois University; Stanley E. Smith, Arizona State University; Jan Quarles, University of Georgia; Pamela J. Creedon, Ohio State University; Joel P. Bowman, Western Michigan University; Thomas H. Bivins, University of Oregon; Joseph T. Nolan, University of North Florida; Frankie A. Hammond, University of Florida; Bruce Joffe, George Mason University; Larissa Grunig, University of Maryland; Maria P. Russell, Syracuse University; and Melvin L. Sharpe, Ball State University.

Finally, the single most important reason to push ahead with new and better editions of this tome—aside, of course, from the never-ending quest for higher scholarship—is the three-headed, whip-cracking, free-spending but ever-loving Rosemary, Raina, and David Seitel. They're the best.

Fraser P. Seitel

About the Author

Fraser P. Seitel is a veteran of close to three decades in the practice of public relations. In 1992, after serving for a decade as senior vice president and director of public affairs for Chase Manhattan Bank, Mr. Seitel formed Emerald Partners, a management and communications consultancy, and also became senior counselor at the world's largest public affairs firm, Burson-Marsteller. In his practice, Mr. Seitel continues to counsel corporations, nonprofits, associations, and individuals in the areas for which he had responsibility at Chase—media relations, speech writing, consumer relations, employee communications, financial communications, philanthropic activities, and strategic management consulting.

Mr. Seitel has supplemented his professional public relations career with steady teaching assignments at Fairleigh Dickinson University, Pace University, New York's Professional Development Institute, Chicago's Ragan Communications Workshops, and Colorado's Estes Park Institute. Over the course of his career, Mr. Seitel has taught thousands of public relations professionals.

After studying and examining many texts in public relations, he concluded that none of them "was exactly right." Therefore, in 1980, he wrote the first edition of *The Practice of Public Relations* "to give students a feel for how exciting this field really is." In nearly two decades of use at hundreds of colleges and universities, Mr. Seitel's book has introduced generations of students to the excitement, challenge, and uniqueness of the practice of public relations.

CHAPTER ONE

What Is Public Relations?

In the waning years of the twentieth century, spin is in.[1]

And for professionals in the practice of public relations, that ain't particularly good news.

PUBLIC RELATIONS, SIMPLY DEFINED, IS THE PRACTICE of doing the right thing—of performing—and communicating the substance of that performance. Public relations as a field has grown immeasurably—in numbers and respect—over the last two decades and today is clearly a *growth industry.*

- In the United States alone, public relations is a multibillion dollar business practiced by nearly 200,000 professionals, according to the U.S. Bureau of Labor Statistics. Furthermore, the bureau ranks public relations as one of the fastest growing industries, with job growth between 1994–2005 projected at a nearly 47 percent increase.
- In a study of the chief executive officers of 200 organizations in the United States, Canada, and the United Kingdom, communications in general and the practice of public relations in particular were valued highly.[2]
- Approximately 200 colleges and universities in the United States and many more overseas offer a public relations sequence or degree program. Many more offer public relations courses. In the vast majority of college journalism programs, public relations sequences rank first or second in enrollment.

- In the twenty-first century, while industries from banking to utilities to retailing are vulnerable to seismic movements, the public relations profession is expected to thrive, with more and more organizations interested in communicating their story.[3]
- The U.S. government has 9,000 communications workers employed by the United States Information Agency alone. Another 1,000 communications specialists work in the Department of Defense. The 20 largest public relations agencies generate nearly $2 billion in fee income annually.[4]

The field's strength stems from its roots: "A democratic society where people have freedom to debate and to make decisions—in the community, the marketplace, the home, the workplace, and the voting booth. Private and public organizations depend on good relations with groups and individuals whose opinions, decisions, and actions affect their vitality and survival."[5]

So pervasive has the influence of public relations become in our society that some even fear it as a pernicious force; they worry about "the power of public relations to exercise a kind of thought control over the American public."[6]

Which brings us to spin.

Spin has come to mean the twisting of messages to create the appearance of performance, which may or may not be true. Distortion, obfuscation, even downright lying are fair game as far as spin is concerned.

Consider the following:

- Democrat William Jefferson Clinton is reelected president of the United States as he deftly dodges charges of illegal real estate investments in Arkansas, sexual harassment of government workers, and campaign finance irregularities.
- Unsuccessful Republican presidential candidate Bob Dole flip-flops on issues from the deficit to abortion to win favor with the voters. Meanwhile, Speaker of the House Newt Gingrich "befriends" arch liberal Jesse Jackson to help soften his image as an inflexible reactionary conservative.
- Newsweek journalist Joe Klein, who rails against truth-defying politicians, is himself caught in a lie about his authorship of the anti-Clinton best-seller, *Primary Colors*. Klein and his editor, who also lied to protect his subordinate's anonymity, try to explain away their canard.
- Presidential strategist Dick Morris, architect of Clinton's "family values" initiative, is exposed on the eve of his client's convention nomination as having allowed a prostitute to listen in on conversations with the president, fathered an illegitimate child, and, perhaps worst of all, signed a book deal in violation of White House policy. He is promptly fired, and then, just as promptly, attempts to make a comeback.
- Finally, as President Clinton delivers his State of the Union address in February 1997, the nation is transfixed, not on the president's speech but on the Santa Monica liable verdict in the trial of a fallen football hero, who continues to spin his innocence in the grisly murder of his ex-wife and a friend.

All of this has implications for the practice of public relations. Indeed, *The New York Times* headlines its review of a popular book on the field, *How Public Relations Tries to Keep the World Spinning.*[7] In such an era of spin and consequent unrelenting questioning by the media and the public, individuals and organizations must not only be sensitive to but also highly considerate of their actions and communication with many influential publics.

PROMINENCE OF PUBLIC RELATIONS

In the twentieth century, the prominence of public relations has never been greater. On the other hand, the wave of downsizings, layoffs, mergers, and outright firings across America and the world has taken its toll on the public relations profession. The pervasive retrenchment of organizations has weighed heavily on public relations professionals. Many have lost their jobs, and the environment for the public relations people who remain employed has become decidedly less enjoyable or secure.

So the conundrum for public relations as the century draws to a close is that, on the one hand, the field has never been more accepted, respected, or high paying but, on the other hand, jobs are less plentiful, less predictable, and certainly less pleasant.

- President Clinton twice rode into office by deftly using the public relations techniques of town meetings, satellite press conferences, and message-rebuttal swat teams. Many consider communications and a deft knowledge of using the media the president's greatest asset. Meanwhile, a third political party in the United States, led by billionaire industrialist H. Ross Perot, has made miraculous strides, largely through public relations techniques such as using television talk shows to speak directly to the American public.
- Similarly in Great Britain, new Labour Party Prime Minister Tony Blair uses Clintonesque public relations approaches to give that perpetually losing party newfound life.
- In the business world, Louis Gerstner, the chairman of IBM recruited in 1993 to resuscitate the once great computer company, made his first official move the replacement of IBM's longtime vice president of communications. Gerstner deemed the public relations function so important that he insisted it be staffed immediately by his own person. In subsequent years, the company regained its former aura and clout.
- Salaries for public relations executives continued to rise in both corporations and agencies, with the very top performers earning in the seven figure range.
- In the nonprofit world, America's largest charity, United Way, steadily regained its former respectability, after its chairman was fined and imprisoned in the wake of a stunning public relations scandal.

So public relations has made real progress in shedding old misconceptions, and it has acquired new responsibilities and inherited an increasing amount of power, prestige, and pay.

However, along with its new stature, the practice of public relations is faced with unprecedented pressure.

- The most difficult pressure on public relations professionals is the new job insecurity that has afflicted the field in the 1990s. Although public relations jobs are expected to grow in the years ahead, nonetheless organizations are becoming more rigorous in their scrutiny of the function. Just as public relations salaries have increased in the 1990s, so has the reality of decreasing job security.
- The very name public relations is being challenged by such euphemisms as public affairs, corporate communications, integrated marketing, public information, and a variety of other terms.
- Critics have intensified as the field has grown, with at least one newsletter, *PR Watch,* established to "exposing" nefarious public relations practice.
- As public relations positions have achieved greater credibility and heightened stature, competition from other fields has become more intense. Today the profession finds it-

self vulnerable to encroachment by people with non public relations backgrounds, such as lawyers, marketers, and general managers of every stripe. Ironically, the most prominent public relations person in America in the 1990s is the chief lawyer of General Motors, Harry Pearce, who took on the powerful NBC Network and won (see Case Study, chapter 18).

- The lack of leadership among public relations professionals continues to plague the field. Few practitioners are seen as leaders. No wonder cries of "PR for PR" are heard constantly.
- Many in public relations also are concerned about the preponderance of women in the field, the lack of equal pay for equal work among these women, and the paucity of minority practitioners.
- The field's focus on mastering the new technology of the Internet and World Wide Web is both a blessing and a curse. On the one hand, public relations professionals need to understand the implications and uses of cyberspace. On the other hand, working with the new technology is but one of many skill sets that practitioners should use.[8]
- Finally, public relations continues to be hampered by a general lack of understanding among senior managers of its purpose and value. Even today—nearly a century after the first American public relations professional rose to prominence—many in management still don't understand what public relations is all about.[9]

Despite its considerable problems—in attaining leadership status, in finding its proper role in society, in disavowing spin and earning enduring respect—the practice of public relations has never been more prominent. After less than 100 years as a formal, integrated, strategic thinking process, public relations has become part of the fabric of modern society.

DEFINING PUBLIC RELATIONS

The CEO who thunders, "I don't need public relations!", is a fool. He or she doesn't have a choice. Every organization has public relations, whether it wants it or not. The trick is to establish good public relations. That's what this book is all about—professional public relations, the kind you must work at.

Public relations affects almost everyone who has contact with other human beings. All of us, in one way or another, practice public relations daily. For an organization, every phone call, every letter, every face-to-face encounter is a public relations event.

To be sure, public relations is not yet a profession like law, accounting, or medicine, in which all practitioners are trained, licensed, and supervised. Nothing prevents someone with little or no formal training from hanging out a shingle as a public relations specialist. Such frauds embarrass professionals in the field and, thankfully, are becoming harder and harder to find.

As the field has increased in prominence, it also has grown in professional stature. The International Association of Business Communicators, a broad-based group that started with an internal communications focus, has 12,500 members. The Public Relations Society of America, with a national membership of nearly 18,500 in 109 national chapters, has accredited about one-third of its members through a standardized examination. The society has also investigated legal licensing—similar to that of the accounting and legal professions—for public relations practitioners.

THE REST OF THE STORY

SO LONG, GEORGE

Figure 1–1
FOB/public relations outcast turned broadcaster, George Stephanopoulos.

No event in the last decade of the twentieth century signaled the growing importance of the practice of public relations more than the White House demotion of George Stephanopoulos in 1993 (Figure 1–1).

When Bill Clinton became president, no adviser was a closer FOB (friend of Bill) than Stephanopoulos. As director of communications for the Clinton–Gore campaign, Stephanopoulos was rewarded when the president named him White House communications director, charged with improving the administration's relations with the news media.

From the start, Stephanopoulos was a disaster in the role.

His first act was to close off the corridor outside his office to reporters. Reporters complained of a lack of access to the president. Stephanopoulos's press briefings developed an air of tension and mistrust. By June, well aware of the critical nature of the chief White House public relations person, President Clinton reluctantly replaced his friend with, of all things–a Ronald Reagan Republican!

David Gergen, a former Reagan communications director and speech writer for Presidents Nixon and Ford, was recruited to undo the damage Stephanopoulos had done. Within a month, under the watchful eye of Gergen, President Clinton's relations with the media improved and reporters' access to the president increased.

Within months, the early image of a bumbling president was replaced by that of a man in control of the budget, health care, and other domestic issues. Gergen's in-depth, yet invisible, public relations hand paid off remarkably well, and the corridor outside the communications director's office was reopened to one and all.

Ironically, at the start of President Clinton's second administration, with Gergen now back in the media, he was joined by a most unlikely new "journalist"—none other than new *ABC News* analyst, author, and all-around journalistic commentator, George Stephanopoulos.

The society's main objective is to increase the field's professionalism. It has a code of standards (see Appendix A), which focuses strongly on the practitioner's ethical responsibilities.

Whereas marketing and sales have as their primary objective selling an organization's products, public relations attempts to sell the organization itself. Central to its concern is the public interest.

Advertising also generally aims to sell products through paid means. Good public relations, on the other hand, cannot be bought; it must be earned. The credibility derived from sound public relations work may far exceed that gained through paid advertising.

The earliest college teachers of public relations exhorted students to learn new ways of using knowledge they already had—a different viewpoint, as if one moved to one side and looked at everything from unfamiliar angles. Project yourself into the minds of people you are trying to reach and see things the way they do. Use everything you've learned elsewhere—English, economics, sociology, science, history—you name it.[10]

Two decades later, it is still widely thought that a broad background is essential to manage public issues effectively. Although specific definitions of public relations may differ, most who practice it agree that good public relations requires a firm base of theoretical knowledge, a strong sense of ethical judgment, solid communication skills, and, most of all, an uncompromising attitude of professionalism.

What, then, is public relations? Many people seem to have a pretty good idea, but few seem to agree. American historian Robert Heilbroner describes the field as "a brotherhood of some 100,000, whose common bond is its profession and whose common woe is that no two of them can ever quite agree on what that profession is."[11]

The reason for the confusion is understandable. On the one hand, the scope of activities taken on by public relations professionals is limitless. The duties of a practitioner in one organization may be completely different from those of a colleague in another organization. Yet both are engaged in the practice of public relations. Beyond this, because public relations is such an amorphous, loosely defined field, it is vulnerable to entry to anyone self-styled as a "public relations professional."

In 1923, the late Edward Bernays described the function of his fledgling public relations counseling business as one of providing "information given to the public, persuasion directed at the public to modify attitudes and actions, and efforts to integrate attitudes and actions of an institution with its publics and of publics with those of that institution."[12]

Today, although a generally accepted definition of public relations still eludes practitioners, there is a clearer understanding of the field. One of the most ambitious searches for a universal definition was commissioned in 1975 by the Foundation for Public Relations Research and Education. Sixty-five public relations leaders participated in the study, which analyzed 472 different definitions and offered the following 88-word sentence:

> Public relations is a distinctive management function which helps establish and maintain mutual lines of communications, understanding, acceptance, and cooperation between an organization and its publics; involves the management of problems or issues; helps management to keep informed on and responsive to public opinion; defines and emphasizes the responsibility of management to serve the public interest; helps management keep abreast of and effectively utilize change, serving as an early warning system to help anticipate trends; and uses research and sound and ethical communication techniques as its principal tools.[13]

In 1980, the Task Force on the Stature and Role of Public Relations, chartered by the Public Relations Society of America, offered two definitions that project an image of the field at the highest policy-making level and encompass all its functions and specialties:

> Public relations helps an organization and its publics adapt mutually to each other.
> Public relations is an organization's efforts to win the cooperation of groups of people.[14]

DEFINING BY FUNCTIONS

Communications professor John Marston suggested that public relations be defined in terms of four specific functions: (1) research, (2) action, (3) communication, and (4) evaluation.[15] Applying the R-A-C-E approach involves researching attitudes on a particular issue, identifying action programs of the organization that speak to that issue, communicating those programs to gain understanding and acceptance, and evaluating the effect of the communication efforts on the public.

Public relations professor Sheila Clough Crifasi has proposed extending the R-A-C-E formula into the five-part R-O-S-I-E to encompass a more managerial approach to the field. R-O-S-I-E prescribes sandwiching the functions of objectives, strategies, and implementation between research and evaluation. Indeed, setting clear objectives, working from set strategies and implementing a predetermined plan is a key to sound public relations practice.

Both R-A-C-E and R-O-S-I-E echo one of the most widely repeated definitions of public relations, developed by Denny Griswold, founder of *Public Relations News*, a leading newsletter for practitioners:

> Public relations is the management function which evaluates public attitudes, identifies the policies and procedures of an individual or an organization with the public interest, and plans and executes a program of action to earn public understanding and acceptance.[16]

The key words in this definition are two: management and action. Public relations, if it is to serve the organization properly, must report to top management. Public relations must serve as an honest broker to management, unimpeded by any other group. For public relations to work, its advice to management must be unfiltered, uncensored, and unexpurgated. This can only be achieved if the public relations department reports to the CEO. Although marketing promotes a specific product, public relations promotes the entire institution.

Nor can proper public relations take place without appropriate action. No amount of communications—regardless of its persuasive content—can save an organization whose performance is substandard. Performance, that is, action, must precede publicity. Indeed, in 1993, when Pepsi Cola was accused of allowing syringes to be placed in its cans, the company was so certain of the integrity of its manufacturing process that it "cried foul" immediately and was promptly vindicated. Pepsi could never have responded so quickly or triumphed so convincingly if its performance had been at all suspect. The same was true in General Motors' rebuttal of NBC's *Dateline* charges of "exploding trucks." (Both the Pepsi and GM cases are included in this book.)

Public relations, then, boils down to a process, as educator Melvin Sharpe has put it, that "harmonizes" long-term relationships among individuals and organizations in society.[17] Professor Sharpe applies five principles to this process:

1. Honest communication for credibility
2. Openness and consistency of actions for confidence
3. Fairness of actions for reciprocity and goodwill
4. Continuous two-way communication to prevent alienation and to build relationships
5. Environmental research and evaluation to determine the actions or adjustments needed for social harmony

Stated yet another way, the profession is described by public relations professor Janice Sherline Jenny as "the management of communications between an organization and all entities that have a direct or indirect relationship with the organization, i.e. its publics."

The goal of effective public relations, then, is to harmonize internal and external relationships so that an organization can enjoy not only the goodwill of all of its publics, but also stability and long life.

INTERPRETING MANAGEMENT TO THE PUBLIC

Public relations practitioners are basically interpreters. On the one hand, they must interpret the philosophies, policies, programs, and practices of their management to the public; on the other hand, they must convey the attitudes of the public to their management.

To accomplish these tasks accurately and truthfully, practitioners must gain attention, understanding, acceptance, and ultimately, action from target publics. But first, they have to know what management is thinking.

Good public relations can't be practiced in a vacuum. No matter what the size of the organization, a public relations department is only as good as its access to management. For example, it's useless for a senator's press secretary to explain the reasoning behind an important decision without first knowing what the senator had in mind. So, too, an organization's public relations staff is impotent without firsthand knowledge of the reasons for management's decisions and the rationale for organizational policy.

The public relations department in a profit-making or nonprofit enterprise can counsel management. It can advise management. It can even exhort management to take action. But management must call the shots on organizational policy. Practitioners must fully understand the whys and wherefores of policy and communicate these ideas accurately and candidly to the public. Anything less can lead to major problems.

INTERPRETING THE PUBLIC TO MANAGEMENT

The flip side of the coin is interpreting the public to management. Simply stated, this task means finding out what the public really thinks about the firm and letting management know. Regrettably, recent history is filled with examples of public relations departments failing to anticipate the true sentiments of the public.

- In the 1960s, General Motors paid little attention to an unknown consumer activist named Ralph Nader, who spread the message that GM's Corvair was unsafe at any speed. When Nader's assault began to be believed, the automaker assigned professional detectives to trail him. In short order, General Motors was forced to acknowledge its act of paranoia and the Corvair was eventually sacked, at great expense to the company.
- In the 1970s, as both the price of gasoline and oil company profits rose rapidly, the oil companies were besieged by an irate gas-consuming public. When, at the height of the criticism, Mobil Oil purchased the parent of the Montgomery Ward department store chain, the company was publicly battered.
- In 1980, Ronald Reagan rode to power on the strength of his ability to interpret what was on the minds of the electorate. To his critics, President Reagan was a man of mediocre intellect and limited concentration. But to his supporters, Reagan was the "great communicator" who led the nation to eight years of unprecedented worldwide acclaim.
- In the 1990s, Reagan's successor in the White House, George Bush, turned out to be a less skillful communicator. Despite an overwhelming Gulf War victory and unprecedented popularity, President Bush suffered a stunning electoral defeat in 1992 at the hands of another savvy communicator, Governor Bill Clinton of Arkansas. While Bush stumbled, Clinton kept his candidacy focused on one single, unwavering message: "It's the economy, stupid." Candidate Clinton became President Clinton largely

on the strength of correctly interpreting to the American public the importance of that key theme. Clinton's communications skills improved measurably into his second term.

The savviest institutions in the 1990s—be they government, corporate, or nonprofit—understand the importance of effectively interpreting their management and organizational philosophy, policies, and practices to the public and, even more important, interpreting how the public views their organization back to management.

THE PUBLICS OF PUBLIC RELATIONS

The term *public relations* is really a misnomer. Public relations, or relations with the publics, would be more to the point. Practitioners must communicate with many different publics—not just the general public—each having its own special needs and requiring different types of communication. Often the lines that divide these publics are thin, and the potential overlap is significant. Therefore, priorities, according to organizational needs, must always be reconciled (Figure 1–2).

Technological change—particularly satellite links for television, the Internet and World Wide Web, and the computer generally—has brought greater interdependence to people and organizations, and there is growing concern in organizations today about managing extensive webs of interrelationships. Indeed, managers have become interrelationship conscious.

Internally, managers must deal directly with various levels of subordinates, as well as with cross relationships that arise when subordinates interact with one another. Externally, managers must deal with a system that includes government regulatory agencies, labor unions, subcontractors, consumer groups, and many other independent—but often related—organizations. The public relations challenge in all of this is to manage effectively the communications between managers and the various publics, which often pull organizations in different directions.

Definitions differ on precisely what constitutes a public. One time-honored definition states that a public arises when a group of people (1) face a similar indeterminate situation, (2) recognize what is indeterminate and problematic in that situation, and (3) organize to do something about the problem.[18] In public relations, more specifically, a public is a group of people with a stake in an issue, organization, or idea.

Publics can also be classified into several overlapping categories:

1. **Internal and external** Internal publics are inside the organization: supervisors, clerks, managers, stockholders, and the board of directors. External publics are those not directly connected with the organization: the press, government, educators, customers, the community, and suppliers.
2. **Primary, secondary, and marginal** Primary publics can most help—or hinder— the organization's efforts. Secondary publics are less important, and marginal publics are the least important of all. For example, members of the Federal Reserve Board of Governors, who regulate banks, would be the primary public for a bank awaiting a regulatory ruling, whereas legislators and the general public would be secondary.
3. **Traditional and future** Employees and current customers are traditional publics; students and potential customers are future ones. No organization can

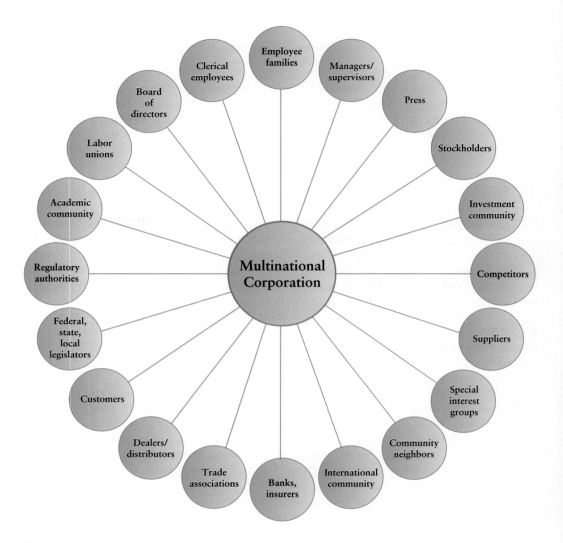

Figure 1–2   Twenty key publics of a typical multinational corporation.

afford to become complacent in dealing with its changing publics. Today, a firm's publics range from women to minorities to senior citizens to homosexuals. Each might be important to the future success of the organization.

4. **Proponents, opponents, and the uncommitted**   An institution must deal differently with those who support it and those who oppose it. For supporters, communications that reinforce beliefs may be in order. But changing the opinions of skeptics calls for strong, persuasive communications. Often, particularly in politics, the uncommitted public is crucial. Many a campaign has been decided because the swing vote was won over by one of the candidates.

The typical organization is faced with a myriad of critical publics with whom it must communicate on a frequent and direct basis. It must be sensitive to the self-interests, desires, and concerns of each public. It must understand that self-interest groups today are

---

DRAWING THE LINE ON QUESTIONABLE CLIENTS

In the final years of the 1990s, the essence of public relations practice—with management, journalists, and colleagues—comes down to one word: integrity. Once a public relations professional has lost that quality, he or she has lost the game.[20]

Ethical choices in public relations must be made daily.

On the one side are those who believe, like former public relations professor James D. Sodt, that "Honestly advocating an unpopular or even wrong position serves the public interest in helping to resolve the issue."[21] On the other side are those who suggest that "If the trend continues of public relations people becoming image mercenaries, accepting any client regardless of character or conscience, as long as he or she pays the freight, then all of us will lose."[22] Even before the O.J. Simpson case perplexed the public in this regard, an earlier lightning rod for this issue of ethics in the 1990s was the huge public relations firm Hill & Knowlton. Early in the decade, Hill & Knowlton found itself under fire for deciding to accept such clients as the controversial Church of Scientology, the restrictive nation of China, and the antiabortion United States Conference of Catholic Bishops.

Hill & Knowlton attracted the greatest controversy when it represented Citizens For Free Kuwait in the fall of 1990. Hill & Knowlton's job was to stimulate U.S. public support for the war against Iraq. As part of its initiative, the firm distributed a video news release of a young Kuwaiti woman's testimony before Congress. The woman told of unspeakable Iraqi army atrocities, including the "dumping" of babies from incubators in Kuwaiti hospitals. The testimony of the woman, identified only as "Naryah," was riveting. The videotape was aired on stations throughout the country, and public support for the Kuwaiti plight was achieved.

Months later, it was revealed that Naryah was actually the daughter of the Kuwaiti ambassador. She had, in fact, never witnessed the Iraqi atrocities of which she spoke. Indeed, she hadn't been in Kuwait at the time. The subsequent controversy over Naryah's videotaped testimony raised the question of public relations counsel representing issues and individuals of questionable veracity.

Stated another way, Are there clients whom public relations people shouldn't represent? Where do you draw the line?

---

themselves more complex. Therefore, the harmonizing actions necessary to win and maintain support among such groups should be arrived at in terms of public relations consequences.[19] Whereas management must always speak with one voice, its communications inflection, delivery, and emphasis should be sensitive to all its constituent publics.

SUMMARY

Ethics, truth, credibility—these values are what good public relations is all about. Coverup, distortion, and subterfuge are the antitheses of good public relations.

Much more than customers for their products, managers today desperately need constituents for their beliefs and values. In the 1990s, the role of public relations is much more to guide management in framing its ideas and making its commitments. The counsel that management will need must come from advisers who understand public attitudes, public moods, public needs, and public aspirations.

Winning this elusive goodwill takes time and effort. Credibility can't be won overnight, nor can it be bought. If management policies aren't in the public's best interest, no amount of public relations can obscure that reality. Public relations is not effective as a temporary defensive measure to compensate for management misjudgment. (See the Exxon Case Study at the end of chapter 2.) If management errs seriously, the best—and only—public relations advice must be to get the story out immediately. (See Texaco Case Study at the end of this chapter.)

One public relations professional who probably summed up the opinion of many colleagues about exactly what it is he does for a living was Peter F. Jeff, a Michigan practitioner who wrote to a local editor:

> A public relations professional is a bridge builder, not a drum beater—building long-term relationships between a company or organization and its publics based on two-way communication, i.e., listening and speaking. A public relations professional serves as an interpreter, helping the company adapt and adjust to the political, social, and economic climate . . . and assisting the public in more fully understanding the company.[23]

No less an authority than Abraham Lincoln once said: "Public sentiment is everything . . . with public sentiment nothing can fail. Without it, nothing can succeed. He who molds public sentiment goes deeper than he who executes statutes or pronounces decisions. He makes statutes or decisions possible or impossible to execute."

Stated another way, no matter how you define it, the practice of public relations has become an essential element in the conduct of relationships in the 1990s.

DISCUSSION STARTERS

1. Why has the practice of public relations become so pervasive in the 1990s?
2. Why are others—lawyers, accountants, general managers, and so on—interested in doing public relations?
3. Why is the practice of public relations generally misunderstood by the public?
4. Why isn't there one all-encompassing definition of the field?
5. Explain the approach toward defining public relations by the nature of its functions.
6. Explain the approach toward defining public relations as a harmonizing process.
7. Why is a public relations professional fundamentally an interpreter?
8. What are the four overlapping categories of publics?
9. What is the essence of proper public relations practice?
10. Has public relations truly rid itself of charlatan practitioners? Will it ever?

NOTES

1. Randall Rothenberg, "The Age of Spin," *Esquire* (December 1996): 73.
2. James G. Grunig, "IABC Study Shows CEO Value PR," *IABC Communication World* (August 1990): 5.

3. Ronald B. Liebert, "How Safe is Your Job?" *Fortune* (April 1, 1996): 76.
4. Jack O'Dwyer, "1996 PR Fee Income of 50 Firms," *O'Dwyer's PR Services Report* (March 1996): 5.
5. "The Design for Undergraduate Public Relations Education," a study cosponsored by the public relations division of the Association for Education and Journalism and Mass Communication, the Public Relations Society of America, and the educators' section of PRSA, 1987, 1.
6. Jeff Blyskal and Marie Blyskal, *PR: How the Public Relations Industry Writes the News* (New York: William Morrow, 1985), 61.
7. Deborah Stead, "How Public Relations Tries to Keep the World Spinning," *The New York Times*, November 3, 1996, B8.
8. Roger W. W. Baker, "Lurking and Seeding Within the Web," *The Public Relations Strategist* (Winter 1996): 42.
9. Philip Lesly, "The Balkanizing of Public Relations," *The Public Relations Strategist* (Fall 1996): 43.
10. Berton J. Ballard, lecture at San Jose State University, San Jose, CA, 1948. Cited in Pearce Davies, "Twenty-Five Years Old and Still Growing," *Public Relations Journal* (October 1977): 22–23.
11. Cited in Scott M. Cutlip and Allen H. Center, *Effective Public Relations*, 6th ed. (Upper Saddle River, NJ: Prentice Hall, 1985), 5.
12. Edward L. Bernays, *Crystallizing Public Opinion* (New York: Liveright, 1961).
13. Rex F. Harlow, "Building a Public Relations Definition," *Public Relations Review* 2, no. 4 (Winter 1976): 36.
14. Philip Lesly, "Report and Recommendations: Task Force on Stature and Role of Public Relations," *Public Relations Journal* (March 1981): 32.
15. John E. Marston, *The Nature of Public Relations* (New York: McGraw-Hill, 1963), 161.
16. Denny Griswold, *Public Relations News*, 127 East 80th Street, New York, NY 10021.
17. This definition was developed by Dr. Melvin L. Sharpe, professor and coordinator of the Public Relations Sequence, Department of Journalism, Ball State University, Muncie, IN 47306.
18. John Dewey, *The Public and Its Problems* (Chicago: Swallow Press, 1927).
19. Sharpe, loc. cit.
20. "Leaders, Not Lap Dogs, Needed to Ensure PR's Future," *O'Dwyer's PR Services Report*, (January 1993): 17–18.
21. James D. Sodt, "Why I Would Represent the Serbs," *The Public Relations Strategist* (Spring 1995): 34.
22. Fraser P. Seitel, "Walking the Public Relations High Wire in the 90's," speech delivered to the Raymond Simon Institute for Public Relations, Utica College— Syracuse University, April 1, 1992.
23. Peter F. Jeff, "Dissent! Public Relations," *Grand Rapids Press*, March 2, 1990.

SUGGESTED READINGS

Albrecht, Karl. *At America's Service*, Homewood, IL: Dow Jones, 1988.
Baskin, Otis W., and Craig E. Aronoff. *Public Relations: The Profession and the Practice*, 2nd ed. Dubuque, IA: Wm. C. Brown, 1988.

"SPIN DOCTORS"

TOP OF THE SHELF

STUART EWEN

PR! A SOCIAL HISTORY OF SPIN

NEW YORK: BASIC BOOKS, 1996

History professor Stuart Ewen's history of the practice of public relations is not particularly flattering. The link between "truth" and "hype," according to the professor, is not altogether clear. More often than not, he writes, the history of public relations is a recounting of "virtual factuality," in which the construction of "reality" has become a fact of American life.

The book recounts tales of AT&T using advertising to sway previously uncooperative newspaper editors; Standard Oil of New Jersey launching a communications offensive to defuse revelations it colluded with the Nazis; and Ronald Reagan using public relations "techniques" to transform him from a B actor to President of the United States.

Professor Ewen's conclusion, that public relations systematically has manipulated public opinion over the course of nine decades may not be either right or fair—but it's worth reading, if only to find out how the adversaries think.

Cantor, Bill (Chester Burger, ed.). *Experts in Action: Inside Public Relations*, 2nd ed. White Plains, NY: Longman, 1989.

Center, Allen H., and Patrick Jackson. *Public Relations Practices: Managerial Case Studies and Problems*, 4th ed. Upper Saddle River, NJ: Prentice Hall, 1990.

Cutlip, Scott M., Allen H. Center, and Glen M. Broom, *Effective Public Relations*, 7th ed. Upper Saddle River, NJ: Prentice Hall, 1994. (Without question, the first and still most comprehensive text book in the field.)

Dozier, David M. *Manager's Guide to Excellence in Public Relations and Communication Management.* Hillsdale, NJ: Lawrence Erlbaum Associates, 1995.

Dwyer, Thomas. *Simply Public Relations: Public Relations Made Challenging, Complete and Concise.* Stillwater, OK: New Forums, 1992.

Haberman, David, and Harry Dolphin. *Public Relations: The Necessary Art.* Iowa City: Iowa State University Press, 1988.

Hausman, Carl, and Phillip Benoit. *Positive Public Relations.* Blue Ridge Summit, PA: Tab Books, 1989.

Hiebert, Ray Eldon, editor. *Precision Public Relations.* White Plains, NY: Longman, 1988.

Jenkins, Frank. *Public Relations*, 4th ed. Philadelphia: Trans-Atlantic, 1992.

Newsom, Doug, Alan Scott, and Judy Van Slyke Turk. *This Is PR: The Realities of Public Relations*, 5th ed. Belmont, CA: Wadsworth, 1993.

Reilly, Robert T. *Public Relations in Action*, 2nd ed. Upper Saddle River, NJ: Prentice Hall, 1987.

Saffir, Leonard. *Power Public Relations: How to Get PR to Work for You.* Lincoln wood, IL: NTC Business, 1992.

Sharpe, Melvin L., and Sam Black, eds. "Special Issue: International Public Relations," *Public Relations Review* 18, no. 2 (Summer 1992).

Wood, Robert J. *Confessions of a PR Man*. Scarborough, Ontario: New American Library of Canada, Ltd., 1989.

Wragg, David. *Public Relations Handbook*. Colchester, VT: Blackwell Business, 1992.

CASE STUDY

Texaco and the Black Jellybeans

After less than five months in the saddle, Texaco Chairman Peter I. Bijur was hardly ready for the front page story in the November 4, 1996 *New York Times* that accused senior Texaco officials of "belittling the company's minority employees with racial epithets."

The story described, in gruesome detail, the conversations of Texaco finance department executives, who talked of their disgust with inferior minority workers and their plans to destroy documents demanded in a federal discrimination lawsuit. Worst of all for Texaco, the conversations weren't heresay or the product of someone's vague recollection—they were tape recorded by one of the participants.

Richard Lundwall, senior coordinator of personnel services in Texaco's finance department, would slip a tiny tape recorder into his jacket to make sure his minutes of the meetings with Texaco treasurer Robert Ulrich and senior assistant treasurer J. David Keough were accurate. He never told his colleagues about the tape recordings.

Incriminating Evidence

Who Mr. Lundwall did tell about the recordings were plaintiffs' attorneys, hired two years earlier by Texaco employees in a $520 million discrimination lawsuit. The suit, brought on behalf of 1,500 black employees, claimed that they were denied promotions and advancement opportunities because of their race.

Mr. Lundwall, "downsized" after the last fateful meeting, was evidently so outraged at his own firing, he forked over the telltale tapes to the company's adversaries. In the process, not only did he reportedly "spill the beans" on his finance department colleagues, but also on himself.

For example, when the talk turned to minorities. . . .

MR. ULRICH: "This diversity thing. You know how the black jelly beans agree."
MR. LUNDWALL: "That's funny. All the black jelly beans seem to be glued to the bottom of the bag."
MR. ULRICH: "You can't have just we and them. You can't just have black jelly beans and other jelly beans. It doesn't work."
MR. LUNDWALL: Yeah. But they're perpetuating the black jelly beans."
Or when the talk turned to tampering with evidence. . . .
MR. ULRICH: "I just don't want anybody to have a copy of that."
MR. LUNDWALL: "Good. No problem."
MR. ULRICH: "There's no point in even keeping the restricted version anymore. All it could do is get us in trouble. . . . I would not keep anything."
MR. LUNDWALL: Let me shred this thing and any other restricted version like it."

Not surprisingly, the attorneys suing Texaco were more than willing to turn over "transcripts" of the recordings—but not the tape recordings themselves—to *The New York Times*. And while the *Times* was careful to report that the transcripts "appear" to have captured senior Texaco officers using the word, "nigger," and conspiring to destroy evidence, the effect of the page one story was immediate and categorical.

Texaco, most presumed, was guilty.

Especially convinced were the Texaco managers bringing the lawsuit, some of whom the *Times* quoted. "It sounded like a Klan meeting," sniffed one. "I wasn't at all surprised," huffed another, adding that a lot of the words on the tapes were similar to "what I heard in the office."

With Texaco now firmly in the national spotlight, ensuing television coverage and newspaper and magazine editorials universally corroborated Texaco's guilt.

Some pointed out the particularly repulsive dialogue repeated by the *Times*, in which one participant said, "I'm still struggling with Hanukkah, and now we have Kwanzaa." The National Association for the Advancement of Colored People called for a Justice Department investigation. Civil rights activists Jesse Jackson and Al Sharpton called for a nationwide boycott of Texaco products (Figure 1–3).

Immediate Action

Chairman Bijur (Figure 1-4), obviously stunned by the sudden catastrophe, reacted just as swiftly in voicing his outrage over the remarks. On November 6, two days after the *Times* story—and before listening to the quoted tapes or knowing firsthand what they

Figure 1–3 Black demonstrators outside a Texaco service station in Washington, DC, were typical of protests that the company drew from the disclosure of allegedly racist remarks.

Figure 1–4   Texaco Chairman Peter Bijur publicly apologized for alleged racist statements made by several executives and then paid out $176 million in settlement.

said—Bijur apologized for the incident, first at a midday press conference and then in an evening appearance on ABC's *Nightline*. And then, in rapid succession, Bijur took additional immediate steps to defuse the crisis.

- He agreed to form a special panel to examine Texaco's "diversity programs in their entirety."
- He unveiled an advertising campaign headlined, "Where we go from here . . ." asking readers to help make Texaco "a company of limitless opportunity" and a leader "in according respect to every man and woman." The campaign appeared mainly in local weekly publications with smaller circulations than general interest newspapers and magazines.

- He hired minority advertising firm UniWorld Group to refine and deliver its targeted message.
- He also acted against the participants at the incriminating meetings. Both Lundwall's and Ulrich's medical, insurance, and other retirement benefits were cut off. And two other meeting participants, still at the company, were suspended.
- Finally, in the most controversial action emanating from the *Times'* tapes, Bijur agreed to a $176 million payment to settle the discrimination lawsuit. In the wake of his actions, Bijur was hailed as a "hero," particularly in handling the company's crisis and communicating his refusal to allow such racist tactics to exist at Texaco.

Tale of the Tape

While Bijur was acting, Texaco's own law firm was carefully examining the extremely fuzzy tapes finally given over by the plaintiffs' attorneys. A week after the initial story, Texaco announced that the tapes revealed that the word "nigger" had not been used at all. Further, it was revealed that the term "jellybeans," which had caused so much commotion, was not a pejorative Texaco concoction, but rather was a term used in diversity sensitivity programs at the company.

After listening to digitally enhanced excerpts from the tapes, some debated whether comments by the Texaco officials were, in fact, racist at all. True, they were resentful. "They're perpetuating an us/them atmosphere," one official complained on the tape, referring to an incident where some black workers refused to stand for the national anthem. "I walked out; I'm sorry . . . and would apologize to nobody for walking out of there."

Also at issue on the tapes were the views of the officers that the company promoted for affirmative action and not merit reasons. On the other hand, the tapes didn't necessarily reveal that the officials in question were against hiring or promoting capable minority workers. One official suggested recruiting at colleges such as Howard and Temple, with primarily black students who are advanced "simply on the basis of scholastic merit."

In the months following the Texaco crisis and Bijur's actions, critics of the chairman's settlement began to emerge. Some questioned the haste of Bijur's voluntarily awarding the $176 million. Others wondered about the chairman's agreement to delegate hiring and promotion decisions to a special panel, with three of its seven members appointed by the plaintiffs and three by Texaco. If Texaco disagreed with any of the panel's actions, it had to seek relief from a federal judge presiding over the agreement. Finally, some wondered whether the chairman's hasty actions would, in fact, exacerbate racial tensions between black and white Texaco workers.

As the crisis subsided to the back pages of the newspapers, it was still unclear whether in acting swiftly and conclusively to stem the racial crisis at Texaco, Chairman Bijur was a hero or a sellout.

QUESTIONS

1. Was Texaco's chairman a hero or a sellout?
2. What did public relations have to do with it?
3. What alternative actions and potential outcomes might Bijur have considered?

P.S.   Texaco was not the only one that paid for the black jellybean controversy. In March 1997, whistle blower Lundwall, the former executive who came forward with the secret tape recordings, was indicted on a charge of obstruction of justice "to corruptly destroy, conceal and withhold" evidence in the race discrimination case. For his initiative, Mr. Lundwall faced 10 years in prison and a fine of $250,000.

For further information about the Texaco case, see Sally Goll Beatty, "Texaco's Image Repair Effort Draws Fire," *The Wall Street Journal*, November 27, 1996, B2; Robert A. Bennett, "Texaco's Bijur: Hero or Sellout?" *The Public Relations Strategist* (Winter 1996): 18–20; Kurt Eichenwald, "Texaco Executives, On Tape, Discussed Impeding a Bias Suit," *The New York Times*, November 4, 1996, A1–D4; Kurt Eichenwald, "The First Casualties in Scandal at Texaco," *The New York Times*, November 7, A1–D10; Kurt Eichenwald, "N.A.A.C.P. Wants U.S. Inquiry Into Texaco," *The New York Times*, November 8, 1996, B6; Kurt Eichenwald, "The Two Faces of Texaco," *The New York Times*, November 10, 1996, Sect. 3–1–10,11; Peter Fritsch and Allanna Sullivan, "Texaco's New Chairman Navigates PR Crisis," *The Wall Street Journal*, B1, 2; "Texaco: Lessons From a Crisis-in-Progress," *Newsweek*, December 2, 1996, 44.

VOICE OF EXPERIENCE

MICHAEL D. McCURRY

Mike McCurry was named assistant to the president and presidential press secretary in January 1995. A veteran press secretary and Democratic strategist, Mr. McCurry served as chief spokesman for the state department before joining President Clinton's staff. Mr. McCurry began his career on the staff of the United States Senate, working from 1976 to 1983 for Senators Harrison A. Williams Jr. of New Jersey and Daniel Patrick Moynihan of New York. He has been a Democratic communications advisor and strategist in four presidential campaigns.

WHAT IS THE PRIMARY FUNCTION OF THE PRESIDENT'S PRESS SECRETARY?

Newspaper magnate Edward Wyllis Scripps once said that the press exists "to comfort the afflicted and afflict the comfortable." The White House Press Office exists to keep the president's daily afflictions as comfortable as possible.

The Press Office works for the American people. We transmit the truth every day to the American people about the work of the president, his staff, and his administration. We work for the president, but we also work for the press corps. We cannot help our boss unless we adequately serve our many bosses in the press. Our goal is to keep the president happy, provide good service to the press corps, and keep the White House story unerringly aimed at the truth, for better or worse.

WHAT IS YOUR PRIMARY MISSION?

The mission of the White House Press Office is to provide accurate, truthful, and timely information to the American public in a way that advances the program of the president of the United States, consistent with the needs of a White House Press Corps that is ever vigilant in protecting the American people's "right to know."

WHAT IS YOUR DAILY ACCESS TO THE PRESIDENT?

I usually drop by his office immediately before each of my daily briefings to see if anything newsworthy is bubbling. When I began this job, I made it clear that to successfully communicate to the press the specifics of the president's initiatives and message, I need access to the president. I sit in on meetings I think the press will be interested in, and I often discuss issues directly with the president.

HOW WOULD YOU CHARACTERIZE YOUR RELATIONSHIP WITH PRESIDENT CLINTON?

I didn't have a personal relationship with him before I came to work at the White House. Since arriving here, I have spent a great deal of time with him—on flights on Air Force One, at meetings, and even during "down time" at the White House. President Clinton has a wonderful sense of humor and an incredible interest in his staff and their lives. He respects the opinion of his staff—even when we disagree with him.

HOW DO YOU REGARD THE WHITE HOUSE PRESS CORPS?

The White House press corps is a group of well-informed, perceptive, and extremely capable reporters. Most of them have been at the White House longer than I have; many have been here longer than President Clinton. In fact, one of the sharpest reporters around, Helen Thomas of UPI, has covered the White House since the Kennedy Administration. They keep me on my toes in their demands to protect the American people's "right to know."

WHAT ARE THE MOST IMPORTANT ATTRIBUTES OF A PRESIDENTIAL PRESS SECRETARY?

First, accuracy and quickness of response. If the press secretary relays even the slightest inaccuracy, his or her credibility is tarnished and the media have no further reason to trust him. This can end a career of a press secretary, not to mention make the president appear dishonest. It is critical for the press secretary to be trusted by the press. Second, appreciation for deadlines is another important attribute of a presidential press secretary.

WHAT HAS BEEN YOUR TOUGHEST ASSIGNMENT?

Handling a complicated issue that requires a detailed explanation—such as the nuances of the administration's efforts to regulate the tobacco advertising aimed at children.

HOW DOES PRESIDENT CLINTON FEEL ABOUT THE MEDIA?

I think he has learned, over the years, to appreciate them more. Like most presidents, President Clinton believes that his work is often mischaracterized by the media. But his relationship with the media has improved over the last few years. One reason for this new attitude is the increase in informal, off-the-record sessions between the president and the press, which has allowed each a clearer view of the other's intentions. Both have a common "boss"—the American people and are obliged therefore to seek the truth in serving the peoples' priorities. In this sense, the two have quite a bit in common.

WHAT IS THE MOST REWARDING PART OF YOUR JOB?

The daily briefings with the press corps. I relish the daily challenge. I enjoy anticipating the questions I will be asked. Satisfying their seemingly insatiable appetite for knowledge and details is the biggest reward.

HOW DOES ONE BECOME WHITE HOUSE PRESS SECRETARY?

Familiarity with campaigns, background in politics and journalism, the ability to think quick on your feet, talk fast, and stay ahead of the headlines. Plus being in the right place at the right time counts for a lot.

CHAPTER TWO

The Evolution
of Public Relations

IN THE YEAR 2000 PUBLIC RELATIONS WILL still be less than 100 years old. Public relations as a modern American phenomenon is much younger than other disciplines. The relative youthfulness of the practice means that the field is still evolving, and its status is improving daily. Indeed, the professionals entering the practice today are by and large superior in intellect, training, and even experience to their counterparts decades ago.

The strength of the practice of public relations today is based on the enduring commitment of the public to participate in a free and open democratic society. At least four trends are related to the evolution of public relations: (1) the growth of big institutions; (2) the increasing incidence of change, conflict, and confrontation in society; (3) the heightened awareness and sophistication of people everywhere as a result of technological innovations in communications; and (4) the increased importance of public opinion in the twenty-first century for positive democratic means as well as a use by those who would repress other people (Figure 2–1).

- The size of today's society has played a significant role in the development of public relations. The days of the mom and pop grocery store, the tiny community college, and the small local bank are rapidly disappearing. In their place have emerged Wal-Marts, Home Depots, and Staples Super Stores, statewide community college systems with populous branches in several cities, and multistate banking networks. As instit-

Figure 2–1 The communications revolution sweeping the world fueled evil forces as well as good. Terrorists, knowledgeable of the power of the media to broadcast their message instantaneously around the world, used their acts of destruction to spread their beliefs.

utions have grown larger, the public relations profession has evolved to interp
large institutions to the publics they serve.

- The increasing incidence of change, conflict, and confrontation in society
  other reason for the evolution of public relations. Women's rights, gay r
  mal rights, consumerism and environmental awareness; downsizings a
  and resultant unhappiness with large institutions; and the extraordinary grow..g
  impact of the Internet and cyberspace have all contributed materially to the need
  for more and better communications and the existence of more and better communicators.

- A third factor in the development of public relations has been the heightened awareness
  of people everywhere. First came the invention of the printing press. Later it was the per-
  vasiveness of mass communications: the print media, radio, and television. Then it was
  the development of cable, satellite, videotape, video discs, video typewriters, portable
  cameras, word processors, fax machines, the World Wide Web, and all the other communications technologies that have helped fragment audiences and create Marshall
  McLuhan's "global village."

In a world in which the image of a lone protester blocking a line of tanks in Beijing's Tiananmen Square can be flashed around the world to be seen on the evening
news; when a hostage standoff in Peru can be witnessed in real time by people in their
living rooms in Bangor, Maine; when a dictator in the Persian Gulf can be interviewed
live by a reporter in Washington, there can be no doubt that the communications revolution has arrived.

- Finally, the outbreak of democracy in Latin America, Eastern Europe, the former Soviet Union, and South Africa has heightened the power of public opinion in the world.
  Just as increasing numbers of Americans made their voices heard through the civil
  rights movements, various consumer movements, the women's rights movement, and
  political movements throughout the ages, so too have oppressed peoples around the
  world risen up and spoken out. Accordingly, the practice of public relations, as a facilitator in understanding more clearly and managing more effectively in the midst of
  such democratic revolution, has increased in prominence.

ANCIENT BEGINNINGS

Although modern public relations is a twentieth-century phenomenon, its roots are ancient. Leaders in virtually every great society throughout history understood the importance of influencing public opinion through persuasion. For example, the Babylonians of
1800 B.C. hammered out their messages on stone tablets so that farmers could learn the
latest techniques of harvesting, sowing, and irrigating.[1] The more food the farmers grew,
the better the citizenry ate and the wealthier the country became—a good example of
planned persuasion to reach a specific public for a particular purpose; in other words,
public relations.

Later on, the Greeks put a high premium on communication skills. The best speakers,
in fact, were generally elected to leadership positions. Occasionally, aspiring Greek politicians enlisted the aid of Sophists (individuals renowned for both their reasoning and their
rhetoric) to help fight verbal battles. Sophists would gather in the amphitheaters of the

day and extol the virtues of particular political candidates. Thus, the Sophists set the stage for today's lobbyists, who attempt to influence legislation through effective communications techniques. From the time of the Sophists, the practice of public relations has been a battleground for questions of ethics. Should a Sophist or a lobbyist or a public relations professional "sell" his or her talents to the highest bidder, regardless of personal beliefs, values, and ideologies? When modern-day public relations professionals agree to represent repressive governments in Serbia or Nazi sympathizers in Switzerland or when dyed-in-the-wool Republicans like David Gergen switch sides to join staunch Democrats like Bill Clinton, these ethical questions remain very much a focus of modern public relations.[2]

The Romans, particularly Julius Caesar, were also masters of persuasive techniques. When faced with an upcoming battle, Caesar would rally public support through assorted publications and staged events. Similarly, during World War I, a special U.S. public information committee, the Creel Committee, was formed to channel the patriotic sentiments of Americans in support of the U.S. role in the war. Stealing a page from Caesar, the committee's massive verbal and written communications effort was successful in marshaling national pride behind the war effort. According to a young member of the Creel Committee, Edward L. Bernays (later considered by many to be the father of public relations), "This was the first time in our history that information was used as a weapon of war."[3]

Even the Catholic Church had a hand in the creation of public relations. In the 1600s, under the leadership of Pope Gregory XV, the church established a college of propaganda to "help propagate the faith." In those days, the term propaganda did not have a negative connotation; the church simply wanted to inform the public about the advantages of Catholicism. Indeed, the roots of public relations lie in the development of propaganda, defined neutrally.[4] Today, the pope and other religious leaders maintain communications staffs to assist relations with the public. Indeed, the chief communications official in the Vatican maintains the rank of Archbishop of the Church. (See the interview in chapter 3.)

EARLY AMERICAN EXPERIENCE

The American public relations experience dates back to the founding of the Republic. Influencing public opinion, managing communications, and persuading individuals at the highest levels were at the core of the American Revolution. The colonists tried to persuade King George III that they should be accorded the same rights as Englishmen. "Taxation without representation is tyranny!" became their public relations slogan to galvanize fellow countrymen.

When King George refused to accede to the colonists' demands, they combined the weaponry of sword and pen. Samuel Adams, for one, organized committees of correspondence as a kind of revolutionary Associated Press to disseminate speedily anti-British information throughout the colonies. He also staged events to build up revolutionary fervor, like the Boston Tea Party, in which colonists, masquerading as Indians, boarded British ships in Boston Harbor and pitched chests of imported tea overboard—as impressive a media event as has ever been recorded sans television. Indeed, Adams's precept, "Put the enemy in the wrong and keep him there," is as solid persuasive advice today as it was more than two centuries ago.[5]

Thomas Paine, another early practitioner of public relations, wrote periodic pamphlets and essays that urged the colonists to band together. In one essay contained in his Crisis papers, Paine wrote poetically: "These are the times that try men's souls. The summer soldier and the sunshine patriot will, in this crisis, shrink from the service of their country." The people listened, were persuaded, and took action—testifying to the power of early American communicators.

LATER AMERICAN EXPERIENCE

The creation of the most important document in our nation's history, the Constitution, also owed much to public relations. Federalists, who supported the Constitution, fought tooth and nail with anti-Federalists, who opposed it. Their battle was waged in newspaper articles, pamphlets, and other organs of persuasion in an attempt to influence public opinion. To advocate ratification of the Constitution, political leaders like Alexander Hamilton, James Madison, and John Jay banded together, under the pseudonym Publius, to write letters to leading newspapers. Today those letters are bound in a document called *The Federalist Papers* and are still used in the interpretation of the Constitution.

After ratification, the constitutional debate continued, particularly over the document's apparent failure to protect individual liberties against government encroachment. Hailed as the Father of the Constitution, in 1791 Madison framed the Bill of Rights, which ultimately became the first ten amendments to the Constitution. Fittingly, the first of those amendments safeguarded, among other things, the practice of public relations: "Congress shall make no law respecting an establishment of religion, or prohibiting the free exercise thereof; or abridging the freedom of speech, or of the press, or the rights of the people peaceably to assemble, and to petition the government for a redress of grievances." In other words, people were given the right to speak up for what they believed in and the freedom to try to influence the opinions of others. Thus was the practice of public relations ratified.[6]

Into the 1800s

The practice of public relations continued to percolate in the nineteenth century. Among the more prominent—yet negative—antecedents of modern public relations that took hold in the 1800s was press agentry. Two of the better-known—some would say notorious—practitioners of this art were Amos Kendall and Phineas T. Barnum.

In 1829, President Andrew Jackson selected Kendall, a writer and editor living in Kentucky, to serve in his administration. Within weeks, Kendall became a member of Old Hickory's "kitchen cabinet" and eventually became one of Jackson's most influential assistants.

Kendall performed just about every White House public relations task. He wrote speeches, state papers, and messages and turned out press releases. He even conducted basic opinion polls and is considered one of the earliest users of the "news leak." Although Kendall is generally credited with being the first authentic presidential press secretary, his functions and role went far beyond that position.

Among Kendall's most successful ventures in Jackson's behalf was the development of the administration's own newspaper, the *Globe*. Although it was not uncommon for the governing administration to publish its own national house organ, Kendall's deft editorial touch refined the process to increase its effectiveness. Kendall would pen a Jackson news release, distribute it for publication to a local newspaper, and then reprint the press clipping in the *Globe* to underscore Jackson's nationwide popularity. Indeed, that popu-

THE REST OF THE STORY

WHAT HATH BARNUM WROUGHT?

P.T. Barnum's methods to achieve publicity for his museum attractions and circus acts pales in comparison to the efforts of today's entertainment publicists to promote new movies.

With studios investing tens of millions of dollars in movies, which must score at the box office immediately to return the hundreds of millions studios seek, the element of publicity is as important as any other in the movie marketing mix.

So today's movie publicists play hardball.

In one 1996 study, more than half of 61 entertainment writers and film critics said the major Hollywood film studios "put more pressure on them to play by their rules." Nearly one-third said they had been "black listed" for not playing the studio's publicity rules.[7]

One writer reported being blacklisted by Disney for trashing the movie, *Beauty and the Beast*. The negative review got the writer barred from future Disney screenings, interviews, and junkets.

The study also reported that entertainment publicists make journalists sign agreements as to where a story may run and which sensitive subjects may not be broached in celebrity interviews. For example, if Woody Allen doesn't wish to talk about Mia Farrow or Roseanne has no inclination to discuss Tom Arnold or Madonna wishes not to discuss Dennis Rodman, so be it. If a journalist raises the issue—he's outa' there.

The same holds true for celebrities "wanting the cover of a magazine." Unless you can guarantee the cover of *Movieline* or *Entertainment Weekly* or even *Newsweek* or *Time*—John Travolta or Arnold Schwarzenegger or even Howard Stern may not agree to the interview. Such is the publicity clout that today's show biz-dominated culture commands. When a movie like the 1996 thriller *Independence Day* can command upwards of $20 million in a weekend opening, favorable publicity becomes a pivotal profitability variable.

In the dawn of the twenty-first century then, in the area of entertainment at least, it is the public relations publicist—in the best traditions of P.T. Barnum—who holds all the cards.

larity continued unabated throughout Jackson's years in office, with much of the credit going to the president's public relations adviser.*

Most public relations professionals would rather not talk about P. T. Barnum as an industry pioneer. Barnum, some say, was a huckster, whose motto might well have been, "The public be fooled." More sanguine defenders suggest that while Barnum may have had his faults, he nonetheless was respected in his time as a user of written and verbal public relations techniques to further his museum and circus.

Like him or not, Barnum was a master publicist. In the 1800s, as owner of a major circus, Barnum generated article after article for his traveling show. He purposely gave his star performers short names—for instance, Tom Thumb, the midget, and Jenny Lind, the singer—so that they could easily fit into the headlines of narrow newspaper columns. Barnum also staged bizarre events, such as the legal marriage of the fat lady to the thin

---

*Kendall was decidedly not cut from the same cloth as today's neat, trim, buttoned-down press secretaries. On the contrary, Jackson's man was described as "a puny, sickly looking man with a weak voice, a wheezing cough, narrow and stooping shoulders, a sallow complexion, silvery hair in his prime, slovenly dress, and a seedy appearance" (Fred F. Endres, "Public Relations in the Jackson White House," *Public Relations Review* 2, no. 3 [Fall 1976]: 5–12).

man, to drum up free newspaper exposure. And although today's practitioners scoff at Barnum's methods, some press agents still practice his techniques. Nonetheless, when today's public relations professionals bemoan the specter of shysters and hucksters that still overhangs their field, they inevitably place the blame squarely on the fertile mind and silver tongue of P. T. Barnum.

Emergence of the Robber Barons

The American Industrial Revolution ushered in many things at the turn of the century, not the least of which was the growth of public relations. The twentieth century began with small mills and shops, which served as the hub of the frontier economy, giving way to massive factories. Country hamlets, which had been the centers of commerce and trade, were replaced by sprawling cities. Limited transportation and communications facilities became nationwide railroad lines and communications wires. Big business took over, and the businessman was king.

The men who ran America's industries seemed more concerned with making a profit than with improving the lot of their fellow citizens. Railroad owners such as William Vanderbilt, bankers such as J. P. Morgan, oil magnates such as John D. Rockefeller, and steel impresarios such as Henry Clay Frick ruled the fortunes of thousands of others. Typical of the reputation acquired by this group of industrialists was the famous—and perhaps apocryphal—response of Vanderbilt when questioned about the public's reaction to his closing of the New York Central Railroad: "The public be damned!"

Little wonder that Americans cursed Vanderbilt and his ilk as robber barons who cared little for the rest of society. Although most who depended on these industrialists for their livelihood felt powerless to rebel, the seeds of discontent were being sown liberally throughout the culture. It was just a matter of time before the robber barons got their comeuppance.

Enter the Muckrakers

When the ax fell on the robber barons, it came in the form of criticism from a feisty group of journalists dubbed muckrakers. The muck that these reporters and editors raked was dredged from the scandalous operations of America's business enterprises. Upton Sinclair's novel *The Jungle* attacked the deplorable conditions of the meat-packing industry. Ida Tarbell's *History of the Standard Oil Company* stripped away the public facade of the nation's leading petroleum firm. Her accusations against Standard Oil Chairman Rockefeller, many of which were grossly untrue, nonetheless stirred up public attention.

Magazines such as McClure's struck out systematically at one industry after another. The captains of industry, used to getting their own way and having to answer to no one, were wrenched from their peaceful passivity and rolled out on the public carpet to answer for their sins. Journalistic shock stories soon led to a wave of sentiment for legislative reform.

As journalists and the public became more anxious, the government got more involved. Congress began passing laws telling business leaders what they could and couldn't do. Trust busting then became the order of the day. Conflicts between employers and employees began to break out, and newly organized labor unions came to the fore. The Socialist and Communist movements began to take off. Ironically, it was "a period when free enterprise reached a peak in American history, and yet at that very climax, the tide of public opinion was swelling up against business freedom, primarily because of the breakdown in communications between the businessman and the public."[8]

For a time, these men of inordinate wealth and power found themselves limited in their ability to defend themselves and their activities against the tidal wave of public condemnation. They simply did not know how to get through to the public effectively. To tell their side of the story, the business barons first tried using the lure of advertising to silence journalistic critics; they tried to buy off critics by paying for ads in their papers. It didn't work. Next, they paid publicity people, or press agents, to present their companies' positions. Often, these hired guns painted over the real problems and presented their client's view in the best possible light. The public saw through this approach.

Clearly, another method had to be discovered to get the public to at least consider the business point of view. Business leaders were discovering that a corporation might have capital, labor, and natural resources, yet be doomed to fail if it lacked intelligent management, particularly in the area of influencing public opinion. The best way to influence public opinion, as it turned out, was through honesty and candor. This simple truth was the key to the accomplishments of American history's first successful public relations counselor, Ivy Lee.

IVY LEE: A FATHER OF MODERN PUBLIC RELATIONS

Ivy Ledbetter Lee was a former Wall Street reporter who plunged into publicity work in 1903. Lee believed in neither Barnum's the-public-be-fooled approach nor Vanderbilt's the-public-be-damned philosophy. For Lee, the key to business acceptance and understanding was that the public be informed. Lee firmly believed that the only way business could answer its critics convincingly was to present its side honestly, accurately, and forcefully.[9] Instead of merely appeasing the public, Lee thought a company should strive to earn public confidence and good will. Sometimes this task meant looking further for mutual solutions. At other times, it even meant admitting that the company was wrong. Hired by the anthracite coal industry in 1906, Lee set forth his beliefs in a Declaration of Principles to newspaper editors:

> This is not a secret press bureau. All our work is done in the open. We aim to supply news. This is not an advertising agency; if you think any of our matter ought properly to go to your business office, do not use it. Our matter is accurate. Further details on any subject treated will be supplied promptly, and any editor will be assisted most cheerfully in verifying any statement of fact. . . . In brief, our plan is frankly and openly, on behalf of business concerns and public institutions, to supply to the press and public of the United States prompt and accurate information concerning subjects which are of value and interest.

In 1914, John D. Rockefeller, Jr., who headed one of the most maligned and misunderstood of America's wealthy families, hired Lee. As Lee's biographer Ray Eldon Hiebert has pointed out, Lee did less to change the Rockefellers' policies than to give them a public hearing.[10] For example, when the family was censured scathingly for its role in breaking up a strike at the Rockefeller-owned Colorado Fuel and Iron Company, the family hired a labor relations expert (at Lee's recommendation) to determine the causes of an incident that had led to several deaths. The result of this effort was the formation of a joint labor–management board to mediate all workers' grievances on wages, hours, and working conditions. Years later, Rockefeller admitted that the public relations outcome of the Colorado strike "was one of the most important things that ever happened to the Rockefeller family."[11]

In working for the Rockefellers, Lee tried to humanize them, to feature them in real-life situations such as playing golf, attending church, and celebrating birthdays. Simply, Lee's goal was to present the Rockefellers in terms that every individual could understand and appreciate. Years later, despite their critics, the family came to be known as one of the nation's outstanding sources of philanthropic support.

Ironically, even Ivy Lee could not escape the glare of public criticism. In the late 1920s, Lee was asked to serve as adviser to the parent company of the German Dye Trust, which, as it turned out, was an agent for the policies of Adolf Hitler. When Lee realized the nature of Hitler's intentions, he advised the Dye Trust cartel to work to alter Hitler's ill-conceived policies of restricting religious and press freedom. For his involvement with the Dye Trust, Lee was branded a traitor and dubbed "Poison Ivy" by members of Congress investigating un-American activities. The smears against him in the press rivaled the most vicious ones against the robber barons.[12]

Despite his unfortunate involvement with the Dye Trust, Ivy Lee is recognized as the individual who brought honesty and candor to public relations. Lee, more than anyone before him, transformed the field from a questionable pursuit (i.e., seeking positive publicity at any cost) into a professional discipline designed to win public confidence and trust through communications based on openness and truth.

THE GROWTH OF MODERN PUBLIC RELATIONS

Ivy Lee helped to open the gate. After he established the idea that firms have a responsibility to inform their publics, the practice began to grow in every sector of American society.

Government

During World War I, President Woodrow Wilson established the Creel Committee under journalist George Creel. Creel's group, composed of the nation's leading journalists, scholars, press agents, and other assorted press celebrities, mounted an impressive effort to mobilize public opinion in support of the war effort and to stimulate the sale of war bonds through Liberty Loan publicity drives. Not only did the war effort get a boost, but so did the field of public relations. The nation was mightily impressed with the potential power of publicity as a weapon to encourage national sentiment and support.

During World War II, the public relations field received an even bigger boost. With the Creel Committee as its precursor, the Office of War Information (OWI) was established to convey the message of the United States at home and abroad. Under the directorship of Elmer Davis, a veteran journalist, the OWI laid the foundations for the United States Information Agency as America's voice around the world.

World War II also saw a flurry of activity to sell war bonds, boost the morale of those at home, spur production in the nation's factories and offices, and, in general, support America's war effort as intensively as possible. By virtually every measure, this full-court public relations offensive was an unquestioned success.

The proliferation of public relations officers in World War II led to a growth in the number of practitioners during the peace that followed. One reason companies saw the need to have public relations professionals to "speak up" for them was the more combative attitude of President Harry Truman toward many of the country's largest institutions. For example, in a memorable address over radio and television on April 8, 1952, President Truman announced that, as a result of a union wage dispute, "the government would take over the steel plants." The seizure of the steel mills touched off a series of historic events that reached into Congress and the Supreme Court and stimulated a massive public relations campaign, the likes of which had rarely been seen outside the government.

Counseling

The nation's first public relations firm, the Publicity Bureau, was founded in Boston in 1900 and specialized in general press agentry. The first Washington, DC, agency was begun in 1902 by William Wolff Smith, a former correspondent for the *New York Sun* and the *Cincinnati Inquirer*. Two years later, Ivy Lee joined with George Parker to begin a public relations agency that was later dissolved. Lee reestablished the agency in New York in 1919 and brought in T. J. Ross as a partner.

John W. Hill entered public relations in 1927 after a dozen years as a journalist. Together with William Knowlton, Hill founded Hill & Knowlton, Inc., in Cleveland. Hill soon moved East, and Knowlton dropped out of the firm. However, the agency quickly became one of the largest public relations operations in the world, with 1,050 employees in 20 countries and 20 U.S. cities. Hill stayed active in the firm for half a century and mused about the field's beginnings:

> In 1927, public relations was just in its infancy. Think of the contrast of the present with fifty years ago. Less than a handful of counseling firms anywhere in the world and barely a handful of practitioners tucked away and lost in the offices of a very few large corporations—far removed from the executive suite.[13]

In addition to Hill, Creel Committee Associate Chairman Carl Byoir launched his own public relations counseling firm in 1930. Ironically, 56 years later, Byoir's firm, Carl Byoir & Associates, merged with Hill & Knowlton to become the largest public relations company in the world.

Besides Byoir and Hill, Earl Newsom and Pendleton Dudley also founded early firms. Newsom, who began Newsom & Company in 1935, generally limited his public relations practice to counseling companies like Ford, General Motors, and Jersey Standard. In his otherwise critical treatment of public relations, *The Image Merchants*, author Irwin Ross paid tribute to Newsom's success:

> The goal of a good many public relations men is someday to attain the lonely eminence of Earl Newsom. His fees are high; his clients include some of the most august names in the corporate roster; and his work involves pure "consultation."[14]

Another early counselor, Harold Burson, emphasized marketing-oriented public relations, "primarily concerned with helping clients sell their goods and services, maintain a favorable market for their stock, and foster harmonious relations with employees."[15] Today, Burson-Marsteller ranks as the world's largest public relations agency.

In the 1990s, the counseling business saw the emergence of international super agencies. Hill & Knowlton, Burson-Marsteller, and Shandwick all boasted worldwide networks with thousands of employees linked to serve clients with communications services throughout the world. As the decade draws to an end, a proliferation of Internet public relations firms ushered the counseling end of the business into a new century.

Corporations

Problems in the perception of corporations and their leaders dissipated in the United States after World War II. Opinion polls of that period ranked business as high in public esteem. People were back at work, and business was back in style.

Smart companies—General Electric, General Motors, American Telephone & Telegraph (AT&T), for example—worked hard to preserve their good names through both words and actions. Arthur W. Page became AT&T's first public relations vice president in 1927. Page was a pacesetter, helping to maintain AT&T's reputation as a prudent and proper corporate citizen. Indeed, Page's five principles of successful corporate public relations are as relevant now as they were in the 1930s:

1. To make sure management thoughtfully analyzes its overall relation to the public
2. To create a system for informing all employees about the firm's general policies and practices
3. To create a system giving contact employees (those having direct dealings with the public) the knowledge needed to be reasonable and polite to the public
4. To create a system drawing employee and public questions and criticism back up through the organization to management
5. To ensure frankness in telling the public about the company's actions.[16]

Paul Garrett was another person who felt the need to be responsive to the public's wishes. A former news reporter, he became the first director of public relations for General Motors in 1931. Garrett once reportedly explained that the essence of his job was to convince the public that the powerful auto company deserved trust, that is, "to make a billion-dollar company seem small."

Education

One public relations pioneer who began as a publicist in 1913 was Edward L. Bernays, nephew of Sigmund Freud and author of the landmark book *Crystallizing Public Opinion* (see page 45). Bernays was a giant in the public relations field for nearly the entire century. In addition to contributing as much to the field as any other professional in its history, Bernays was a true public relations scholar. He taught the first course in public relations in 1923. Bernays's seminal writings in the field were among the first to disassociate public relations from press agentry or publicity work. As Bernays wrote later:

> At first we called our activity "publicity direction." We intended to give advice to clients on how to direct their actions to get public visibility for them. But within a year we changed the service and its name to "counsel on public relations." We recognized that all actions of a client that impinged on the public needed counsel. Public visibility of a client for one action might be vitiated by another action not in the public interest.[17]

Historian Eric Goldman credited Bernays with "[moving] along with the most advanced trends in the public relations field, thinking with, around, and ahead of them."[18]

Bernays was also at least indirectly responsible for encouraging the development of another public relations phenomenon that would take on added impetus in the 1990s—the emergence of women in the field. Bernays's associate (and later, wife), Doris E. Fleischman, helped edit a leaflet, called *Contact*, that helped American leaders understand the underpinnings of the new profession Bernays represented. Fleischman's important assistance in spreading the Bernays doctrine was an early contribution to a field that, in the 1990s, showed women clearly in the majority among public relations professionals.

PUBLIC RELATIONS COMES OF AGE

As noted earlier, public relations really came of age as a result of the confluence of four general factors in our society: (1) the growth of large institutions and their sense of responsibility to the public; (2) the increased changes, conflicts, and confrontations among interest groups in society; (3) the heightened awareness of people brought about by increasingly sophisticated communications technology everywhere; and (4) the spread of global democracy.

Growth of Large Institutions

Ironically, the public relations profession received perhaps its most important thrust when business confidence suffered its most severe setback. The economic and social upheaval caused by the Great Depression of the 1930s provided the impetus for corporations to seek public support by telling their stories. Public relations departments sprang up in scores of major companies, among them Bendix, Borden, Eastman Kodak, Eli Lilly, Ford, General Motors, Standard Oil, Pan American, and U.S. Steel. The role that public relations played in helping regain post-Depression public trust in big business helped project the field into the relatively strong position it enjoyed during World War II.

The Truman years marked a challenging period for public relations, with government questioning the integrity of large business corporations. The ebbing and flowing conflict between government and business is unique to America. In other nations—Japan and Germany most prominently—government and business work more in concert to achieve common goals. In the United States, many businesses, both large and small, complain that government overregulation frustrates their ability to prosper. Businesses of every size have recognized that aggressively communicating corporate products and positions can help win public receptivity and support and ward off government intrusion.

Change, Conflict, and Confrontation

Disenchantment with big institutions peaked in the 1960s. The conflicts during the early part of the decade between private economic institutions—especially large corporations—and various disenfranchised elements of society arose from long-standing grievances. As one commentator put it: "Their rebellion was born out of the desperation of those who had nothing to lose. Issues were seen as black or white, groups as villainous or virtuous, causes as holy or satanic, and leaders as saints or charlatans."[19]

The social and political upheavals of the 1960s dramatically affected many areas, including the practice of public relations. The Vietnam War fractured society. Ralph Nader began to look pointedly at the inadequacies of the automobile industry. Women, long denied equal rights in the workplace and elsewhere, began to mobilize into activist groups such as the National Organization of Women (NOW). Environmentalists, worried about threats to the land and water by business expansion, began to support groups such as the Sierra Club. Minorities, particularly blacks and Hispanics, began to petition and protest for their rights. Homo-

A QUESTION OF ETHICS

WATERGATE: A BLACK EYE FOR PUBLIC RELATIONS

On August 8, 1974, President Richard M. Nixon resigned in disgrace and humiliation. His administration had been tarnished by illegal wiretapping, illegal surveillance, burglary, and unlawful use of the law. The president and his men were toppled by the most profound political scandal in the nation's history, which grew out of a series of break-ins at the Democratic national headquarters in a Washington, DC, apartment building named Watergate.

Figure 2–2 Watergate's dubious cast of characters stimulated this takeoff on the promotional work done for the movie *That's Entertainment*.

Nixon and his advisers steadfastly refused, throughout the long and arduous—and publicly televised—Watergate crisis, to acknowledge any role in the break-in.

President Nixon's response, in particular, was incredible in its obstinacy.

- He ordered preparation of an "Enemies List" of journalists who had written negatively about Watergate.

■ He discussed lying about the reasons for the Watergate break-in and another break-in at the office of the psychiatrist Daniel Ellsberg, an administration enemy who had leaked secret Pentagon papers to *The New York Times*.

■ He fired Archibald Cox, the special prosecutor appointed to get to the bottom of Watergate (Figure 2–2).

■ Attorney General Elliott Richardson refused to carry out Nixon's order, and he, himself, resigned. And Richardson's deputy, William Ruckelshaus, also refused to carry out the order, and Nixon fired him.

■ Nixon's relationship with the media, never good, deteriorated to the point of no return. At one heated press conference, he responded pointedly to a question posed by CBS correspondent Dan Rather, "I am not a crook."

Ultimately, as a nation painfully watched on in horror, Nixon's aides appeared at a televised Senate hearing and finally admitted to their role in the break-ins and their subsequent efforts to "cover up."

Nixon's resignation was unprecedented in the nation's history. And many blamed his downfall on one thing—an overriding concern about public relations.

Observers argued that the president and his advisers were so consumed with covering up the facts—with public relations—that they orchestrated their own downfall. In point of fact, what Nixon and his henchmen wrought was the exact opposite of proper public relations.

Nonetheless, no event in recent history has given the practice of public relations a blacker eye than Watergate.

---

sexuals, senior citizens, birth control advocates, and social activists of every kind began to challenge the legitimacy of large institutions. Not since the days of the robber barons had large institutions so desperately needed professional communications help.

Heightened Public Awareness

The 1970s and 1980s brought a partial resolution of these problems. Many of the solutions came from the government in the form of affirmative action guidelines, senior citizen programs, consumer and environmental protection acts and agencies, aids to education, and myriad other laws and statutes.

Business began to contribute to charities. Managers began to consider community relations a first-line responsibility. The general policy of corporations confronting their adversaries was abandoned. In its place, most large companies adopted a policy of conciliation and compromise.

This new policy of social responsibility continued into the 1990s. Corporations came to realize that their reputations are a valuable asset to be protected, conserved, defended, nurtured, and enhanced at all times. In truth, institutions in the 1990s had little choice but to get along with their publics.

By 1994, 93 million American homes had television, with 61 percent of U.S. homes wired for cable.

As the world moves into the twenty-first century, the potential of two-way communications has arrived. Not only have cable, satellite, fax, computer, and videodisc technologies revolutionized the information transmission and receiving process, but the emergence of cyberspace and the Internet and the World Wide Web promise to radically intensify the spread of communications even further in the new millennium.

As a result of all this communication, publics have become much more segmented, specialized, and sophisticated. Public relations professionals have had to discard many of the traditional methods used to reach and influence these publics. Today organizations face the new reality of communicating with their key publics instantaneously, real time, all the time. Optimizing communications in this environment is a daunting public relations challenge.

Global Democracy in the Twenty-First Century

As the world moves into the twenty-first century, democracy has run rampant. The Berlin Wall's destruction was transmitted live around the world. So was the dissolution of the Union of Soviet Socialist Republics. In 1993, two longtime archenemies, Nelson Mandela and Nicholas DeKlerck, stood together to share the Nobel Peace Prize as free elections were held in South Africa. Three years later, two equally ardent enemies, Israeli leader Benjamin Netanyahu and Palestinian leader Yassir Arafat also came together to hammer out a peace proposal for their perpetually warring lands. Today, with the world now truly "safe for democracy," the public relations challenge has grown in intensity.

PUBLIC RELATIONS EDUCATION

As the practice of public relations has developed, so too has the growth of public relations education. In 1951, 12 schools offered major programs in public relations. Today well in excess of 200 journalism or communication programs offer concentrated study in public relations, with nearly 300 others offering at least one course dealing with the profession. Although few data are available on public relations programs in business schools, the number is increasing, especially those related to marketing.

As the debate continues about where public relations education should appropriately be housed—either in business or journalism schools—the best answer is that both should offer public relations courses.[20] In business, the practice of public relations has become an integral part of the way companies operate. Therefore, business students should be exposed to the discipline's underpinnings and practical aspects before they enter the corporate world. In journalism, with upwards of 70 percent of daily newspaper copy emanating from public relations-generated releases, journalists, too, should know what public relations is all about before they graduate. Wherever it is housed, the profession's role as an academic pursuit has continued to gain strength. This educational dimension has, in turn, contributed to the new respect accorded public relations in modern society.

SUMMARY

Today public relations is big, worldwide business.

- The Public Relations Society of America, organized in 1947, boasts a growing membership of 18,500 in 107 chapters nationwide.

- The Public Relations Student Society of America, formed in 1968 to facilitate communications between students interested in the field and public relations professionals, has 5,000 student members at 180 colleges and universities.
- More than 5,400 U.S. companies have public relations departments.
- Close to 6,000 public relations agencies exist in the United States, some billing hundreds of millions of dollars per year.
- More than 500 trade associations have public relations departments.
- Top communications executives at major companies and agencies draw six-figure salaries.

The scope of modern public relations practice is vast. Press relations, web relations, employee communications, public relations counseling and research, local community relations, audiovisual communications, contributions, and numerous other diverse activities fall under the public relations umbrella. Because of this broad range of functions, many public relations practitioners today seem preoccupied with the proper title for their calling—public relations, external affairs, corporate communications, public affairs, corporate relations, ad infinitum. They argue that the range of activities involved offers no hope that people will understand what the pursuit involves unless an umbrella term is used.[21]

Practitioners also worry that as public relations becomes more prominent, its function and those who purportedly practice it will be subject to increasingly intense public scrutiny. Greater minority membership in the field, particularly with respect to African Americans, is a recurring objective.[22] Then too, the high-profile scandals of Speaker of the House Newt Gingrich, presidential policy advisor Dick Morris, and even President Bill Clinton have cast a pall over the profession—just as Watergate did two decades earlier.

Despite these concerns, the practice of public relations enters the twenty-first century as a potent, persuasive force in society. Clearly, the public relations field today—whatever it is called and by whomever it is practiced—is in the spotlight. Its senior-most officers serve as members of the management committees that set policy for our great organizations.[23] Its professionals command higher salaries. Its counselors command increased respect. And its practice is taught in increasing numbers, not only in American colleges and universities but around the world.

With close to 200,000 men and women in the United States alone practicing public relations in some form, the field has become solidly entrenched as an important, influential, and professional component of our society.

DISCUSSION STARTERS

1. What societal factors have influenced the spread of public relations?
2. Why do public relations professionals think of P. T. Barnum as a mixed blessing?
3. What is the significance to the practice of public relations of American revolutionary hero Samuel Adams?
4. What did the robber barons and muckrakers have to do with the development of public relations?
5. Why are Ivy Lee and Edward Bernays considered two of the fathers of public relations?
6. What impact did the Creel Committee and the Office of War Information have on the development of public relations?

7. What was the significance of Arthur Page to the development of corporate public relations?
8. Identify and discuss the significance of some of the earliest public relations counselors.
9. What are some of the yardsticks indicating that public relations has arrived in the latter stages of the twentieth century?
10. What are some of the issues that confront public relations in the twenty-first century?

NOTES

1. Scott M. Cutlip, Allen H. Center, and Glen M. Broom, *Effective Public Relations*, 6th ed. (Upper Saddle River, NJ: Prentice Hall, 1985): 23.
2. James D. Sodt, "Why Would I Represent the Serbs," *The Public Relations Strategist* (Spring 1995): 32.
3. Edward L. Bernays, speech at the University of Florida Public Relations Symposium, Gainesville, FL, February 1, 1984.
4. Paul Swift, "The Antecedents," *Public Relations Quarterly* (Summer 1996): 6.
5. Frank Winston Wylie, "Book Reviews," *Public Relations Review* (Fall 1996): 312.
6. Harold Burson, speech at Utica College of Syracuse University, Utica, NY, March 5, 1987.
7. "Film Writers Complain About PR Pressure," *Jack O'Dwyer's Newsletter*, November 27, 1996, 3.
8. Ray Eldon Hiebert, *Courtier to the Crowd: The Story of Ivy L. Lee and the Development of Public Relations* (Ames: Iowa State University Press, 1966).
9. Rex Harlow, "A Public Relations Historian Recalls the First Days," *Public Relations Review* (Summer 1981): 39–40.
10. Cited in Sherman Morse, "An Awakening in Wall Street," *American Magazine* 62 (September 1906): 460.
11. Hiebert, loc. cit.
12. Cited in Alvin Moscow, *The Rockefeller Inheritance* (Garden City, NY: Doubleday, 1977), 23.
13. John W. Hill, *The Making of a Public Relations Man* (New York: David McKay, 1963), 69.
14. Irwin Ross, *The Image Merchants* (Garden City, NY: Doubleday, 1959), 85.
15. Burson, loc. cit.
16. Cited in Noel L. Griese, "The Employee Communications Philosophy of Arthur W. Page," *Public Relations Quarterly* (Winter 1977): 8–12.
17. Edward L. Bernays, "Bernays' 62 Years in Public Relations," *Public Relations Quarterly* (Fall 1981): 8.
18. David L. Lewis, "The Outstanding PR Professionals," *Public Relations Journal* (October 1970): 84.
19. James E. Grunig, "Teaching Public Relations in the Future," *Public Relations Review* (Spring 1989): 16.
20. J. David Pincus, "Changing How Future Managers 'View' Us," *The Public Relations Strategist* (Spring 1997).
21. "Diverse Titles Splinter Image of Field: Report of PRSA's Special Committee on Terminology," *Public Relations Reporter* (April 20, 1987): Tips & Tactics.

TOP OF THE SHELF

SCOTT M. CUTLIP

THE UNSEEN POWER—PUBLIC RELATIONS, A HISTORY

HILLSDALE, NJ: LAWRENCE ERLBAUM ASSOCIATES, 1994

Scott Cutlip is the public relations field's most eminent historian, and this is the field's most eminent historical treatise.

Cutlip traces the roots of public relations practice through the sermons of Georgia preacher John Wesley to the efforts of Massachusetts residents to raise money for their new Harvard College to the more sophisticated techniques of Sam Adams and his colleagues to help mobilize their countrymen to create a new country.

Cutlip's history is particularly rich in chronicling the work of the field's pioneers, Ivy Lee and Edward Bernays, and its latter-day developers in corporations and agencies who paved the way for today's modern practice. The author recounts tales of many of the field's most colorful characters and many of the field's ugliest episodes, from Exxon's disastrous response to the Valdez oil spill to Dow Corning's questionable response to its silicone gel breast implant problem.

Cutlip's 808 pages may not be easy sledding, but for a student interested in the antecedents of today's practice of public relations, few books are as rich in historical flavor.

22. Marilyn Kern-Foxworth, "Status and Roles of Minority PR Practitioners," *Public Relations Review* (Fall 1989): 39.
23. Harold Burson, "Introduction: The Maturation of Public Relations," *Journal of Corporate Public Relations-Northwestern University* (1994–1995): 6.

SUGGESTED READINGS

Arnold, James E. and Consultants. *Issues and Trends in the 1990's*. PRSA Counselors Academy, 1992.

Bernays, Edward L. *Crystallizing Public Opinion*, New York: Liveright Publishing Corp., 1961.

Bernays, Edward L. *The Later Years: PR Insights, 1956–1958*. Rhinebeck, NY: H & M, 1987.

Burson, Harold. "A Decent Respect to the Opinion of Mankind." Speech delivered at the Raymond Simon Institute for Public Relations (Burson-Marsteller, 866 Third Ave., New York, NY 10022), March 5, 1987. This speech highlights public relations activities that have influenced the United States from colonial times to the present day.

Cutlip, Scott M. *Public Relations History from the 17th to the 20th Century*. Hillsdale, NJ: Lawrence Erlbaum Associates, Inc., 1995. A companion work to the "Top of the Shelf" inclusion.

International Encyclopedia of Communications (4 vols.). New York: Oxford University Press, 1989.

Newsom, Doug, Alan Scott, and Judy Van Slyke Turk. *This Is PR: The Realities of Public Relations*, 5th ed. Belmont, CA: Wadsworth, 1993.

Pratte, Paul Alfred. *Gods Within the Machine.* Westport, CT: Praeger Publishers, 1995. Chronicles the history of the American Society of Newspaper Editors and its role in developing a free press.

Public Relations News (1201 Seven Locks Road, Potomac, MD 61130). Weekly.

Public Relations Quarterly (P.O. Box 311, Rhinebeck, NY 12572).

Public Relations Review (10606 Mantz Rd., Silver Spring, MD 20903).

PR Reporter (P.O. Box 600, Exeter, NH 03833-0600). Weekly.

Public Relations Strategist (PRSA, 33 Irving Place, New York, NY 10003). Monthly.

CASE STUDY

EXXON CORPORATION'S BAD GOOD FRIDAY

In the history of public relations practice, few events have been handled as questionably, received as much global notoriety, and had such far-reaching implications on the profession as those involving the Exxon Corporation on a Friday morning in 1989.

At 8:30 A.M. on March 24, 1989—Good Friday, no less—Lawrence G. Rawl, chairman and chief executive of the Exxon Corporation, one of the world's largest companies, was in his kitchen sipping coffee when the phone rang.

"What happened? Did it lose an engine? Break a rudder?" Rawl asked the caller.

"What happened" was that an Exxon tanker had run aground and was dumping gummy crude oil into the frigid waters of Prince William Sound, just outside the harbor of Valdez, Alaska.

What was about to happen to Mr. Rawl and his company—and to the environment—was arguably the worst environmental disaster in the history of the United States.

The facts, painfully portrayed in media across the country, were these: The Exxon Valdez, a 978-foot tanker, piloted by a captain who was later revealed to be legally drunk, ran aground on a reef 25 miles southwest of the port of Valdez. The resulting rupture caused a spill of 250,000 barrels, the largest spill ever in North America, affecting 1,300 square miles of water, damaging some 600 miles of coastline, and murdering as many as 4,000 Alaskan sea otters. The disaster also enshrined the name of Exxon in the all-time Public Relations Hall of Shame.

Exxon's dilemma broke down roughly into five general categories.

To Go or Not to Go

The first problem that confronted Exxon and its top management after news of the Good Friday spill had broken was whether Chairman Rawl should personally fly to Prince William Sound to demonstrate the company's concern. This was what Union Carbide chairman, Warren Anderson, did when his company suffered a devastating industrial explosion in Bhopal, India. It was also what Ashland Oil's chairman, John R. Hall, did when his company suffered an oil spill earlier in 1989.

If Rawl went to Alaska, the reasoning went, he might have been able to reassure the public that the people who run Exxon acknowledged their misdeed and would make amends. What could be a better show of concern than the chairman flying to the local scene of the tragedy?

On the other hand, a consensus of executives around Rawl argued that he should remain in New York. "What are you going to do?" they asked. "We've already said we've done it, we're going to pay for it, and we're responsible for it." Rawl's more effective role, said these advisers, was right there at Exxon headquarters in Manhattan.

In the end, the latter view triumphed. Rawl didn't go to Alaska. He left the cleanup in "capable hands" and sent a succession of lower-ranking executives to Alaska to deal with the spill. As he summarized in an interview one year after the Prince William Sound nightmare, "We had concluded that there was simply too much for me to coordinate from New York. It wouldn't have made any difference if I showed up and made a speech in the town forum. I wasn't going to spend the summer there; I had other things to do."

Rawl's failure to fly immediately to Valdez struck some as shortsighted. Said one media consultant, "The chairman should have been up there walking in the oil and picking up dead birds."

Where to Establish Media Central

The second dilemma that confronted Exxon was where to establish its media center.

This decision started, correctly enough, with Exxon senior managers concluding that the impact of the spill was so great that news organizations should be kept informed as events unfolded. Exxon, correctly, wanted to take charge of the news flow and give the public, through the news media, a credible, concerned, and wholly committed corporate response.

It decided that the best place to do this would be in Valdez, Alaska, itself. "Just about every news organization worth its salt had representatives in Valdez," said Exxon's publicity chief. "But in retrospect, we should have sent live broadcasts of news conferences to several points around the country."

The problem was that Valdez was a remote Alaskan town with limited communications operations. This complicated the ability of Exxon to disseminate information quickly. As *Oil & Gas Journal* stated later: "Exxon did not update its media relations people elsewhere in the world. It told reporters it was Valdez or nothing."

Additionally, there was a four hour time difference between Valdez and New York. Consequently, "Exxon statements were erratic and contradictory," said the publisher of another oil bulletin. The phone lines to Valdez quickly became jammed, and even Rawl couldn't find a knowledgeable official to brief him. That left news organizations responsible for keeping the public informed cut off from Exxon information during the early part of the crisis. Because news conferences took place at unsuitable viewing hours for television networks and too late for many morning newspapers, predictable accusations of an Exxon "cover-up" resulted. Said one Exxon official about the decision to put the center in Valdez, "It didn't work."

Rapidity of Response

A cardinal rule in any crisis is: Keep ahead of the information flow. Try not to let events get ahead of you. Keep in front of the information curve. Here Exxon had serious problems.

First, it took Chairman Rawl a full week to make any public comment on the spill. When he did, it was to blame others: The U.S. Coast Guard and Alaskan officials were "holding up" his company's efforts to clean up the spill. But Rawl's words were too little, too late. The impression persisted that, in light of the delay in admitting responsibility, Exxon was not responding vigorously enough.

A full 10 days after the crisis, Exxon placed an advertisement in 166 newspapers. To some readers, the ad seemed self-serving and failed to address the many pointed questions raised about Exxon's conduct.

"It seems the company was a bit too relaxed in its capabilities," offered the president of the Public Relations Society of America. Meanwhile, one group that wasn't relaxed was the Alaska state legislature, which enacted a tax increase on oil from the North Slope fields within weeks of the Exxon spill. Congressional committees in Washington moved just as quickly to increase liability limits and potential compensation for oil-spill damage and to increase the money available through the industry-financed Offshore Oil Pollution Compensation Fund.

When Exxon hesitated, its opponents seized the initiative. Concluded another public relations executive, "They lost the battle in the first 48 hours."

How High the Profile

Exxon's response in the face of this most challenging crisis in its history was, to put it mildly, muted.

From an operations and logistics viewpoint, Exxon did a good job. The company immediately set up animal rescue projects, launched a major cleanup effort, and agreed to pick up a substantial percentage of the cost. But it made the mistake of downplaying the crisis in public.

Exxon's public statements sometimes contradicted information from other sources. At one point, an Exxon spokesman said that damage from the oil spill would be minimal. Others watching the industry said the damage was likely to be substantial.

Chairman Rawl, an otherwise blunt and outspoken CEO, seemed defensive and argumentative in his public comments. In one particularly disastrous personal appearance on *CBS Morning News*, Rawl glared at interviewer Kathleen Sullivan and snapped: "I can't give you details of our cleanup plan. It's thick and complicated. And I haven't had a chance to read it yet. The CEO of a major company doesn't have time to read every plan."

Exxon's attempts to calm the public also were criticized. Its ad drew fire for not expressing enough concern. It hired an outside firm to do a series of video news releases to show how the company was cleaning up the spill. At an estimated cost of more than $3 million, a 13-minute tape was shown at the corporation's annual meeting. The video, called *Progress in Alaska*, attracted intense criticism from those attending the conference, as well as from the press. The film implied, argued *Boston Globe* reporter Robert Lenzner, that "The brutal scenes of damage to Alaskan waters seen nightly on television news programs were false." *USA Today* called the tape "Exxon's worst move of the day." When the consultant who devised the video wrote an op-ed article in *The New York Times* defending Exxon's approach in Alaska, the Alaskan representative to the National Wildlife Federation responded with a blistering letter to the editor, noting that the consultant omitted in his article that the spill had resulted in the death of more than 15,000 sea birds and numerous otters and eagles.

Exxon then added an environmental expert to its board of directors, but only after pension funds, which control a large chunk of its stock, demanded such a response.

Dealing with the Aftermath

Finally, Exxon was forced to deal with all the implications of what its tanker had wrought in Valdez.

The company became embroiled in controversy when Exxon USA sent a $30,000 contribution to the Alaska Public Radio Network, which covered the crisis on a daily basis. The network, sniffing "conflict of interest," flatly turned down Exxon's attempted largesse. Subsequently, a special appropriations bill was introduced in the Alaskan legislature to forward an identical amount to Alaska Public Radio.

The accident and the company's reaction to it also had consequences for the oil industry. Plans to expand drilling into the Alaskan National Wildlife Refuge were shelved by Congress, and members called for new laws increasing federal involvement in oil spills.

The company's employees, too, felt confused, embarrassed, and betrayed. Summarizing the prevailing mood at the company, one Exxon worker said, "Whenever I travel now, I feel like I have a target painted on my chest."

In 1994, more than five years after the tanker ran aground, Exxon went to court in Anchorage to defend itself against $15 million in civil claims. Early in 1996, the company still battled its past demons, as the company and its new chairman, Lee R. Raymond, were accused of making "side deals" with plaintiffs in the case—even though they denied, under oath, that they had done so.

Finally, in November 1996, seven years after the Exxon Valdez ran aground, a weary Exxon announced to the world that it was closing the books on its unforgettable disaster. Total cost to Exxon: $2.5 billion.

The lessons of the Exxon Valdez's Good Friday oil spill would not soon be forgotten by corporate managers. The episode, predicted one, "will become a textbook example of what not to do when an unexpected crisis thrusts a company into the limelight." Said another, Exxon's response "is fast becoming the stuff of PR legend."

QUESTIONS

1. What would you have recommended Chairman Rawl do upon learning of the Prince William Sound oil spill?
2. How would you have handled the media in this case?
3. What would have been your "timing" in terms of public relations responses in this case?
4. What would be your overall public relations strategy—i.e., aggressive, low-key, etc.—if you were Exxon's public relations director?
5. Do you think this case will ever qualify as a "textbook example" of what not to do in a crisis?

For further information about the Exxon Valdez case, see Richard Behar, "Exxon Strikes Back," *Time* (26 March, 1990): 62–63; Claudia H. Deutsch, "The Giant with a Black Eye," *The New York Times*, 2 April 1989, B1–4; E. Bruce Harrison, with Tom Prugh, "Assessing the Damage," *Public Relations Journal* (October 1989): 40–45; John Holusha, "Exxon's Public-Relations Problem," *The New York Times*, 21 April 1989, D1–4; Peter Nulty, "Exxon's Problem: Not What You Think," *Fortune* (April 23, 1990): 202–204; James Lukaszewski, "How Vulnerable Are You? The Lessons from Valdez," *Public Relations Quarterly* (Fall 1989): 5–6; Phillip M. Perry, "Exxon Falters in PR Effort Following Alaskan Oil Spill," *O'Dwyer's PR Services Report*, (July 1989): 1;16–22; Allanna Sullivan, "Rawl Wishes He'd Visited Valdez Sooner," *The Wall Street Journal*, 30 June 1989, B7; Joseph B. Treaster, "With Insurers' Payment, Exxon Says Valdez Case is Ended," *The New York Times* (1 November 1996): B2; and Paul Wiseman, "Firm Finds Valdez Oil Fowls Image," *USA Today* (26 April 1990): B1.

EDWARD L. BERNAYS

Edward L. Bernays, who died in 1995 at the age of 103, was a public relations patriarch. A nephew of Sigmund Freud, Bernays pioneered the application of the social sciences to public relations. In partnership with his late wife, he advised presidents of the United States, industrial leaders, and legendary figures from Enrico Caruso to Eleanor Roosevelt. This interview was conducted with the legendary counselor in his ninety-eighth year.

WHEN YOU TAUGHT THE FIRST PUBLIC RELATIONS CLASS, DID YOU EVER ENVISION THE FIELD GROWING TO ITS PRESENT STATURE?

I gave the first course in public relations after *Crystallizing Public Opinion* was published in 1923. I decided that one way to give the term "counsel on public relations" status was to lecture at a university on the principles, practices, and ethics of the new vocation. New York University was willing to accept my offer to do so. But I never envisioned at that time that the vocation would spread throughout the United States and then throughout the free world.

WHAT WERE THE OBJECTIVES OF THAT FIRST PUBLIC RELATIONS COURSE?

The objectives were to give status to the new vocation. Many people still believed the term counsel on public relations was a euphemism for publicity man, press agent, flack. Even H. L. Mencken, in his book on the American language, ranked it as such. But in his Supplement to the American Language, published some years later, he changed his viewpoint and used my definition of the term.

WHAT ARE THE MOST SIGNIFICANT FACTORS THAT HAVE LED TO THE RISE IN PUBLIC RELATIONS PRACTICE?

The most significant factor is the rise in people power and its recognition by leaders. Theodore Roosevelt helped bring this about with his Square Deal. Woodrow Wilson helped with his New Freedom, and so did Franklin Delano Roosevelt with his New Deal. And this tradition was continued as time went on.

DO YOU HAVE ANY GRIPES WITH THE WAY PUBLIC RELATIONS IS PRACTICED TODAY?

I certainly do. The meanings of words in the United States have the stability of soap bubbles. Unless words are defined as to their meaning by law, as in the case of professions—for instance, law, medicine, architecture—they are in the public domain. Anyone can use them. Recently, I received a letter from a model agency offering to supply me with a "public relations representative" for my next trade fair at which we might exhibit our client's products. Today, any plumber or car salesman or unethical character can call himself or herself a public relations practitioner. Many who call themselves public relations practitioners have no education, training, or knowledge of what the field is. And the public equally has little understanding of the meaning of the two words. Until licensing and registration are introduced, this will continue to be the situation.

WHAT PLEASES YOU MOST ABOUT CURRENT PUBLIC RELATIONS PRACTICE?

What pleases me most is that there are, indeed, practitioners who regard their activity as a profession, an art applied to a science, in which the public interest, and not pecuniary motivation, is the primary consideration; and also that outstanding leaders in society are grasping the meaning and significance of the activity.

HOW WOULD YOU COMPARE THE CALIBER OF TODAY'S PUBLIC RELATIONS PRACTITIONER WITH THAT OF THE PRACTITIONER OF THE PAST?

The practitioner today has more education in his subject. But, unfortunately, education for public relations varies with the institution where it is being conducted. This is due to the lack of a standard definition. Many institutions of higher learning think public relations activity consists of skillful writing of press releases and teach their students accordingly. This is, of course, not true. Public relations activity is applied social science to the social attitudes or actions of employers or clients.

WHERE DO YOU THINK PUBLIC RELATIONS WILL BE 20 YEARS FROM NOW?

It is difficult to appraise where public relations will be 20 years from now. I don't like the tendency of advertising agencies gobbling up large public relations organizations. That is like surgical instrument manufacturers gobbling up surgical medical colleges or law book publishers gobbling up law colleges. However, if licensing and registration take place, then the vocation is assured a long lifetime, as long as democracy's.

CHAPTER THREE

Public Opinion

PUBLIC OPINION IS AN ELUSIVE AND FRAGILE commodity. And because it is, the practice of public relations will be around forever.

Doubt that?

Consider the following from the annals of just one year, 1996.

- America West Airlines turned around a plane loaded with passengers to pick up the California Angels baseball team, whose Arizona charter flight was canceled. The passengers were summarily dumped; the ballplayers chauffeured skyward.
- Southwest Elementary School of Lexington, North Carolina, attracted nationwide publicity when it suspended a first grade boy for kissing a girl classmate.
- Marge Schott, owner of baseball's Cincinnati Reds, who earlier was suspended from baseball for using racist language, expressed disappointment over cancellation of the opening day game after umpire John Mc-Sherry collapsed and died of a heart attack in the first inning.
- Baltimore Oriole second baseman Roberto Alomar spit in the face of another umpire and then suggested that the arbiter hadn't been the same since the death of his young son to a rare disease.
- American Society of Composers, Authors, and Publishers distributed a letter to summer camps, including the Girl Scouts, informing them that a fee was required to use any of its members' copyrighted songs.
- *Newsweek* columnist Joe Klein was exposed as the anonymous author of the best-selling roman à clef Bill Clinton expose, *Primary Colors*, even though the writer had steadfastly denied in print—including in his own magazine—that he was "Anonymous."
- WPIX-FM in Latham, New York, received national attention for revealing the identity of its "Ugliest Bride," triggering a $300,000 lawsuit from the humiliated woman.[1]

And these, as tennis star Andre Agassi once said, were but "scratching the iceberg."

The point is not that 1996 was a bad year for baseball people, authors, kissing first graders and brides, but rather that individuals and organizations today—both large and small—need assistance in dealing with the delicate commodity of public opinion.

On the other hand, there is Michael Jordan. Mr. Jordan, the most widely recognized athlete in the world, is perhaps as skillful at managing his public image as any individual on the planet. In recent years, Mr. Jordan has suffered the tragic murder of his father, an ill-fated attempt at playing professional baseball, and assorted accusations of gambling and selfishness. Nonetheless, the revered basketball star continues to enjoy a sky high image (Figure 3-1).

Meanwhile, Jordan's teammate, Dennis Rodman, enjoys an equally well-known prominence, but his is as negative as Jordan's is pure (Figure 3–2).

Such are the peculiarities of public opinion.

Usually it's difficult to move people toward a strong opinion on anything. It's even harder to move them away from an opinion once they reach it. Recent research, in fact, indicates that mass media appeals may have little immediate effect on influencing public opinion.

Nonetheless, the heart of public relations work lies in attempting to affect the public opinion process. Most public relations programs are designed either to (1) persuade people to change their opinion on an issue, product, or organization, (2) crystallize uninformed or undeveloped opinions, or (3) reinforce existing opinions.

So public relations professionals must understand how public opinion is formed, how it evolves from people's attitudes, and how it is influenced by communication. This chapter discusses attitude formation and change and public opinion creation and persuasion.

Figure 3–1   No other individual in the waning years of the twentieth century came close to rivaling the popular appeal of basketball star/marketing conglomerate Michael Jordan. When Jordan temporarily retired from basketball in 1993, people everywhere still yearned to "be like Mike." And corporate sponsors Nike, Kelloggs, and a host of others continued to support their superstar, who returned triumphantly to star on the court, in the movies, and in society.

FREEK JOB.

Figure 3–2   No other sports figure in the waning years of the twentieth century evoked more strident opinions—many not nice—as Jordan's Chicago Bulls teammate Dennis Rodman. Whether dressing in women's clothes, authoring tell-all books, kicking a cameraman in the groin, or hosting an MTV grunge retrospective, the irrepressible Rodman was a public opinion lightning rod.

WHAT IS PUBLIC OPINION?

Public opinion, like public relations, is not easily explained. Newspaper columnist Joseph Kraft called public opinion "the unknown god to which moderns burn incense." Edward Bernays called it "a term describing an ill-defined, mercurial, and changeable group of individual judgments."[2] And Princeton professor Harwood Childs, after coming up with no fewer than 40 different, yet viable definitions, concluded with a definition by Herman C. Boyle: "Public opinion is not the name of something, but the classification of a number of somethings."[3]

   Splitting public opinion into its two components, public and opinion, is perhaps the best way to understand the concept. Simply defined, public signifies a group of people who share a common interest in a specific subject—stockholders, for example, or employees or community residents. Each group is concerned with a common issue—the price of the stock, the wages of the company, or the building of a new plant.

An opinion is the expression of an attitude on a particular topic. When attitudes become strong enough, they surface in the form of opinions. When opinions become strong enough, they lead to verbal or behavioral actions.

A forest products company executive and an environmentalist from the Sierra Club might differ dramatically in their attitudes toward the relative importance of pollution control and continued industrial production. Their respective opinions on a piece of environmental legislation might also differ radically. In turn, how their organizations respond to that legislation—by picketing, petitioning, or lobbying—might also differ.

Public opinion, then, is the aggregate of many individual opinions on a particular issue that affects a group of people. Stated another way, public opinion represents a consensus. And that consensus, deriving as it does from many individual opinions, really begins with people's attitudes toward the issue in question. Trying to influence an individual's attitude—how he or she thinks on a given topic—is a primary focus of the practice of public relations.

WHAT ARE ATTITUDES?

If an opinion is an expression of an attitude on a particular topic, what then is an attitude? Unfortunately, that also is not an easy question to answer. It had been generally assumed that attitudes are predispositions to think in a certain way about a certain topic. But recent research has indicated that attitudes may more likely be evaluations people make about specific problems or issues. These conclusions are not necessarily connected to any broad attitude.[4] For example, an individual might favor a company's response to one issue but disagree vehemently with its response to another. Thus, that individual's attitude may differ from issue to issue.

Attitudes are based on a number of characteristics.

1. Personal—the physical and emotional ingredients of an individual, including size, age, and social status.
2. Cultural—the environment and lifestyle of a particular country or geographic area, such as Japan versus the United States or rural America versus urban America. National political candidates often tailor messages to appeal to the particular cultural complexions of specific regions of the country.
3. Educational—the level and quality of a person's education. To appeal to the increased number of college graduates in the United States today, public communication has become more sophisticated.
4. Familial—people's roots. Children acquire their parents' tastes, biases, political partisanships, and a host of other characteristics. Some pediatricians insist that children pick up most of their knowledge in the first seven years, and few would deny the family's strong role in helping to mold attitudes.

5. Religious—a system of beliefs about God or the supernatural. Religion is making a comeback. In the 1960s many young people turned away from formal religion. In the late 1990s, even after several evangelical scandals, religious fervor has reemerged.
6. Social class—position within society. As people's social status changes, so do their attitudes. For example, college students, unconcerned with making a living, may dramatically change their attitudes about such concepts as big government, big business, wealth, and prosperity after entering the job market.
7. Race—ethnic origin, which today increasingly helps shape people's attitudes. The history of blacks and whites in America has been stormy, with peaceful coexistence often frustrated. Nonetheless, minorities in our society, as a group, continue to improve their standard of living. And in so doing, African Americans, Latinos, Asians, and others have retained pride in and allegiance to their cultural heritage.

These characteristics help influence the formation of attitudes. So, too, do other factors, such as experience, economic class, and political and organizational memberships. Again, recent research has indicated that attitudes and behaviors are situational—influenced by specific issues in specific situations. Nonetheless, when others with similar attitudes reach similar opinions, a consensus, or public opinion, is born.

HOW ARE ATTITUDES INFLUENCED?

Strictly speaking, attitudes are positive, negative, or nonexistent. A person is for something, against it, or neutral. Studies show that for any one issue, most people don't care much one way or the other. A small percentage express strong support, and another small percentage express strong opposition. The vast majority are smack in the middle—passive, neutral, indifferent. Former Vice President Spiro T. Agnew called them "the silent majority." In many instances—political campaigns being a prime example—this silent majority holds the key to success because they are the group most readily influenced by a communicator's message.

It's hard to change the mind of a person who is staunchly opposed to a particular issue or individual. Likewise, it's easy to reinforce the support of a person who is wholeheartedly in favor of an issue or an individual. Social scientist Leon Festinger discussed this concept when he talked about cognitive dissonance. He believed that individuals tend to avoid information that is dissonant or opposed to their own points of view and tend to seek out information that is consonant with, or in support of, their own attitudes.[5] An organization might attempt to remove dissonance to reach its goals. For example, in the face of stinging government attacks against cigarette smoking, Phillip Morris took the initiative by proposing an ambitious program to restrict cigarette sales to minors. The Federal Trade Commission, arch enemy of tobacco, ignored the Phillip Morris ideas.[6]

As Festinger's theory intimates, the people whose attitudes can be influenced most readily are those who have not yet made up their minds. In politics this group is often referred to as the swing vote. Many elections have been won or lost on last-minute appeals to these politically undecided voters. In addition, it is possible to introduce information that may cause dissonance in the mind of a receiver.

Understanding this theory and its potential for influencing the silent majority is extremely important for the public relations practitioner, whose objective is to win support through clear, thoughtful, and persuasive communication. Moving a person from a latent state of attitude formation to a more aware state and finally to an active one becomes a matter of motivation.

MOTIVATING ATTITUDE CHANGE

People are motivated by different factors, and no two people respond in exactly the same way to the same set of circumstances. Each of us is motivated by different drives and needs.

The most famous delineator of what motivates people was Abraham Maslow. His hierarchy of needs helps define the origins of motivation, which, in turn, help explain attitude change. Maslow postulated a five-level hierarchy:

1. The lowest order is physiological needs: a person's biological demands—food and water, sleep, health, bodily needs, exercise and rest, and sex.
2. The second level is safety needs: security, protection, comfort and peace, and orderly surroundings.
3. The third level is love needs: acceptance, belonging, love and affection, and membership in a group.
4. The fourth level is esteem: recognition and prestige, confidence and leadership opportunities, competence and strength, intelligence and success.
5. The highest order is self-actualization, or simply becoming what one is capable of becoming. Self-actualization involves self-fulfillment and achieving a goal for the purposes of challenge and accomplishment.[7]

According to Maslow, the needs of all five levels compose the fundamental motivating factors for any individual or public.

In the 1990s, as people once again get involved in causes—from abortion to animal rights to environmentalism—motivating attitude change becomes more important (Figure 3–3). Many activist groups, in fact, borrow heavily from psychological research on political activism to accomplish attitude change. Six cardinal precepts of political activism are instructive in attempting to change attitudes:

1. Don't use graphic images unless they are accompanied by specific actions people can execute. Many movements—the gay rights campaign, for one, and the antiabortion movement, for another—began by relying heavily on graphic images of death and destruction. But such images run the risk of pushing people away rather than drawing them in. Disturbing presentations rarely lead to a sustained attitude change.
2. Go to the public instead of asking the public to come to you. Most people will never become directly involved in an activist campaign. They will shy away. But by recognizing the limits of public interest and involvement, you can develop realistic strategies to capitalize on public goodwill without demanding more than people are willing to give.
3. Don't assume that attitude change is necessary for behavior change. A large body of psychological research casts doubt on the proposition that the best way to change behavior is to begin by changing attitudes. Indeed, the relationship between attitudes and behavior is often quite weak. Therefore, informing smokers of the link between cigarettes and cancer is far easier than getting them to kick the habit.

Figure 3–3 By the late 1990s, even rock groups were tapping into the peculiarities of public opinion. In 1996, the well spoken, relatively clean cut California group Dishwalla caused an instant public opinion uproar with the song, "Counting Blue Cars," which featured the lyrics, "Tell me all your thoughts on God . . . I'd really like to meet her." Christian fundamentalists reacted with unbridled opprobrium to this alternative perspective of religion. Dishwalla's tune, meanwhile, shot up the charts thanks to the controversy.

4. Use moral arguments as adjuncts, not as primary thrusts. Moral views are difficult to change. It is much easier to gain support by stressing the practical advantages of your solution rather than the immorality of your opponent's. For example, it is easier to convert people to a meatless diet by discussing the health benefits of vegetables than by discussing whether the Bible gives people dominion over animals.

5. Embrace the mainstream. In any campaign, people from all walks of life are necessary to win widespread approval. No campaign can be won if it is dubbed radical or faddish. That is why the involvement of all people must be encouraged in seeking attitude change.

6. Don't offend the people you seek to change. Research on persuasion shows that influence is usually strongest when people like the persuader and see the persuader as similar to themselves. It is impossible to persuade someone whom you have alienated. Or, as my mother used to say, "You can attract more flies with honey than you can with vinegar." The same applies to people.[8]

POWER OF PERSUASION

Perhaps the most essential element in influencing public opinion is the principle of persuasion. Persuading is the goal of the vast majority of public relations programs. Persuasion theory has myriad explanations and interpretations. Basically, persuasion means getting another person to do something through advice, reasoning, or just plain arm twisting. Books have been written on the enormous power of advertising and public relations as persuasive tools.

Social scientists and communications scholars take issue with the view of many public relations practitioners that a story on network news or the front page of *The New York Times* has a tremendous persuasive effect. Scholars argue that the media have a limited effect on persuasion—doing more to reinforce existing attitudes than to persuade toward a new belief. There is little doubt, however, that the persuasiveness of a message can be increased when it arouses or is accompanied by a high level of personal involvement. In other words, an individual who cares about something and is in fundamental agreement with an organization's basic position will tend to be persuaded by a message supporting that view.

According to the persuasion theory of Michael Ray—the hierarchies of effects—there are at least three basic orderings of knowledge, attitude, and behavior relative to persuasion:

1. When personal involvement is low and little difference exists between behavioral alternatives, knowledge changes are likely to lead directly to behavioral changes.
2. When personal involvement is high but behavioral alternatives are indistinguishable, behavioral change is likely to be followed by attitudinal change, similar to Festinger's cognitive dissonance approach.
3. When personal involvement is high and clear differences exist among alternatives, people act in a more rational manner. First, they learn about the issue. Second, they evaluate the alternatives. Then they act in a manner consistent with their attitudes and knowledge.[9]

To these complex theories of persuasion is added the simpler, yet no less profound, notion of former Secretary of State Dean Rusk: "One of the best ways to persuade others is to listen to them." No matter how one characterizes persuasion, the goal of most communications programs is, in fact, to influence a receiver to take a desired action.

How Are People Persuaded?

Saul Alinsky, a legendary radical organizer, had a simple theory of persuasion.

"People only understand things in terms of their own experience. . . . If you try to get your ideas across to others without paying attention to what they have to say to you, you can forget about the whole thing."[10] In other words, if you wish to persuade people, you must cite evidence that coincides with their own beliefs, emotions, and expectations.

What Kinds of "Evidence" Persuade People?

1. Facts—Facts are indisputable. Although it is true, as they say, that "statistics sometimes lie," nonetheless empirical data are a persuasive device in hammering home a point of view. This is why any good public relations program will always start with research—the facts.

2. Emotions—Maslow was right. People do respond to emotional appeals—love, peace, family, patriotism. Ronald Reagan was known as "the great communicator" largely as a result of his appeal to emotion. Even when the nation was outraged in 1983, when 200 American soldiers died in a terrorist attack in Lebanon, President Reagan reversed the skepticism by talking of one wounded U.S. marine lying in a Lebanese bed.

That Marine, and all those others like him, living and dead, have been faithful to their ideals, they've given willingly of themselves so that a nearly defenseless people in a region of great strategic importance to the free world will have a chance someday to live lives free of murder and mayhem and terrorism.[11]

Such is the persuasive power of emotional appeals.

3. Personalizing—People respond to personal experience.
   - When Jesse Jackson talks about poverty, even those who don't agree with his politics, listen to the man who rose from the ghetto.
   - When Sarah Brady crusades about gun control, people understand that her husband, President Reagan's former press secretary, was permanently handicapped by a bullet intended for the president.
   - When baseball pitcher Jim Abbott talked about dealing with adversity, people marveled at a star athlete born with only one arm.

   Again, few can refute knowledge gained from personal experience.

4. Appealing to "you"—The one word that people never tire of hearing is "you." "What is in this for me?" is the question that everyone asks. So one secret to persuading is constantly to think in terms of the audience, constantly to refer to "you."

   As simple as these four precepts are, they are difficult to grasp—particularly for business leaders, who frown on emotion or personalizing or even appealing to an audience. Some consider it "beneath them" to show human emotion. This, of course, is a mistake. The power to persuade—to influence public opinion—is the measure not only of a charismatic but an effective leader.[12]

INFLUENCING PUBLIC OPINION

Public opinion is a lot easier to measure than it is to influence. However, a thoughtful public relations program can crystallize attitudes, reinforce beliefs, and occasionally change public opinion. First, the opinions to be changed or modified must be identified and understood. Second, target publics must be clear. Third, the public relations professional must have in sharp focus the "laws" that govern public opinion—as amorphous as they may be.

In that context, the 15 Laws of Public Opinion, developed many years ago by social psychologist Hadley Cantril, remain pertinent:

1. Opinion is highly sensitive to important events.
2. Events of unusual magnitude are likely to swing public opinion temporarily from one extreme to another. Opinion doesn't become stabilized until the implications of events are seen in some perspective.
3. Opinion is generally determined more by events than by words—unless those words are themselves interpreted as an event.

4. Verbal statements and outlines of courses of action have maximum importance when opinion is unstructured and people are suggestible and seek some interpretation from a reliable source.

5. By and large, public opinion doesn't anticipate emergencies—it only reacts to them.

6. Opinion is basically determined by self-interest. Events, words, or any other stimuli affect opinion only insofar as their relationship to self-interest is apparent.

7. Opinion doesn't remain aroused for a long period of time unless people feel that their self-interest is acutely involved or unless opinion—aroused by words—is sustained by events.

8. Once self-interest is involved, opinions aren't easily changed.

9. When self-interest is involved, public opinion in a democracy is likely to be ahead of official policy.

10. When an opinion is held by a slight majority or when opinion is not solidly structured, an accomplished fact tends to shift opinion in the direction of acceptance.

11. At critical times, people become more sensitive to the adequacy of their leadership. If they have confidence in it, they are willing to assign more than usual responsibility to it; if they lack confidence in it, they are less tolerant than usual.

12. People are less reluctant to have critical decisions made by their leaders if they feel that somehow they themselves are taking part in the decision.

13. People have more opinions and are able to form opinions more easily on goals than on methods to reach those goals.

14. Public opinion, like individual opinion, is colored by desire. And when opinion is based chiefly on desire, rather than on information, it is likely to shift with events.

15. By and large, if people in a democracy are provided with educational opportunities and ready access to information, public opinion reveals a hard-headed common sense. The more enlightened people are to the implications of events and proposals for their own self-interest, the more likely they are to agree with the more objective opinions of realistic experts.[13]

POLISHING THE CORPORATE IMAGE

Most organizations today and the people who manage them are extremely sensitive to the way they are perceived by their critical publics. This represents a dramatic change in corporate attitude from years past. In the 1960s, 1970s, and well into the 1980s, only the most enlightened companies dared to maintain anything but a low profile. Management, frankly, was reluctant to step out publicly, "to stand up for what it stood for."

In the 1990s, however, organizations—particularly large ones—have had little choice but to go public.

Consider the following:

- Bedrock American companies, heretofore the symbols of pristine and silent management decorum, were crucified for lackluster executives, inefficient organizations, and, ultimately, falling profits. In rapid succession, the chairmen of General Motors, American Express, and IBM were beheaded in brutally public bloodlettings. So sensitive were big companies to public approval that some didn't wait to announce management problems. Early in 1993, the nation's twenty-fifth largest industrial company,

THE REST OF THE STORY

WHEN BARBIE TALKED, WOMEN WENT BONKERS

One of the quickest and savviest corporate reactions to negative public opinion came in late 1992 when Los Angeles-based Mattel Inc. reacted to criticism about its talking Barbie doll, which uttered the phrase "math class is tough" (Figure 3–4).

Figure 3–4   The alleged perpetrator.

No sooner were the words out of Teen Talk Barbie's mouth than the American Association of University Women attacked the math comment as "sexist" in a report on how schools shortchange girls.

This was no trivial matter to Mattel. Each year, the company makes nearly $2 billion in sales of its nearly 40-year-old Barbie, the company's largest business.

Mattel immediately announced that it was removing the offensive computer chip from the Barbie repertoire and offered to swap a new chip for anyone who bought an offending doll.

In a letter to the president of the association, Mattel President Jill E. Barad said the company made a mistake.

In hindsight, the phrase "math class is tough," while correct for many students both male and female, should not have been included. We didn't fully consider the potentially negative implications of this phrase, nor were we aware of the findings of your organization's report.

Way 'ta go, Barbie![14]

Tenneco, announced that its high-profile chairman, Michael H. Walsh, was suffering from brain cancer. The announcement was made by Walsh himself.[15]

- Four days later, the board of directors of Brinker International convened a hastily called meeting to name and announce a new chairman and CEO to replace the company's well-known leader, Norman E. Brinker, who had been rendered unconscious in a jarring collision during a polo match.[16]
- However, not one to learn from the misfortunes of others, in 1994 when Walt Disney Co. CEO Michael Eisner underwent emergency quadruple bypass surgery, the company was typically tight-lipped about status and prognosis. "We're not discussing it," sniffed the firm's communications chief.[17] What compounded the issue was that Eisner had no successor in place.
- Two years later, in 1996, Disney again found itself in the succession soup, when touted super agent Michael Ovitz, whom Eisner had plucked as his successor, was canned less than a year after joining the team. Ovitz was paid an outrageous $36 million in severance pay for the humiliation. And Disney had more noncommunicative egg on its face.

Most organizations today understand clearly that it takes a great deal of time to build a favorable image for a corporation but only one slip to create a negative public impression. In other words, the corporate image is a fragile commodity. Yet, most firms also believe that a positive corporate image is essential for continued long-term success.

As Ray D'Argenio, the former communications director of United Technologies, put it, "Corporate communications can't create a corporate character. A company already has a character, which communications can reinforce"[18] (Figure 3–5).

BEWARE THE TRAPS OF PUBLIC OPINION

Analyzing public opinion is not as easy as it looks. Once a company wins favorable public opinion for a product or an idea, the trick is to maintain it (Figure 3–7). The worst thing to do is sit back and bask in the glory of a positive public image; that's a quick route to image deterioration (Figure 3–8).

Public opinion is changeable, and in assessing it, communicators are susceptible to a number of subtle yet lethal traps.

- Cast in stone—This fallacy assumes that just because public opinion is well established on a certain issue, it isn't likely to change. Not true. Consider an issue such as women's liberation. In the early 1960s, people laughed at the handful of women raising a ruckus about equal rights, equal pay, and equal treatment. By the early 1970s, women's liberation pervaded every sector of our culture, and nobody laughed. In the space of a decade, public opinion about the importance of this issue had shifted substantially.
- Gut reaction—This fallacy assumes that if management feels in its corporate gut that the public will lean strongly in a certain direction, then that must be the way to go. Be careful. Some managements are so cut off from the real world that their knee-jerk reactions to issues often turn out to be more jerk than anything else. One former auto company executive, perhaps overstating the case, described the problem this way: "There's no forward response to what the public wants today. It's gotten to be a total insulation from the realities of the world." Certainly, manage-

**Brighten
Your Corner**

Have you
noticed the
great difference
between the
people you
meet?
Some are as
sunshiny as
a handful of
forget-me-nots.
Others come on
like frozen mackerel.
A cheery, comforting
nurse can
help make a
hospital stay
bearable.
An upbeat secretary
makes visitors
glad they came
to see you.
Every corner of the
world has its clouds,
gripes, complainers,
and pains in the
neck—because many
people have
yet to
learn that
honey works better
than vinegar.
You're in control
of *your* small
corner of the
world.
Brighten it . . .
You *can*.

Figure 3–5   Although many companies attempted to construct a differentiable corporate image through advertising, few succeeded as well as United Technologies, which kept its messages succinct, savvy, and sparkling.

A QUESTION OF ETHICS

THE DOWNSIZING POSTER BOY

Figure 3–6 AT&T's CEO was one of those portrayed a bit harshly by *Newsweek*.

No corporate issue in the latter days of the twentieth century evoked greater debate than the wave of downsizings, cutbacks, and outright firings that spread across the United States and the world at the end of the 90s.

Wall Street and steadily higher quarterly profits seemed the objective for any public company. The casualty, more often than not, in attaining that goal was a steadily declining corporate workforce. Companies throughout the United States threw workers out of work.

In 1996, *The New York Times* ran a 37,000-word front page series on downsizing. *Newsweek* ran the photos of several well-known CEOs on its cover, under the headline "Corporate Killers." (Figure 3–6)

And the "poster boy" of corporate downsizers was AT&T Chairman Robert Allen. Allen, a straight-backed, austere patrician happened to be in the wrong place at the wrong time. A lifetime employee of Ma Bell, the CEO presided over the announced layoff of 40,000 workers, while receiving a pay package of $18 million.

The media, the nation, and, needless to say, many AT&T employees were outraged at the chutzpah. Worst of all, Allen seemed to go into "hiding" in the face of the public opinion backlash.

Until one day, he was ambushed by the scourge of every company, *60 Minutes*.

"Mr. Allen," he was asked by his ambusher, correspondent Leslie Stahl, "how can you justify a pay package of millions and millions of dollars when you're firing thousands and thousands of people?"

"Look, I didn't come here to answer those questions," replied the cornered chairman, in a barely audible voice. And then he feebly offered, "In point of fact, I didn't receive a pay package worth 'millions and millions of dollars.' "

Whether he did or not, Allen's timid response begged several questions. Why couldn't he justify what he earned? Why wasn't he willing to defend his salary? And what about the firings? Why not discuss why they were necessary? How "ethical" was it to fire so many and be paid so much?

In later days, after the *60 Minutes* debacle, the AT&T chief became more visible, trying to recoup his lost credibility.

But it was too little too late.

Several months later, AT&T tapped a little-known executive from the printing industry to succeed the embattled CEO, prior to Allen's intended retirement date. And only months after that, Allen suffered a heart attack, as the company continued to suffer. Might he have been able to handle the spotlight better had he been more publicly attuned?

Figure 3–7 The key to a corporate image that gets through to people is a combination of simplicity, unity, and balance. These excerpts from the corporate identity manual of David's Lemonade, the creation of Fulton + Partners, Inc., are examples of a clear corporate image.

ment's instincts in dealing with the public may be questionable at times. Generally, gut-reaction judgments should be avoided in assessing public opinion.

- General public—There may well be a public at large, but there's no such thing as the general public. Even the smallest public can be subdivided. No two people are alike, and messages to influence public opinion should be as pointed as possible rather than scatter shot. Sometimes individuals may qualify as members of publics on both sides of an issue. In weighing the pros and cons of lower speed limits, for example, many people are both drivers and pedestrians. Categorizing them into one general group can be a mistake.
- Words move mountains—Perhaps they do sometimes, but public opinion is usually influenced more by events than by words. For example, in 1995, pro-choice advocates saw their cause aided by the tragic killings of abortion doctors and workers at abortion clinics by antiabortion sympathizers.
- Brother's keeper—It's true that most people will rise up indignantly if a fellow citizen has been wronged. But they'll get a lot more indignant if they feel they themselves have been wronged. In other words, self-interest often sparks public opinion. An organization wishing to influence public opinion might be well advised to ask initially, "What's in this for the people whose opinion we're trying to influence?"

Figure 3–8 The Xerox Company has a unique name and logo problem. The Xerox name is so widely used that it must fight a continual battle to have the name treated as a proper adjective with a capital X, rather than a verb with a lowercase x—thus the frustration expressed in this ad.

SUMMARY

Influencing public opinion remains at the heart of professional public relations work. Perhaps the key to realizing this objective is anticipating or keeping ahead of trends in our society. Anticipating trends is no easy task. But in the new millennium, trend watching has developed into a veritable cottage industry. One self-styled prognosticator riding the crest of trend analysis was John Naisbitt, whose book *Megatrends 2000* claimed to predict the new directions that would influence American lives in the next century. Among them are the following:

- Inflation and interest rates will be held in check.
- There will be a shift from welfare to workfare.
- There will be a shift from public housing to home ownership.

AUCTIONEER'S REPUTATION ON THE BLOCK

Sotheby's of New York and London is the bluest of the blue blood auction firms.

In 1996, the world's oldest and most prestigious auction house was chosen to preside over the auction of the possessions of Jacqueline Kennedy Onassis.

Sotheby's reputation, in fact, is perhaps more pristine than any other organization in the world. Until the winter of 1997.

That's when a British author went undercover to accuse Sotheby's of smuggling, fabricating documentation, and rigging auctions. Specifically, using hidden cameras and tape recorders, the author found the firm breaking art preservation laws in countries like Italy and India by paying smugglers for stolen antiquities from tombs and places of worship.

Sotheby's sniffed that the reports were basically "innuendo" and "speculation."

But they also were recorded by a camera concealed in the reporter's crystal brooch.

After the Italian government launched an investigation and *60 Minutes* viciously trashed the renowned auctioneer, Sotheby's accepted the resignation of its director in Italy and suspended another executive in London.

Nonetheless, the reputation of Sotheby's, so meticulously honed over so many years, had taken a serious public opinion wallop.[19]

- There will be a shift from sports to the arts as the primary leisure preference.
- Consumers will demand more customized products.
- The media will amplify bad economic news.
- The rise of the Pacific Rim will be seen in terms of economic dominance.
- Asia will add 80 million more people.
- CEOs in a global economy will become more important and better known than political figures.[20]

Some might argue that there is nothing revolutionary in these megatrends (and they might well be right). Nonetheless, such trends deserve to be scrutinized, analyzed, and evaluated by organizations in order to deal more effectively with the future.

As public relations counselor Philip Lesly once pointed out, "The real problems faced by business today are in the outside world of intangibles and public attitudes."[21] To keep ahead of these intangibles, these public attitudes, and these kernels of future public opinion, managements will turn increasingly to professional public relations practitioners for guidance.

DISCUSSION STARTERS

1. What is public opinion?
2. What are attitudes, and on what characteristics are they based?
3. How are attitudes influenced?

4. What is Maslow's hierarchy of needs?
5. Explain the law of cognitive dissonance.
6. How difficult is it to change a person's behavior?
7. What are Cantril's Laws of Public Opinion?
8. What kinds of "evidence" persuade people?
9. How did the issue of corporate downsizing affect public opinion in the late 1990s?
10. What are the traps of public opinion?

NOTES

1. "Agency Picks Worst PR Blunders of Year," *Jack O'Dwyer's Newsletter*, January 8, 1997, 2.
2. Cited in Edward L. Bernays, *Crystallizing Public Opinion* (New York: Liveright, 1961), 61.
3. Cited in Harwood L. Childs, *Public Opinion: Nature, Formation, and Role* (Princeton, NJ: Van Nostrand, 1965), 15.
4. James E. Grunig and Todd Hunt, *Managing Public Relations* (New York: Holt, Rinehart & Winston, 1984), 130.
5. Leon A. Festinger, *A Theory of Cognitive Dissonance* (New York: Harper & Row, 1957), 163.
6. "Olive Branch or Smoke Screen?", *Reputation Management* (July/August 1996): 9.
7. Abraham Maslow, *Motivation and Personality* (New York: Harper & Row, 1954).
8. S. Plous, "Toward More Effective Activism," *The Animal's Agenda* (December 1989): 24–26.
9. John V. Pavlik, *Public Relations: What Research Tells Us* (Newbury Park, CA: Sage, 1987), 74.
10. Saul D. Alinsky, Rules for Radicals (New York: Vintage Books, 1971), 81.
11. Ronald W. Reagan, Address by the President to the Nation, October 27, 1983.
12. Robert L. Dilenschneider, *Power and Influence* (New York: Prentice Hall, 1990), 5.
13. Hadley Cantril, *Gauging Public Opinion* (Princeton, NJ: Princeton University Press, 1972), 226–230.
14. "Teen Talk Barbie Turns Silent on Math," *The New York Times*, October 20, 1992, p. 5.
15. Thomas C. Hayes, "Tenneco's Chief Has Brain Cancer," *The New York Times*, January 21, 1993, D1, D20.
16. Thomas C. Hayes, "Brinker Names New Chief," *The New York Times*, January 25, 1993, D1, D3.
17. Fraser P. Seitel, "Who's Runnin' The Company?" *Public Relations Tactics*, September 1994, 13.
18. Ray D'Argenio, speech at the Communications Executive of the Year Luncheon, sponsored by Corpcom Services, December 10, 1981.
19. "Sotheby's Reputation on the Block," *Newsweek*, February 17, 1997, 63.
20. John Naisbitt and Patricia Aburdene, *Megatrends 2000* (New York: Morrow, 1990).
21. Philip Lesly, "How the Future Will Shape Public Relations—and Vice Versa," *Public Relations Quarterly* (Winter 1981–82): 7.

THE NEW YORK TIMES

NEW YORK: THE NEW YORK TIMES COMPANY

THE WALL STREET JOURNAL

NEW YORK: DOW JONES & COMPANY, INC.

Public relations can be practiced only by understanding public opinion, and the best forums in which to study it are *The New York Times* and *The Wall Street Journal*. Their pages daily reveal the diverse views of pundits, politicians, and plain people. *The Times* is arguably the primary source of printed news in the world. *The Journal*, likewise, is the primary printed source of the world's business and investment news—an area of increasingly dominant importance.

Both papers, through their opinion pages and in-depth stories, express the attitudes of leaders in politics, business, science, education, journalism, and the arts, on topics ranging from abortion rights to genetic engineering to race relations. Occasionally, *The Times* and *The Journal* supplement their usual coverage with public opinion polls to gauge attitudes and beliefs on particularly hot issues. The *Sunday Times*, with features that include the magazine sections "Week in Review" and "Business Forum" is an important resource for public relations professionals. *The Times* also is now printed in color.

To influence public opinion, counselors must first understand it. Two excellent sources with which to begin the quest are *The New York Times* and *The Wall Street Journal*. Read these papers daily, and you'll keep abreast of popular thought on major issues and trends.

SUGGESTED READINGS

Creedon, Pamela J., *Women in Mass Communications: Challenging General Values.* Newbury Park, CA: Sage, 1989.

Garbett, Thomas F. *How to Build a Corporation's Identity and Project Its Image.* Lexington, MA: Lexington Books, 1988.

Gilbert, Dennis A. *Compendium of American Public Opinion.* New York: Facts on File, 1988.

Glasser, Theodore L. and Charles T. Salmon. *Public Opinion and the Communication of Consent.* New York: Guiford Press, 1995. Anthology of articles spanning the history of the role of public opinion from ancient to contemporary times.

Knapp, Mark L. and Anita L. Vangelisti. *Interpersonal Communication and Human Relationships.* Boston: Allyn & Bacon, 1992.

Lipset, Seymour Martin, and William Schneider. *The Confidence Gap: Business, Labor and Government in the Public.* New York: Free Press, 1988.

Lukaszewski, Jim. *Influencing Public Attitudes.* Leesburg, VA: Issue Action Publications, 1993.

McCombs, Maxwell, et al. *Contemporary Public Opinion: Issues and the News.* Hillsdale, NJ: Lawrence Erlbaum Associates, 1991.

McGill, Michael. *American Business and the Quick Fix.* New York: Holt & Co., 1988.

Mercer, Laurie and Jennifer Singer. *Opportunity Knocks: Using PR.* Radnor, PA: Chilton, 1989.

Nager, Norman and Richard Truitt. *Strategic Public Relations Counseling.* White Plains, NY: Longman, 1987; University Press of America, 1991.

Pratkanis, Anthony and Elliot Aronson. *Age of Propaganda: The Everyday Use and Abuse of Persuasion.* New York: W. H. Freeman, 1992.

Sauerhaft, Stan and Chris Atkins. *Image Wars.* New York: Wiley, 1989.

Selame, Elinor and Joseph Selame. *The Company Image: Building Your Identity and Influence in the Marketplace.* New York: John Wiley & Sons, 1988.

CASE STUDY

Pepsi Punctures the Great Syringe Soda Scare

Pepsi-Cola's worst nightmare began inauspiciously enough on June 10, 1993, when an elderly Fircrest, Washington, couple claimed that they had discovered a syringe floating inside a can of Diet Pepsi.

For the next two weeks, the 50,000 people of Pepsi-Cola—from CEO and corporate communications staff to independent bottlers—worked round the clock to mount a massive public relations offensive that effectively thwarted a potential business disaster for its 95-year-old trademark and a potential devastating blow to one of the world's foremost consumer reputations.

The Pepsi case is a tribute to sound communications thinking and rapid, decisive public relations action in the face of imminent corporate catastrophe.

The day after the Fircrest complaint, a nearby Tacoma woman reported finding another hypodermic needle in a can of Diet Pepsi. The story of the two tampered cans—initially labeled "some sort of sabotage" by the local Pepsi bottler—ran on the *Associated Press* wire nationwide and sent shock waves throughout the country.

Pepsi, while immediately forming a crisis management team, headed by its president and CEO, Craig Weatherup, nonetheless chose to "hold its powder" publicly while first assessing all pertinent facts about the two incidents and devoting attention to the Seattle plant. Pepsi's perceived reluctance to confront the problem in a dramatic way—while it worked "behind the scenes"—drew initial fire from so-called crisis experts. One management communications professor warned, "They are underestimating the potential for rumors to feed off one another." Another crisis management counselor said, "This will be a terrible mistake if it turns out they should have acted in light of later events."

On June 13, the commissioner of the Food and Drug Administration (FDA), David A. Kessler, warned consumers in Washington, Oregon, Alaska, Hawaii, and Guam "to inspect closely cans of Diet Pepsi for signs of tampering and to pour the contents into a glass or cup before drinking."

In the face of criticism and with copycat tamperings accelerating, Pepsi held its ground. Although critics urged the company to recall its products, the company continued to insist that its cans were virtually tamperproof. "We are 99% sure that you cannot open one and reseal it without its being obvious," the company assured its customers.

Because there was "no health risk to either of the two consumers who filed the complaints or to the general public," Pepsi urged its bottlers and general managers not to remove the product from shelves.

On June 14, Pepsi issued an internal "consumer advisory" to its bottlers and general managers, reporting the results of its initial research on the reported claims:

- The syringes that were found are those commonly used by diabetics for insulin. We do not have syringes of this type in any of our production facilities.
- All cans used for Pepsi-Cola products are new packages. They are not reused or refilled at any time. There are two visual inspections during production: The first before cans are filled, the second while cans are on the filling line. The cans are then sealed.

Pepsi's strong inference was that first, the speed and security of its bottling production process made it extremely unlikely that any foreign object could appear in an unopened Pepsi container and second, what was being inserted wasn't being put into cans at the factory.

By June 14, the nation was awash in copycat Pepsi-Cola tamperings. Pepsi was barraged with reports of syringes in its cans from Louisiana to New York, from Missouri to Wyoming, from Pennsylvania to Southern California. Adding to Pepsi's nightmare was a media feeding frenzy the likes of which the company had never before encountered.

- "A 'Scared' Firm Fights to Save Its Good Name"—*New York Post*
- "FDA Warns Diet-Pepsi Drinkers"—*Associated Press*
- "Diet Pepsi Drinkers Warned of Debris"—*USA Today*
- "No Program for a Recall of Diet Pepsi"—*The New York Times*

Pepsi tampering stories dominated the national media, leading the evening news and network morning programs for three days. Local crews throughout the nation positioned themselves at local Pepsi bottling plants. Pepsi-Cola's president and six-person public relations staff put in 20-hour days in the company's Somers, New York, headquarters, each fielding 80 to 100 inquiries daily. The company was besieged by syringe-tampering mania.

Late on the evening of June 15, Pepsi received its first break.

A man in central Pennsylvania was arrested on the charge that he had fraudulently reported finding a syringe in a can of Pepsi.

With the first arrest made, Pepsi seized the offensive.

Media Relations
Pepsi's media strategy centered on one medium—television. Downplaying traditional print media—"the press conference is a dinosaur"—Pepsi-Cola's communications executives launched daily satellite feeds to the nation's electronic media to get out Pepsi's side of the tampering allegations.

- An initial video news release (VNR) picturing the high-speed can-filling lines, with voice-over narration by a plant manager, conveyed the message of a manufacturing process built on speed, safety, and integrity, in which tampering with products would be highly unlikely. The goal was to show that the canning process was safe. The initial VNR was seen by 187 million viewers (more than watched the 1993 Super Bowl) on 399 stations in 178 markets across the United States.
- A second VNR, picturing Pepsi President Weatherup and additional production footage, reported the first arrest for a false claim of tampering. It made four critical points: (1) complaints of syringes reported to be found in Diet Pepsi cans in other

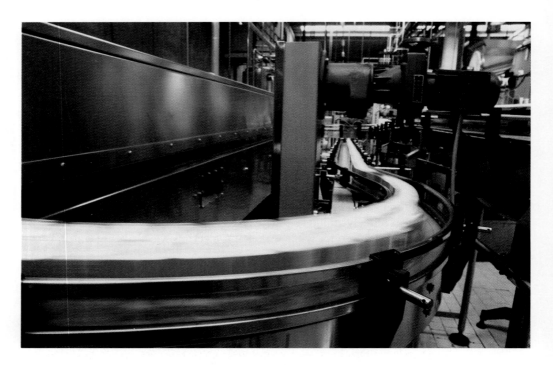

Figure 3–9 The subject of Pepsi's first VNR to reassure the public about its processing speed and safety was this rapid glimpse of a Pepsi bottling plant.

cities are unrelated; (2) tampering appears to be happening after cans are opened; (3) the soft drink can is one of the safest packages for consumer food products; and (4) a recall is not warranted. This Pepsi-produced VNR was seen by 70 million viewers on 238 stations in 136 markets.

- A third VNR, narrated by President Weatherup, presented a segment from a convenience store surveillance video in which a woman was caught inserting a syringe into an open Diet Pepsi can. Weatherup thanked consumers for their support, reported additional arrests, and reaffirmed Pepsi's decision not to recall its product. This surveillance video was broadcast to 95 million viewers on 325 stations in 159 markets and, in effect, "broke the back" of the Pepsi syringe scare.
- In addition to the VNRs, Pepsi's media offensive included appearances by the company's president and a product safety expert on as many talk shows as could be fit into their schedules—each of the three major network evening newscasts, ABC's *Nightline*, CNN's *Larry King Live*, and so on.

Pepsi's video media blitz was unparalleled in corporate public relations history.

Government Relations

Meanwhile, Pepsi cooperated fully with Commissioner Kessler and the FDA. While other consumer firms have adopted an adversarial position toward the watchdog agency, Pepsi embraced the FDA's investigation.

It was the FDA's Office of Criminal Investigation (OCI), in fact, that reported the breakthrough in the arrest of the man in central Pennsylvania. In addition to the FDA's "consumer alert" in the Pacific Northwest, Commissioner Kessler issued a statement on the tampering and the possibility of copy-cats. Later, Kessler appeared with Weatherup on *Nightline* and took the unprecedented step of declaring that "calm is in order . . . a recall is not necessary."

On June 17, Commissioner Kessler held a press conference in Washington, DC, unequivocally characterizing the controversy as a hoax—the product of "misguided individual acts, magnified and multiplied by the attendant glare of the media, and a predictable outbreak of copy-cat behavior."

On June 21, Pepsi President Weatherup wrote to President Clinton, thanking him for the "excellent work" of Kessler and the FDA "in pursuing the recent product tampering hoax."

Employee Relations

In the area of employee relations—with its staff and bottlers—Pepsi adopted a policy of full and immediate disclosure as soon as it had discerned the pertinent facts.

Consumer advisories were dispatched at least once a day, usually twice or three times on each day of the crisis, letting bottlers and general managers in Pepsi's 400 field locations know what was going on, what had been reported, what the government was doing, and how the company was responding.

SCENES OF AN ALLEGED PRODUCT TAMPERING

FRAME: 08:32:15

An opened can of Diet Pepsi, held by a Colorado woman, appears to be lowered behind the counter of a convenience store, out of the clerk's line of sight.

FRAME: 08:32:27

The woman fumbles with her purse and pulls out what appears to be a syringe.

FRAME: 08:32:34

The woman appears to place the syringe in the opened can of Diet Pepsi while keeping it behind the counter.

FRAME: 08:32:39

The woman places the can back on the counter then asks the clerk for a cup into which she pours the Diet Pepsi and allegedly discovers the syringe.

Figure 3–10   The evidence ending the Pepsi tampering hoax was this surveillance video of a woman caught stuffing a syringe into a Pepsi can.

Managers were advised on how to "communicate with employees and customers" in the form of "Product Tampering Guidelines," as well as in procedures for reporting alleged tamperings.

President Weatherup also personally wrote to bottlers and general managers periodically during the crisis to keep them advised of breaking developments. When the surveillance video was found, Weatherup sent all Pepsi bottlers, by overnight mail, a videotape of Commissioner Kessler's news conference, along with the surveillance footage.

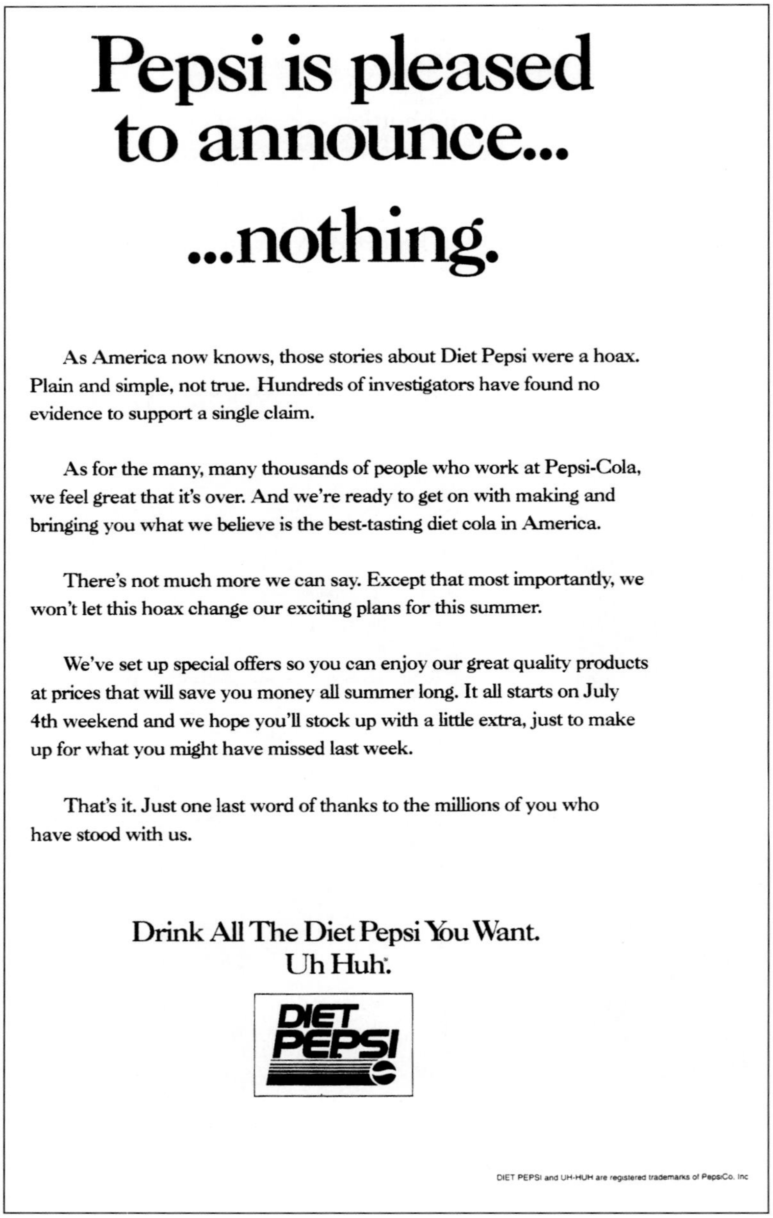

Pepsi is pleased to announce...

...nothing.

As America now knows, those stories about Diet Pepsi were a hoax. Plain and simple, not true. Hundreds of investigators have found no evidence to support a single claim.

As for the many, many thousands of people who work at Pepsi-Cola, we feel great that it's over. And we're ready to get on with making and bringing you what we believe is the best-tasting diet cola in America.

There's not much more we can say. Except that most importantly, we won't let this hoax change our exciting plans for this summer.

We've set up special offers so you can enjoy our great quality products at prices that will save you money all summer long. It all starts on July 4th weekend and we hope you'll stock up with a little extra, just to make up for what you might have missed last week.

That's it. Just one last word of thanks to the millions of you who have stood with us.

Drink All The Diet Pepsi You Want.
Uh Huh.

DIET PEPSI and UH-HUH are registered trademarks of PepsiCo. Inc

Figure 3–11 With its crisis proven to be a hoax, Pepsi triumphantly proclaimed its victory with this ad.

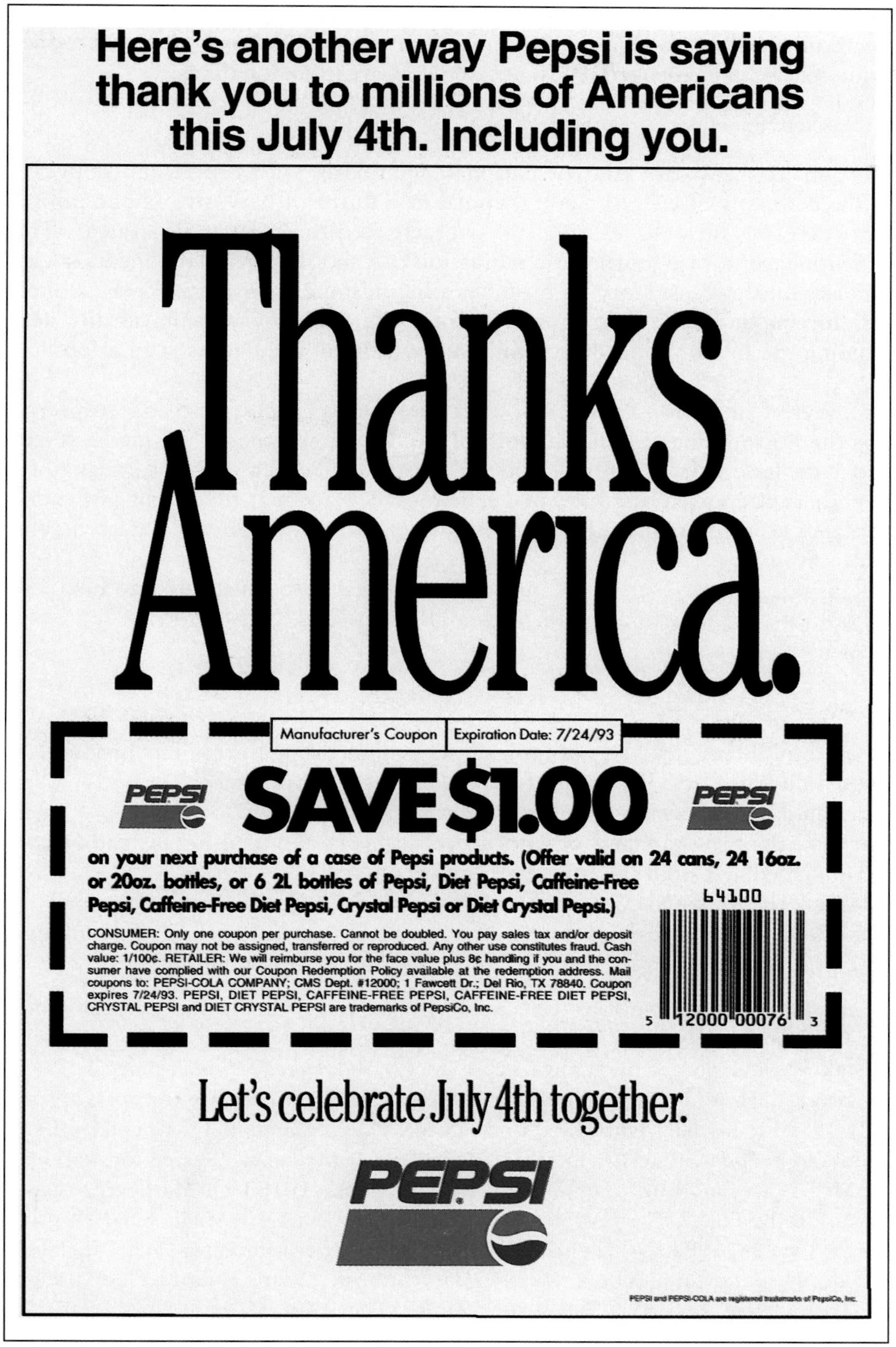

Figure 3–12 Case closed. Uh huh!

"Please share it with your customers," the Pepsi president suggested.

By June 18, just one week—and what seemed like one millennium—after its product and reputation had been challenged, Pepsi declared victory in national ads:

Pepsi is pleased to announce . . . nothing.

What had begun as the worst kind of national nightmare, with critics and copycats threatening the company at every juncture, ended in a flurry of pervasive public praise. "Media-smart Pepsi" is how *Advertising Age* characterized the company's strategy. The *Milwaukee Sentinel*, in a rare journalistic admission of candor, labeled the media's leap to sensationalism on the Pepsi story "a mistake, a big mistake." *Business Week* credited the company for making "the right moves, Baby." The company was universally heralded for holding the line on a product recall and putting on the line its reputation and credibility.

Perhaps sweetest of all for Pepsi-Cola, after the FDA/OCI's arrest of 55 suspected hoaxers, was the bottom-line aftermath: Not only had Pepsi weathered the media storm and emerged with its credibility intact, but the impact on Pepsi's sales was negligible. President Weatherup reported that sales had fallen just 3 percent at the height of the crisis, approximately $30 million. By July and August, Pepsi sales were up 7 percent, the best summer in five years.

All in all, as one industry periodical put it, "Pepsi's response constituted nothing less than 'a textbook case' of how to come through a PR crisis."

QUESTIONS

1. Do you think Pepsi erred by not immediately volunteering to recall its product?
2. How would you assess Pepsi's overall public relations strategy?
3. How would you assess Pepsi's government relations strategy?
4. What were the pros and cons of ignoring print media and focusing instead on electronic media? Could this strategy backfire on Pepsi?
5. What were the pros and cons of using Pepsi's president as chief spokesperson?
6. What public relations lessons can be drawn from Pepsi's experience for handling future product tampering cases?

For further information about the Pepsi-Cola syringe scare case, see Claudia Carpenter, "A 'Scared' Firm Fights to Save Its Good Name," *New York Post*, June 17, 1993, 25; Gerry Hinckley, "'Big Mistake' Acknowledged on Syringe–Pepsi Story," *Milwaukee Sentinel*, June 21, 1993; Thomas K. Grose, "How Pepsico Overcame Syringe Challenge," *TJFR Business News Reporter*, July 1993, 1; Michael Janofsky, "Under Siege, Pepsi Mounts a TV Counter Offensive," *The New York Times*, June 17, 1993, D-1; Charles M. Madigan, "Recipe for National Scare: Pepsi, Media, Me-Too-Ism," *The Record*, June 21, 1993, D-1; Tom Mashberg, "Pepsi Puts Reputation on the Line," *The Boston Globe*, June 17, 1993, A-1; "Media-Smart Pepsi," *Advertising Age*, June 28, 1993, 26; "Public Relations Victory Sweep for Pepsi-Cola Officials," *Washington Post News Service*, June 20, 1993; Gary Strauss, "Scare Fails to Flatten Pepsi Sales," *USA Today*, June 23, 1993, B-1; Laura Zinn, "The Right Moves, Baby," *Business Week*, July 5, 1993, 30.

ARCHBISHOP JOHN P. FOLEY

John P. Foley was ordained as an archbishop and named president of the Pontifical Commission for Social Communications at the Vatican by Pope John Paul II in 1984. In this capacity, he is the highest-ranking public relations official in the Vatican. Archbishop Foley began his communications career writing radio plays as a teenager. He continued his writing, radio, and television work in secondary school. On being ordained to the priesthood, he was assigned to the *Catholic Standard and Times* newspaper. He became editor of the paper and later served as English language press secretary for Pope John Paul II's trip to Ireland and the United States in 1979.

WHAT IS THE CHURCH'S ATTITUDE TOWARD PUBLIC RELATIONS?

The church has always been interested in public relations in the wide sense of the term. Also, one can say that the church has been involved in most communications media at the beginning—the first printed book was the Bible; Marconi himself developed Vatican Radio; among the first and still among the most widely transmitted satellite broadcasts are the papal ceremonies of Christmas, Holy Week, and Easter.

At the Vatican, press information that had previously been made available through *L'Osservatore Romano*, the Vatican daily, began to be made available through a special press office during the Second Vatican Council (1962–1965). This press office of the Holy See has become a permanent fixture at the Vatican, and the director of the press office makes public the official statements of the Holy See. Contact with the electronic and film media is done through the Pontifical Council for Social Communications, which also makes arrangements for the satellite transmission of papal ceremonies. Naturally, there has been growing contact with the media over the years and an increased professionalism in such public relations contacts.

The Congregation for Catholic Education has also asked that all those preparing for the priesthood be trained in basic communications skills—for example, preparing press releases and responding to media queries.

WHAT IS THE MAKEUP OF THE VATICAN COMMUNICATIONS STAFF?

First, the 15 staff members of this council authorize and provide technical assistance for about 1,500 audiovisual projects each year, promote Catholic communications work throughout the world, maintain contact with the three international Catholic communications organizations—one for press, one for radio-TV, and a third for cinema—maintain the Vatical film library, and prepare communications policy documents. There are also the more than 300 people of Vatican Radio, which broadcasts in more than 30 languages around the world; the somewhat smaller staff of *L'Osservatore Romano*, which publishes a daily newspaper in Italian and weekly editions in Italian, English, French, Spanish, German, and Portuguese and a monthly edition in Polish; the dozen staff members of the Vatican Television Center, a production facility that documents the public activity of the pope and coproduces programs for TV stations and networks around the world; and the Press Office of the Holy See and Vatican Information Service, for contact with the media in Rome and elsewhere.

WHAT IS YOUR NORMAL WORKING DAY?

Normal working day—Monday through Saturday: rise between 5:30 and 6 A.M. for prayer and Mass. Arrive at office at about 7:30 A.M. Review mail, in Italian, English, Spanish, French, Portuguese, German, and Dutch—someone else tells me what the German and Dutch correspondence says—and respond to letters; regular 9 A.M. meeting with top staff; appointments starting at 10 A.M. with communicators, bishops, ambassadors, technicians, etc., etc. Lunch: 2 P.M., often a working lunch. Afternoon—desk work and planning and meetings, in office or at home. Dinner—8 P.M., often a working dinner. Almost every day, it is necessary to speak four languages—Italian, English, Spanish, and French.

HOW ACTIVE IS THE POPE IN COMMUNICATIONS ACTIVITY?

Pope John Paul II has a great interest in communications and is a natural communicator through his obvious authenticity and through his symbolic gestures. And he is, obviously, a major news maker. He does not, however, do anything specifically for the media, except the recording of an occasional radio or TV message before making a pastoral visit to a particular country. He is open to full coverage of all his public activity, however, and he does visit on the plane with journalists who accompany him on his international trips. He is most willing to meet with groups of communicators who come to Rome and to offer a specific message on the media. He is a very warm and expressive person, and this seems to be communicated well in the media, especially in television and in photos.

HOW EXTENSIVE IS THE POPE'S SPEAKING SCHEDULE?

The Secretariat of State forms, among other things, a research staff for the pope in gathering material for the preparation of speeches by the pope. In the 15 years of his pontificate, during the 175 trips the pope has made outside of Rome, the pope has made 2,728 speeches. The pope generally makes between 20 and 25 speeches a week here in Rome.

WHAT HAS BEEN YOUR MOST SIGNIFICANT
PUBLIC RELATIONS CHALLENGE?

I would say that my biggest challenge is to get communicators to take seriously the religious and spiritual dimension of human life. These aspects of life—the validity and effectiveness, and indeed the importance, of spiritual and religious motivation in human activity—seem foreign to secular journalists. Without acceptance of the reality of such spiritual and religious motivation, how do you account for those who suffered for their faith under Communist oppression—and indeed, the thirst for religious liberty, which was in part responsible for the collapse of Communism?

Allied to this is a certain amount of frustration in getting news people to recognize "good news"—as when the media, until the last minute, virtually ignored the presence of 250,000 young people for the World Day of Youth in Denver in August 1993 and focused on dissent and problems in the church. I do not say that dissent and problems should not be covered; I do say that there is a story behind the presence of 250,000 enthusiastic and generous young people from around the world in Denver, which should not be overlooked or ignored. The reporting of such good news can also contribute to an improvement in social morale and can offer encouragement and models for imitation to others. I do not say that bad news should be covered up; I do say that good news is indeed news and should not be ignored.

Thus, my biggest challenge is to get people to accept the importance or reality of the spiritual and religious dimension of human life and to convince them not to ignore the good news—what the Baptist evangelist and educator Russell Conwell called the "acres of diamonds" in our own backyard.

CHAPTER FOUR

Ethics

SEVERAL YEARS AGO, SOCIOLOGIST RAYMOND BAUMHART ASKED business people, "What does ethics mean to you?" Among their replies:

Ethics has to do with what my feelings tell me is right or wrong.
Ethics has to do with my religious beliefs.
Being ethical is doing what the law requires.
Ethics consists of the standards of behavior our society accepts.
I don't know what the word means.

The meaning of ethics is hard to pin down, and the views many people have about ethics are uncertain. Nonetheless, ethical dilemmas are all around us. In many sectors of society today, institutions are sending out mixed signals about the value of moral conduct.

Consider the following:

- In 1997, the highest levels of the U.S. government were dogged by infuriating ethical scandals.

  President Clinton was accused of offering the Lincoln bedroom in the White House as a "reward" for significant campaign contributions, and Vice President Al Gore was accused of soliciting Democratic contributions from the White House, in violation of federal law.

  Special Prosecutor Kenneth Starr doggedly investigated President and Mrs. Clinton's questionable investment in the Whitewater real estate development in Arkansas.

  President Clinton's chief media strategist Dick Morris was forced to resign when it was revealed he regularly hired a Washington prostitute, who "listened in" on telephone strategy sessions with the president.

  Vice President Gore attended a campaign meeting in a California Buddhist temple, claiming he was "unaware" that funds were being raised for his Democratic reelection campaign. In point of fact, the temple meeting was a "fund raiser," just the tip of an effort to enlist millions in campaign contributions from Asian influence seekers.

On the other side of the aisle, Republican Speaker of the House Newt Gingrich was reprimanded and heavily fined by a Congressional Ethics Committee for using an educational course as a "front" for raising campaign contributions.

- Journalism, too, was plagued by ethical transgressions.

ABC News commentator Barbara Walters did a glowing report on *Sunset Boulevard* creator Andrew Lloyd Webber on her *20/20* program in late 1996. Ms. Walters made no mention of her investment of $100,000 in the very same Broadway production she lauded.[1]

Newsweek columnist Joe Klein was exposed as the author of a best-selling "fictional" work, which trashed President Clinton and others. Klein insistently denied he was the "Anonymous" author of *Primary Colors*, until he was forced to admit the lie.[2]

NBC TV News, which prided itself as the model of objectivity and impartiality, was revealed to have rigged crash tests to ensure that a General Motors truck self-destructed on cue before rolling cameras. Only the tenacity of GM itself forced NBC to admit its abuse of investigative journalistic power.

- Profit-making and nonprofit-making organizations also could not escape ethical scandal.

The nation's leading cigarette manufacturers were hauled before Congress and the courts in the late 90s, charged with knowing all along—but not admitting—that cigarette smoking was harmful and addictive (see Case Study, chapter 16). Finally, one major manufacturer, Liggett, admitted that it had known for years that smoking was addictive.[3]

The Prudential Insurance Company, known as "the Rock" of financial integrity, was itself "rocked" by a scandal involving its sales people in unscrupulous practices.

The American Express Company, among the world's largest and most prestigious corporations, contributed $8 million to settle a dispute with a former top executive after acknowledging that the corporation had tried to discredit the man by linking him to illegal activities.

Wal-Mart, for years a proponent of a "Buy America" program, was exposed as hiring underage workers to produce garments in Latin America and Asia. Even worse, tearful Wal-Mart partner Kathie Lee Gifford, a pristine TV personality, was accused of fronting for the slavish child laborers, who manufactured the garments bearing her name.[4]

United Way of America, the nation's largest nonprofit group, was humiliated when its president was found to be spending the organization's funds on lavish expenses and nepotism.

- Even the public relations profession came under its share of ethical scrutiny.

In 1996, public relations veteran John Scanlon was targeted by federal prosecutors for "obstructing justice," for dishing the dirt on a former cigarette company executive who went public with charges against Scanlon client Brown & Williamson Tobacco Corp.

In 1997, New York public relations firm Kekst & Co. was chastised for agreeing to represent the banks of Switzerland, who were disclosed as having secretly sympathized with the Nazis during and after the Holocaust.

What's going on here?

Pollster Richard Wirthlin has discovered that "For most organizations, image is determined not only by what goods and services are provided, but also by the persona of the corporation. The first imperative of leadership is 'honesty.' "[5]

So, what constitutes ethics for an organization? Sadly, there is no one answer. Ethical guidelines are just that—guidelines. They don't necessarily provide right answers, just educated guesses. And reasonable people can and do disagree about what is moral, ethical, and right in a given situation.

Nonetheless, when previously respected business, government, and religious leaders, as well as other members of society, are exposed as cheaters, con artists, and even crooks, those who would look up to and be influenced by such people are correctly appalled. Little wonder then that societal pressure in the area of ethics has never been more intense. In public relations no issue is more critical than ethics—of both the practice and the practitioner.

The bigness of most institutions today—where mega mergers are commonplace among business organizations, hospitals, media firms, public relations agencies, and other institutions—immediately makes them suspect. All have become concerned about their individual cultures—the values, ideals, principles, and aspirations that underlie their credibility and viability. As the internal conscience of many organizations, the public relations department has become a focal point for the institutionalization of ethical conduct. Increasingly, management has turned to public relations officers to lead the internal ethical charge, to be the keeper of the organizational ethic.

ETHICS IN SOCIETY

What exactly are ethics? Roughly translated, an individual's or organization's ethics come down to the standards that are followed in relationships with others—the real integrity of the individual or organization.

A discussion of the many classical theories of ethics lies beyond the scope of this book. Philosophers throughout the ages have debated the essence of ethics. To Aristotle, the golden mean of moral virtue could be found between two extreme points of view. Kant's categorical imperative recommended acting "on that maxim which you will to become a universal law." Mill's principle of utility recommended "seeking the greatest happiness for the greatest number." And the traditional Judeo-Christian ethic prescribes "loving your neighbor as yourself." Indeed, this Golden Rule makes great good sense in the practice of public relations.

Public relations people, in particular, must be ethical. They can't assume that ethics are strictly personal choices without relevance or related methodology for resolving moral quandaries. Rather, as the Code of Professional Standards of the Public Relations Society of America states (Appendix A), practitioners must be scrupulously honest and trustworthy, acting at all times in the public interest, which, by definition, also represents the best interests of individual organizations. Indeed, if the ultimate goal of the public relations professional is to enhance public trust of an organization, then only the highest ethical conduct is acceptable.

The essence of the Public Relations Society of America Code of Standards and that of the International Association of Business Communicators (Figure 4–1) is that honesty and fairness lie at the heart of public relations practice. In light of the field's public nature, these codes underscore the importance of members promoting and maintaining "high standards of public service and ethical conduct." Inherent in these standards of the profession is the understanding that ethics have changed and continue to change as society changes. Over time, views have changed on such areas as minority discrimination, double standards in the treatment of women, pollution of the environment, destruction of endangered species and natural resources, lack of concern for human rights, and on and on. Again, honesty and fairness are two critical components that will continue to determine the ethical behavior of public relations professionals.[6]

The first question that public relations must pose in any management discussion is "Are we doing the right thing?" Often the public relations professional will be the only member of management with the nerve to pose such a question. Sometimes this means saying "no" to what the boss wants to do. The bottom line for public relations professionals must always be what is in the best interests of the organization.

In the 1990s, this is easier said than done.

● Hill & Knowlton, one of the world's largest public relations firms, as noted, was embarrassed in recent years by taking on clients, such as the antiabortion National Con-

IABC CODE OF ETHICS

The IABC Code of Ethics has been developed to provide IABC members and other communication professionals with guidelines of professional behavior and standards of ethical practice. The Code will be reviewed and revised as necessary by the Ethics Committee and the Executive Board.

Any IABC member who wishes advice and guidance regarding its interpretation and/or application may write or phone IABC headquarters. Questions will be routed to the Executive Board member responsible for the Code.

Communication and Information Dissemination

1. *Communication professionals will uphold the credibility and dignity of their profession by encouraging the practice of honest, candid and timely communication.*

The highest standards of professionalism will be upheld in all communication. Communicators should encourage frequent communication and messages that are honest in their content, candid, accurate and appropriate to the needs of the organization and its audiences.

2. *Professional communicators will not use any information that has been generated or appropriately acquired by a business for another business without permission. Further, communicators should attempt to identify the source of information to be used.*

When one is changing employers, information developed at the previous position will not be used without permission from that employer. Acts of plagiarism and copyright infringement are illegal acts; material in the public domain should have its source attributed, if possible. If an organization grants permission to use its information and requests public acknowledgment, it will be made in a place appropriate to the material used. The material will be used only for the purpose for which permission was granted.

Standards of Conduct

3. *Communication professionals will abide by the spirit and letter of all laws and regulations governing their professional activities.*

All international, national and local laws and regulations must be observed, with particular attention to those pertaining to communication, such as copyright law. Industry and organizational regulations will also be observed.

4. *Communication professionals will not condone any illegal or unethical act related to their professional activity, their organization and its business or the public environment in which it operates.*

It is the personal responsibility of professional communicators to act honestly, fairly and with integrity at all times in all professional activities. Looking the other way while others act illegally tacitly condones such acts whether or not the communicator has committed them. The communicator should speak with the individual involved, his or her supervisor or appropriate authorities – depending on the context of the situation and one's own ethical judgment.

Confidentiality/Disclosure

5. *Communication professionals will respect the confidentiality and right-to-privacy of all individuals, employers, clients and customers.*

Communicators must determine the ethical balance between right-to-privacy and need-to-know. Unless the situation involves illegal or grossly unethical acts, confidences should be maintained. If there is a conflict between right-to-privacy and need-to-know, a communicator should first talk with the source and negotiate the need for the information to be communicated.

6. *Communication professionals will not use any confidential information gained as a result of professional activity for personal benefit or for that of others.*

Confidential information can be used to give inside advantage to stock transactions, gain favors from outsiders, assist a competing company for whom one is going to work, assist companies in developing a marketing advantage, achieve a publishing advantage or otherwise act to the detriment of an organization. Such information must remain confidential during and after one's employment period.

Professionalism

7. *Communication professionals should uphold IABC's standards for ethical conduct in all professional activity, and should use IABC and its designation of accreditation (ABC) only for purposes that are authorized and fairly represent the organization and its professional standards.*

IABC recognizes the need for professional integrity within any organization, including the association. Members should acknowledge that their actions reflect on themselves, their organizations and their profession.

Printed with the assistance of the Mead Corporation and Brown & Kroger Printing, Dayton, OH

Figure 4–1 The International Association of Business Communicators adopted these seven tenets to guide the professional behavior of its members.

ference of Catholic Bishops, the controversial Church of Scientology, and the scandalized Bank of Credit and Commerce International.

- One of the nation's best-known public relations counselors, Robert Dilenschneider, was slapped with a $50 million lawsuit for turning against a former client and seizing control of his business.[7]
- Kekst & Co., another of the nation's most successful public relations firms, was found to be representing both Paramount and Viacom in the latter's attempt to buy the former. What complicated the situation was that another hopeful acquirer, QVC, announced its willingness to pay the shareholders more for Paramount than Viacom—thus compromising the integrity of the Kekst initiative.[8]
- Political public relations counselor Edward Rollins boasted to a media group that he had "bribed" black leaders in New Jersey to stay away from the polls so that his employer, Governor Christine Todd Whitman, could be reelected.

Examples like these point out the difficulty, in an increasingly competitive society, of maintaining high ethical standards in public relations practice specifically and in business in general.

ETHICS IN BUSINESS

For many people today, regrettably, the term business ethics is an oxymoron. Its mere mention stimulates thoughts of disgraced financiers like Ivan Boesky and Michael Milken illegally raking in millions of dollars with insider stock tips or of tobacco companies being charged by congressional committees for withholding damaging data on the addictive properties of cigarettes.

Fraud, price gouging, discrimination, runaway pollution—all these allegations have made headlines in recent years. And American business, perhaps the most ethical business system in the world, has been shocked—so much so that in 1987 the former Securities and Exchange Commission chairman, John Shad, donated $23 million to begin a program at Harvard Business School to make the study of ethics an integral part of the curriculum.*

In one significant study, a leading business group, the Business Roundtable, pointed out the "crucial role of the chief executive officer and top managers in establishing a strong commitment to ethical conduct and in providing constant leadership in tending and reviewing the values of the organization."[9] The Roundtable study debunked the myth that there is an inherent contradiction between ethics and profits. On the contrary, it emphasized that there is a strong relationship between acting ethically, maintaining a good reputation for fair and honest business, and making money.

Another study of key business leaders, conducted by the accounting firm Touche Ross, corroborated the notion that a majority of business leaders—63 percent—"believe that a business enterprise actually 'strengthens' its competitive position by maintaining

---

*Ironically Mr. Shad himself was the subject of an embarrassing ethical dilemma. He was called in to head Drexel Burnham Lambert after the firm was fined and discredited for junk bond indiscretions led by Milken. Shad was duly mortified when Drexel Burnham went belly up in 1989.

high ethical standards." Only 14 percent said that a company with high ethical standards was a "weaker competitor."[10] The Touche Ross research on more than 1,000 business leaders also turned up other interesting findings about the current state of business ethics:

- Intense concentration on short-term earnings is a major threat to American business ethics today. Respondents ranked this threat almost equal to that posed by decay in cultural and social institutions.
- Respondents ranked the United States as having higher standards of business ethics than any other country—noting high standards also in the United Kingdom, Canada, Switzerland, and Germany.
- Among industries, respondents ranked commercial banking, utilities, and drugs, pharmaceuticals, and cosmetics as the three most ethical.
- Among all professions, respondents ranked the clergy, teachers, engineers, and accountants as the four most ethical.[11]

In the waning years of the 1990s, the outbreak of downsizings and mergers and cutbacks helped create a serious "trust gap" between employers and workers.[12] Where once workers "trusted" the ethics of their employers, in the twenty-first century, this is likely to be much less the case, as business struggles with declining employee loyalty.

CORPORATE CODES OF CONDUCT

One manifestation of the increased attention to corporate ethics is the growth of internal codes of conduct. Codes of ethics, standards of conduct, and similar statements of corporate policies and values have proliferated in recent years. The reasons corporations have adopted such codes vary from company to company.

- To increase public confidence—The scandals concerning overseas bribery and domestic political campaign contributions during the 1970s led to a decline of public trust and confidence in business. Many firms responded with written codes of ethics.
- To stem the tide of regulation—As public confidence declined, government regulation of business increased. Some estimated the cost to society of compliance with regulations at $100 billion per year. Corporate codes of conduct, it was hoped, would serve as a self-regulation mechanism.
- To improve internal operations—As companies became larger and more decentralized, management needed consistent standards of conduct to ensure that employees were meeting the business objectives of the company in a legal and ethical manner.
- To respond to transgressions—Frequently when a company itself was caught in the web of unethical behavior, it responded with its own code of ethics. For example, Fiat, Italy's biggest private company, sought to extricate itself from a huge corruption scandal in the country by issuing the first Italian corporate code of ethical conduct for employees.[13]

Ralph Waldo Emerson once wrote that "an organization is the lengthened shadow of a man." Today, many corporate executives realize that just as an individual has certain responsibilities as a citizen, a corporate citizen has responsibilities to the society in which it is privileged to operate (Figure 4–2).

Corporate codes of conduct are not without their critics. Some ethics specialists say that what is contained in the codes doesn't really address ethics in general. A Washington

Dear Colleague:

Lockheed Martin aims to "set the standard" for ethical business conduct. We will achieve this through six virtues: Honesty, Integrity, Respect, Trust, Responsibility, and Citizenship.

Honesty: to be truthful in all our endeavors; to be honest and forthright with one another and with our customers, communities, suppliers, and shareholders.

Integrity: to say what we mean, to deliver what we promise, and to stand for what is right.

Respect: to treat one another with dignity and fairness, appreciating the diversity of our workforce and the uniqueness of each employee.

Trust: to build confidence through teamwork and open, candid communication.

Responsibility: to speak up – without fear of retribution – and report concerns in the work place, including violations of laws, regulations and company policies, and seek clarification and guidance whenever there is doubt.

Citizenship: to obey all the laws of the United States and the other countries in which we do business and to do our part to make the communities in which we live better.

You can count on us to do everything in our power to meet Lockheed Martin's standards. We are counting on you to do the same. We are confident that our trust in you is well placed and we are determined to be worthy of your trust.

DANIEL M. TELLEP   NORMAN R. AUGUSTINE   BERNARD L. SCHWARTZ

Figure 4–2   The principles enumerated here represent the obligations that Lockheed Martin Company believes it has to its public.

State University study of ethical codes at 200 Fortune 500 companies found that while 75 percent failed to address the company's role in civic and community affairs, consumer relations, environmental safety, and product safety, more than 75 percent dealt with conflicts of interest—which can affect the bottom line.[14] Such skepticism notwithstanding, formal ethical codes, addressing such topics as confidentiality of corporate information, misappropriation of corporate assets, bribes and kickbacks, and political contributions, have become a corporate fact of life.

CORPORATE SOCIAL RESPONSIBILITY

Closely related to the ethical conduct of an organization is its social responsibility, which has been defined as a social norm. This norm holds that any social institution, including the smallest family unit and the largest corporation, is responsible for the behavior of its members and may be held accountable for their misdeeds.

In the late 1960s, when this idea was just emerging, initial responses were of the knee-jerk variety. A firm that was threatened by increasing legal or activist pressures and harassment would ordinarily change its policies in a hurry. Today, however, organizations and their social responsibility programs are much more sophisticated. Social responsibility is treated just like any other management discipline: Analyze the issues, evaluate performance, set priorities, allocate resources to those priorities, and implement programs that deal with issues within the constraints of the organization's resources. Many companies have created special committees to set the agenda and target the objectives.

Social responsibility touches practically every level of organizational activity, from marketing to hiring, from training to work standards. When a worldwide company, like Texaco, discovers violations of its social responsibility code (see Case Study, chapter 1), it has no alternative but to take prompt and forceful action. A partial list of social responsibility categories might include the following:

- Product lines—dangerous products, product performance and standards, packaging, and environmental impact
- Marketing practices—sales practices, consumer complaint policies, advertising content, and fair pricing
- Employee services—training, counseling and placement services, transfer procedures, and educational allowances
- Corporate philanthropy—contribution performance, encouragement of employee participation in social projects, and community development activities
- Environmental activities—pollution-control projects, adherence to federal standards, and evaluation procedures for new packages and products
- External relations—support of minority enterprises, investment practices, and government relations
- Employment diversity in retaining and promoting minorities and women—current hiring policies, advancement policies, specialized career counseling, and opportunities for special minorities such as the physically handicapped
- Employee safety and health—work environment policies, accident safeguards, and food and medical facilities

More often than not, organizations have incorporated social responsibility into the mainstream of their practice. Most firms recognize that social responsibility, far from

A QUESTION OF ETHICS

SHAM OR SHAMU: THE PUSH TO FREE WILLY

In the 1990s, an increasing number of Americans opposed placing marine mammals in captivity. Helping to fuel the fire was a wildly successful and sympathetic movie, *Free Willy*, in which a young boy released a three-ton captive whale, as misty-eyed theatergoers cheered appreciatively.

On one side of the debate stood groups like the Fund for Animals and In Defense of Animals, who argued that dolphins and so-called killer whales or orcas weren't meant to swim in contained tanks in amusement parks. Rather, these groups argued, such unnatural treatment leads to an inordinate amount of dolphin and whale deaths.

Adding to the anticaptivity charge was the revelation that in the 1980s, theme park Sea World provided tour guides with an instruction package that read, in part, "If people ask you about a particular animal that you know has passed away, please say, 'I don't know.' "

Sea World answered critics by explaining that this practice was eliminated after Anheuser-Busch purchased Sea World in 1989.

Other aquariums around the nation, such as the Shedd Aquarium in Chicago, initiated public relations offensives to point out that "There is evidence that many species of dolphins live as long in aquariums as they do in the wild, if not longer." Nonetheless through the mid-nineties, animal activists increased their protests to keep the pressure on aqua exhibitors.

Indeed, in confronting an issue such as this, the question must be raised, "What are the ethical implications in displaying dolphins in such unnatural habitats?"*

*Gary Robbins, "Truth Unclear in Dolphin Debate," *The Sunday Record*, November 28, 1993, A–12.

---

being an add-on program, must be a corporate way of life. Beyond this, some studies have indicated that those organizations that practice social responsibility over time rank among the most profitable and successful firms in society.

ETHICS IN GOVERNMENT

Politics has never enjoyed an unblemished reputation when it comes to ethics. And in the final years of the twentieth century, politics has developed a particularly sleazy reputation.

The 1997 campaign financing scandal was symptomatic of the ethical problems afflicting politics. President Clinton handily turned back Republican challenger Bob Dole in the 1996 election campaign. Nonetheless, after the election, it was revealed that the Democrats used questionable judgment to entice huge contributions, particularly from representatives of nations like Indonesia, China, and Korea. Amidst calls for a new "Special Prosecutor" to coexist with the one already hired to investigate Whitewater, people couldn't help but question the ethics of a political process that depends on costly television advertising to get elected.

THE REST OF THE STORY

Figure 4–3 From political guru to public relations casualty, former Clinton advisor turned talk show host, Dick Morris.

SHORT, SAD SAGA OF THE POLITICAL SAGE

No advisor symbolized better the "political ethics"—or lack thereof—of the late 1990s as Dick Morris (Figure 4–3).

As a strategist for national and local candidates, it apparently made no difference to Morris as to which side or inclination his candidates represented. Just as long as they "showed him the money," Morris was content, working for right wingers, like Senators Jesse Helms and Trent Lott, and left leaners, like Senator Howard Metzenbaum and President Bill Clinton.

The latter, of course, was Morris' primary client. Indeed, when President Clinton's popularity sagged in the middle of his first term, he turned immediately to his old strategist to bail him out. Morris suggested that the president adopt a less liberal, more middle-of-the-road platform. The president took the advice and made great progress.

Advisor Morris, however, let his access and power get the best of him. He flaunted his status, was nasty to others around him, and claimed credit for virtually anything that the administration did right. But in a classic case of "what goes around comes around," in what should have been his finest hour, consultant Morris crashed and burned.

On the eve of President Clinton's party "coronation" in Chicago, in the fall of 1996, it was revealed in rapid order that presidential confidante Morris had been less than highly ethical with his employer. To wit:

■ He secretly signed a lucrative book contract, without telling the White House and in violation of administration ethical standards.

■ He regularly employed a DC prostitute and let his "friend" listen in on the extension, as he counseled the president and the first lady on matters of national import.

■ He alienated most of the president's other associates, so that when it came time to "stick up for Dick," few allies rushed to defend their fallen comrade.

Poor Dick.

As he, himself, sadly lamented in his $2.5 million autobiography, "I began life weighing only two pounds, eleven ounces and spent my first three months in incubators, untouched by anyone, even my mother. Only after years of therapy did I begin to understand how this early deprivation affected my personality thereafter."

> Poor, whiny Dick.
> Ultimately, Morris was forced to resign from the president's employ. His wife announced she was leaving him. And in the most ignominious sign of how utterly impoverished his life had now become, Dick Morris became a radio talk show host.

The sleaze factor in government, of course, is nothing new.

In 1993, Oregon Republican Senator Robert Packwood was the subject of embarrassing publicity regarding unseemly sexual advances that Packwood had made to women over decades in politics. On the other side of the political aisle, Illinois Congressman Mel Reynolds was hounded out of office for similar transgressions with an underaged campaign worker. Still earlier, President Bush was plagued by skepticism about his role in secret Iran-Nicaraguan Contra negotiations. President Reagan suffered an embarrassing scandal in his Housing and Urban Development Department and lobbying violations by several key assistants. Five U.S. senators in the winter of 1990 were accused of serious ethical violations in support of Charles Keating, a convicted savings and loan operator. Four years later, four of the "Keating Five" senators were gone from the Senate.

In the twenty-first century, the public should be less willing to tolerate such ethical violations from their elected officials. It is likely that ethics in government will become an even more important issue as fed-up voters insist on representatives who are honest, trustworthy, and ethical.

ETHICS IN JOURNALISM

The Society of Professional Journalists is quite explicit on the subject of ethics (Figure 4–4).

Journalists at all times will show respect for the dignity, privacy, rights and well-being of people encountered in the course of gathering and presenting the news.

1. The news media should not communicate unofficial charges affecting reputation or moral character without giving the accused a chance to reply.
2. The news media must guard against invading a person's right to privacy.
3. The media should not pander to morbid curiosity about details of vice and crime.

And so on.

Unfortunately, what is in the code often doesn't reflect what appears in print or on the air. More often than not, journalistic judgments run smack into ethical principles.

• In the 1990s, the proliferation of "tabloid television programs," from *A Current Affair* to *Inside Edition* to *Hard Copy*, and sleazy talk shows, from Jerry Springer to Maury Povich to Jenny Jones compromised journalism significantly. The most outrageous example of the depths to which television, in particular, had sunk, occurred in 1996 when a "guest" on the *Jenny Jones Show* murdered a fellow program participant, after the man revealed a "secret crush" on his neighbor on national television (Figure 4–5).

THE SOCIETY OF PROFESSIONAL JOURNALISTS, SIGMA DELTA CHI

Code OF Ethics

THE SOCIETY of Professional Journalists, Sigma Delta Chi believes the duty of journalists is to serve the truth.

WE BELIEVE the agencies of mass communication are carriers of public discussion and information, acting on their Constitutional mandate and freedom to learn and report the facts.

WE BELIEVE in public enlightenment as the forerunner of justice, and in our Constitutional role to seek the truth as part of the public's right to know the truth.

WE BELIEVE those responsibilities carry obligations that require journalists to perform with intelligence, objectivity, accuracy and fairness.

To these ends, we declare acceptance of the standards of practice here set forth:

RESPONSIBILITY:

The public's right to know of events of public importance and interest is the overriding mission of the mass media. The purpose of distributing news and enlightened opinion is to serve the general welfare. Journalists who use their professional status as representatives of the public for selfish or other unworthy motives violate a high trust.

FREEDOM OF THE PRESS:

Freedom of the press is to be guarded as an inalienable right of people in a free society. It carries with it the freedom and the responsibility to discuss, question and challenge actions and utterances of our government and of our public and private institutions. Journalists uphold the right to speak unpopular opinions and the privilege to agree with the majority.

ETHICS:

Journalists must be free of obligation to any interest other than the public's right to know the truth.

1. Gifts, favors, free travel, special treatment or privileges can compromise the integrity of journalists and their employers. Nothing of value should be accepted.

2. Secondary employment, political involvement, holding public office and service in community organizations should be avoided if it compromises the integrity of journalists and their employers. Journalists and their employers should conduct their personal lives in a manner which protects them from conflict of interest, real or apparent. Their responsibilities to the public are paramount. That is the nature of their profession.

3. So-called news communications from private sources should not be published or broadcast without substantiation of their claims to news value.

4. Journalists will seek news that serves the public interest, despite the obstacles. They will make constant efforts to assure that the public's business is conducted in public and that public records are open to public inspection.

5. Journalists acknowledge the newsman's ethic of protecting confidential sources of information.

ACCURACY AND OBJECTIVITY:

Good faith with the public is the foundation of all worthy journalism.

1. Truth is our ultimate goal.

2. Objectivity in reporting the news is another goal, which serves as the mark of an experienced professional. It is a standard of performance toward which we strive. We honor those who achieve it.

3. There is no excuse for inaccuracies or lack of thoroughness.

4. Newspaper headlines should be fully warranted by the contents of the articles they accompany. Photographs and telecasts should give an accurate picture of an event and not highlight a minor incident out of context.

5. Sound practice makes clear distinction between news reports and expressions of opinion. News reports should be free of opinion or bias and represent all sides of an issue.

6. Partisanship in editorial comment which knowingly departs from the truth violates the spirit of American journalism.

7. Journalists recognize their responsibility for offering informed analysis, comment and editorial opinion on public events and issues. They accept the obligation to present such material by individuals whose competence, experience and judgment qualify them for it.

8. Special articles or presentations devoted to advocacy or the writer's own conclusions and interpretations should be labeled as such.

FAIR PLAY:

Journalists at all times will show respect for the dignity, privacy, rights and well-being of people encountered in the course of gathering and presenting the news.

1. The news media should not communicate unofficial charges affecting reputation or moral character without giving the accused a chance to reply.

2. The news media must guard against invading a person's right to privacy.

3. The media should not pander to morbid curiosity about details of vice and crime.

4. It is the duty of news media to make prompt and complete correction of their errors.

5. Journalists should be accountable to the public for their reports and the public should be encouraged to voice its grievances against the media. Open dialogue with our readers, viewers and listeners should be fostered.

PLEDGE:

Journalists should actively censure and try to prevent violations of these standards, and they should encourage their observance by all newspeople. Adherence to this code of ethics is intended to preserve the bond of mutual trust and respect between American journalists and the American people.

Figure 4–4 The Society of Professional Journalists has elaborated in some detail on the ethical guidelines that should govern all journalists.

Figure 4–5 Television's ethical nadir came in 1996, when a mortified "Jenny Jones Show" guest, Johnathan Schmitz, murdered a male neighbor, who had revealed an amorous affection for him before a national TV audience.

- So-called more "legitimate" TV news programs also weren't immune from ethical scandal. The problems of NBC-TV News and, in particular, its *Dateline* program tarnished the reputation of television news in general. *Dateline's* bogus presentation of exploding General Motors trucks was but one example of the blurring of the distinction between news and entertainment.
- In print journalism, when a Steele County, Minnesota, woman's description of a bloody fight between two men was broadcast over the police radio band, she begged an Owatonna People's Press reporter not to use her name. She feared reprisal from either or both of the men. The next day's story reported her name, address, and an account of what she had seen. The following day one of the men was found stabbed to death, and the other was arrested not far from the woman's home.
- In 1990, the banking reporter and business editor of the *St. Petersburg* (Florida) *Times* resigned under pressure when it was disclosed that they dealt in the stocks of companies they wrote about. Because the *Times'* policy cautions reporters to "avoid even the appearance of a conflict and to ask their supervisors if they have doubts about an investment," the two men were let go.
- And, of course, as noted, the 1996 lying episode involving *Newsweek's* Joe Klein was perhaps the most major blot on the record of "journalistic ethics."

Figure 4–6   The topic of journalistic ethics in the 1990s has become such an important one that newsletters like this one have begun to emerge.

The point is that a sense of ethics helps an individual make moral decisions, and journalists have to make their decisions with speed and certainty. They can't usually afford to say maybe, and they can never say, "We'll have time to get back to this when the dust settles." Their decisions must meet a deadline. Usually, the principles, values, and ideals that get reported depend largely on the individual doing the reporting (Figure 4–6).

ETHICS IN PUBLIC RELATIONS

In light of numerous misconceptions about what the practice of public relations is or isn't, it is imperative that practitioners emulate the highest standards of personal and professional ethics. Within an organization, public relations practitioners must be the standard bearers of corporate ethical initiatives. By the same token, public relations consultants must always counsel their clients in an ethical direction—toward accuracy and candor and away from lying and hiding the truth.

The Public Relations Society of America has been a leader in the effort to foster a strong sense of ethics among its membership. Its Code of Professional Standards is a model in the attempt to promulgate high standards of public service and ethical conduct. In recent years, this code has been tested on a variety of issues, ranging from noncompetition agreements with the employees of a public relations firm, to the protection of public relations campaign proposals to prospective clients, to paying employees and consultants finder's fees to obtain new accounts.

A study by the Foundation for Public Relations Research and Education, covering the years 1950 to 1985, revealed a strong adherence in the field to the ethical code originally adopted in 1950. During that period, 168 issues and complaints were registered and investigated. Articles of the code most frequently cited were these:

- A member shall deal fairly with clients or employers—past, present, and potential—with fellow practitioners, and with the general public.
- A member shall adhere to truth and accuracy and to generally accepted standards of good taste.
- A member shall conduct his or her professional life in accord with the public interest.
- A member shall not intentionally communicate false or misleading information and is obligated to use care to avoid communication of false or misleading information.
- A member shall not engage in any practice that tends to corrupt the channels of communication or the processes of government.

The foundation concluded that the code, with its enforcement provisions, is a good one: "It has been, can be, and will be improved. It is a vibrant, living document that depends, as our future and that of public relations depends, on constant understanding and application by the society's members."[15]

Among the general public, the relatively strong state of public relations ethics apparently is being recognized more. In an ethics survey by The Pinnacle Group, business persons ranked public relations practitioners fifth among occupations in terms of ethics. Public relations counselors ranked ahead of lawyers, funeral home operators, and advertising professionals. In the same survey, senior high school students ranked public relations professionals seventh in terms of ethics, with doctors, dentists, accountants, and yes, even lawyers, outpacing public relations people.[16]

▲▲▲▲▲▲▲

THE REST OF THE STORY

HITTING THE "ETHICAL WALL"

Perhaps the most persuasive sign that society had hit an "ethical wall" as the twentieth century ended was the announcement from Green Bay, Wisconsin, after the Green Bay Packers won the 1997 Super Bowl. Along with all the mugs and T-shirts, banners and hats commemorating the Packers' triumph was a new product: Packer condoms. The green-and-gold condom, called the "Sport a Legend," was approved by the Federal Drug Administration. Somewhere Coach Vince Lombardi is spinning in his grave.

SUMMARY

The success of public relations in the twenty-first century and beyond will depend largely on how the field responds to the issue of ethical conduct. Public relations professionals must have credibility in order to practice. They must be respected by the various publics with whom they interact. To be credible and to achieve respect, public relations professionals must be ethical. It is that simple.

The final arbiter in assessing whether ethics is important is the public (Figure 4–7). And above all, the public is concerned with the credibility of an organization and of those who serve it. In light of this, the key job for public relations professionals is to "advise clients to adapt to changing conditions and societal expectations, rather than to try to manipulate the environment for the good of the organization."[17] For public relations practice in general and individual public relations professionals in particular, credibility in the next few years will depend on how scrupulously they observe and apply, in everything they do, the principles and practice of ethics.

DISCUSSION STARTERS

1. How would you define ethics?
2. How would you describe the state of ethics in business, government, and journalism?
3. How important are ethics in the practice of public relations?
4. What two concepts underscore ethical conduct in public relations?
5. Compare the ethical codes of the Society of Professional Journalists and the Public Relations Society of America.
6. What is corporate social responsibility?
7. What are corporate codes of conduct?
8. What was the ethical dilemma in the case of Dick Morris?
9. Is the public more or less tolerant of ethical violators today?
10. What is the significance, in terms of ethical practice, of Mike Milken and Ivan Boesky?

Figure 4-7   In 1987, a provocative series of three *Associated Press* photographs showed Pennsylvania treasurer R. Budd Dwyer motioning to reporters, putting a pistol in his mouth, and actually firing the shot that claimed his life. The first picture in the series is shown here; however, the other two are so graphic that ethical standards—not to mention good taste—precluded their presentation in this text.

NOTES

1. "ABC Admits Walters Had 'Sunset' Stake," *The New York Times* (February 20, 1997): Metro 2.
2. Joe Klein, "A Brush With Anonymity," *Newsweek* (July 29, 1996): 76.
3. Warren E. Leary, "Cigarette Company Developed Tobacco With Stronger Nicotine," *The New York Times* (June 22, 1994): A1–14.
4. "Making the Fashion Industry Sweat," *Reputation Management* (September/October 1996): 33.
5. Fraser P. Seitel, "Ethics and Decency," *United States Banker* (April 1993): 58.
6. See Melvin L. Sharpe, "Exploring Questions of Media Morality," *Journal of Mass Media Ethics*, no. 1 (1989): 113–115.
7. Paul Tharp, " 'Double-crossing' PR Supremo Sued for $50 M," *The New York Post* (September 22, 1993): 33.
8. James Cox, "Kekst Under Fire in Paramount Fight," *USA Today* (October 12, 1993): B2.
9. "An Overview of a Landmark Roundtable Study of Corporate Ethics," *Roundtable Report* (February 1988): 1.
10. "Ethics in American Business," Touche Ross (January 1988).
11. Ibid.
12. "The Dream in Danger," *The Public Relations Strategist* (Spring 1995): 43.
13. Alan Cowell, "Fiat, in Scandal, Adopts Ethics Code," *The New York Times* (May 11, 1993).
14. Amanda Bennett, "Ethics Codes Spread Despite Skepticism," *The Wall Street Journal* (July 15, 1988): 18, 19.
15. Public Relations Society of America, study of ethical files, 1950–85, Foundation for Public Relations Research and Education, April 17, 1987, New York.
16. Business Ethics Survey, Minneapolis, MN.: The Pinnacle Group, Inc. (September 27, 1989).
17. Kathie A. Leeper, "Public Relations Ethics and Communitarianism: A Preliminary Investigation," *Public Relations Review* (Summer 1996): 175.

SUGGESTED READINGS

Badaracco, Joseph. *Business Ethics: Roles and Responsibilities.* Burr Ridge, IL: Irwin Professional Publishing, 1995. Cases, readings and text aimed at the moral responsibilities of business executives.

Baker, Lee. *The Credibility Factor: Putting Ethics to Work in Public Relations.* Homewood, IL: Business One Irwin, 1992.

Beaucamp, Tom, and Norman E. Bowie, eds. *Ethical Theory and Business*, 3d ed. Upper Saddle River, NJ: Prentice Hall, 1988.

Behrman, Jack N. *Essays on Ethics in Business and the Professions.* Upper Saddle River, NJ: Prentice Hall, 1988.

Blanchard, Kenneth and Norman Vincent Peale. *The Power of Ethical Management.* New York: Fawcett Crest, 1991.

TOP OF THE SHELF

JOHN STAUBER AND SHELDON RAMPTON

TOXIC SLUDGE IS GOOD FOR YOU: LIES, DAMN LIES AND THE PUBLIC RELATIONS INDUSTRY

MONROE, ME: COMMON COURAGE PRESS, 1996

Stand back, public relations lovers. This book is lethal. *Toxic Sludge*, its publisher claims, "blows the lid off today's multibillion dollar propaganda-for-hire industry." The book focuses on the activities of corporations to persuade the public, particularly in controversial areas like smoking and the environment.

The authors—surprise!—have great disdain and disgust toward the practice of public relations and take particular relish in pointing fingers at the nation's largest public relations firms, Burson-Marsteller, Hill & Knowlton and Ketchum—"the invisible men who control our political debates and public opinion."

This clearly is an unflattering, diabolical, dare I say "somewhat biased" swipe at the public relations profession. But if "knowing the enemy makes one more knowledgeable," then by all means read it.

Corporate Ethics: A Prime Business Asset. New York: Business Roundtable, February 1988. Members of TBR supplied information to develop this report on policy and practice in company conduct.

Dilenschneider, Robert L. *Power and Influence: Mastering the Art of Persuasion.* New York: Prentice Hall, 1990.

Donaldson, Thomas. *Ethics in the Global Market.* London, England: Oxford Press, 1989.

Ethics in American Business. New York: Deloitte & Touche, January 1988. This report on ethical behavior is based on a poll of key business leaders.

Ferre, James. *Public Relations Ethics: A Bibliography.* Boston: G. K. Hall, 1991.

Fink, Conrad C. *Media Ethics.* Needham, MA: Allyn and Bacon, 1995.

Henderson, Verne E. *What's Ethical in Business.* New York: McGraw-Hill, 1992.

McElreath, Mark P. *Managing Systematic and Ethical Public Relations.* Dubuque, IA: Wm. C. Brown, 1993.

"An Overview of a Landmark Roundtable Study of Corporate Ethics." *Roundtable Report.* New York: Business Roundtable,

Posner, Ari. "The Culture of Plagiarism." *New Republic* (April 18, 1988): 19–24.

"PR Groups Combine on Code of Ethics." *Jack O'Dwyer's Newsletter* (May 18, 1988).

Schick, Thomas A. "Technician Ethics in Public Relations." *Public Relations Quarterly* (Spring 1996): 30–35.

Sevareid, Eric. "Ethics and the Media." *Across the Board.* New York: Conference Board, 1988, 12–13.

Speck, Bruce W. "Writing Professional Codes of Ethics to Introduce Ethics in Business Writing," *Bulletin of the Association for Business Communications,* no. 3 (1990).

Trevino, Linda K. and Katherine A. Nelson. *Managing Business Ethics: Straight Talk About How to Do it Right.* New York: John Wiley & Sons, 1995. Discusses not only what business ethics are, but also why business should care.

Walton, Clarence. *The Moral Manager.* New York: Harper Business, 1990.

Ward, Gary. *Developing and Enforcing a Code of Business Ethics.* Babylon, NY: Pilot, 1989.

Weaver, Paul H. *The Suicidal Corporation.* New York: Simon & Schuster, 1988.

Young, Thomas A. "Ethics in Business: Business of Ethics," *Vital Speeches* (15 September 1992): 725–730.

CASE STUDY

ETHICAL FALL FROM GRACE

The Grace family had ruled the roost of W.R. Grace Company for more than 100 years, ever since Peter Grace's great grandfather founded the company in 1854. Peter, himself, was chief executive officer for decades, maintaining a corporate fiefdom that few other families enjoyed.

Over the years, Peter expanded the company into everything from bath products to gourmet foods to bull semen. Peter appointed his sons to management positions in the company and handpicked the board of directors. And he rewarded them—lavishly. On top of their regular fees, the directors, their companies, and their relatives collected additional payments of more than $60 million over a 10-year period, according to proxy statements.

At the same time, Peter Grace was one of the nation's most outspoken business leaders. He regularly spoke of corporate waste and government mismanagement. President Reagan was so impressed with his friend's no nonsense manner that he appointed Grace to head a commission to rid government of overregulation. The panel, which became known as the Grace Commission, recommended dozens of ways that the government could save money.

Soon after the panel began, it was joined by another swashbuckling businessman, J.P. Bolduc. Almost immediately, Messrs. Grace and Bolduc developed a mutual admiration society. This was the beginning of the end for Mr. Grace and his dynasty.

Like a Son

Grace developed an almost paternal affection for Bolduc—a condition that didn't sit well with Peter's real sons. Grace allowed Bolduc to manage some of his investments and become involved in several Grace charities. In short order, Grace hired Bolduc to assist him in running the company. By 1992, J.P. Bolduc was president and chief operating officer of W.R. Grace.

Bolduc immediately went to work, slashing costs at Grace and trimming the company's far flung empire. Some of the "trimming" was at the expense of his predecessor's favorite units, like the bull semen operation. Nonetheless, Bolduc's moves raised profits and won praise from the analysts. In 1993, Bolduc was named chief executive officer, the first non-Grace to head the company.

And Chairman Grace, who by this time had been diagnosed with cancer and was receiving chemotherapy treatments, began to seethe. He didn't want the company his family had founded and whose board he still ruled to be taken over by this brash outsider.

But Bolduc was now in charge, so much so that he considered W.R. Grace, "his" company. And he wanted the chairman—and his sons—out of the picture.

Tightening the Screws

Bolduc began to squeeze Grace and his sons out of the picture. He disallowed the chairman and his sons use of the corporate Gulfstream IV jet. He cut Grace's personal staff to four from ten. He even threatened to disclose unauthorized and questionable loans made to Peter Grace's son, Peter. In the face of this threat, Chairman Peter Grace resigned from the company.

Even though the former chairman remained on the board, W.R. Grace was now unequivocally Bolduc's company.

That's why in March 1995, employees and outsiders alike were shocked when CEO Bolduc abruptly resigned, reportedly for "differences in style and philosophy" with others on the board. The announcement was careful, legalistically crafted.

But why, people wondered, would the heir-apparent to a multibillion dollar company forsake his job? What possible "differences in style and philosophy" could cause him to abandon everything?

The company refused to elaborate on Bolduc's reasons, except to acknowledge that the former CEO would be paid $20 million in severance pay and benefits. Predictably, he, too, wasn't elaborating.

Sexual Harassment

And then the ethical roof fell in for the CEO, his predecessor and the company.

No one, neither the company nor Mr. Bolduc, had bothered to explain the two words that encapsulated the real reasons for the CEO's departure: sexual harassment.

Grace's nondisclosure triggered a blistering page one story in *The Wall Street Journal* that painted a portrait of a dysfunctional company, run by a selfish family and megalomaniacal successor.

Chairman Grace, the story charged, had borrowed liberally from stockholder assets—treating them as his own—to fund his personal nursing care, security guards, apartments and cooks. President Bolduc, the story alleged, was accused of numerous and serious incidents of sexual improprieties with Grace staff members. The matter had been reported to the board, which hired a former federal judge to investigate. When the judge's report confirmed the suspicions, Bolduc was asked to resign.

The devastating *Journal* story also reported a board of directors that was either ignorant or scared or simply out-of-touch with reality. In one memorable disclosure, the article noted:

> One director, Charles H. Erhart, Jr., said in an interview yesterday that the board had learned of allegations of sexual harassment against Mr. Bolduc by female employees. (When Mr. Erhart was called again later at the same home phone number, he denied having ever spoken to a *Wall Street Journal* reporter.)

So much for "differences in style and philosophy."

In the wake of the *Journal* revelation, W.R. Grace & Co. dramatically altered its "official explanation" of why Bolduc departed, saying that "he was forced to resign because directors believed he had sexually harassed female employees."

Immediately thereafter, the Grace company became a sieve. Anonymous charges and countercharges were hurled at the various parties. Peter Grace died shortly thereafter, his sons all left W.R. Grace, and J.P. Bolduc slunk off into $20 million oblivion. A once mighty company had become a shell of its former self, its reputation for honesty and integrity in ruins, its image for propriety and ethical conduct, materially tarnished.

QUESTIONS

1. What was wrong with the way Peter Grace apparently ran his company?
2. How do you assess the statement issued in explanation of J.P. Bolduc's departure from W.R. Grace?
3. What should the company have said relative to Bolduc's departure?
4. Was there any way Grace might have avoided the public pain brought about by the Bolduc situation?

For further information see Robert A. Bennett, "Autocratic Fall From Grace," *The Public Relations Strategist*, Spring 1996, 7–11; Cathy Booth, Tom Curry, and Jane Van Tassel, "Sex, Lies and W.R. Grace," *Time*, April 10, 1995, 58; Kenneth N. Gilpin, "Peter Grace, Ex-Company Chief, Dies at 81," *The New York Times*, April 21, 1995; Leslie Kaufman-Rosen, "More Grace Under Fire," *Newsweek*, April 10, 1995, 44; James P. Miller, Thomas M. Burton, and Randall Smith, "W.R. Grace Is Roiled by Flap Over Spending and What to Disclose," *The Wall Street Journal*, March 10, 1995, A1, 6; and Fraser P. Seitel, "How to Avoid a Fall from Grace," *Ragan Report,* July 10,1995, 2.

BONUS CASE STUDY

CNA DOES THE RIGHT THING

The flipside of the Grace case occurred two years later, in March 1997, when two female employees of the CNA Life Insurance Company began complaining about offensive sexual remarks made by one individual at the company. Who?

The president and highest ranking executive.

The women turned to the president's deputy for assistance, but nothing happened. So, as a final resort, they went to the insurance company's parent, the giant CNA Financial Corporation.

After a brief investigation, CNA announced the resignations of both the president and his deputy, saying that the president had made "offensive comments," which it did not describe, and that the deputy had failed to take action.

Stark Contrast to Grace

The CEO of the parent corporation personally apologized to both women. No legal action was taken against the company as a result of the complaints. Nor was a complaint filed with the Equal Employment Opportunity Commission.

The swift and public action stood in stark contrast to the backing and filling on the part of W.R. Grace, Mitsubishi Motors Corporation, and others when faced with similar accusations.

Experts hailed the enlightened attitude of CNA.

Said one sexual harassment consultant, "A few years ago, a corporation very well might have tried to cover this up or they might have just laughed it off as horseplay."

Indeed, while the battles at the Grace company lasted several very public months, after two days of newspaper coverage, the CNA incident was over. And the company was considered a model of proper ethical conduct.

Summarized the public relations officer for CNA, "We've done the right thing here. Everyone should recognize that we do not tolerate this sort of thing."

QUESTION

1. How did CNA's response to sexual harassment differ from that of W. R. Grace?

For further information, see Joseph B. Treaster, "2 Executives in Harassment Case at CNA," *The New York Times*, March 5, 1997, D1–22.

VOICE OF EXPERIENCE

BARBARA LEY TOFFLER

Barbara Ley Toffler is one of the nation's best-known authorities on the subject of ethics. Director of Arthur Andersen's Ethics and Responsible Business Practices consulting services, Toffler was a founding partner of Resources for Responsible Management in Boston and a lecturer at the Yale School of Organization and Management. She served on the faculty of the Harvard Business School for eight years. She is the author of *Managers Talk Ethics: Making Tough Choices in a Competitive Business World*, published in 1991.

ARE THERE ANY ABSOLUTES IN DEALING WITH ETHICS?

In the United States one has to start with the Judeo-Christian tradition. We believe that truth telling is an absolute. But, unfortunately, life today is a complicated exercise. For instance, what if telling the truth is harmful to someone else's sense of self-esteem? In most situations we're faced with competing claims—loyalty to an organization versus responsibility to the public, for example. Sometimes fulfilling one claim means having to compromise another. I dislike the negative implications of the term situational ethics, but, in reality, that's what usually applies.

WHAT IS THE STATE OF ETHICS IN BUSINESS?

Private industry clearly is struggling with ethical issues. Many companies are paying serious attention to creating an ethical environment in their firms and encouraging employees to act with integrity. The smart companies are those that take ethics seriously and realize that ethics can't be tacked on. It must be integrated into business goals, business practices, and the way that employees conduct themselves.

HOW DO YOU SOLVE AN ETHICAL PROBLEM IN AN ORGANIZATION?

First, you've got to talk to the key people, those who run the organization. Next, you must meet with other groups and elicit their views on issues and problems in the organization. Then you must consider the environment in which the organization operates and what issues loom on the horizon. Then, like a doctor, you've got to diagnose the company and its problems so that you can both suggest preventive medicine and design and implement responses to existing conditions.

WHAT IS THE STATE OF ETHICS IN GOVERNMENT?

I wouldn't say the public sector is less ethical than others. But one of the most fascinating things I've noticed is that the public sector managers with whom I've dealt don't tend to think about ethics in terms of their own behavior. Rather, they think first about the constituencies they serve. A private sector manager, by contrast, focuses first on his or her behavior and is therefore more self-reflective. The reason that public sector people run into more difficulty in this area is not that they are less ethical, but rather they often don't know where to look.

WHAT IS THE STATE OF ETHICS IN RELIGION?

People who do pastoral counseling today struggle terribly with ethics and probably have the most difficulty in dealing successfully with ethical problems in complex situations. As professionals in religion, they feel obligated to enact that which is absolutely ethical. The stresses of dealing in a complex world make this particular charge difficult, if not impossible. A theologian might say, "I don't like any of the choices, so I won't decide." Well, often neither do we like our choices, but we must make a decision. A manager must always decide and act, and therein lies the ethical dilemma.

WHAT IS THE STATE OF ETHICS IN PUBLIC RELATIONS?

Public relations people have as difficult a job as anyone in society. Their role is to manage all of the boundaries between the organization and the outside world and within the organization itself. Consequently, they struggle mightily with difficult ethical problems all the time. If anything, they tend to err on the side of loyalty to and protection of the organization, which is their primary charge. Is that unethical? Again, it all depends.

HOW DOES ONE BEGIN TO ACT ETHICALLY?

First, spend time thinking about how others view the world. One critical word in ethics is respect. In fact, the Golden Rule falls a bit short. What it should say is, "Do unto others as you would have them do unto you—if you were they." It takes empathy and understanding to settle conflicts. Another key word is competence. A manager can't be ethical unless he or she is also competent. Frankly, a great deal of unethical behavior in our society is attributable to incompetent people. Finally, because most ethical situations involve competing claims and complex situations where people can't simply apply what they believe, acting ethically also demands imagination. By imagination I don't mean creating stories to cover things up. Rather, I mean using an active, creative imagination to arrive at positive solutions that are also ethical.

CHAPTER FIVE

Research

EVERY PUBLIC RELATIONS PROGRAM OR SOLUTION SHOULD begin with research. Most don't, which is a shame.

The four-step R-A-C-E and six-step R-O-S-I-E approaches to public relations problem solving, alluded to in chapter 1, both start with research. Because public relations is still a misunderstood and amorphous function to many, public relations recommendations must be grounded in hard data whenever possible. In other words, before recommending a course of action, public relations professionals must analyze audiences, assess alternatives, and generally do their homework. In other words, most clients are less interested in what their public relations advisors think than in what they know. And the only way to know what to do is by researching first. Indeed, research has become the essential first step in the practice of modern public relations.

Instinct, intuition, and gut feelings all remain important in the conduct of public relations work; but management today demands more—measurement, analysis, and evaluation at every stage of the public relations process. In an era of scarce resources, management wants facts and statistics from public relations professionals to show that their efforts contribute not only to overall organizational effectiveness but also to the bottom line. Why should we introduce a new employee newspaper? What should it say and cost? How will we know it's working? Questions like these must be answered through research.

In a day when organizational resources are precious and companies don't want to spend money unless it enhances results, public relations programs must contribute to meeting business objectives.[1] That means that research must be applied to help segment market targets, analyze audience preferences and dislikes, and determine which messages might be most effective with which audiences. Research then becomes essential in helping realize management's goals.

Research should be applied in public relations work both at the initial stage, prior to planning a campaign, and at the final stage, to evaluate a program's effectiveness. Early research helps to determine the current situation, prevalent attitudes, and difficulties that the program faces. Later research examines the program's success, along with what else still needs to be done. Research at both points in the process is critical.

Even though research does not necessarily provide unequivocal proof of a program's effectiveness, it does allow public relations professionals to support their own intuition. It's little wonder, then, that the idea of measuring public relations work has steadily gained acceptance.[2]

WHAT IS RESEARCH?

Research is the systematic collection and interpretation of information to increase understanding (Figure 5–1).[3] Most people associate public relations with conveying information; although that association is accurate, research must be the obligatory first step in any project. A firm must acquire enough accurate, relevant data about its publics, products, and programs to answer these questions:

- How can we identify and define our constituent groups?
- How does this knowledge relate to the design of our messages?
- How does it relate to the design of our programs?
- How does it relate to the media we use to convey our messages?
- How does it relate to the schedule we adopt in using our media?
- How does it relate to the ultimate implementation tactics of our program?

It is difficult to delve into the minds of others, whose backgrounds and points of view may be quite different from one's own, with the purpose of understanding why they think as they do. Research skills are partly intuitive, partly an outgrowth of individual temperament, and partly a function of acquired knowledge. There is nothing mystifying about them. Although we tend to think of research in terms of impersonal test scores, interviews, or questionnaires, they are only a small part of the process. The real challenge lies in using research—knowing when to do what, with whom, and for what purpose.

TYPES OF PUBLIC RELATIONS RESEARCH

In general, research is conducted to do three things: (1) describe a process, situation, or phenomenon; (2) explain why something is happening, what its causes are, and what effect it will have; and (3) predict what probably will happen if we do or don't take ac-

Figure 5–1 An early research effort, albeit a futile one, was the return of the biblical scouts sent by Moses to reconnoiter the land of Canaan. They disagreed in their reports, and the Israelites believed the gloomier versions. This failure to interpret the data correctly caused them to wander another 40 years in the wilderness. (An even earlier research effort was Noah's sending the dove to search for dry ground.)

tion. Most research in public relations is either theoretical or applied. Applied research solves practical problems; theoretical research aids understanding of a public relations process.

Applied Research

In public relations work, applied research can be either strategic or evaluative. Both applications are designed to answer specific practical questions.

- *Strategic research* is used primarily in program development to determine program objectives, develop message strategies, or establish benchmarks. It often examines the tools and techniques of public relations. For example, a firm that wants to know how employees rate its candor in internal publications would first conduct strategic research to find out where it stands.
- *Evaluative research,* sometimes called summative research, is conducted primarily to determine whether a public relations program has accomplished its goals and objectives. For example, if changes are made in the internal communications program to in-

crease candor, evaluative research can determine whether the goals have been met. A variant of evaluation can be applied during a program to monitor progress and indicate where modifications might make sense.

Theoretical Research

Theoretical research is more abstract and conceptual than applied research. It helps build theories in public relations work in areas such as why people communicate, how public opinion is formed, and how a public is created.

Knowledge of theoretical research is important as a framework for persuasion and as a base for understanding why people do what they do.

Some knowledge of theoretical research in public relations and mass communications is essential for enabling practitioners to understand the limitations of communication as a persuasive tool. Attitude and behavior change have been the traditional goals in public relations programs, yet theoretical research indicates that such goals may be difficult or impossible to achieve through persuasive efforts. According to such research, other factors are always getting in the way.

Researchers have found that communication is most persuasive when it comes from multiple sources of high credibility. Credibility itself is a multidimensional concept that includes trustworthiness, expertise, and power. Others have found that a message generally is more effective when it is simple because it is easier to understand, localize, and make personally relevant. According to still other research, the persuasiveness of a message can be increased when it arouses or is accompanied by a high level of personal involvement in the issue at hand.

The point here is that knowledge of theoretical research can help practitioners not only understand the basis of applied research findings, but also temper management's expectations of attitude and behavioral change resulting from public relations programs.

METHODS OF PUBLIC RELATIONS RESEARCH

Observation is the foundation of modern social science. Scientists, social psychologists, and anthropologists make observations, develop theories, and, hopefully, increase understanding of human behavior. Public relations research, too, is founded on observation. Three primary forms of public relations research dominate the field.

- **Surveys** are designed to reveal attitudes and opinions—what people think about certain subjects.
- **Communication audits** often reveal disparities between real and perceived communications between management and target audiences. Management may make certain assumptions about its methods, media, materials, and messages, whereas its targets may confirm or refute those assumptions.
- **Unobtrusive measures**—such as fact finding, content analysis, and readability studies—enable the study of a subject or object without involving the researcher or the research as an intruder.

Each method of public relations research offers specific benefits and should be understood and used by the modern practitioner.

Surveys

Survey research is one of the most frequently used research methods in public relations. Surveys can be applied to broad societal issues, such as determining public opinion about a political candidate, or to the most minute organizational problem, such as whether shareholders like the quarterly report. Surveys come in two types.

1. **Descriptive surveys** offer a snapshot of a current situation or condition. They are the research equivalent of a balance sheet, capturing reality at a specific point in time. A typical public opinion poll is a prime example.
2. **Explanatory surveys** are concerned with cause and effect. Their purpose is to help explain why a current situation or condition exists and to offer explanations for opinions and attitudes. Frequently, such explanatory or analytical surveys are designed to answer the question "Why?" Why are our philanthropic dollars not being appreciated in the community? Why are employees not believing management's messages? Why is our credibility being questioned?

Surveys generally consist of four elements: (1) the sample, (2) the questionnaire, (3) the interview, and (4) the analysis of results. (Direct mail surveys, of course, eliminate the interview step.) Because survey research is so critical in public relations, we will examine each survey element in some detail.

THE SAMPLE The sample, or selected target group, must be representative of the total public whose views are sought. Once a survey population has been determined, a researcher must select the appropriate sample or group of respondents from whom to collect information. Sampling is tricky. A researcher must be aware of the hidden pitfalls in choosing a representative sample, not the least of which is the perishable nature of most data. Survey findings are rapidly outdated because of population mobility and changes in the political and socioeconomic environment. Consequently, sampling should be completed quickly.

Two cross-sectional approaches are used in obtaining a sample: random sampling and nonrandom sampling. The former is more scientific, the latter more informal.

RANDOM SAMPLING In random sampling, two properties are essential—equality and independence in selection. Equality means that no element has any greater or lesser chance of being selected. Independence means that selecting any one element in no way influences the selection of any other element. Random sampling is based on a mathematical criterion that allows generalizations from the sample to be made to the total population. There are four types of random or probability samples.

1. **Simple random sampling** gives all members of the population an equal chance of being selected. First, all members of the population are identified, and then as many subjects as are needed are randomly selected—usually with the help of a computer. Election polling uses a random approach; although millions of Americans vote, only a few thousand are ever polled on their election preferences. The Nielson national television sample, for example, consists of 4,000 homes. The Census Bureau uses a sample of 72,000 out of 93 million households to obtain estimates of employment and other population characteristics.

    How large should a random sample be? The answer depends on a number of factors, one of which is the size of the population. In addition, the more similar the population elements are in regard to the characteristics

THE REST OF THE STORY

MEASURING PRESS COVERAGE

Through the decades, the most tried and true public relations measurement technique was to "measure" press clipping inches to justify to employers the success of a particular program.

The Rowland Company, a New York-based public relations agency, has revolutionized this most standard of public relations measurements. The Rowland Publicity Index applies numerical values to the following evaluative criteria.

PHYSICAL CHARACTERISTICS

1. Length of article
    How long is the article?
    Is it a brief mention or an extensive story?
    What portion of the article is relevant to the topic?
A brief mention receives a score of 1. An average clipping, one-quarter page, receives a 3 rating. A one-half page article receives a 5; a cover story, a 10.
2. Position
    Where does the story appear in the publication? On the page?
    Is it a main story, for example, page one?
    Is there a "teaser" on the front page for the story?
A 4 or 5 would be given to a story on the front section above the fold. A story would receive a strong 5 rating if a teaser ran on the front page and the article runs on the front page of a section.
3. Graphics
    How big is the headline? One line or two?
    Is there a complementary photo?
    What is the size and quality of the photo?
    Is there a sidebar or similar element?
This score is the average of the individual ratings for the headline, photo, and related items.

MESSAGE, CONTEXT, OBJECTIVES

1. Key message
    Were the promotion's key messages included in the article?
    Were they up front or buried in the back?
    Was a spokesperson quoted?
    Were the messages present in the headline or cutline?
Assessment of the key messages depends on the written marketing plan and stated public relations objectives for most important messages. An article taken verbatim from a news release merits a 10 rating. An article that contains no key messages merits a 1.
2. Context
    Does the story mention a product? In a positive or negative way?
    Does the story offer a substitution for a product?
    Is the story critical of the organization or industry?
    Does the article have a positive or negative tone?
A positive article earns a 10 and a negative piece just a 1 or 2.

3. Achieved objectives
    Did the article accomplish what we set out to achieve?
    Was it covered as a stand-alone or included in a wrap-up mention with other ideas?
    What was the overall impact of the article?
Again, this depends on the stated objectives of the campaign. Articles based word-for-word on a news release receive a 10 rating.*

*For further information, see "PR Execs Measure the Worth of Traditional Measurements," PR News, February 10, 1997, 7.

being studied, the smaller the sample required. In most random samples, the following population-to-sample ratios apply, with a 5 percent margin of error:

POPULATION	SAMPLE
1,000	278
2,000	322
3,000	341
5,000	355
10,000	370
50,000	381
100,000	383
500,000	383
Infinity	384

   Random sampling owes its accuracy to the laws of probability, which are best explained by the example of a barrel filled with 10,000 marbles—5,000 green ones and 5,000 red ones. If a blindfolded person selects a certain number of marbles from the barrel—say, 400—the laws of probability suggest that the most frequently drawn combination will be 200 red and 200 green. These laws further suggest that with certain margins of error, a very few marbles can represent the whole barrel, which can correspond to any size—for example, that of city, state, or nation.

2. **Systematic random sampling** is closely related to simple random sampling, but it uses a random starting point in the sample list. From then on, the researcher selects every nth person in the list. As long as every person has an equal and independent chance to be selected on the first draw, then the sample qualifies as "random" and is equally reliable to simple random sampling. Random digit dialing, for example, which solves the problem of failing to consider unlisted numbers, may use this technique.

3. **Stratified random sampling** is a procedure used to survey different segments or strata of the population. For example, if an organization wants to determine the relationship between years of service and attitudes toward the company, it may stratify the sample to ensure that the breakdown of respondents accurately reflects the makeup of the population. In other words, if more than half of the employees have been with the company more than 10

years, more than half of those polled should also reflect that level of service. By stratifying the sample, the organization's objective can be achieved.

4. **Cluster sampling** involves first breaking the population down into small heterogeneous subsets, or clusters, and then selecting the potential sample from the individual clusters or groups. A cluster may often be defined as a geographic area, such as an election district.

NONRANDOM SAMPLING Nonrandom samples come in three types—convenience, quota, and volunteer.

1. **Convenience samples,** also known as accidental, chunk, or opportunity samples, are relatively unstructured, rather unsystematic, and designed to elicit ideas and points of view. Journalists use convenience samples when they conduct person-on-the-street interviews. The most common type of convenience sample in public relations research is the focus group. Focus groups generally consist of 8 to 12 people, with a moderator encouraging in-depth discussion of a specific topic. Focus groups generate concepts and ideas rather than validate hypotheses.

2. **Quota samples** permit a researcher to choose subjects on the basis of certain characteristics. For example, the attitudes of a certain number of women, men, blacks, whites, rich, or poor may need to be known. Quotas are imposed in proportion to each group's percentage of the population. The advantage of quota sampling is that it increases the homogeneity of a sample population, thus enhancing the validity of a study. However, it is hard to classify interviewees by one or two discrete demographic characteristics. For example, a particular interviewee may be black, Catholic, female, under 25, and a member of a labor union all at the same time, making the lines of demographic demarcation pretty blurry. (A derivative of quota sampling is called purposive sampling.)

3. **Volunteer samples** use willing participants who agree voluntarily to respond to concepts and hypotheses for research purposes.[4]

THE QUESTIONNAIRE Before creating a questionnaire, a researcher must consider his or her objective in doing the study. What you seek to find out should influence the specific publics you ask, the questions you raise, and the research method you choose. After determining what you're after, consider the particular questionnaire design. Specifically, researchers should observe the following in designing their questionnaire:

1. Keep it short. Make a concerted attempt to limit questions. It's terrific if the questionnaire can be answered in 5 minutes.

2. Use structured, not open-ended, questions. People would rather check a box or circle a number than write an essay. But leave room at the bottom for general comments or "Other." Also, start with simple, nonthreatening questions before getting to the more difficult, sensitive ones. This approach will build respondent trust as well as commitment to finishing the questionnaire.

3. Measure intensity of feelings. Let respondents check "very satisfied," "satisfied," "dissatisfied," or "very dissatisfied" rather than "yes" or "no." One popular approach is the semantic differential technique shown in Figure 5–2.

4. Don't use fancy words or words that have more than one meaning. If you must use big words, make the context clear.

Dictaphone

1	2	3	4	5
High price				Low price

1	2	3	4	5
Not reliable				Reliable

1	2	3	4	5
Bulky				Compact

1	2	3	4	5
Inconvenient				Convenient

1	2	3	4	5
Bad service				Good service

1	2	3	4	5
Not likely to buy				Likely to buy

Stowe

1	2	3	4	5	6	7	8	9	10
Hard to get to									Easy to get to

1	2	3	4	5	6	7	8	9	10
Severe weather									Moderate weather

1	2	3	4	5	6	7	8	9	10
Few levels of skiing									Many levels of skiing

1	2	3	4	5	6	7	8	9	10
Relatively easy trails									Very difficult trails

1	2	3	4	5	6	7	8	9	10
Poor trail grooming									Excellent trail grooming

1	2	3	4	5	6	7	8	9	10
Long liftlines									Short liftlines

1	2	3	4	5	6	7	8	9	10
Few apres-ski activities									Many apres-ski activities

1	2	3	4	5	6	7	8	9	10
Poor lodging facilities									Excellent lodging facilities

1	2	3	4	5	6	7	8	9	10
Poor overall resort value									Excellent overall resort value

Figure 5–2 In questionnaires, one common device to measure intensity of feelings is the semantic differential technique, which gives respondents a scale of choices from the worst to the best. These semantic differential scales for portable dictating equipment and for ski lodges are typical.

5. Don't ask loaded questions. "Is management doing all it can to communicate with you?" is a terrible question. The answer is always no.
6. Don't ask double-barreled questions. "Would you like management meetings once a month, or are bimonthly meetings enough?" is another terrible question.
7. Pretest. Send your questionnaire to a few colleagues and listen to their suggestions.
8. Attach a letter explaining how important the respondents' answers are, and let recipients know that they will remain anonymous. Respondents will feel better if they think the study is significant and their identities are protected. Also, specify how and where the data will be used.
9. Hand-stamp the envelopes, preferably with unique commemorative stamps. Metering an envelope indicates assembly-line research, and researchers have found that the more expensive the postage, the higher the response rate. People like to feel special.
10. Follow up your first mailing. Send a reminder postcard three days after the original questionnaire. Then wait a few weeks and send a second questionnaire, just in case recipients have lost the first.
11. Send out more questionnaires than you think necessary. The major weakness of most mail surveys is the unmeasurable error introduced by nonresponders. You're shooting for a 50 percent response rate; anything less tends to be suspect.
12. Enclose a reward. There's nothing like a token gift of merchandise or money— a $2 bill works beautifully—to make a recipient feel guilty for not returning a questionnaire.[5]

Appendix B gives an example of a survey questionnaire.

THE INTERVIEW Interviews can provide a more personal, firsthand feel for public opinion. Interview panels can range from focus groups of randomly selected average people to Delphi panels of so-called opinion leaders. Interviews can be conducted in a number of ways, including face to face, telephone, mail, and drop-off techniques.

Focus Groups This approach is used with increasing frequency in public relations today. Such interviews can be conducted one-to-one or through survey panels. These panels can be used, for example, to measure buying habits or the impact of public relations programs on a community or organizational group. They can also be used to assess general attitudes toward certain subjects, such as new products or advertising.

With the focus group technique, a well-drilled moderator leads a group through a discussion of opinions on a particular product, organization, or idea. Participants represent the socioeconomic level desired by the research sponsor—from college students to office workers to millionaires. Almost always, focus group participants are paid for their efforts. Sessions are frequently videotaped and then analyzed, often in preparation for more formal and specific research questionnaires.

Focus groups should be organized with the following guidelines in mind:

1. **Define your objectives and audience.** The more tightly you define your goals and your target audience, the more likely you are to gather relevant information. In other words, don't conduct a focus group with friends and family members, hoping to get a quick and inexpensive read. Nothing of value will result.

2. **Recruit your groups.** Recruiting participants takes several weeks, depending on the difficulty of contacting the target audience. Contact is usually made by phone, with a series of questions to weed out employees of competitors, members of the news media (to keep the focus group from becoming a news story), and those who don't fit target group specifications. Persons who have participated in a group in the past year should also be screened out; they may be more interested in the money than in helping you find what you're looking for.

3. **Choose the right moderator.** Staff people who may be excellent conversationalists are not necessarily the best focus group moderators. The gift of gab is not enough. Professional moderators know how to establish rapport quickly, how and when to probe beyond the obvious, how to draw comments from reluctant participants, how to keep a group on task, and how to interpret results validly.

4. **Conduct enough focus groups.** One or two focus groups usually are not enough. Four to six are better to uncover the full range of relevant ideas and opinions. Regardless of the number of groups, however, you must resist the temptation to add up responses. That practice gives the focus group more analytical worth than it deserves.

5. **Use a discussion guide.** This is a basic outline of what you want to investigate. It will lead the moderator through the discussion and keep the group on track.

6. **Choose proper facilities.** The discussion room should be comfortable, with participants sitting around a table that gives them a good view of each other. Observers can use closed-circuit TV and one-way mirrors, but participants should always be told when they are being observed.

7. **Keep a tight rein on observers.** Observers should rarely be in the same room with participants; the two groups should ordinarily be separated. Observers should view the proceedings seriously; this is not "dinner and a show."

8. **Consider using outside help.** Setting up focus groups can be time-consuming and complicated. Often the best advice is to hire a firm recommended by the

American Marketing Association or the Marketing Research Association so that the process, the moderator, and the evaluation are as professional as possible.[6]

Telephone Interviews   In contrast to personal interviews, telephone interviews suffer from a high refusal rate. Many people just don't want to be bothered. Such interviews may also introduce an upper-income bias because lower-income earners may lack telephones. However, the increasing use of unlisted numbers by upper-income people may serve to mitigate this bias. Telephone interviews must be carefully scripted so that interviewers know precisely what to ask, regardless of a respondent's answer. Calls should be made at less busy times of the day, such as early morning or late afternoon.

With both telephone and face-to-face interviews, it is important to establish rapport with the interview subject. It may make sense to begin the interview with nonthreatening questions, saving the tougher, more controversial ones—on income level or race, for example—until last. Another approach is to depersonalize the research by explaining that others have devised the survey and that the interviewer's job is simply to ask the questions.

MAIL INTERVIEWS This is the least expensive approach, but it often suffers from a low response rate. You are aiming for a 50 percent response rate. Frequently, people who return mail questionnaires are those with strong biases either in favor of or (more commonly) in opposition to the subject at hand. As noted, one way to generate a higher response from mail interviews is through the use of self-addressed, stamped envelopes or enclosed incentives such as dollar bills or free gifts.

Drop-Off Interviews   This approach combines face-to-face and mail interview techniques. An interviewer personally drops off a questionnaire at a household, usually after conducting a face-to-face interview. Because the interviewer has already established some rapport with the interviewee, the rate of return with this technique is considerably higher than it is for straight mail interviews.

Delphi Panels   The Delphi technique is a more qualitative research tool that uses opinion leaders—local influential persons, national experts, and so on—often to help tailor the design of a general public research survey. Designed by the Rand Corporation in the 1950s, the Delphi technique is a consensus-building approach that relies on repeated waves of questionnaires sent to the same select panel of experts. Delphi findings generate a wide range of responses and help set the agenda for more meaningful future research. Stated another way, Delphi panels offer a "research reality check."[7]

ANALYSIS OF RESULTS After selecting the sample, drawing up the questionnaire, and interviewing the respondents, the researcher must analyze the findings. Often a great deal of analysis is required to produce meaningful recommendations.

The objective of every sample is to come up with results that are valid and reliable. A margin of error explains how far off the prediction may be. A sample may be large enough to represent fairly the larger universe; yet, depending on the margin of sampling error, the results of the research may not be statistically significant. That is, the differences or distinctions detected by the survey may not be sizable enough to offset the margin of error. Thus, the margin of error must always be determined.

This concept is particularly critical in political polling, where pollsters are quick to acknowledge that their results may accurately represent the larger universe, but normally with a 2 or 3 percent margin of error. Thus, the results could be as much as 3 percent more or less for a certain candidate. Consequently, a pollster who says a candidate will win with 51 percent of the vote really means that the candidate could win with as much as 54 percent or lose with as little as 48 percent of the vote.

Political polls are fraught with problems. They cannot predict outcomes scientifically. Rather, they freeze attitudes at a certain point in time, and people's attitudes obviously change with the tide of events. Perhaps the most notorious political poll was that of the *Literary Digest* in 1936, which used a telephone polling technique to predict that Alf Landon would be the nation's next president. Landon thereupon suffered one of the worst drubbings in American electoral history at the hands of Franklin Roosevelt. It was probably of little solace to the *Literary Digest* that most of its telephone respondents, many of whom were Republicans wealthy enough to afford phones, did vote for Landon.

The point made here is that in analyzing results, problems of validity, reliability, and levels of statistical significance associated with margins of error must be considered before recommendations based on survey data are offered.

Communication Audits

An increasingly important method of research in public relations work is the communications audit. Such audits are used frequently by corporations, schools, hospitals, and other organizations to determine how the institution is perceived by its core constituents. Communications audits help public relations professionals understand more clearly the relationships between management actions and objectives, on the one hand, and communications methods to promote those objectives, on the other.

Communication audits are typically used to analyze the standing of a company with its employees or community neighbors; to assess the readership of routine communication vehicles, such as annual reports and news releases; or to examine an organization's performance as a corporate citizen. Communication audits often provide benchmarks against which future public relations programs can be applied and measured.

Communication audits typically are used to provide information on how to solve the following problems:

- Bottlenecked information flows
- Uneven communication workloads
- Employees working at cross-purposes
- Hidden information within an organization that is not being used, to the detriment of the institution
- Conflicting or nonexisting notions about what the organization is and does.[8]

The most effective communication audits start with a researcher who (1) is familiar with the public to be studied, (2) generally understands the attitudes of the target public toward the organization, (3) recognizes the issues of concern to the target public, and (4) understands the relative power of the target public vis-à-vis other publics.

Unobtrusive Methods

Of the various unobtrusive methods of data collection available to public relations researchers, probably the most widely used is simple fact finding. Facts are the bricks and mortar of public relations work; no action can be taken unless the facts are known, and the fact-finding process is continuous.

Each organization must keep a fact file of the most essential data with which it is involved. For example, such items as key organization statistics, publications, management

A QUESTION OF ETHICS

THE CREDIBILITY-SAVING AUDIT

In 1993, a taxpayer-funded bank set up to aid Eastern Europe was rocked by scandal when it was revealed that the bank's president had spent millions of dollars of taxpayers' money on such "necessities" as shaded carpets, a marbled lobby, mirrored ceilings, and trips by private jet to exotic places.

Embarrassing publicity plagued the new bank for about six months, until the board could take no more. It summarily fired President Jacques Attali and commissioned an audit to restore the bank's credibility. Auditors Coopers & Lybrand revealed a president who spared no expense either in furnishing his bank or in feathering his nest. The audit revealed hundreds of millions of dollars on extravagances, such as special gray glass for conference rooms, a specially designed ceiling, and 57 presidential flights over a two-year period that had cost the bank—and the taxpayers—nearly $2 million. The auditors found that a private jet based in Paris often flew empty to London for the sole purpose of picking up President Attali.

The audit report, in a word, was devastating, but bank directors seemed ambivalent. Said one, "The audit report has to bring credibility back to the board."

Is this a reasonable expectation for a single piece of research?

For further information, see Janet Guyon, "European Aid Bank Hopes Audit Chief's Departure Will End Chaos," *The Wall Street Journal*, July 19, 1993.

---

biographies and photos, press clippings, media lists, competitive literature, pending legislation, organizational charters and bylaws should be kept on file and updated. Even better, computerized listings of such facts offer easier access when research is called for in these areas.

Another unobtrusive method is content analysis, the primary purpose of which is to describe a message or set of messages. For example, an organization with news releases that are used frequently by local newspapers can't be certain, without research, whether the image conveyed by its releases is what the organization seeks. By analyzing the news coverage, the firm can get a much clearer idea of the effectiveness of its communications. Such content analysis might be organized according to the following specific criteria:

- **Frequency of coverage**—How many releases were used?
- **Placement within the paper**—Did releases appear more frequently on page 1 or 71?
- **People reached**—What was the circulation of the publications in which the releases appeared?
- **Messages conveyed**—Did the releases used express the goals of the organization, or were they simply informational in content?
- **Editing of releases**—How much did the newspaper edit the copy submitted? Were desired meanings materially changed?
- **Attitude conveyed**—Was the reference to the organization positive, negative, or neutral?

Another unobtrusive method, the readability study, helps a communicator determine whether messages are written at the right educational level for the audience. Typical measures include the Flesch Formula, the FOG Index, and the SMOG Index—all based on the concept that the greater the number of syllables in a passage, the more difficult and less readable the text.[9]

Clearly, there is nothing particularly mysterious or difficult about unobtrusive methods of research. Such methods are relatively simple to apply, yet they are essential for arriving at appropriate modifications for an ongoing public relations program.

EVALUATION

No matter what type of public relations research is used, results of the research and the research project itself should always be evaluated. Evaluation is designed to determine what happened and why.

Evaluation of public relations programs depends on several things:

- **Setting measurable public relations program objectives.** Goals should specify who the target publics are, what impact the program seeks to have on those publics, and when the results are expected.
- **Select the most appropriate outcomes.** At one end of outcome evaluation is a measurement of the press clipping a program received; that is, the number of column inches or air time devoted to the program. At the other end of the evaluative spectrum is a "content analysis" of the messages conveyed as a result of the program. This is a more sophisticated evaluation of program effectiveness.
- **Determine the optimum data-gathering mechanism.** Again, raw program records and observation are a rudimentary but acceptable method of evaluative measurement. Better would be attitude pre-and-post testing to determine if a particular program helped facilitate a shift in attitudes toward a program, company, or issue.

In any event, in evaluating after the fact, researchers can learn how to improve future efforts. Were the target audiences surveyed the right ones? Were the research assumptions applied to those audiences correct? Were questions from research tools left unanswered?

Again, research results can be evaluated in a number of ways. Perhaps the most common in public relations is a seat-of-the-pants evaluation, in which anecdotal observation and practitioner judgment are used to estimate the effectiveness of the public relations program. Such evaluation might be based on feedback from members of a key public, personal media contacts, or colleagues, but the practitioner alone evaluates the success of the program with subjective observation.

More scientific evaluation results from public relations opinion polls and surveys and fact-finding research, such as content analysis, in which the numerical tabulation of results is evaluated and often combined with seat-of-the-pants observation. One of the most effective evaluative techniques to determine the success of a program is to pretest target audiences before the public relations program is implemented and then posttest after the program is completed.

Comparing the results of the two tests enables a more scientific assessment of the program's success.

An ongoing system for monitoring public relations activities is yet another way to evaluate programs. Monitoring a public relations campaign, for example, may indicate necessary changes in direction, reallocation of resources, or redefinition of priorities. Another way to evaluate is to dissect public programs after the fact. Such postmortem evaluation can provide objective analysis when a program is still fresh in one's mind. This can be extremely helpful in modifying the program for future use.

In the fiercely competitive, resource-dear twenty-first century, the need to evaluate public relations results—in as scientific a manner as possible—will increasingly become the standard mandate of management.

THE REST OF THE STORY

FIGURES AND FACES—LIE

If you don't believe the old maxim that "figures lie and liars figure," consider the following: In often-repeated research, randomly selected participants are shown the following two faces and asked, "Which woman is lovelier?"

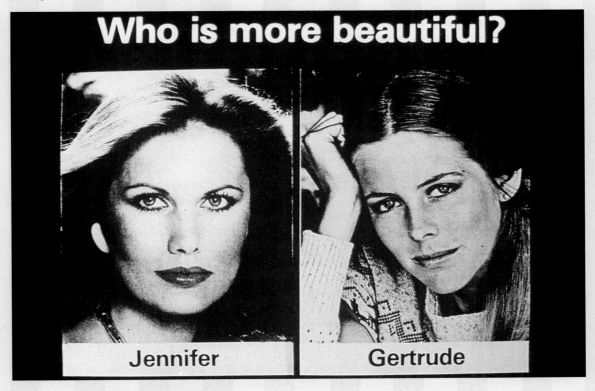

Invariably, the answer is split 50-50.

However, when each woman is named—one "Jennifer" and the other "Gertrude"—respondents overwhelming vote for Jennifer as the more beautiful woman. That is how pervasive the antibeauty bias against the name Gertrude is. (Sorry all you Gertrudes out there!)

Shown by this is the point that audiences and researchers can't help but introduce their own biases, and this factor always should be taken into account in evaluating public relations research.

USING OUTSIDE RESEARCH HELP

Despite its occasional rough spots, in recent years public relations research has made substantial gains in quantifying the results of public relations activities. Counseling firms have even organized separate departments to conduct attitude and opinion surveys as well as other types of research projects.

Ketchum Public Relations, for example, has devised a computer-based measurement system that evaluates public relations results on both a quantitative and qualitative basis. The Ketchum system focuses on the differences in placement of publicity, that is, where in a periodical publicity has a better chance of being noticed. Although the Ketchum system cannot predict attitudinal or behavioral change, it is a step forward in providing practitioners with a mechanism to assess the extent to which their publicity has been seen.

It often makes sense to use outside counsel for research assistance. Once a firm is hired, public relations professionals should avoid the temptation of writing the questions or influencing the methodology. The best contribution a public relations practitioner can make to an outside-directed research endeavor is to state the objectives of the project clearly and then stand back and let the pros do the job.[10]

Often, before turning to outside consultants, the best first step is to determine whether research has already been done on your topic. Because research assistance is expensive, it makes little sense to reinvent the wheel. It is much wiser to piggyback on existing research.

SUMMARY

Research is a means of both defining problems and evaluating solutions. The day of the seat-of-the-pants practitioner is over. Even though intuitive judgment remains a coveted and important skill, management must see measurable results.

Nonetheless, informed managements recognize that public relations may never reach a point at which its results can be fully quantified. Management confidence is still a prerequisite for active and unencumbered programs. However, such confidence can only be enhanced as practitioners become more adept in using research.

Frankly, practitioners don't have a choice. With efficiency driving today's bottom line and public relations unfortunately viewed as "nebulous" by many in top management, it will become increasingly incumbent on public relations people to "prove" their value through measuring their contribution to the organization's goals.[11]

DISCUSSION STARTERS

1. Why is research important in public relations work?
2. What are several methods of public relations research?
3. What are the four elements of a survey?
4. What is the difference between random and stratified sampling?
5. What are the keys to designing an effective questionnaire?

6. What are the several rules of thumb in organizing focus groups?
7. What is a communication audit?
8. What is the most widely used unobtrusive method of public relations research?
9. Why is evaluation important in public relations research?
10. How essential do you think research will be in the future for public relations practice?

NOTES

1. Jennifer Nedeff, "The Bottom Line Beckons: Quantifying Measurement in Public Relations," *Journal of Corporate Public Relations–Northwestern University* (1996–1997): 34.
2. Lisa Richter and Steve Drake, "Apply Measurement Mindset to Programs," *Public Relations Journal* (January 1993): 32.
3. John V. Pavlik, *Public Relations: What Research Tells Us* (Newbury Park, CA: Sage, 1987), 16.
4. Walter K. Lindenmann, "Opinion Research: How It Works; How to Use It," *Public Relations Journal* (January 1977): 13.
5. Walter K. Lindenmann, *Attitude and Opinion Research: Why You Need It/How to Do It*, 3d ed. (Washington, DC: Council for Advancement and Support of Education, 1983), 35–38.
6. David L. Nasser, "How to Run a Focus Group," *Public Relations Journal* (March 1988): 33–34.
7. "The Delphi: A Forecasting Methodology You Can Use to Generate Expert Opinion on Any Subject," *PR Reporter* (June 29, 1992): 3.
8. Seymour Hamilton, "Selling the CEO on a Communication Audit," *IABC Communication World* (May 1988): 33.
9. Pavlik, op. cit., 39.
10. Andrea L. Simpson, "Ten Rules of Research," *Public Relations Quarterly* (Summer 1992): 27–28.
11. Nedeff, op. cit.

SUGGESTED READINGS

Attitude and Opinion Research: Why You Need It/How to Do It, 3d ed. Washington, DC: Case (11 Dupont Circle, 20036), 1983.

Awards, Honors, Prizes. Detroit: Gale Research Co., 1990.

Barabba, V. P., and G. Zaltman. *Hearing the Voice of the Market: Competitive Advantage Through Creative Use of Market Information*. New York: McGraw-Hill, 1991.

Barzun, Jacques, and Henry F. Graff. *The Modern Researcher*, 5th ed. Ft. Worth, TX: HBJ College Publications, 1992.

Blakenship, A. B. and George Breen. *State of the Art Marketing Research*. Lincolnwood, IL: NTC Business, 1992.

Bradburn, Norman and Seymour Sudman. *Polls and Surveys*. San Francisco: Jossey-Bass, 1988.

Breen, George and A. B. Blakenship. *Do-It-Yourself Marketing Research,* 3d ed. New York: McGraw-Hill, 1991.

TOP OF THE SHELF

GLEN M. BROOM AND DAVID M. DOZIER

USING RESEARCH IN PUBLIC RELATIONS: APPLICATIONS TO PROGRAM MANAGEMENT

UPPER SADDLE RIVER, NJ: PRENTICE HALL, 1990

JOHN V. PAVLIK

PUBLIC RELATIONS: WHAT RESEARCH TELLS US

NEWBURY PARK, CA: SAGE, 1987

Research is an essential component of any communications program. Two texts that contribute to the understanding of this important public relations function are *Using Research in Public Relations: Applications to Program Management* and *Public Relations: What Research Tells Us.*

In *Using Research in Public Relations*, Glen Broom and David Dozier, leading public relations researchers, explain the value of conducting basic quantitative and qualitative analyses to help achieve communications goals. Such research, they contend, can substantiate a practitioner's hunches and enhance the credibility of the profession. The authors also present the research methods counselors employ: statistical inference, focus groups, sampling, and content analysis, among others. To show how these tools influence and enhance public relations work, Broom and Dozier use several case studies.

In similar fashion, John Pavlik, a communications professor at Penn State University, explores the uses of research in the profession, as well as common research techniques, in *Public Relations: What Research Tells Us*. He also examines what methodical research can reveal about the profession itself—that is, what scientific evidence discloses about the field and its effects on the journalism people consume. Pavlik discusses these and similar issues by citing numerous media studies.

Sound research can yield benefits to public relations strategies at all phases, from development to execution to evaluation. For expert instruction on the public relations–research relationship, read *Using Research in Public Relations* and *Public Relations: What Research Tells Us.*

Brody, E. W. and Gerald C. Stone. *Public Relations Research*. New York: Praeger, 1989.

Broom, Glen M. and David M. Dozier. *Using Research in Public Relations: Applications to Program Management*. Upper Saddle River, NJ: Prentice Hall, 1990.

Crispell, Diane. *The Insider's Guide to Demographic Know-How*. Chicago: Probus, 1992.

Emmert, Philip and Larry Baker. *Measurements of Communication Behavior*. White Plains, NY: Longman, 1989.

Fowler, Floyd J. Jr. *Survey Research Methods*, 2nd ed. Newbury Park, CA: Sage Publications, 1993.

Fuld, Leonard. *Monitoring the Competition: Finding Out What's Really Going On Over There*. New York: John Wiley & Sons, 1988.

Hamilton, Seymour. "Selling the CEO on a Communication Audit." *Communication World* (May 1988): 33, 34.

Hardy, Hugh S., ed. *The Politz Papers: Science and Truth in Marketing Research*. Chicago: American Marketing Association, 1990.

Lehman, Carol M., William Himstreet, and Wayne Baty. *Business Communications*, 11th ed. Cincinnati, OH: South-Western College Publishing, 1996.

Lindolf, Thomas R. *Qualitative Communication Research Methods*. Thousand Oaks, CA: Sage Publications, 1995. Updated review of research methods in communication.

The Markets Directory. Dobbs Ferry, NY: Dobbs Directories, 1991.

Martel, Myles. *Mastering the Art of Q & A*. Homewood, IL: Dow Jones-Irwin, 1988.

Nasser, David L. "How to Run a Focus Group." *Public Relations Journal* (March 1988): 33, 34.

New Technology and Public Relations. New York: Institute for PR Research and Education, 1988.

Rossi, Peter H. and Howard E. Freeman. *Evaluation: A Systematic Approach*, 5th ed. Newbury Park, CA: Sage Publications, 1993.

Rubenstein, Sondra Miller. *Surveying Public Opinion*. Belmont, CA: Wadsworth Publishing, 1995.

Shaw, Robert and Merlin Stone. *Database Marketing*. New York: John Wiley & Sons, 1989.

Soares, Eric. *Cost-Effective Marketing Research*. Westport, CT: Quorum, 1988.

Stempel, Guido and Bruce Westley. *Research Methods in Mass Communication*, 2nd ed. New York: Prentice Hall, 1989.

Sudman, Seymour. *Thinking About Answers: The Application of Cognitive Process to Survey Methodology*. San Francisco: Jossey-Bass, 1995.

CASE STUDY

RESEARCHING A POSITION FOR ALAN LOUIS GENERAL

The administrator at Alan Louis General Hospital confronted a problem that he hoped research could help solve. Alan Louis General, although a good hospital, was smaller than most of Bangor, Maine's, other hospitals and less well-known. In its area alone, it competed with 20 other medical facilities. Alan Louis needed a "position" that it could call unique to attract patients to fill its beds.

For a long time, the Alan Louis administrator, Sven Rapcorn, had believed in the principle that truth will win out. Build a better mousetrap, and the world will beat a path to your door. Erect a better hospital, and your beds will always be 98 percent filled. Unfortunately, Rapcorn learned, the real world seldom recognizes truth at first blush.

In the real world, more often than not, perception will triumph. And because people act on perceptions, those perceptions become reality. Successful positioning, Rapcorn learned, is based on recognizing and dealing with people's perceptions. And so, Rapcorn set out with research to build on existing perceptions about Alan Louis General.

As a first step, Rapcorn talked to his own doctors and trustees to gather data about their perceptions, not only of Alan Louis General, but also of other hospitals in the community. From this effort, pictures of each major competitor began to emerge. For example, the University Health Center had something for everybody—exotic care, specialized care, and basic, bread-and-butter care. Bangor General was a huge, well-respected hospital whose reputation was so good that only a major tragedy could shake its standing in the community.

Mercy Hospital was known for its trauma center. And so on. As for Alan Louis itself, doctors and trustees said that it was a great place to work, that excellent care was provided, and that the nursing staff was particularly friendly and good. The one problem, everyone agreed, was that "nobody knows about us."

The second step in Rapcorn's research project was to test attributes important in health care. Respondents were asked to rank eight factors in order of importance and to tell Rapcorn and his staff how each of the surveyed hospitals rated on those factors. The research instrument used a semantic differential scale of 1 to 10, with 1 the worst and 10 the best possible score. Questionnaires were sent to two groups: 1,000 area residents and 500 former Alan Louis patients.

The third step in the research was to tabulate the results. Among area residents who responded, the eight attributes were ranked accordingly:

1. Surgical care—9.23
2. Medical equipment—9.20
3. Cardiac care—9.16
4. Emergency services—8.96
5. Range of medical services—8.63
6. Friendly nurses—8.62
7. Moderate costs—8.59
8. Location—7.94

After the attributes were ranked, the hospitals in the survey were ranked for each attribute. On advanced surgical care, the most important feature to area residents, Bangor General ranked first, with University Health Center a close second. Alan Louis was far down on the list. The same was true of virtually every other attribute. Indeed, on nursing care, an area in which its staff thought Alan Louis excelled, the hospital came in last in the minds of area residents. Rapcorn was not surprised. The largest hospitals in town scored well on most attributes; Alan Louis trailed the pack.

However, the ranking of hospital scores according to former Alan Louis patients revealed an entirely different story. On surgical care, for example, although Bangor General still ranked first, Alan Louis came in a close second. And its scores improved similarly on all other attributes. In fact, in nursing care, where Alan Louis came in last on the survey of area residents, among former patients its score was higher than that of any other hospital. It also ranked first in terms of convenient location and second in terms of costs, range of services, and emergency care.

The fourth step in Rapcorn's research project was to draw some conclusions. He reached three conclusions:

1. Bangor General was still number one in terms of area hospitals.
2. Alan Louis ranked at or near the top on most attributes, according to those who actually experienced care there.
3. Former Alan Louis patients rated the hospital significantly better than the general public did.

In other words, thought Rapcorn, most of those who try Alan Louis like it. The great need was to convince more people to try the hospital.

(handwritten margin note: Because the patients may not have been to the other facilities)

But how could this be accomplished with a hospital? Other marketers generate trial by sending free samples in the mail, offering cents-off coupons, holding free demonstrations, and the like. Hospitals are more limited in this area. Rapcorn's challenge was to launch a communications campaign to convince prospects to see other area hospitals in a different, less favorable light and/or to give people a specific reason to think about trying Alan Louis. In other words, he needed to come up with a communications strategy that clearly differentiated Alan Louis—admittedly, among the smallest of area hospitals— from the bigger, less personal hospitals. Rapcorn was confident that the data he had gathered from the research project were all he needed to come up with a winning idea.

QUESTIONS

1. What kind of communications program would you launch to accomplish Rapcorn's objectives?
— 2. What would be the cornerstone—the theme—of your communications program?
③ What would be the specific elements of your program?
4. In launching the program, what specific steps would you follow—both inside and outside the hospital—to build support?

VOICE OF EXPERIENCE

KATHLEEN LADD WARD

Kathleen Ladd Ward is a pubic relations strategist with 30 years experience in public relations, marketing communications, and research. Before founding K. Ladd Ward & Company in 1981, Ward held key positions in communications research, advertising copy writing, and market research with Doremus and Kenyon & Eckhardt in New York City. An eminent public relations researcher, Ward chairs the Research Committee of the Public Relations Society of America and chaired that society's first and second national Forum on Research.

HOW IMPORTANT IS RESEARCH IN PUBLIC RELATIONS PRACTICE?

Research is the crucial first step in public relations. It is essential to evaluating an organization's reputation and repairing it if need be. It is essential in evaluating stakeholder relationships and assessing how successful the organization is in achieving its mission.

HOW DOES PUBLIC RELATIONS RESEARCH DIFFER FROM OTHER TYPES OF RESEARCH?

Research for public relations is different than public opinion or marketing research, because the ultimate use of the information is different. Those other research approaches only need to identify people's preferences at a particular point in time. Our information needs require research that will tell us why people think and feel the way they do, in their own words, so we can address their concerns.

IS IT POSSIBLE TO MEASURE PUBLIC RELATIONS "SUCCESS"?

Of course—so long as we have done the preliminary research that enables us to determine appropriate public relations goals, objectives, strategies, and tactics. Without that preprogram research, we have nothing to measure our work against, so we can't possibly know, or prove, how good a job we've done.

WHAT MEASUREMENTS ARE MOST USEFUL FOR PUBLIC RELATIONS?

There are two kinds of measurements: outputs and outcomes. Evaluating the outputs—publicity placements and the like—helps us evaluate our activities. Evaluating outcomes tells us the impact of that output on the target audience.

WHAT IS THE MOST EFFECTIVE PUBLIC RELATIONS RESEARCH TECHNIQUE?

The most effective research technique depends on the need. What strategic information are we after? Who is our target audience? How difficult will it be to reach them? Do we need statistically projectible data? Or will opinion leaders be an appropriate resource? There are advantages and disadvantages to every methodology. We have to pick and choose according to need.

HOW DO YOU ANSWER PEOPLE WHO CLAIM PUBLIC RELATIONS IS PRIMARILY INTUITIVE?

I ask, "Whose intuition?" And "How can you be sure your organization's reputation and relationships are everything they need to be to succeed? How can you be sure you're coming up with the most effective strategies to be successful? How do you know you're saying the right things to the right people? And how do you know you're spending your budget wisely, no wishfully?"

WHAT IS THE TWENTY-FIRST CENTURY OUTLOOK FOR PUBLIC RELATIONS RESEARCH?

That depends on the people who practice public relations. To the extent practitioners appreciate the importance of research, learn to use it, and learn to sell it, our profession will become more strategic. That, in turn, will enable public relations to achieve its promise and prove its value. And members of our profession can then take their rightful place at the senior management table. It is up to public relations practitioners.

CHAPTER SIX

Communication

EVERY ORGANIZATION IN AMERICA TOOK NOTICE IN January 1996 when AT&T announced it would reduce its payroll by nearly 40,000 jobs over three years. The reaction was as vicious as it was rapid. AT&T was pilloried with negative publicity, and Chairman Robert Allen, as noted in chapter three, became the "poster boy" for ruthless corporate firings of lower and middle level employees that enriched the pockets of high-ranking executives.

Although Wall Street positively loved these kinds of expense reductions, other companies took notice of the pain inflicted on AT&T, and the language used to announce layoffs immediately changed.

To wit:

- When they announced their merger in the spring of 1996, Bell Atlantic and Nynex pointedly passed up an opportunity to announce the elimination of 3,000 "overlapped" jobs. Rather, the company insisted, "new markets will open up for the merged company, saving the workers from layoffs."
- A short time later, SBC Communications Inc. merged with Pacific Telesis Group and spoke of creating 1,000 jobs at the new headquarters "over what otherwise would have been the case if the merger had not occurred."
- A month after that, Conagra Inc., a large food processor, in acknowledging that it would be laying off 6,500 employees, quickly added that "our employment has grown by 10,000 since 1992, and we aren't eliminating as many jobs as we've created."[1]

Thereafter, companies were even more careful how they referred to "firing" workers. Softer terms, such as "downsizing" or "rightsizing" or "retrenching" or "reconfiguring" began to creep into the kinder and gentler corporate lexicon.

The lesson here was obvious: Entering the twenty-first century, communications must be handled with great care.

The public relations practitioner is a professional communicator. More than anyone else in an organization, the practitioner must know how to communicate. This knowledge sets the public relations professional apart from other employees.

Fundamentally, communication is a process of exchanging information, imparting ideas, and making oneself understood by others. Importantly, it also includes understanding others in return. Indeed, understanding is critical to the communications process. If one person sends a message to another, who disregards or misunderstands it, then communication hasn't taken place. But if the idea received is the one intended, then communication has occurred. Thus, a boss who sends subordinates dozens of memos isn't necessarily communicating with them. If the idea received is not the one intended, then the sender has done little more than convert personal thoughts to words—and there they lie.

Although all of us are endowed with some capacity for communicating, the public relations practitioner must be better at it than most. Indeed, the effectiveness of public relations professionals is determined by their own ability to communicate and to counsel others on how to communicate. Before public relations practitioners can earn the respect of management and become trusted advisors, they must demonstrate a mastery of many communications skills—writing, speaking, listening, promoting, and counseling. Just as the controller is expected to be an adept accountant, and the legal counsel is expected to be an accomplished lawyer, the public relations professional is expected to be an expert communicator.

COMMUNICATIONS THEORY

Books have been written on the subject of communications theory. Consequently, we won't attempt to provide an all-encompassing discussion on how people ensure that their messages get through to others. But, in its most basic sense, communication commences with a source, who sends a message through a medium to reach a receiver, who, we hope, responds.

One early theory of communication, the two-step flow theory, stated that an organization would beam a message first to the mass media, which would then deliver that message to the great mass of readers, listeners, and viewers for their response. This theory may have given the mass media too much credit. People today are influenced by a variety of factors, of which the media may be one but not necessarily the dominant one. Another theory, the concentric-circle theory, developed by pollster Elmo Roper, assumed that ideas evolve gradually to the public at large, moving in concentric circles from great thinkers to great disciples to great disseminators to lesser disseminators to the politically active to the politically inert. This theory suggests that people pick up and accept ideas from leaders, whose impact on public opinion may be greater than that of the mass media. The overall study of how communication is used for direction and control is called cybernetics.

One key element in communication—and particularly in public relations—is feedback. In cybernetic theory, feedback is communication that helps a source control a receiver's behavior. However, just as a thermostat gives indications as to how to adjust temperature, so too, feedback doesn't necessarily imply "active communication" from a receiver. By contrast, in a theoretical communications approach called the "two-way symmetric model," dialogue is key—from both senders and receivers. In this model of public relations communication, both senders and receivers have an equal chance of persuading and being persuaded.[2]

Although there are numerous models of communication, one of the most fundamental is the S-M-R approach. This model suggests that the communication process begins with the source (S), who issues a message (M) to a receiver (R), who then decides what action to take, if any, relative to the communication. This element of receiver action, or feedback, underscores that good communication always involves dialogue between two or more parties. The S-M-R model has been modified to include additional elements: (1) an encoding stage, in which the source's original message is translated and conveyed to the receiver, and (2) a decoding stage, in which the receiver interprets the encoded message and takes action. This evolution from the traditional model has resulted in the S-E-M-D-R method, which illustrates graphically the role of the public relations function in modern communications; both the encoding (E) and the decoding (D) stages are of critical importance in communicating any public relations message.

The Source

The source of a message is the central person or organization doing the communicating. The source could be a politician giving a campaign speech, a school announcing curriculum changes, or even, as one superior court judge in Seattle ruled, a topless go-go dancer in the midst of gyrating.

Although the source usually knows how it wants the message to be received, there is no guarantee that it will be understood that way by the receiver. In many cases—a public speech, for example—the speaker is relatively limited in ability to influence the interpretation of the message. Gestures, voice tone, and volume can be used to add special importance to certain remarks, but whether the audience understands what is intended may ultimately depend on other factors, particularly the encoder.

The Encoder

What the source wants to relate must be translated from an idea in the mind to a communication. In the case of a campaign speech, a politician's original message may be subject to translation or reinterpretation by at least three independent encoders.

1. The politician may consult a speech writer to help put ideas into words on paper. Speech writers become encoders in first attempting to understand the politician's message clearly and then in translating that message effectively into language that an audience will understand and, hopefully, accept.

2. Once the speech is written, it may be further encoded into a news release. In this situation, the encoder—perhaps a different individual from the speech writer—selects what seem to be the most salient points of the speech and provides them to media editors in a fairly brief format.

3. A news editor may take the news release and retranslate it before reporting it to the voters, the ultimate audience for the politician's message. Thus, the original message in the mind of the politician has been massaged three separate times before it ever reaches the intended receivers. Each time, in all likelihood, the particular encoder has added new subjective shadings to the politician's original message. The very act of encoding depends largely on the encoder's personal experience.

WORDS/SEMANTICS Words are among our most personal and potent weapons. Words can soothe us, bother us, or infuriate us. They can bring us together or drive us apart. They can even cause us to kill or be killed. Words mean different things to different people, depending on their backgrounds, occupations, education, or geographic locations. What one word means to you might be dramatically different from what that same word means to your neighbor. The study of what words really mean is called semantics, and the science of semantics is a peculiar one indeed.

Figure 6–1   Pennsylvania snack food maker Snyder of Berlin was quick to take advantage of the pervasive use of the term couch potato by cooking up a "potato couch" for use in a promotion for Thunder Crunch, its newest line of potato chips. The spud sofa was a most "ap-peeling" promotion. (Sorry.)

Words are perpetually changing in our language. What's in today is out tomorrow. What a word denotes according to the dictionary may be thoroughly dissimilar to what it connotes in its more emotional or visceral sense. Even the simplest words—liberal, conservative, profits, consumer activists—can spark semantic skyrockets. Many times, without knowledge of the territory, the semantics of words may make no sense. Take the word *cool*. In American vernacular a person who is cool is good. A person who is "not so hot" is bad. So cool is the opposite of "not so hot." But wait a minute; "not so hot" must also be the opposite of hot. Therefore, in a strange and convoluted way, cool must equal hot. (If you get my drift.)

Entering the twenty-first century, public relations professionals must constantly be alert to alterations in the language. In 1995, when football legend Orenthal J. Simpson became a national cause celebre as an accused murderer, the orange juice industry downplayed its signature abbreviation, "O.J.," until the dust settled. On the other hand, when the term "couch potato" came into vogue to signify an inveterate television watcher, a Pennsylvania potato chip maker was quick to capitalize (Figure 6–1).

Words used in the encoding stage have a significant influence on the message conveyed to the ultimate receiver. Thus, the source must depend greatly on the ability of the encoder to accurately understand and effectively translate the true message—with all its semantic complications—to the receiver.

THE REST OF THE STORY

WHEN IN ROME . . .

It's hard enough to understand English words if you speak the language, but if English isn't your first language, it's even more confounding to understand why when words are apparently put together in the proper construction—they don't exactly mean what they should.

Here are a few overseas examples.

- In a Paris hotel elevator: "Please leave your values at the front desk."
- Outside a Hong Kong tailor shop: "Ladies may have a fit upstairs."
- In a Zurich hotel: "Because of the impropriety of entertaining guests of the opposite sex in the bedroom, it is suggested that the lobby be used for this purpose."
- In a Bangkok dry cleaners: "Drop your trousers here for best results."
- In a Bucharest hotel: "The lift is being fixed for the next day. During that time, we regret that you will be unbearable."
- In a Rome laundry: "Ladies, leave your clothing here and spend the afternoon having a good time."
- Advertisement of donkey rides in Thailand: "Would you like to ride on your own ass?"
- In an Acapulco hotel: "The manager has personally passed all the water served here."
- In a Copenhagen Airport: "We take your bags and send them in all directions."
- In a Budapest zoo: "Please do not feed the animals. If you have any suitable food, give it to the guard on duty."

The Message

Once an encoder has taken in the source's ideas and translated them into terms a receiver can understand, the ideas are then transmitted in the form of a message. The message may be carried in a variety of communications media: speeches, newspapers, news releases, press conferences, broadcast reports, and face-to-face meetings. Communications theorists differ on what exactly constitutes the message, but here are three of the more popular explanations.

1. **The content is the message.** According to this theory, which is far and away the most popular, the content of a communication—what it says—constitutes its message. According to this view, the real importance of a communication—the message—lies in the meaning of an article or in the intent of a speech. Neither the medium through which the message is being communicated nor the individual doing the communicating is as important as the content.

2. **The medium is the message.** Other communications theorists—the late Canadian professor Marshall McLuhan being the best known—argue that the content of a communication is not the message at all. According to McLuhan, the content is less important than the vehicle of communication.

   McLuhan's argument stemmed largely from the fact that many people today are addicted to television. He said that television is a "cool" medium—that is, someone can derive meaning from a TV message without working too hard. On the other hand, reading involves hard work to grasp an idea fully; thus, newspapers, magazines, and books are "hot" media. Furthermore, McLuhan argued, a television viewer can easily become part of that which is being viewed. This has particular implications as television becomes more and more interactive.

   One direct outgrowth of this medium-is-the-message theory was the development of the friendly team style of local television news reporting. Often called the eyewitness approach, this format encouraged interaction among TV newscasters in order to involve viewers as part of the news team family.

   The medium of television has become particularly important to the president of the United States. Commencing with the cool, polished television demeanor of John F. Kennedy and proceeding through modern-day presidents, television has become the great differentiator in terms of presidential popularity. Ronald Reagan, a former movie actor and media spokesman for General Electric, was a magnificent master of the TelePrompTer. Reagan's televised speeches were studies in proper use of the medium. George Bush, less good than his predecessor, nonetheless had his moments. And Bill Clinton, while not as polished as Reagan with prepared speeches, nonetheless is skilled in using the medium to suggest a committed, concerned, and undeniably human commander-in-chief.

3. **The person is the message.** Still other theorists argue that it is neither the content nor the medium that is the message, but rather the speaker. For example, Hitler was a master of persuasion. His minister of propaganda, Josef Goebbels, used to say, "Any man who thinks he can persuade, can

persuade." Hitler practiced this self-fulfilling communications prophecy to the hilt. Feeding on the perceived desires of the German people, Hitler was concerned much less with the content of his remarks than with their delivery. His maniacal rantings and frantic gestures seized public sentiment and sent friendly crowds into a frenzy. In every way, Hitler himself was the primary message of his communications.

Today, in a similar vein, we often refer to a leader's charisma. Frequently, the charismatic appeal of a political leader may be more important than what that individual says. President Clinton, for example, can move an audience by the very inflection of his words. Likewise, Jesse Jackson can bring a group to its feet merely by shaking a fist or raising the pitch of his voice. And accomplished speakers, from retired military leaders like Colin Powell and Norman Schwarzkopf, to business consultants like Tom Peters and Stew Leonard, to sports coaches like Pat Riley and Bill Parcells, can also rally listeners with their personal charismatic demeanor.

Often people cannot distinguish between the words and the person who speaks them. The words, the face, the body, the eyes, the attitude, the timing, the wit, the presence—all form a composite that, as a whole, influences the listener. As political consultant turned television executive Roger Ailes has put it, it comes down to the "like" factor in communication. Ailes points out that some candidates get votes just because people like them. "They forget that you're short, or you're fat, or you're bald . . . they say 'I like that guy.' "[3] In such cases, the source of the communication becomes every bit as important as the message itself.

THE REST OF THE STORY

ARE YOU SURE YOU SAW WHAT YOU THOUGHT YOU SAW?

First read the sentence that follows:

FINISHED FILES ARE THE RESULT OF YEARS OF SCIENTIFIC STUDY COMBINED WITH THE EXPERIENCE OF MANY YEARS.

Now, count the *Fs* in the sentence. Count them only once, and do not go back and count them again.

QUESTION

How many *Fs* are there?

ANSWER

There are six *Fs*. However, because the capital F in OF sounds like a capital V, it seems to disappear. Most people perceive only three Fs in the sentence. Our conditioned, habitual patterns (mental blocks) restrict us from being as alert as we should be. Frequently, we fail to perceive things as they really are.

The Decoder

After a message has been transmitted, it must be decoded by a receiver before action can be taken. This stage is like the encoding stage in that the receiver takes in the message and translates it into his or her own common terms. Obviously, language again plays a critical role. The decoder must fully understand the message before acting on it; if the message is unclear or the decoder is unsure of its intent, there's probably little chance that the action taken by the receiver will be the action desired by the source. Messages must be understood in common terms.

How a receiver decodes a message depends greatly on that person's own perception. How an individual looks at and comprehends a message is a key to effective communications (Figure 6–2). Remember that everyone is biased; no two people perceive a message identically. Personal biases are nurtured by many factors, including stereotypes, symbols, semantics, peer group pressures, and—especially in today's culture—the media.

STEREOTYPES Everyone lives in a world of stereotypical figures. Yuppies, Midwesterners, feminists, bankers, blue-collar workers, PR types, and thousands of other characterizations cause people to think of certain specific images. Public figures, for example, are typecast regularly. The dumb blond, the bigoted right winger, the computer geek, and the shifty, used-car salesman are the kinds of stereotypes our society—particularly television—perpetuate.

Like it or not, most of us are victims of such stereotypes. For example, research indicates that a lecture delivered by a person wearing glasses will be perceived as "signifi-

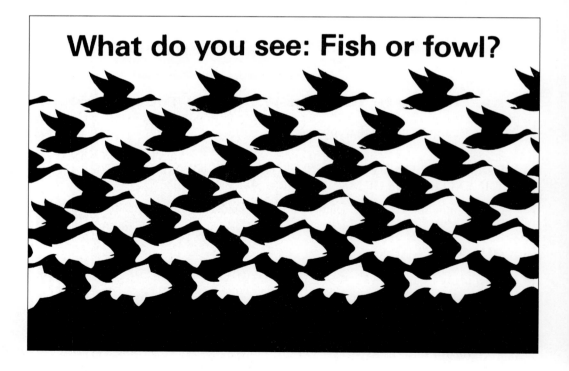

Figure 6–2 Often what we see may not be what others see. (Hint: There are both white fish and black fowl.)

THE REST OF THE STORY

DECODING LANGUAGE AT THE PENSION OFFICE

These 11 extracts supposedly emanate from genuine letters sent to the pensions office of some company, somewhere, sometime. Although crude, they were written in good faith by their authors. Try to decode them.

1. I can't get sick pay. I have six children. Can you tell me why this is?
2. This is my eighth child. What are you going to do about it?
3. Mrs. Morris has no clothes and has not had any for a year. The clergy have been visiting her.
4. Unless I get my husband's money quickly, I shall be forced to lead an immoral life.
5. I am sending you my marriage certificate and six children. I had seven and one died, which was baptized on a half sheet of paper by the Rev. Thomas.
6. In answer to your letter, I have given birth to a little boy weighing 10 pounds. Is this satisfactory?
7. You have changed my little girl into a little boy. Will this make any difference?
8. I have no children as my husband is a bus driver and works all day and night.
9. Milk is wanted for my baby as the father is unable to supply it.
10. I want money as quick as you can send it. I have been in bed with my doctor all week, and he does not seem to be doing me any good.
11. Sir, I am glad to say that my husband, reported missing, is now dead.

---

cantly more believable" than the same lecture delivered before the same audience by the same lecturer without glasses. The stereotyped impression of people with glasses is that they are more trustworthy and more believable.

SYMBOLS The clenched-fist salute, the swastika, and the thumbs-up sign all leave distinct impressions on most people. Marshaled properly, symbols can be used as effective persuasive elements (Figure 6–3). The Statue of Liberty, the Red Cross, the Star of David, and many other symbols have been used traditionally for positive persuasion. On the other hand, when unrelated Middle Eastern terrorists selected American targets to sabotage in the 1990s, they chose to bomb the World Trade Center early in the decade and shoot up the Empire State Building later in the decade. No doubt, these locations were chosen because of their "symbolic" value as American icons.

SEMANTICS Public relations professionals make their living largely by knowing how to use words effectively to communicate desired meanings. Occasionally, this is tricky because the same words may hold contrasting meanings for different people. In 1995, when President Clinton tried to enact sweeping new health care reform, Republicans and the insurance industry scuttled the effort by painting the issue as an effort to sabotage the health benefits of the elderly. Especially vulnerable are popular and politically sensitive phrases such as capital punishment, law and order, liberal politician, right winger, and on and on, until you reach the point where the Oakridge Mall in San Jose, California, demanded that the gourmet hamburger restaurant on its premises, with a logo depicting a

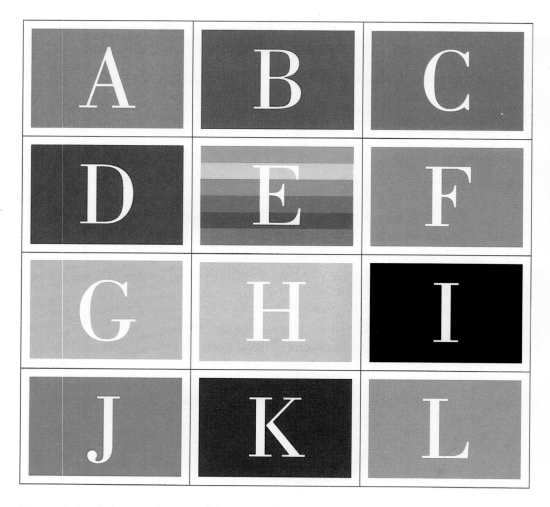

Figure 6–3   Color can be one of the most effective "symbols" in society. For example, some of the most well-known corporations in the world have spent hundreds of millions of dollars over the years to familiarize you with the the 12 corporate colors above. Can you match each shade with the company that "owns" it?

smiling hamburger with a monocle and top hat, either change its "suggestive name" or leave the mall. The restaurant's name? Elegant Buns.

In the 1990s, the label "terrorists," a misnomer that the media have bestowed on those who hijack planes and blow up buildings, may play right into the hands of those who attack innocent civilians. Behavioral science studies show that such people seek the aura of power. Labeling them as terrorists concedes that they are, in fact, achieving their aims.[4] The same can be argued about those rap music artists, who preach a philosophy of violence and hate. Such gangster rappers claim that they are "telling it like it is" or "reporting what we see in the streets." But when reporters and record company executives give credence to such misguided rhetoric, they become just as guilty for the often unfortunate consequences that result; for example, the killings in the late 1990s of enemy rap artists, Tupac Shakur and Notorious B.I.G.[5]

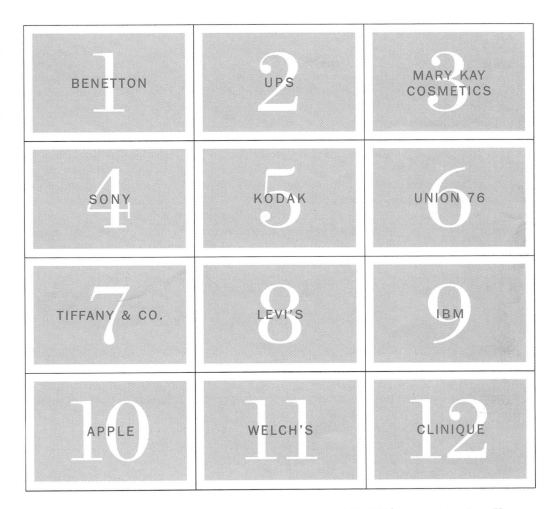

Figure 6–3 (continued) Answers: 1-J Benetton green, 2-K UPS brown, 3-L Mary Kay Cosmetics pink, 4-I Sony black, 5-H Kodak yellow, 6-A Union 76 orange, 7-F Tiffany & Co. light blue, 8-C Levi's red, 9-B IBM blue, 10-E Apple spectrum, 11-D Welch's purple, 12-G Clinique light green.

Because language and the meanings of words change constantly, semantics must be handled with extreme care. Good communicators always consider the consequences of the words they plan to use before using them.

PEER GROUPS In one famous study, students were asked to point out, in progression, the shortest of three lines.

A   ————————————————

B   ————————————

C   ——————————————

Although line B is obviously the shortest, each student in the class except one was told in advance to answer that line C was the shortest. The object of the test was to see whether the one student would agree with his peers. Results generally indicated that, to a statistically significant degree, all students, including the uncoached one, chose C. Peer pressure prevails.

MEDIA The power of the media—particularly as an agenda setter or reinforcement mechanism—is also substantial. A common complaint among lawyers is that their clients cannot receive fair trials because of pretrial publicity leading to preconceived verdicts from potential jurors who read newspapers and watch television.

In one famous case in North Carolina, army officer Jeffrey MacDonald was put on trial for the savage killing of his wife and two children. The officer claimed that he was innocent and that a band of hippies had stabbed him and killed his family. State newspapers publicized the case extensively, running photographs of the soldier and commentary about the circumstances of the murders. Neither the soldier nor his lawyer would talk to the press. A random telephone survey taken a week before the trial indicated that most people thought the soldier was guilty. Several weeks later, however, the army dropped the murder charges against him when it couldn't make a case. Ironically, nine years later, the man was convicted of those murders, subsequently released, and then found guilty on appeal.

It is clear that people often base perceptions on what they read or hear, without bothering to dig further to elicit the facts. Although appearances are sometimes revealing, they are often deceiving.

The Receiver

You really aren't communicating unless someone is at the other end to hear and understand what you're saying. This situation is analogous to the old mystery of the falling tree in the forest: Does it make a noise when it hits the ground if there's no one there to hear it? Regardless of the answer, communication doesn't take place if a message doesn't reach the intended receivers and exert the desired effect on those receivers.

Even if a communication is understood clearly, there is no guarantee that the motivated action will be the desired one. In fact, a message may trigger several different effects.

1. **It may change attitudes.**   This result, however, is very difficult to achieve and rarely happens.
2. **It may crystallize attitudes.**   This outcome is much more common. Often a message will influence receivers to take actions they might already have been thinking about taking but needed an extra push to accomplish. For example, a receiver might want to contribute to a certain charity, but seeing a child's photo on a contribution canister might crystallize his or her attitude sufficiently to trigger action.
3. **It might create a wedge of doubt.**   Communication can sometimes force receivers to modify their points of view. A persuasive message can cause receivers to question their original thinking on an issue.
4. **It may do nothing.**   Often communication results in no action at all. When the American Cancer Society waged an all-out campaign to cut into cigarette sales, the net impact of the communication campaign was hardly significant.

Feedback is critical to the process of communication. A communicator must get feedback from a receiver to know what messages are or are not getting through and how to structure future communications. Occasionally, feedback is ignored by professional communicators, but this is always a mistake.

SLUMMING IN RAPLAND

Figure 6–4 Rap superstar Notorious B.I.G., aka Biggie Smalls aka Arnold Wallace, met an early and violent death in 1997.

I got my black shirt on,
I got my black gloves on,
I got my ski mask on,
I'm 'bout to bust some shots off,
I'm 'bout to dust some cops off,
Die, die, die, pig, die.

Thus begins the ballad of "Cop Killer," part of the "Body Count" gangsta rap album recorded by the rap music artist Ice-T and distributed by Time Warner.

The song's release in the summer of 1992 and its subsequent defense on free-speech grounds by Time Warner triggered a predictable outcry among business-people and the general public alike. Philadelphia's municipal pension fund announced plans to sell $1.6 million of Time Warner stock to protest the company's decision to distribute the rapper's album. One corporate CEO said he found Time Warner's behavior "offensive as a corporation. I hope it kills them."

Time Warner's public response was muted. Gerald Levin, the company's chairman, when asked what the firm's "standards of acceptability" were, answered with a prepared statement: "Time Warner is a home for journalists and artists who have significant messages to tell. They do it with journalistic and artistic integrity. Time Warner will finance, support and disseminate their work. That's what the company is."

Later, Mr. Levin defended Ice-T's album and gangsta rap in general as "the CNN of the streets."

That defense lasted until the presidential campaign of 1995 made Time Warner and its sponsorship of gangsta rap, a page one issue. Candidate Bob Dole in a most public speech in the heart of Hollywood, lambasted the company for its ethical failings, "You have sold your souls, but must you debase our nation and threaten our children for the sake of corporate profits?"

Dole's harsh words resonated with Time Warner. The company, in fact, treated the whole debate in a 14-page cover report in its own magazine, *Time*. One excerpt from that article read:

> "No company likes to be told it is contributing to the moral decline of a nation. . . . At Time Warner, however, such questions are simply the latest manifestation of a soul-searching that has embroiled the company since the conglomerate was born in 1990."

Although Time Warner executives reportedly were upset that candidate Dole had singled them out, in the wake of the attacks, the company underwent a great deal of soul searching about its under-contract gangsta rappers, such as Snoop Doggy Dogg, Tupac Shakur, and Dr. Dre. Quietly in 1996, after the blast from candidate Dole and former Education Secretary William Bennett, Time Warner sold back its $125 million stake in rap label Death Row Records.

Ultimately, the controversy died down, but not before Time Warner had fired the second ranking executive in its music division and recruited as its new president, respected African American banker Richard Parsons.

In 1997, the recording, marketing and promotion of gangsta rap took a fatal turn, when two arch enemies, Tupac Shakur and Notorious B.I.G. aka Biggie Smalls, were both shot and killed after late night parties (Figure 6–4).

Ironically, in 1990, at the time of the merger between Time and Warner, it was Chairman Levin who said, "Our good name is our basic asset. This company has a higher obligation than simply making money."

To which, a cynic world must ask, How does promoting gangsta rap help realize that "higher obligation"?

For further information about the Time Warner gangsta rap controversy, see Richard M. Clurman, "Pushing All the Hot Buttons," *The New York Times*, November 29, 1992, Arts & Leisure section, 16–17; Ted Field, "Slumming in Rapland," *The Wall Street Journal*, March 18, 1997, A23; Joe Klein, "Off to the Culture War," *Newsweek*, June 12, 1995, 28; Phil Kuntz, "Time Warner, a Big Donor to Democratic Camp Becomes Easy, Convenient Target for Bob Dole," *The Wall Street Journal*, June 5, 1995, A16; Mark Landler, "Time Warner, Under Its Own Spotlight," *The New York Times*, June 12, 1995, D4.; Roger Salquist, "Time Warner's Hard Line Takes Hits," *The Wall Street Journal*, July 23, 1992, B-1, 8; Tom Unger, "In Defense of Free Speech," *Public Relations Journal*, August 1992, 6; Jonathan Yardley, "The Music Industry's Lame Song and Dance Over Free Speech," *The Washington Post*, July 27, 1992, B6.

Whether the objectives of a communication have been met can often be assessed by such things as the amount of sales, number of letters, or number of votes obtained. If individuals take no action after receiving a communication, feedback must still be sought. In certain cases, although receivers have taken no discernible action, they may have understood and even passed on the message to other individuals. This person-to-person relay of received messages creates a two-step flow of communications: (1) vertically from a particular source and (2) horizontally from interpersonal contact. The targeting of opinion leaders as primary receivers is based on the hope that they will distribute received messages horizontally within their own communities.

SUMMARY

As society eases into the twenty-first century, some communications consultants believe the future of communication may be a "step back in time." The advent of narrow casting and communicating to more targeted, smaller audiences will mean a return to more direct communication between people. By combining the new technology—cable, Internet telemarketing, floppy disks, CD-ROM, and all the rest—people will need the help of public relations professionals to communicate effectively.[6]

There is no trick to effective communication. In addition to some facility with techniques, it is knowledge, hard work, and common sense that are the basic guiding principles. Naturally, communication must follow performance; organizations must back up what they say with action. Slick brochures, engaging speeches, intelligent articles, and a good press may capture the public's attention, but in the final analysis, the only way to obtain continued public support is through proper performance.

THE REST OF THE STORY

WHAAAT?

Extra credit for anyone who can decode the following sentence:

> We respectfully petition, request, and entreat that due and adequate provision be made, this day and the date herein after subscribed, for the satisfying of this petitioner's nutritional requirements and for the organizing of such methods as may be deemed necessary and proper to assure the reception by and for said petitioner of such quantities of baked products as shall, in the judgment of the aforesaid petitioner, constitute a sufficient supply thereof.*

WHAAAT?

---

*Give us this day our daily bread.

HUH?

Perhaps this one is easier to decode.*

1. The Lord is my external-internal integrative mechanism.
2. I shall not be deprived of gratifications for my visogeneric hungers or my need dispositions.
3. He motivates me to orient myself toward a nonsocial object with affective significance.
4. He positions me in a nondecisional situation.
5. He maximizes my adjustment.

---

*1. The Lord is my shepherd.
2. I shall not want.
3. He leadeth me besides the still waters.
4. He maketh me to lie down in green pastures.
5. He restoreth my soul.

DISCUSSION STARTERS

1. Above all else, the public relations practitioner is what?
2. Describe the process of communication.
3. Why do words like liberal, conservative, profits, and consumer activist spark semantic skyrockets?
4. What communications vehicle did President Reagan and President Bush use to maximum effectiveness?
5. What is meant by the "symmetric model" of communication?
6. Describe the S-E-M-D-R approach to communication.
7. How does perception influence a person's decoding?
8. Why is feedback critical to the communications process?
9. What common mistakes do people make when they communicate?
10. Why do some communications consultants believe that the future of communications may be a "step back in time"?

NOTES

1. Louis Uchitelle, "The New Buzz: Growth is Good," *The New York Times*, June 18, 1996, B1.
2. James E. Grunig and Todd Hunt, *Managing Public Relations*, (New York: Holt, Rinehart and Winston, 1984), 23.
3. "The 'Like Factor' in Communications," *Executive Communications* (February 1988): 1.
4. "Semantics Power," *Public Relations Reporter* (April 4, 1988): 4.
5. Brent Staples, "The Politics of Gangster Rap," *The New York Times*, August 27, 1993.
6. "Communication May Step Back in Time '90s," *IABC Communication World* (February 1990): 9.

SUGGESTED READINGS

Agee, W. *Introduction to Mass Communication*, 9th ed. New York: Harper & Row, 1988.

Ailes, Roger and Jon Kraushar. *You Are the Message*. Homewood, IL: Dow Jones-Irwin, 1988.

Bateman, David and Norma Sigband. *Communicating in Business*, 3rd ed. Glenview, IL: Scott-Foreman, 1989.

Bell, Arthur H. *Tools for Technical and Professional Communication*. Lincolnwood, IL: NTC Publishing Group, 1995.

Bittner, John. *Mass Communications*, 5th ed. Upper Saddle River, NJ: Prentice Hall, 1989.

Bovee, Courtland L. and John V. Thill. *Business Communication Today*, 3rd ed. New York: McGraw-Hill, 1992.

Brody, E. W. *Managing Communication Processes: From Planning to Crisis Response*. Wesport, CT: Praeger, 1991.

Corman, Steven R., et al. *Foundations of Organization Communication*. White Plains, NY: Longman, 1990.

Diamant, Lincoln. *Broadcast Communications Dictionary*, 3rd ed. Lincolnwood, IL: NTC Business, 1991.

Dilenschneider, Robert L. *A Briefing for Leaders: Communication as the Ultimate Exercise of Power*. New York: Harper Business, 1992.

Fraser, Edith A. *Glossary of Common Acronyms and Terms of Modern Human Resource Management*. Orangeburg, NY: Implementation Support Associates.

Goldhaber, Gerald. *Organizational Communication*, 4th ed. Madison, WI: Brown and Benchmark, 1993.

Grunig, James E., ed. *Excellence in Public Relations and Communications Management*. Hillsdale, NJ: Lawrence Erlbaum Associates, 1992.

Hewes, Dean E., ed. *The Cognitive Bases of Interpersonal Communication*. Hillsdale, NJ: Lawrence Erlbaum Associates, 1995.

International Encyclopedia of Communication, Vol. 4. New York: Oxford University Press, 1989.

Johnson, Hans. *Professional Communications—For a Change*. New York: Prentice Hall, 1990.

TOP OF THE SHELF

RICHARD WEINER

WEBSTER'S NEW WORLD DICTIONARY OF MEDIA AND COMMUNICATIONS

NEW YORK: PUBLIC RELATIONS PUBLISHING COMPANY, 1996

Renowned public relations practitioner Richard Weiner has compiled the definitive compendium of the language of advertising, broadcasting, film, journalism, printing, marketing, and public relations.

On one page, you can find the answers to questions that have dogged you for eons, such as the derivation of the "twang box" (a sound effects device), the identity of a "tweenie" (a 600-watt spotlight), and a TVF (a made-for-TV film).

If you're ever concerned about not understanding the terminology in a particular medium of communication, this book provides all the jargon, abbreviations, acronyms, nicknames, and other nourishing tidbits to convey communications expertise in virtually any media-related area, from the Internet to the printing press.

Kreps, Gary L. *Organizational Communications*, 2nd ed. White Plains, NY: Longman, 1990.

Leeds-Hurwitz, Wendy. *Social Approaches to Communication*. New York: Guilford Press, 1995.

Ragan Report. Chicago: Ragan Communications. Weekly. Pointed commentary on current communications issues; particularly pointed columnists.

Sigman, Stuart J., ed. *The Consequentiality of Communication*. Hillsdale, NJ: Lawrence Erlbaum Associates, 1995. Goes beyond the "effects" of communication, exploring the procedures, dynamics and structures.

Thill, John V. and Courtland L. Bovee, *Excellence in Business Communication*, 3rd ed. New York: McGraw-Hill, 1996.

Windahl, Sven and Benno Signitzer. *Using Communications Theory: An Introduction to Planned Communications*. Newbury Park, CA: Sage Publications, 1991.

CASE STUDY

BOXED IN AT JACK IN THE BOX

Food poisoning is a food company's worst nightmare. When hundreds of customers complain of symptoms and three children die, the firm faces communications and other problems that are severe. Thus in January 1993, when Jack in the Box, a subsidiary of Food Maker, Inc., was beseiged by customers in the Northwest who suddenly became ill after eating the company's hamburgers, the firm momentarily panicked.

Complaints began in Seattle and spiraled immediately. All told, some 800 people complained of food poisoning symptoms, with 477 infected by the painful—and occasionally deadly—*Escherichia coli* 0157:H7, a bacteria that damages the kidneys.

Of those who complained, 144 were hospitalized. A majority of the seriously ill were children, who had to undergo kidney dialysis for weeks. Three children died, but only one was directly linked to Jack in the Box.

Immediately upon being apprised of the situation, Jack in the Box voluntarily stopped selling all hamburger products in Washington State.

"Although this is an isolated case, we are taking every precaution to ensure that we meet and exceed health department standards," said the company's vice president in announcing the voluntary halt.

Three days later, as press reports of additional cases of bacterial infection emerged, Jack in the Box rushed its president to Seattle for a morning news conference. President Robert Nugent began the session by saying: "I would like to express my deepest sympathies to those who have been stricken—especially the children. I pray that they all have a speedy and complete recovery." President Nugent went on to describe the stellar historical record of Jack in the Box in Washington and then acknowledged that, "The problem is in fact due to contaminated hamburger."

However, the president suggested that the source of the contaminated hamburger wasn't Jack in the Box but rather a Northwest meat supplier with whom the company dealt. Further, said President Nugent, although Jack in the Box was accused of "violating the state's cooking procedures," the facts were the following: "Our cooking procedures were established to comply with all federal and state regulations and have been in use for over 30 years. . . . While the Washington State Health Department recently, and we think appropriately, upgraded their temperature regulations for hamburger, it is clear that Jack in the Box was not properly informed of this change."

At the height of the controversy, Food Maker, Inc., dismissed its long-time public relations firm, describing the breakup as "differences in strategic direction."

In the ensuing weeks, Jack in the Box established an 800 number for the public to receive direct information about the bacteria outbreak. It announced the hiring of a new supplier of hamburger meat for its restaurants in the western United States. And Food Maker announced record first-quarter earnings, despite the Jack in the Box dilemma, to try to reassure the investment community.

The company's rebound was short-lived. A few weeks later, at Food Maker's annual meeting, President Nugent was obliged to make an embarrassing disclosure. He corrected his earlier statement that the company "hadn't received" new state food heating regulations from government officials. Rather, according to Nugent, the rules were "on file" at Food Maker's San Diego corporate headquarters. The Jack in the Box restaurant in Tacoma, Washington, site of the poisonings, also apparently had received a copy of the regulations in the mail.

Nugent said that a company vice president failed to alert top management of the new cooking regulations, which weren't adhered to. Had the new regulations, which required cooking hamburger patties at 155°F, been followed, the *E. coli* bacteria in the meat may have been killed.

As the gravity of the Jack in the Box situation began to sink in, Food Maker's stock plummeted and the company hit hard times. By June, 40 lawsuits in Washington, California, Idaho, and Nevada had been filed against Food Maker. The company immediately settled with the family of a 17-month-old boy whose death was attributed to a secondary infection picked up from another child who had eaten at Jack in the Box.

Jack in the Box now sought to recover from its early missteps. It announced a program to pay the hospital costs of all customers hospitalized as a result of eating contaminated hamburgers. Said President Nugent: "We are committed to meeting all of our responsibilities in connection with this devastating situation. We are prepared to pay all hospital costs for our customers who have been affected by this tragedy."

As 1993 drew to a close, Food Maker and Jack in the Box aggressively sought to explain to customers, through ads and corporate literature, how the contamination had occurred and how the incidents were isolated. At the same time, the company continued to promote its program to pay the medical costs for all those sickened from eating at its restaurants.

Slowly, Jack in the Box began to reemerge from its nightmare, resigned to the long-term challenge of reassuring clients that its stores and its products were safe.

QUESTIONS

1. Was Jack in the Box's management right in reacting so quickly to the contamination problem?
2. How would you assess the strategy of spreading the blame for the contaminated hamburger?
3. How harmful to the Jack in the Box case was the inaccurate statement about the company's failure to receive new state hamburger cooking regulations?
4. What is your overall assessment of how Food Maker handled this communications challenge? What kinds of communications should the firm adopt in attempting to restore its credibility?

For further information about the Jack in the Box case, see "Jack in the Box's Worst Nightmare," *The New York Times*, February 6, 1993, 35, 37; "Last Patient Is Released in Jack in the Box Case," *The New York Times*, June 30, 1993, A14; and Calvin Sims, "Burger Chain Confronts Nightmare," *The New York Times*, July 16, 1993, 39, 51.

VOICE OF EXPERIENCE

FRANKIE A. HAMMOND

Frankie Hammond is associate professor in the Department of Public Relations in the College of Journalism and Communications at the University of Florida, where she has taught since 1974. During a five-year period as director of development and placement for the college, Professor Hammond helped more than 1,000 graduates launch their professional careers in public relations, advertising, journalism, and telecommunications. A former reporter and editor, Professor Hammond is a past president of the North Florida chapter of the Public Relations Society of America and served two terms on the society's Education Section Board.

How Would You Describe Today's Public Relations Students?

Today's students appear to be more career-driven than their earlier counterparts. They are ambitious and eager to join the workforce. But at the same time, they exhibit more altruism; they want to give something back to society. Current students' interests expand beyond the workplace, and money no longer seems to be a prime motivator.

What Advice Do You Give Those Who Want to Become Public Relations Practitioners?

Learn anything you can about everything you can. Then write. Rewrite. And rewrite some more. Sharpen your problem-solving capabilities. Get practical experience while you're in school and during the summers. Participate in the Public Relations Student Society of America. Take advantage of every opportunity to improve yourself and your skills.

Why Should A Student Be Interested in a Career in Public Relations?

Public relations is such a multifaceted endeavor that any individual should be interested in it. The opportunities for personal and professional growth offer a lifetime of interesting work, interesting people, and a lot of enjoyment.

How Does One Land a Job in the Field?

Solid writing ability, common sense, and good judgment are always in demand. There are many entry-level jobs for well-rounded, enthusiastic, skilled, and persistent new graduates.

What Distinguishes a Good Public Relations Practitioner?

Judgment and ethics, backed by communications skills and a familiarity with the social and behavioral forces that make people tick. An understanding of the public relations process and how it impacts on and is impacted by society is a must. The ability to view problems as opportunities and having a good sense of humor are also important.

What Is the Most Significant Challenge Confronting Public Relations Today?

The constant change in the environment in which public relations operates, and therefore the constant change in its practice, is undoubtedly the most significant challenge today. The successful practitioner must adapt to meet the societal, economic, and political changes in the world or become an anachronism.

If You Had Your Career to Start Over Again, What Would You Do?

Basically, I would do what I have done. I have had a variety of interesting experiences as the result of a willingness to take advantage of opportunities and new directions as they came up. It's added a broader perspective to my thinking, as well as a lot of fun.

WHAT WILL THE STATE OF PUBLIC RELATIONS BE LIKE IN THE YEAR 2000?

Virtually every organization will have a public relations effort because the organization's survival will depend on it. The need for and appreciation of public relations will increase as the field continues its shift from primarily communications toward more emphasis on counseling and advising. The number of practitioners in top-level jobs will increase by the turn of the century, with more and more CEOs named from the ranks of practitioners.

CHAPTER SEVEN

Management

THE PROSPECT OF "LIFETIME EMPLOYMENT" IN THE twenty-first century will all but disappear. The decade of the 1990s has been characterized by unprecedented turbulence for the working class. Acquisitions, mergers, downsizings, layoffs, spinoffs, plant and company closings, and all the rest have had a great impact on the security of jobs and the loyalty of workers. The turmoil that has afflicted organizations from companies to hospitals, and from government agencies to schools, has badly damaged the so-called "social contract" between employer and employee. As a consequence, workers feel more expendable and more distrustful of management than at any time in recent memory.[1]

Among those who feel increasingly vulnerable in their positions are public relations people. In a phrase, public relations positions are no longer secure.

Like most other organizational pursuits in an era of rising costs, shrinking resources, and increased competition, public relations must compete for its survival. In the twenty-first century, top management will insist that public relations be run as a management process.

Like other management processes, professional public relations work emanates from clear strategies and bottom line objectives that flow into specific tactics, each with its own budget, timetable, and allocation of resources. Stated another way, public relations today is much more a planned, persuasive social/managerial science than a knee-jerk, damage-control reaction to sudden flare-ups.

On the organizational level, as public relations has enhanced its overall stature, it has been brought increasingly into the general management structure of institutions. Indeed, the public relations function works most effectively when it reports directly to top management.

On the individual level, public relations practitioners are increasingly expected to have mastered a wide variety of technical communications skills, such as writing, editing, placement of articles, production of printed materials, and video programming. At the same time, by virtue of their relatively recent integration into the general management process, public relations professionals are expected to be fluent in management theory and technique. In other words, public relations practitioners themselves must be, in every sense of the word, managers.

REPORTING TO TOP MANAGEMENT

The public relations function, by definition, must report to top management. Often, alas, this is not the case, and public relations is subordinated to advertising or marketing or legal or human resources. This is a shame because, as noted in chapter 1, public relations must be the interpreter of the organization—its philosophy, policy, and programs. These emanate from top management. Therefore, public relations must report to those who run the organization.

Increasingly, the public relations director reports directly to the CEO. The job of the public relations director consists of promoting the entire organization. If the public rela-

---

THE REST OF THE STORY

MANAGEMENT TRANSLATION: "HIT THE ROAD, JACK"

As companies try to put a positive "spin" on firing people, here is the new downsizing lexicon that has emerged.

Company	*Euphemism*
AT&T	Force management program
Bank of America	Release of resources
Bell Labs	Involuntary separation from payroll
Digital Equipment Corp.	Involuntary severance
General Motors	Career-transition program
Harris Bank-Chicago	Rightsizing the bank
National Semiconductor	Reshaping
Newsweek	Reduction in force (RIF)
Pacific Bell	Elimination of employment security policy
Procter & Gamble	Strengthening global effectiveness
Stouffer Foods Corp.	Schedule adjustments
Tandem Computer	Focused reduction
Wal-Mart	Normal payroll adjustment

tions chief were to report to the director of marketing or advertising, the job would become one of promoting specific products. There's a big difference. Thus, if public relations is made subordinate to any other discipline—marketing, advertising, legal, administration, whatever—then its independence, credibility, and, ultimately, value as an objective, honest broker to management will be jeopardized.

Whereas the marketing and advertising groups must, by definition, be defenders of their specific products, the public relations department has no such mandated allegiance. Public relations, rightfully, should be the corporate conscience. An organization's public relations professionals should enjoy enough autonomy to deal openly and honestly with management. If an idea doesn't make sense, if a product is flawed, if the general institutional wisdom is wrong, it is the duty of the public relations professional to challenge the consensus.

This is not to say that advertising, marketing, and all other disciplines shouldn't enjoy a close partnership with public relations. Clearly, they must. All disciplines must work to maintain their own independence while building long-term, mutually beneficial relationships for the good of the organization. However, public relations should never shirk its overriding responsibility to enhance the organization's credibility by ensuring that corporate actions are in the public interest.

MANAGEMENT THEORY OF PUBLIC RELATIONS

In recent years, public relations has developed its own theoretical framework as a management system. The work of communications professors James Grunig and Todd Hunt, while not the only relevant management theory, nonetheless has done much to advance this development.[2] Grunig and Hunt suggest that public relations managers perform what organizational theorists call a boundary role; they function at the edge of an organization as a liaison between the organization and its external and internal publics. In other words, public relations managers have one foot inside the organization and one outside. Often, this unique position is not only lonely but also precarious.

As boundary managers, public relations people support their colleagues by helping them communicate across organizational lines both within and outside the organization. In this way, public relations professionals also become systems managers, knowledgeable about and able to deal with the complex relationships inherent in the organization.

- They must consider the relationship of the organization to its environment—the ties that unite business managers and operations support staff, for example, and the conflicts that separate them.
- They must work within organizational confines to develop innovative solutions to organizational problems. By definition, public relations managers deal in a different environment from that of their organizational colleagues. Public relations people deal with perceptions, attitudes, and public opinion. Other business managers deal in a more empirical, quantitative, concrete domain. Public relations managers, therefore, must be innovative, not only in proposing communications solutions, but also in making them understandable and acceptable to colleagues.
- They must think strategically. Public relations managers must demonstrate their knowledge of the organization's mission, objectives, and strategies. Their solutions must answer the real needs of the organization. They must reflect the big picture. Business managers will care little that the company's name was mentioned in the morning paper unless they can recognize the strategic rationale for the reference.

- Public relations managers also must be willing to measure their results. They must state clearly what they want to accomplish, systematically set out to accomplish it, and measure their success. This means using such accepted business school techniques as management by objectives (MBO), management by objectives and results (MOR), and program evaluation and research technique (PERT).
- Finally, as Grunig and Hunt point out, in managing an organization's public relations system, practitioners must demonstrate comfort with the various elements of the organization itself: (1) functions, the real jobs of organizational components; (2) structure, the organizational hierarchy of individuals and positions; (3) processes, the formal decision-making rules and procedures the organization follows; and (4) feedback, the formal and informal evaluative mechanisms of the organization.[3]

Such a theoretical overview is important to consider in properly situating the practice of public relations as a management system within an organization.

PLANNING FOR PUBLIC RELATIONS

Like research, planning for public relations is essential not only to know where a particular campaign is headed but also to win the support of top management. Indeed, one of the most frequent complaints about public relations is that it is too much a seat-of-the-pants activity, impossible to plan and difficult to measure. Clearly, planning in public relations must be given greater shrift. With proper planning, public relations professionals can indeed defend and account for their actions.

Before organizing for public relations work, practitioners must consider objectives and strategies, planning and budgets, and research and evaluation. The broad environment in which the organization operates must dictate overall business objectives. These, in turn, dictate specific public relations objectives and strategies. And once these have been defined, the task of organizing for a public relations program should flow naturally.

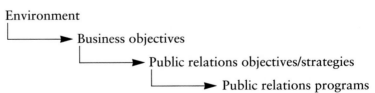

Setting objectives, formulating strategies, and planning are essential if the public relations function is to be considered equal in stature to other organizational components. Planning requires thinking. Planning a short-term public relations program to promote a new service may require less thought and time than planning a longer-term campaign to win support for a public policy issue. However, in each case, the public relations plan must include clear-cut objectives to achieve organizational goals, strategies to reach those objectives, tactics to implement the strategies, and measurement to determine whether the tactics worked.

Among the most important aspects of public relations practice is setting clear goals, objectives, and targets for the tactics applied. Public relations activities are meaningless unless designed to accomplish certain measurable goals.

For example, consider the following elementary public relations plan:

I. *Environment*

We need to increase product sales in the local market. Currently we are number three in the market, running close behind the second-place supplier but far behind the market leader.

II. *Business objectives*

Our goal is to build market share for our product in the local area. We seek to surpass the number two provider and edge closer to number one.

III. *Public relations objectives*

- Confirm our company's solid commitment to local customers.
- Convince potential customers that our company offers the staff, expertise, products, and responsiveness that match their needs.
- Position our company as formidable competition to the two market leaders.

IV. *Public relations strategies*

Position our company as the expert in the market through company-sponsored surveys and research directed at local decision makers; media placement of company-related articles; speaking platforms of company executives; and company-sponsored seminars to demonstrate our expertise.

V. *Public relations programs/tactics*

- Seek media placements and bylined articles discussing company products for local media.
- Solicit profile features and interviews with company officials on an exclusive basis with leading trade publications.
- Sponsor a quarterly survey of local companies. Mail the survey to local decision makers, focus on a current topic of concern, and offer information and comment from the customer's view.
- Sponsor four seminars a year for emerging product-using companies in the local area. Tailor each seminar to particular audiences—women, minorities, small businesses, specific industries, not-for-profit groups, etc. Seminars should feature company experts and well-known outside speakers. Thus, they should reinforce our commitment to the local market and also stimulate publicity.
- Launch a company speakers bureau wherein company speakers address important groups throughout the area.

After the adoption of such public relations programs, the success or failure of the campaign must be evaluated. In devising the public relations plan along these lines, an organization is assured that their public relations programs will reinforce and complement their overall business goals.

MANAGING BY PUBLIC RELATIONS OBJECTIVES

An organization's goals must define what its public relations goals will be, and the only good goals are ones that can be measured. Public relations objectives and the strategies that flow from them, like those in other business areas, must be results-oriented. As the baseball pitcher Johnny Sain used to say, "Nobody wants to hear about the labor pains, but everyone wants to see the baby."

So, too, must public relations people think strategically. Strategies are the most crucial decisions of a public relations campaign. They answer the general question "How will we manage our resources to achieve our goals?" The specific answers then become the public relations tactics used to implement the strategies. Ideally, strategies and tactics should profit from pretesting.

As for objectives, good ones stand up to the following questions:

- Do they clearly describe the end result expected?
- Are they understandable to everyone in the organization?
- Do they list a firm completion date?
- Are they realistic, attainable, and measurable?
- Are they consistent with management's objectives?[4]

Increasingly, public relations professionals are managing by objectives, adopting MBO and MOR techniques to help quantify the value of public relations in an organization. The two questions most frequently asked by general managers of public relations practitioners are "How can we measure public relations results?" and "How do we know whether the public relations program is making progress?" MBO can provide public relations professionals with a powerful source of feedback. MBO and MOR tie public relations results to management's predetermined objectives. Even though procedures for implementing MBO programs differ, most programs share four points:

1. Specification of the organization's goals, with objective measures of the organization's performance.
2. Conferences between the superior and the subordinate to agree on achievable goals.
3. Agreement between the superior and the subordinate on objectives consistent with the organization's goals.
4. Periodic reviews by the superior and the subordinate to assess progress toward achieving the goals.

Again, the key is to tie public relations goals to the goals of the organization and then to manage progress toward achieving those goals. The goals themselves should be clearly defined and specific, practical and attainable, and measurable.

The key to using MBO effectively in public relations work can be broken down into seven critical steps:

1. Defining the nature and mission of the work
2. Determining key result areas in terms of time, effort, and personnel
3. Identifying measurable factors on which objectives can be set
4. Setting objectives/determining results to be achieved
5. Preparing tactical plans to achieve specific objectives, including:
   - Programming to establish a sequence of actions to follow
   - Scheduling to set time requirements for each step
   - Budgeting to assign the resources required to reach the goals
   - Fixing individual accountability for the accomplishment of the objectives
   - Reviewing and reconciling through a testing procedure to track progress
6. Establishing rules and regulations to follow
7. Establishing procedures to handle the work.[5]

BRITISH AIR'S IMAGE SHAKEUP

Early in 1992, British Airways announced several management changes, including the resignation of its popular chairman and its chief public relations officer. The latter reportedly had taken part in unethical practices to undermine the airline's primary competitor.

The trouble began when the flamboyant founder of Virgin Atlantic Airlines, Richard Branson, accused British Air of conducting a smear campaign against them and of using unethical and perhaps illegal measures to win away Virgin's customers and to monitor the airline's activities. British Air's director of public affairs was named in numerous reports in the British press as a key participant in the campaign to win passengers away from Virgin.

In a campaign reminiscent of the American Express Company's attempts to defame the reputation of former partner Edmond Safra, British Air allegedly orchestrated scurrilous stories about Branson's character and activities.

Ultimately, Branson sued.

To settle the matter, in 1993 British Airways paid Virgin and Branson $945,000 in damages and assumed $3,000,000 in legal expenses.

Shortly thereafter, British Air's Chairman Lord King, who had presided over the company for nearly 12 years and led it through its privatization by the government, was replaced by Sir Colin Marshall as the airline's CEO.

Lord King was replaced despite his protests that "lower-level employees," acting without the knowledge and approval of the board and top management, were responsible for the dirty tricks.

Shortly after seizing the reins at British Air, Sir Colin adopted an aggressive, forthright, and personalized campaign to win public approval of British Air's proposed investment in US Air.

One presumes that the new management of British Air was hopeful that the new, more candid communications approach would help wash away the ethical stain that developed during the prior management's regime. Is such a strategy sensible?

BUDGETING FOR PUBLIC RELATIONS

Forecasting expected activities has always been one of the most uncertain tasks in public relations. Many argue that "measurement" in a practice like public relations is, by definition, an imperfect art. As a consequence, many public relations operations almost routinely overrun planned budget targets.[6]

Nonetheless, like any other business activity, public relations programs must be based on sound budgeting. After identifying objectives and strategies, the public relations professional must detail the particular tactics that will help achieve those objectives. No organization can spend indiscriminately. And without a realistic budget, no organization can succeed. Likewise, public relations activities must be disciplined by budgetary realities.

The key to budgeting may lie in performing two steps: (1) estimating the extent of the resources—both personnel and purchases—needed to accomplish each activity and (2) estimating the cost and availability of those resources.[7] With this information in hand, the development of a budget and monthly cash flow for a public relations program becomes easier. Such data also provide the milestones necessary to audit program costs on a routine basis and to make adjustments well in advance of budget crises.

Most public relations programs operate on limited budgets. Therefore, whenever possible, adaptable programs—which can be readily recycled and redesigned to meet changing needs—should be considered. For example, television, magazine, and newspaper advertising generally are too expensive for most public relations budgets. On the other hand, special events, personalized literature, direct mail, personal contacts, and promotional displays are the kinds of inexpensive communications vehicles that can be easily duplicated.[8]

One way to ensure that budgets are adhered to is to practice the process of open bidding for public relations materials and suppliers. An open bidding process allows several vendors to demonstrate how they would fulfill the specifications enumerated for the job. These specifications should take into account programmatic considerations in terms of both quality and quantity. Public relations budgets should be reasonable—ordinarily, a fraction (10 percent or so)—of advertising budgets and flexible enough to withstand mid-course corrections and unexpected cost overruns.

Most public relations agencies treat client costs in a manner similar to that used by legal, accounting, and management consulting firms: The client pays only for services rendered, often against an established monthly minimum for staff time. Time records are kept by every employee—from chairperson to mail clerk—on a daily basis to be sure that agency clients know exactly what they are paying for. Hourly charges for public relations agency employees can range from low double figures per hour to upwards of $350 to $400 an hour for agency superstars.

PREPARING THE PUBLIC RELATIONS CAMPAIGN PLAN

The public relations campaign puts all of the aspects of public relations planning—objectives, strategies, research, tactics, and evaluation—into one cohesive framework. The plan specifies a series of "whats" to be done and "hows" to get them done—whatever is necessary to reach the objectives.

Again, the public relations plan must track the strategies and objectives of the organization. Accordingly, the "blueprint" for the public relations campaign should be the R-A-C-E or R-O-S-I-E approaches to public relations, defined in chapter 1. Time should be taken in advance to determine what public relations approaches and activities are most likely to reach organizational goals. Every aspect of the public relations plan should be designed to be meaningful and valuable to the organization.

The skeleton of a typical public relations campaign plan resembles the following:

1. **Backgrounding the problem** —This is the so-called situation analysis, background, or case statement that specifies the major aims of the campaign. It can be a general statement that refers to audiences, known research, the organization's positions, history, and the obstacles faced in reaching the desired goal. A public relations planner should divide the overriding goal into several subordinate objectives, which are the "whats" to be accomplished.

2. **Preparing a proposal** —The second stage of the campaign plan sketches broad approaches to solve the problem at hand. It outlines the strategies— the "hows"—and the public relations tools to be used to fulfill the objectives. The elements of the public relations proposal may vary, depending on subject matter, but generally include the following:
   - *Situational analysis*—description of the challenge as it currently exists, including background on how the situation reached its present state.
   - *Scope of assignment*—description of the nature of the assignment: what the public relations program will attempt to do.
   - *Target audiences*—specific targets identified and divided into manageable groups.
   - *Research methods*—specific research approach to be used.
   - *Key messages*—specific selected appeals: What do we want to tell our audiences? How do we want them to feel about us? What do we want them to do?
   - *Communications vehicles*—tactical communications devices to be used.
   - *Project team*—key players who will participate in the program.
   - *Timing and fees*—a timetable with proposed costs identified.

The specific elements of any proposal depend on the unique nature of the program itself. When an outside supplier submits a proposal, additional elements—such as cancellation clauses, confidentiality of work, and references—should also be included.

3. **Activating the plan**—The third stage of a campaign plan details operating tactics. It may also contain a time chart specifying when each action will take place. Specific activities are defined, people are assigned to them, and deadlines are established. This stage forms the guts of the campaign plan.

4. **Evaluating the campaign**—To find out whether the plan worked, evaluation methods should be spelled out here.
   - Did we implement the activities we proposed?
   - Did we receive appropriate public recognition for our efforts?
   - Did attitudes change—among the community, customers, management— as a result of our programs?

   Pre- and post-testing of audience attitudes, quantitative analysis of event attendance, content analysis of media success, surveys, sales figures, staff reports, letters to management, and feedback from others—the specific method of evaluative testing is up to the practitioner. But the inclusion of a mechanism for evaluation is imperative.[9]

A public relations campaign plan should always be spelled out—in writing—so that planners can keep track of progress and management can assess results. And although planning in public relations is important and should be taken more seriously than it presently is by public relations professionals, the caveat of management gurus Thomas Peters and Robert Waterman must always be considered: "The problem is that the planning becomes an end in itself."[10] In public relations this cannot be allowed. No matter how important planning may be, public relations is assessed principally in terms of its action, performance, and practice.

IMPLEMENTING PUBLIC RELATIONS PROGRAMS

The duties and responsibilities of public relations practitioners are as diverse as the publics with whom different institutions deal. Basically, public relations tasks can be divided into four broad categories:

1. *Advice* —provided to management on organizational decisions and policies, to ensure that they are consistent with the public interest.
2. *Communications service* —including the outward communication of information to various external publics and the inward communication of corporate philosophy, policies, and programs to the employees.
3. *Public issues research and analysis* —identifying, evaluating, and communicating to management, the external information that may be most relevant to organizational policies and programs.
4. *Public relations action programs* —designed to generate goodwill through comprehensive programs focused on a particular issue or audience.[11]

Specific public relations tasks are as varied as the organizations served. Here is a partial list of public relations duties:

- Reaching the employees through a variety of internal means, including newsletters, television, and meetings. Traditionally, this role has emphasized news-oriented communications rather than benefits-oriented ones, which are usually the province of personnel departments.
- Coordinating relationships with the print and electronic media, which includes arranging and monitoring press interviews, writing news releases and related press materials, organizing press conferences, and answering media inquiries and requests. A good deal of media relations work consists of attempting to gain favorable news coverage for the firm.
- Coordinating activities with legislators on local, state, and federal levels. This includes legislative research activities and public policy formation.
- Orchestrating interaction with the community, perhaps including open houses, tours, and employee volunteer efforts designed to reflect the supportive nature of the organization to the community.
- Managing relations with the investment community, including the firm's present and potential stockholders. This task emphasizes personal contact with securities analysts, institutional investors, and private investors.
- Supporting activities with customers and potential customers, with activities ranging from hard-sell product promotion activities to "soft" consumer advisory services.
- Coordinating the institution's printed voice with its public through reprints of speeches, annual reports, quarterly statements, and product and company brochures.

- Coordinating relationships with outside specialty groups, such as suppliers, educators, students, nonprofit organizations, and competitors.
- Managing the institutional—or nonproduct—advertising image as well as being called on increasingly to assist in the management of more traditional product advertising.
- Coordinating the graphic and photographic services of the organization. To do this task well requires knowledge of typography, layout, and art.
- Conducting opinion research, which involves assisting in the public policy formation process through the coordination and interpretation of attitudinal studies of ke publics.
- Managing the gift-giving apparatus, which ordinarily consists of screening and evaluating philanthropic proposals and allocating the organization's available resources.
- Coordinating special events, including travel for company management, corporate celebrations and exhibits, dinners, groundbreakings, and grand openings.
- Management counseling, which involves advising administrators on alternative options and recommended choices in light of public responsibilities.

ORGANIZING THE PUBLIC RELATIONS DEPARTMENT

Once an organization has analyzed its environment, established its objectives, set up measurement standards, and thought about appropriate programs and budgets, it is ready to organize a public relations department. Departments range from one person operations—even in billion dollar enterprises, such as far-flung Reliance Insurance Company of New York—to other huge companies, such as General Motors, with a staff of hundreds around the world, responsible for relations with the press, investors, civic groups, employees, and governments around the world.

Today, many corporate public relations departments typically have suffered the ravages of downsizing and decentralization. The former has led to the shrinkage of once large operations. The latter has led to the formation of decentralized, line-oriented departments to complement smaller central units. The two together have led many corporate public relations people to fear for the security of positions they once took for granted.[12] What's the best way to organize for public relations in an organization? There is no one answer. However, again, the strongest public relations department is one led by a communications executive who reports directly to the CEO. This is eminently preferable to reporting to a legal or financial or administrative executive, who may tend to "filter" top management messages.[13]

In government, public relations professionals typically report directly to department heads. In universities, the public relations function is frequently coupled with fund-raising and development activities. In hospitals, public relations is typically tied to the marketing function.

As for the names of the departments in which public relations is housed, organizations use a wide variety of names for the function. Ironically, the trend today seems to be away from use of the traditional term public relations and toward corporate communications. In one comprehensive analysis, about 30 percent of the organizations surveyed still use public relations, whereas corporate communications or just plain communications is used by nearly 20 percent. About 8 percent use public affairs, and another 8 percent use advertising/public relations. Among the other titles in use are corporate relations and public information.

THE REST OF THE STORY

PR SALARIES GOING UP, UP, UP!

Public relations may once have been a corporate backwater, but at least in terms of executive salaries, it is a stepchild no longer.

Today an increasing number of public relations executives around the country earn upwards of $200,000 in salary and bonus. Some agency heads and corporate directors earn much more than that.

In 1997, the individual presumed to be the "highest paid corporate public relations person" resigned his post. Tod R. Hullin stepped down as senior vice president of communications and public affairs at Time Warner, Inc. after six years at the company. In 1996, Hullin's salary, according to the Time Warner proxy statement, was $525,000 and his bonus, $550,000. In other words, the Time Warner public relations chief earned in excess of $1 million per year, not including his $35,000 options to buy Time Warner stock. Not too shabby.

Public relations agency salaries, too, have been ascending. As agencies have grown with the downsizing of corporations and the subcontracting of public relations work, they have been willing to pay higher wages to their employees.

However, the rule of thumb in agency work is to produce three times your compensation in client billings. So if an agency professional earning $50,000 a year doesn't bill clients for $150,000 a year—the next step could be the door.

Such is the downside of making more money in public relations.

ORGANIZING THE PUBLIC RELATIONS AGENCY

The biggest difference between an external agency and an internal department is perspective. The former is outside looking in; the latter is inside looking out (often literally for itself). Sometimes the use of an agency is necessary to escape the tunnel-vision syndrome that afflicts some firms, in which a detached viewpoint is desperately needed. An agency unfettered by internal corporate politics might be better trusted to present management with an objective reading of the concerns of its publics.

An agency has the added advantage of not being taken for granted by a firm's management. Unfortunately, management sometimes has a greater regard for an outside specialist than for an inside one. This attitude frequently defies logic but is nonetheless often true. Generally, if management is paying (sometimes quite handsomely) for outside counsel, it tends to listen carefully to the advice.

Agencies generally organize according to industry and account teams. Larger agencies are divided into such areas as health care, sports, fashion, technology, finance, and so on. Account teams are assigned specific clients. Team members bill clients on an hourly basis, with most firms, as noted, intending to retain two-thirds of each individual's hourly billing rate as income. In other words, if an account executive bills at a rate of $300 per hour—and many senior counselors do—the firm expects to retain $200 of that rate toward its profit. In recent years, as clients have begun to manage resources more rigorously, agencies have gotten much more "systematic" in measuring success and in keeping customers from "migrating" to a competitor. Indeed, if not actively and directly addressed on an ongoing basis, customer satisfaction will, inevitably decline.[15]

Public relations agencies today, as noted, are huge businesses. The top six agencies earn net fees in excess of $100 million per year, and the largest firm, Burson-Marsteller, earns more than $200 million in net fees per year. The stakes and costs of the public relations agency business have become so high that seven of the top ten public relations agencies are subsidiaries of advertising agencies (Table 7–1).

Public relations counsel is, by definition, a highly personalized service. A counselor's prescription for a client depends primarily on what the counselor thinks a client needs and how that assessment fits the client's own perception of those needs. Often an outsider's fresh point of view is helpful in focusing a client on particular problems and opportunities and on how best to conquer or capitalize on them.

On the other hand, because outside agencies are just that—outside—they are often unfamiliar about details affecting the situation of particular companies and with the idiosyncrasies of company management. The good external counselor must constantly work to overcome this barrier. The best client–agency relationships are those with free-flowing communications between internal and external public relations groups so that both resources are kept informed about corporate policies, strategies, and tactics. A well-oiled, complementary department–agency relationship can result in a more positive communications approach for an organization.

WHAT'S IT PAY?

Without question the communications function has increased in importance and clout. Top communications professionals in many large corporations today draw compensation packages well into six figures. Entry-level jobs for writers and editors generally fall into the $20,000+ range. Managers of public relations units, press relations, consumer relations, financial communications, and the like may earn anywhere from $40,000 to $100,000. Public relations directors may range in salary from $30,000 to upward of $300,000.

The median public relations salary, according to a landmark study by the Public Relations Society of America, is slightly more than $49,000 a year (Table 7–2).[16] Men and women, however, seem to be paid differently, with men's salaries found to be 45 percent higher, on average, than women's.

Among other findings, the study determined:

- Public relations salaries are markedly higher in the Northeast and the West than in the Midwest or South.

TABLE 7–1

1996 PR FEE INCOME OF 50 FIRMS SUPPLYING DOCUMENTATION TO O'DWYER'S DIRECTORY OF PUBLIC RELATIONS FIRMS

(A) means ad agency related	1996 Net Fees	Employees	% Fee Change from 1995
1. Burson-Marsteller (A)	$233,344,022	1,863	+10.1
2. Shandwick	190,300,000	1,969	+6.9
3. Hill and Knowlton (A)	160,800,000	1,320	+13.9
4. Porter Novelli International (A)	121,178,280	1,175	+25.0
5. Edelman Public Relations Worldwide	111,680,350	1,151	+24.8
6. Fleishman-Hillard	107,494,000	786	+20.0
7. Ketchum Public Relations (A)	74,836,000	614	+16.3
8. GCI Group including GTFH PR (A)	52,293,330	445	+17.4
9. Ogilvy Adams & Rinehart (A)	48,544,000	410	+17.7
10. Manning, Selvage & Lee (A)	47,925,000	370	+25.7
11. Bozell Sawyer Miller Group (A)	43,900,000	276	+8.0
12. Ruder Finn	41,870,165	366	+26.6
13. Cohn & Wolfe (A)	25,034,552	198	+35.9
14. Financial Relations Board	20,224,882	209	+23.7
15. Morgen-Walke Assocs.	16,504,604	126	+30.9
16. Cunningham Communication	15,661,623	109	+38.8
17. The Weber Group (A)	14,595,156	156	+18.6
18. Powell Tate	14,324,343	70	+15.0
19. The Kamber Group	11,250,000	95	+28.1
20. Technology Solutions	10,795,000	121	+44.5
21. MWW/Strategic Communications	10,479,000	92	+24.0
22. Pacific/West Communications Group	9,734,000	55	+22.1
23. Gibbs & Soell	9,605,000	97	+5.4
24. Stoorza, Ziegaus & Metzger	8,884,417	71	-4.6
25. Dewe Rogerson	8,725,427	69	+21.0
26. Dan Klores Assocs.	7,428,839	46	+48.0
27. Interscience (A)	7,341,458	40	+29.0
28. SCIENS Worldwide PR (formerly NCI PR) (A)	7,066,779	50	+52.0
29. EvansGroup PR Division (A)	7,013,993	64	+17.0
30. Dix & Eaton	6,787,312	51	+24.7
31. Makovsky & Co.	6,504,000	58	+24.6
32. Noonan/Russo Communications	6,400,000	34	+25.0
33. Padilla Speer Beardsley	5,920,220	59	+24.2
34. Earle Palmer Brown Cos. (A)	5,824,196	50	-16.9
35. KCSA Public Relations	5,720,350	39	+18.8
36. Nelson Communications Group	5,624,940	45	- 0.04
37. Wilson McHenry Co.	5,394,026	40	+31.8
38. Cramer-Krasselt Public Relations (A)	5,130,000	47	+21.0
39. Blanc & Otus	5,079,647	44	+4.7
40. Karakas, VanSickle, Ouellette (A)	4,933,132	45	+45.0
41. Morgan & Myers	4,849,673	56	+33.6
42. The Tierney Group	4,836,786	33	+15.2
43. Bender, Goldman & Helper	4,743,368	52	+6.2
44. Dennis Davidson Assocs.	4,605,175	61	+19.0
45. Dye, Van Mol & Lawrence	4,571,156	69	+11.3
46. Ryan-McGinn	4,549,521	23	+66.3
47. Public Communications	4,386,601	46	+15.4
48. Edward Howard & Co.	4,255,626	40	+6.1
49. MCC	4,235,324	41	+75.0
50. William Silverman and Co.	4,223,378	31	+21.7

TABLE 7–2 Overall Public Relations Salaries

SALARIES OVERALL: PRSA MEMBERS & NON-MEMBERS

	Total Respondents %	Total %	PRSA Members APR %	Non-APR %	Non-Members %
Total Respondents	100	100	100	100	100
Less than $45,000	42	40	23	46	43
Less than $15,000	3	1	2	*	4
$15,000 - $24,999	8	4	2	5	10
$25,000 - $34,999	14	17	6	21	13
$35,000 - $44,999	17	18	13	19	17
$45,000 - $74,999	33	34	42	31	3
$45,000 - $54,999	15	16	20	15	14
$55,000 - $64,999	11	11	14	11	11
$65,000 - $74,999	8	7	9	6	
$75,000 or more	21	22	31	19	20
$75,000 - $99,999	11	11	16	10	10
$100,000 - $149,999	8	7	10	7	8
$150,000 or more	3	3	4	3	3
No answer	4	5	5	4	4
Median	**$49,070**	**$49,830**	**$58,840**	**$46,370**	**$48,660**

* Less than .5%

- Investor relations is the highest paying public relations specialty, with a median salary of more than $72,000.
- The lowest paying public relations jobs are found in government, health care and non-profit organizations, with the median salaries approximately $43,000 for each (Table 7–3).
- There is little difference between median salaries in public relations agencies and corporations.
- Members of the Public Relations Society of America have higher salaries than non-members.
- The larger the number of public relations professionals employed at a specific business location, the higher the median salary.
- Entry level salaries are basically the same from industry-to-industry, generally in the low $20,000 range (Table 7–4). Since "getting in the door" is often the toughest part of employment in the public relations profession, a lower entry level salary may be sufficient relative to the potential earnings power later on.

TABLE 7–3 Public relations salaries by organization

SALARIES BY ORGANIZATION TYPE			
	P.R. Firms	**Corporations**	**Government Health Care/ Non-Profit**
	%	%	%
Total Respondents	100	100	100
Less than $45,000	39	39	53
Less than $15,000	2	3	1
$15,000 - $24,999	9	9	5
$25,000 - $34,999	12	13	22
$35,000 - $44,999	16	15	25
$45,000 - $74,999	24	36	32
$45,000 - $54,999	11	15	16
$55,000 - $64,999	6	12	9
$65,000 - $74,999	6	8	7
$75,000 or more	29	21	12
$75,000 - $99,999	11	11	8
$100,000 - $149,999	11	8	5
$150,000 or more	7	2	*
No answer	8	4	2
Median	**$51,340**	**$50,770**	**$43,260**

* Less than .5%

TABLE 7–4 Entry-level public relations salaries

SALARIES BY TYPE OF ORGANIZATION			
	PR Firm	**Corporation**	**Government/ Health Care/Non-Profit**
	%	%	%
Total Respondents	100	100	100
Less than $15,000	7	6	3
$15,000 - $19,999	27	19	19
$20,000 - $24,999	37	29	39
$25,000 - $29,999	7	20	19
$30,000 or more	6	17	14
No answer	16	9	5
Median	**$21,110**	**$23,550**	**$23,210**

WHAT MANNER OF MAN/WOMAN?

What kind of individual does it take to become a competent public relations professional?

In order to make it, a public relations professional ought to possess a set of specific technical skills as well as an appreciation of the proper attitudinal approach to the job. On the technical side, these seven skills are important:

1. **Knowledge of the field**—the underpinnings of public relations, culture and history, philosophy, and social psychology.
2. **Communications knowledge**—the media and the ways in which they work, communications research, and, most important, the writing process.
3. **Technological knowledge**—the computer, the Net, the World Wide Web, cyberspace, all are vitally important (see chapter 10).
4. **Knowledge of what's going on around you**—current events and factors that influence society: literature, language, politics, economics, and all the rest—from Herzegovina to Hebron, from a unified Germany to a divided Zaire; from Dr. Kevorkian to Dr. Dre; from Michael Jordan to Michael Bolton to Skankin Pickle. A public relations professional must be, in the truest sense, a Renaissance man or woman.
5. **Business knowledge**—how business works, a bottom-line orientation, and a knowledge of one's company and industry.
6. **Knowledge of bureaucracy**—how to get things done in a bureaucratic organization, how to use and gain power for the best advantage, and how to maneuver in a politically charged environment.
7. **Management knowledge**—how public policy is shaped and what pressures and responsibilities fall on senior managers.

In terms of attitude, public relations professionals ought to possess the following four characteristics:

1. **Communications orientation**—a bias toward disclosing rather than withholding information. Public relations professionals should want to communicate with the public. They should practice the belief that the public has a right to know.
2. **Advocacy**—a desire to be advocates for their employers. Public relations people must stand up for what their employers represent. Although they should never distort, lie, or hide facts, occasionally it may be in an organization's best interest to avoid comment on certain issues. If practitioners don't believe in the integrity and credibility of their employers, their most honorable course is to quit.
3. **Counseling orientation**—a compelling desire to advise senior managers. As noted, top executives are used to dealing in tangibles, such as balance sheets, costs per thousand, and cash flows. Public relations practitioners understand the intangibles, such as public opinion, media influence, and communications messages. Practitioners must be willing to support their beliefs—often in opposition to lawyers or personnel executives. They must even be willing to disagree with management at times. Far from being compliant, public relations practitioners must have the gumption to say "no."
4. **Personal confidence**—a strong sense of honesty and ethics, a willingness to take risks, and, not unimportant, a sense of humor. Public relations professionals must have the courage of their convictions and the personal confidence to represent proudly a curious—yet critical—role in any organization.

In recent years many more women have joined the public relations ranks. Women now account for just under half of all practitioners but, according to the research, still earn substantially less than men.

The issue of increased feminization, as noted, is a particularly thorny one for the practice of public relations. University public relations sequences across the country report a preponderance of female students, outnumbering males by as much as 80 percent. In public relations practice, too, women now outnumber men. However, the ranks of women executives in public relations, as opposed to their male counterparts, are still woefully thin. Hence the picture of, on the one hand, public relations becoming a "velvet ghetto" of women workers and, on the other hand, a profession in which women have not achieved upper-management status. This is a paramount concern to the profession.*

In addition to gender gap problems, there is the issue of minority public relations professionals. According to the Bureau of Labor Statistics, only 7 percent of public relations professionals are minorities—one-third less than the national average for minorities in professional fields. To help more minorities enter the field, the Public Relations Society of America has launched a program of scholarships and internships at public relations agencies for minority professionals. And in 1997, the society named educator Debbie Miller (see chapter 20), as its first African American president.

SUMMARY

In recent years, the practice of public relations has become accepted not only as part of the marketing mix, but as part of the management process of any well-run organization.

Public relations objectives and goals, strategies, and tactics must flow directly from the organization's overall goals. Public relations strategies must reflect organizational strategies, and tactics must be designed to realize the organization's business objectives.

So, despite its stereotypes and demographic idiosyncrasies, public relations requires neither a false smile nor a glad hand. Rather, it demands a solid grounding in all aspects of professional communications, human relations, and judgmental and learning skills. Most of all, it takes hard work.

DISCUSSION STARTERS

1. Describe the elements of a public relations plan.
2. How does MBO relate to public relations?
3. How are public relations objectives derived?
4. What elements go into framing a public relations budget?
5. What are the four general steps in preparing a public relations campaign plan?
6. What activities constitute the four broad categories of public relations practice?

*The public relations salary "gender gap" is an area of hot debate in the field, with at least one researcher claiming that the Public Relations Society of America figures that show men making more than women fail to take into account that "men are usually older and more experienced." (James G. Hutton, "Exploding the Myth of the Public Relations Gender Gap," *The Public Relations Strategist*, Fall 1996, 49.

7. What is the ideal reporting relationship for a director of public relations?
8. What are the technical skills that a public relations professional should possess?
9. What kinds of attitudinal characteristics should a public relations professional possess?
10. What is meant by the term velvet ghetto?

NOTES

1. "The Dream in Danger," *The Public Relations Strategist*, Spring 1995, 44.
2. James E. Grunig and Todd Hunt, *Managing Public Relations* (New York: Holt, Rinehart and Winston, 1984), 89–97.
3. Ibid.
4. Richard H. Truitt, "Wanted: Hard-Headed Objectives," *Public Relations Journal* (August 1969): 12, 13.
5. George L. Morrisey, *Management by Objectives and Results for Business and Industry*, 2d ed. (Reading, MA: Addison-Wesley, 1977), 9.
6. H. Lawrence Smith, "Accountability in PR: Budgets and Benchmarks," *Public Relations Quarterly* (Spring 1996): 15.
7. Jack Tucker, "Budgeting and Cost Control: Are You a Businessman or a Riverboat Gambler?" *Public Relations Journal* (March 1981): 15.
8. Donald T. Mogavero, "When the Funds Come Tumbling Down," *Public Relations Journal* (October 1981): 13.
9. Anthony Fulginiti, "How to Prepare a Public Relations Plan," *Communication Briefings* (May 1985): 8a, b.
10. Thomas J. Peters and Robert H. Waterman, Jr., *In Search of Excellence* (New York: Harper & Row, 1982), 40.
11. Charles H. Prout, "Organization and Function of the Corporate Public Relations Department," in *Lesly's Handbook of Public Relations and Communications* (Chicago, IL: Probus Publishing Company, 1991), 228–729.
12. "PR Opinion Items," *Jack O'Dwyers Newsletter*, March 19, 1997, 8.
13. Prout, op. cit., 6.
14. Kenneth D. Makovsky, "Seven Strategies to Ensure Quality Control," *Public Relations Strategist* (Summer 1996): 19.
15. Salary Survey of Public Relations Professionals, New York: The Public Relations Society of America, 1996.

SUGGESTED READINGS

Berquist, William. *Building Strategic Relationships*. San Francisco: Jossey-Bass, 1995.
Brody, E. W. *Professional Practice Development*. New York: Praeger, 1989.
Brody, E. W. *Public Relations Programming and Production*. New York: Praeger, 1988.
Careers in Public Relations. New York: *Public Relations Society of America*.
Case, John. *Open-Book Management*. New York: Harper Business, 1995. Innovative approach to business and financial management, where everybody is privy to everything.
Center, Allen H. and Jackson, Patrick. *Public Relations Practices, Managerial Case Studies & Problems,* 5th ed. Upper Saddle River, NJ: Prentice Hall, 1995.

JACK TROUT AND STEVE RIVKIN

THE NEW POSITIONING

NEW YORK: McGRAW-HILL, 1996

One key to effective management is "positioning" the organization or operation so that it is "differentiated" from others. Most managers fall short, when it comes to separating their institutions from what the authors call "the muddled middle" of organizational mediocrity.

In this twenty-first century update to the strategy of "positioning," these two marketing veterans explain first how the mind works and doesn't work in forming attitudes and opinions and second, what must be done to deal with changing or reinforcing attitudes in people's minds.

For the first time in positioning literature, a chapter here is devoted to "The Positioning Power of PR," advising managers that public relations techniques can play an even more critical role than advertising in effectively positioning an organization.

Champy, John. *Reengineering Management: The Mandate for New Leadership.* New York: Harper Business, 1995. Best seller that focuses on the need for new leadership from the top down.

Galbraith, Jay R. *Designing Organizations.* San Francisco: Jossey-Bass, 1995.

Godin, Seth. *Wisdom Inc.* New York: Harper Business, 1995. Names 30 business virtues to turn ordinary people into extraordinary leaders.

Grunig, James E. *Excellence in Public Relations and Communications Management.* Hillsdale, NJ: Lawrence Erlbaum Associates, 1992.

Hammer, Michael. *Beyond Reengineering.* New York: Harper Business, 1995. Another best seller that explains what needs to be done after an organization reengineers itself.

Harris, Thomas L. *Choosing and Working with Your Public Relations Firm.* Lincolnwood, IL: NTC Business, 1992.

Hart, Norman. *Effective Corporate Relations: Applying Public Relations in Business and Industry.* New York: McGraw-Hill, 1988.

Hendrix, Jerry A. *Public Relations Cases,* 2nd ed. Belmont, CA: Wadsworth, 1992.

Hills, Curtis. *How to Save Your Clients from Themselves.* Phoenix, AZ: Olde & Oppenheim, 1988.

Jefkins, Frank. *P.R. Techniques.* Portsmouth, NH: William Heinemann, 1988.

Joyce, William F. *Megachange.* Burr Ridge, IL: Irwin Professional Publishing, 1995. Explores the new logic for radically transforming organizations.

Kotter, John P. *The New Roles.* New York: The Free Press, 1995. Rewrites rules for success in management.

Marsteller, William. *Creative Management.* Lincolnwood, IL: NTC Business, 1992.

Mitchell, Howard. *What Every Account Executive Should Know About Public Relations.* American Association of Advertising Agencies, 1989.

Nager, Norman R. and Allen T. Harrell. *Public Relations: Management by Objectives.* Lanham, MD: University Press of America, 1991.

Olins, Wally. *Corporate Identity*. Cambridge: Harvard Business School Press, 1990.

Ries, Al. *Focus*. New York: Harper Business, 1995. The future of American business depends on "focus," according to this marketing guru.

Ross, Joel E. *Total Quality Management: Text, Cases and Readings*. Delray Beach, FL: St. Lucie Press, 1992.

Rukeyser, Louis and John Cooney. *Louis Rukeyser's Business Almanac*. New York: Simon & Schuster, 1991.

Simon, Raymond. *Cases in Public Relations Management*. Lincolnwood, IL: NTC Publishing Group, 1994.

Slater, Robert. *The New GE: How Jack Welch Revived an American Institution*. Homewood, IL.: Business One Irwin, 1992.

Thomsett, Michael C. *The Little Black Book of Product Management*. New York: AMACOM, 1990.

Toffler, Alvin and Heidi Toffler. *Creating a New Civilization*. Atlanta, GA: Turner Publishing Inc., 1995. Creates a blueprint for managing change that transcends one single organization.

Tomasko, Robert M. *Downsizing: Reshaping the Corporation for the Future*. New York: AMACOM, 1990.

Weinstein, David A. *How to Protect Your Business, Professional and Brand Names*. New York: John Wiley & Sons, 1990.

CASE STUDY

DOW CORNING IN THE CRUCIBLE

The sprawling Dow Corning Corporation campus sits peacefully amidst the rolling fields of Midland, Michigan. Thousands of employees, most of them Dow Corning veterans, arrive early, work diligently, and devote themselves happily to a company they consider almost family.

But the pastoral tranquility of the campus and the friendly devotion of the workers belie a turbulent and uncertain reality.

Dow Corning and its management are involved in a public war of claims and counterclaims, accusations and denials, and public relations judgments that may mean billions of dollars in losses and ultimately, the viability of the company itself.

With $5 billion in assets, 50,000 customers, 9,600 products, 8,700 employees and operations on four continents—Dow Corning is in Chapter 11 bankruptcy, its future by no means clear.

The company is being sued for billions of dollars by attorneys representing thousands of women, who claim that silicone gel-filled breast implants, manufactured by Dow Corning and others, have caused, among other ailments, autoimmune disease. Stated simply, Dow Corning and the others are charged with manufacturing dangerous devices, foisted on unsuspecting women.

CBS Hatchet Job

Dow Corning's precarious situation, which started in the 1960s and has continued through four decades, is the ultimate public relations management crisis.

Breast implants first came on the market in the early 1960s, and the Food and Drug

Administration began approving the devices in 1976. Given the long track record of breast implants, the FDA presumed that they were reasonably safe. In 1988, however, the FDA announced that breast-implant manufacturers would henceforth have to submit evidence of safety.

Two years later, on December 10, 1990, Dow Corning was thrust into a spotlight from which it has still not recovered. On her CBS television show, *Face to Face with Connie Chung,* the moderator trotted out a parade of women, seemingly terrified and victimized, who claimed that their silicone breast implants had given them autoimmune disease. Although several supportive breast implant users as well as favorable doctors were interviewed for the Chung show, none made it on air. Connie Chung never called Dow Corning for comment or participation on the program (Figure 7–1).

After the national television broadcast, Dow Corning said nothing publicly but quickly put together a 30-second commercial, with women who could speak positively about their experience with breast implants. The company planned to air the spots around the country to follow the rebroadcast of the Chung show and bought time on CBS-owned and operated stations.

A few hours before the program was scheduled to be broadcast, however, the CBS stations notified Dow Corning that the spot would not run, because it would open them up to "equal time considerations" they couldn't honor.

The Roof Caves In

After the Chung rebroadcast, the roof caved in for Dow Corning.

Congress held public hearings. Ralph Nader's Public Citizen group pressed the issue in the media and the courts. A San Francisco jury awarded more than $7 million to a woman who claimed that her Dow Corning breast implants had caused her to have

Figure 7–1   Connie Chung "lowered the boom" on Dow Corning in 1990.

mixed connective tissue disease. And in April 1992, FDA Commissioner David Kessler banned the sale of silicone gel-filled breast implants, except for use in clinical trials of breast reconstruction after cancer surgery.

The ban, Dr. Kessler took pains to point out, was not because breast implants had been found dangerous—indeed Dow Corning insisted that the implants were safe. He banned the sale, Dr. Kessler explained, because the manufacturers had not "proved scientifically that the products were safe."

This fine distinction—that there was no evidence of danger—was lost on the million or so women who already had implants. Why would the FDA ban a product if it wasn't dangerous? Predictably, women panicked.

Large numbers came forward complaining of various illnesses caused by their breast implants. Media-seeking doctors and scientists popped up with evidenceless theories explaining how breast implants affected the immune system. The media, in response, jumped on the story with a vengeance. Plaintiff's attorneys, capitalizing on the budding crop of "expert witnesses" and media attention, successfully converted the trickle of breast implant lawsuits into a flood.

Low Key Response

Through the trauma, there was an eerie silence from the people in Midland, Michigan.

Dow Corning management insisted that their product was fundamentally safe.

But they wanted to reconfirm that fact with undisputed scientific evidence. Dow Corning committed to spend tens of millions of dollars—upwards of $30 million through 1997—to sponsor independent university research to do the necessary epidemiology studies that would answer the safety questions.

And while the company proceeded with the painstaking and prolonged task of scientific research, the media had a field day, in effect, issuing a constant drumbeat of "corporate guilt."

Dow Corning stuck to its guns with a reasoned, low key public relations response that built up gradually (Figure 7–2):

- In 1991, it released to the general public more than 10,000 pages of proprietary information on silicone breast implants.
- In 1992, it made available complete sets of its FDA breast implant application to medical schools.
- That same year, it distributed 90 documents—nearly 1,400 pages of internal company memos and scientific studies about the safety aspects of its breast implant product.
- Later, it began to hold news conferences to rebut false allegations, and its new chairman, Richard Hazleton, began to make himself available to the media, including one stormy session facing angry breast implant users on *The Oprah Winfrey Show*.

Too Little, Too Late

But Dow Corning's actions couldn't stem the onrushing tide.

In 1993, Dow Corning exited the breast implant business.

In 1994, breast implant manufacturers, desperate to limit their losses, agreed to the largest class-action settlement in history, with $4.25 billion to be set aside for all women with breast implants. The lawyers' take would be $1 billion. Not unsurprisingly, nearly half of all women with breast implants registered for the settlement, with half of them claiming to be suffering from implant-related illnesses.

With so many women opting out of the settlement and deciding to continue with their lawsuits and their attorneys' exorbitant demands, Dow Corning filed for Chapter 11 bankruptcy protection in May 1995. The settlement collapsed shortly thereafter.

Figure 7–2   Dow Corning CEO Richard Hazleton(r) and Public Relations Director T. Michael Jackson.

In December 1996, Dow Corning filed a proposed $3 billion bankruptcy reorganization plan, $2 billion of which could potentially be set aside to cover breast implant claims. The Dow Corning plan was met by derision among plaintiffs' attorneys, who argued that the settlement fell far short of what was needed.

By 1997, Dow Corning's fate once again rested with the courts.

CEO Hazleton, reflecting on the controversy and the decisions that management made throughout, said, "I feel like all of us have done the best we could under the circumstances. Obviously, there are a lot of lessons that everybody has learned that I hope we all take to heart to prevent something like this from ever happening again."

QUESTIONS

1. What's your opinion of how *Face to Face with Connie Chung* handled the breast implant story?
2. What options did Dow Corning have in responding to the story?
3. How would you characterize Dow Corning's public relations strategy?
4. What other strategic public relations options did Dow Corning management have in answering the silicone breast implant charges?
5. What should the company's public relations strategy be going forward?

HAROLD BURSON

Harold Burson is chairman of Burson-Marsteller, a worldwide public relations firm with 2,500 employees and 50 offices in 27 countries. He was CEO of Burson-Marsteller from its founding in 1953 until January 1988. Burson is a legendary public relations practitioner and lecturer as well as the recipient of virtually every major honor awarded by the profession.

HOW HAS THE BUSINESS OF PUBLIC RELATIONS CHANGED OVER TIME?

Public relations has, over time, become more relevant as a management function for all manner of institutions—public and private sector, profit and not-for-profit. CEOs increasingly recognize the need to communicate to achieve their organizational objectives. Similarly, they have come to recognize public relations as a necessary component in the decision making process. This has enhanced the role of public relations both internally and for independent consultants.

HOW CAN A PUBLIC RELATIONS FIRM INFLUENCE PUBLIC OPINION?

The public relations function can be divided into two principal classes of activity: the strategic and the implementing. Public relations firms play a major role on behalf of clients in both areas. In the realm of the strategic, a public relations firm brings to a client an independent perspective based on broad organizational experience with a wide spectrum of clients and problems. The public relations firm is not encumbered with the many internal considerations that frequently enter into the corporate or institutional decision making process. In implementing programs, the public relations firm has a broad range of resources, both functional and geographic, that can be brought to bear on a client's problem. Furthermore, the public relations firm can usually be held to more specific accountability—both in terms of results and costs.

WHAT CONSTITUTES THE IDEAL PUBLIC RELATIONS MAN OR WOMAN?

Public relations today covers so broad a range of activity that it is difficult to establish a set of specifications for all the kinds of people wearing the public relations mantle. Generally, I feel four primary characteristics apply to just about every successful public relations person I know.

1. They're smart—bright, intelligent people; quick studies. They ask the right questions. They have that unique ability to establish credibility almost on sight.
2. They know how to get along with people. They work well with their bosses, their peers, their subordinates. They work well with their clients and with third parties like the press and suppliers. They are emotionally stable—even (especially) under pressure. They use the pronoun we more than I.

3. They are motivated, and part of that motivation involves an ability to develop creative solutions. No one needs to tell them what to do next; instinctively, they know. They don't fear starting with a blank sheet of paper. To them, the blank sheet of paper equates with challenge and opportunity.

4. They can write; they can articulate their thoughts in a persuasive manner.

HOW DO ETHICS APPLY TO THE PUBLIC RELATIONS FUNCTION?

In a single word, pervasively. Ethical behavior is at the root of what we do as public relations professionals. We approach our calling with a commitment to serve the public interest, knowing full well that the public interest lacks a universal definition and knowing that one person's view of the public interest differs markedly from that of another. We must therefore be consistent in our personal definition of the public interest and be prepared to speak up for those actions we take.

HOW WOULD YOU ASSESS THE FUTURE OF PUBLIC RELATIONS?

More so than ever before, those responsible for large institutions whose existence depends on public acceptance and support recognize the need for sound public relations input.

At all levels of society, public opinion has been brought to bear in the conduct of affairs both in the public and private sectors. A once-popular president failed in his reelection efforts; numerous CEOs of major corporations have been deposed following initiatives undertaken by the media, by public interest groups, by institutional stockholders—all representing failures that stemmed from a lack of sensitivity to public opinion.

Accordingly, my view is that public relations is playing and will continue to play a more pivotal role in the decision making process than ever before.

The sources of public relations counsel may well become less structured and more diverse, simply because of the growing pervasive understanding that public tolerance has become so important in the achievement of any goals that have a recognizable impact on society.

CHAPTER EIGHT

Public Relations Writing

EVEN IN THE AGE OF THE COMPUTER, writing remains the key to public relations.

The practice of public relations distinguishes professional communicators from amateurs. All of us know how to write and speak. But public relations professionals should write and speak better than their colleagues. Communication—that is, effective writing and speaking—is the trade last of the practice of public relations.

What this means is that the ability to write easily, coherently, and quickly distinguishes the public relations professional from others in an organization. It's not that the skills of counseling and judgment aren't just as important; some experts argue that these skills are far more important than knowing how to write. Maybe. But not knowing how to write—how to express ideas on paper—may reduce the opportunities to ascend the public relations success ladder.

General managers usually have finance, legal, engineering, or sales backgrounds, where writing is not stressed. But when they reach the top, they are expected to write articles, speeches, memos, and testimony. They then need advisers, who are often their trusted public relations professionals. That's why it's imperative that public relations students know how to write—even before they apply public relations techniques to cyberspace. Even beginning public relations professionals are expected to have mastery over the written word. Chapters 8 and 9, properly preceding a discussion of Public Relations and the Internet, focus on what public relations writing is all about.

What does it take to be a public relations writer? For one thing, it takes a good knowledge of the basics. Although practitioners probably write for a wider range of purposes and use a greater number of communications methods than do other writers, the principles remain the same, whether writing an annual report or a case history, an employee newsletter, or a public speech. This chapter and the next will explore the fundamentals of writing: (1) discussing public relations writing in general and news releases in particular, (2) reviewing writing for reading, and (3) discussing writing for listening.

WRITING FOR THE EYE AND THE EAR

Writing for a reader differs dramatically from writing for a listener. A reader has certain luxuries a listener does not have. For example, a reader can scan material, study printed words, dart ahead, and then review certain passages for better understanding. A reader can check up on a writer; if the facts are wrong, for instance, a reader can find out pretty easily. To be effective, writing for the eye must be able to withstand the most rigorous scrutiny.

On the other hand, a listener gets only one opportunity to hear and comprehend a message. If the message is missed the first time, there's usually no second chance. This situation poses a special challenge for the writer—to grab the listener quickly. A listener who tunes out early in a speech or a broadcast is difficult to draw back into the listening fold.

Public relations practitioners—and public relations students—should understand the differences between writing for the eye and the ear. Although it's unlikely that any beginning public relations professional would start by writing speeches, it's important to understand what constitutes a speech and how it's prepared and then be ready for the assignment when opportunity strikes. Because writing lies at the heart of the public relations equation, the more beginners know about writing, the better they will do. Any practitioner who doesn't know the basics of writing and doesn't know how to write is vulnerable and expendable.

FUNDAMENTALS OF WRITING

Few people are born writers. Like any other discipline, writing takes patience and hard work. The more you write, the better you should become, provided you have mastered the basics. Writing fundamentals do not change significantly from one form to another.

What are the basics? Here is a foolproof, three-part formula for writers, from the novice to the novelist.

1. **The idea must precede the expression.**   Think before writing. Few people can observe an event, immediately grasp its meaning, and sit down to compose several pages of sharp, incisive prose. Writing requires ideas, and ideas require thought. Ideas must satisfy four criteria:
   - They must relate to the reader.
   - They must engage the reader's attention.
   - They must concern the reader.
   - They must be in the reader's interest.

Sometimes ideas come quickly. At other times, they don't come at all. But each new writing situation doesn't require a new idea. The trick in coming up with clever ideas lies more in borrowing old ones than in creating new ones. What's that, you say? Is your author encouraging "theft"? You bet! The old cliche, "Don't reinvent the wheel," is absolutely true when it comes to good writing. Never underestimate the importance of maintaining good files.[1]

2. **Don't be afraid of the draft.** After deciding on an idea and establishing the purpose of a communication, the writer should prepare a rough draft. This is a necessary and foolproof method for avoiding a mediocre, half-baked product. Writing, no matter how good, can usually be improved with a second look. The draft helps you organize ideas and plot their development before you commit them to a written test. Writing clarity is often enhanced if you know where you will stop before you start. Organization should be logical; it should lead a reader in a systematic way through the body of the text. Sometimes, especially on longer pieces, an outline should precede the draft.

3. **Simplify, clarify, aim.** In writing, the simpler the better. The more people who understand what you're trying to say, the better your chances for stimulating action. Shop talk, jargon, and "in" words should be avoided. Clear, normal English is all that's required to get an idea across. In practically every case, what makes sense is the simple rather than the complex, the familiar rather than the unconventional, and the concrete rather than the abstract. Clarity is another essential in writing. The key to clarity is tightness; that is, each word, each passage, each paragraph must belong. If a word is unnecessary, a passage redundant, a paragraph vague—get rid of it. Writing requires judicious editing; copy must always be reviewed with an eye toward cutting.

Finally, writing must be aimed at a particular audience. The writer must have the target group in mind and tailor the message to reach them. To win the minds and deeds of a specific audience, one must be willing to sacrifice the understanding of certain others. Writers, like companies, can't expect to be all things to all people.

Television journalist Bill Moyers offers this advice for good writing:

> Strike in the active voice. Aim straight for the enemy: imprecision, ambiguity, and those high words that bear semblance of worth, not substance. Offer no quarter to the tired phrase or overworn idiom. Empty your knapsack of all adjectives, adverbs, and clauses that slow your stride and weaken your pace. Travel light. Remember the most memorable sentences in the English language are also the shortest: "The King is dead" and "Jesus wept."[2]

FLESCH READABILITY FORMULA

Through a variety of writings, the late Rudolf Flesch staged a one-man battle against pomposity and murkiness in writing.* According to Flesch, anyone can become a writer. He suggested that people who write the way they talk will be able to write better. In other words, if people were less inclined to obfuscate their writing with 25-cent words

---

*Among the more significant of Flesch's books are *Say What You Mean*, *The Art of Plain Talk*, *The Art of Readable Writing*, and *How to Be Brief: An Index to Simple Writing*.

and more inclined to substitute simple words, then not only would communicators communicate better, but receivers would receive more clearly.

In responding to a letter, Flesch's approach in action would work as follows: "Thanks for your suggestion, Tom. I'll mull it over and get back to you as soon as I can." The opposite of the Flesch approach would read like this: "Your suggestion has been received; and after careful consideration we shall report our findings to you." See the difference?

There are countless examples of how Flesch's simple dictum works.

- Few would remember William Shakespeare if he had written sentences like "Should I act upon the urgings that I feel or remain passive and thus cease to exist?" Shakespeare's writing has stood the test of centuries because of sentences such as "To be or not to be?"
- A scientist, prone to scientific jargon, might be tempted to write, "The biota exhibited a 100 percent mortality response." But, oh, how much easier and infinitely more understandable to write, "All the fish died."
- One of President Franklin D. Roosevelt's speech writers once wrote, "We are endeavoring to construct a more inclusive society." FDR changed it to "We're going to make a country in which no one is left out."
- Even the most famous book of all, the Bible, opens with a simple sentence that could have been written by a twelve-year-old: "In the beginning, God created the heaven and the earth."

Flesch gave seven suggestions for making writing more readable.

1. Use contractions like it's or doesn't.
2. Leave out the word that whenever possible.
3. Use pronouns like I, we, they, and you.
4. When referring back to a noun, repeat the noun or use a pronoun. Don't create eloquent substitutions.
5. Use brief, clear sentences.
6. Cover only one item per paragraph.
7. Use language the reader understands.

To Flesch the key to all good writing was getting to the point. Stated another way, public relations writers should remember their A's and B's:

- Avoid big words.
- Avoid extra words.
- Avoid cliches.
- Avoid Latin.
- Be specific.
- Be active.
- Be simple.
- Be short.
- Be organized.
- Be convincing.
- Be understandable.[3]

In addition to Flesch, a number of other communications specialists have concentrated on how to make writing more readable. Many have developed their own instruments to measure readability. The most prominent, the Gunning Fog Index, designed by Robert Gunning, measures reading ease in terms of the number of words and their difficulty, the number of complete thoughts, and the average sentence length in a piece of copy. Good writing can't be confusing or unclear. It must be understandable.

NONREADABILITY

Although Rudolf Flesch stressed the "readability" of writing, everyday we see numerous examples of writing that seeks to be anything but readable. To wit, the following, "Accident Report."

The party of the first part hereinafter known as Jack and the party of the second part hereinafter known as Jill ascended or caused to be ascended elevation of undetermined height and degree of slope, hereinafter referred as "hill." Whose purpose it was to obtain, attain, procure, secure, or otherwise, gain acquisition to, by any and/or all means available to them a receptacle or container, hereinafter known as "pail," suitable for the transport of a liquid whose chemical properties shall be limited to hydrogen and oxygen, the proportions of which shall not be less than or exceed two parts for the first mentioned element and one part for the latter. Such a combination will hereinafter be called "water." On the occasion stated above, it has been established beyond a reasonable doubt that Jack did plunge, tumble, topple, or otherwise be caused to lose his footing in a manner that caused his body to be thrust in a downward direction. As a direct result of these combined circumstances, Jack suffered fractures and contusions of his cranial regions. Jill, whether due to Jack's misfortune or not, was known to also tumble in a similar fashion after Jack. (Whether the term, "after," shall be interpreted in a spatial or time passage sense, has not been determined.)

THE BEAUTY OF THE INVERTED PYRAMID

Newspaper writing is the Flesch formula in action. Reporters learn that words are precious and are not to be wasted. In their stories every word counts. If readers lose interest early, they're not likely to be around at the end of the story. That's where the inverted pyramid comes in. Newspaper story form is the opposite of that for a novel or short story. Whereas the climax of a novel comes at the end, the climax of a newspaper story comes at the beginning. A novel's important facts are rolled out as the plot thickens, but the critical facts in a newspaper story appear at the start. In this way, if readers decide to leave a news article early, they have already gained the basic ideas.

Generally, the first tier, or lead, of the inverted pyramid is the first one or two paragraphs, which include the most important facts. From there, paragraphs are written in descending order of importance, with progressively less important facts presented as the article continues—thus, the term inverted pyramid. (See Figure 8–1 for an exception to the inverted pyramid style.)

```
FACTS FACTS FACTS FACTS FACTS FACTS
 CTS FACTS FACTS FACTS FACTS FAC
  TS FACTS FACTS FACTS FACTS FA
   FACTS FACTS FACTS FACTS F
    FACTS FACTS FACTS FACTS
     CTS FACTS FACTS FAC
      TS FACTS FACTS FA
       FACTS FACTS F
        FACTS FACT
         CTS FAC
          TS FA
           V
```

PalmCoast   **NEWS RELEASE**

ITT COMMUNITY DEVELOPMENT CORPORATION
CORPORATE RELATIONS
PALM COAST, FLORIDA 32051
(904) 445-5000

ITT

105**88   FOR IMMEDIATE HOLIDAY ENJOYMENT

CONTACT: CAL MASSEY 904/445-2653

(Individual versions sent to media contacts)

Linda Chase and Family

TO ENJOY HAPPY HOLIDAY SEASON

     PALM COAST, FL -- Palm Coast media relations guy Cal Massey introduced the
world's first (possibly not) sing-along press release today, in order to wish
Linda Chase and family happiness during the holidays and new year, and in order
to embarrass himself and his profession for the fifth consecutive holiday
season.

(Sung to the tune of "Jingle Bell Rock")

         Writer's block/writer's block/writer's block rock...
         The brain said goodbye/and left nothing but schlock...
         Norm-al-ly you get/a witty release...
         But this year/the PR guy's blocked!

                 Dum-de-dum-dum...

         Writer's block/writer's block/writer's block rock...
         Hope your holiday's fun/and you get more than socks...
         Rhy-ming is tough/when there's nothing but -ock...
         But this year/it's all that we've got!

                 A little as-son-ance...

         Writer's block/writer's block/writer's block rock...
         It's been a great year/with good news 'round the clock...
         Palm Coast is growing/and not without thought...
         Except for/the PR guy, BLOCKED!

                 Big finish, now...

         Writer's block/writer's block/writer's block rock...
         I'm taking a few days/so don't be too shocked...
         If very soon/you receive in your mail...
         Next year's/release in a box!

                 My brain's rested...

         Dum-de-dum/dum-de-dum/dum-de-dum-dum...

The final refrain: I hope the media representatives I have had the pleasure of
working with over the years enjoy a relaxing holiday and new year graced by a
light touch --- Cal Massey/Manager, Media Services/ITT Community Development
Corporation.

Figure 8–1 As a holiday exception to the inverted pyramid news release, Palm Coast Media Services manager Cal Massey dispatched this sing-along press release, tailored to each of his primary media contacts.

The lead is the most critical element, usually answering the questions concerning who, what, why, when, where, and occasionally how. For example, the following lead effectively answers most of the initial questions a reader might have about the subject of the news story.

Michael Jordan announced yesterday in Chicago that he will play one more year with the Chicago Bulls and then retire from basketball.

That sentence tells it all; it answers the critical questions and highlights the pertinent facts. It gets to the point quickly without a lot of extra words. In only 22 words it captures and communicates the essence of what the reader needs to know.

After the lead, the writer must select the next most important facts and array them in descending order, most important facts higher in the story. In this way, the inverted pyramid style is more the "selection and organization" of facts than it is an exercise in creative "writing."

This same style of straightforward writing forms the basis for the most fundamental and ubiquitous of all public relations tools—the news release.

THE NEWS RELEASE

The news release, a valuable but much-maligned device, is the granddaddy of public relations writing vehicles. Most public relations professionals swear by it. Some newspaper editors swear about it. But everyone uses the release as the basic interpretive mechanism to let people know what an organization is doing. There is no better, clearer, more persuasive way to announce news about an organization, its products and their applications than by issuing a news release.[4] That's why the news release deserves special attention as a public relations writing vehicle.

A news release may be written as the document of record to state an organization's official position—for example, in a court case or in announcing a price or rate increase. More frequently, however, releases have one overriding purpose—to influence a publication to write favorably about the material discussed. Each day, in fact, professionals send releases to editors in the hope of stimulating favorable stories about their organizations.

Most news releases are not used verbatim. Rather, they may stimulate editors to consider covering a story. In other words, the release becomes the point of departure for a newspaper, magazine, radio, or television story. Why then do some editors and others describe news releases as "worthless drivel"?[5] The answer, says researcher Linda Norton of the University of Oklahoma's Herbert School of Journalism, is threefold:

1. **Releases are poorly written.**   Professor Norton found that most news releases are written in a more complicated and difficult-to-read style than most newspaper stories. "This could be the result of pressure from administrators as they review and critique press releases," she reasoned.
2. **Releases are rarely localized.**   Newspapers focus largely on hometown or regional developments. The more localized a news release, the greater the chance it has of being used. However, according to Professor Norton, "Practitioners may not want to do the additional work that localization requires." This is a bad decision because research indicates that a news release is 10 times more likely to be used if it is localized.
3. **Releases are not newsworthy.**   This is the grand dilemma. An editor will use a public relations release only if he or she considers it news. If it's not newsworthy, it won't be used. What determines whether something is news? Professor Norton suggests five requisites:

   - Impact
   - Oddity
   - Conflict
   - Known principal
   - Proximity

Research indicates that the vast majority of public relations releases don't contain any of these elements, limiting their chances of "seeing the light of print."[6]

With these findings as backdrop, it is not surprising that research also indicates that only 3 to 8 percent of all news releases are published.[7] Nonetheless, each day's *Wall Street Journal*, *New York Times*, *USA Today*, and daily publications around the nation, are filled with stories generated by public relations professionals.

So the fact is that the news release—despite the harsh reviews of some—remains the single most important public relations vehicle.

News Value

The key challenge for public relations writers is to ensure that their news releases reflect news (Figure 8–2). What is "news"? That's an age-old question in journalism. Traditionally, journalists said that when "a dog bites a man, it's not news." But when

Figure 8–2 A news release is worthless unless it gets published. The key to getting published is to ensure that the release is newsworthy. This release of a revolutionary 24-hour-a-day payments system qualifies as news.

"a man bites a dog, that's news." The best way to learn what constitutes "news value" is to scrutinize the daily press and broadcast news reports and see what they use for news. In a general sense, news releases ought to include the following elements of "news."

- Have a well-defined reason for sending the release.
- Focus on one central subject in each release.
- Make certain the subject is newsworthy in the context of the organization, industry, and community.
- Include facts about the product/service/issue being discussed.
- Provide the facts, "factually"—with no puff, no bluff, no hyperbole.
- Rid the release of unnecessary jargon.
- Include appropriate quotes from principals—but avoid inflated superlatives that do little more than boost management egos.
- Include product specifications, shipping dates, availability and price; all pertinent information for telling the story.

THE GLOBAL SETTLEMENT FUND. INC.

FOR IMMEDIATE RELEASE   Contact: Doff Meyer
                                              212-222-3436

        GLOBESET™, WORLD'S FIRST ROUND-THE-CLOCK,

     MULTI-CURRENCY PAYMENT SYSTEM, BEGINS OPERATION

The Global Settlement Fund, Inc. (GlobeSet™), the world's

first 24-hour-a-day, multi-currency payment system, has begun

operation as a new form of margin collateral for futures

trades. A mutual fund as well as a payment system, GlobeSet

seeks to earn income for its shareholders.

Unlike traditional collateral management and payment systems,

GlobeSet is the world's first system to offer the following

features:

    · Payments using GlobeSet shares are instantaneous and

       final.

    · Payments using GlobeSet shares can be made 24 hours a

       day, every business day, 7 a.m. Monday, Tokyo time,

       through 8 p.m. Friday, New York time.

    · GlobeSet is designed to accept payments in multiple

       currencies — initially United States Dollars,

       Japanese Yen and British Pound Sterling.

                    --- more ---

Figure 8–2   Continued

THE REST OF THE STORY

JUST THE FACTS

Writing in news release style is easy. It is less a matter of formal writing than it is of selecting, organizing, and arraying facts in descending sequence.

Here are 10 facts:

Fact 1: Attorney General Janet Reno will speak in Lansing, Michigan tomorrow.

Fact 2: She will be keynote speaker at the annual convention of the American Bar Association.

Fact 3: She will speak at 8 P.M. in the Michigan State University Field House.

Fact 4: Her speech will be a major one.

Fact 5: Her topic will be capital punishment.

Fact 6: She will also address university law classes while she is in Lansing.

Fact 7: She will meet with the university's chancellor while she is in Lansing.

Fact 8: She is serving her second term as attorney general under President Clinton.

Fact 9: She is a former Florida prosecutor.

Fact 10: She has, in the past, steadfastly avoided addressing the subject of capital punishment.

Organize these facts into an American Bar Association news release for tomorrow morning's Lansing newspaper.

- Include a brief description of the company (aka "boilerplate") at the end of the release, what it is and what it does.
- Write clearly, concisely, forcefully.[8]

Format

The format of a news release is important. Because the release is designed to be used in print, it must be structured for easy use by an editor. Certain mechanical rules of thumb should be followed (Figure 8–3):

- **Spacing**—News releases should always be typed and double-spaced on 8½ by 11 inch paper. No editor wants to go rummaging through a handwritten release or a single-spaced, oversized piece of paper. Although most releases are typed on only one side, in these days of environmental concern, releases typed on both sides of a page are acceptable.

Press Contacts:
Dave Boelio, Imark Technologies: 908-464-1878
Patricia M. Samson, SilverPlatter Information, Inc.: 800-343-0064, X189
Trade Press: Mark Bruce, GHB Communications: 203-321-1242
Investment Press: Joe Procopio, The Poretz Group: 703-506-1778

Imark's NET-MAX™ Opens Up Pay-Per-Use Revenue Stream

SilverPlatter Launches Search by Search™ with NET-MAX™ at ALA Summer Conference

*Reston, VA—June 25, 1997—*Imark Technologies, Inc. (NASDAQ: MAXX) and SilverPlatter Information, Inc. announced today that SilverPlatter will launch Search by Search™, a new pay-as-you-go Internet service that relies on Imark's NET-MAX™ software, at the American Library Association (ALA) Annual Conference in San Francisco, June 28 - July 1, 1997.

Search by Search™ provides direct access to a collection of widely used databases covering over ten subject areas in such disciplines as Arts & Humanities, Engineering, Medicine & Health Science, Social Sciences, and many others. The service enables users to access Search by Search™ on an "as needed basis," paying only for what they use.

Search by Search™ is the first transaction-based service available from SilverPlatter. Previously, the company's popular databases were only accessible on a subscription basis. A new form of information distribution is now opening for the 33,000 active subscribers to SilverPlatter products. These users and others who need only occasional access to these databases can be accommodated with this new "pay-per-use" pricing option. With NET-MAX™, users can establish credit card or purchase order accounts with a minimum commitment of $500.00.

-- More --

IMARK Technologies, Inc.
11480 Sunset Hills Road · Reston, VA 20190-5208 703.925.3400 fax:703.925.3430 www.imarktech.com

Figure 8–3 Even in the age of cyberspace, the news release is still the best vehicle to explain clearly the news of the day. This high-tech announcement illustrates proper news release format, from spacing to identification, from margins to headlines, from slug lines to overall appearance.

Imark Technologies FAQ

What tools are available for maximizing my revenues on the Internet?
Effective pricing plays a major role in giving publishers the opportunity to achieve greater market penetration and maximize revenues. At Imark, we counsel our clients not to choose one price plan over another, but to offer flexible pricing schemes including subscription, pay-per-use, advertising, premiums, and special offers to meet customers' needs. With Imark's tools, it is possible to charge by customer category, by searches, by records, by abstracts, by chapters, by session, etc.

My customers are used to flat-rate subscriptions. By changing my pricing strategy, don't I risk actually losing revenues?
Fortunately, it is not an either/or proposition. By **combining** flat-rate subscription with other pricing metrics, you will open up the market for your products beyond the universe of customers that now have access. More choices mean broader appeal; broader appeal means more business. Examples abound. For instance, some restaurants that offer an "all you can eat" buffet also have an a la carte menu.

Will I need to reengineer my whole business in order to take advantage of electronic commerce and variable pricing?
No. Imark has integrated the NET-MAX transaction system with an impressive list of developers and publishing software companies that can help you make Internet commerce and pay-per-use a practical reality. By using software and services from an Imark partner such as **Dataware Technologies**, **SilverPlatter Information**, and **Folio Corporation**, content providers can save valuable development time. Imark has partners in hosting and development that can assist you with programming and design needs as well.

Why isn't everyone offering pay-per-use?
Actually, per-document pricing is beginning to gather steam among many online publishers and aggregators such as SilverPlatter, OCLC, and others. In the financial services sector, pay-per-use is now a part of most companies' marketing strategy. Perhaps the biggest reason is that pay-per-use for Web applications is a new capability. Technologies have not been widely available, until now, to make pay-per-use pricing practical and efficient.

As a publisher, does my information need to be formatted or stored in any special way in order to use NET-MAX ™?
Your information should be in database form and it is preferred that you deliver it from a secure Web server with a CGI program capable of denying access to content.

Does Imark host content for publishers?
No. Imark does not offer hosting services, but we have partners who specialize in this area. We would be happy to help you find an excellent hosting service should you require one.

(over)

Imark Technologies, Inc. • *(800) 236-2901*

Figure 8–3   Continued

SilverPlatter Information and **Imark Technologies, Inc**. have collaborated on a new Web-based service called *SEARCH BY SEARCH*™, providing access to a growing collection of databases. With no annual subscription costs, you pay only for what you use. Using SilverPlatter's familiar WebSPIRS™ gateway and integrating the transaction capabilities of NET-MAX™ from Imark, Search by Search offers on-demand account information and usage statistics in a secure environment.

Information providers taking part in this new service are:

Public Affairs Information Service

Willow Tree Press

Human Relations Area Files

IFI/Plenum Data Corporation

Diogenes

American Association of Retired Persons

Cambridge Scientific Abstracts

National Association of Social Workers

American Society of Health-System Pharmacists

National Library of Medicine

ERIC Processing and Reference Facility

Pierian Press

National Technical Information Service

Government Printing Office

American Economic Association

Sociological Abstracts

Access Innovations

Council on Exceptional Children

IFIS Publishing

Responsive Database Services

H.W. Wilson Company

Information Today, Inc.

CAB INTERNATIONAL

Imark Technologies, Inc. ● *(800) 236-2901*

Figure 8–3   Continued

- **Paper**—Inexpensive paper stock should be used. Reporters win Pulitzer Prizes with stories written on plain copy paper. Nothing irritates an editor more than seeing an expensively embossed news release while watching newspapers die due to soaring newsprint costs.
- **Identification**—The name, address, and telephone number of the release writer should appear in the upper part of the release in case an editor wants further information. It's a good idea to list two names, with office and home telephone numbers.
- **Release date**—Releases should always be dated, either for immediate use or to be held until a certain later date, often referred to as an embargoed date. In this day of instant communication, however, newspapers frown on embargoes. And only in the most extreme cases—for example, proprietary or confidential medical or government data—will newspapers honor them. Frequently, a dateline is used on releases; it is the first line of the release and tells where the story originated.
- **Margins**—Margins should be wide enough for editors to write in, usually about one to one and a half inches.
- **Length**—A news release is not a book. It should be edited tightly so that it is no more than two to two and a half pages long. Words and sentences should be kept short.
- **Paragraphs**—Paragraphs should also be short, no more than six lines at most. A single sentence can suffice as a paragraph. Because typographical composers may type exactly what they see, words should not be broken at the end of a line. Likewise, paragraphs should be completed before a new page is begun to ensure that a lost page in the news or composing room will not disrupt a particular thought in the release.
- **Slug lines**—Journalistic shorthand, or slug lines, should appear on a release—such things as "more" at the bottom of a page when the release continues to another page and "30" or "###" to denote the end of the release. Page numbers and one-word descriptions of the topic of the release should appear on each page for quick editorial recognition.
- **Headlines**—Headlines are a good idea and help presell an editor on the gist of the news release that follows. Releases should be folded with the headline showing.
- **Proofreading**—Grammar, spelling, and typing must be perfect. Misspellings, grammatical errors, or typos are the quickest route to the editorial wastebasket.
- **Timing**—News release writers must be sensitive to editorial deadlines. Newspapers, magazines, and broadcast stations work under constant deadline pressure. Because stale news is no news, a release arriving even a little late may just as well never have been mailed. This is particularly the case today, where faxes and E-mail deliver documents immediately. But . . .
- **Internet prudence**—Most journalists still don't use technology for primary news collection. That means that neither e-mailing releases nor stating the lead over voice mail nor messengering a disc—will guarantee that a reporter will even see a release. The best advice is to check a particular reporter's preferred way to receive news releases before dispatching them.

Style

The style of a news release is almost as critical as its content. Sloppy style can break the back of any release and ruin its chances for publication. Style must also be flexible and evolve as language changes.

One element of style that has evolved over the years relates to sexism in writing. Dealing with gender has become more important for a writer and also more difficult.

No matter how hard a writer tries to be evenhanded in treating men and women in print, he or she is bound to offend someone. The Washington Press Club has published guidelines for the elimination of sexual bias in the media. Among its highlights are these rules:

1. Terms referring to a specific gender should be avoided when an alternative term will do. Use *business executive* instead of businessman and *city council member* for councilman.
2. Where neither a gender-free term nor any term accurately designating gender is yet in common use, continue to employ the old terminology—for example, *Yeoman* First Class Yael Morris or Maureen Re, a telephone company *lineman*.
3. No occupational designation should include a description of the person's gender unless it is pertinent to the story. For example, don't use *woman lawyer* or *male nurse*.
4. Avoid terms like *man-made* for synthetic, *man on the street* for ordinary citizen, *manpower* for workforce, *man and wife* for husband and wife, and *co-ed* for student.

Despite such attempts to eliminate sexism in writing style, satisfying everyone is a nearly impossible task for any writer.

Most public relations operations follow the style practiced by major newspapers and magazines rather than that of book publishers. This news style is detailed in various guides published by such authorities as the *Associated Press* and the *New York Times*.

Because the press must constantly update its style to conform to changing societal concepts, news release style is subjective and everchanging. However, a particular firm's style must be consistent from one release to the next. The following are examples of typical style rules:

- **Capitalization**—Most leading publications use capital letters sparingly; so should you. Editors call this a *down style* because only the most important words begin with capital letters.
- **Abbreviations**—Abbreviations present a many-faceted problem. For example, months, when used with dates, should be abbreviated, such as Sept. 2, 1999. But when the day of the month is not used, the month should be spelled out, such as September 1999. Days of the week, on the other hand, should never be abbreviated. In addition, first mention of organizations and agencies should be spelled out, with the abbreviation in parentheses after the name, such as Securities and Exchange Commission (SEC).
- **Numbers**—There are many guidelines for the spelling out of numbers, but a general rule is to spell out numbers through nine and use figures for 10 and up. Yet figures are perfectly acceptable for such things as election returns, speeds and distances, percentages, temperatures, heights, ages, ratios, and sports scores.
- **Punctuation**—The primary purpose of punctuation is to clarify the writer's thoughts, ensure exact interpretation, and make reading and understanding quicker and easier. Less punctuation rather than more should be the goal. The following are just some of the punctuation marks a public relations practitioner must use appropriately.

  1. The colon introduces listings, tabulations, and statements and takes the place of an implied "for instance."
  2. The comma is used in a variety of circumstances, including before connecting words, between two words or figures that might otherwise be misunderstood, and before and after nonrestrictive clauses.

3. In general, exclamation points should be resisted in releases. They tend to be overkill!

4. The hyphen is often abused and should be used carefully. A single hyphen can change the meaning of a sentence completely. For example, "The six-foot man eating tuna was killed" means the man was eating tuna; it should probably be punctuated "The six-foot, man-eating tuna was killed."

5. Quoted matter is enclosed in double or single quotation marks. The double marks enclose the original quotation, whereas the single marks enclose a quotation within a quotation.

- **Spelling**—Many words, from adviser to zucchini, are commonly misspelled. The best way to avoid misspellings is to have a dictionary always within reach. When two spellings are given in a dictionary, the first spelling is always preferred.

These are just a few of the stylistic stumbling blocks that writers must consider. In the news release, style should never be taken lightly. The style, as much as any other part of the release, lets an editor know the kind of organization that issued the release and the competence of the professional who wrote it.

THE REST OF THE STORY

INFLATED CORPORATE STYLE

Even in the twenty-first century, corporate jargon—especially in news releases—is often unbearable. In some companies, in fact, things have gotten so "inflated" that words in corporatespeak can be interchangeable.

In case you wind up working for one of these companies, feel free to mix and match from any of these three columns with any of these 42 words in any order.* (They'll think you're smart!)

1. overarching	visionary	objectives
2. strategic	support	alternatives
3. special	customer-oriented	expectations
4. specific	stretch	mechanisms
5. core	planning	assessment
6. long term	marketing	update
7. defined	service	model
8. technology-based	process	product
9. formal	fundamental	centralization
10. exceptional	sales	incentive
11. value-based	budget	initiatives
12. executive	operating	feedback
13. immediate	discretionary	infrastructure
14. interactive	tracking	proposition

*Eileen Kinsella, "After All, What's a News Article But a Formalized Update Process?" *The Wall Street Journal* (August 1, 1996): C1.

Content

Again, the cardinal rule in release content is that the end product be newsworthy. The release must be of interest to an editor and readers. Issuing a release that has little chance of being used by a publication serves only to crush the credibility of the writer.

When a release is newsworthy and of potential interest to an editor, it must be written clearly and concisely, in proper newspaper style. It must get to the facts early and answer the six key questions. From there it must follow inverted pyramid structure to its conclusion. For example, consider the following lead for the Janet Reno news release posed earlier in this chapter.

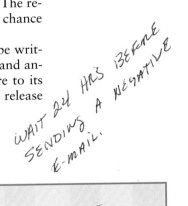

WAIT 24 HRS BEFORE SENDING A NEGATIVE E-MAIL.

A QUESTION OF ETHICS

LEAKING THE GLEEFUL DISASTER MEMO

The best thing anyone can do after writing an internal memo is to avoid sending it unless absolutely necessary. Consider the case of Jeffrey W. Greenberg and Hurricane Andrew.

On August 24, 1992, one of the worst hurricanes in U.S. history, Hurricane Andrew, struck Florida with such vengeance that 17 people were killed and upwards of $8 billion in damages was recorded.

Nonetheless, on the same day that Andrew hit Florida, Mr. Greenberg, executive vice president of the insurance giant American International Group and the son of Chairman Maurice Greenberg, suggested in a memo to company presidents and regional vice presidents that they call their "underwriters together and explain the significance of the hurricane."

Greenberg the younger continued in his two-paragraph memo: "This may cause the industry the biggest storm loss ever. This is an opportunity to get price increases now. We must be the first."

Although few could argue with the facts and reasoning suggested by Mr. Greenberg, several observers questioned (1) his choice of words and (2) his timing.

One such critic was Florida Insurance Commissioner Tom Gallagher, who, on reading about the leaked Greenberg memo, immediately issued an order freezing insurance rates and warning companies against "greed-motivated rate hikes" in the aftermath of Hurricane Andrew.

Gallagher said his department would reject any efforts by the insurance industry to "capitalize on the misfortune of Hurricane Andrew's victims. We have heard reports that some in the insurance business see Hurricane Andrew as an opportunity to raise rates unfairly." This practice, Gallagher warned, would not be tolerated.

AIG Chairman Greenberg blasted back that his son's memo had been taken out of context. He pointed out that commercial and industrial insurance rates "have been inadequate for some time." And he argued that the sense of the memo was correct—that rates should be higher so that insurance companies can remain financially strong to respond to future disasters.

Right or wrong, the errant memo's damage had been done. Had he to do it over again, might Mr. Greenberg have worded the memo differently?

For further information, see "Limits Are Urged on Insurers After Storm," *The New York Times* (September 8, 1992): D-4; and Thomas S. Mulligan, "Insurer Uses Hurricane to Promote Rate Hike," *Los Angeles Times* (September 5, 1992): D-1.

> LANSING, MICHIGAN—Attorney General Janet Reno will deliver a major address on capital punishment at 8 P.M. tomorrow in the Michigan State University Field House before the annual convention of the American Bar Association.

This lead answers all the pertinent questions: who (Attorney General Janet Reno), what (a major address on capital punishment), where (Michigan State University Field House), when (tomorrow at 8 P.M.), and why (American Bar Association is holding a convention). In this case, how is less important. But whether the reader chooses to delve further into the release or not, the story's gist has been successfully communicated in the lead.

To be newsworthy, news releases must be objective. All comments and editorial remarks must be attributed to organization officials. The news release can't be used as the private soapbox of the release writer. Rather, it must appear as a fair and accurate representation of the news that the organization wishes to be conveyed.

News releases can be written about almost anything. Three frequent subjects are product and institutional announcements, management changes, and management speeches.

THE ANNOUNCEMENT

Frequently, practitioners want to announce a new product or institutional development, such as construction plans, earnings, mergers, acquisitions, or company celebrations. The announcement release should have a catchy yet significant lead to stimulate an editor to capitalize on the practitioner's creative idea.

> "Tennis whites," the traditional male court uniform, will yield to bright colors and fashion styling this spring as Jockey spearheads a new wave in tennis fashion with the introduction of a full line of tennis wear for men.

Typically, in an announcement release, after the lead identifies the significant aspects of the product or development, a spokesperson is quoted for additional product information. Editors appreciate the quotes because they then do not have to interview a company official.

> The new, lightweight plastic bottle for Coca-Cola began its national rollout today in Spartanburg, S.C. This two-liter package is the nation's first metric plastic bottle for soft drinks.

> "We are very excited about this new package," said John H. Ogden, president, Coca-Cola U.S.A. "Our two-liter plastic bottle represents an important advancement. Its light weight, toughness, and environmental advantages offer a new standard of consumer benefits in soft drink packaging."

The subtle product "plug" included in this release is typical of such announcements. Clearly, the organization gains if the product's benefits are described in a news story. But editors are sensitive to product puffery, and the line between legitimate information and puffery is thin. One must always be sensitive to the needs and concerns of editors. A professional avoids letting the thin line of product information become a short plank of puffery.

THE MANAGEMENT CHANGE

Newspapers are often interested in management changes, but editors frequently reject releases that have no local angle. For example, the editor of the Valdosta, Georgia, *Citizen* has little reason to use this announcement:

NEW YORK, NY, SEPT. 5, 1999—Ronald O. Schram has been named manager of the hosiery department at Bloomingdale's Paramus, NJ, store.

On the other hand, the same release, amended for local appeal, would almost certainly be used by the *Citizen*.

NEW YORK, NY, SEPT. 5, 1999—Ronald O. Schram, son of Mr. and Mrs. Siegfried Schram of 221 Starting Lane, Valdosta, has been named manager of the hosiery department at Bloomingdale's Paramus, NJ, store.

Sometimes one must dig for the local angle. For example, suppose Mr. Schram was born in Valdosta but went to school in Americus, Georgia. With this knowledge, the writer might prepare the following release, which would have appeal in the newspapers of both Georgia cities.

NEW YORK, NY, SEPT. 5, 1999—Ronald O. Schram, son of Mr. and Mrs. Siegfried Schram of 221 Starting Lane, Valdosta, and a 1976 graduate of Americus High School, was named manager of the hosiery department of Bloomingdale's Paramus, NJ, store.

Penetrating local publications with the management change release is relatively easy once the local angle has been identified, but achieving publication in a national newspaper or magazine is much harder. *The Wall Street Journal*, for example, will not use a management change announcement unless the individual has attained a certain level of responsibility, usually corporate vice president or higher, in a major firm. In other words, if a release involves someone who has not attained senior executive status at a listed company, forget it, at least as far as *The Wall Street Journal* is concerned.

For national consumption it is the importance or uniqueness of the individual or company that should be emphasized. For example, an editor might not realize that the following management change is unique:

WASHINGTON, DC, JUNE 6, 1998—Howie Barmad of Jersey City, NJ, today was promoted to the rank of admiral in the United States Navy.

However, the same release stands out clearly for its news value when the unique angle is played up.

WASHINGTON, DC, JUNE 6, 1998—Howie Barmad, born in Yugoslavia, today was named the first naturalized admiral in the history of the United States Navy.

One can never go wrong by being straightforward in a news release, but a local or unique angle to help sell the story to an editor should always be investigated.

THE MANAGEMENT SPEECH

Management speeches are another recurring source of news releases. The key to a speech news release is selecting the most significant portion of the talk for the lead. A good speech generally has a clear thesis, from which a lead naturally flows. Once the thesis is identified, the remainder of the release simply embellishes it.

BOONEVILLE, MO, OCT. 18, 1998—Booneville Mining Company is "on the verge of having several very profitable years," Booneville Mining President J. Kenneth Krafchik said today.

Addressing the Booneville Chamber of Commerce, the Missouri mining company executive cited two reasons for the positive projections: The company's orders are at an all-

How can kids grow in classrooms like this?

Washington's schools now have the fourth largest class sizes in the nation. And this crisis is only getting worse. In just five years, 100,000 new students will jam our already overcrowded schools.

Crowded classrooms may be a great place to rub elbows, but they're a tough place to get an education. Why? Because students don't always get the individual attention they need: there are just too many kids.

Our children need more space. Space to learn, grow and prepare for the future. If we don't do something to reduce class sizes today, our kids won't be ready for tomorrow.

Give Our Kids Room To Grow.

 Washington Education Association

33434 Eighth Avenue South
Federal Way, Washington 98003
206 941 6700

Washington Education Association   News Release

March 31, 1989

For more information: Teresa Moore, Washington Education
                         Association, (206) 941-6700

FOR IMMEDIATE RELEASE

'GIVE OUR KIDS ROOM TO GROW' CAMPAIGN STARTS

FEDERAL WAY, WA -- What do sardines in a can and many of Washington's public school children have in common? They're both in a tight spot.

"Overcrowded classrooms are making it more and more difficult for kids to learn," said Terry Bergeson, President of the Washington Education Association. "Washington has the 4th largest class size in the nation. Our children are too important to the future of the state to allow this overcrowding to continue."

Bergeson's comments were made as the W.E.A. launched a media campaign to heighten awareness statewide about school overcrowding.

"We're taking our message to the streets, into people's homes," Bergeson said. "When the people become aware of just how large many classes are, they'll demand that our kids be given room to grow."

One year ago, W.E.A. members agreed to sponsor and raise funds for a statewide information campaign about Washington's K-12 public schools.

more ... more

Figure 8–4   A news release, derived from a speech by the president of the Washington Education Association on classroom overcrowding, was complemented by this provocative advertisement.

time high, and its overseas facilities have "turned the corner" on profitability in the current year.

Normally, if the speech giver is not a famous person, the release should not begin with the speaker's name but rather with the substance of the remarks. If the speaker is a well-known individual, leading with the name is perfectly legitimate.

Federal Reserve Chairman Alan Greenspan called today for a "new attitude toward business investment and capital formation."

The body copy of a speech release should follow directly from the lead. Often, the major points of the speech must be paraphrased and consolidated to conform to a two-page release. In any event, it is frequently a significant challenge to convert the essence of a management speech to news-release form (Figure 8–4).

THE IMPORTANCE OF EDITING

Editing is the all-important final touch for the public relations writer. In a news release, a careful self-edit can save the deadliest prose. An editor must be judicious. Each word, phrase, sentence, and paragraph should be weighed carefully. Good editing will "punch up" dull passages and make them sparkle. For instance, "The satellite flies across the sky" is dead, but "The satellite roars across the sky" is alive.

In the same context, good editing will get rid of passive verbs. Invariably, this will produce shorter sentences. For example, "The cherry tree was chopped down by George Washington" is shorter and better than "George Washington chopped down the cherry tree."

A good editor must also be gutsy enough to use bold strokes—to chop, slice, and cut through verbiage, bad grammar, misspellings, incorrect punctuation, poorly constructed sentences, misused words, mixed metaphors, non sequiturs, cliches, redundancies, circumlocutions, and jargon. Sentences like "She is the widow of the late Marco Picardo" and "The present incumbent is running for re-election" are intolerable to a good editor.

THE REST OF THE STORY

DEOBFUSCATING OBFUSCATORY PROVERBS

Test your editing skills by tightening up these annoyingly verbose proverbs.

1. Avian entities of identical plummage inevitably congregate.
2. Pulchritude possesses profundity of a merely cutaneous nature.
3. It is fruitless to become lachrymose over precipitately departed lacteal fluid.
4. It is inefficacious to indoctrinate a superannuated canine with innovative maneuvers.
5. Eschew the implement of correction and vitiate the scion.
6. Visible vapors that issue from ignited carbonaceous materials are a harbinger of simultaneous or imminent conflagration.
7. Lack of propinquity causes an effulgence of partiality in the cardiac area.
8. A revolving mass of lithic conglomerate does not accumulate a congery of small green bryophitic plants.
9. Presenter of the ultimate cachinnation thereby obtains the optimal cachinnation.
10. Ligneous or petrous projectiles may have the potential to fracture my osseous structure, but perjorative appellations remain eternally innocuous.

ANSWERS

1. Birds of a feather flock together.
2. Beauty is only skin deep.
3. There's no use crying over spilt milk.
4. You can't teach an old dog new tricks.
5. Spare the rod and spoil the child.
6. Where there's smoke, there's fire.
7. Absence makes the heart grow fonder.
8. A rolling stone gathers no moss.
9. He who laughs last laughs best.
10. Sticks and stones may break my bones, but names can never hurt me.

Probably the two most significant writing and editing supports for a practitioner are a good unabridged dictionary and a thesaurus. To these might be added *Bartlett's Familiar Quotations*, the *World Almanac*, and an encyclopedia. Editing should also concentrate on organizing copy. One release paragraph should flow naturally into the next. Transitions in writing are most important. Sometimes it takes only a single word to unite two adjoining paragraphs. Such is the case in the following example, which uses the word size.

The machine works on a controlled mechanism, directed by a series of pulleys. It is much smaller than the normal motor, requiring less than half of a normal motor's components.

Not only does the device differ in size from other motors, but it also differs in capacity.

Writing, like fine wine, should flow smoothly and stand up under the toughest scrutiny. Careful editing is a must.

SUMMARY

Writing is the essence of public relations practice. The public relations professional, if not the best writer in his or her organization, must at least be one of the best. Writing is the communications skill that differentiates public relations professionals from others.

Some writers are born. But writing can be learned by understanding the fundamentals of what makes interesting writing; by practicing different written forms; and by working constantly to improve, edit, and refine the written product. When an executive needs something written well, one organizational resource should pop immediately into his or her mind—public relations.

DISCUSSION STARTERS

1. What is the difference between writing for the ear and for the eye?
2. What are several of the writing fundamentals one must consider?
3. What is the essence of the Flesch method of writing?
4. What is the inverted pyramid and why does it work?
5. What is the essential written communications vehicle used by public relations professionals?
6. Why is the format of a news release important to a public relations professional and the organization?
7. What are common purposes of news releases?
8. Should a news release writer try to work his or her own editorial opinion into the release?
9. What is the key to writing a release on a management speech?
10. What is the purpose of editing?

NOTES

1. Fraser P. Seitel, "Steal!" *United States Banker* (1992): 44.
2. Bill Moyers, "Watch Your Language," *The Professional Communicator* (August–September, 1985): 6.
3. Fraser P. Seitel, "Getting It Write," *United States Banker* (December 1991): 54.
4. G.A. Marken, "Press Releases: When Nothing Else Will Do, Do It Right," *Public Relations Quarterly* (Fall 1994): 9.
5. "J-Prof Says PR Releases Are 'Worthless,' " *Jack O'Dwyer's Newsletter* (July 14, 1993): 4.
6. "Researcher Finds Complaints Against Press Releases Are Justified," *Editor and Publisher* (May 8, 1993): 42, 52.
7. Linda P. Morton, "Producing Publishable Press Releases," *Public Relations Quarterly* (Winter 1992–1993): 9–11.
8. Marken, op. cit., 10.

SUGGESTED READINGS

Bivins, Thomas. *Handbook for Public Relations Writing.* Lincolnwood, IL: National Textbook Company, 1991.

Bivins, Thomas and William E. Ryan. *How to Produce Creative Publications: Traditional Techniques and Computer Applications.* Lincolnwood, IL: NTC Publishing Group, 1992.

Block, Mervin. *Writing Broadcast News—Shorter, Sharper, Stronger.* Chicago: NTC Publishing Group, 1992.

Cormier, Robin A. *Error-Free Writing: A Lifetime Guide to Flawless Business Writing.* Alexandria, VA: EEI Press, 1995.

Crystal, David. *The Cambridge Encyclopedia of the English Language.* Cambridge, England: Cambridge University Press, 1995.

Fensch, Thomas. *Sports Writing Handbook*, 2nd ed., Hillsdale, NJ: Lawrence Erlbaum Associates, 1995. Updates a special type of writing for sports information.

King, Janice. *Writing High-Tech Copy that Sells.* New York: John Wiley & Sons, 1995. A guide to preparing persuasive promotional materials for high technology products and services.

Lesikar, Raymond V. *Report Writing for Business*, 9th ed. Burr Ridge, IL: Irwin Professional Publishing, 1995.

Meyer, Herbert and Jill Meyer. *How to Write.* Washington, DC: Storm King Press, 1991.

Newsome, Douglas and Bob Carrell. *Public Relations Writing: Form and Style.* 2nd ed. Belmont, CA: Wadsworth, 1988.

Rayfield, Robert., et al. *Public Relations Writing: Strategies and Skills.* Dubuque, IA: William C. Brown, 1991.

Simon, Raymond and Joseph Zappala. *Public Relations Workbook: Writing & Techniques.* Lincolnwood, IL: NTC Publishing Group, 1996.

Smith, Peggy. *Letter Perfect: A Guide to Practical Proofreading.* Alexandria, VA: EEI Press, 1995.

Strunk, W. and E. B. White. *Elements of Style.* New York: Macmillan, 1979.

MERRY ARONSON AND DONALD E. SPETNER

THE PUBLIC RELATIONS WRITER'S HANDBOOK

NEW YORK: LEXINGTON BOOKS, 1993

"While always acting as an advocate for the client or company and always having a specific point of view, the true professional does not exaggerate, equivocate, or misrepresent the facts."

Thus begins *The Public Relations Writer's Handbook*, which offers step-by-step advice on the wide range of writing required by public relations professionals. Using examples from both successful public relations campaigns and hypothetical clients, the authors instruct readers on the ins and outs of writing effective public relations copy.

The authors, two contemporary public relations professionals, discuss such modern public relations challenges as attracting television and radio coverage, launching new products to the press, responding to unfavorable media coverage, writing management speeches, ensuring attendance at special events, creating press kits, and managing public relations projects.

Part of this handbook's appeal is the practical examples relevant to today's public relations. Relatively little attention is paid to more anachronistic practices, such as arranging plant tours and preparing floats for the holiday parade. Whether writing for print or broadcast purposes, *The Public Relations Writer's Handbook* is a most useful guide for any professional.

Success in Newsletter Publishing and Hotline. Newsletter Association (1341 G. St., NW, Washington, DC 20007). Biweekly.

Thomsett, Michael C. *The Little Black Book of Business Words.* New York: AMACOM, 1991.

Tucker, Kerry, Doris Derelian, and Donna Rouner. *Public Relations Writing: An Issue Driven Behavioral Approach,* 3rd ed. Upper Saddle River, NJ: Prentice Hall, 1997.

Wilcox, Dennis L., and Lawrence W. Nolte. *Public Relations Writing and Media Techniques.* New York: Harper College Press, 1990.

Williams, Patrick. *How to Create Winning Employee Publications.* Bartlesville, OK: Joe Williams Communications, 1990.

Yale, David R. *The Publicity Handbook: How to Maximize Publicity for Products, Services and Organizations.* Lincolnwood, IL: NTC Publishing Group, 1991.

CASE STUDY

THE RAINA NEWS RELEASE

Background: The Raina, Inc., Carborundum plant in Blackrock, Iowa, has been under pressure in recent months to remedy its pollution problem. Raina's plant is the largest in Blackrock, and even though the company has spent $1.3 million on improving its pollution-control equipment, black smoke still spews from the plant's smokestacks, and waste products are still allowed to filter into neighboring streams. Lately, the pressure on Raina has been intense.

- On September 7, J. J. Kelinson, a private citizen, called to complain about the "noxious smoke" fouling the environment.
- On September 8, Mrs. Janet Greenberg of the Blackrock Garden Club called to protest the "smoke problem" that was destroying the zinnias and other flowers in the area.
- On September 9, Clarence "Smoky" Salmon, president of the Blackrock Rod and Gun Club, called to report that 700 people had signed a petition against the Raina plant's pollution of Zeus Creek.
- On September 10, WERS Radio editorialized that "the time has come to force area plants to act on solving pollution problems."
- On September 11, the Blackrock City Council announced plans to enact an air and water pollution ordinance for the city. The council invited as its first witness before the public hearing Leslie Sludge, manager of the Raina Carborundum Blackrock plant.

News Release Data
1. Leslie Sludge, manager of Raina's Carborundum Blackrock plant, appeared at the Blackrock City Council hearing on September 11.
2. Sludge said Raina had already spent $1.3 million on a program to clean up pollution at its Blackrock plant.
3. Raina received 500 complaint calls in the past three months protesting its pollution conditions.
4. Sludge said Raina was "concerned about environmental problems, but profits are still what keeps our company running."
5. Sludge announced that the company had decided to commit another $2 million for pollution-abatement facilities over the next three months.
6. Raina is the oldest plant in Blackrock and was built in 1900.
7. Raina's Blackrock plant employs 10,000 people, the largest single employer in Blackrock.
8. Raina originally planned to delay its pollution-abatement program but speeded it up because of public pressure in recent months.
9. Sludge said that the new pollution-abatement program would begin in October and that the company projected "real progress in terms of clean water and clean air" as early as two years from today.
10. Five years ago, Raina, Inc., received a Presidential Award from the Environmental Protection Agency for its "concern for pollution abatement."
11. An internal Raina study indicated that Blackrock was the "most pollutant laden" of all Raina's plants nationwide.
12. Sludge formerly served as manager of Raina's Fetid Reservoir plant in Fetid Reservoir, New Hampshire. In two years as manager of Fetid Reservoir, Sludge was able to convert it from one of the most pollutant-laden plants in the system to the cleanest, as judged by the Environmental Protection Agency.
13. Sludge has been manager of Blackrock for two months.
14. Raina's new program will cost the company $2 million.
15. Raina will hire 100 extra workers especially for the pollution-abatement program.
16. Sludge, 35, is married to the former Polly Usion of Wheeling, West Virginia.
17. Sludge is author of the book *Fly Fishing Made Easy.*

18. The bulk of the money budgeted for the new pollution-abatement program will be spent on two globe refractors, which purify waste destined to be deposited in surrounding waterways, and four hyperventilation systems, which remove noxious particles dispersed into the air from smokestacks.

19. Sludge said, "Raina, Inc., has decided to move ahead with this program at this time because of its long-standing responsibility for keeping the Blackrock environment clean and in response to growing community concern over achieving the objective."

20. Former Blackrock plant manager Fowler Aire was fired by the company in July for his "flagrant disregard for the environment."

21. Aire also was found to be diverting Raina funds from company projects to his own pockets. In all, Aire took close to $10,000, for which the company was not reimbursed. At least part of the money was to be used for pollution control.

22. Aire, whose whereabouts are presently not known, is the brother of J. Derry Aire, Raina's vice president for finance.

23. Raina's Blackrock plant has also recently installed ramps and other special apparatus to assist handicapped employees. Presently, 100 handicapped workers are employed in the Raina Blackrock plant.

24. Raina's Blackrock plant started as a converted garage, manufacturing plate glass. Only 13 people worked in the plant at that time.

25. Today the Blackrock plant employs 10,000, covers 14 acres of land, and is the largest single supplier of plate glass and commercial panes in the country.

26. The Blackrock plant was slated to be the subject of a critical report from the Private Environmental Stabilization Taskforce (PEST), a private environmental group. PEST's report, "The Foulers," was to discuss "the 10 largest manufacturing polluters in the nation."

27. Raina management has been aware of the PEST report for several months.

QUESTIONS

1. If you were assigned to draft a news release to accompany Sludge to the Blackrock City Council meeting on September 11, which items would you use in your lead (i.e., who, what, why, where, when, how)?

2. Which items would you avoid using in the news release?

3. If a reporter from the *Blackrock Bugle* called and wanted to know what happened to former Blackrock manager Fowler Aire, what would you tell him?

WILLIAM C. ADAMS

William C. Adams is an associate professor in the School of Journalism and Mass Communication at Florida International University. Prior to joining FIU in 1990, Adams spent 25 years in corporate public relations, including management positions with Amoco Corporation, Phillips Petroleum Company, and ICI Americas. He has written and lectured extensively on all facets of organizational communications.

HOW IMPORTANT IS WRITING IN PUBLIC RELATIONS?

Good writing is the essence of public relations. It's the lifeblood of our profession and is often what sets us apart from others in the organizations we serve. It's also a balancing act. By "good," I'm referring to well-thought-out, grammatically correct, targeted, purposeful, and effective writing. Writing to communicate effectively both inside and outside the organization is the most critical thing a student can learn when studying the many elements of public relations.

By "balancing act," I mean that public relations writers are both translators and interpreters of concepts and ideas, while also being the organization's advocates/persuaders. It's skillfully achieving that fine balance between news and advocacy that gets your writing looked at and read by internal and external audiences alike.

WHAT'S THE QUALITY OF TODAY'S PUBLIC RELATIONS WRITING?

Unfortunately, much of it is not very good. And what is good—or even passable—is often mundane and perfunctory, devoid of even a whiff of humor or cleverness. News releases, for example, too often miss their target audiences, are loaded with jargon and legalese, aren't newsy and interesting, or offer nothing but hype. Many simply are not well written. (Ask any journalist.)

The same goes for other public relations communications tools, such as newsletters, brochures, memos, and even letters. I see too much sloppiness in sentence construction, a lack of smooth-flowing transition between paragraphs and thoughts, and an overall carelessness in editing and proofing (and don't blame Spell-Check!).

ARE NEWS RELEASES STILL WORTHWHILE?

It depends upon whom you ask. Some reporters and editors claim never to use news releases, while others find them indispensable for covering their beats. The trick, much like targeting audiences you wish to reach with your communications program, is to find out who prefers what. For example, one writer on a specific beat may prefer "fact sheets" or even a phone call, while another wants news releases.

Research has shown that the reasons most releases don't get used is because they have poor-quality writing, are full of hype, or are not newsy enough. A well-prepared, professional-appearing, and targeted release has an excellent chance of being used—or at least getting the reporter's or editor's attention. A daily newspaper columnist once told one of my public relations writing classes not to "bother him" with "junk mail" (news releases) when they went out into the "real world." They were stunned until a reporter from that same newspaper followed by saying, "Don't believe him . . . he couldn't write his column without help from public relations people and their news releases."

So What's the Key to Writing an Effective News Release?

You and the reporters and editors should ask basically the same questions: "Is it news?" "Is it timely?" "Is it localized?" The newsperson asks a critical fourth question: "Is it important to my readers/listeners/viewers?" If the answer to all four of the questions is "yes," there's an excellent chance that your release will be used, or at least provide a basis from which a reporter will call you for further information.

Also important as a "use factor" is a well-crafted informational lead and the overall quality of the release itself, which includes grammar, punctuation, sentence structure, and style—free from jargon and hype.

What's the Secret to Effective Public Relations Writing?

Clarity and conciseness are the keys to successful public relations writing (correct grammar goes without saying). You also must be able to grab a journalist's attention with a newsy and interesting opening statement (it is a "pitch," after all), followed with a reason that reporter should be interested in your story idea.

Does Writing Remain Important Throughout a Public Relations Career?

The answer is a solid "yes." Even at the managerial level, writing remains a crucial part of the public relations profile.

First of all, to get to that level of success, public relations managers generally move through the "technician" stage, wherein they hone their communication skills, increasing their value to the organization.

Writing well is an art, however, and often scares young people just entering the profession. For example, once after speaking to a group of students, I was approached by a potential public relations major who asked, timidly: "If I go into PR, do I have to do all that writing stuff?" The answer remains "yes."

CHAPTER NINE

Writing for the Eye and Ear

WRITING FOR READING EMPHASIZES THE WRITTEN WORD. Writing for listening emphasizes the spoken word. The two differ significantly. Writing for the eye traditionally has ranked among the strongest areas for public relations professionals. Years ago, most practitioners entered public relations through print journalism. Accordingly, they were schooled in the techniques of writing for the eye, not the ear. Today, of course, a background in print journalism is not necessarily a prerequisite for public relations work. Just as important today is writing for the ear—writing for listening. The key to such writing is to write as if you are speaking. Use simple, short sentences, active verbs, contractions, and one- and two-syllable words. In brief, be brief.

This chapter will focus on two things: First, the most frequently used communication vehicles designed for the eye, beyond the news release; and second, the most widely used methods for communicating through the ear, particularly speeches and presentations. Communicating via computer will be the focus of chapter 10 and through the medium of video, the focus of chapter 11.

Today's public relations professional must be conversant in writing for both the eye and the ear.

THE MEDIA KIT

Beyond the news release, the most ubiquitous print vehicle in public relations work is the media or press kit. Press kits incorporate several communications vehicles for potential use by newspapers and magazines. A bare-bones media kit consists of a news release, backgrounder, biography, photo, often today a CD-ROM and perhaps one or two other items. The kit is designed to answer all of the most likely questions that the media might ask about the organization's announcement. The kit is designed to be all the media need to understand and portray an announcement.

Media kits may also require fact sheets or Q & A (question-and-answer) sheets. The public relations professional must weigh carefully how much information is required in the media kit. Journalists don't appreciate being overwhelmed by too much copy and too many photos.

In preparing a media kit, public relations professionals must keep the following points in mind:

- Be sure the information is accurate and thorough and will answer a journalist's most fundamental questions.
- Provide sufficient background information material to allow the editor to select a story angle.
- Don't be too commercial. Offer balanced, objective information.
- Confine opinions and value judgments to quotes from credible sources.
- Never lie. That's tantamount to editorial suicide.
- Visually arresting graphics may mean the difference between finding the item in the next day's paper or in the same day's wastebasket.

Figure 9–1 shows the press kit used to launch the nationwide tour of one of our country's "most critical natural resources," the California Raisins.

THE BIOGRAPHY

Next to the news release, the most popular tool is the biography, often called the biographical summary or just plain bio. The bio recounts pertinent facts about a particular individual. Most organizations keep a file of bios covering all top officers. Major newspapers and wire services prepare standby bios on well-known people for immediate use on breaking news, such as sudden deaths.

Straight Bios

The straight bio lists factual information in a straightforward fashion in descending order of importance, with company-oriented facts preceding more personal details. For example, the straight biography of international business philanthropist David Rockefeller might begin this way:

> David Rockefeller, an international businessman and philanthropist, became chairman of the board of directors and chief executive officer of the Chase Manhattan Bank, N.A. in New York on March 1, 1969, and of the Chase Manhattan Corporation upon its formation on June 4, 1969.
>
> During his career with Chase Manhattan, Rockefeller gained a worldwide reputation as a leading banker and spokesman for the business community. He spearheaded the bank's expansion both internationally and throughout the metropolitan New York area and helped the bank play a significant role as a corporate citizen.
>
> Rockefeller joined the Chase National Bank as an assistant manager in the foreign department in 1946. He was appointed an assistant cashier in 1947, second vice president in 1948, and vice president in 1949.

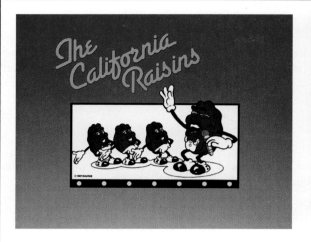

news from the grapevine...

FROM: KETCHUM PUBLIC RELATIONS
55 Union Street
San Francisco, CA 94111
Hilary Hanson
(415) 984-6385
David Emanuel
(415) 984-6326

FOR IMMEDIATE RELEASE

CELEBRATED CALIFORNIA DANCING RAISINS HIT THE ROAD THIS SUMMER
ON ACTION-PACKED SUMMER VACATION

FRESNO, Calif. -- Guess who's packing their bags for a summer vacation across America?

Rumor has it through the grapevine that it's not Chevy Chase filming a new sequel. . .It's the California Dancing Raisins -- those entertaining characters who have captured the hearts of Americans and become celebrities overnight since their top-rated commercials began airing two years ago. The Raisins are planning a whirlwind 6,500-mile road trip stopping in 27 U.S. cities this summer to visit America's favorite landmarks, receive keys to major cities, inform fans of their new national fan club and entertain young and old alike with their famous Grapevine dance.

(more)

55 Union Street • San Francisco, CA 94111

---

news from the grapevine...

FACT SHEET
CALIFORNIA RAISIN ADVISORY BOARD

The Ad Campaign

- The California Dancing Raisin campaign was voted the most popular television commercial in 1987 by consumers, according to research by Video Storyboard Tests, Inc.

- Three Claymation raisin commercials have been produced since 1986: "Lunch Box," "Late Show" and "Playing With Your Food." A fourth television ad will premiere this fall, airing nationwide beginning in October, starring Ray Charles and a hip new cast of Claymation Raisins.

- A 30-second commercial featuring the Claymation Raisin characters takes an average of three months to produce; it takes one full day of work to create one second of footage. Claymation is the process of creating animation with clay. Produced by Will Vinton, Claymation requires 25 frames of film or individual pictures to create one second of a commercial.

The Raisin Industry

- Approximately 350,000 tons of raisins are produced annually, generating $400 million dollars in sales.

- The California Raisin Advisory Board (CALRAB) represents the U.S. raisin industry, which is composed of 23 raisin packers and more than 5,000 raisin growers in the San Joaquin Valley.

- The California Raisin industry produces virtually the entire domestic supply and almost one-third of the world's supply of raisins.

- Raisins are harvested in late August. Skilled farm workers carefully hand-pick the grapes and place them on clean paper trays in the fields between the rows of vines. They are allowed to dry naturally for days in the sun. After about three weeks of exposure, the grapes become delicious and nutritious juicy raisins.

(more)

55 Union Street • San Francisco, CA 94111

Figure 9–1 When the California Raisin Advisory Board wanted to promote its product across the country, it launched a nationwide tour of the beloved California Raisins, announced via this media kit.

From 1950 to 1952, he was responsible for the supervision of Chase's business in Latin America, where, under his direction, new branches were opened in Cuba, Panama, and Puerto Rico, plus a representative office in Buenos Aires.

On the other hand, each individual organization with which Mr. Rockefeller is involved might adapt his biography a bit differently, to emphasize its own relationship with him (Figure 9–2).

Narrative Bios

The narrative bio, on the other hand, is written in a breezier, more informal way. This style gives spark and vitality to the biography to make the individual come alive.

David Rockefeller, who has been described as a man possessed of "a peculiar blend of enterprise, prudence, knowledge, and dedication," is the world's premier business statesman.

THE ROCKEFELLER UNIVERSITY
1230 YORK AVENUE   NEW YORK, NEW YORK 10021-6399
(212) 327-8080   FAX (212) 327-8900

OFFICE OF THE PRESIDENT

David Rockefeller

Mr. David Rockefeller, Chairman of the Chase Manhattan Bank's International Advisory Committee, became Executive Committee Chairman of The Rockefeller University Board of Trustees in 1975, after serving first as member of the board (1940 to 1950), president then chairman of the board (1950 to 1975).

A graduate of Harvard University (B.S., 1936) and University of Chicago (Ph.D. in economics, 1940), Mr. Rockefeller served as an intelligence officer in North Africa and Southern France, and was an assistant military attaché in Paris at the time he was demobilized as captain in 1945. One year later, Mr. Rockefeller joined the former Chase National Bank as assistant manager in the foreign department, and subsequently became vice president (1949); senior vice president (1952); executive vice president (1955); vice chairman of the board of directors (1957); and president and chairman of the executive committee of the board of directors (1961). He retired as chairman in 1981.

Mr. Rockefeller, whose grandfather, John D. Rockefeller, founded The Rockefeller Institute for Medical Research, is involved in many business activities and not-for-profit organizations spanning a broad range of international, governmental, civic and cultural issues. He served as chairman of the Council of Foreign Relations from 1970 to 1985 and continues to be an active member. In addition, he was instrumental in creating the International Executive Service Corps and helped to found the Trilateral Commission in 1973. Mr. Rockefeller is chairman of the Americas Society and its affiliate, the Council of the Americas. In addition, he is Chairman Emeritus of the Museum of Modern Art, where he has served as a trustee since 1948, and as Chairman from 1962 to 1972 and 1987 to 1993.

Figure 9–2   Both straight and narrative biographies are adapted to fit the particular organization issuing them. In this case, David Rockefeller's role with The Rockefeller University takes prominence.

His mother was the former Abby Aldrich, daughter of Senator Nelson Aldrich of Rhode Island. She had met John D. Rockefeller Jr., the shy son of multimillionaire John D. Rockefeller, when he was an undergraduate at Brown University in Providence.

John D. Rockefeller Jr. was anxious that his children not be spoiled by the fortune his father had created and therefore put them on strict allowances. The household atmosphere was deeply religious, with one of the children reading the scriptures each morning before breakfast. Mrs. Rockefeller was an exceptional woman, with a strong interest in the arts. She and David were very close.

The narrative bio, in addition to bringing to life the individual discussed, doubles as a speech of introduction when the individual described serves as a featured speaker. In effect, the narrative bio becomes a speech.

THE BACKGROUNDER

Background pieces, or backgrounders, provide additional information to complement the shorter news release. Backgrounders can embellish the announcement, or can discuss the institution making the announcement, the system behind the announcement, or any other appropriate topic that will assist a journalist in writing the story (Figure 9–3).

Backgrounders are longer and more general in content than the news release. For example, a two-page release announcing the merger of two organizations may not permit much description of the companies involved. A four- or five-page backgrounder provides editors with more depth on the makeup, activities, and history of the merging firms. Backgrounders are usually not used in their entirety by the media but are excerpted.

Subject matter dictates backgrounder style. Some backgrounders are written like a news release, in a snappy and factual manner. Others take a more descriptive and narrative form.

Example One: News Release Style

BACKGROUNDER—SWENSEN'S ICE CREAM COMPANY

The original Swensen's Ice Cream Shoppe was established in 1948 by Earle Swensen at the corner of Union and Hyde in San Francisco.

In 1963 Mr. Swensen licensed the company's predecessor, See Us-Freeze, Inc., later known as United Outlets, Inc., to use Swensen's trade names, trade secrets, recipes, and methods of operation as the basis for Swensen's franchise system. The license agreement was modified in June 1975 and permits the company to use the licensed property and franchise Swensen's shops in all areas of the world except the city and county of San Francisco.

Example Two: Descriptive, Narrative Style

BACKGROUNDER—SICKLE CELL DISEASE

The man was a West Indian black, a twenty-year-old student in a professional school in Illinois. One day in 1904, he came to James B. Herrick, an eminent Chicago cardiologist, with symptoms Herrick had never seen before and could not find in the literature. The patient had shortness of breath, a disinclination for exercise, palpitation, jaundice, cough,

Life Savers 'Round America Tour

CONTACT: Chuck Wallington
Planters LifeSavers Co.
919/741-7671

Sari Seiken
Burson-Marsteller
212/614-4021

A LIFELONG HERITAGE: LIFESAVERS® CANDIES

In 1912, candy maker Clarence Crane was searching for a sweet that could withstand the Cleveland, Ohio, summer heat better than his chocolates could. His answer was hard candy mints.

At that time, mints were primarily sold in Europe -- in square, pillow shapes. To set himself apart, Crane created a circular mint with a hole in the middle. Since it looked like a miniature life preserver, Crane named his product Life Savers® and registered the trademark.

A Peppermint Product

Tying into the life preserver idea, the original campaign for the new peppermint candies was "For That Stormy Breath." After a near capsize (caused by packaging problems), a New York advertising man bought the product and set the company for smooth sailing. Within a few years, the Mint Products Company had made a quarter million dollars.

- more -

Life Savers Heritage/page 2 of 2

World War I put a temporary freeze on production and expansion but, a year after the war ended, mint sales increased more than 200 percent. In 1920, Wint-O-Green was introduced, to be followed by three other mint flavors.

In 1924, the company created fruit flavored drops, consisting of sugar syrups and flavor essences. Flavors included Lemon, Orange and Lime. Over the years, approximately 40 flavors have been launched, discontinued or revived according to consumer preference.

Today, all Life Savers candies are made in Holland, Michigan. The plant produced 568 million rolls of Life Savers in 1991 and expects to make 644 million rolls this year.

Company Expansion

Life Savers candies are made and marketed by the LifeSavers Division of the Nabisco Foods Group. With headquarters in Winston-Salem, N.C., the division's well-known brands include Life Savers® hard-roll candy, Life Savers® Holes, Bubble Yum®, Care*Free® and Fruit Stripe® gums.

# # #

Figure 9–3 This backgrounder accompanied the 80th birthday of Life Savers candies. It is written in a breezier, narrative style, to coincide with the subject matter—Laughin' Lemon, Outlandish Orange, Perky Pineapple, Looney Lime, and Wacky Wild Cherry.

dizziness, headache, leg ulcers, scars from old leg ulcers, many palpable lymph nodes, pale mucous membranes, muscular rheumatism, severe upper abdominal pain, dark urine, and anemia. Blood smears showed many odd-shaped cells, but what arrested the eye was the presence of numerous sickle-shaped cells.

Herrick kept the patient under observation for many years. He did not suspect that he was looking at a disease that afflicted millions of people, including thousands of blacks in America.

In devising a backgrounder, a writer enjoys unlimited latitude. As long as the piece catches the interest of the reader/editor, any style is permissible.

THE FEATURE

Closely related to the backgrounder is the feature story. Features in magazines or newspapers are the opposite of news items. They're often light and humorous. One of the foremost sources of feature writing is *The Wall Street Journal.* Each business day the *Journal's* front page is dominated by three "leader" articles, most written in a time-tested feature-writing style. Basically, the *Journal* system separates each story into three distinct parts, sometimes labeled the *D-E-E system* (description, explanation, evaluation).

Description

The typical *Journal* story begins by describing an existing situation, often with a light touch, in such a way that readers are drawn directly into the story.

In Texas on business last week, Susan Binion took a day off and drove with her sister-in-law to South Padre Island to relax. As the car got closer to the island's famed beaches, relaxation receded. "Guys started hanging out their car windows hollering stuff at us," says Ms. Binion, a 37-year-old mother of three. "I looked at my sister-in-law and said, 'I wonder if this is spring break.'"[1]

Explanation

The second part of the *Journal* feature explains how a situation, trend, or event came to be. It is often historical in nature, citing dates, places, and people from the past. It often relates how other factors (economic, sociopolitical, or environmental) may have come to bear on the topic.

In the dark ages before MTV, spring break was confined to only a few resort areas such as Fort Lauderdale, Fla. Indeed, for many collegians, Fort Lauderdale was synonymous with spring break—an association that the city grew to view as a tourist detraction. To erase its image as party central, the city some years ago enacted strict drinking laws and tough enforcement. Other spring-break towns followed, forcing the college scene to disperse.[2]

Evaluation

The final section of the *Journal* feature evaluates the meaning of what is contained in the first two parts. It often focuses on the future, frequently quoting sociologists, psychologists, or other experts on what is likely to happen to the subject discussed or the larger societal meaning.

> A spokesman for the city's convention bureau insists Clearwater isn't a spring-break site—but John Feeney is one of many regular tourists who begs to differ. "There's not much beach and a lot of bodies," says Mr. Feeney, 40, who visits his in-laws there once a year. But he makes the best of things: He has taught his teenage son to suck in his gut as he walks past the coeds; as for himself, he says, "It's really exciting to be reliving the old days, even though you don't look like a college student anymore."[3]

In public relations the D-E-E approach often works in feature writing assignments.

THE CASE HISTORY

The case history is frequently used to tell about a customer's favorable use of a company's product or service. Generally, the case history writer works for the company whose product or service is involved. Magazines, particularly trade journals, often welcome case histories, contending that one person's experience may be instructive to another.

Case history articles generally follow a five-part formula:

1. They present a problem experienced by one company but applicable to many other firms.
2. They indicate how the dimensions of the problem were defined by the company using the product.
3. They indicate the solution adopted.
4. They explain the advantages of the adopted solution.
5. They detail the user company's experience after adopting the solution.

Incorporating the D-E-E approach into the case-history writing process may interest an editor in a particular product or service. Done skillfully, such a case history is soft sell at its best—beneficial to the company and interesting and informative to the editor and readers.

THE BYLINER

The bylined article, or byliner, is a story signed and ostensibly authored by an officer of a particular firm. Often, however, the byliner is ghostwritten by a public relations professional. In addition to carrying considerable prestige in certain publications, byliners allow corporate spokespeople to express their views without being subject to major reinterpretation by the publication.

Perhaps the major advantage of a byliner is that it positions executives as experts. The fact that an organization's officer has authored an informed article on a subject means that not only are the officer and the organization credible sources, but also, by inference, that they are perhaps more highly regarded on the issues at hand than their competitors. Indeed, the ultimate audience exposed to a byliner may greatly exceed the circulation of the periodical in which the article appears. Organizations regularly use byliner reprints as direct mail pieces to enhance their image with key constituent groups.

THE MEMORANDUM

Humorist Art Buchwald tells of the child who visited his father's office. When asked what his dad did, the son replied, "He sends pieces of paper to other people, and other people send pieces of paper to him." Most people who work know a great deal about memoranda. In many organizations, the memo is the most popular form of communication. Memos are written for a multitude of purposes and take numerous forms. Even though almost everyone gets into the memo-writing act, writing memos correctly takes practice and hard work.

The key to writing good memos is clear thinking. Many memos reflect unclear thinking and are plagued by verbosity and fuzzy language. Inverted pyramid style is often a good way to compose a memo. More often, rewriting turns out to be the key.

Public relations people are expected to write good memos. This is no easy feat. The key is to keep in mind the six primary elements of a meaningful memo:

1. **State the issue.**   Don't dilly dally. Memos don't require preambles. Get right to the issue at hand.
2. **Back it up with data.**   Put the issue into a clear, snappy context so that the recipient understands your thought processes.
3. **Present alternatives.**   List all the possibilities that must be considered before rendering a decision. Again, brevity is a virtue.
4. **Offer your solution/recommendation.**   Be decisive. Stick your neck out. Suggest a clear course of action.
5. **Back it up with detail.**   Explain, again briefly, why you believe the action you've recommended is justifiable.
6. **Call for the question.**   Always end with a question that demands action.

Don't leave things up in the air. Too often, memos end by drifting into space. Avoid this. Make the recipient get back to you by asking a question to which he or she must respond, such as "Do you agree with this?" or "Can we move on this?"[4]

THE PITCH LETTER

The pitch letter is a sales letter, pure and simple. Its purpose is to interest an editor or reporter in a possible story, interview, or event. Figure 9–4 offers an example of two excellent pitch letters for the same product. Although letter styles run the gamut, the best are direct and to the point, while being catchy and evocative.

Some have questioned the utility of the pitch letter, replacing it with a straightforward "media alert" format to grab the attention of editors and news directors. The new format eschews the use of long paragraphs in favor of short, bulleted items highlighting the "5W's" used by journalists: who, what, when, where, and why. The premise of the media alert is that it "talks to the media in a language it has been trained to accept."[5]

Such criticism notwithstanding, a good pitch letter—especially one with a provocative lead—can hit a reader right between the eyes. For example, Father Bruce Ritter, the founder of New York's Covenant House, who moved to Australia after being accused of financial mismanagement and sexual improprieties, nonetheless was the master of the legendary pitch letter. One of Father Bruce's most famous pitch letters began this way:

Please read what I have to tell you.
Children are being sold.

National Lampoon

This Is Your Last Chance . . .

Say good-bye, sweetheart. This is it! You can kiss the $7.95 one-year subscription to the *National Lampoon* good-bye just as you've said *au revoir* and *harry verderchi* to the fifty-cent gallon of gas, the ten-cent cigar, and the twenty-cent bus ride.

The price is going up and we're giving you fair warning. We're not saying exactly how much we're going to charge for the new one-year subscription but — it's less than the gross national product of Yugoslavia and more than a rubdown in a midget massage parlor.

The reasons for the increase in price are numerous in addition to greed:

1. The cost of paper has skyrocketed. All right, let's examine that. What does it mean to a magazine operation? Well, our editors drink a lot of coffee and this means an increase in the price of coffee cups. They throw paper airplanes around the room while trying to think of funny things to say. Up your cost of paper airplanes by 50 percent.

2. The cost of typewriters has increased. This doesn't affect us since no one on our staff knows how to type.

3. The cost of manufacturing has increased. This means that our editor in chief will be paying more for his Mercedes-Benz this year, and that means more for you to kick in. Would you ask the editor in chief of the world's most widely read adult humor magazine to drive around in last year's Mercedes-Benz?

4. The price of grain is spiraling. (We don't know what that means, but it is an exact quote from the *Wall Street Journal* so it must be important.)

O.K., put this all together and it means — raise the subscription prices. No more $7.95. So, this is it. This is your last chance. From here on in, it's clipsville. You pay more.

If you really want to save, take out a two- or three-year subscription. The savings are so big that we actually lose money every time you or anyone else subscribes for two or three years. We do it only because our subscription manager is insecure and he wants to know that he'll have at least a handful of people around for a long time.

No more message. If you want the latest in yocks, mirth, and lovable satire, subscribe today and subscribe at these pre-inflation prices.

Sincerely,

Herbert Hoover
Herbert Hoover
Subscription Manager

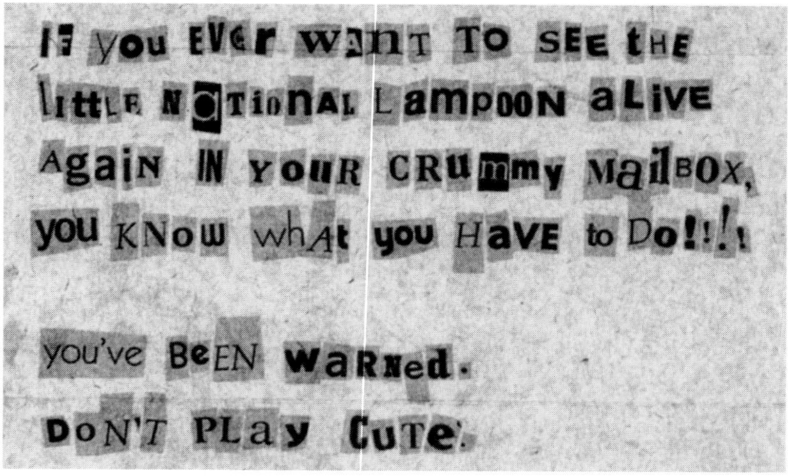

Figure 9–4 This letter from the subscription department of the *National Lampoon* magazine may not be a "public relations pitch letter" per se, but it is exactly the kind of enticing, catchy and evocative letter necessary to capture the interest of a prospect.

Their bodies and spirits are being corrupted.
They are forced into a life of abuse and degradation.
Where?
India? Uganda? Peru?
No!
Right here in New York, the Big Apple, Fun City.
Covenant House began as a response to the needs of these children of the streets. Will you join with me in helping to carry out this work?

Such unbridled, heart-tugging language is typical of a good, compassionate pitch letter.

Pitch letters that sell generally contain several key elements. First, they open with a grabber, an interesting statement that impels the reader to read on. Next, they explain why the editor and/or publication should be interested in the pitch, or invitation. Finally, they are personally written to specific people, rather than being addressed to "editor" (which is the journalistic equivalent of "occupant").

OTHER TOOLS

Other public relations tools, such as the round-up article, the fact sheet, and the Q & A, may be helpful in certain infrequent situations.

The Round-Up Article

Although many publications discourage publicity about a single company, they encourage articles that summarize, or round-up, the experiences of several companies within an industry. These trend articles may be initiated by the publications themselves or at the suggestions of public relations people. Weaker or smaller companies, in particular, can benefit from being included in a round-up story with stronger, larger adversaries. Thoroughly researching and drafting round-up articles is a good way to secure articles that mention the practitioner's firm in favorable association with top competitors. *The Wall Street Journal* and *USA Today*, in particular, are regular users of round-ups.

The Fact Sheet

Fact sheets are short documents that compactly profile an organization. They generally support the information in news releases and backgrounders. Editors find fact sheets helpful as a quick supply of resource material for articles. Fact sheets are designed to provide an editor with a quick thumbnail sketch of an organization, individual, or event. For example, a typical one-page corporate fact sheet includes a brief description of the company and its product lines, the names of its top managers, its location, current sales figures, leading products, and a summary of its history. How is all this possible in a one-page sketch? Figure 9–5 shows how.

Figure 9–5 Another variation on the fact sheet theme is this submission by Pillsbury in recognition of its Dough Boy's 25th birthday.

The Q & A

The question-and-answer form, or Q & A, often substitutes for or complements a fact sheet in conveying easy-to-follow information. In the Q & A, the writer lists frequently asked questions about the subject and then provides appropriate answers. A skillfully written Q & A can often substitute for a personal interview between an editor and a company official.

PHOTOGRAPHIC SUPPORTS

Photos or artistic renderings, when used properly, enhance brochures, annual reports, and even news releases. Any practitioner involved with printed material should know the basics of photography. Although a detailed discussion of photographic terms and techniques is beyond the scope of this book, public relations practitioners should be relatively conversant with photographic terminology and able to recognize the attributes of good photos:

1. Photos should be taken "live," in real environments with believable people, instead of in studios with stilted models.
2. They should focus clearly on the issue, product, image, or person that the organization wishes to emphasize, without irrelevant, visually distracting clutter in the foreground or background.
3. They should be eye-catching, using angles creatively—overhead, below, to the side—to suggest movement.
4. They must express a viewpoint—an underlying message.
5. Most of all, photos must make a visual impact. The best photos are those that remain in a person's mind long after written appeals to action have faded. These are the photos that are "worth 10,000 words."[6]

THE POSITION PAPER

Another writing vehicle public relations people are frequently called on to write is the "position paper," also called the "white paper." Position papers are longer documents, written primarily for internal background purposes, which rigorously document the facts and assumptions that lead to a particular "position" that the organization is suggested to take. Such documents form the basis of review and discussion and ultimately serve as the nucleus for a corporate position. After such a position is ratified by management, a "sanitized" position paper may be made available for distribution to opinion leaders and the general public.

THE STANDBY STATEMENT

Organizations sometimes take actions or make announcements they know will lead to media inquiries or even public protests. In such cases, firms prepare concise statements to clarify their positions, should they be called to explain. Such standby statements generally are defensive. They should be brief and unambiguous so as not to raise more questions than they answer. Such events as executive firings, layoffs, price increases, and extraordinary losses are all subject to subsequent scrutiny by the media and are therefore proper candidates for standby statements.

THE SPEECH

Speechwriting has become one of the most coveted public relations skills. Increasingly, speechwriters have used their access to management to move up the organizational ladder. The prominence they enjoy is due largely to the importance top executives place on

---

THE REST OF THE STORY

DON'T—REPEAT—DON'T USE "DO NOT"

In writing standby statements, public relations practitioners should keep in mind that publications sometimes mistakenly drop words in print. Invariably, the most important words are the ones dropped.

For example, the public relations officer of the labor union who issues the statement "We do not intend to strike" may have his quote appear in the next day's paper as "We do intend to strike"—the *not* having been inadvertently dropped by the paper. A slight yet significant change.

The remedy: Use contractions. It's pretty hard to drop a significant word or distort the intended meaning when the statement is "We don't intend to strike."

---

making speeches. Today's executives are called on by government and special-interest groups to defend their policies, justify their prices, and explain their practices to a much greater degree than ever before. In this environment, a good speech writer becomes a valuable—and often highly paid—asset.

A speech possess five main characteristics:

1. **It is designed to be heard, not read.**   The mistake of writing for the eye instead of the ear is the most common trap of bad speeches. Speeches needn't be literary gems, but they ought to sound good.
2. **It uses concrete language.**   The ear dislikes generalities. It responds to clear images. Ideas must be expressed sharply for the audience to get the point.
3. **It demands a positive response.**   Every word, every passage, every phrase should evoke a response from the audience. The speech should possess special vitality—and so, for that matter, should the speaker.
4. **It must have clear-cut objectives.**   The speech and the speaker must have a point—a thesis. If there's no point, then it's not worth the speaker's or the audience's time to be there.
5. **It must be tailored to a specific audience.**   An audience needs to feel that it is hearing something special. The most frequent complaint about organizational speeches is that they all seem interchangeable—they lack uniqueness. That's why speeches must be targeted to fit the needs of a specific audience. Beyond adhering to these five principles and before putting words on paper, a speechwriter must have a clear idea of the process—the route—to follow in developing the speech.

THE SPEECHWRITING PROCESS

The speechwriting process breaks down into four components: (1) preparing, (2) interviewing, (3) researching, and (4) organizing and writing.

Preparing

One easy way to prepare for a speech is to follow a 4W checklist. In other words, answer the questions who, what, where, and when.

- **Who**—The who represents two critical elements: the speaker and the audience. A writer should know all about the speaker: manner of speech, use of humor, reaction to an audience, background, and personality. It's almost impossible to write a speech for someone you don't know.

    The writer should also know something about the audience. What does this audience think about this subject? What are its predispositions toward the subject and the speaker? What are the major points with which it might agree? The more familiar the writer is with the who of a speech, the easier the writing will be.
- **What**—The what is the topic. The assigned subject must be clearly known and well-defined by the writer before formal research is begun. If the writer fails to delineate the subject in advance, much of the research will be pointless.
- **Where**—The where is the setting. A large hall requires a more formal talk than a roundtable forum. Often, the location of the speech—the city, state, or even a particular hall—bears historic or symbolic significance that can enhance a message.
- **When**—The when is the time of the speech. People are more awake in the morning and get sleepier as the day progresses, so a dinner speech should be kept short. The when also refers to the time of year. A speech can always be linked to an upcoming holiday or special celebration.

Interviewing

Interviewing speakers in advance is essential. Without that chance, the results can be dismal. A good interview with a speaker often means the difference between a strong speech and a poor one. Stated another way, the speechwriter is only as good as his or her access to the speaker.

In the interview the speechwriter gets some time—from as little as 15 minutes to over an hour—to observe the speaker firsthand and probe for the keys to the speech. The interview must accomplish at least three specific goals for the speech writer:

1. **Determine the object of the talk**—The object is different from the subject. The subject is the topic, but the object is the purpose of the speech—that is, what exactly the speaker wants the audience to do after he or she is finished speaking. Does the speaker want them to storm City Hall? To love big business? To write their congressional representatives? The interviewer's essential question must be "What do you want to leave the audience with at the conclusion of your speech?" Once the speaker answers this question, the rest of the speech should fall into place.
2. **Determine the speaker's main points**—Normally, an audience can grasp only a few points during a speech. These points, which should flow directly from the object, become touchstones around which the rest of the speech is woven. Again, the writer must determine the three or four main points during the interview.
3. **Capture the speaker's characteristics**—Most of all, during the interview, the writer must observe the speaker. How comfortable is the speaker with

humor? How informal or deliberate is he or she with words? What are the speaker's pet phrases and expressions? The writer must file these observations away, recall them during the writing process, and factor them into the speech.

Researching

Like any writer, a speechwriter sometimes develops writer's block: the inability to come up with anything on paper. One way around writer's block is to adopt a formalized research procedure.

1. **Dig into all literature, books, pamphlets, articles, speeches, and other writings on the speech subject.** Prior speeches by the speaker are also important documents to research. A stocked file cabinet is often the speechwriter's best friend.
2. **Think about the subject.** Bring personal thoughts to bear on the topic. Presumably, the speaker has already discussed the topic with the writer, so the writer can amplify the speaker's thoughts with his or her own.
3. **Seek out the opinions of others on the topic.** Perhaps the speaker isn't the most knowledgeable source within the organization about this specific subject. Economists, lawyers, accountants, doctors, and other technical experts may shed additional light on the topic. Outside sources, particularly politicians and business leaders, are often willing to share their ideas when requested.

Organizing and Writing

Once preparation, interviewing, and research have been completed, the fun part begins. Writing a speech becomes easier if, again, the speech is organized into its four essential elements: introduction, thesis, body, and conclusion.

INTRODUCTION Writing a speech introduction is a lot like handling a bar of soap in the shower: The first thing to do is get control. An introduction must grab the audience and hold its interest. An audience is alert at the beginning of a talk and is with the speaker. The writer's job is to make sure the audience stays there.

The speechwriter must take full advantage of the early good nature of the audience by making the introduction snappy. Audience members need time to settle in their seats, and the speaker needs time to get his or her bearings on the podium. Often, the best way to win early trust and rapport with the audience is to ease into the speech with humor.

THESIS The thesis is the object of the speech—its purpose or central idea. A good thesis statement lets an audience know in a simple sentence where a speech is going and how it will get there. For example, its purpose can be to persuade:

The federal government must allow home football games to be televised.

Another thesis statement might be to reinforce or crystallize a belief:

Sunday football viewing is among the most cherished of winter family home entertainments.

The purpose of yet another thesis statement might merely be to entertain:

Football viewing in the living room can be a harrowing experience. Let me explain.

In each case, the thesis statement lets the audience know early what the point of the speech will be and leads listeners to the desired conclusion.

BODY The speech body is just that—the general body of evidence that supports the three or four main points. Although facts, statistics, and figures are important elements, writers should always attempt to use comparisons or contrasts for easier audience understanding. For example:

> In a single week, 272 million customers passed through the checkout counters of American supermarkets. That's equal to the combined populations of Spain, Mexico, Argentina, France, West Germany, Italy, Sweden, Switzerland, and Belgium.

Such comparisons dramatically hammer points home to a lazy audience.

CONCLUSION The best advice on wrapping up a speech is to do it quickly. As the old Texas bromide goes, "If you haven't struck oil in the first 20 minutes, stop boring." Put another way, the conclusion must be blunt, short, and to the point. It may be a good idea to review orally the major points and thesis one last time and then stop.

THE SPOKEN WORD

Because speeches are meant to be heard, the writer should take advantage of tools that emphasize the special qualities of the spoken word. Such devices can add vitality to a speech, transcending the content of the words themselves. Used skillfully, these devices can elevate a mediocre speech into a memorable one.

Speeches are meant to be heard. Therefore, the speech writer should take advantage of tools—figures of speech—that emphasize the special qualities of the spoken word:

- **Alliteration,** the repetition of initial sounds in words.
- **Antithesis,** using sharply opposed or contrasting ideas in the same passage.
- **Metonymy,** substituting one term for another closely associated one to give a passage more figurative life.
- **Metaphor** and **simile,** which figuratively connect concepts that have little literal connection.
- **Personification,** which gives life to animals, inanimate objects, or ideas.
- **Repetition,** using the same words or phrases over and over again.
- **Humor** that is relevant, fresh, and in good taste.

A derivative of speechwriting is constructing "talking points"—highlights of a speech that a manager can allude to in speaking more extemporaneously. The key to speechwriting, as to any other kind of writing, is experience. As speechwriting has become a more competitive, highly paid, and sought-after pursuit in public relations, it has become increasingly difficult for an interested novice to break in. But don't be dismayed. Most political candidates or nonprofit community organizations are more than willing to allow beginners to try their hand at drafting speeches. Although the pay for such endeavors may be limited—or nonexistent—such voluntary efforts are a good way to learn the ropes of speechwriting.

Few other activities in public relations offer as much fulfillment—in both psychological and monetary rewards—as speechwriting.

MAKING AN EFFECTIVE PRESENTATION

A business presentation is different from a speech. A presentation generally is designed to sell a product, service, or idea. Everyone, somewhere along the line, must deliver a presentation. Like any other speaking device, an effective presentation depends on following established guidelines. Here are 10 points worth pursuing prior to presenting:

1. **Get organized.** Before considering your presentation, consider the 4Ws of speechwriting. Who are you addressing? What are you trying to say? Where and when should something happen?

2. **Get to the point.** Know your thesis. What are you trying to prove? What is the central purpose of your presentation?

3. **Be logical.** Organize the presentation with some logic in mind. Don't skip randomly from one thought to another. Lead from your objective to your strategies to the tactics you will use to achieve your goal.

4. **Write it out.** Don't wing it. If Jay Leno and David Letterman write out their ad libs, so should you. Always have the words right in front of you.

5. **Anticipate the negatives.** Keep carping critics at bay. Anticipate their objections and defuse them by examining and dismissing vulnerabilities in the presentation.

6. **Speak, don't read.** Sound as if you know the information. Practice before the performance. Make the presentation part of you. Reading suggests uncertainty. Speaking asserts assurance.

7. **Be understandable.** Speak with clarity and concreteness so that people understand you. If you want to make the sale, you must be clear.

8. **Use graphics wisely.** Audiovisual supports should do just that—support the presentation. Graphics should be used more to tease than to provide full information. And graphics shouldn't be crammed with too much information. This will detract from the overall impact of the presentation. Because many audiovisual channels are available to a presenter (see Appendix D), it may be wise to seek professional help in devising compelling graphics for a presentation.

9. **Be convincing.** If you aren't enthusiastic about your presentation, no one else will be. Be animated. Be interesting. Be enthusiastic. Sound convinced that what you're presenting is an absolute necessity for the organization.

10. **STOP!** A short, buttoned-up presentation is much more effective than one that goes on and on. At his inaugural, U.S. President William Henry Harrison delivered a two-hour, 6,000-word address into a biting wind on Pennsylvania Avenue. A month later, he died of pneumonia. The lesson: When you've said it all, shut up!

Is learning how to make an effective presentation really worth it? Well, when General Norman Schwarzkopf retired after the Gulf War, he marched into the speaking world at $80,000 per speech.[7] That was $20,000 less than former President George Bush began charging when he ventured into the speech market in 1994. In the 1990s, in fact, about the only two celebrities not particularly interested in public speaking were golf champions Arnold Palmer and Jack Nicklaus. They each asked $45,000 per speech "because they really don't want to speak"—or, one presumes, need to do so.[8]

THE REST OF THE STORY

EVERY PICTURE TELLS A STORY

As executive speech making has become more important, a plethora of counseling firms have sprung up to advise executive speakers on how to create and deliver winning speeches. Communispond, Inc., developed one of the most novel concepts.

Because most executives are neither comfortable at a podium nor confident in their ability to perform before a large audience, Communispond came up with the concept of drawing pictures to replace formal written speeches. Essentially, after gathering all available evidence and support material and outlining in words what they want to cover, Communispond-trained executives are encouraged to draw pictures, called ideographs, to reflect accurately the subject at hand. For example, a corporate speaker who wants to express the notion that the ship of American capitalism is still being fired on by entrenched socialist salvos around the world might sketch an ideograph similar to the one here.

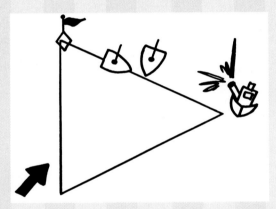

In this way, Communispond-trained speakers are taught to use their nervousness to convey natural, human conviction. In other words, not constrained by lifeless written copy, an executive is free, as Communispond puts it, "to speak as well as you think."

Although not right for everyone, Communispond's unique approach, when mastered, allows for a much more extemporaneous and lively discourse than the average prepared text. Fortunately, however (at least as far as corporate speech writers are concerned), most executives still insist on the security blanket of a full written text.

A QUESTION OF ETHICS

BEAVIS AND BUTT-HEAD BATTLE BACKLASH

Another indication that the world is coming to an end was the popularity in the 1990s of two inane MTV cartoon characters, the irrepressible Beavis and Butt-Head.

Each evening, millions of MTV viewers turned on Beavis and Butt-Head to hear their heroes repeat over and over again "Heh-heh-heh. Heh, heh, heh, cool." Or, if the contrary mood struck them, "Heh-heh-heh. Heh-heh-heh, sucks."

Earlier in the decade, the two cartoon culprits came under attack after an Ohio mother blamed Beavis and Butt-Head's habit of lighting fires and saying "Fire is good" for causing the death of her two-year-old daughter after her five-year-old son set their trailer home ablaze.

The Senate Commerce Committee lambasted the cartoon duo and demanded that MTV take action.

MTV responded immediately. In a prepared statement, the network called the Ohio fire a "terrible tragedy" and promised to "reexamine issues regarding Beavis and Butt-Head."

This "reexamination" led to an immediate shift by MTV of Beavis and Butt-Head to a later (10:30 P.M.) starting time. MTV added that it would seek "to come up with a different concept for new episodes of the series that could be on earlier." By the end of the decade, Beavis and Butt-Head were back on top, starring in their own feature film. Nonetheless, in voluntarily moving the MTV show to a later starting time, what was MTV admitting about Beavis and Butt-Head?

SUMMARY

Skillful writing lies at the heart of public relations practice. Basically, public relations professionals are professional communicators. Ergo, each person engaged in public relations work must be adept at writing.

In today's overcommunicated society, everyone from newspaper editors to corporate presidents complains about getting too much paper. So, before a professional even thinks of putting thoughts on paper, he or she must answer the following questions:

1. Will writing serve a practical purpose? If you can't come up with a purpose, don't write.
2. Is writing the most effective way to communicate? Face-to-face or telephone communication may be better and more direct than writing.
3. What is the risk? Writing is always risky; just ask a lawyer. Once it's down in black and white, it's difficult or impossible to retract. So, think before you write.
4. Are the timing and the person doing the writing right? Timing is extremely important in writing. A message, like a joke, can fall flat if the timing is off. The individual doing the writing must also be considered. A writer should always ask whether he or she is the most appropriate person to write.

The pen—or, more likely, the personal computer—is a powerful weapon. Like any other weapon, writing must be used prudently and properly to achieve the desired result.

DISCUSSION STARTERS

1. What are the essential elements of a media kit?
2. What is the difference between a straight biography and a narrative biography?
3. What is a backgrounder?
4. What are the benefits of a round-up story?
5. When might an organization require a standby statement?
6. What are the essential characteristics of a speech?
7. What questions does one ask to begin the speechwriting process?
8. What are the elements that constitute an effective presentation?
9. What is the purpose of using "figures of speech" in a presentation and what types are useful?
10. What are possible pitfalls that must be considered before writing anything?

NOTES

1. Lisa Miller, "Seeking Only a Bit of Peace and Quiet, Hapless Travelers Hear 'It's Spring Break!' " *The Wall Street Journal* (March 21, 1997) B1.
2. Ibid.
3. Loc. cit., B10.
4. Fraser P. Seitel, "Meaningful Memos," *United States Banker* (November 1993): 77.
5. "Farewell to the Pitch Letter," *Public Relations Journal* (July 1990): 13.
6. G. A. Marken, "Public Relations Photos . . . Beyond the Written Word," *Public Relations Quarterly* (Summer 1993): 7–12.
7. Randall Poe, "Talk Isn't Cheap," *Across the Board* (September 1992): 19–24.
8. "One Speech Writer's Complaint," *The Effective Speech Writer's Newsletter* (October 6, 1989): 1.

SUGGESTED READINGS

Ailes, Roger and John Krausher. *You Are the Message*. Homewood, IL: Dow Jones-Irwin, 1988.

Arrendondo, Lani. *How to Present Like a Pro*. New York: McGraw-Hill, 1991.

Bakshian, Jr., Aaron. *The American Speaker*. Washington, DC: Georgetown Publishing House, 1995. Written by a former Ronald Reagan speechwriter, this book receives more ingenious self-promotion than probably any work in the history of the world. But it does have its qualities, among them excellent anecdotes from a number of excellent public speakers.

Decker, Bert. *You've Got To Be Believed To Be Heard*. New York: St. Martin's Press, 1992. One of America's foremost speech coaches shares his secrets.

Detz, Joan. *How to Write and Give a Speech*. New York: St. Martin's Press, 1992.

Executive Speaker (P.O. Box 292437, Dayton, OH 45429). Newsletter.

Executive Speechmaker. New York: Institute for Public Relations Research and Education, 1980 (310 Madison Ave. 10017).

TOP OF THE SHELF

HENRY EHRLICH

WRITING EFFECTIVE SPEECHES

NEW YORK: PARAGON HOUSE, 1992

Henry Ehrlich, one of the nation's most gifted business speech writers, knows the difference between writing for the ear and the eye. This volume explains all a beginner needs to know about writing an effective speech.

Among the topics the author explores are the following:

- The difference between writing for yourself and for someone else
- How to write a speech for a member of the opposite sex
- New ways to begin a speech
- Tackling an unfamiliar subject
- Assessing an audience
- Phrasing, coaching the speaker, typing the script, and adding visual cues

Perhaps most appealing, the author confronts his subject with large doses of humor, developed over years of experience. He suggests effective ways to use humor and anecdotes, as well as how to organize lighter speeches, such as awards presentations, speaker introductions, and motivational talks.

All in all, Henry Ehrlich's contribution to speechwriting literature is as inspirational as it is instructive. (Besides, how can you dislike a guy who suggests to a bank president that he add a little levity to his speech by "imitating Marilyn Monroe"?)

Fettig, Art. *How to Hold an Audience in the Hollow of Your Hand.* Battle Creek, MI: Growth Unlimited, 1988.

Filson, Brent. *Executive Speeches.* Williamstown, MA: Williamstown Publishing Company, 1991.

Hanson, Garth A. *Say It Right: A Guide to Effective Oral Business Presentations.* Burr Ridge, IL: Irwin Professional Publishing, 1995.

Kaplan, Burton. *The Corporate Manager's Guide to Speechwriting.* New York: Free Press, 1988.

Radio Interview Guide. New York: Book Promotions, 1988 (26 E. 33rd St.).

Rafe, Stephen. *The Executive's Guide to Successful Presentations.* Warrentown, VA: S/RC, 1991.

Richardson, Linda. *Winning Group Sales Presentations.* Homewood, IL: Dow Jones-Irwin, 1991.

Robinson, James W. *Winning Them Over.* Rocklin, CA: Prima Publishing and Communications, 1987.

Roesch, Roberta. *Smart Talk.* New York: AMACOM, 1989.

Sarnoff, Dorothy. *Never Be Nervous Again.* New York: Crown, 1988.

Smith, Terry C. *Making Successful Presentations,* 2nd ed. New York: John Wiley & Sons, 1991.

Speechwriter's Newsletter (Available from Ragan Communications, 407 S. Dearborn, Chicago, IL 60605).

Thomserr, Michael C. *The Little Black Book of Business Speaking.* New York: AMA-COM, 1989.

United Press International. *Broadcast Stylebook.* (220 E. 42nd Street, New York, NY 10017.) This is not a rule book, but it suggests methods and treatment for properly preparing news copy, with examples of wire copy and brief comments on correct and incorrect methods of news wire copy preparation. It's designed to help people write the kind of copy used by an announcer.

Variety (Available from 475 Park Ave. South, New York, NY 10016; published weekly on Wednesday.) This paper publishes news, features, and commentary each week on every aspect of show business, with extensive reviews of productions around the world.

CASE STUDY

Illinois Power's Reply

For three decades, no network news program rivaled the incredible impact of CBS-TV's *60 Minutes*. Watched each Sunday night by more than 20 million Americans, *60 Minutes* still ranks as one of the most popular programs in the nation and the show most feared by public relations professionals. When *60 Minutes* comes calling, scandal, or at least significant problems, can't be far behind.

Such was the thinking at Illinois Power Company (IP) in Decatur in the fall of 1979, when *60 Minutes* sent reporter Harry Reasoner to find out why the company's Clinton nuclear reactor project was behind schedule and over budget.

What followed—the exchange between Reasoner and IP—still ranks as history's most classic confrontation between television and corporate public relations professionals.

Because IP suspected that *60 Minutes* wanted to do a hatchet job, the company agreed to be interviewed only if it, too, videotaped the *60 Minutes* filming on its premises. In other words, IP would videotape the videotapers; it would report on the reporters; it would meet *60 Minutes* on its own terms. Reasoner and his producer reluctantly agreed to the arrangement.

And so in early October, IP's executive vice president sat for an hour-and-a-half interview before the *60 Minutes*—and the IP—cameras. He answered Reasoner's questions straightforwardly and comprehensively. And he and his company prepared for the worst.

Which is precisely what they received.

On November 25, *60 Minutes* broadcast a 16-minute segment on the Clinton plant, charging IP with mismanagement, missed deadlines, and costly overruns that would be passed on to consumers. Viewers saw three former IP employees accuse the utility of making no effort to control costs, allowing slipshod internal reporting, and fabricating estimates of construction completion timetables. One of the accusers was shown in silhouette with a distorted voice because, as reporter Reasoner intoned, "He fears retribution." To add salt to the IP wound, the 90-minute interview with the company's executive vice president merited less than 2 minutes of edited, misleading air time.

Worst of all, 24 million Americans viewed the crucifixion in their living rooms.

The day after the CBS story, IP's stock fell a full point on the New York Stock Exchange in the busiest trading day in the company's history. Rather than responding as most companies do—with bruised feelings, a scorched reputation, and feeble cries of "foul" to its stockholders—IP lashed back with barrels blazing. Within days of the broadcast, IP produced *60 Minutes/Our Reply*, a 44-minute film incorporating the entire *60 Minutes* segment, punctuated by insertions and narrative presenting the company's rebuttal.

The rebuttal included videotape of CBS film footage not included in the program, much of which raised serious questions about the integrity of the material CBS used. The rebuttal also documented the backgrounds and possible motives of the three former employees CBS quoted, all of whom had been fired for questionable performance. One of the former employees, in fact, was the leader of the local antinuclear group opposing IP.

Initially, the reply tape was aired to a relatively small audience: the company's employees, customers, shareholders, and investors. But word traveled quickly that IP had produced a riveting, broadcast-quality production, so true to the *60 Minutes* format—ticking stopwatch and all—that it could easily be mistaken for the original. Within a year, close to 2,500 copies of the devastating rebuttal had been distributed to legislators, corporate executives, journalists, and others. Excerpts were broadcast on television stations throughout the nation, and the IP production became legendary. As *The Wall Street Journal* put it, "The program focuses new attention on news accuracy. . . . Although even a telling, polished, counter-program like Illinois Power's can't reach the masses of a national broadcast, the reply tape has proven effective in reaching a significant 'thinking' audience."

Even CBS was impressed. The producer of the original *60 Minutes* segment called the rebuttal highly sophisticated, especially for a company that had first seemed to him to be a "down-home cracker barrel" outfit. The IP tape soon spawned imitators. Companies such as Chevron, Union Carbide, Commonwealth Edison, and many others began experimenting with defensive videotaping in dealing with television journalists.

Although *60 Minutes* admitted to some sloppiness in its reporting and to two minor factual inaccuracies, it essentially stood by its account. Complained CBS executive producer Don Hewitt, "We went in as a disinterested party and did a news report. They made a propaganda film for their side, using our reporting for their own purposes."

Perhaps. But one irrefutable result of the dramatic confrontation between the huge national network and the tiny local utility was that IP—by turning the television tables on the dreaded *60 Minutes*—had earned its place in public relations history.*

QUESTIONS

1. Do you agree with IP's original decision to let *60 Minutes* in despite the suspicion that the program would be a hatchet job? What might have happened if IP turned down the *60 Minutes* request?
2. If *60 Minutes* had turned down IP's request to videotape the Reasoner interviews, would you have still allowed the filming?
3. Presume that IP didn't tape the *60 Minutes* filming on its premises. What other communications options might the company have pursued to rebut the *60 Minutes* accusations?
4. Do you think IP did better by allowing *60 Minutes* in to film or would they have been better off keeping CBS out?

*Sandy Graham, "Illinois Utility Sparks Widespread Interest with Its Videotape," *The Wall Street Journal* (April 12, 1980): 23. For further information on the IP case, see Punch, Counterpunch: "60 Minutes" vs. Illinois Power Company (Washington, DC: Media Institute, 1981), and "Turning the Tables on '60 Minutes,' " *Columbia Journalism Review* (May–June 1980): 7–9.

◆◆◆◆◆◆◆
VOICE OF EXPERIENCE

SHIRLEY CARTER

Shirley Staples Carter is professor and chairperson of the Department of Mass Communications and Journalism at Norfolk State University, Norfolk, VA. Prior to that, she was associate professor/director and former inaugural chairperson of the Department of Communications and Visual Arts at the University of North Florida. Carter directs the university's efforts to plan and develop new communications technologies, such as instructional television fixed-services delivery systems, other broadcast initiatives, and cable and community education. Carter's experience spans two decades in higher education administration and teaching. She is the first African-American female to serve as a department chairperson in journalism/mass communications at a mainstream university.

WHAT DOES IT TAKE TO BECOME AN EFFECTIVE PRINT WRITER?

We need to return to the basics, which include reading, listening, and observing skills. As our society prepares for the explosion of the information superhighway, the effective print writer should incorporate visual elements into the writing task as well.

WHAT DOES IT TAKE TO BECOME AN EFFECTIVE WRITER FOR THE SPOKEN WORD?

The same, basically. We must be literate in terms of the environment, our society, political systems, and evolution. The broadcast writer must be able to stir the imagination of the listener if the medium is audio or evoke the desired response or emotion in the viewer if the medium is video.

HOW IMPORTANT IS IT FOR A PUBLIC RELATIONS STUDENT TO HONE HIS OR HER WRITING SKILLS?

It is extremely important. The most important tool for the public relations professional is writing. And perhaps one of the great challenges of the new information society is that writers must be versatile and knowledgeable about how to communicate with multicultural audiences or markets.

WHAT IS THE CALIBER OF PUBLIC RELATIONS STUDENTS TODAY?

They are a diverse lot. Some are more mature, more focused, and tend to be highly specialized in their career aspirations, for example, international relations, government relations, public affairs, sports marketing, political communications. They expect a tremendous technological impact on the industry and society in general, and they are beginning to understand, thanks to the global reach of CNN and other factors, that our world is getting smaller. Some have a great deal of potential, even if their notions about what public relations is (an easy job) and what public relations requires (a pretty smile) are erroneous. These qualities in our students make public relations education especially challenging and exciting.

WHAT IS THE STATUS OF MINORITIES IN PUBLIC RELATIONS?

There are still too few, as in other communications and related fields. Minorities account for less than 5 percent of mid-level jobs in mid-management; they are virtually invisible in senior management. We can do more at the grass-roots level to attract minorities to the public relations industry. University programs might focus as much on retention efforts as on recruitment and encourage minority student participation in organizations such as Public Relations Student Society of America and mainstream public relations internships. Professionals can take this one step further by mentoring and nurturing minorities interested in public relations careers. Now is the best time to prepare for the changes already taking shape in the workplace, the shifting demographics, the increasing black and Latino consumer markets, and expanding global opportunities.

WHAT IS THE FUTURE FOR MINORITIES IN PUBLIC RELATIONS?

I think the future is quite bright. The opportunities will definitely be there, but we need students who are fully prepared to take advantage of them. Education and awareness will be the key determinants. The responsibility of minority students is to develop essential skills such as writing, mastery of a foreign language, and appreciation of foreign cultures, and to attain a strong liberal arts background and computer literacy. Minority students should also seek exposure to public relations career opportunities and be keenly aware of the possibilities open to them as a result of ethnic, global, and technological changes in our society.

CHAPTER TEN

Public Relations and The Net

"CYBERSPACE." AH, WHAT AN OVERUSED WORD. In the best traditions of "interface" and "quality" and "empowerment" and "excellence," cyberspace has taken its place among the hottest buzz words of the day—a veritable panacea for solving the world's ills. (See Cyberspace Glossary, appendix E)

In public relations, as in other fields, nothing seems more important, as the world enters the twenty-first century, than mastering the interactive workplace; cyberspace, the Internet, the World Wide Web. The computer apparently rules, and all else seems to pale by comparison.

Not so fast, buckaroo.

Although the computer has unleashed tremendous potential power for public relations and other communications disciplines, particularly in the areas of research and access to information, its promise has thus far exceeded its payoff. By the end of the 1990s, there were many signs the early Web bloom was off the rose.

- America Online (AOL), the nation's largest online provider, closed down its Global Network Navigator operations, the first commercial Web site, in 1996 after failing to make it work.
- CMP Publications slashed the staff of its Web magazine, also started with great fanfare, from 200 workers to 65.
- Time Warner, the nation's largest media company, acknowledged that its Pathfinder Web site was losing between $5 and $10 million a year.[1]

That's the discouraging news.

The better news is that no area of public relations work is "hotter" in the new millennium than the development of Web sites, Intranet operations, and the general harnessing of the Web to communicate with target publics. Although the wonders of the Web are only evolving, attention to the computer and what it can provide the public relations practitioner are the topics that dominate discussion.

GROWING USE OF THE INTERNET

Almost one in four American adults—nearly 50 million people—have used the Internet. Another 12 million annually take the Internet plunge.

More than half log on from home, and about 30 percent are in the 25-to-34-year-old population, the fastest growing segment of the on-line population. Although women comprise 45 percent of users, males are heavier Internet users by three-to-one. Nearly half of all users in this early stage of Web development rate their overall on-line satisfaction as "very good" or "excellent."[2] Internet users, predictably are generally smart and affluent. Nearly 50 percent have completed college. Mean annual income of Internet users is $62,000 (Figure 10–1).[3]

The burgeoning growth of the World Wide Web is not without its downside. Although the Internet increases in popularity every day, it is bogged down—gridlocked—by too many users, contributing a continuous and unrestrained stream of communication, much labeled "shovelware," or, literally translated, unadulterated garbage.[4] The number of pages on the Web has mushroomed from a few thousand in 1992 to an estimated 50 million. In terms of how clogged it is, government scientists have warned that the Internet is in a "dangerous state." The danger lies largely in the inverse correlation between volume of information available compared to that which is useful. The most celebrated of the Web's overuse problems came in 1996, when an embarrassed AOL had to issue refunds when the unlimited access payment plan it introduced caused horrible access problems.[5]

Among those unamused by the Web's problems was veteran journalist Brit Hume, who said, "The Net is such a mess and the World Wide Web has so much junk on it." Echoed Bloomberg Wire Service founder Michael Bloomberg, "The Internet hysteria is a creature of hype and hero worship."[6]

Nor has the Internet thus far become a roaring success in profitability terms.

Although traffic on the world's computer network is booming, most firms that provide the Net's infrastructure—the telecommunications lines and access services—lose

Figure 10–1   America's Employers (http://www.americasemployers.com), developed by consultants CRC America, assists corporations and job seekers in locating employment. There is no charge for job seekers to use this online service, which features tips on job searching and interviewing, company databases and even online interviews with prospective employers.

THE REST OF THE STORY

WHO USES THE NET AND WHY?

Here's the answer.

- 40.5 percent of all households in the United States have a computer.
- 34 percent of those households use the Internet.
- Mean income is $62,000.
- Nearly 50 percent have completed college or have graduate degrees.
- 94 percent use e-mail.
- 34 percent use the Net to play games.
- 54 percent use the Net to buy products.
- 34 percent think Web advertising is effective.
- 60 percent say the Internet reduces family television watching time.
- 80 percent are "deeply concerned" about privacy issues.
- 78 percent favor controlling what children can see on the Internet.

Source: "Who is Using the Internet?" *Ragan's Interactive PR*, June 21, 1996, 8.

money in the business. Some of the nation's largest advertising agencies, quick to set up "interactive divisions," have either cut them back or abandoned them entirely. The "hope" for the future is that as Web usage continues to grow, higher volume will bring increased profitability.[7]

Nonetheless, despite its detractors and its early fits and starts, the fact is the World Wide Web is but in its infancy. There is no question that in the twenty-first century, the Internet will become an increasingly powerful communications vehicle and a growingly important vehicle for public relations practitioners.

NET EFFECT ON PUBLIC RELATIONS

Compared to some other industries, such as stock brokerage and advertising, public relations professionals have been relatively slow to use the Internet to advance their own messages and those of their clients.[8] Nonetheless, for three reasons in particular, use of the Net by public relations practitioners inevitably will grow in the future.

- First, the demand to be educated versus being sold. Today's consumers are smarter, better educated, and more media savvy. They know when they are being hustled by self-promoters and con artists. So communications programs must be grounded in education-based information, rather than blatant promotion. The Net is perhaps the world's greatest potential repository of such information.

- Second, the need for real-time performance. The world is moving quickly. Everything happens instantaneously, in real-time. As media visionary Marshall McLuhan predicted four decades ago, in the twenty-first century the world has become a "global village," wired for immediate communications. Public relations professionals can use this to their advantage to structure their information to respond instantly to emerging issues and market changes.
- Third, the need for customization. There used to be three primary television networks. Today, there are more than 500 television channels. Today's consumers expect more focused, targeted, one-on-one communications relationships. More and more, organizations must broadcast their thoughts to narrower and narrower population segments. The Net offers such narrowcasting to reporters, analysts, opinion leaders, and consumers.[9]

Such is the promise of the Internet to the practice of public relations. In terms of broad use of cyberspace by public relations professionals, electronic mail or e-mail is probably the most pervasive internal mechanism. In a growing number of organizations, e-mail, delivered on-line and immediately, has replaced traditional print publications and the even more recent fax technology as a rapid delivery information vehicle. An outgrowth of e-mail—Intranets or internal Web sites—are another growing phenomenon (Figure 10–2).

Another rapidly expanding use of the Net by public relations professionals is the creation and maintenance of Web sites to profile companies, promote products, or position issues. Federal Express, for example sets two goals for its Web site: To do business and to provide up-to-date unfiltered news.[10]

Figure 10–2 E-mail and a Web address have become necessities for company and agency communicators in the twenty-first century.

Managing ones own Web site gives an individual or institution the flexibility and freedom of getting "news out" without having it filtered by an intermediary, which is the case in normal journalistic channels. Public relations people, therefore, can use Web sites to disseminate information, without the fear of being edited by someone else. In 1997, when Boulder, Colorado police investigated the brutal murder of 6-year-old beauty queen JonBenet Ramsey, the public relations agency hired by the little girl's family took the unusual step of creating a Ramsey family Web site to provide their side of developments.

Beyond the creation of Web sites, public relations practitioners are using the Net to communicate to the media and the financial community. Again, while these uses are still in their nascent stage, there is no question that mastering the intricacies and technologies of cyberspace will be a twenty-first century requisite for every public relations professional.

MOVING TO E-MAIL

E-mail is far and away the most pervasive computer-oriented organizational communications vehicle. In some companies, e-mail is well on the way toward replacing print-based newsletters, bulletins, and internal announcements.

At Tandem Computers, for example, five on-line newsletters have replaced traditional internal print products. Such vehicles are both more immediate and more interactive than print counterparts. Employees can "feed back" to what they've read or heard instantaneously. The organization, in turn, can apprise itself quickly of relevant employee attitudes and opinions. Such on-line vehicles also lend an element of timeliness that employee magazines and newspapers often have a hard time meeting.

Externally, e-mail can be used to sell products and services. Advertising giant J. Walter Thompson marketed the Ford Taurus automobile with a comprehensive e-mail campaign, including online brochures, flyers, and chat room for prearranged cyber conferences. The latter was set up much as a call-in radio show, with designers answering consumer questions about the new car.

With e-mail growing rapidly throughout industry and society in general, it is not inconceivable to imagine that e-mail will soon become the internal communications medium of choice.

ORGANIZING A WEB SITE

Web sites are proliferating. No self-respecting company, trade association, nonprofit agency, political candidate or entrepeneur today can afford to be without his or her or its own Web site (Figure 10–3). Or at least, that's the common wisdom. Accordingly, in many such sites, the haste to establish a Home Page becomes embarrassingly obvious. Many Web sites are uninteresting, redundant, unnourishing and dull.

How should one create a winning Web site? By first asking and answering several strategic questions.

1. What is our goal?
   To extend the business? Sell more products? Make more money? Win support for our position? Turn around public opinion? Introduce our

A QUESTION OF ETHICS

AOL: ARROGANCE ON THE LOOSE

In fall 1996, the nation's largest on-line access provider, America Online, faced a marketing problem. With its stock and the number of its subscribers soaring and people buying into its confident—even brash—predictions of nonstop growth, what could it do for an encore to keep the momentum moving?

Its answer: Charge customers a flat $19.95 monthly fee for unlimited use. AOL reasoned that once it introduced this kind of unlimited access bargain, clients would rush to sign up. And boy, was AOL right!

Within days, AOL access lines were jammed, with piggish customers logging on the Net and then staying there forever. Others, who had signed up and paid their money to AOL, had to suffer interminable delays or couldn't get on at all. Worse, it was virtually impossible to get through to the company—either on the phone or the Net—to complain. The company, it seemed, could care less about its customers.

So AOL customers threatened lawsuit. Throughout the country, they petitioned their states attorneys general to do something about AOL's failure to respond to the constant busy signals. In January 1997, the company announced it would give "millions of dollars of credits and refunds as compensation for network traffic jams." Attorneys general around the nation thumped their chests with pride and proclaimed the AOL agreement as "wholly satisfactory."

BUT WAS IT?

In point of fact, AOL had pulled a fast one on the clueless government gumshoes. Although the company had agreed to "refund millions," it insisted that the only way you could claim your refund was by phone. Refund-seeking subscribers were forced to call a jammed 800 number that contained no recorded information about refunds but instead offered a slew of bewildering sales messages and a frustrating menu of options. Said one fed-up AOL subscriber, "I called the number and held on for 40 minutes. It's a mess. . . . We just want to get our money back."

Despite this growing consumer consternation, AOL Chairman Stephen M. Case blissfully declared on-line that the refund program was "a great success." The contented CEO went on to say: "The feedback I got today from members was favorable. People wanted to know what steps we were going to take to satisfy our customers and we told them."

The stock market loved Mr. Case's fancy footwork, recognizing that even though customers were angry, the politicians were confused; the company didn't stand to lose "millions" at all. So the stock went up. But the consuming public, as usual, was a lot smarter than its elected representatives.

The next day, AOL subscribers around the nation cried "foul," claiming the announced settlement was a sham. "On-Line Ire Is Not Pacified by Agreement," headlined *The New York Times* on the first page of its Business Day section. Consumers demanded remedial action to the remedial action.

And so, the several attorneys general, who, the day before had been quick to take credit for the AOL agreement, now headed back to the drawing board, chagrined and humiliated but wiser that even in cyberspace, a company can publicly champion the ethical course, but easily get diverted along the way.

For further information, see Steven Kevy, "Is AOL Out of Lines?" *Newsweek*, February 10, 1997, 51; Steve Lohr, "Refunds Planned by America Online in Internet Jam," *The New York Times*, January 30, 1997, A1; and Seth Schiesel, "On-Line Ire Is Not Pacified by Agreement," *The New York Times*, January 31, 1997, D1.

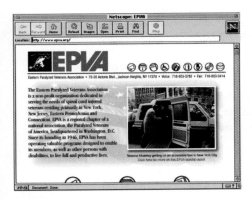

Figure 10–3 The Eastern Paralyzed Veterans Association EPVA (http://www.epva.org), a non profit organization serving veterans with a spinal cord injury or disease, residing primarily in the eastern United States, uses its Web site as a communications vehicle.)

company? Without the answers to these fundamental questions, the "what" and "how" of a Web site are inconsequential. Just as in any other pursuit in public relations, the overriding goal must be established first.

2. What content will we include?
   The reason many Web sites are tedious and boring—and they are!—is that little forethought has gone into determining the content of a site. Simply cramming chronological news releases onto a Home Page won't advance an organization's standing with its publics. Rather, content must be carefully considered, in substance and organization, before proceeding with a Web site. Too often, a site's content appears to be an afterthought.

3. How often will we edit?
   Usually, the answer to this question is: Not often enough. Stale news and the lack of updating are common Web site problems. Another is overwriting. By and large, the writing on the Web is horrible. People seem to feel that because the Web is "free," they can write endlessly. Of course, they can. But no one will read it. So an editorial process to cull information down to its most essential parts is a necessity for a good Web site.

4. How will we enhance design?
   Like it or not, the "style" of the site is most important. If a Home Page isn't attractive, it won't attract many "hits." Good design makes complicated things understandable, and this is essential in a Web site. The Web is a largely "visual" medium, so great care should be taken to professionally design a site.

5. How interactive will it be?
   Traditional communications is unidirectional, one way. You read or view it, and that's where the process stops. A Web site, on the other hand, should be bidirectional. Communication can be translated into an interactive vehicle, a game, an application, or an e-mail chat vehicle. This is what distinguishes good Web sites from mediocre ones (Figure 10–4).

6. How will we track use?
   As in any other communications project, the use of a Web site must be measured. The most basic form of cyberspace measurement is "hits" to the site. But like measuring press clippings, this doesn't tell you whether your information is being appreciated, acted on, or even read. It is the site itself that allows direct "conversations" with customers and potential customers to find

out what they really think. Measuring Web site performance, therefore, should be a multifaceted exercise that includes such analysis as volume during specific times of day, kind of access, specific locations on the site to which visitors are clicking first, and the sequencing through the site that visitors are following.

7. Who will be responsible?
Managing a Web site, if it is done correctly, must be someone's full-time job. Often, companies subordinate it to someone—usually in the public relations department—who has many other "more important" responsibilities. Wrong.

Much better is to treat the Web site as a first line of communication to the public, which requires full-time attention (Figure 10–5).[11]

The variety of content available on organizational Web sites varies considerably. Standard fare includes annual reports, news releases, corporate profile, products, and personality biographies.

- AT&T, with one of the more advanced Home Pages, includes a section called "AT&T in the News," which is updated daily and includes the latest headlines involving the company. AT&T also provides a sampling of its two dozen different internal newsletters.
- Edelman Public Relations includes on its site a Global News Web, which allows a visitor to choose from a variety of information topics—technology to health and medicine—and to be connected to the latest developments in the chosen area in which Edelman clients are involved.

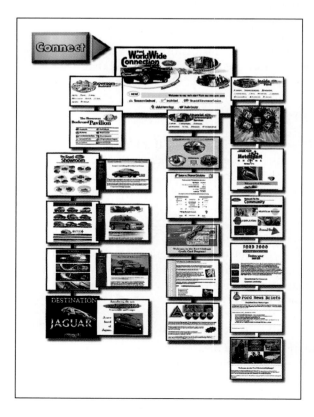

Figure 10–4 Ford Motor Company's Web site allows visitors to access a showroom to "sample" cars, a dealer locator to find the closest Ford dealer, and several corporate pages to research financial and company information.

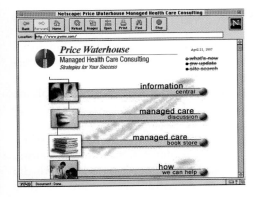

Figure 10–5   The Price Waterhouse Managed Care Web site (http://www.pwmc.com) was developed and managed by PW information technology executive Mark Huppert. It is continuously updated and includes a bookstore, discussion forums, video clips, white papers and reports.

- Some organizations use "known personalities" to spark their Web sites. Personalities increase traffic to a site. This is why Sportsline USA Inc. features spokesman Shaquille O'Neal on its site, and Ragu Spaghetti Sauce features its fictitious, recipe-toting "Mama" on its Home Page.[12]

Stated simply, it is often the "creativity and forethought" that public relations professionals apply to a Web page that determines its success or failure.

MEDIA RELATIONS ON THE NET

The boosters of the Internet claim that "communicating via e-mail is fast becoming a norm, particularly for the media."[13] Not exactly. The vast majority of reporters today do their leg work, their fact finding, and the bulk of their interviewing and reporting the old-fashioned way—by digging into literature, talking to sources, and composing from notes. But things are changing, and journalists are becoming computerized.

One 1994 study of 725 writers, reporters, and editors found that 16 percent used on-line services daily, and one-third said they signed on at least weekly. The study found that media use of on-line services for research and news gathering is increasing, and that editors said they were more likely to use the information provided on-line by nonprofits than they were that provided by profit-making companies.[14] This suggests that an organization's "credibility" problems can't be solved by merely going on-line.

Even though many reporters complain that their e-mail has become as crowded as their voice mail, which became as crowded as the little pink telephone reminder slips on their desk, on-line media relations can be effective in a number of areas.

- Press kits can become digital. Packaging electronic press kits means providing reporters with the video, sound, and screen shots that can be easily translated on-line. Computer literate reporters may appreciate receiving a less-bulky kit electronically or even on CD Rom. Hollywood, in particular, has turned to interactive press kits to promote upcoming movies. Such kits, which can cost upwards of $30,000 to produce, often include a direct response mechanism to promote reporter feedback.[15]
- Products can be launched through the Net. As the Net becomes the "preferred method of communication" among young people, products catering to youthful age groups can be announced in cyberspace. Marvel Comics, for example, launched its "Generation X"

comic book at a late night cyberconference. Working with commercial on-line services, Marvel provided electronic graphics and information to launch the new publication.[16]

- Interviews, too, can be conducted on-line. E-mail interviews, for example, allow more time to answer questions in a more thoughtful way. E-mail interviews save an interviewee—and a reporter—the time and expense of meeting face-to-face. The downside, of course, is a lack of spontaneity in dealing through the computer. Often, telephone follow up is necessary after an e-mail interview.

Some editors and journalists, of course, are slow to change. Media relations is still a matter of personal relationships and trust. Cyberspace will never replace those factors. But the Net can be helpful in expediting dealings with the media. And to deal with the media in cyberspace, a new, more Net-compatible set of writing and communications skills will be needed.

PRODUCT PROMOTION ON THE NET

The Internet provides a virtual laboratory to mesh public relations, advertising, and marketing techniques to promote products. On the positive side, buyers and potential buyers can access your information directly. On the negative side, you are competing with hundreds of thousands of other information providers for a visitor's attention. So promotional messages must be evocative, eye-catching, and brief.

One emerging product promotion device is the "adlink." The adlink is a small display advertisement that promotes another site or page. The adlink may be less than a square inch or may stretch across the screen in a rectangular block. Usually, the adlink promotes another site with a tantalizing line of copy and bit of art. In addition, the adlink will automatically hyperlink, for example, connect you to the site referenced. Adlink "hits" are easily measured to determine their effectiveness. They can serve as excellent entry points for production promotional messages.

THE REST OF THE STORY

SCOOPING YOURSELF NETSTYLE

In March 1997, the *Dallas Morning News* became the first paper in history to "scoop itself" by reporting a jailhouse confession on its Web site, seven hours before its newspaper hit the streets.

The Internet confession by Timothy McVeigh, accused and later convicted of bombing an Oklahoma federal building and causing hundreds to be killed, was unprecedented.

Why would the paper scoop itself? Said its executive editor, "We put the story on the Web site because it was, in our view, extraordinarily important."

But McVeigh's attorney argued that the newspaper rushed to print the story on the Net, because if it waited, he would have sought a temporary injunction from publishing the report.

Whatever the reason, the *Dallas Morning News* precedent is likely to be repeated far more frequently in the twenty-first century as newspapers wrestle with the question: Who gets the story first?

On-line discussion groups provide another winning source of product promotion. The Internet is flooded with news groups, which specialize in different subject areas. Smart organizations research news groups to see if their company's name, product's name, or specialty area is being mentioned. If it is, they respond by e-mailing participants with product information, thus increasing awareness and hopefully, sales. On the flip-side, companies regularly monitor news groups to see if "negative information" is being spread about products. This is what Mrs. Fields Inc. did in 1996, when a rumor that the company contributed cookies to O.J. Simpson's criminal case victory party spread on the Net. Mrs. Fields promptly squelched the inaccurate report. As computer giant Intel found (see Case Study at the end of the chapter), the worst thing you can do is assume Internet news groups lack product clout.

Creating individual product Home Pages is yet another way to promote product recognition and sales on the Net. Reader's Digest promotes its *Family Handyman* magazine by providing a forum for do-it-yourselfers to share tips and learn from professionals on the magazine's Home Page. Three hundred people visit the site each week, and only 10 percent are subscribers. Thus most learn about the product from use of the Web site.

INVESTOR RELATIONS ON THE NET

Public companies are coming to recognize and use the Internet as a more controlled communications mechanism to reach potential investors. For the little investor, who has seen the flow of corporate information increasingly be directed towards analysts or brokers or institutions—the Internet is an informational blessing.

The government that "watches over" securities markets is less convinced. Securities regulators are worried about the anonymous nature of on-line information and the ability of people whose interests stray far from fairness and transparency to misinform and corrupt the market for information.[17]

Companies meanwhile have begun to verge into the investor relations Internet area more aggressively. One study indicated that the majority of annual report producers are thinking of adapting traditional publications to Internet use. Although the printed document remains the most prominent communications vehicle for most companies, electronic annual reports are becoming more important for several reasons.

- Electronic versions are more easily integrated with other communications. Analysts can "pull out" financial data and spreadsheets in electronic reports, which don't depend on stapled pages. The electronic medium can "reshape" the report to the touch of the key, making analysis and study much easier.
- Electronic reports are less static than print reports. Electronic reports can help companies "come to life" before a stockholder or prospect. Graphics can be enhanced, and sound and motion added. Not only might this provide a clearer portrait of a company but also might help "sell" it to the viewer.
- Electronic versions are longer lasting. No longer will investors be forced to keep dog-eared copies of the printed annual report in their files. Access to last year's report can be attained through the push of a button. Indeed, it is not too far fetched to assume that in the twenty-first century, print annual reports will be subordinated to electronic versions.

In its purest form, using the Net for investor relations can assure all stockholders, and not just large ones, an equal opportunity for access to corporate news and information.

THE REST OF THE STORY

MICROSOFT BUYS THE CHURCH

Microsoft's Bill Gates is the richest man in America. He earned that distinction by being one of the first of his generation to spot the immense power and potential of the computer and cyberspace. So if the word spreads that Wild Bill wants to buy something, like say the Catholic Church, people may believe it.

And if the word spreads on Bill's own medium, the Internet, you *know* they'll believe it.

And so, when the following "news story" hit the Net in 1995, cyberites didn't question its authenticity.

MICROSOFT BIDS TO ACQUIRE THE CATHOLIC CHURCH

VATICAN CITY (AP)—In a joint press conference in St. Peter's Square this morning, Microsoft Corporation and the Vatican announced that the Redmond, WA,-based software giant will acquire the Roman Catholic Church in exchange for an unspecified number of shares of Microsoft common stock. If the deal goes through, it will be the first time a corporation has acquired a major world religion.

With the acquisition, Pope John Paul II will become president of the combined company's new Religious Software Division, according to Microsoft chairman Bill Gates.

"We expect a lot of growth in the religious market in the next 5 to 10 years," said Gates. "The combined resources of Microsoft and the Catholic Church will allow us to make religion easier and more understandable for a broader range of people."

Through the Microsoft Network, the company's new online service, "we will make the sacraments available for the first time," Gates said.

A new software application, Microsoft Church, will include a macro language that you can program to download indulgences and special graces when you are away from your computer.

An estimated 17,000 people attended the announcement in St. Peter's Square, watching on a 60-foot screen. The event was broadcast by satellite to 700 sites worldwide.

Only it really wasn't. Cuz' it was all pretend, the fictitious outpouring of a weirded out Netnick. But . . . with the Web rumor mill grinding hard and fast, a lot of people believed it. And Microsoft had to resort to issuing an official statement denying it was seeking to acquire the Roman Catholic Church. As a Microsoft spokesperson dourly concluded, "Given the seriousness of the issue, it's not something we wanted to be associated with."

Besides Microsoft would never actually "buy" the Catholic Church, would it?

Well . . .

INTRANETS, EXTRANETS, AND CD-ROMs

Three additional cyberspace communications vehicles—Intranets, extranets, and CD-ROMs—deserve additional reference.

Intranets are another rapidly expanding phenomenon among U.S. companies. One 1996 study indicated that 63 percent of U.S. businesses either had deployed or were planning to deploy an intranet. What is an intranet?

Generally defined, an intranet is an internal vehicle, which integrates communication with workflow, process management, infrastructure, and all other aspects of completing a job. Intranets allow communicators, management, and employees to exchange information quickly and effectively, much more quickly and effectively than any similar vehicle. Intranets, in other words, are Internets for specific organizations, designed to provide the necessary proprietary information to improve productivity.[18]

Organizations ranging from Ford to Exxon to Xerox to Levi-Strauss to the Mayo Clinic are relying on intranets to communicate. The largest supplier of intranet technology, Netscape Communications, sells more Web servers for internal intranets than for external Internets. By communicating through their intranets, such organizations try to create an "ownership culture," in which all members share in comprehensive knowledge about the firm. In other words, with an intranet, every employee can learn about company finances, update project schedules, exchange messages on computer bulletin boards, consult more frequently, and engage in live "chat sessions" for brainstorming and work teams.

An extranet, on the other hand, allows a company to use the Internet to communicate information to targeted external groups, such as investors, vendors, key customers, left-handed playing piano players, East Coast rap artists, 320-pound offensive tackles, whatever. In segmenting the information in such a focused fashion—and protecting its dissemination through a complex series of firewalls—the targeted audience is assured that the data will remain confidential to it alone. Only approved individuals can access the information by using an assigned i.d. and password, restricted to extranet users exclusively.

CD-ROMs have become so important in public relations work that the Public Relations Society of America created a special award category in its 1996 competition. CD-ROM stands for Compact Disc Read Only Memory, which means you can read information from it but can't change that information.

CD-ROMs boast great storage capacity, capable of holding 650 megabytes of information—the equivalent of 451 floppy discs. CD-ROMs can supply 72 minutes of sound and 20 minutes of video, not to mention text and graphics, to tell a full and rich story about a product, company, candidate, or issue.

Public relations professionals have begun to dispatch CD-ROMs in place of print handouts and video tapes. Indeed, while the VCR created the industry of bringing movies home and allowed greater access to information, the CD-ROM does the same thing but introduces one exciting extra element—interaction.

WRITING FOR THE NET

Writing for online readership differs in several significant ways from writing for other media.

- Online readers don't have the luxury of putting the printed document down for awhile and then coming back to it. They must be given information quickly and concisely. No meandering around a point.
- Writing must be "warmer" than other media. The computer screen can be a cold medium. People have a hard time reading on a screen to begin with, so if they're not engaged, they won't read. So engage them with lighter, more pointed, more interesting prose.
- Finally, writing for the Net is much closer to *USA Today* than to *The New York Times*. Items should be brief, hitting the major points and concluding. Does this mean rewriting in transferring print data to Net data? You bet.

SUMMARY

American industry's late nineties dash into cyberspace has sarcastically been compared to the gold rush of the nineteenth century, when prospectors panned for—but rarely discovered—the elusive commodity that would make them rich.[19]

And while the digital miners thus far have met with spotty success, the Net's impact on the public relations field promises to be profound.

The traditional skills of writing and media and communications knowledge will continue to be essential for the public relations practitioner in the twenty-first century, but added to them will be the necessity of understanding technology, of being proficient in negotiating the Net. The arrival and continued ascension of the Internet as a research engine and marketing tool has altered the career landscape for public relations professionals.[20] The best practitioners in the new century will combine a working knowledge of traditional communications skills and new technological understanding and proficiency.

With 75 percent of U.S. companies already on the Internet, virtually all of corporate America will soon be interactive. That suggests an increased need for public relations professionals, who can counsel on matters of the Net. Such high-tech public relations agencies have begun to prosper, serving computer companies across the nation and the globe. Opportunities to work with the cyberspace communications/public relations needs of organizations should accelerate in the new century.

On the other hand, as the initial euphoria over the wonders of the Web and the intrigue of the Internet wear off, expectations of the possibilities of the new technologies will become more realistic. In an economic downturn, for example, some suggest that the first corporate casualties will be Web sites, more than 1,000 of which are being added each day.[21] Perhaps. But there can be no doubt that the development of the Internet as a pursuit for some and a tool for many will have enormous and long-lasting impact on the practice of public relations in the twenty-first century.

DISCUSSION STARTERS

1. Why is "cyberspace" such a hot buzz word in public relations today?
2. What are the "downsides" to the growth of the World Wide Web?
3. Why will the use of the Net by public relations people grow in the future?
4. What is the most pervasive computer-oriented communications vehicle?
5. What are the purposes of a corporate Web site?
6. What are the elements that constitute an effective Web site?
7. What is the general attitude of the media toward using the Net?
8. How has the Net impacted investor relations?
9. What is the difference between the Intranet and extranet?
10. How important to public relations will cyberspace be in the twenty-first century?

NOTES

1. Don Clark, "Facing Early Losses, Some Web Publishers Begin to Pull the Plug," *The Wall Street Journal* (January 14, 1997): A1.

2. Mike Snider, "Growing On-Line Population Making Internet 'Mass Media,' " *USA Today* (February 19, 1997): A1.

3. "Who is Using the Internet," *Ragan's Interactive Public Relations* (June 21, 1996): 8.

4. Bart Ziegler, "Slow Crawl on the Internet," *The Wall Street Journal* (August 23, 1996): B1.

5. Steve Lohr, "Refunds Planned by America Online in Internet Jam," *The New York Times* (January 30, 1997): 1.

6. Michael Bloomberg, "Have We Become Intermesmerized?" *Across the Board* (January 1997): 16.

7. Bart Ziegler, "Net is Rarely Pipeline to Profit," *The Wall Street Journal* (August 23, 1996): B1.

8. Nancy Ross, "Public Relations and the Internet," a survey of communications professionals, The Dilenschneider Group, New York, NY, January 1997.

9. Lawrence Weber, "Internet Rewrites Rules of Public Relations Game," *PR Tactics* (November 1996): 20.

10. "Cyberspace's Value as PR Tool Touted," *Jack O'Dwyer's Newsletter* (June 6, 1996): 7.

11. Phaedra Hise, "Seven Common Mistakes in Developing Web Sites," *@ Issue* (Fall 1996): 26–31.

12. "Getting Personal: Using Personalities to Make Web Sites More Compelling," *Ragan's Interactive Public Relations* (July 19, 1996): 1.

13. "Take Media Relations Back to Online Basics," *Ragan's Interactive Public Relations* (March 1, 1997): 1.

14. Steven S. Ross and Don Middleberg, The Media in Cyberspace (a national survey of journalists), New York, NY, February 2, 1995.

15. "How Hollywood Uses Interactive Press Kits to Promote Movies," *Ragan's Interactive Public Relations"* (April 5, 1996): 2.

16. Jerry Walker, "How to Use Cyberspace to Launch a Product," *O'Dwyer's PR Services Report* (January 1995): 92.

17. Bill Barnhart, "Nothing But Net: A Commentary on the Impact of the Internet on Investor Relations," *Journal of Corporate Public Relations-Northwestern University* (1996–1997): 16.

18. "What Do Intranets Look Like?" *Technology Workshop for Editors* (January 1997): 1.

19. Seth Schiesel, "Payoff Still Elusive in Internet Gold Rush," *The New York Times* (January 2, 1997): C17.

20. Gene Koprowski, "Landing a PR or Marketing Job Now Requires Technical Proficiency," *Ragan's Interactive PR* (October 1, 1995): 7.

21. "Web Sites May be the First Projects Cut at the Next Economic Downturn," *Ragan's Interactive Public Relations* (April 26, 1996): 1.

SUGGESTED READINGS

Eddings, Joshua. *How the Internet Works.* New York: Ziff-Davis, 1994.

Fitzsimmons, Martha, ed. *Media, Democracy and the Information Highway.* New York: Freedom Forum Media Studies Center, 1993.

Gates, Bill, Nathan Myhrvold, and Peter Rinearson. *The Road Ahead.* New York: Viking Press, 1996.

NICHOLAS NEGROPONTE

BEING DIGITAL

NEW YORK: ALFRED A. KNOPF, 1995

This is the first logical choice in embarking onto the Internet. This book, beyond all others, puts the computer and cyberspace and the Internet and the World Wide Web in perspective. "Computing," writes M.I.T. guru Negroponte, "is not about computers any more. It is about living." And so it is. As Professor Negroponte points out, "Bits are the DNA of information," rapidly replacing atoms as the basic commodity of human interaction. The author spends much of this book explaining why yesterday's "mass media" have evolved into today's more personalized "two-way street of communication."

Negroponte, as much as Microsoft's Bill Gates or Intel's Andy Grove, is a legendary figure in the cyberspace age. His is essential reading for the student of public relations in the changes that will fundamentally alter how we learn, how we work, how we entertain ourselves, and how the practice of public relations will be refined in the future. In other words, this book, which illuminates and entertains simultaneously, is "must reading."

Interactive Public Relations, bi-weekly published by Ragan Communications, 212 West Superior St., Chicago, IL 60610. Updates on public relations progress on the Net.

Krol, E. *The Whole Internet.* Sebastopol, CA: O'Reilly & Associates, 1992.

Marlow, Eugene. Electronic Public Relations. Belmont, CA: Wadsworth, 1996.

M Booth & Associates. *Promoting Issues & Ideas: A Guide to Public Relations for Non-profit Organizations.* New York: The Foundation Center, 1996. Excellent explanation of advantages of and requirements for designing a web site for nonprofit organizations.

Pavlick, John V. *New Media Technology: Cultural and Commercial Perspectives.* Boston: Allyn & Bacon, 1995.

Pitter, Keiko and Robert Minato. *Every Student's Guide to the World Wide Web.* New York: McGraw-Hill, 1996.

SpinWARE. Miami, FL: SpinWARE Software Publishing, Inc., 1996. A computer software designed for public, media, and investor relations professionals. Assists in tracking media lists, distributing press releases and other messages by mail and fax, analyzing press clippings, and organizing schedules.

Thornburg, David D. *Edutrends 2010.* San Carlos, CA: Starstrong Publications, 1992.

Thornburg, David D. *Putting the Web to Work.* San Carlos, CA: Starstrong Publications, 1996.

Vivian, John. *The Media of Mass Communications,* 4th ed. Boston: Allyn & Bacon, 1997.

CASE STUDY

"NO-TELL" INTEL LEARNS SILENCE ISN'T GOLDEN

> "The Internet is like a 20-foot tidal wave coming, and we are in kayaks."
>
> *Andy Grove, Chairman, Intel Corp.*

Next to Bill Gates, Intel CEO Andy Grove is as respected a technological guru as anyone. But thanks to IBM CEO Lou Gerstner, Grove today has a far greater understanding of the practice of public relations than he did prior to December 12, 1994. That was the day his particular "kayak" sunk.

On December 12, 1994, IBM announced it would halt shipment of its highest-powered PCs, containing Intel's flawed Pentium chip, because it was revealed that Intel had "significantly underestimated" Pentium's potential for errors. IBM's shocking news release made the front page of every newspaper in the nation. It also forced Intel to deal with what some labeled the "Exxon Valdez public relations nightmare" of the technology industry.

Intel's public relations naivete, coupled with a muted response from primary Pentium user Dell Computer Corp., and a much more vigorous response from IBM, vividly illustrated varying communications strategies. Each major company—IBM, Dell, and Intel—adopted a different approach to its cyberspace crisis.

IBM's High Profile

Intel's problems began six months before IBM went public. In June 1994, a Lynchburg (VA) College math professor discovered the numbers on his Pentium computer simply didn't compute. Intel advised the professor that he was one out of two million Pentium users at the time to report the "obscure problem." The professor told some friends, who posted the news on the Internet and thereby casually notified 30 million people. Predictably, the Net was abuzz with the flaw in the mightiest of chips.

Intel wasn't prepared for the cyber backlash.

Despite this unwanted Internet notoriety, Intel concluded that the flaw would impact "a typical spreadsheet user once every 27,000 years." Consequently, the company decided not to notify consumers or offer a recall. Growing consumer grumbling notwithstanding, Intel may well have gotten away with its stonewalling had IBM not blown the whistle.

The tidal wave of negative publicity on the Net and in the media following IBM's announcement stunned Intel.

"We had no choice but to go public," said IBM's media relations officer. "Once our research concluded the likelihood of error using the chip, we owed it to our customers to let them know."

IBM's research determined that the flaw would create inaccuracies in mathematical calculations 90 times more frequently than Intel had acknowledged. IBM's CEO Gerstner chose to personally "go public" to make this point.

Industry competitors, however, questioned the "public spirited" motivation of IBM, where only 5 percent of computers sold were Pentium-based.

Huffed one competitor, "IBM's public relations broadside was obvious. Their future is in the chip business. They did this to further their own position and weaken Intel's."

Dell's Low Profile

Dell Computer, Intel's largest Pentium client, adopted a more moderate course in the wake of the chip problem. Its public relations initiatives were confined first to working with Intel to learn how its customers might be affected, and second, to notify its customer about the problem.

In contrast to IBM, Dell made no public announcement. "We decided early on that we didn't want to be the Pentium 'poster child' splashed prominently in the headlines at war with Intel," said Dell's public relations manager.

So Dell quietly contacted its customers and worked with them, either to seek replacement chips or work around the problem.

"We know our customers well," the public relations director said, "We want them to be delighted with our products and will do whatever it takes to satisfy them. Being in the public limelight isn't really our highest priority."

Intel's No Profile

As for Intel, the Pentium problem proved not to be the company's finest public relations moment.

In June, when the problem was first reported, Intel chose to downplay its significance. In October, leaks and commentary on the Internet became more intense about Intel's problem and its failure to disclose more details. Nonetheless, the company dug in its heels and insisted that anyone who wanted a replacement chip "must prove that the new chip was needed."

At the same time, Intel chose not to throttle down its prominent $80 million "Intel Inside" national advertising campaign, designed to make its corporate name and its Pentium chip the "quality standards" of the computer industry.

By the time IBM's public bombshell hit in December, Intel was ready for a fall.

IBM struck, and Intel remained tight-lipped. Initially, it lashed back at IBM and started a brief "war of words." Next lawsuits against Intel were commenced by consumers in three states.

And then, finally, a chastened Andy Grove saw the light. On December 21, 1994, the company ran full-page newspaper ads apologizing for its poor job in handling consumer complaints. The company also announced that it would offer customers a free replacement Pentium upon request with no questions asked. In the end, the public relations lesson cost Intel millions of dollars in reserves set aside to handle the problem.

"It was the right thing to do, both morally and ethically," Chairman Grove concluded. "Our earlier policy seemed arrogant and uncaring."

QUESTIONS

1. Was it ethical for IBM to "go public" with the Pentium problem?
2. Was Dell right in maintaining a silent public posture?
3. How should Intel have responded to the professor who reported the glitch?
4. How should Intel have responded publicly? In its ads? To IBM?
5. What should Intel have done upon being apprised of the Pentium problem?

For further information about Intel's Pentium chip, see Lou Dolinar, "IBM: Chips are Down for Pentium," *New York Newsday*, A4; Kevin Maney, "Intel May Get Chip on Its Shoulder," *USA Today*, December 13, 1994, 3B; Kevin Maney, "IBM Won't Sell PCs With Flawed Intel Chip," *USA Today*, December 13, 1994, A1; John Markoff, "Intel's Crash Course on Consumers," *The New York Times*, December 21, 1994, D1, 6; John Markoff, "In About-Face, Intel Will Swap Its

Flawed Chip," *The New York Times*, December 21, 1994, A1, D6; Bart Ziegler and Don Clark, "Computer Giants' War Over Flaw in Pentium Jolts the PC Industry," *The Wall Street Journal*, December 13, 1994, A1,10; Aaron Zitner, "IBM Stops Selling Computers with Flawed Intel Chip," *The Boston Globe*, December 13, 1994, A1, 49.

VOICE OF EXPERIENCE

LAWRENCE WEBER

Larry Weber is chairman of Weber Public Relations Worldwide (WPRW), the tenth largest public relations agency in the world and a subsidiary of McCann Erickson Worldwide, the world's largest multinational advertising agency. Weber is widely recognized as one of the public relations industry's foremost visionaries in applying technology to transform the practice of public relations.

HOW IMPORTANT IS THE INTERNET IN THE PRACTICE OF PUBLIC RELATIONS?

The Internet will be as important to public relations as television was to the advertising industry. Public relations is changing. To educate different constituencies about a certain point of view, the Internet will increasingly be the avenue of choice. As the bandwidth of the Internet fully expands, public relations professionals will have the amazing ability to implement things like visual press releases and on-line chat sessions with senior executives or government officials. The Internet will have the greatest impact anything has had on public relations to date.

WHAT SKILLS WILL BE MOST IMPORTANT FOR THE PRACTITIONER OF 2010?

The public relations practitioner must acquire a base understanding of the technology available to facilitate the communications between constituencies. Content is king, so what is being said and how it is presented is extremely important. It's not important to have the thickest press kit. Rather, it is what is said in e-mail, how the information is presented in the virtual press room, and how new technology tools are used. The public relations professional needs to have a continued focus on the quality of the message and a commitment to openness, thoughtfulness, and education—not hype. We must use the empowerment that new technology gives us to accomplish great marketing and other goals.

HOW DOES TECHNOLOGY FIT WITH PUBLIC RELATIONS AS A "RELATIONSHIP BUSINESS"?

Public relations is still about gaining people's trust and building relationships, even though the mechanism for building these relationships has changed. People today are moving more quickly, doing more telecommuting, and recognizing the additional business opportunities from distant parts of the world. We have to rely on technology as the facilitator to get things accomplished in a world that moves very, very fast. The best business relationships are based on the principle of value. The challenge for us is learning how to apply technology to add greater value to a relationship, be it with an employee, customer, supplier, or reporter.

WHAT NEW USES OF TECHNOLOGY DO YOU FORESEE IN PUBLIC RELATIONS?

We are moving away from broadcasting of a one-way communication to an interacting mode. Across that spectrum, the new uses of technology are almost endless. There are a multitude of technologies emerging that help public relations professionals service their clients better. There are proprietary databases, such as a drilldown database of writers and targeted information, as well as online sources of news and information. The public relations professional needs to have the smartest desktop available to provide clients with the service they expect.

HOW IMPORTANT WILL THE NET BE TO MEDIA RELATIONS?

The Internet already is and will increasingly become an important tool for journalists. Journalists will begin taking more advantage of the Internet, from conducting research and using the Net to obtain searches, to communicating with key influencers on their beat—analysts as well as executives of the companies they cover. Journalists are no longer writing simply for the newspaper, but for the paper's Web site as well. Any professional who can digitize, store, and disseminate not just information, but relevant intelligence to a journalist, is likely to become that journalist's preferred information source.

HOW IMPORTANT WILL THE NET BE TO INTERNAL COMMUNICATIONS?

All nets, including the Internet, intranets, and extranets, will have significant impact on internal communications. The old-fashioned means of communications were restricted by time, space, and form. Employees no longer depend upon chats by the water cooler, the shareholder meeting, or the office bulletin board for information. The Internet provides immediate access. But again, the effectiveness of this medium depends on the quality of the content. Information will no longer reside in a binder at the bottom of a drawer or in the monthly paper-based company newsletter. Employees will have immediate access to the information they need, through the Internet or the company intranet, and they will be able to provide immediate feedback.

WHAT IS THE INTERNET'S POTENTIAL FOR THE PRACTICE OF PUBLIC RELATIONS?

If our job is to gain faster, positive acceptance of the ideas, products, and legislation we represent, we are going to have to understand how to market those properly with the right technologies. Public relations will be at the highest level—advertising will become a more tactical element as people become more entrenched with information-based marketing. Public relations people then will rise to the top because they are the ones schooled in audience identification and analysis and in changing and building popular opinion. With the Internet, we have the ultimate tool. We'll see a change in structure, where corporate communications people are right in the inner circle of the management of a company and its marketing.

CHAPTER ELEVEN

Publicity and the Media

WHEN YOU MENTION THE PRACTICE OF PUBLIC relations to most people—be they politician or office worker, hospital employee or trade association executive, foreman on the assembly line or CEO—their thoughts instinctively turn to the press and publicity. Whereas students and practitioners of public relations know that the field represents much more than simply securing publicity in the media, nonetheless to most people, public relations means publicity. The media and the practice of public relations are inextricably intertwined.

And therein lies the problem.

As society enters the twenty-first century and the mass media are increasingly challenged by new channels of communication, from interactive TV to Internet access for everything from medical diagnoses to financial services, the relationship between the mass media and the public has become more strained. To hold existing readers and viewers and attract new mass media clients in such a newly competitive marketplace, reporters and editors have had to become more controversial in their coverage, more hard-edged in reporting on establishment institutions.

Because public relations professionals are, in most institutions, the first line of defense and explanation, it is the public relations practitioner who meets the reporter head on. And in the twenty-first century, reporters are looked upon much less favorably than they used to be.

- A 1994 L.A. Times Mirror survey revealed that 66 percent of Americans believe that news reports dwell excessively on disasters, misdeeds, and failure.

- In the same survey, 71 percent agreed that "the news media get in the way of society solving its problems."[1]
- Not surprisingly, daily newspaper readership has plummeted, from 69 percent of adults in 1972 to 50 percent or less today. Viewership of nightly network news has fallen from 75 percent in 1970–1971 to 54 percent in 1994–1995.[2]
- Meanwhile, the media are getting sued for stupefying amounts and are regularly losing libel verdicts. ABC's *20/20* program lost two huge libel verdicts in Miami, Florida, and Greensboro, North Carolina, in the space of two days in 1996 (see chapter 12, A Question of Ethics). NBC-TV News settled a threatened libel suit in 1997 with Richard Jewell, a security guard, about whom it strongly—and wrongly—suggested may have planted a bomb at the Atlanta 1996 Olympics that led to two deaths and many injuries.[3] The *Wall Street Journal* lost the largest media libel verdict in history, $227 million (later reduced) in 1997. A week later, Wall Street investor Julian Robertson announced his intent to sue *Business Week* because of that magazine's nasty portrait of him, for a tidy $1 billion.[4]
- Even journalists are condemning the lack of objectivity in their own profession. In 1996, veteran CBS News reporter Bernard Goldberg wrote a scathing article in the *Wall Street Journal*, charging that "media elites," including some of his own CBS colleagues, have such a "liberal bias that is so blatantly true that it's hardly worth discussing anymore."[5]

Clearly, the mass media have become more vigilant and that means that the practice of public relations, which must deal firsthand with the media, faces new challenges in ensuring that clients are treated "fairly."

POWER OF PUBLICITY

Whether the mass media have lost relative influence to other proliferating alternative communications vehicles or not, the fact remains that securing positive publicity through the mass media is still a critical activity for most public relations professionals. Moreover, public relations professionals still regard the mass media as an institution of awesome power.

This chapter focuses on how to coexist with the media, particularly the print media with whom public relations professionals deal the most (chapter 12 addresses the electronic media). We explore here what it takes to work with the media to convey the most effective impression for an organization, that is, attracting positive publicity.

Because publicity, as we will see, is generally regarded as more credible than advertising, establishing a good working relationship with the media—despite the media's more aggressive, some would argue, hostile, tone—remains essential for successful communications programs. Traditionally, dealing with the media has been a primary responsibility of public relations professionals. And as noted, the practice of public relations has been most closely associated—for better or worse—with the function of media publicity. Accordingly, media relations has developed into a career specialty for many in the field.

When the media go to bat for an organization or individual, the rewards can be substantial. On the other hand, when the media take aim at a particular individual or institution, the results can be devastating.

Recent U.S. history is studded with examples of people and organizations whose power and influence have been cut short because of extensive and critical media attention.

- In 1991, when IBM Chairman John Akers fulminated in an internal memo that his troops were becoming "too damn comfortable . . . standing around the water cooler waiting to be told what to do," the word leaked to the press and the ensuing headlines weren't pleasant. A year later, Akers was shown the door by his board.[6] His replacement as CEO, Lou Gerstner, by contrast, was hailed in the media as "Big Blue's savior."
- In 1993, two federal law enforcement agencies warned their agents that "loose and often uninformed comments to the press" would jeopardize their efforts to solve the bombing at the World Trade Center in New York City and the armed standoff at the Branch Davidian headquarters in Waco, Texas. The directors of both agencies—the FBI at the World Trade Center and the Bureau of Alcohol, Tobacco, and Firearms in Waco—eventually were replaced.[7] Four years later, the FBI was back in the soup, as the media zeroed in on the agency, for a forensics laboratory found guilty of skewing evidence against high profile defendants, from O.J. Simpson to the Oklahoma City Federal Office Building bomber.
- In 1996, Speaker of the House Newt Gingrich, having enjoyed media acclaim for engineering a "Republican revolution," was vilified by the press for ethical violations. In 1997, when Gingrich borrowed $300,000 from failed presidential candidate Bob Dole to pay his fine, the media crucified him again.
- Likewise in 1997, President and Mrs. Clinton continued to be dogged by a media, energized two years earlier when a First Family friend and government attorney, Vincent Foster, was found dead. Allegations of a cover-up in the financing of the Arkansas Whitewater Development Corporation refused to die, while each day brought front page headlines of additional campaign funding questions. Even the President's constant and vociferous denials couldn't shake the press from bird-dogging him and First Lady Hillary throughout the Clinton presidency (see the Case Study in chapter 16).

The vigilance of the media in exposing fraud, deception, and questionable practices in society is a tradition (Figure 11–1). The media's crowning achievement was the exposure of the Watergate break-in, which eventually led to the resignation of President Richard Nixon. The success of the *Washington Post* in getting to the bottom of Watergate encouraged journalists to focus on power abuses in all areas of society. Over the years since Watergate, investigative reporting has gained a solid foothold, particularly on television, where one picture is worth a thousand words. The cream of the TV investigative crop, of course, is *60 Minutes*, among the nation's most widely watched shows for the better part of three decades. But even *60 Minutes* is not without its faults. According to CBS anchorman Dan Rather, "We make mistakes so often, violating the basics of accuracy, clarity, or fairness, that sometimes it shatters me. If with our budget and our staff and time we make so many mistakes in exposé material, what's it like under less luxurious circumstances?"[8]

What indeed? So-called tabloid journalism in the latter part of the 1990s took its toll on media relations. Those who had been burned by the half-truths and preconceived biases of the tabloids counseled others not to cooperate at all with such "pretend journalists."[9] One casualty was the so-called legitimate media, which seemed to succumb to the competition for titillation by lowering its standards. Indeed, with the spate of gossip columnists and tell-all talk shows in the latter part of the 1990s—from Howard Stern to Jenny Jones, from *A Current Affair* to *Inside Edition*, from *Hard Copy* to the *National Enquirer*—the spread of tattletale journalism has put an added burden on public relations professionals, who, as the primary voice of management, seek fair and unbiased treatment of their organizations in the media.

The Sanctions Debate: 3

"We turned out the lights, but the game went on"

Several weeks ago, we examined the U.S. government's use of economic sanctions as a tool of first resort in the conduct of foreign policy. But are they effective or just a "moral high"? Some examples from recent history are illuminating.

■ Following the Turkish invasion of Cyprus in 1974, the U.S. imposed economic sanctions on Turkey that lasted four years. The Turks, arguing that they needed to protect the Turkish Cypriots, kept their forces on the island, while U.S. sanctions petered out.

■ After Russia invaded Afghanistan, the U.S. imposed a grain embargo on the Soviet Union and boycotted the 1980 Moscow Olympics to strike out at the Soviet economy and image. The U.S.S.R. simply turned to other suppliers, and U.S. farmers lost a major customer for their products. And, despite the absence of the U.S. and other boycotting nations, the Games went on.

■ In 1994, the U.S. applied economic sanctions against Haiti in an attempt to oust that country's military dictatorship. But change only came after the U.S. dispatched troops to that country—long after the Haitian people had suffered economic deprivation from the U.S. boycott.

■ In 1985, the U.S. and other nations imposed economic and athletic sanctions against South Africa to protest its apartheid policy. After years of resistance on the part of the white minority government, apartheid died a bloodless death and South Africa made a smooth transition to majority rule. Clearly, sanctions played a role—though they probably had less impact than <u>internal</u> factors such as escalating black resistance and increased urbanization.

Significantly, the sanctions imposed against South Africa had the additional force of being multilateral, while the three "failures" were largely unilateral. This pattern has continued over the past 20 years as the U.S. has increasingly gone it alone—especially to protest human rights violations. The tactic has become a handy alternative to war or inaction—especially with Congress where members find it plays well with local constituencies who have strong ties to a targeted country. But does it work?

What, for example, does the U.S. gain by threatening to deny most-favored-nation trading status to China? Not much. The Chinese resent it as an affront to their sovereignty. And they have a wide choice of other markets for their trade. Imposing economic sanctions on China could actually hurt the U.S., by reducing its influence in this economically burgeoning and strategically critical nation. Diminished trade would hurt the U.S. economy—and American consumers—far more than it would the Chinese; increased contact with U.S. companies and Western values promises to narrow the social and political gap currently dividing us from a country that only recently emerged from isolation.

As America considers its foreign policy alternatives, we hope it will be mindful that while sanctions may provide some temporary emotional satisfaction, they rarely achieve their aims. Rather, as in the case of the 1980 grain embargo and Olympic boycott of Russia, the U.S. felt it had turned out the lights, only to find that the Games went on. In today's global economy where there are many players, the game will go on—with or without the United States.

 **Mobil** The energy to make a difference.

Figure 11–1 Over the years, the nation's largest oil companies have had their share of problems with investigative reporting. As one way of fighting back, Mobil has reserved op-ed space in *The New York Times* every Thursday since the mid 1960s.

THE REST OF THE STORY

KLEIN AS IN "LYIN"

Add "journalistic ethics" to your list of oxymorons.

The nation's number one best-selling book in 1996 was a scathing, loosely disguised tell-all tale about President Clinton's 1992 campaign. Called *Primary Colors*, the book told the story of a leering and unprincipled candidate who would stop at nothing to get elected. What made the novel even more titillating was that the identity of its author was a secret. "The book was written by 'Anonymous,' " said publisher Random House, "and that's all we will reveal."

For months, journalists tried to uncover the identity of "Anonymous." One suspect was Joe Klein (Figure 11-2), *Newsweek* political columnist. For months, both Klein and his editor, Maynard Parker, vociferously denied the charge. As proof, Parker allowed another *Newsweek* columnist to suggest in print that the identity of Anonymous was a former speechwriter for New York Governor Mario Cuomo. Klein himself was interviewed by CBS and others and each time laughed off the possibility that he could be "Anonymous."

Then in July, the *Washington Post* analyzed the handwriting of edits on the book's original manuscript. And the cat was out of the bag.

Joe Klein, trusted journalist and friend, announced to a press conference of stunned colleagues, "My name is Joe Klein, and I wrote *Primary Colors*." Just as bad, Klein's editor, Parker, knew all about the ruse.

Figure 11–2   Joe Klein(L) aka Anonymous.

But how could a columnist, whose only asset is his "credibility," blatantly lie to his fellow reporters. Said Klein, "There are times I've had to lie to protect a source. I put that in this category."

His colleagues weren't buying it.

CBS News, for which Klein served as a commentator and to whom he had lied, canned him. *Newsweek* granted him a "leave of absence," which looked to be more permanent. The *New York Times* huffed in an editorial, "People interested in preserving the core values of serious journalism have to view his actions and words as corrupt."

On the other hand, the disgraced author did pocket $6 million for the exercise. And all it cost him, summarized *Times'* columnist Maureen Dowd, "was [a] few friendships . . . and his credibility".

WHAT RESEARCH TELLS US ABOUT THE MEDIA

The relationship between journalists and public relations people has never been an easy one. The former often accuse the latter of withholding information. The latter often accuse the former of left-leaning one-sided reporting. Research corroborates an uneasy relationship between those who interview and those who are being interviewed. In one 1987 telephone survey of 100 top-level executives, 59 percent of those polled claimed that they "invariably get misquoted" by the press. "Journalistic ignorance" was cited by 39 percent, with 25 percent saying that journalists were guilty of an "overemphasis on the negative." Another 22 percent cited "sensationalist tendencies," and 12 percent cited clear-cut "bias" among members of the press.[10]

A 1986 study of so-called elite journalists working for major news organs in Washington, D.C., and New York found evidence to support a liberal bias among journalists. The authors concluded that evidence "does not imply a conspiracy to exclude conservative voices, but merely reflects the human tendency to turn more often to those you trust, and to trust most those who think most like you do." They suggest that when it comes time to find expert commentary on policy issues, it is the liberal left that most often provides that commentary. As proof, they cited investigations of articles on welfare reform, consumer protection, nuclear energy, and other issues for which liberal sources were quoted significantly more than conservative ones.[11]

Recent studies show that neither journalists nor public relations people hold the strongly negative views that may once have been common. According to several studies, there seems to be a fairly high level of mutual respect within the two camps: Journalists tend to think that most public relations people do a good job and vice versa.

As for the general public, a 1995 survey showed that 50 percent of Americans feel the media are in conflict with their goals. In 17 years, daily newspaper readership has dropped from 69 to 50 percent. Likewise, nightly network news viewing, with the growth of cable, the Internet and other alternatives, has plummeted from 75 to 54 percent over the same period.[12]

Predictably, as the news gets harder edged and more sensationalized, and in the face of increased competition for readers and viewers, the American public seems less enamored with journalists than they were in the days when avuncular CBS anchor Walter Cronkite was regularly voted "the most trusted man in America."

OBJECTIVITY IN THE MEDIA

Total objectivity in reporting is unattainable; it would require complete neutrality and near-total detachment in reporting a story. Most people start with biases and preconceived notions about almost any subject. Reporting, then, is subjective. Nevertheless, scholars of journalism believe that reporters and editors should strive for maximum objectivity (Figure 11–3).

THE JOURNALIST'S Creed

I believe IN THE PROFESSION OF JOURNALISM.

I BELIEVE THAT THE PUBLIC JOURNAL IS A PUBLIC TRUST; THAT ALL CONNECTED WITH IT ARE, TO THE FULL MEASURE OF THEIR RESPONSIBILITY, TRUSTEES FOR THE PUBLIC; THAT ACCEPTANCE OF A LESSER SERVICE THAN THE PUBLIC SERVICE IS BETRAYAL OF THIS TRUST.

I BELIEVE THAT CLEAR THINKING AND CLEAR STATEMENT, ACCURACY, AND FAIRNESS ARE FUNDAMENTAL TO GOOD JOURNALISM.

I BELIEVE THAT A JOURNALIST SHOULD WRITE ONLY WHAT HE HOLDS IN HIS HEART TO BE TRUE.

I BELIEVE THAT SUPPRESSION OF THE NEWS, FOR ANY CONSIDERATION OTHER THAN THE WELFARE OF SOCIETY, IS INDEFENSIBLE.

I BELIEVE THAT NO ONE SHOULD WRITE AS A JOURNALIST WHAT HE WOULD NOT SAY AS A GENTLEMAN; THAT BRIBERY BY ONE'S OWN POCKETBOOK IS AS MUCH TO BE AVOIDED AS BRIBERY BY THE POCKETBOOK OF ANOTHER; THAT INDIVIDUAL RESPONSIBILITY MAY NOT BE ESCAPED BY PLEADING ANOTHER'S INSTRUCTIONS OR ANOTHER'S DIVIDENDS.

I BELIEVE THAT ADVERTISING, NEWS AND EDITORIAL COLUMNS SHOULD ALIKE SERVE THE BEST INTERESTS OF READERS; THAT A SINGLE STANDARD OF HELPFUL TRUTH AND CLEANNESS SHOULD PREVAIL FOR ALL; THAT THE SUPREME TEST OF GOOD JOURNALISM IS THE MEASURE OF ITS PUBLIC SERVICE.

I BELIEVE THAT THE JOURNALISM WHICH SUCCEEDS BEST—AND BEST DESERVES SUCCESS—FEARS GOD AND HONORS MAN; IS STOUTLY INDEPENDENT, UNMOVED BY PRIDE OF OPINION OR GREED OF POWER, CONSTRUCTIVE, TOLERANT BUT NEVER CARELESS, SELF-CONTROLLED, PATIENT, ALWAYS RESPECTFUL OF ITS READERS BUT ALWAYS UNAFRAID, IS QUICKLY INDIGNANT AT INJUSTICE; IS UNSWAYED BY THE APPEAL OF PRIVILEGE OR THE CLAMOR OF THE MOB; SEEKS TO GIVE EVERY MAN A CHANCE, AND, AS FAR AS LAW AND HONEST WAGE AND RECOGNITION OF HUMAN BROTHERHOOD CAN MAKE IT SO AN EQUAL CHANCE; IS PROFOUNDLY PATRIOTIC WHILE SINCERELY PROMOTING INTERNATIONAL GOOD WILL AND CEMENTING WORLD-COMRADESHIP; IS A JOURNALISM OF HUMANITY, OF AND FOR TODAY'S WORLD.

Walter Williams

DEAN SCHOOL OF JOURNALISM, UNIVERSITY OF MISSOURI, 1908-1935

Figure 11–3 "The Journalist's Creed" was written after World War I by Dr. Walter Williams, dean of the School of Journalism at the University of Missouri.

THE FALL OF "FAIRNESS"

To many business CEOs, sitting for an interview with a reporter is the communications equivalent of root canal. CEOs approach the media with fear and loathing. Journalists respond by claiming that if you are fair to them, they will reciprocate.

But sometimes, it doesn't quite work that way.

Take the case of Wall Street legend Julian Robertson.

In 1980, Robertson began his Tiger Management hedge fund company with $8 million to invest. By 1996, he had built that figure to about $8 billion. Over those years, Robertson kept a healthy distance from the press, despite their great interest in his operation.

In 1995, however, the investor received a persuasive note from the venerable *Business Week* magazine, commending Tiger for having "achieved a significant rebound" from a poor 1994 and asking for a chance to "tell the full story" about Robertson's firm. Trusting the publication to be "fair," the Tiger chieftain agreed to "open up" the company to *Business Week*, directing all of the firm's top managers to meet individually with the magazine's reporter.

Robertson, himself, sat for three interviews and two sets of photographs in New York and Paris. And when Tiger completed its best January in history, a 17 percent increase at the start of 1996, the firm was hopeful the story would explain how it was able to regain its stellar performance after two sub-par years.

And then the bottom fell out.

The magazine didn't produce the story after Tiger's resounding January, but instead waited till April, after Tiger suffered a disappointing March. The cover story that resulted—published on April Fool's Day no less!—was a good, old-fashioned hatchet job. "The Fall of the Wizard of Wall Street" screamed the cover. Inside, the story predicted Robertson's "unraveling" and documented the comments of a parade of seemingly disgruntled former employees, who complained about their former leader's management style.

Understandably, Robertson and his colleagues were stunned by the one-sided treatment, particularly after they had cooperated so willingly with the magazine.

Robertson's friends and associates—many of the most powerful names on Wall Street—leapt to his defense with a letter to *Business Week*. The letter was also signed by the seven former Tiger employees mentioned in the article, although *Business Week* curiously deleted this reference in reprinting the letter.

As for Robertson himself, he said nothing publicly until Tiger completed one of its best years ever in 1996.

Then the hedge-fund master sat for two other interviews with *Barron's* and *Institutional Investor* magazines, which both hailed his "comeback." "His performance makes the [*Business Week*] article look silly," summarized *Barron's* in its story headlined "Still a Winner."

And there the issue would have ended had not Robertson, in the spring of 1997, announced plans to sue *Business Week* for the tidy sum of $1 billion for "false and derogatory statements." When journalists shuddered at the amount, the "reannointed wizard's" spokesman said the money was not nearly as important as defending the principle of "fairness."

By virtue of their role, the media views officials, particularly business and government spokespersons, with a degree of skepticism. Reporters shouldn't be expected to accept on faith the party line. By the same token, once a business or government official effectively substantiates the official view and demonstrates its merit, the media should be willing to report this accurately, without editorial distortion.

Stated another way, the relationship between the media and the establishment should be one of healthy adversaries rather than of bitter enemies. Unfortunately, this is not always the case. According to one network anchorman, the fault lies with the First Amendment, which discourages critical analysis by the press of the press. Says NBC's Tom Brokaw: "In American journalism, we generally are inclined to call attention to almost everyone's failings but our own. When criticism is directed at us, we are very likely to develop a glass jaw."[13] Author Janet Malcolm takes an even dimmer view: "Every journalist who is not too stupid or too full of himself to notice what is going on knows that what he does is morally indefensible. He is a kind of confidence man, preying on people's vanity, ignorance, or loneliness, gaining their trust and betraying them without remorse."[14] Whew!

Fortunately, such journalists are in the minority. Most want to get the facts from all sides, and they acknowledge and respect the public relations practitioner's role in the process. If they are dealt with fairly, they will reciprocate in kind. However, some executives fail to understand the essential difference between the media and their own organizations. The reporter wants the "story" whether bad or good. Organizations, on the other hand, want things to be presented in the best light. Because of this difference, some executives consider journalists to be adversaries, and they fear and distrust the media.

Thoughtful journalists, of course, abhor the enemy tag. They implore officials in business and government to continue to talk to the media and to explain complex issues so that the public can better understand them. According to Lewis H. Young, former editor-in-chief of *Business Week* magazine: "The chief executive officer has to learn to be comfortable with the press. And the only way to be comfortable with the press is to get to meet media people, to talk to them, to go out for lunch with them, go out to dinner with them, and get used to the kinds of things that they're going to ask about, what they're interested in."[15] Based on the deep-seated distrust that some business and government people reserve for the media, Young's wish is no easy task.

With the media and the public still on different philosophical wavelengths, the challenge for public relations professionals remains to foster a closer relationship between their organizations and those who present the news. The key, once again, is fairness, with each side accepting—and respecting—the other's role and responsibility. Often the relationship works well. Other times, it doesn't work at all.

DEALING WITH THE MEDIA

It falls on public relations professionals to orchestrate the relationship between their organizations and the media. To be sure, the media can't ordinarily be manipulated in our society. They can, however, be confronted in an honest and interactive way to convey the organization's point of view in a manner that may merit being reported. First, an organization must establish a formal media relations policy (Figure 11–4). Second, an organization must establish a philosophy for dealing with the media, keeping in mind the following 10 principles:

1. **Flexibility is key.** Having a plan to deal with the media is fine, but an organization must remain flexible, dealing with media inquiries on a case-by-case basis and not being locked into an overly restrictive policy.

Organization and Policy Guide

Unit with Primary Responsibility for Review Corporate Communications

It is frequently in Chase's best interest to take advantage of interest from the media to further the reputation and services of the bank. In dealing with the media, Chase officers must be careful to protect the best interests of the bank, particularly with regard to the area of customer confidence.

The following policies will serve as a guideline for media relationships. Specific questions regarding the media should be addressed to the Public Relations Division.

Inquiries from the Media

Most journalists call the Public Relations Division when they need information about the bank or wish to arrange an interview with a bank officer. Many times, public relations officers are able to handle inquiries directly. Occasionally, however, more complex questions require input from appropriate bank officers. In these cases, inasmuch as journalists are often under deadline pressures, it is important that bank officers cooperate as fully and respond as promptly as possible. Such cooperation enhances Chase's reputation for integrity with the news media.

Less frequently, reporter inquiries will go directly to line officers. In this case, either one of two responses may be appropriate:

1. If a journalist seeks simple, factual information such as Chase's current rate on a particular savings instrument or the factual details of a new bank service, officers may provide it directly.

2. If a reporter seeks Chase policy or official opinion on such subjects as trends in interest rates, legislation, etc., responses should be reviewed with the Public Relations Division. If an officer is unfamiliar with a particular policy or requires clarification of it, he or she should always check first with the Public Relations Division before committing the bank in print.

In talking with a reporter, it is normally assumed that whatever a bank officer says may be quoted and attributed directly to him or her by name as a spokesperson for the bank. An officer not wishing to be quoted must specify that desire to the journalist.

Figure 11–4 This media relations policy of The Chase Manhattan Bank is typical of that found in many large organizations. Relationships with the media are generally encouraged, with the public relations division taking overall responsibility for all of the bank's relationships with journalists.

Most reporters with whom the bank deals will respect an officer's wishes to maintain anonymity. Most journalists recognize that it is as important for them to honor the wishes of their sources at the bank as it is for the bank to disseminate its comments and information to the public through the news media. Chase's policy toward the media should be one of mutual trust, understanding and benefit.

Interviews With the Media

In order to monitor the bank's relationships with journalists, all requests for interviews with bank officers by journalists must be routed through the Public Relations Division.

As a rule, public relations officers check the credentials of the journalist and determine the specific areas of inquiry to be examined. The public relations officer will then decide whether the interview is appropriate for the bank. When the decision is affirmative, the public relations officer will discuss subject matter with the recommended interviewee and together they will decide on a course of action and Chase objectives for the interview.

A member of the public relations staff is normally present during any face-to-face interview with an officer of the bank. The purpose of the public relations staffer's attendance is to provide assistance in handling the interview situation as well as to aid the reporter with follow-up material.

When a reporter calls an officer directly to request an interview, the officer should check with the Public Relations Division before making a commitment.

Authorized Spokespersons

Vice presidents and above are normally authorized to speak for the bank on matters in their own area of responsibility.

Normally, officers below the level of vice president are not authorized to speak for attribution on behalf of the bank except where they are specialists in a particular field, such as technical directors, economists, etc.

Exceptions may be made in special situations and in concert with the Public Relations Division.

Written Material for the Media

Chase articles bylined by officers may either be written by the officer approached or by a member of the public relations staff. If an officer decided to author his or her own article, the public relations division must be consulted for editing, photographic support and policy proofing.

Occasionally, customers or suppliers may wish to include Chase in an article or advertisement they are preparing. This material too must be routed through the Public Relations Division for review.

Figure 11–4   Continued

2. **Provide the media with only one voice.** The media prefer many spokespersons, but an organization should stick to one. He or she should be available to one and all in the press, and everyone in the organization should understand that it is this person's job alone to convey information to the outside world.

3. **Don't volunteer the chief as spokesperson.** The media insist on speaking to the top person. Sometimes this makes sense. Normally, though, exposing the chief executive to the media is the worst thing one can do. It is much better to offer a trained spokesperson who is knowledgeable and experienced in dealing with the idiosyncrasies of reporters and the media.

4. **Don't always take the lawyer's advice.** A lawyer's job is to protect the organization from challenge in a court of law. However, a lawyer's advice often may not be responsive to the likely perception of the institution in another critical court—the "court of public opinion." The smart manager always weighs legal advice against public relations advice.

5. **Don't wait until you've got all the facts.** If you wait for all the data, you may still be sitting after the public has branded you "guilty as charged." Often, it

THE REST OF THE STORY

CONFESSIONS OF A MEDIA MAVEN

Dealing with the media for fun and profit, even for an experienced public relations hand, is a constant learning experience. Often, such learning is achieved the hard way.

In the 1980s, many of the nation's largest banks were a bit jittery about negative publicity on their loans to lesser developed countries. One of the most vociferous bank bashers was Patrick J. Buchanan, a syndicated columnist who later became President Reagan's communications director and still later campaigned for president.

After one particularly venomous syndicated attack on the banks, a certain young and impetuous bank public affairs director wrote directly to Buchanan's editor asking whether he couldn't "muzzle at least for a little while" his wild-eyed columnist. The letter's language, in retrospect, was perhaps a bit harsh.

Some weeks later, in a six-column article that ran throughout the nation, Buchanan wrote in part:

Another sign that the banks are awaking to the reality of the nightmare is a screed that lately arrived at this writer's syndicate from one Fraser P. Seitel, vice president of Chase Manhattan.

Terming this writer's comments "wrong," "stupid," "inflammatory," and "the nonsensical ravings of a lunatic," Seitel nevertheless suggested that the syndicate "tone down" future writings, "at least 'til the frenetic financial markets get over the current hysteria."*

The columnist went on to describe the fallacy in bankers' arguments and ended by suggesting that banks begin immediately to cut unnecessary frills—such as directors of public affairs!

Moral: Never get into a shouting match with somebody who buys ink by the barrel.

Secondary moral: Just because you write a textbook doesn't mean you know everything!

---

*Patrick J. Buchanan, "The Banks Must Face Up to Losses on Third World Loans," *New York Post* (July 12, 1984): 35.

makes sense to launch a preemptive rebuttal to media charges. This shows the public that you're not going to accept unfounded accusations.

6. **Don't answer every question.** The fact that the media ask doesn't mean you have to answer. You have no obligation to answer every question. And you should answer only those questions you are prepared to handle.

7. **Squawk if you're wronged.** If the media print inaccuracies, blast them. Call the reporter and demand a correction. Correct the public record. If you don't, the inaccuracy will go uncorrected for so long that eventually it will become a "media fact."

8. **Don't keep journalists at arm's length.** As noted, a journalist's job is to get a story, whatever that entails. The public relations professional's job is to be an advocate for the institution. As long as both understand and respect each other's position, cooperating with a journalist can often be in an organization's best interest.

9. **Share information with allies.** Limiting information to those who need to know can be counterproductive. Employees, customers, and even stockholders can serve as valuable allies in dealing with the public and the media. They should be kept aware of the organization's position on issues of media interest.

10. **You can lose the media battle but still win the longer term credibility war.** Sometimes, especially if you're wrong, the most sensible thing to do is admit it. Had Richard Nixon done this over Watergate, he might have served his full second term. There is nothing as refreshing as hearing an official admit, "We made a mistake. We'll make restitution. It won't happen again." That's how an organization retains its credibility.[16]

SECURING PUBLICITY

Publicity, through news releases and other methods, is designed to broaden knowledge and positive recognition of an organization, its personnel, and its activities. Publicity is most often gained by dealing directly with the media, either by initiating the communication or by reacting to inquiries. Publicity differs dramatically from advertising, despite the fact that most people confuse the two.

Advertising possesses the following characteristics:

1. You pay for it.
2. You control what is said.
3. You control how it is said.
4. You control to whom it is said.
5. To a degree, you control where it is put in a publication or on the air.
6. You control the frequency of its use.

Publicity, on the other hand, offers no such controls. Typically, publicity is subject to review by news editors, who may decide to use all of a story, some of it, or none of it. When it will run, who will see it, how often it will be used are all subject, to a large degree, to the whims of a news editor. However, even though publicity is by no means a sure thing, it does offer two overriding benefits that enhance its appeal, even beyond that of advertising:

- First, although not free, publicity costs only the time and effort expended by public relations personnel and management in attempting to place it in the media. Therefore, relatively speaking, its cost is minimal, especially when compared with the costs of advertising and assessed against potential returns.

• Second and more important, publicity, which appears in news rather than in advertising columns, carries the implicit endorsement of the publication in which it appears. In other words, publicity is perceived as objective news rather than self-serving promotion, which translates into the most sought-after commodity for an organization—credibility.

This is the true value of publicity over advertising.

VALUE OF PUBLICITY

Publicity holds much value for an organization. In light of the implicit third-party endorsement that publicity carries, it is often regarded as news and therefore as more credible than advertising. For any organization, then, publicity makes great sense in the following areas:

• **Announcing a new product or service.**   Because publicity can be regarded as news, it should be used before advertising commences. A new product or service is news only once. Once advertising appears, the product is no longer news. Therefore, one inflexible rule—that most organizations, alas, break—is that publicity should precede advertising.

• **Reenergizing an old product.**   When a product has been around for a while, it's difficult to make people pay attention to advertising. Therefore, publicity techniques—staged events, sponsorships, and so on—may pay off to rejuvenate a mature product. The Sharps Beer Truck is a good example (Figure 11–5).

• **Explaining a complicated product.**   Often there isn't enough room in an advertisement to explain a complex product or service. Insurance companies, banks, mutual funds, and so on, all of which offer products that demand thoughtful explanation, may find advertising space too limiting. Publicity, on the other hand, allows enough room to tell the story.

• **Little or no budget.**   Often, organizations don't have the budget to accommodate advertising. To make an impact, advertising requires frequency—the constant repetition of ads so that readers eventually see them and acknowledge the product. In the case of Samuel Adams Lager Beer, for example, the company lacked an advertising budget to promote its unique brew. So it used public relations techniques to spread the word about this different-tasting beer. Over time, primarily through publicity about its victories at beer-tasting competitions, Samuel Adams grew in popularity. Today, its advertising budget is robust. But the company's faith in publicity endures.

• **Enhancing the organization's reputation.**   Advertising is, at its base, self-serving. When a company gives to charity or does a good deed in the community, taking out an ad is the wrong way to communicate its efforts. It is much better for the recipient organization to commend its benefactor in the daily news columns.

• **Crisis response.**   In a crisis, publicity techniques are the fastest and most credible means of response. In 1996, when Texaco was charged with racism, the company took to the public airwaves to dispel the criticism. Earlier, when Pepsi-Cola suffered its tampering scare, the company launched an immediate publicity response. Only when the crisis was resolved and Pepsi had won did the company authorize ads thanking its employees and customers for their loyalty amid the turmoil.

Figure 11–5 The Sharps Beer Truck, which traveled from town to town, attracting curious onlookers and plenty of publicity photos, proved an excellent way to reinvigorate a mature product.

These are just a few of the advantages of publicity over advertising. A smart organization, therefore, will always consider publicity a vital component in its overall marketing plan.

AVENUES OF PUBLICITY

Many vehicles can be used for publicity purposes, from skywriting to Pennysavers to the bull horn at a political rally.

The vehicle that remains the most frequent target of public relations professionals is the newspaper. Even though the electronic media and the Internet have become increasingly important, the news of the day is still dictated by daily newspapers. In fact, the first thing a TV news director does when he or she reaches the office in the morning is to check the local paper to set the TV news agenda. On the national level, the *New York Times*, *Wall Street Journal*, and *Washington Post* generally set the "news agenda."

Newspapers provide more diversity and depth of coverage than TV or radio. It may be for this reason that approximately 60 million copies of daily newspapers are sold each day. Newspapers range from giant dailies with circulations approaching 2 million to small weekly papers written, edited, and produced by a single individual. There are approximately 1,650 daily newspapers in the United States, most of which appear in the afternoon (Table 11–1).

TABLE 11–1

TOP 25 U.S. NEWSPAPERS BY CIRCULATION

Rank	Newspaper	Circulation (9/30/96)	Gain/Loss from 9/30/95
1	Wall Street Journal	1,783,500	20,400
2	USA Today	1,591,600	68,000
3	New York Times	1,071,100	−10,400
4	Los Angeles Times	1,029,100	−21,800
5	Washington Post	789,200	−4,500
6	New York Daily News	734,300	3,700
7	Chicago Tribune	680,500	−3,800
8	Newsday	564,800	n/a
9	Houston Chronicle	554,300	3,900
10	Chicago Sun-Times	496,000	7,600
11	San Francisco Chronicle	487,000	−2,300
12	Dallas Morning News	478,200	−22,200
13	Boston Globe	471,000	−27,800
14	New York Post	429,600	15,900
15	Philadelphia Inquirer	427,200	−42,200
16	Newark Star-Ledger	405,900	−30,800
17	Cleveland Plain Dealer	386,300	10,500
18	Phoenix Arizona Republic	382,100	16,100
19	San Diego Union-Tribune	372,100	−7,600
20	Minneapolis/ St. Paul Star-Tribune	366,000	n/a
21	Detroit Free Press	363,400	n/a
22	Orange County Register (Santa Ana)	353,800	3,900
23	Miami Herald	344,400	−23,100
24	Portland Oregonian	338,600	−4,900
25	Denver Post	334,400	31,131

Source: Business Wire, December 1996.

In recent years, with operating costs skyrocketing and many Americans leaving the central cities for the suburbs, some urban papers have folded. Traditional competition between morning and evening newspapers has diminished in these cities. And it is true that newspaper readership has remained at the same general level for decades and, most disturbing, a large proportion of young adults in the 20 to 40 age bracket aren't newspaper subscribers.[17]

Occasionally, the same publishing firm owns both papers. The huge Rochester-based Gannett chain, for example, owns 97 daily newspapers reaching 6 million readers, as well as 8 TV stations and 15 radio stations. In 1982, Gannett launched its most ambitious project to date with the publication of USA Today, a truly national newspaper, transmitted from Rosslyn, Virginia, to major American cities via satellite. The paper costs Gannett upward of $50 million per year. The full-color newspaper lists daily news from all 50 states; offers national weather, sports, and business; and downplays international news. USA Today has become "America's hometown newspaper." Some critics still charge that USA Today's abbreviated articles are fast-food journalism and derisively label the publication "McPaper." Nevertheless, its circulation has reached 1.59 million, second only to that of the the Wall Street Journal.

Despite the loss of journalistic competition in many cities, the newspaper is still a primary target for media relations activities. To practitioners and their managements, penetrating the daily with positive publicity is a critical challenge. To many corporate managements, favorable publicity in *The New York Times* is a special achievement. To politicians, a complimentary story in the *Washington Post* is equally cherished. In other communities, a positive piece in the local daily is just as rewarding.

Not to be overlooked in media relations are the suburban newspapers, the small-city dailies, and the nearly 7,500 weekly newspapers. All are targets for news releases and story ideas. When an organization has a branch or plant in an area, these local media contacts can be of critical importance, particularly for consumer product publicity.

PLACING PUBLICITY

How does a public relations practitioner "place" a story in a newspaper? How does he or she convert publicity to news? After getting the release written, the following hints may help achieve placement:

1. **Know deadlines.**   Time governs every newspaper. *The New York Times* has different deadlines for different sections of the paper, with its business section essentially closing down between 6:00 and 7:00 P.M. News events should be scheduled, whenever possible, to accommodate deadlines. An old and despised practice (at least by journalists) is to announce bad news close to deadline time on Friday afternoon, the premise being that newspaper journalists won't have time to follow up on the story and that few people will read Saturday's paper anyway. Although this technique may work on occasion, it leaves reporters and editors hostile.

2. **Generally write, don't call.**   Reporters are barraged with deadlines. They are busiest close to deadline time, which is late afternoon for morning newspapers and morning for afternoon papers. Thus, it's preferable to mail or send news releases by messenger rather than try to explain them over the telephone. Follow-up calls to reporters to "make sure you got our release" also should be avoided. If reporters are unclear on a certain point, they'll call to check.

3. **Direct the release to a specific person or editor.**   Newspapers are divided into departments: business, sports, style, entertainment, and the like. The release directed to a specific person or editor has a greater chance of being read than one addressed simply to "editor." At smaller papers, one person may handle all financial news. At larger papers, the financial news section may have different editors for banking, chemicals, oil, electronics, and many other specialties. Public relations people should know who covers their beat and target releases accordingly.

   Public relations professionals should also know the differences in the functions of newspaper personnel. For example, the publisher is the person responsible for overall newspaper policy. The editorial editor is generally responsible for editorial page content, including the opinion-editorial (op-ed) section. The managing editor is responsible for overall news content. These three should rarely, if ever, be called to secure publicity. That leaves the various section editors and reporters as key contacts for public relations practitioners.

4. **Make personal contact.**   Knowing a reporter may not result in an immediate story, but it can pay residual dividends. Those who know the

THE REST OF THE STORY

ANSWERING THE MEDIA

How well would you do if you were asked to go toe to toe with a reporter? Take this yes-or-no quiz, borrowed from the *Public Relations Reporter*, and find out. Answers are given below.

1. When addressing a print reporter or electronic medium moderator, should you use his or her first name?
2. Should you ever challenge a reporter in a verbal duel?
3. Are reporters correct in thinking that they can ask embarrassing questions of anyone in public office?
4. Should you answer a hypothetical question?
5. Should you ever say, "No comment"?
6. When a reporter calls on the telephone, should you assume that the conversation is being taped?
7. Do audiences remember most of the content of a TV interview 30 minutes after it is broadcast?
8. Should you ever admit you had professional training to handle the media?
9. If you don't know the correct answer to a reporter's question, should you try to answer it anyway?

BONUS QUESTION:

What did Henry Kissinger say at the start of his press briefings as secretary of state?

ANSWERS

1. Yes. In most cases, using first names is the best strategy. It makes the discussion much more conversational and less formal than using "Mr." or "Ms."
2. No. Most people should try to gain goodwill in an interview. This is rarely achieved by getting into an acrimonious debate.
3. Yes. Journalists must be suspicious of any claim by a public person that he or she is telling not only the truth, but the whole truth. Anyone in public office must be prepared to respond to such questions.
4. No. Avoid hypothetical questions. Rarely can you win by dealing with them.
5. No. It is tantamount to taking the Fifth Amendment against self-incrimination. You appear to be hiding something.
6. Yes. Many state laws no longer require the "beep" that signals a taped call. Always assume that everything you say is being recorded and will be used.
7. No. Studies have found that audiences remember only 60 percent of the content after 30 minutes. They remember 40 percent at the end of the day and 10 percent by the end of the week.
8. Yes. By all means. You should point out that good communication with the public is a hallmark of your organization and that you're proud it has such a high priority.
9. No. Don't be afraid to say, "I don't know." Offer to find the answer and get back to the interviewer. Don't dig yourself into a hole you can't get out of.

Bonus answer: "Does anyone have any questions . . . for my answers?"

local weekly editor or the daily city editor have an advantage over colleagues who don't. Also, when a reporter uses your story idea, follow up with a note of commendation—particularly on the story's accuracy.

5. **Don't badger.** Newspapers are generally fiercely independent about the copy they use. Even a major advertiser will usually fail to get a piece of puffery published. Badgering an editor about a certain story is bad form, as is complaining excessively about the treatment given a certain story. Worst of all, little is achieved by acting outraged when a newspaper chooses not to run a story. Editors are human beings, too. For every release they use, dozens get discarded. If a public relations person protests too much, editors will remember.

6. **Use exclusives sparingly.** Sometimes public relations people promise exclusive stories to particular newspapers. The exclusive promises one newspaper a scoop over its competitors. For example, practitioners frequently arrange to have a visiting executive interviewed by only one local newspaper.

   Although the chances of securing a story are heightened by the promise of an exclusive, the risk of alienating the other papers exists. Thus, the exclusive should be used sparingly.

7. **When you call, do your own calling.** Reporters and editors generally don't have assistants. Most do not like to be kept waiting by a secretary calling for the boss. Public relations professionals should make their own initial and follow-up calls. Letting a secretary handle a journalist can alienate a good news contact. And above all, be pleasant and courteous.

Although cynics continue to predict "the end of reading as we know it," newspapers and magazines continue to endure. Although some predicted a decline in the magazine business in the 1990s, today approximately 11,002 are published in the United States. They range from the mainstream *Time* and *Newsweek*, to the gossipy *People* and *US*, to publications further afield, such as *OUT*, catering to the upscale gay and lesbian market, and *Chile Pepper*, the bimonthly that covers peppers of all types.

The fact remains that dealing with the print media is among the most essential technical skills of the public relations professional. Ergo, anyone who practices public relations must know how to deal with the print press.

WIRE SERVICES

Traditionally, two news-gathering organizations—the Associated Press (AP) and United Press International (UPI)—formed the backbone of the nation's news delivery system, supplying up-to-the-minute dispatches from around the world to both the print and electronic media. These wire services traditionally competed to deliver the most accurate news first, however, the AP now serves more than 15,000 worldwide clients—newspapers, magazines, TV, and radio stations—through 220 bureaus around the country and the world, and UPI, which has experienced financial problems, has far fewer subscribers and is but a shadow of its former self. Both wire services report in a simple, readable, understandable style.

Staging an equally intense rivalry on the financial side are three primarily business wires—Dow Jones, Reuters, and the upstart, Bloomberg Financial News. These wires specialize in business-oriented news. Reuters, based in London, is both a worldwide business service and a general news service. Dow Jones, whose flagship publication is the *Wall Street Journal*, also has an international affiliate in AP-Dow Jones. Bloomberg, begun by a former Wall Street investor, Michael Bloomberg, operates a multimedia operation from its Park Avenue headquarters.

When a company releases news that may influence the decision of an investor to hold, sell, or buy the company's stock, it is required to release the information promptly to the broadest group of investors. In this instance, Dow Jones, Reuters, Bloomberg and the local press are notified simultaneously. Dow Jones, Reuters and Bloomberg news wires, like those of the AP and UPI, are found in newspaper offices, brokerage firms, banks, investment houses, and many corporate offices throughout the country.

Additionally, commercial wire services, such as PR News Wire and Business Wire, distribute public relations material to news outlets nationwide. Unlike the AP and UPI, these commercial wires charge organizations a fee for running news release stories verbatim. Business Wire, for example, will charge a flat fee of $300 to $500 for a 400-word release, with an additional fee of $95 to $125 for 100 more words. These commercial wires can tailor their services to fit categories or geographies—across the United States and around the world. Such commercial wires are an effective backup, ensuring that announcements at least reach news outlets.

Feature syndicates, such as North American Newspaper Alliance and King Features, are another source of editorial material for newspapers and magazines. They provide subscribing newspapers with a broad spectrum of material, ranging from business commentaries to comic strips to gossip columns. Some of their writers—such as Art Buchwald, Dave Barry, and Jane Bryant Quinn—have built national reputations. Many such columnists depend heavily on source material provided by public relations personnel.

Media Directories

Another publicity support is the media directory, which describes in detail the various media.

1. *Gale's Directory of Publications* lists about 20,000 publications, including daily and weekly newspapers, as well as general circulation, trade, and special interest magazines. Gale's also includes the names, addresses, and phone numbers of publication editors.
2. *Bacon's Publicity Checker* provides data on almost 5,000 U.S. and Canadian trade and business publications that are organized in some 100 categories—from accounting and advertising to woolens and yachting. Bacon's includes editors' names, addresses, and phone numbers.
3. *Broadcasting Yearbook* contains information on radio and TV stations in the United States, Canada, and Latin America. It also lists key personnel, along with their addresses and telephones.
4. *Editor & Publisher Yearbook* lists newspapers across the United States (daily, weekly, national, black, college and university, foreign language) and their personnel.
5. *Working Press of the Nation* is a five-volume publication. It lists locations and editorial staff for newspapers, magazines, radio, television, feature syndicates, and house magazines.

6. Specialized directories—from *Hudson's Washington News Media Directory* and *Congressional Staff Guide* to the *Anglo-Jewish Media List*—and various state media directories, published by state press or broadcasters' associations, are also excellent resources for publicity purposes. Appendix G offers a comprehensive list of leading media directories compiled from *O'Dwyer's PR Services Report*.

MEASUREMENT ASSISTANCE/

After an organization has distributed its press materials, it needs an effective way to measure the results of its publicity. A variety of outside services can help.

Press Clipping Bureaus

Some agencies monitor company mentions in the press. These press clipping bureaus can supply newspaper and magazine clippings on any subject and about any company. The two largest, Burrelle's and Luce, each receive hundreds of newspapers and magazines daily. Both services dispatch nearly 50,000 clippings to their clients each day. Burrelle's, for example, employs about 800 people and subscribes to about 1,700 daily newspapers, 8,300 weeklies, 6,300 consumer and trade magazines, and various other publications.

These bureaus may also be hired in certain regions to monitor local news or for certain projects that require special scrutiny. Most charge monthly fees that are around $200 in addition to clipping charges of about $1.00 per article. For a practitioner who must keep management informed of press reports on the firm, the expense is generally worthwhile.

Broadcast Transcription Services

Specialized transcription services have been created to monitor broadcast stories. A handful of such broadcast transcription services exist in the country, with Radio-TV Reports and the Video Monitoring Service the largest, with offices in several cities. These firms monitor major radio and TV stations around the clock, checking for messages on client companies. After a client orders a particular segment of a broadcast program, Radio-TV Reports either prepares a typed transcript or secures an audiotape. Costs for transcripts are relatively high.

Content Analysis Services

A more sophisticated analysis of media results is supplied by firms that evaluate the content of media mentions on clients. Firms such as Ketchum Public Relations and PR Data use computer analysis to find positive and negative mentions about organizations. Although this measurement technique is rough and somewhat subjective, it helps an organization obtain a clearer idea of its portrayal by the media. However, such press-clipping computer analysis stops short of being a true test of audience attitudes.

████████████████
THE REST OF THE STORY

THE END OF THE WORLD AS THEY WRITE IT

When the end of the world arrives, here's how the various media may cover it:

- *USA Today:* WE'RE DEAD
- The *Wall Street Journal:* DOW PLUMMETS AS WORLD ENDS
- *Playboy:* GIRLS OF THE APOCALYPSE
- *Sports Illustrated:* GAME OVER
- *TV Guide:* DEATH AND DAMNATION: NIELSON RATINGS SOAR
- *Martha Stewart Living:* PLANNING THE PERFECT LAST SUPPER
- *Inc. Magazine:* 10 WAYS YOU CAN PROFIT FROM THE APOCALYPSE
- *National Enquirer:* O.J. AND NICOLE, TOGETHER AGAIN*

Speechwriter's Newsletter, April 1, 1997, 6.

HANDLING INTERVIEWS

Public relations people coordinate interviews for both print and broadcast media. Most executives are neither familiar with nor comfortable in such interview situations. For one thing, reporters ask a lot of searching questions, some of which may seem impertinent. Executives aren't used to being put on the spot. Instinctively, they may resent it, and thus the counseling of executives for interviews has become an important and strategic task of the in-house practitioner as well as a lucrative profession for media consultants.

In conducting interviews with the media the cardinal rule to remember is that such interviews are not "intellectual conversations." Neither the interviewee or the interviewer seek a lasting friendship. Rather, the interviewer wants only a "good story." And the interviewee wants only to convey his or her key messages.

Accordingly, the following 10 dos and don'ts are important in newspaper, magazine, or other print interviews:

1. **Do your homework in advance.** An interviewee must be thoroughly briefed—either verbally or in writing—before the interview. Know what the interviewer writes, for whom, and his or her opinions. Also, determine what the audience wants to know.
2. **Relax.** Remember that the interviewer is a person, too, and is just trying to do a good job. Building rapport will help the interview.
3. **Speak in personal terms.** People distrust large organizations. References to "the company" and "we believe" sound ominous. Use "I" instead. Speak as an individual, as a member of the public, rather than as a mouthpiece for an impersonal bureaucracy.
4. **Welcome the naive question.** If the question sounds simple, it should be answered anyway. It may be helpful to those who don't possess much knowledge of the organization or industry.

5. **Answer questions briefly and directly.**   Don't ramble. Be brief, concise, and to the point. An interviewee shouldn't get into subject areas about which he or she knows nothing. This situation can be dangerous and counterproductive when words are transcribed in print.

6. **Don't bluff.**   If a reporter asks a question that you can't answer, admit it. If there are others in the organization more knowledgeable about a particular issue, the interviewee or the practitioner should point that out and get the answer from them.

7. **State facts and back-up generalities.**   Facts and examples always bolster an interview. An interviewee should come armed with specific data that support general statements. Again, the practitioner should furnish all the specifics.

8. **If the reporter is promised further information, provide it quickly.**   Remember, reporters work under time pressures and need information quickly to meet deadlines. Anything promised in an interview should be granted soon. Forgetting (conveniently) to answer a request may return to haunt the organization when the interview is printed.

9. **There is no such thing as being off the record.**   A person who doesn't want to see something in print shouldn't say it. It's that simple. Reporters may get confused as to what was off the record during the interview. And although most journalists will honor an off-the-record statement, some may not. It's not generally worthwhile to take the risk. Occasionally, reporters will agree not to attribute a statement to the interviewee but to use it as background. Mostly, though, interviewees should be willing to have whatever they say in the interview appear in print.

10. **Tell the truth.**   Telling the truth is the key criterion. Journalists are generally perceptive; they can detect a fraud. So don't be evasive, don't cover up, and, most of all, don't lie. Be positive, but be truthful. Occasionally, an interviewee must decline to answer specific questions but should candidly explain why. This approach always wins in the long run. Remember, in an interview, your integrity is always on the line. Once you lose your credibility, you've lost everything.[18]

PRESS CONFERENCES

Press conferences, the convening of the media for a specific purpose, are generally not a good idea (Figure 11–6). Unless an organization has real news to communicate, press conferences can flop. Reporters don't have the time for meetings that offer little news. They generally don't like to shlep across town to hear news they could have received through a release. Before attempting a conference, ask this question: Can this information be disseminated just as easily in a news release? If the answer is yes, the conference should be scratched.

Eventually, though, every organization must face the media in a conference—in connection with an annual meeting or a major announcement or a presentation to securities analysts. The same rules and guidelines that hold true for a one-on-one interview hold true for dealing with the press in conference. Be honest, forthright, and fair. Follow these additional guidelines in a press conference:

1. **Don't play favorites; invite representatives from all major news outlets.**
   Normally, it makes sense to alert wire services, which in turn may have the

"Just tell the press the Ambassador feels it would be inappropriate to comment until he's had time to study the complete text."

Figure 11–6   For some, "meeting the press" isn't a particularly pleasant prospect.

resources to advise their print and broadcast subscribers. For example, the AP carries daily listings, called the day book, of news events in major cities.

2. **Notify the media by mail well in advance of the conference and follow up by phone.**   Ordinarily, the memo announcing the event should be straightforward and to the point, listing the subject, date, time, and place, as well as the speaker and the public relations contact's name, title, and phone number. If possible, the memo should reach the editor's desk at least 7 to 10 days before the event. Also, the day before the event, a follow-up phone call reminder is wise.

3. **Schedule the conference early in the day.**   Again, the earlier in the business day, the better, particularly for TV consumption.

4. **Hold the conference in a meeting room, not someone's office.**   Office auditoriums and hotel meeting rooms are good places for news conferences. Chairs should be provided for all reporters, and space should be allowed for TV crews to set up cameras. The speaker at the conference should preside from either a table or a lectern so that microphones and tape recorders can be placed nearby.

5. **The time allotted for the conference should be stated in advance.**   Reporters should be told at the beginning of the conference how much time they will have. Then no one can complain later.

6. **Keep the speaker away from the reporters before the conference.**   Mingling prior to the conference will only give someone an edge. Keep all reporters on equal footing in their contact with the speaker.

7. **Prepare materials to complement the speaker's presentation.**   The news conference is an apt place for a press kit, which should include all the pertinent information about the speaker, the subject, and the organization.

8. **Let the reporters know when the end has come.**   Just before the stated time has elapsed, the practitioner should announce to the reporters that the next question will be the last one. After the final question, the speaker should thank the reporters for coming and should take no more questions. After the conference, some reporters (particularly broadcast journalists) may want to ask follow-up questions individually. Do so only if all reporters have an opportunity to share in the one-on-one format.

THE REST OF THE STORY

AW SHADDUP!

Nothing is sweeter to public relations people than learning that even the untouchables holding the microphone occasionally don't know when to "stifle themselves."

■ In 1997, NBC-TV News anchor Tom Brokaw, evidently unaware that a satellite feed was still operating, let slip some disparaging comments about CBS rival Dan Rather, for which he later apologized.

■ Earlier, Rather's colleague, the veteran *60 Minutes* newsman Mike Wallace was caught—and taped—by a rolling camera making disparaging, off-color remarks about California minorities about whom he was reporting.

■ In the winter of 1990, network interviewer and Miss America judge Larry King answered another interviewer's question by denouncing Miss Pennsylvania as the "ugliest contestant in the pageant." A devastated Miss Pennsylvania demanded an apology, which was quickly volunteered. Poor Larry was at it again some weeks later when he asked, on a national broadcast, if a certain pro football holdout had "a drug problem." The player didn't. But that didn't prevent him and his agent from blasting King for raising the question before 15 million viewers.

■ And finally one other cable commentator joined King in the "foot-in-mouth" derby for making what sounded suspiciously like anti-Semitic remarks about Israel's views on a possible war in the Middle East. The commentator, who was denounced by friend and foe alike, had earlier defended a Nazi gas chamber operator being prosecuted for war crimes. The bombastic broadcaster's name? Patrick J. Buchanan, the self-same journalist and Presidential candidate who once long ago picked on a poor, defenseless public affairs director.

Moral: What goes around, comes around.

SUMMARY

As is true of any other specialty in public relations work, the key to securing publicity is professionalism. Because management relies principally on public relations professionals for expertise in handling the media effectively, practitioners must not only know their own organization and management, but must also be conversant in and respectful of the role and practice of journalists.

This means all that has been discussed in this chapter must be practiced—from sending journalists information that is "newsworthy"; to knowing how to reach reporters most expeditiously be it messenger, e-mail, or fax; to understanding that journalists have become more pressured to produce material that is "entertaining" and therefore more potentially flammable for most organizations.

At the same time, all public relations practitioners should understand that their role in the news-gathering process has become more respected by journalists. As Fred Andrews, the former business/finance editor of *The New York Times*, once said, "PR has gotten more professional. PR people can be a critical element for us. It makes a difference how efficiently they handle things, how complete the information is that they have at hand. We value that and understand all the work that goes into it."[19] Indeed, the best public relations/journalist relationship today—the only successful one over the long term—must still be based on mutual understanding, trust, and respect.

DISCUSSION STARTERS

1. What is the difference between advertising and publicity?
2. What is the current state of the newspaper industry?
3. Why should public relations professionals be familiar with newspaper deadlines?
4. How has dealing with the media changed in the late 1990s?
5. What is the difference between public relations and publicity?
6. What are the general interest, financial, and commercial wire services?
7. How can public relations professionals keep track of the publicity they receive for their organizations?
8. What are the several dos and don'ts of interviews?
9. Are press conferences advisable in most cases?
10. What are five recommended ways to work with the media?

NOTES

1. Bennett Daviss, "Of the People, By the People, For the People," *Ambassador* (March 1997): 33.
2. Mike Tharp, "The Media's New Fix," *U.S. News & World Report* (March 18, 1996): 73.
3. Ellen Alderman and Caroline Kennedy, "The Legacy of Richard Jewell," *Columbia Journalism Review* (April 1997): 27.

4. Patrick M. Reilly, "Investor Files Papers Signaling Intent to Sue Business Week for $1 Billion," *The Wall Street Journal* (April 4, 1997): A4.
5. Bernard Goldberg, "Op Ed," *The Wall Street Journal* (February 13, 1996).
6. Fraser P. Seitel, "Loose Lips," *U.S. Banker* (October 1991): 81.
7. Howard Kurtz, "Federal Agents Warned on Comments to Media," *The Washington Post* (March 10, 1993): A-12.
8. Kevin Goldman, "TV Network News Is Making Re-Creation a Form of Recreation," *The Wall Street Journal* (October 30, 1989): A4.
9. Debra Coudert Sweeney, "Not Dealing with Tabloid Television," *The Public Relations Strategist* (Summer 1995): 46.
10. Judith A. Mapes, "Top Management and the Press—The Uneasy Relationship Revisited," *Corporate Issues Monitor*, Egon Zehnder International, vol. 11, no. 1 (1987): 2.
11. S. Robert Lichter, Stanley Rothman, and Linda S. Lichter, *The Media Elite: America's New Powerbrokers* (Bethesda, MD: Adler & Adler, 1986).
12. Tharp, op. cit.
13. "What's News?" *New York University Magazine* (Fall 1989): 16–17.
14. Janet Malcolm, "The Journalist and the Murderer," *The New Yorker* (March 13, 1989): 38.
15. Lewis H. Young, "The Media's View of Corporate Communications in the '80s," *Public Relations Quarterly* (Fall 1981): 10.
16. Fraser P. Seitel, "Confronting the Media," *U.S. Banker* (January 1989): 53.
17. "Daily Newspaper Circulations Still Plugging Along to Nowhere," *Business Wire Newsletter* (December 1996): 1.
18. Robert T. Gilbert, "What to Do When the Press Calls," *The Wall Street Journal* (June 17, 1996).
19. "Getting into the Times: How Andrews Views PR," *Across the Board* (August 1989): 21.

SUGGESTED READINGS

American Society of Journalists and Authors Directory (1501 Broadway, New York, NY 10036). Freelance writers.

Bacon's Media Alerts. Chicago: Bacon Publishing Co. (332 S. Michigan 60604). Bimonthly.

Beals, Melba. *Expose Yourself: Using the Power of Public Relations to Promote Your Business and Yourself*. San Francisco: Chronicle, 1990.

Chancellor, John and Walter R. Mears, *The New News Business: A Guide to Writing and Reporting*. New York: HarperCollins, 1995.

Charity, Arthur. *Doing Public Journalism*. New York: Guilford Press, 1995.

Crossen, Cynthia. *Tainted Truth: The Manipulation of Facts in America*. New York: Simon & Schuster, 1994.

Doty, Dorothy I. *Publicity and Public Relations*. Hauppauge, NY: Barron, 1990.

Downing, John et al. *Questioning the Media*, 2nd ed. Thousand Oaks, CA.: Sage Publications, 1995.

Engel, James F. et al. *Promotional Strategy: Managing the Marketing Communications Process*. Homewood, IL: Business One Irwin, 1990.

TOP OF THE SHELF

PAUL H. WEAVER

NEWS AND THE CULTURE OF LYING: HOW JOURNALISM REALLY WORKS

NEW YORK: THE FREE PRESS, 1994

This book may speak for the vast majority of business people in the nation, who viscerally distrust the news media.

The news media and the government, according to the author, have created a charade that serves their own interests but misleads the public. What has emerged, says business journalist Weaver, is nothing less than a "culture of lying—a discourse and behavior of officials seeking to enlist the powers of journalism in support of their goals, and of journalists seeking to co-opt public and private officials into their efforts to find and cover stories of crisis and emergency response."

Weaver argues that the "substance" of most stories is sacrificed by journalists, hungry to provide entertaining copy to titillate the masses. This has a particularly deleterious impact on government, according to Weaver. "The result," he says, "is to distort the constitutional role of government into an institution that must continually resolve or appear to resolve crises."

Gottschalk, Jack A. *Promoting Your Professional Services*. Homewood, IL: Business One Irwin, 1991.

Hiebert, Ray E., Donald F. Ungurait, and Thomas W. Bohn. *Mass Media VI*. White Plains, NY: Longman, 1991.

International Directory of Special Events and Festivals. Chicago: Special Events Reports (213 W. Institute Place 60610).

Klein, Barry. *Guide to Free Product Publicity Sources*. West Nyack, NY: Todd Publications, 1992.

Kremer, John. *How to Make the News: A Step-By-Step Guide to National Publicity*. Fairfield, IA: Open Horizons, 1991.

Lewis, Peter Y. and Jerry Booth. *The Invisible Medium: Commercial, Public and Community Radio*. Washington, DC: Howard University Press, 1990.

Lichter, Robert and Robert Noyes. *Good Intentions Make Bad News*. Lanham, MD: University Press of America, 1995. Outlines how campaign journalism has evolved in the last quarter century.

Media News Keys (40–29 27th St., Long Island City, NY 11101). Weekly.

Miller, Peter G. *Media Power: How Your Business Can Profit from the Media*. Chicago: Dearborn, 1991.

National Research Bureau. *Working Press of the Nation*. (Available from the author, 242 N. 3rd St, Burlington, IA 52601.) Each volume covers a different medium—newspapers, magazines, radio-TV, feature syndicates, and in-house newsletters.

Nelson, Joyce. *Sultans of Sleaze: Public Relations and the Media*. Monroe, ME: Common Courage Press, 1992. A different—purists would say "jaundiced"—view of public relations and the media.

Network Futures (Television Index, 40–29 27th St., Long Island City, New York 11101). Monthly.

Newsletter on Newsletters (P.O. Box 311, Rhinebeck, NY 12572). Weekly.

O'Dwyer, Jack, ed. *O'Dwyer's Directory of Corporation Communications*. New York: J. R. O'Dwyer, 1994. This guide provides a full listing of the public relations departments of nearly 3,000 companies and shows how the largest companies define public relations and staff and budget for it.

O'Dwyer, Jack, ed. *O'Dwyer's Directory of PR Firms*. New York: J. R. O'Dwyer, 1997. This directory lists 1,200 public relations firms. In addition to providing information on executives, accounts, types of agencies, and branch office locations, the guide provides a geographical index to firms and cross indexes more than 8,000 clients.

Perry, David. *Media How-To Guidebook*. San Francisco: Media Alliance, 1991.

PR Aids' Party Line. (Available from 221 Park Ave. South, New York, NY 10003.) This information service weekly, published on Monday, lists editorial placement opportunities in all media, including network and local radio and TV.

Public Relations, Inc. (221 Park Ave. South, New York, NY 10003). A computerized media system lets a client select local broadcast media by market, type of programming, power of radio stations, network for TV, and department (news, program, women's interest, public service, etc.).

Rosenblum, Mort. *Who Stole the News?* New York: John Wiley & Sons, 1993.

Schudson, Michael. *The Power of News*. Cambridge: Harvard University Press, 1995. Describes news coverage as a culture with its own conventions.

Shimp, Terence. *Promotion Management and Marketing Communications*. Ft. Worth, TX: Dryden, 1990.

Silverblatt, Art. *Media Literacy*. Westport, CT: Praeger Publishers, 1995.

Veciana-Suarez, Ana. *Hispanic Media: Impact and Influence*. Washington, D.C.: The Media Institute, 1990.

Weiner, Richard. *Dictionary of Media and Communications*. New York: Simon & Schuster, 1990.

What to Do When the Media Contact You. (New York State Bar Association, Dept. of Communications and Public Affairs, One Elk St., Albany, NY 12207).

Yale, David. *The Publicity Handbook*. Lincolnwood, IA: NTC Business, 1991.

CASE STUDY

WACO

The first—and probably most remembered—bona fide nightmare of both halves the Clinton Administration arrived in February 1993 when four federal agents were killed in the line of duty while attempting to arrest the leader of an obscure religious sect, the Branch Davidians, in Waco, Texas.

Over the next two months, FBI and Bureau of Alcohol, Tobacco and Firearms (ATF) agents attempted to negotiate with Branch Davidian leader David Koresh to release the 86 individuals, including two dozen children, literally imprisoned behind the compound's walls.

For 51 days, TV viewers around the world witnessed a standoff between the American government and the leader of the fringe religious group. Each day, spokesmen from the FBI or ATF would cryptically update the world on "progress."

On Monday, April 19, the showdown came to a grim conclusion. At 12:05 P.M., the first wisps of smoke were seen coming from several windows of the compound. Until then, armored vehicles had been battering the building's sides all morning, injecting tear gas through a long boom. Ultimately, a raging fire commenced.

At 12:13 P.M. the FBI called the Waco Fire Department for help. Two fire trucks were dispatched and arrived about 15 minutes later. It was another 21 minutes before the authorities allowed the fire trucks onto the compound. The reason for the delay, the FBI said, was that the Davidians were armed with automatic weapons.

When the firefighters were finally allowed to enter the compound, there was no one left to save. Thirty-mile-an-hour winds coupled with the flimsy wooden construction of compound buildings created a tinder box. All that remained at the grisly scene were charred bodies and skeletal remains of 86 people.

"The American people are shocked," said New York's Governor Mario M. Cuomo. "This is an awful tragedy and the American people want an explanation." In particular, the question that dominated the dialogue was, "Why did the children have to die?"

That question—and all others surrounding the debacle—were fielded by Attorney General Janet Reno, the appointed Waco spokesperson for the Clinton Administration.

The Attorney General argued that "reports of child abuse inside the compound" had led her to order Federal authorities to act quickly. Reno also volunteered to one and all that she took "full responsibility" for the action on the cultist compound.

Indeed, during the first 24 hours after the Waco raid, President Clinton remained mysteriously unavailable. Reno said she had spoken with the President, who agreed with her decision.

Two days after the destruction, President Clinton reemerged to conduct a news conference on Waco. "Why," he was asked, did he choose to "distance himself for 24 hours?" The President replied that he was "bewildered" by the accusation. "The only reason I made no public statement yesterday," he said, "is that I had nothing to add to what was being said."

Later it was revealed that not only was there no proof of "child abuse within the compound," but also that the FBI, apparently unwilling to rotate a new force of agents to continue to monitor the stalemate with Koresh, decided to push the issue to a conclusion. Attorney General Reno, so the story went, willingly acquiesced.

News organizations rushed to "pick apart" the Administration's story on Waco. Where first Reno was hailed for "stepping up" to the responsibility of the raid, later she was ostracized. Journalists and others began openly to question the logic of her decision to raid the compound.

With the government steadfastly maintaining a "no other alternative" explanation, reporters began to quote law enforcement experts and others who questioned the timing and justification of the raid. "I think they haven't made the public case for the necessity to do what they did," argued one legal scholar in *The New York Times*.

Each day, it seemed, brought a new element of doubt about the necessity of the raid.

The situation for the Administration steadily deteriorated. Justice Department Spokesman Carl Stern, a former NBC newsman, acknowledged that while there had in fact been "accounts of child beatings" at the compound, he could recall no assertions that there had been any incidents of abuse. Later, it was disclosed that the FBI and ATF had squabbled over jurisdiction in the Waco matter. To heighten the controversy, Koresh's lawyer claimed that his client "would have been ready soon to give himself up if the government had just waited."

In the final analysis, Waco stood as one of the Clinton Administration's darkest hours. Every time that some other government in the world successfully rescued hostages—as Peru President Alberto Fujimori's did in Lima in 1997—people were reminded of the botched attempt at Waco. Summarized one law school professor: "The question is, could we have done anything differently? And the answer is, 'I would have exhausted all the alternatives before launching the fatal raid.'"

QUESTIONS

1. How would you assess the public relations handling of Waco?
2. What could have been done to avoid public squabbling between the FBI and ATF?
3. In a crisis like Waco, what media relations philosophy and approach should be used?
4. Do you agree with the decision to appoint Janet Reno as the public relations focal point after the raid on Waco?
5. How would you characterize President Clinton's public performance after the raid?
6. Had you been the President's communications advisor, what strategy and tactics would you have suggested be adopted immediately after the raid on Waco?

VOICE OF EXPERIENCE

ANDREW S. EDSON

Andrew S. Edson is president and chief operating officer of Andrew Edson & Associates, Inc., an independent New York-based corporate and financial relations consultancy. He also serves as senior counselor to Manning, Selvage & Lee, one of the world's 10 largest public relations companies. Edson founded his firm in 1996 after a 28-year career in both the corporate and consulting ranks.

HOW WOULD YOU DEFINE PUBLIC RELATIONS?

Advertising is what you pay for. Good public relations is what you pray for.

HOW DOES ONE DEAL EFFECTIVELY WITH THE MEDIA?

By being a student of the media. You must be a voracious reader, viewer, and listener to comprehend how the press works and how best to approach reporters. Above all, be honest. If you don't know the answer, admit it. Be cooperative.

HOW IMPORTANT ARE MEDIA CONTACTS?

Not as important as they once were. We are living in an era of voice and mail messages, e-mail pitches, website downloading. Fewer journalists are "breaking bread" or certainly not indulging in a two-martini lunch. Still, if you can meet a reporter, even for a cup of coffee or with an executive in tow, it helps humanize the experience and gets a relationship started.

WHAT IS THE PROPER RELATIONSHIP BETWEEN A JOURNALIST AND A PUBLIC RELATIONS PRACTITIONER?

Some say at "arm's length" while others make it a habit of getting to know a journalist on an almost personal and social basis. The distinction between proper and improper relies a lot on common sense. Then, too, the Code of Ethics of the Public Relations Society of America addresses this and merits reviewing before engaging in a meaningful media relations program.

HOW DO YOU PUBLICIZE A CLIENT?

By not engaging in publicity for the mere sake of publicity. Initially, it's best to develop a clear plan with stated goals, strategies to achieve them, tactical elements, a timetable and a measurement yardstick. Know the strengths and weaknesses of the client as you create the plan and implement it. Start out slowly and don't overpromise results or build undue expectations. I always err to the conservative.

ARE CLIENTS UNDERSTANDING WHEN THEY DON'T ATTRACT PUBLICITY?

Generally, especially if you haven't overpromised. You do not control the media. You are dealing in the court of public opinion, and frequently the results are not what you had hoped for. Consider alternatives if you don't realize sought-after publicity. We now have cyber media, new media, corporate and institutional advertising, all of which requires skilled public relations practitioners. Gimmicks and press agentry are largely passe.

WHAT SPECIAL TIPS CAN YOU OFFER IN DEALING WITH THE MEDIA?

Courtesy and responsiveness seem to be a thing of the past. Being adversarial should not be part of the job description. Saying thank you, sending a note of appreciation and following up, where and when required—all go a long way to establish and maintain a relationship with a reporter.

HOW CAN YOU STAY CURRENT WITH AN EVER-EXPANDING MEDIA UNIVERSE?

With difficulty, but it can be done. The world is shrinking. You can now see and hear news happening almost anywhere in the world. Satellite, cable, and the Internet have seen to that. But you can never stop learning or asking questions. That's what makes this profession unique and every day different.

CHAPTER TWELVE

Electronic Media

ON THE FINAL DAY OF THE 1997 Masters Golf Tournament in Augusta, Georgia, veteran golfer Fuzzy Zoeller zinged 21-year-old superstar winner Tiger Woods with dopey, blithely delivered comments that smacked of racism. Even though the comments were witnessed by several reporters, Zoeller's comments, about the "little boy" winner preferring "fried chicken and collard greens" for the Masters Champions Dinner, didn't become a national cause celebre until a full week later, when CNN aired the offensive comments on a Sunday golf program.

Immediately thereafter, KMart dropped Zoeller as a spokesman, Zoeller dropped out of the next tournament, and the story became page one copy across the nation.[1]

In other words, the "news" didn't become the "news" until television proclaimed it as such. And the Fuzzy-Tiger brouhaha was typical of the amazing power of television.

As society rolls into the twenty-first century, few communications forces are more pervasive and prominent than the electronic media.

Television and radio are everywhere.

- In 1997, when Peruvian forces stormed the Japanese ambassador's residence in Lima to free hostages trapped for months, the images of the rescue were beamed instantaneously around the world.
- In 1996, when a late night bomb exploded in Atlanta during the summer Olympics, to update developments American networks went "live" immediately.
- In 1994, when Heisman Trophy winner O. J. Simpson led Los Angeles police on a low-speed freeway journey, following the murder of his former wife and a friend, Americans across the nation observed every excruciating mile.

- And when *Time* magazine chose its "25 Most Influential Americans" in the spring of 1997, a scruffy-haired, former alcoholic drug addict turned radio commentator, Don Imus, headed the list.

In other words, the power of the electronic media is awesome. According to a 1992 Roper Poll, at least 81 percent of all Americans received most of their news from television, and fully 54 percent received all of their news from television. Moreover, Americans reported that they were more likely to believe news received from television than from newspapers or other print media.[2] What makes this so disconcerting—some would say scary—is that the average 30-minute TV newscast would fill, in terms of words, only one-half of one page of the average daily newspaper!

Moreover, in recent years, TV news has been wracked by scandals—from NBC's *Dateline* exploding General Motors trucks (see chapter 18) to ABC's *Prime Time Lives* contaminated Food Lion supermarket story (see chapter 12). TV news has even felt heat from its own ranks. In 1996, as noted in chapter 11, CBS newsman Bernard Goldberg wrote a scathing commentary in the *Wall Street Journal*, criticizing his own colleagues for their "liberal bias."[3]

Nonetheless, despite its problems, to many Americans, television is the news. The growth of video in the United States has been astounding. In 1950, 3.8 million persons, or 9 percent of the population, possessed a television set. Twenty years later, the number had grown to 60 million, or 96 percent of the population. And by 1993, 93 million homes, or 98 percent, possessed televisions.

In 1950, the average number of channels received by homes in the United States was about three. By 1970, seven channels were available. By 1992, the number was 35 channels, which included cable. And some predict that by the end of this decade, the information superhighway will usher in the era of 500-channel TV.[4]

At the same time, radio has experienced a rebirth. In the latter half of the 1990s, so-called "talk radio" dominated the airwaves. Of the nation's 11,000 radio stations, approximately 1,000 offer conversation on controversial topics, raging from sex to nutrition to politics. As *The New York Times* put it, "Talk radio is cost-free, travel-free and time-efficient, and reaches millions of Americans who don not normally keep Foreign Affairs by their bedsides."[5]

Given the extent to which the electronic media dominate society, it is incumbent on public relations people to become more resourceful in understanding how to deal with them.

TV NEWS—PERVASIVE, INVESTIGATIVE, INFLAMMATORY

Video news, in particular, has overwhelmed society.

In the last years of the twentieth century, no situation comedy, ensemble drama, miniseries, movie, or documentary dominates American TV the way news and talk do.[6] From the televised O. J. Simpson criminal trial to devastating floods in the Dakotas to the outbreak of war in Zaire and Bosnia, to the trials and travails of assorted sordid characters from Michael Jackson to Dennis Rodman to Susan Smith to Marshall Applewhite and the Hale-Bopp Comet, television news covered every gruesome detail.

One key factor in the rise of TV news around the world has been the growth of the Cable News Network (CNN). Entrepreneur Ted Turner's brainchild—which competitors mocked as "Chicken Noodle Network" when it began more than a decade ago—today boasts a domestic U.S. audience of upward of 60 million, international viewership in more than 7 million homes and 250,000 hotel rooms, news bureaus in 25 world capitals, and availability in more than 100 countries.[7]

Indeed, during the last great battle involving U.S. soldiers, when Americans were trapped in Kuwait in the fall of 1990, the troops watched CNN to determine their next move. So did President Bush. And so, too, did Iraqi President Sadaam Hussein, who crafted statements especially for CNN to send back via satellite to American officials.

The growth of cable television has created enormous new publicity placement possibilities for public relations professionals.

Cable networks on the air or in the planning stages offer something for everyone— from the Food Channel to the Cable Health Club, from the Game Show Channel to the Military Channel, from the World African Network to National Empowerment Television.

Dealing with such narrow casting—targeting one's message to a specific public—will become increasingly important as the new century approaches.[8]

On the other hand, the push toward investigation and more inflammatory reporting on television has created additional problems for public relations professionals assigned to ensure their organizations are treated with fairness.

- News magazine programs such as *60 Minutes*, *20/20*, and *Dateline NBC*, which package scintillating news in entertainment formats, were copied by CNN and even local cable stations.
- Talk shows such as *Oprah Winfrey*, *Sally Jesse Raphael*, and *Larry King Live*, have become standard stomping grounds for politicians, authors, and anyone else seeking to sell a product or an issue.
- Talk show knock-offs, specializing in sleaze and starring such questionable "talents" as Jenny Jones, Montel Williams, and Maury Povich, have proliferated.
- Reality-based shows such as *Unsolved Mysteries* and *Rescue 911*, which stage reenactments of real-life events, have appeared.
- Also gaining in popularity are "screaming commentary" programs, such as the inane *McLaughlin Group* and tabloid TV programs, such as *Hard Copy*, *A Current Affair*, and *Inside Edition*, which try to top each other with lurid tales of agony and woe.

The growth of all of these newslike programs has helped blur the boundary of legitimate news programming.

The 1993 attempt by *Dateline NBC* to rig an explosion of a General Motors truck and the stunning 1997 verdict against ABC's *Prime Time Live* in its hidden camera report on supermarket chain Food Lion were perhaps the worst examples of TV journalism run amuck.

As pressure increases on TV news to provide "better pictures and more sensational footage," the incidents of "credibility stretching" have become more pronounced. And corporations and others have begun to fight back with a legal vengeance.

● In 1995, *ABC News* publicly apologized to Philip Morris for a *Day One* report that stated cigarette companies add extra nicotine to their cigarettes. Philip Morris sued, and ABC backed off (Figure 12–1).

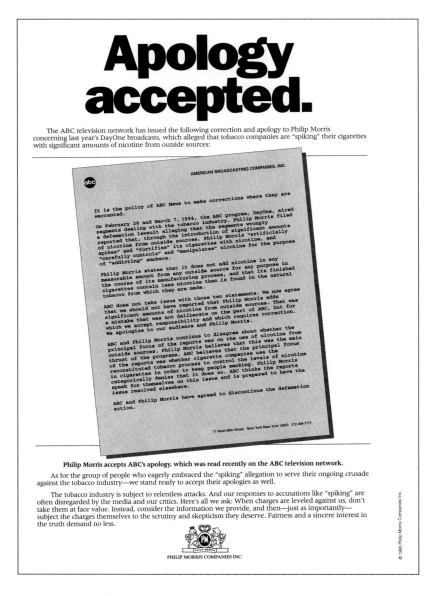

Figure 12–1   Philip Morris reveled in ABC's apology for a *Day One* report that claimed the cigarette company "spiked" its product with addictive nicotine.

- In 1996, NBC was roundly criticized for pretending to present Atlanta Olympics events as "live," when the action was really taped, sometimes hours earlier.
- Also in 1996, ABC's *20/20* lost a $10 million libel verdict to a Florida financier accused of securities fraud.
- In 1997, *Dateline NBC* was sued by a trucking company for fraud, claiming NBC promised to produce a "positive" story on the trucking industry, which instead turned into an attack. Summarized the vice president of NBC-TV News: "There's no question that the atmosphere is that people now think lawsuits will benefit them. We expect to get more lawsuits thrown at us."[9]

The sagging state of objectivity in TV news was summarized by one of broadcasting's own, NBC's Katie Couric: "Some news coverage has become more salacious, more sensationalistic, less intelligent, more giving people what they want to hear or what you think they want to hear, rather than what you think they need to or should ideally hear."[10] The "dumbing down" of TV news has put added pressure on public relations people to deal cautiously when contemplating coverage of the organizations they represent.

HANDLING TV INTERVIEWS

Although appearing on television may indeed be "dangerous for one's health," it nonetheless can also be most persuasive. Accordingly, as television has become a more potent channel of news, executives from all fields are being called on to air their views on news and interview programs. For the uninitiated and the unprepared, a TV interview can be a harrowing experience. This is particularly true now, when even TV veterans like Dan Rather warn of "sleaze and glitz replacing quality and substance" on the airwaves.[11] To be effective on TV takes practice. Executives must accept guidance from public relations professionals on how to act appropriately in front of a camera that never blinks. The following dos and don'ts may help:

1. **Do prepare.**   Preparation is the key to a successful broadcast appearance. Executives should know the main points they wish to make before the interview begins. They should know the audience. They should know who the reporter is and something about the reporter's beliefs. They should also rehearse answering tough hypothetical questions before entering the studio.

2. **Do be yourself.**   Interviewees should appear relaxed. Smiles are appropriate. Nonverbal signs of tension (clenching fists, gripping the arms of a chair, or tightly holding one hand with the other) should be avoided. Gesturing with the palms opened, on the other hand, suggests relaxation and an eagerness to discuss issues. Giggling, smoking, or chewing gum should be avoided (unless you are ex-quarterback Terry Bradshaw!). Proper posture also is important.

3. **Do be open and honest.**   Television magnifies everything, especially phoniness. If facts are twisted, it will show. On TV, a half-truth becomes a half-lie. Credibility must be established early.

4. **Do be brief.**   TV and radio have no time for beating around the bush. Main points must be summarized at the beginning of sentences. Language must be understandable. Neither the reporter nor the public is familiar with technical jargon, so avoid it.

A QUESTION OF ETHICS

FAKES, LIES AND VIDEOTAPE: FOOD LION VS. ABC

Although TV news defenders put a brave face on the February 1996 $5.5 million punitive damage award against ABC TV for its 1992 hidden-camera expose of the Food Lion supermarket chain, the fact is broadcast news may never be the same (Figure 12–2).

FOOD LION

P.O. Box 1330   Salisbury,   North Carolina   28145-1330   Telephone 704-633-8250

FOOD LION VS. CAPITAL CITIES/ABC, INC.
A BACKGROUNDER

In September, 1992, Food Lion, Inc., one of the nation's top-performing grocery companies with more than 1,000 stores in 14 states, filed suit against Capital Cities/ABC, Inc., and four producers of its *PrimeTime Live* program, for fraud, deceptive trade practices, civil conspiracy and breach of duty of loyalty.

The case went to trial December 9, in the U.S. District Court for the Middle District of North Carolina, Winston-Salem Division, in Greensboro, North Carolina.

This is the story of how *PrimeTime Live* created its segment on Food Lion.

WHAT YOU SEE IS NOT WHAT THEY GOT

In April of 1992, producers for *PrimeTime Live* began surreptitiously videotaping various operations at Food Lion supermarkets in North Carolina and South Carolina. Two producers had obtained jobs at Food Lion stores with falsified applications, work histories and references and secretly shot almost 36 hours of video with hidden miniature cameras. Another nine hours of hidden-camera video was filmed by ABC in other Food Lion stores.

From those 45 hours of videotape, about ten minutes was used in a November 5, 1992 *PrimeTime Live* segment that alleged widespread labor law violations and unsanitary conditions in Food Lion stores and attributed the conditions to management pressure to reduce costs and raise profits.

An examination of the unedited footage provides an extraordinary look at how a network news magazine can create false impressions. In this case, the video provides a nearly complete record of ABC's time inside Food Lion, and shows that:

- ABC producers and editors used a combination of staged events and selective editing to fit a preconceived story line and systematically create a story to deceive the public;

- ABC producers did not carry out their obligations to Food Lion even though they accepted employment — in critical positions and to perform key tasks — and wages from Food Lion. Their failure to perform their duties hindered the effectiveness of other Food Lion employees and, by not making a good-faith effort to perform their Food Lion jobs, the producers violated the legal responsibility all employees owe their employer.

Backgrounder/Page 2 of 7

- This failure to perform work, combined with the deliberate staging of events, coaxing and baiting of fellow employees into negative postures, and failure to carry out explicit directions from Food Lion supervisors or co-workers, created the appearance of misdeeds at Food Lion, which were then filmed and blamed on Food Lion.

THE EDITOR'S HAND IS QUICKER THAN THE VIEWER'S EYE

The unedited videotapes provide many examples of ABC's producers intentionally deceptive story-generating strategies. Among the instances of selectively editing to create a false impression are:

- **Aired:** Footage showing a Food Lion employee sliding around on a floor while the narrator described it as being slick with grease.
  Edited Out: Footage showing that the employee was actually sliding playfully on some soapy water that had been spilled while cookware was being washed at the sink.

- **Aired:** Footage showing a tray of rice pudding being held (by the ABC producer) under the nose of an employee, who agrees with her that it does not smell good. The implication is that the pudding is for sale to customers.
  Edited Out: Footage showing that the tray was actually in a work area away from customers, awaiting disposal, after having been removed hours earlier from a sales counter. And, footage showing the ABC producer actually prompted the Food Lion employee twice before the employee agreed that the pudding didn't smell good.

- **Aired:** Footage showing a Food Lion employee recalling an incident in which she was reluctant to cook a batch of chicken because she believed it had been already out of date when it was put into the marinade the night before.
  Edited Out: Footage before and after these comments in which the employee makes it clear she did not cook the chicken, including comments that she went to the manager, who told her to throw the chicken out.

- **Aired:** Footage showing a market manager working quickly and saying that he runs out of time each day.
  Edited Out: Footage following this in which the producer asks whether "they" give him enough time to do his work. He replies: "Oh, yeah. We get enough time." Also edited out were approximately 10 minutes preceding this question during which this manager took time away from his own duties to teach the producer how to trim meat.

Figure 12–2   Food Lion's 1996 court victory issued a "chilling" warning for TV news investigative methods.

In issuing the verdict, the Greensboro, North Carolina jury opened a new line of legal attack against the news media and put hidden-camera journalism on trial. Although Food Lion vehemently denied the truth of the expose, which accused the chain of selling rat-gnawed cheese and expired meat, its case focused on the ethics of ABC's news gathering methods.

The federal jury found that ABC's *Prime Time Live* producers had trespassed and committed fraud, including submitting false resumes to get into the store's meat department, where hidden cameras allegedly filmed employees putting tainted meat out for sale.

Food Lion said that two ABC producers had obtained jobs at its stores with falsified applications, work histories and references and secretly shot almost 36 hours of video with hidden miniature cameras. Another nine hours of hidden-camera video was filmed by ABC in other Food Lion stores. From their 45 hours of videotape, ABC eventually aired about 10 minutes that alleged widespread labor law violations and unsanitary conditions in Food Lion stores and attributed the conditions to management pressure to reduce costs and raise profits.

In defending its suit, Food Lion obtained "outtakes" from ABC that clearly showed its employees acting responsibly and rejecting the suggestions in some cases of the confederate ABC workers themselves to leave the contaminated food out.

Among its claims, Food Lion contended the following differences between what was aired and what was edited out.

- *Aired:* Footage showing a Food Lion employee sliding around on a floor while a narrator described it as being slick with grease.
  Edited Out: Footage showing the employee sliding playfully on soapy water that had been spilled while cookware was being washed at the sink.

- *Aired:* Footage showing a tray of rice pudding held by an ABC producer under the nose of an employee, who agrees it "doesn't smell good."
  Edited Out: Footage showing the tray was actually in a work area away from customers, awaiting disposal, after having been removed hours earlier from a sales counter.

- *Aired:* Footage showing a Food Lion employee recalling an incident in which she was reluctant to cook a batch of chicken because it was already out of date when it was put into the marinade the night before.
  Edited Out: Footage before and after the aired comments, in which the employee makes it clear that her manager told her to throw out the questionable chicken.

- *Aired:* Footage showing a market manager working quickly and saying that he runs out of time each day.
  Edited Out: Footage following this in which the ABC producer asks whether "they" give him enough time to get his work done. "Oh yeah, we get enough time."

Food Lion contended throughout that ABC engaged its report at the suggestion of the United Food and Commercial Workers Union, which was engaged in bitter lawsuits against the nonunionized Food Lion chain. When the ABC report aired, Food Lion was one of the nation's fastest-growing grocery concerns. After the program was broadcast, Food Lion closed dozens of stores, fired hundreds of employees, and saw its sales decline by $4.6 billion and its earnings by $233 million in less than two years.

Journalists seemed split on the "ethics" of the ABC–Food Lion controversy and verdict. *Newsweek* media critic Jonathan Alter said the court was "slamming the media for doing its job in exposing risks to public health." But *Washington Post* reporter Richard Harwood saw an essential difference between TV investigative journalism and that used by the print media, "Journalistic practices that would get you fired from the *Chicago Tribune* or *New York Times*—surreptitious eavesdropping or assuming a false identity—are standard techniques on network news magazines."

Was the ABC–Food Lion report fair and ethical? What do you think?

For further information on the ABC-Food Lion case, see Russ Baker, "Damning Undercover Tactics as 'Fraud,'" *CJR*, March/April 1997, 28; James Boylan, "Punishing the Press," *CJR*, March/April 1997, 24; "Food Lion Verdict Shocks Media Experts," *Jack O'Dwyer's Newsletter*, February 5, 1997, 2; and William S. Weiss, "Food Lion Jury Roars at 'Primetime Live,'" *PR Tactics*, April 1997, 5.

5. **Do play it straight; be careful with humor.**   An interviewee can't be giddy, vacuous, or irreverent. Attempts to be a comic may be interpreted as foolishness. Natural and relaxed use of appropriate humor may be a big plus in getting a point across. If humor doesn't come naturally, interviewees should play it straight. That way, they won't look stupid.

6. **Do dress for the occasion.**   Bold patterns, checks, or pinstripes should be avoided; so should jewelry that shines or glitters. Skirts should fall easily below a woman's knees. Men's socks should be high enough to prevent a gap between socks and pants. Colors of shirts, socks, suits, and accessories generally should be muted.

7. **Don't assume the interviewer is out to get you.**   Arguments and hostility come through clearly on TV. In a discussion on a controversial subject with a professional interviewer, the guest frequently comes out looking like the villain. Therefore, all questions, even naive ones, should be treated with respect and deference. If an interviewee becomes defensive, it will show.

8. **Don't think everything you say will be aired.**   TV is a quick and imperfect medium. A guest might be interviewed for 45 minutes and appear as a 10-second segment on a newscast. That's why an interviewee must constantly hammer home his or her main points.

9. **Don't let the interviewer dominate.**   Interviewees can control the interview by varying the length and content of their responses. If a question requires a

We used to say no comment.

Coors

Toll Free Numbers (800) 525-3786
Colo. Only (800) 332-3725

Corporate Communications Dept.

(303) 279-6565 Ext. 2555

Adolph Coors Company. Golden. Colorado 80401

Now we're asking for your questions.

For years at Adolph Coors Company we were quiet about our business. We paid our people to tell the media, "No comment."

Not that we had anything to hide. Just the opposite. Since that first barrel of Coors beer was brewed in 1873 we've taken great pride in the quality of our product, in our concern for the community, the environment, the world around us. We've always had a good story to tell. We were just a little shy in telling it.

But that's all changed. Now we're asking for your questions. We realize that as competition in the brewing industry gets stiffer, a company who is bent on surviving must be willing to talk to the media. Openly and frankly. About anything. Coors' responsibility for the environment, brewing processes, contributions, relations with minority groups.

So call us toll free. Give us a chance to answer your questions. We'll give you the facts.

Coors

Figure 12–3   Typical of an enlightened attitude toward TV and other media is this ad by Adolph Coors Company, a firm that once was criticized in the media for its policy of silence.

complicated answer, the interviewee should acknowledge that before getting trapped in an incomplete and misleading response. If interviewees make mistakes, they should correct them and go on. If they don't understand the question, they should ask for clarification.

10. **Don't say "No comment."**   "No comment" sounds evasive, and most Americans assume it means "guilty" (Figure 12–3). If interviewees can't answer certain questions, they should clearly explain why. Begging off for competitive or proprietary reasons is perfectly alright as long as some explanation is offered.

11. **Do stop.**   One common broadcast technique is to leave cameras running and microphones open even after an interviewee has responded to a question. Often the most revealing, misleading, and damaging statements are made by interviewees embarrassed by the silence. Don't fall for the bait. Silence can always be edited out later. Interviewers know this and interviewees should, too, especially before getting trapped.

These are just a few hints in dealing with what often becomes a difficult situation for the uninitiated. The best advice for a TV interviewee is to be natural, straightforward, and, most of all, prepared.

IMPORTANCE OF ORGANIZATIONAL VIDEO

Given the domination of the TV culture today, organizational communicators must turn increasingly to video to communicate with a wide range of audiences, from employees to customers to shareholders to legislators.

Internally, an increasing number of companies are creating employee video magazines. Firms like Bell Atlantic and Philip Morris find corporate videos useful to help a widely dispersed employee body understand corporate objectives, on the one hand, and individual department activities, on the other. Videos also can serve as a stimulus for interaction, response, and discussion at employee meetings.

The use of video as an external marketing and lobbying tool also is expanding. Many organizations create videos to introduce new products to potential clients. Videos also are used extensively to present issues to legislators. And sometimes, video annual reports are used to give shareholders a more "lively" view of the organization. Although video annual reports enjoyed fleeting popularity in the mid-1980s and then disappeared, some believe they will make a comeback in the years ahead, "coming through a modem to your computer terminal on demand."[12]

A variety of video vehicles are available to corporate public relations professionals, however, the most pervasive are video news releases (VNRs), public service announcements (PSAs), and satellite media tours (SMTs).

VIDEO NEWS RELEASES

The video news release is by far the most pervasive external video vehicle used by public relations professionals. It is also the most controversial.

A VNR, simply stated, is a print news release put on video. Its aim is to achieve maximum exposure on television news. VNRs, incorporated into local TV newscasts, are designed to run from 30 to 90 seconds. VNRs have proliferated because of the growth of local news programming.

In the early 1980s, as news staffs were cut and air time for news programming was expanded with cable television, the golden age of VNRs began. With news programs hungry for information, the companies sponsoring VNRs found they were used often. By the early 1990s, VNRs had become big business. In 1991, more than 4,000 were produced—10 for every day of the week. And today, as VNRs have proliferated, the competition to place them on the air has increased. Indeed with upward of 150 video firms producing VNRs, the "hit rate" of VNR placements has declined measurably.

VNRs are not for everyone. In general, an organization should consider producing one when it has hard, visual news to promote. The best VNRs are those that cover breaking news stories, the kind broadcasters would cover for themselves if they had the resources. Timely stories with good visual impact are delivered directly to TV newsrooms by satellite. Satellite feeds of unedited footage—called B-roll—include a written preamble-story summary and sound bites from appropriate spokespersons. The TV stations then assemble the stories themselves, using as much or as little of the VNR footage as they see fit.

Such breaking news stories are superior to evergreen VNRs, which concern non-breaking news features. In the "old days"—1990 and earlier—evergreen stories may well have been used by local stations (Figure 12–4). Today, with news stations better staffed and VNR competition increased, evergreens have decidedly less chance of being used.

Figure 12–4   The top electronic publicity event of 1996 was a video news release, produced by Golin/Harris Communications, of the introduction of McDonald's Arch Deluxe sandwich. A giant crane unveiled a foam version of the sandwich, encasing the famed Cinerama Dome on Hollywood's Sunset Boulevard. The VNR received a whopping 233 million impressions.

What does promise to become increasingly popular is the on-line VNR, in which a VNR is downloaded directly to the Internet. More and more, organizations will want video news on the Net.

Generally, an organization should consider producing a VNR when:

- It is involved in a legitimate medical, scientific, or industrial breakthrough.
- The video will clarify or provide a new perspective on issues in the news.
- The video will help a news department create a better story.
- The video can be used as background footage while a station's reporter discusses pertinent news copy.
- The organization can provide unusual visual footage that stations themselves can't get.
- The VNR provides an interview segment that stations, again, can't get on their own.[13]

VNR Caveats: Expensive and Controversial

As noted, VNRs are not without risks.

For one thing, they are expensive. They must be created, produced, packaged, and distributed professionally. Budgets for VNRs can range from $5,000 to $100,000, depending on their complexity. In Pepsi-Cola's case in 1993, the quarter of a million dollar VNR expense to distribute videos defusing the tampering crisis was well worth it. A nationally distributed VNR costs a minimum of $20,000.[14]

Nonetheless, before one creates a VNR—and because a good one is expensive—the following questions must be asked:

1. Is this VNR needed?
2. How much time do we have?
3. How much do we have to spend to make the VNR effective?
4. What obstacles must be considered, including bad weather, unavailability of key people, and so on?
5. Is video really the best way to communicate this story?

Then, too, there is the controversy surrounding VNRs in general. In 1992, *TV Guide*, angered primarily by the Kuwaiti VNR distributed by Hill & Knowlton to build support for the Desert Storm offensive, labeled VNRs "fake news—all the PR that news can use." *TV Guide's* researchers reported that although broadcasters used elements from VNRs, rarely were they labeled so that viewers could know their sponsor's identity.

On the heels of the *TV Guide* controversy, the PR Service Council for VNR Producers issued a "Code of Good Practice" for VNRs, which called for putting the source of the material on every VNR issued. Still, the controversy persists. Despite their problems, the fact remains that if an organization has a dramatic and visual story, using VNRs may be a most effective and compelling way to convey its message to millions of people.

PUBLIC SERVICE ANNOUNCEMENTS

The public service announcement (PSA) is a TV or radio commercial, usually 10 to 60 seconds long, that is broadcast at no cost to the sponsor. Nonprofit organizations such as the Red Cross and United Way are active users of PSAs (Figure 12–5). Commercial organizations, too, may take advantage of PSAs for their nonprofit activities, such as

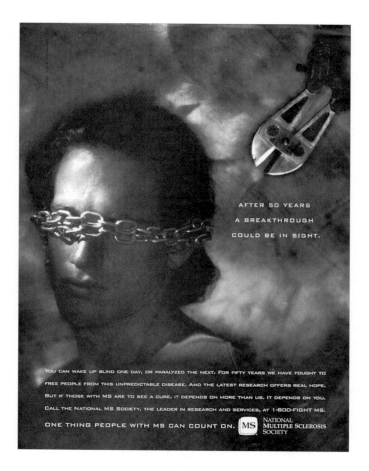

AFTER 50 YEARS
A BREAKTHROUGH
COULD BE IN SIGHT.

YOU CAN WAKE UP BLIND ONE DAY, OR PARALYZED THE NEXT. FOR FIFTY YEARS WE HAVE FOUGHT TO
FREE PEOPLE FROM THIS UNPREDICTABLE DISEASE. AND THE LATEST RESEARCH OFFERS REAL HOPE.
BUT IF THOSE WITH MS ARE TO SEE A CURE, IT DEPENDS ON MORE THAN US. IT DEPENDS ON YOU.
CALL THE NATIONAL MS SOCIETY, THE LEADER IN RESEARCH AND SERVICES, AT 1-800-FIGHT MS.
ONE THING PEOPLE WITH MS CAN COUNT ON. **MS** NATIONAL MULTIPLE SCLEROSIS SOCIETY

Figure 12–5 PSAs can be prepared for broadcast or
print purposes and used by the media at no cost.

blood bank collections, voter registration drives, health testing, and the like. The spread
of local cable TV stations has expanded the opportunity for placing PSAs on the air.
Nevertheless, radio PSAs are still far more widely used.

Unlike news releases, PSAs are generally written in advertising-copy style—punchy
and pointed. The essential challenge in writing PSAs is to select the small amount of information to be used, discard extraneous information, and persuade the listener to take
the desired action. The following is a typical 30-second PSA:

> The challenge of inflation has never been more serious than it is today.
> The need for strong national leadership has never been more pressing than it is
> today.
> Americans must tell their elected leaders to stop spending and regulating and start
> listening to the people.
> But they won't until you demand it.
> Until you demand that they stop overspending, stop crippling our economy with
> needless regulation, stop suffocating America with outrageous taxes.

You can make a difference.
This message brought to you by Hooter Valley National Bank.

According to survey research, broadcasters use three primary criteria in determining which PSAs make the air: (1) sponsorship, (2) relevance of the message to the community, and (3) message design. In terms of sponsorship, the reputation of the sponsor for honesty and integrity is critical. As to the relevance of the message, urgent social problems, such as health and safety issues and education and training concerns, all rank high with broadcasters. In message design, the more imaginative, original, and exciting the message, the better the chance of its getting free play on the air.

SATELLITE MEDIA TOURS

The twenty-first century equivalent to the sit down, in-studio interview is the satellite media tour (SMT), which is a series of preset interviews, conducted via satellite, between an organization's spokesperson and TV station personalities across the nation or around the world.

An SMT originates with a subject speaking from one location, who is then whisked electronically from station to station where he or she enjoys on-air, one-on-one discussions. A derivative of the in-studio SMT is a remote SMT, which originates on location from a site outside the studio.

Corporate executives, celebrities, and "experts" of every stripe have taken advantage of the privatization of satellites and down-link dishes at local TV stations by conducting these rapid-fire "personalized" television interviews.

A successful SMT relies on the immediate relevance of an organization's issue and message. In addition, several steps must be taken to ensure the viability of an SMT:

1. **Defining objectives.** As in any public relations program, the organization's objectives must first be considered. What is the "news hook" required to interest stations? Who is the target audience? In which markets do we want interviews? What stations do we prefer? Within which programs on these stations will our interviews play best?

2. **Pitching the SMT.** Television producers must be contacted, first by letter and then by phone, about the availability of the organization's spokesperson. The key issue that must be stressed is news value. Press kits and background material should be sent to the stations at least two weeks in advance of the interview.

3. **Last-minute juggling preparation.** Stations often request time changes. Maintain contact with station personnel, even when placed on a waiting list, so that any scheduling "holes" can be filled if a station cancels an interview close to the SMT date.

4. **Satellite time.** Satellite time needs to be contracted for well in advance to ensure that the SMT is aired when the organization wants.

5. **B-roll.** Background footage—or B-roll video—should be available to further illustrate the topic and enhance the interest of stations.

6. **Availability of dedicated phone lines.** Several dedicated phone lines to communicate with stations should be available, especially in case of interrupted feedback audio—in other words, static.

7. **Spokespeople briefing.** It is essential to brief spokespersons to avoid potential confusion on the names and locations of interviewers during an

SMT. All names should be written out on a studio teleprompter or on large cue cards, which the spokesperson should refer to before the interview. In addition, the spokesperson should become accustomed to the earpiece, because the director's voice can be distracting initially.

8. **Consider controversy.** Don't worry about stirring up a storm—it often makes news.

9. **Avoid becoming too commercial.** Of course the spokesperson is there to "plug" the organization or product, but don't overdo it or you won't be invited back. SMTs can save time and streamline logistics for any organization. But they are expensive—costing $9,000 for a two-hour studio-produced tour reaching 12 to 14 outlets.[15]

VIDEO CONFERENCES

The latest phenomenon of the video revolution is the video conference, which connects audiences throughout the United States or around the world in a satellite-linked meeting.

Although slow to catch on in the early 1990s, long-distance meetings via video conferences are now becoming much more popular. Video conferences may originate from hotel ballrooms or offshore oil platforms, from corporate headquarters or major trade shows. They can be used for information or motivation. All have the benefit of conveying a message—internally to employees or externally to the news media, investors, or consumers—instantly.

In considering a video conference, the following factors should be addressed:

- **Origination site.** Video conferences may originate from a broadcast studio. However, their impact can be increased by choosing a remote location that adds authenticity to the proceedings.
- **Visuals.** Because a video conference is a live TV show, to heighten the visual excitement of the presentation graphics must be considered. In 1993, when General Motors exposed *Dateline NBC's* fraudulent reporting of its trucks, the company used a host of visuals at its media video conference. GM not only made use of extensive video at the conference, it also displayed one of the actual trucks used in the bogus broadcast.
- **Interactivity.** A video conference also may be enhanced by allowing viewers to ask questions. Two-way audio linkups are now common in video conferences. Again, these add a note of immediacy and spontaneity that enhances the interest and impact of the video conference. Video conference technology now is being adopted by corporations, educational institutions, hospitals, and other organizations. In fact, classes broadcast by TV have been a way of life on Alaska's North Slope for many years. So too around the world, the video conference has become a viable alternative for organizations wishing to convey information immediately with impact.

GROWTH OF TALK RADIO

Talk radio has become an influential communications medium in contemporary America. Conservative Rush Limbaugh, off-center Don Imus, and sophomoric Howard Stern attract huge national followings to their daily gabfests.

With many downsized and outsized Americans working from home and many others on the road, the radio has returned as a primary communications medium. All-news, all-sports, and talk have become a steady communications diet for many Americans.

According to *Talk Daily*, a magazine devoted to the talk show industry, approximately half of all adults in the United States tune in talk radio at least occasionally. Part of the appeal of talk radio is that it offers almost every shade of opinion. And it's unfiltered; that is, talk radio cuts out the "middle man." There is no reporter interceding between the listener and the speaker. Communication on talk radio, then, can be considered "purer" than other methods.

Talk radio is also among the only media in which the voices of "everyday people" can be heard immediately. Says talk show host Oliver North, himself no stranger to controversy: "Talk radio is interactive. Listeners know that what they're hearing is authentic."[16] In addition to North, other well-known talk radio figures range from convicted Watergate burglar G. Gordon Liddy to former California Governor Jerry Brown to comedienne Joan Rivers.

Talk radio, of course, is not without considerable controversy. In 1995, it was blamed for stirring up the discontent that led to the tragic Oklahoma City bombing. In 1996, conservative New York City talk show host Bob Grant was unceremoniously canned for wishing aloud that Commerce Secretary Ron Brown wouldn't survive his plane crash. (He didn't.) But controversy attracts listeners, and talk radio is booming.

THE REST OF THE STORY

TALK RADIO RECIPE: DEFLECT, DENY, EVADE, ACT STUPID

In 1996, the Democratic National Committee issued an internal memo to congressional candidates, advising them on what to do when they appear on talk radio. The memo, leaked to the *Wall Street Journal*, included the following tidbits.

- "Some hosts may try to slam you with obscure facts. . . . The key is that you can always change the subject."
- "If a caller raises a 'hot' topic in reference to the president, you can answer, 'I understand that the president is a deeply religious man and he is a regular churchgoer.' "
- To get on the air, "when asked what you want to discuss. . . . make your reservations about the host seem bland."
- "Make sure you know and support the administration's positions."

When apprised of the memo, one talk show host responded, "This is bad advice. Lousy. Bad, bad, bad advice. People are tired of dishonesty."

No matter.

Summarized the Democratic National Committee memo, "No matter how painful the experience, thank the host and say, 'I'm so glad to have had the opportunity to be on your show. . .'"

PENETRATING THE RADIO MARKETPLACE

What makes radio especially effective for public relations people is the sheer number of radio outlets in the United States—there are 11,000 radio stations versus 400 to 600 TV outlets. According to experts, types of organizations that benefit most from radio public relations campaigns are consumer, safety, or health-related.[17]

Four aspects must be considered paramount in penetrating the radio market.

1. **Strong, focused message.**   Stations must be given valuable information that will enhance the lives of listeners.
2. **Localization.**   The local angle is key. The message must be tailored to suit the needs of targeted listeners.
3. **Positive spokespeople.**   Spokespeople must radiate enthusiasm and goodwill. They, after all, are representing the organization and must reflect on it positively.
4. **Timeliness.**   Finally, the message must be timely and topical. Or else, a radio station won't be interested.

Although radio, broadcasting 24 hours a day, is difficult to monitor, the growth in listenership makes the medium a prime choice for public relations professionals.

SUMMARY

The growth of electronic media has made it even more important for public relations professionals to be conversant with TV and radio. Adding to the challenge is the aforementioned trend of "softer news" and heightened "sensationalism." On the other hand, the criticism that tabloid TV has attracted in recent years may mean that producers will be less eager to highlight tattooed strippers, teenage cross-dressers, and lesbian dwarfs in the future.[18]

In any event, it is clear that the electronic revolution has arrived. As generations weaned on TV enter the public relations field, familiarity with broadcast methods will increase.

As cable television stations in particular proliferate, the need for additional programming—for more material to fill news and interview holes—also will expand. This will open the door to a new breed of public relations professional, comfortable with and proficient in the nuances of writing for, dealing with, and mastering the art of video.

DISCUSSION STARTERS

1. Why has video become more important for public relations professionals?
2. How has the definition of news been expanded by video?
3. Is it a good idea for an executive to be spontaneous in a TV interview?
4. How comprehensive should answers be on TV?
5. When should an organization consider using a VNR?
6. Why are VNRs considered controversial?
7. What are the key facets of a PSA?
8. What are the key steps in creating an SMT?

9. What factors must be considered in arranging a video conference?
10. Why is talk radio more important to public relations professionals today?

NOTES

1. Richard Sandomir, "Media Overlooked Zoeller's News," *The New York Times* (April 25, 1997): B21.
2. "The Changing World of Corporate Video," *Inside PR* (June 1992): 13–16.
3. Terry Eastland, "Opining on the News," *Media Critic* (April 1996): 72.
4. "The Hyperactive Highway," *Newsweek* (November 29, 1993): 56.
5. Don Feder, "Why Liberals Find Talk Radio So Threatening," *The American Enterprise* (March/April 1996): 24.
6. Bill Carter, "News Events Become Biggest Television Hits," *The New York Times* (December 30, 1991): 27.
7. Roxanne Roberts, "CNN on Top of the World," *The Washington Post* (August 21, 1990): C1, C10.
8. *Jack O'Dwyer's Newsletter* (January 26, 1994): 3.
9. Kyle Pope, "Trucking Firm Is Suing NBC Over Expose," *The Wall Street Journal* (March 10, 1997).
10. Peter Johnson, "NBC's Couric Reflects on the State of TV News," *USA Today* (February 19, 1997): D3.
11. "Rather to TV News Heads: Fight 'Sleaze and Glitz,' " *O'Dwyer's PR Services Report* (November 1993): 1, 22–26.
12. "The Changing World of Corporate Video," op. cit.
13. Kevin E. Foley, "Ethics and Sigma Are in 'VNR Cartel,' " *O'Dwyer's PR Services Report* (April 1993): 13.
14. "Answering the Most Frequently Asked Questions about Video News Releases," *Interactive Public Relations* (August 1, 1995): 1.
15. "The Experts Reveal the Secrets to Successful Satellite Media Tours," *Interactive Public Relations* (September 1, 1995): 1.
16. Don Feder, op. cit.
17. "Radio is One Way PR Pros Can Reach a Lot of People," *Interactive Public Relations* (August 1, 1995): 8.
18. Jennifer Harper, "Is Tabloid Television Cleaning Up Its Act?" *The Washington Times* (April 13, 1997): 28.

SUGGESTED READINGS

Associated Press. *Broadcast News Stylebook*. (Available from the author, 50 Rockefeller Plaza, New York, NY 10020.) This has a more generalized style than that presented in the UPI style book. Suggestions of methods and treatment for the preparation of news copy and information pertinent to the AP broadcast wire operations are given.

Broadcasting Publications. *Broadcasting*. (Available from the author, 1735 DeSales St., NW, Washington, D.C. 20036; published weekly on Monday.) This basic news magazine for the radio, TV, and cable TV industries reports all activities involved in the entire broadcasting weld.

TOP OF THE SHELF

60 MINUTES CBS TELEVISION NEWS MAGAZINE PROGRAM

For decades, the most widely watched TV program in the nation has been a Sunday night news magazine program that is the subject of fear and loathing of politicians, presidents, and corporate potentates.

60 Minutes, as the saying goes, has been often imitated, never duplicated. The brainchild of news producer Don Hewitt, its correspondents—Mike Wallace, Morley Safer, Dan Rather, Diane Sawyer, Lesley Stahl, Steve Croft, the late Harry Reasoner, Ed Bradley, et. al—have become synonyms for investigative TV journalism.

In its first decade, *60 Minutes* was despised and avoided by most business organizations. They feared the consequences of a national TV skewering, and most refused to be interviewed. Invariably, this cost them, because *60 Minutes* correspondents ordinarily don't accept "not available" or "no comment" for an answer.

In recent years, smart organizations have realized that, in some cases, it makes sense to cooperate with *60 Minutes*, Coors Beer and Johnson & Johnson, for example, found that *60 Minutes* treated them fairly in the midst of terrible crisis.

In the nineties with the plethora of *60 Minutes* copy cats—from respectable shows like ABC's *20/20* to more questionable shows like *Dateline NBC* to downright unrespectable shows like *A Current Affair* and *Hard Copy*—it is incumbent on public relations students to make the viewing of *60 Minutes* a required Sunday evening ritual.

Campbell, Christopher P. *Race, Myths, and the News*. Thousand Oaks, CA: Sage Publications, 1995.

Common Sense Guide to Making Business Videos. (Available from Creative Marketing Corporation, 285 S. 171 St., New Berlin, WI 53151-3511.) Anyone not familiar with business videos will benefit from this booklet, which zeros in on the planning needed to make a successful video.

Critchlow, James. *Radio Hole-in-the-Head/Radio Liberty: An Inside Story of Cost War Broadcasting*. Lanham, MD: University Press of America, 1995. Traces the evolution of Radio Liberty onto the international scene.

Cronkite, Walter. *A Reporter's Life*. New York: Knopf, 1996. Reminiscences of the "most trust man in America."

Daily Variety. (Available from 1400 N. Cahuenga Blvd., Hollywood, CA 90028.) This trade paper for the entertainment industries is centered mainly in Los Angeles, with complete coverage of West Coast production activities; it includes reports from all world entertainment centers.

Jankowski, Gene F. and David C. Fuchs. *Television Today and Tomorrow*. New York: Oxford University Press, 1995.

CASE STUDY

THEY'RE HEEERE!

Suppose you gave a party and *60 Minutes* showed up at the door. Would you let them in? Would you evict them? Would you commit hara-kiri?

Those were the choices that confronted The Chase Manhattan Bank at the American Bankers Association convention in 1988, when *60 Minutes* came to Honolulu to "get the bankers."

The banking industry at the time was taking its lumps. Profits were lagging. Loans to foreign governments weren't being repaid. And it was getting difficult for poor people to open bank accounts.

Understandably, few bankers at the Honolulu convention cared to share their thoughts on camera with *60 Minutes*. Some headed for cover when the cameras approached. Others barred the unwanted visitors from their receptions. In at least one case, a *60 Minutes* cameraman was physically removed from the hall. By the convention's third day, the *60 Minutes* team was decrying its treatment at the hands of the bankers as the "most vicious" it had ever been accorded.

By the third night, correspondent Morley Safer and his *60 Minutes* crew were steaming and itching for a confrontation.

And that's when *60 Minutes* showed up at our party.

For 10 years, with your author as its public affairs director, Chase Manhattan had sponsored a private convention reception for the media. It combined an informal cocktail party, where journalists and bankers could chat and munch hors d'oeuvres, with a more formal, 30-minute press conference with the bank's president. The press conference was on the record, no holds barred, and frequently generated news coverage by the wire services, newspapers, and magazines that regularly sent representatives. No TV cameras were permitted.

But when we arrived at Honolulu's scenic Pacific Club, there to greet us—unannounced and uninvited—were Morley and the men from *60 Minutes*, ready to do battle.

The ball was in our court. We faced five questions that demanded immediate answers.

- First, should we let them in?

  What they wanted, said Safer, was to interview our president about "critical banking issues." He said they had been "hassled" all week and were "entitled" to attend our media reception.

  But we hadn't invited them. And they hadn't had the courtesy to let us know they were coming. But it was true that they were members of the working press. And it was also true that our reception was intended to generate news.

  So we had a dilemma.

- Second, should we let them film the press conference?

  Chase's annual convention press conference had never before been filmed. TV cameras are bulky, noisy, and intrusive. They threatened to sabotage the normally convivial atmosphere of our party. Equally disconcerting would be the glaring TV lights that would have to be set up. The *60 Minutes* crew countered that their coverage was worthless without film. Theirs, after all, was a medium of pictures, and without pictures, there could be no story. As appetizing as this proposition sounded to us, we were worried that if we refused their cameras, what they might film instead would be us blocking the door at an otherwise open news conference. So we had another problem.

- Third, should we let them film the cocktail party?

    Like labor leader Samuel Gompers, TV people are interested in only one thing: "More!" In the case of our reception, we weren't eager to have CBS film the cocktails and hors d'oeuvres part of our party. We were certain the journalists on hand would agree with us. After all, who wants to see themselves getting sloshed on national television when they're supposed to be working?

- Fourth, should we let them film a separate interview with our president? Because few top people at the convention were willing to speak to CBS, *60 Minutes* was eager to question our president in as extensive and uninterrupted a format as possible. Safer wanted a separate interview before the formal press conference started.

    So we also had to deal with the question of whether to expose our president to a lengthy, one-on-one, side-room interview with the most powerful—and potentially negative—TV news program in the land.

- Fifth, should we change our format?

    The annual media reception/press conference had always been an informal affair. Our executives joked with the journalists, shared self-deprecating asides, and generally relaxed. Thus, in light of the possible presence of *60 Minutes*, we wondered if we should alter this laid-back approach and adopt a more on-guard stance.

We had 10 minutes to make our decisions. We also had splitting headaches.

QUESTIONS

1. Would you let *60 Minutes* in?
2. Would you let them film the press conference?
3. Would you let them film the cocktail party?
4. Would you let them film a separate interview with the president?
5. Would you change the format of the party?

VOICE OF EXPERIENCE

MYRON KANDEL

Myron Kandel is one of the country's best-known financial writers and broadcasters. After serving as financial editor of three major newspapers, he switched to TV in 1980 and helped start Cable News Network. He continues to serve as financial editor of *CNN Business News* and on-air economics commentator. Kandel lectures frequently and has taught journalism at Columbia University Graduate School of Journalism and City College of New York. He is the author of *How to Cash In On the Coming Stock Market Boom*, published in 1982.

WHAT IS THE QUALITY OF BUSINESS NEWS COVERAGE ON TV?

Business news, once the wasteland of TV news coverage, has made great strides over a relatively short period of time. It was as recently as June 1980 that Cable News Network began broadcasting the first nightly half-hour business news program in the history of network television. Now, many other news organizations—on cable and public television and in syndication—are offering a wide assortment of business news programming. Up to now, however, the broadcast networks and local television stations have not devoted any real resources or time to such coverage.

WHAT DO JOURNALISTS THINK OF PUBLIC RELATIONS PEOPLE?

It once was conventional wisdom that journalists and public relations people were adversaries. I like to think of them, instead, as fellow communicators with different agendas. As long as each understands the other's goals, the relationship can be productive both ways. Some news people—a declining percentage, I think—still dismiss PR people as mere flacks, trying to foist untrue, misleading, or inappropriate facts or stories on the media. Although there may be some of those types still around, that's an antiquated image. As PR people get more and more professional, that image will continue to diminish.

WHAT KIND OF PUBLIC RELATIONS PERSON DO YOU APPRECIATE?

The PR person I like best is the one who knows what my news organization does, understands our needs, and is responsive to them. Conversely, those I like least don't know enough, or don't care enough, to relate to us specifically. This doesn't mean that a good PR person must necessarily grant our every request. But, first, he or she should know what we do, what kind of programming we're presenting, and who the relevant contacts are. They should understand our time constraints and deadlines and should get back to us accordingly, even if they can't provide a definitive answer. It's always a pleasure to find a PR person who anticipates a need and offers a way to meet it.

A spokesperson who is knowledgeable about his or her organization and has the necessary access to the top to get queries answered impresses me the most. The least impressive are those who obviously don't have the confidence of management to speak for the organization. I'm surprised at how often supposedly professional people are in that situation.

WHAT PROBLEMS HAVE YOU ENCOUNTERED WITH PUBLIC RELATIONS PEOPLE?

I can't remember an occasion where a PR person lied to me deliberately, but there have been instances where they passed on incorrect information because they themselves were misinformed or were kept in the dark. That kind of situation undermines their credibility and sours any relationship that previously existed. Credibility and integrity are two attributes that any professional PR person must safeguard jealously.

ARE MOST REPORTERS HOSTILE TO ORGANIZATIONS?

They often give that impression because they must be probing in their questioning and unwilling to accept statements they're given at face value. Rather than hostile or antiestablishment, they are nonestablishment, and that approach may seem hostile. Some news people do have biases that creep into their reports. As an editor, it's my responsibility to see that this does not happen. If a persistent pattern exists, I would welcome being informed about it. The principal goal of any news organization is to present the news fairly and objectively.

WHAT IS THE STATUS OF THE RELATIONSHIP BETWEEN VIDEO JOURNALISTS AND PUBLIC RELATIONS PEOPLE?

I like to refer to the state of the video journalist-public relations relationship as an uneasy alliance, meaning that although they work together, each side may on occasion have a different objective. Nearly all the time, but not always, they share the goal of truth. They always share a desire for accuracy. The trend in recent years has been toward greater professionalism on both sides and that means more respect and cooperation.

CHAPTER THIRTEEN

Integrated Marketing Communications

MIDWAY THROUGH THE DECADE OF THE NINETIES, one communications wag made the following observation:

> The practices of marketing, advertising and public relations, as we have known them, are dead.
> They died when automobile makers, consumer product firms, computer companies, and many others began to realize that the world had changed. No longer was it possible to make money "the old-fashioned way."[1]

What this perhaps overzealous observer referred to was the irrepressible intertwining of the heretofore separate disciplines of advertising, marketing, sales promotion, and public relations into a sometimes "unholy alliance" to win consumer support. The symbiosis of these different disciplines was dubbed integrated marketing communications. One survey of 200 marketing executives named integration as the most important factor influencing the way marketing strategies would be set in the 1990s.[2]

As integrated marketing becomes more and more the rule in agencies and companies, the need for communications cross-training—to learn the different skills of marketing, advertising, sales promotion, and public relations becomes a requirement for all communicators.

Integrated marketing means approaching communications issues from the customer's perspective. Consumers don't separate promotional material or newspaper advertising or community responsiveness into separate compartments. They lump everything together to make judgments about services and organizations.

Integrated marketing expert Mitch Kozikowski lists six maxims that can guide public relations professionals through the communications cross-training process:

1. Integrated marketing communication is not about ads, direct mail pieces, or public relations projects. It is about understanding the consumer and what the consumer actually responds to. In other words, behavioral change is the communicator's mission. If the customer doesn't act, the communicator—and the communication—have failed.

2. Organizations can't succeed without good relationships with their publics. Organizations need relationships with their customers that go beyond the pure selling of a product or service. They need to build relationships. As the world becomes more competitive in everything from health care to auto repair, from selling insurance to selling cereal, relationship building becomes more critical.

3. Integrated marketing communications requires collaboration on strategy, not just on execution. This means that the entire communications function must be part of the launch of a product, service, campaign, or issue from its inception. In other words, communicators must participate in the planning of a campaign, not just in the implementation of communications vehicles.

4. Strategic plans must be clear on the role that each discipline is to play in solving the problem. The roles of advertising, marketing, and public relations are different. None can do everything by itself. Therefore, although advertising might control the message and marketing and product promotion might provide support, it is public relations that should provide credibility for the product and, even more important, for the organization.

5. Public relations is about relationships. Public relations professionals can become proprietors of integrated marketing communications. Because the essence of public relations is building relationships between an institution and its publics, public relations professionals, perhaps more than any other, should lead the integrated marketing initiative. Public relations professionals have long understood the importance of the two-way communication that builds strong relationships with customers and others. Such an understanding is pivotal to the successful rendering of integrated marketing communications.

6. To be players in integrated marketing communications, public relations professionals need to practice more than the craft of public relations. Simply stated, public relations people must expand their horizons, increase their knowledge of other disciplines, and willingly seek out and participate in interdisciplinary skills building. In other words, public relations professionals must approach their task, in the broadest terms, to enhance customer relationships through a strategy of total communications.[3]

Elements of public relations—among them product publicity, special events, spokesmanship, and similar activities—can enhance a marketing effort. A new discipline—marketing communications—has emerged that uses many of the techniques of public relations. Although some may labor over the relative differences and merits of public relations versus advertising versus marketing versus sales promotion, the fact remains that a smart communicator must be knowledgeable about all of them.

PUBLIC RELATIONS VERSUS MARKETING

Marketing, literally defined, is the selling of a service or product through pricing, distribution, and promotion. Public relations, liberally defined, is the marketing of an organization. Most organizations now realize that public relations can play an expanded role in marketing. In some organizations, particularly service companies, hospitals, and nonprofit institutions, the selling of both individual products and the organization itself are inextricably intertwined.

Stated another way, although the practice of marketing creates and maintains a market for products and services and the practice of public relations creates and maintains a hospitable environment in which the organization may operate, marketing success can be nullified by the social and political forces public relations is designed to confront—and thus the interrelationship of the two disciplines.[4]

In the past, marketers treated public relations as an ancillary part of the marketing mix. They were concerned primarily with making sure that their products met the needs and desires of customers and were priced competitively, distributed widely, and promoted heavily through advertising and merchandising. Gradually, however, these traditional notions among marketers began to change for several reasons.

- Consumer protests about both product value and safety and government scrutiny of the truth of product demands began to shake historical views of marketing.
- Product recalls—from automobiles to tuna fish—generated recurring headlines.
- Ingredient scares began to occur regularly.
- Advertisers were asked how their products answered social needs and civic responsibilities.
- Rumors about particular companies—from fast-food firms to pop rock manufacturers—spread in brushfire manner.
- General image problems of certain companies and industries—from oil to banking—were fanned by a continuous blaze of media criticism.

The net impact of all this was that even though a company's products were still important, customers began to consider a firm's policies and practices on everything from air and water pollution to minority hiring.

Beyond these social concerns, the effectiveness of advertising itself began to be questioned. The increased number of advertisements in newspapers and on the airwaves caused clutter and placed a significant burden on advertisers who were trying to make the public aware of their products. In the 1980s, the trend toward shorter TV advertising spots contributed to three times as many products being advertised on TV as there were in the 1970s. In the 1990s, the spread of cable TV has added yet another multichanneled outlet for product advertising. Against this backdrop, the potential of public relations as an added ingredient in the marketing mix has become increasingly credible.

Indeed, marketing guru Philip Kotler has suggested that to the traditional 4P's of marketing—product, price, place, and promotion—a fifth P, public relations, should be added. Kotler argues that a firm's success depends increasingly on carrying out effective marketing thinking in its relationships with 10 critical players: suppliers, distributors, end users, employees, financial firms, government, media, allies, competitors, and the general public. In other words, public relations.[5]

PRODUCT PUBLICITY

In light of how difficult it now is to raise advertising awareness above the noise of so many competitive messages, marketers are turning increasingly to product publicity as an important adjunct to advertising. Although the public is generally unaware of it, a great deal of what it knows and believes about a wide variety of products comes through press coverage.

In certain circumstances, product publicity can be the most effective element in the marketing mix.[6] For example:

- **Introducing a revolutionary new product.** Product publicity can start introductory sales at a much higher level of demand by creating more awareness of the product.
- **Eliminating distribution problems with retail outlets.** Often, the way to get shelf space is to have consumers demand the product. Product publicity can be extremely effective in creating consumer demand.
- **Small budgets and strong competition.** Advertising is expensive. Product publicity is cheap. Often, publicity is the best way to tell the story.
- **A fine but complicated product.** The use and benefits of many products are difficult to explain to mass audiences in a brief ad. Product publicity, through extended news columns, can be invaluable.
- **Generating new consumer excitement for an old product.** Repackaging an old product for the media can serve as a primary marketing impetus.
- **Tying the product to a unique representative.** "Morris the Cat" was one answer to consumer uninterest in cat food. Ronald McDonald attended the Academy Awards ceremonies. And on April Fool's Day, 1996, Taco Bell "bought" the Liberty Bell before announcing the ruse.[7] Figure 13–1 illustrates yet another unique and memorable representative.

THIRD-PARTY ENDORSEMENT

Perhaps more than anything else, the lure of third-party endorsement is the primary reason smart organizations value product publicity as much as they do advertising. Third-party endorsement refers to the tacit support given a product by a newspaper, magazine, or broadcaster who mentions the product as news. Advertising often is perceived as self-serving. People know that the advertiser not only created the message but also paid for it. Publicity, on the other hand, which appears in news columns, carries no such stigma. When a message is sanctified by third-party editors, it is more

FOR IMMEDIATE RELEASE   CONTACT: Sally Garon/Diane Worton
                     Golin/Harris Communications
                     312/836-7100

OH BOY! PILLSBURY DOUGHBOY TURNS 25!

The Pillsbury Doughboy has grown up! America's most popular and adorable advertising symbol celebrates his 25th birthday this year.

In 1965, the Doughboy popped out of a tube of Pillsbury fresh, ready-to-bake dough for the first time. Soon, he became one of America's most loved and recognized characters and, 25 years later, he still tops the popularity charts. A contest conducted by Advertising Age magazine revealed the Doughboy is America's favorite character symbol.

What's his secret? "At 25, the Doughboy still has an almost magical relationship with consumers," says Michael Paxton, President, Pillsbury Bakery Products Division. "People tell us they trust him and believe in him. He makes the kitchen fun and festive. And, his giggle ... well, who can describe that giggle!

"When he 'popped' onto the scene a quarter century ago, we knew the Doughboy was someone special. He's done so much for us. Now it's our turn to salute him as he celebrates his 25th birthday," says Paxton.

– more –

Pillsbury Inc., Pillsbury Center – M.S. 27A1, 200 S. Sixth Street, Minneapolis, MN 55402 (612)330-4719

Figure 13–1 Among companies that chose unique representatives to earn product publicity as an enhanced marketing effort was food manufacturer Pillsbury. When the Pillsbury Dough Boy turned 25 in 1990, the company celebrated with national publicity-inducing events: cookbooks, recipes, and news releases featuring its cuddly and beloved Poppin' Fresh.

THE REST OF THE STORY

Figure 13–2 Only illustrations, not photographs, were used to depict Airiana, the Human Arrow.

P.T. BARNUM REDUX: THE HUMAN ARROW

The most unique marketing representatives have emerged over time from the circus—particularly the circus made famous by the legendary publicity showman P.T. Barnum.

In the best traditions of Barnum's Tom Thumb and other assorted early twentieth century oddities, the 126th edition of the Ringling Brothers and Barnum & Bailey Circus in 1996 introduced with great hype and hoopla, Airiana, the Human Arrow (Figure 13–2).

Airiana, the star of the show, granted no interviews. Nor did the circus permit her flight to be videotaped. And in television, radio, print and outdoor advertising, she was described as "ethereal and inspiring, mysterious and magnificent," a performer who traverses the ring like a comet "trailing across the darkened sky before passing into the infinity of space."

Actually, Airiana was launched by elastic bands from "the world's largest crossbow," a 5,000-pound, 17-foot-long, 22-foot-high contraption. In the show's finale, Airiana was hurled, according to the show's producers, at a speed of 60 miles an hour into a net 100 feet away.

Yet Airiana and her act remained a mystery. The circus went so far as to issue to news organizations a signed "proclamation" stating that "no camera or recording device will be allowed to be operated within the arena during the final 15 minutes of each performance."

And the circus milked the publicity for all it was worth. It refused to indicate Airiana's last name or her nationality or even—though some journalists speculated—her sex.

Some compared the Airiana phenomenon to Ringling's 1985 introduction of "The Living Unicorns," which turned out to be goats whose horn buds had been surgically shifted together when they were kids.

If there was something similarly strange about Airiana, nobody would say. Somewhere, Phineas T. Barnum was smiling.

---

persuasive than advertising messages, where the self-serving sponsor of the message is identified (Figure 13–3).

Editors have become sensitive to mentioning product names in print. Some, in fact, have a policy of deleting brand or company identifications in news columns. Public relations counselors argue that such a policy does a disservice to readers, many of whom are influenced by what they read and may desire the particular products discussed. Counselors further argue that journalists who accept and print public relations material for its

Figure 13–3   When the *Wall Street Journal* alluded to the Arizona Department of Health Services, 43-foot trailer, the "Ash Kicker," the demand for the $150,000 motorized anti-smoking exhibition skyrocketed.

intrinsic value and then remove the source of the information give the reader or viewer the false impression that the journalist generated the facts, ideas, or photography.

Equally reprehensible are the public relations practitioners who try to place sponsored features without disclosing promotional origins. In other words, some companies will distribute cartoons or stories—either directly or through mail-order services—without identifying the sponsor of the material. Obviously, such a practice raises ethical questions. Understandably, editors do not soon forgive firms that sponsor such anonymous articles.

PUBLIC RELATIONS MARKETING ACTIVITIES

In addition to product publicity, a number of other public relations activities are regularly used to help market products. These activities include article reprints, trade show participation, the use of spokespersons, and cause-related marketing.

Article Reprints

Once an organization has received product publicity in a newspaper or magazine, it should market the publicity further to achieve maximum sales punch. Marketing can be done through article reprints aimed at that part of a target audience—wholesalers, retailers, or consumers—that might not have seen the original article. Reprints also help reinforce the reactions of those who read the original article.

As in any other public relations activity, use of reprints should be approached systematically, with the following ground rules in mind:

1. **Plan ahead, especially if an article has major significance to the organization.** Ideally, reprints should be ordered before the periodical goes to press so that customers can receive them shortly after the article hits the newsstands.

2. **Select target publics and address the recipients by name and title.** This strategy will ensure that the reprint reaches the most important audience.

3. **Pinpoint the reprint's significance.** Accomplish this either by underlining pertinent information in the article, making marginal notes, or attaching a cover letter. In this way, the target audience will readily understand.

4. **Integrate the reprint with other similar articles and information on the same or related subjects.** Often, several reprints can be combined into a single mailing piece. Also, reprints can be integrated into press kits and displays.

Trade Show Participation

Trade show participation enables an organization to display its products before important target audiences. The decision to participate should be considered with the following factors in mind:

1. **Analyze the show carefully.** Make sure the audience is one that can't be reached effectively through other promotional materials, such as article reprints or local publicity. Also, be sure the audience is essential to the sale of the product. For example, how responsible are the attendees for the actual purchase?

2. **Select a common theme.** Integrate public relations, publicity, advertising, and sales promotion. Unify all elements for the trade show and avoid, at all costs, any hint of interdepartmental rivalries.

3. **Make sure the products displayed are the right ones.** Decide well in advance exactly which products are the ones to be shown.

4. **Consider the trade books.** Often, trade magazines run special features in conjunction with trade shows, and editors need photos and publicity material. Always know what special editions are coming up as well as their deadline schedules.

5. **Emphasize what's new.** Talk about the new model that's being displayed. Discuss the additional features, new uses, or recent performance data of the products displayed. Trade show exhibitions should reveal innovation, breakthrough, and newness.

6. **Consider local promotional efforts.** While in town during a trade show, an organization can enhance both the recognition of its product and the traffic at its booth by doing local promotions. This strategy involves visiting trade magazine editors and local media people to stir up publicity for the product during the show.[8]

Use of Spokespersons

In recent years, the use of spokespersons to promote products has increased. Spokespersons shouldn't disguise the fact that they are advocates for a particular product. Their purpose is to air their sponsor's viewpoint, which often means going to bat for a controversial product.

Spokespersons must be articulate, fast on their feet, and thoroughly knowledgeable about the subject. When these criteria are met, the use of spokespersons as an integrated marketing tool can be most effective.

Lately, the use of spokespersons to promote products has become so crazed that professional basketball rookie Allen Iverson not only signed a $50 million multiyear contract for Reebok sportswear, but got stock on top of it. In 1997, after he won the Masters Golf Tournament, Tiger Woods announced that he would "limit" his sponsorships, so he "dipped his toe in the water" by signing a $40 million deal with Nike for athletic shoes and apparel, a $20 million deal with Titleist Cobra for golf clubs and balls, and a $7 million deal with All Star Cafe, the celebrity restaurant chain.[9] Not a bad dip.

Spokespersons come in a variety of sizes, shapes, and occupations. They range from corporate chairmen like Wendy's CEO Dave Thomas, who regularly hawks his hamburgers, to comedians Jay Leno for Doritos brand corn chips and Richard Lewis for Virgin Atlantic Airlines, to more controversial and even unknown spokespersons (Figure 13–4).

The most lucrative field for product spokespersons is sports. In 1996, the Most Wanted Spokespersons List (based on annual contracts) read as follows:

1. Basketball star Michael Jordan, $40 million
2. Basketball star Shaquille O'Neal, $17 million
3. Golfer Arnold Palmer, $15 million
4. Tennis player Andre Agassi, $13 million
5. Golfer Tiger Woods, $10 million
6. Race car driver Dale Earnhardt, $8.5 million
7. Basketball bad boy Dennis Rodman, $8.5 million
8. Race car driver Michael Schumacher, $8 million
9. Tennis player Pete Sampras, $8 million
10. Golfer Jack Nicklaus, $8 million

Especially picky in marketing their images are rock stars. Indeed, when the artist formerly known as Prince, the diminutive Minnesota rocker with the risque lyrics who changed his name to an unpronounceable glyph, was asked for his photo for use in a certain public relations textbook, the author received the following warning from the decidedly unrocklike law firm of Manatt, Phelps, Rothenberg & Tunney.

> Please be advised that our client does not desire to grant you permission to use any picture or likeness of him in connection with your textbook.

So there.

Cause-Related Marketing

Special public relations events also help to market products. Grand opening celebrations, for example, are a staple in the public relations arsenal. They present publicity opportu-

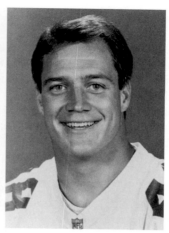

Figure 13–4   Celebrity spokespersons came in all sizes and shapes in the 1990s. The Dallas Cowboys, "America's team," featured all-American spokesperson Daryl "Moose" Johnston. On the other hand, basketball legend Magic Johnson gradually lost endorsements after his retirement because of testing HIV positive. And when two obscure lottery players hit the jackpot, they were recruited by New York LOTTO to tour the state in a stretch limo to promote "the possibilities."

nities and offer businesses a chance to meet customers face-to-face. With the cost of print and broadcast advertising going up each year, companies increasingly are turning to sponsorship of the arts, education, music, festivals, anniversaries, sports, and charitable causes for promotional and public relations purposes.

Such cause-related marketing is popular. Cause-related marketing brings together the fund-raising needs of nonprofit groups with the business objectives of sponsoring companies. Some companies have been called to task for using questionable tactics to promote their products by ostensibly doing good. Perhaps the most blatant example came in the winter of 1990, when Coca-Cola donated 20,000 cases of Coke to American troops in Saudi Arabia. It then promoted the gesture to the national media, which questioned the company's aggressive efforts to seek publicity. Later, Anheuser-Busch donated 22,000 cases of a nonalcoholic beer to the troops in Saudi Arabia and decided, in light of Coke's experience, to soft pedal the announcement.[10]

Despite such false starts, cause-related marketing will continue to grow into the next century. Baby boomers are now middle-aged and more concerned about issues that affect their lives, like saving the rain forests and recycling household trash. This change in itself will drive the creation of events and decision making by corporate sponsors.[11]

In planning special events and cause-related marketing activities, public relations people should first determine what area will best suit their organization's particular marketing objectives—culture, sports, community sponsorship, entertainment, and so on. Once objectives are decided, cause-related marketing can significantly enhance the reception and overall sales of a product or institution.

PUBLIC RELATIONS ADVERTISING

Traditionally, organizations used advertising to sell products. In 1936, though, a company named Warner & Swasey initiated an ad campaign that stressed the power of America as a nation and the importance of American business in the nation's future. Warner & Swasey continued its ads after World War II and thus was born a unique type of advertising—the marketing of an image rather than a product. This technique became known variously as institutional advertising, image advertising, public service advertising, and ultimately public relations advertising.

In the 1970s, opponents of American business began to flex their muscles, with advertisements critical of big business and its practices. Corporations responded with ads of their own that talked about social responsibility, equal employment hiring, minority assistance, and so on. This practice was labeled image advertising.

In the 1980s, the logical extension of image advertising was issues advertising, which advocated positions from the sponsor's viewpoint. Often these concerned matters of some controversy. Organizations, led by the outspoken Mobil Oil, continued the practice of issue ads into the 1990s (Figure 13–5). Indeed, Mobil's practice of placing an issues ad on the Op-Ed page of *The New York Times* and other leading newspapers each Thursday continued into its fourth decade and is still going strong in the latter stages of the 1990s.

Public interest groups have once again seized upon the most pressing issues of the day and are running ads to characterize their questions of business practices (Figure 13–6).

A QUESTION OF ETHICS

A FOUR-LETTER WORD CALLED NIKE

No company in the waning years of the twentieth century represents integrated marketing more than Nike, the West Coast juggernaut that practiced "in-your-face" advertising and thrived on controversy.

Nike savior, Michael Jordan, with supporting players, Spike Lee and Bugs Bunny.

Phil Knight, Nike's unabashed founder, seemed to thrive on the controversial sponsorship climate he created.

- When multisports star Bo Jackson stunned the sports world by revealing that he needed a hip replacement, Knight and Nike stayed with him in a multi million dollar advertising/endorsement campaign. (Jackson rewarded his benefactor when he returned to baseball and promptly hit a homerun in his first at bat!)
- When cry baby tennis star John McEnroe enraged the genteel tennis community, Knight named a building after him at the Nike complex.
- When arch rival Reebok donated millions of dollars to the 1992 U.S. Olympic Committee, Knight-sponsored Michael Jordan, Charles Barkley, and other American Dream Teamers who refused to wear official American team jackets to receive their Olympic gold medals.
- When Tanya Harding was disgraced for helping bang the knees of rival Nancy Kerrigan before the Lillehammer Winter Olympic games in 1994, Knight jumped to her defense.

- In 1996, Knight openly rooted for the Brazilian soccer team to beat the U.S. Why? Because Nike bought the Brazilian team and outfitted it with Nike shoes, while the Americans wore Adidas.
- In 1997, Nike drew the wrath of international soccer officials when its commercials highlighted a French star, whose foul-mouthed, McEnroe-like behavior had gotten him in trouble with rule-making authorities.

Knight and Nike's tentacles stretched across every level of the sports community. The University of Colorado football coach even ordered his players to wear Nike clothing exclusively, after the school signed a $5.6 million deal with Nike in 1996.

With superstar athletes from Neon Deion Sanders to Tiger Woods to the inestimable Michael Jordan all in the Nike camp and with amateur athletes and team also in the Nike clutches—one wondered whether Nike's sophisticated and all-encompassing integrated marketing approach had securely placed loyalty to a shoe company above that to the team, the sport, or even the country.

Where's the rip-off?

The sharp increase in gasoline prices has sparked thousands of words, most of them accusing the oil industry of reaping undeserved profits. Industry spokesmen have attempted to respond, with little apparent success.

So we decided to let the numbers do the talking.

West Texas Intermediate is a benchmark domestic crude oil. We've translated the price per barrel on the spot market to cents per gallon, and tracked the price movement from early July to last Tuesday. Gasoline also trades on the spot market, and we've shown the average spot price of regular unleaded across the U.S.

Finally, we've shown the average price we charged our dealers in 29 key cities for regular unleaded, along with the price for Mobil distributors. The dealers account for 70 percent and the distributors for about 30 percent of our gasoline business.

(All numbers cents/gallon)	CRUDE/PRODUCT PRICES JULY 3, AUGUST 7					
	7/3/90	7/17/90	*7/31/90	**8/2/90	8/7/90	Increase 7/3-8/7
West Texas Intermediate Spot Market Crude	40.2	44.4	48.1	55.5	70.5	+30.3
†Regular Unleaded Spot Market Gasoline	60.4	63.7	62.8	68.9	85.1	+24.7
Average Mobil Price To Dealer Regular Unleaded	74.5	73.6	74.7	75.0	81.2	+ 6.7
Average Mobil Price To Distributor Regular Unleaded	67.8	68.0	69.6	69.8	78.3	+10.5

*OPEC Met July 26-27
**Iraq Invaded Kuwait August 2
†Platt's Low Weighted Average

The table shows that market prices for both crude oil and gasoline rose far more sharply than Mobil's.

One final observation: Much crude is now bought on terms specifying that the price is to be set by the spot market at the time of delivery. So the price of the gasoline you buy today was <u>not</u> set in concrete weeks ago.

Mobil

Figure 13–5   In 1990, when gasoline prices rose quickly and the public once again castigated the oil industry, at least one petroleum firm was ready to answer back.

Figure 13–6   When the nation's tobacco companies were called on the carpet, groups like the Campaign for Tobacco-Free Kids emerged to crystallize the problem for the citizenry.

Purposes of Public Relations Advertising

Traditional public relations, or nonproduct, advertising—as opposed to image or issue positioning—is still widely used. Such advertising can be appropriate for a number of activities:

1. **Mergers and diversifications.**   When one company merges with another, the public needs to be told about the new business lines and divisions. Advertising provides a quick and effective way to convey this message.

2. **Personnel changes.**   A firm's greatest asset is usually its managers, its salespeople, and its employees. Presenting staff members in advertising not only impresses a reader with the firm's pride in its workers, but also helps build confidence among employees themselves.

3. **Organizational resources.**   A firm's investment in research and development implies that the organization is concerned about meeting the future intelligently, an asset that should be advertised. The scope of a company's services also says something positive about the organization.

4. **Manufacturing and service capabilities.**   The ability to deliver quality goods on time is something customers cherish. A firm that can deliver should advertise this capability. Likewise, a firm with a qualified and

attentive servicing capability should let clients and potential clients know about it.

5. **Growth history.**   A growing firm, one that has developed steadily over time and has taken advantage of its environment, is the kind of company with which people want to deal. It is also the kind of firm for which people will want to work. Growth history, therefore, is a worthwhile subject for nonproduct advertising.

6. **Financial strength and stability.**   A picture of economic strength and stability is one that all companies like to project. Advertisements that highlight the company's financial position earn confidence and attract customers and investors.

7. **Company customers.**   Customers can serve as a marketing tool, too. Well-known personalities who use a certain product may be enough to win additional customers. This strategy may be especially viable in advertising for higher priced products such as expensive automobiles or sports equipment.

8. **Organization name change.**   With firms in industries from banking to consumer products to communications now either merging with each other or streamlining their operations, company names change—from Time and Warner Brothers to Time Warner, from Federal Express to Fed Ex, from Kentucky Fried Chicken to KFC. To burnish the new name in people's minds, a name change must be well promoted and well advertised. Only through constant repetition will people become familiar with the new identity.

9. **Trademark protection.**   Companies such as Xerox and Coca-Cola, whose products are household names, are legitimately concerned about the improper generic use of their trademarks in the public domain. Such companies run periodic ads to remind people of the proper status of their marks. In one such ad, a perplexed secretary reminds the boss, "If you had ordered 40 photocopies instead of 40 Xeroxes, we wouldn't have been stuck with all these machines!" (Figure 13–7).

10. **Corporate emergencies.**   Occasionally, an emergency situation erupts—a labor strike, plant disaster, or service interruption. One quick way to explain the firm's position and procedures without fear of distortion or misinterpretation by editors or reporters is to buy advertising space. This tactic permits a full explanation of the reasons behind the problem and the steps the company plans to take to resolve the dilemma.

Public Relations Advertising in the 1990s

As noted, the 1990s signaled something of a reemergence of public relations advertising. In a period of contraction and recession, profit-making organizations must justify their activities. Pressure on nonprofit organizations has intensified their need to prove why they, too, deserve contributions in a period of scarce resources. Hospitals, faced with unprecedented pressure from the public and the federal government to streamline their costs, also must position themselves in a manner that will allow them to stay in business.

You can't Xerox
a Xerox
on a Xerox.

But we don't mind at all if you copy a copy on a Xerox copier.
In fact, we prefer it. Because the Xerox trademark should only identify products made by us. Like Xerox copiers and Xerox printing systems.
As a trademark, the term Xerox should always be used as an adjective, followed by a noun. And it's never used as a verb.

XEROX® is a trademark of XEROX Corporation.

Of course, helping us protect our trademark also helps you. Because you'll continue to get what you're actually asking for.
And not an inferior copy.

XEROX
The Document Company

Figure 13–7   Xerox even into the new century continued to have a hard time identifying its name as a trademark of the Xerox Corporation.

Public relations advertising is one way for organizations to position themselves in the mind of the public.

As organizations enter the twenty-first century, they must keep in mind seven cardinal rules of public relations advertising:

1. **Ads must strengthen the bottom line.**   The institution must keep in mind its own best long-term interest in its advertising. An organization pays for an ad for selfish reasons. Even companies that draw the wrath of others must be credited for one contribution in particular—providing jobs.

2. **Ads must be clear.**   One purpose of public relations advertising is to promote understanding. If message and motives are cloudy, people simply won't understand, no matter how well conceived the ad is (Figure 13–8).

3. **Ads must be supported by top management.**   The more controversial a public relations ad, the better it is. An ad that is watered down is one that is doomed to failure. Top management must be prepared to take the heat and support the advertising.

4. **Ads must persuade.**   Again, this is the basis of advertising. Ads shouldn't just inform—they must be persuasive. When public interest groups opposed Judge Robert Bork's nomination to the Supreme Court in 1987, they initiated a public relations advertising campaign that said in part, "We're one vote away from losing our most fundamental rights . . . choosing

DON'T HIRE A PERSON WITH A DISABILITY
BECAUSE IT'S THE RIGHT THING TO DO.
SUSAN HAS MULTIPLE SCLEROSIS. BUT SHE DOESN'T WANT YOUR SYMPATHY. AND JUDGING
FROM HER JOB PERFORMANCE, SHE DOESN'T NEED IT. MOST PEOPLE WITH DISABILITIES
ARE EXCELLENT EMPLOYEES. 19 OUT OF 20 MANAGERS GIVE EMPLOYEES WITH DISABILITIES
A "GOOD" OR "EXCELLENT" RATING. AND IF AN ACCOMMODATION IS NEEDED, HALF THE TIME
IT'S UNDER $50. SO HIRE A PERSON WITH A DISABILITY. IT'S THE SMART THING TO DO.

ONE THING PEOPLE WITH MS CAN COUNT ON.   NATIONAL
                                            MULTIPLE SCLEROSIS
                                            SOCIETY
                                            1-800-FIGHT-MS

Figure 13–8   The graphic photo and copy for this National Multiple Sclerosis Society ad was typical of a campaign that stated its message clearly.

between sterilization and job loss . . . declaring illegal the use of birth control . . . not being protected from sexual harassment." In other words, they used fear to persuade, and Bork's nomination was defeated.

5. **Ads must sell the persuaded.**   All advertising, especially the public relations variety, must appeal to what the public wants—not what the organization wants. This is a subtle distinction that is often lost on public relations advertisers (Figure 13–9).

6. **Ads must be honest.**   Any advertiser is suspect. All ads begin with a bias. If the organization is to be believed, the ad itself must be scrupulously straightforward and honest. Such was not the case when the head of the United Transportation Union in 1987 ostensibly paid for an ad in *The New York Times* appealing for support to fight a ban on smoking in commuter trains. Several days later, it was revealed that the ad was secretly paid for by the Philip Morris Tobacco Company. A decade later, with smoking bans in effect throughout the nation, such an ad would have been unheard of.

7. **A sense of humor helps.**   Organizations, particularly big ones, can't take themselves too seriously, especially in public relations advertising. Humor disarms a skeptical populace, and a light touch can help to influence readers toward a particular viewpoint (Figure 13–10).

Figure 13–9 Husband and wife animal activists Kim Basinger and Alec Baldwin lent their show biz appeal to People for the Ethical Treatment of Animals for this provocative ad.

INTEGRATED MARKETING FOR THE TWENTY-FIRST CENTURY

Beyond advertising, marketing, and public relations techniques, integrated marketing, too, must keep pace with the ever-changing world of promotional innovations to help sell products and services. Specifically, communications professionals must be familiar with such innovative vehicles as the, infomercials, 900 numbers, and movie product placements.

Infomercials

Infomercials were greeted with universal catcalls in the 1980s when they were introduced as program-length commercials, shamelessly hawking products. Even today, the infomer-

Figure 13–10   The Benetton Company used this unique strategy to collect 500 tons of clothing for needy individuals around the world.

cial remains the Rodney Dangerfield of marketing, shunned and doubted for many reasons—state and federal investigations of infomercial producers, complaints about product performance, and, most important, the belief that a lengthy commercial disguised as a conventional program—like a talk show, complete with theme song and studio audience—unfairly masks what is nothing more than a failed spiel.[12]

Nonetheless, infomercials are growing in popularity for one reason—they work. Between $1 and $2 billion worth of merchandise is sold each year as a result of infomercials. Today even the most well-established organizations run infomercials. And celebrities from Cher to Martin Sheen to Suzanne Somers to Dionne Warwick have joined the growing parade of infomercial pitchmen.

900 Numbers

Establishing a 900 telephone number is another way of publishing and selling information. Such numbers charge callers for the privilege of tuning in to current business news headlines, or stock quotes, or sports information. Just as infomercials were laughed at, 900 numbers were once associated more with parties and steamy adult sex than with mainstream marketing. In the 1990s, though, that situation has changed. At the same time as the government has cracked down on 900 phone services with increased regulations, Fortune 500 corporations, publishers, TV and movie companies, consumer products manufacturers, law firms, counseling services, nonprofit organizations, and even government agencies have joined the 900 marketing cavalcade. With 1996 revenue expected to approach $900 million, 900 numbers are here to stay.[13]

Movie Product Placements

Product placements in films also are proliferating at a rapid rate. The turning point in product plugs occurred two decades ago when M&M/Mars turned down filmmaker Steven Spielberg, when he offered to link M&Ms to the hero of his new movie, *E.T.*. Reese's Pieces, however, took up the movie producer's offer, and the rest is history (Figure 13–11). Corporations from McDonald's to Coca-Cola to General Motors to Microsoft pay huge sums for the privilege of having their product's name mentioned by Sylvester Stallone or Wesley Snipes or Arnold Schwartzenegger. Such product placements in films have become another merchandising resource that communicators should consider as part of their integrated marketing communications strategy.

Figure 13–11 Movie product plugs really caught fire after a certain lovable alien professed his predilection for Reese's Pieces.

SUMMARY

Marketing professor Philip Kotler has said that the days of traditional product marketing may be giving way to a more subtle, social, or public relations marketing. According to Kotler, companies must deal with dwindling resources, inflation that continues to limit buying power, consumers who are becoming more sophisticated, environmental and quality-of-life considerations, and government control.

In other words, what is needed now is an integrated approach to communications, combining the best of marketing, advertising, sales promotion, and public relations. Some public relations people feel threatened by such talk. The thought of working closely with marketing, advertising, direct mail, sales promotion, and database marketing specialists worries them.[14] They fear the subjugation of the practice of public relations to these other disciplines.

Nonetheless, relationship building for organizations of every stripe now holds the key to a successful enterprise. Building lasting relationships rather than selling to transactional customers must be the objective for any intelligent organization.

This implies the need for a communications professional knowledgeable about all aspects of the communications mix. Integrated marketing communications then becomes paramount in preparing public relations professionals for the challenges of the new century.

DISCUSSION STARTERS

1. What is meant by integrated marketing communications?
2. Describe the differences among advertising, marketing, and public relations.
3. What is meant by third-party endorsement?
4. Discuss the phenomenon of the spokesperson.
5. Describe the pros and cons of using someone well-known as a spokesperson.
6. What is cause-related marketing?
7. What is image advertising? Issues advertising?
8. What are the purposes of public relations advertising?
9. What stimulated the reemergence of public relations advertising in the 1990s?
10. What are infomercials? 900 phone numbers?

NOTES

1. Fraser P. Seitel, "Communications Cross-Training," *U.S. Banker* (June 1993): 53.
2. Scot Hume, "Integrated Marketing: Who's in Charge Here?", *Advertising Age* (February 22, 1993): 1, 52.
3. Mitchell Kozikowski, "The Role of Public Relations in Integrated Marketing Public Relations," address presented to the National Conference of the Public Relations Society of America, November 15, 1993, Orlando, FL.
4. "Colloquium of Marketing and PR Spokespersons Agrees Organizations Suffer When Turf Wars Occur," *Public Relations Reporter* (February 13, 1989): 1.

5. Tom Harris, "Kotler's Total Marketing Embraces MPR," *MPR Update* (December 1992): 4.

6. "Marketing PR Can Outperform Advertising, Says Long-Time Counselor Dan Edelman," *Public Relations Reporter* (October 30, 1989): 3.

7. Judann Pollack, "New Marketing Spin: The PR 'Experience,' " *Advertising Age* (August 5, 1996): 33.

8. Susan Friedman, "Tips for Internal and External Trade Show Visitors," *Business Marketing* (June 1995).

9. Kerry Capell, "Tiger, Inc.," *Business Week* (April 28, 1997): 32.

10. Mark Landler and Seth Payne, "Publicity? Why, It Never Even Occurred to Us," *Business Week* (September 24, 1990): 46.

11. "Event Marketing: The Good, the Bad and the Ugly," address by David D'Alessandro at the International Events Group's Annual Event Marketing Conference, March 22, 1993, Chicago.

12. Stuart Elliot, "Some Big Marketers Join Audience for Infomercials," *The New York Times* (June 5, 1992): D9.

13. Sharon McDonald, "Laws Forcing 900 Numbers to Change Tone," *Crain's New York Business* (October 11, 1993): 26.

14. "Integrated Marketing: Is It PR's Nemesis or Salvation?" *O'Dwyer's PR Services Report* (January 1995): 1.

SUGGESTED READINGS

Aaker, David A. *Building Strong Brands*. New York: The Free Press, 1995. Predicts over the next three decades, there will be an unmitigated "battle of the brands."

Albrecht, Karl. *The Only Thing That Matters: Bring the Power of the Customers into the Center of Your Business*. New York: Harper Business, 1992.

Changing World of Marketing: Conference Summary Report No. 92-112. Cambridge, MA: Marketing Science Institute, 1992.

Complete Guide to Creating Successful Brochures. Brentwood, NJ: Asher-Gallent Press, 1988.

Corporate Advertising Practices. New York: Association of National Advertisers, 1991.

Encyclopedia of Telemarketing. New York: Prentice Hall, 1991.

Fowles, Jib. *Advertising and Popular Culture*. Thousand Oaks, CA: Sage, 1995.

Frank, Robert H. and Philip J. Cook. *The Winner Take All Society*. New York: The Free Press, 1995. A critical look at a marketing society that encourages economic waste, growing economic inequality, and senseless consumption.

Goldman, Jordan. *Public Relations in the Marketing Mix*. New York: NTC Business Books, 1992.

Gregory, James R. with Jack G. Wiechmann. *Marketing Corporate Image*. New York: NTC Business Books, 1995.

Harris, Thomas L. *The Marketer's Guide to Public Relations*. New York: John Wiley & Sons, 1993.

Hauman, David J. *The Capital Campaign Handbook: How to Maximize Your Fund-Raising Campaign*. Rockville, MD: Taft Group, 1987 (12300 Twinbrook Parkway, Suite 450, 20852-9830).

TOP OF THE SHELF

DON E. SCHULTZ, STANLEY I. TANNENBAUM, AND ROBERT F. LAUTERBORN

INTEGRATED MARKETING COMMUNICATIONS: PUTTING IT TOGETHER & MAKING IT WORK

NEW YORK: NTC BUSINESS BOOKS, 1996

This book is as good an introduction to integrated marketing communications as any. It shows how to put an integrated program into practice, with guidance on planning, coordinating, and controlling the entire communications process.

What is particularly valuable is the authors' dissection of the core questions in any integrated marketing program: Who controls the program? How should resources be allocated? How can the impact of the program be measured?

Also offered are examples of integrated marketing communications programs in action and how they can work to improve the overall positioning of a company.

How to Handle Public Relations for Your Advertising Agency. New York: American Association of Advertising Agencies, 1991.

Integrated Marketing Communications: A Survey of National Consumer Goods Advertisers. New York: American Association of Advertising Agencies, 1991.

Janul, Daniel S. *Online Marketing Handbook*. New York: Von Nostrand Reinhold, 1995. How to sell, advertise, publicize, and promote prouducts on the Internet.

Lyons, John. *Guts: Advertising from the Inside Out*. New York: AMACOM, 1989.

Magrath, Allan. *Six Imperatives of Marketing: Lessons from the World's Best Companies*. New York: AMACOM, 1992.

Marconi, Joe. *Image Marketing*. New York: NTC Business Books, 1996.

McKenna, Regis. *Relationship Marketing*. Reading, MA: Addison-Wesley, 1991.

McNamara, Jay. *Advertising Agency Management*. Homewood, IL: Dow Jones-Irwin, 1990.

Mingo, Jack. *How the Cadillac Got Its Fins*. New York: Harper Business, 1995. Case histories behind the invention and marketing of famous products.

Ogilvy, David. *Confessions of an Advertising Man*. New York: Macmillan, 1963.

Parmerlee, David. *Preparing the Marketing Plan*. New York: NTC Business Books, 1996.

Ritchie, Karen. *Marketing to Generation X*. New York: Lexington Books, 1995. Foreshadowing the interactive, integrated marketing communications in the twenty-first century.

Savidge, Jack. *Marketing Intelligence: Discover What Your Customers Really Want and What Your Competitors Are Up To*. Homewood, IL: Business One Irwin, 1992.

CASE STUDY

FROM PERKY TO PARIAH: THE SAD SAGA OF KATHIE LEE

Prior to May 1996, the only public charge of which bubbly TV personality Kathie Lee Gifford could be accused was "terminal perkiness."

But in the spring of 1996, everybody's favorite spokesperson was singed—mightily. Charles Kernaghan, executive director of the National Labor Committee Education Fund in Support of Worker and Human Rights in Central America, testified before the U.S. Congress that Kathie Lee was a "pariah." According to the labor leader, Kathie Lee Gifford's Wal-Mart clothing line, which earned more than $300 million for the company and millions for Kathie Lee, was produced by 13-and 14-year-olds, working 20-hour days in factories in Honduras, earning as little as 31 cents an hour.

The clear implication was that Kathie Lee endorsed slave labor.

With her wholesome image beginning to tatter at the seams, Kathie Lee was stunned. The effervescent co-host of the syndicated "Live with Regis and Kathie Lee" sobbed to viewers that she was "unaware" of the conditions under which the Kathie Lee clothing line was produced.

Her antagonist was unimpressed.

"Doesn't she care that abuses were done to make clothes that bear her name?" asked labor leader Kernaghan. "She should accept our invitation and see what conditions are like at these plants with her own eyes."

Around the Corner

As it turned out, Kathie Lee did just that—but not in Honduras; rather she traveled around the corner from her New York City studio.

Within days of the exposé of the Honduran child labor producing Kathie Lee clothes, the *New York Daily News* reported that a midtown Manhattan sweatshop had just shipped 50,000 Kathie Lee blouses to Wal-Mart. Workers reported being paid below minimum wage, cheated out of money due them by their employer, and forced to labor in crowded, sweltering conditions. All in the name of producing the Kathie Lee line.

Now, Kathie Lee was really in the public relations hotseat. "America's Sweetheart" stood in imminent danger of becoming "America's Sweat-Heart."

And that's when the uninformed spokesperson/clothing mogul took the public relations offensive.

- She hired politically well-connected public relations firm Rubenstein & Associates to help resuscitate her sagging image.
- She enlisted New York Governor George Pataki in a drive to put legislative heat on sweatshop owners. The Pataki bill called for the New York attorney general to seize goods produced by exploited workers, denying sweatshop operators of illegal profits.
- Turning to Washington, Kathie Lee next appeared at a press conference with Labor Secretary Robert Reich, both vowing to fight back against oppressive labor conditions for factory workers.
- She scheduled a Washington "Fashion Summit" to talk about labor conditions in the fashion industry.

Kathie Lee, Frank, and a friend.

- In her most bizarre response to the sweatshop flap, Kathie Lee appeared unannounced at the midtown sweatshop itself, carrying peace offerings. With her slightly miffed ex-football star husband, Frank, in tow and surrounded by a phalanx of TV cameras, Kathie Lee handed out $100 bills to any workers she could find who had turned out her goods.

"I have the money to pay them," Frank said, as he surveyed the chaotic scene. "I just need to know who the hell they are." Outside, union activists chanted, "Kath-ie pay my sal-a-ry."

Low Profile

For its part, Wal-Mart, the owner of the goods in question, maintained a decidedly lower profile, staying conveniently off to the side while Kathie Lee took the heat.

Responses of the company, which earlier had been exposed on *Dateline NBC* as using child labor in Bangladesh, were cryptic. At first, Wal-Mart denied the problem in Honduras. Then it claimed that the overseas work had been subcontracted without the company's knowledge.

Other celebrities whose names were also attached to similarly produced garments, including actress Jaclyn Smith and Michael Jordan, also moved out of the line of fire. Said Jordan of charges that his Nike Air Jordans were made by child labor, "I don't know the complete situation. Why should I? I'm trying to do my job. Hopefully, Nike will do the right thing."

To her credit, Kathie Lee seemed committed to doing "the right thing" by leaping forcefully into the child labor fracas. "I'm in a unique and in a strange way privileged, position to implement long-overdue reforms," she declared.

Alas just as the sweatshop issue faded away, Kathie Lee found herself right back in the soup. After lamenting on air that her pedigree pooch had gained a lot of weight and that she was considering giving the dog away, Kathie Lee again was blasted. Friends of Animals wrote to the talking talk show host, offering to rescue the paunchy pooch and find her a "responsible, caring home."

The fur was flying once again around Kathie Lee.

And as if this wasn't enough, in the spring of 1997 loving hubby Frank was caught on videotape in a hotel room with a very un-Kathie looking blond.

Poor Kathie Lee.

QUESTIONS

1. Should celebrities know about the conditions under which the products they sponsor are produced?
2. How would you characterize Kathie Lee's response?
3. Do you think the awarding of $100 bills was a good idea?
4. What other options did she have?
5. How would you characterize Wal-Mart's response to the child labor crisis?

For further information on the Kathie Lee case see Jim Dwyer, "Kathie Lee'll Mend City Sweatshop Ways," *New York Daily News*, May 23, 1996, 3; "Making the Fashion Industry Sweat," *Reputation Management*, September/October 1996, 33; Stephanie Strom, "A Sweetheart Becomes Suspect," *The New York Times*, June 27, 1996, D1; Arlene Vigoda, "Kathie Lee Back in the Doghouse," *USA Today*, August 9, 1996, 2D; Anne Underwood and John Leland, "Perkiness Conquers All," *Newsweek*, June 10, 1996, 94.

VOICE OF EXPERIENCE

STEVE RIVKIN

Steve Rivkin is president of his own communications counseling firm in Glen Rock, New Jersey. Before forming Rivkin & Associates in 1989, he was executive vice president of Trout & Ries, Inc., the prestigious marketing strategy firm known for its pioneering work in positioning. Before joining Trout & Ries, Rivkin worked in public affairs, advertising, and corporate identity for IU International Corporation, a Philadelphia-based conglomerate. He was previously associate editor of *Iron Age Magazine*, a weekly business publication. Rivkin speaks and lectures frequently on communications topics.

WHAT IS INTEGRATED COMMUNICATIONS?

Integrated communications is a new way of looking at the whole. Most of us only see parts—public relations, advertising, sales literature, employee communications, and so forth. Integrated communications is about realigning communications the way the customer sees it—as one flow of information.

Traditional communications is like going into a pharmacy to pick up some items—a package of publicity, a box of direct mail, a carton of advertising.

Integrated communications is more like going to see a team of doctors. Tell them where it hurts—what your communications problem is—and they'll prescribe comprehensive treatment—everything from a remedy through rehabilitation.

WHY DO TODAY'S BUSINESS DEMANDS CALL FOR A NEW COMPOSITION OF COMMUNICATIONS FUNCTIONS?

Because the old lines are blurring. Today, consumers tend to lump all persuasive messages into something they may call advertising. They don't differentiate among messages from TV or magazines or an outdoor display. They don't even differentiate among various functional approaches marketers use, such as advertising, direct mail, sales promotion, public relations, or even advertorials. These are all simply "advertising" or "product messages."

No matter where the message came from, or who created it, or where it appears, it stands for the brand, the company, or the organization.

WHAT WILL HAPPEN TO TRADITIONAL PRACTICES OF MARKETING, ADVERTISING AND PUBLIC RELATIONS?

They'll disappear over time. Specialists in these fields will become generalists in integrated marketing communications.

HOW DO SMART ORGANIZATIONS APPROACH THE NEW REALITIES OF COMMUNICATIONS?

They're looking for synergy. They want the whole of communications to be greater than the sum of its parts.

When all the corporate and product messages are strategically coordinated, the effect is greater than when advertising, sales promotion, naming, PR, packaging, etc. are planned and executed independently. When each is independent, each area competes for budgets and power. And sometimes each area sends out conflicting messages.

WHAT DO YOU ADVISE COMPANIES WITH TRADITIONAL ADVERTISING AND PUBLIC RELATIONS DEPARTMENTS TO DO?

To see the light. To let people out of their boxes.

What you've got now are people trained and then constrained. Their jobs should be to tackle your business problems. Instead, their jobs are to "do public relations" or "do advertising" or "do direct mail."

HOW SHOULD PUBLIC RELATIONS STUDENTS PREPARE FOR INTEGRATED COMMUNICATIONS?

Cross-train your brains. Don't turn up your nose at any one form of communication. What if the database turns out to be a more powerful communications tool than TV ever was?

And always consider communications from the customer's vantage point. That means you should ask (1) what media forms the customer or prospect uses, not simply what is most efficient for the marketer; (2) when your messages might be most relevant to the customer or prospect, not just when you'd prefer to schedule them; and (3) when customers and prospects might be more receptive to your message, not simply when it might be most convenient to deliver that message.

WHAT DOES INTEGRATED COMMUNICATIONS HAVE TO DO WITH POSITIONING AN ORGANIZATION?

Positioning is a touchstone for integrated communications because it starts with the same "outside-in" orientation. Positioning an organization is actually thinking in reverse. Instead of starting with you or your company, you start with the prospect.

Positioning a company means getting into the mind of your prospect with a single, memorable concept or set of ideas about that company. The basic approach of positioning is not to create something new and different, but rather to manipulate what's already there, to retie the connections that already exist.

CHAPTER FOURTEEN

Employees

TODAY THE SINGLE MOST DIFFICULT FUNCTION in the practice of public relations is internal communications, i.e., communicating with employees. The wave of downsizings and layoffs that dominated business and industry both in the United States and worldwide during the latter half of the 1990s, along with the emergence of a technological revolution that has made human resources more expendable, have resulted in employees who are more skeptical, brittle, and dubious. The "trust gap" with management has never been wider.[1] Therefore, the challenge for internal communicators has never been more profound.

In the 1980s, layoffs were greeted with opprobrium in all quarters, as a sign that a company couldn't support growth and had to reduce staff as business declined. In the 1990s, ironically, layoffs were greeted with glee, particularly by the investment community, which interpreted smaller staffs as a sign that the company intended larger profits. "It is unfortunate," said investment banker Felix Rohaytyn, "when a company's stock improves at the expense of its workers."[2]

The days when an employee joined the phone company or the utility company or the bank or the Fortune 500 manufacturer to guarantee job security and lifetime employment are gone forever. Indeed, one of the most significant retrenchment programs was launched by AT&T, once known as "Ma Bell," which summarily fired a whopping 40,000 employees in 1996, while CEO Robert Allen received a whopping pay increase. (Ironically, Allen himself was summarily dumped as AT&T CEO a year later.) Employees who remain in such firms today are less secure, less confident, and therefore less loyal than their predecessors.

All of these changes pose a significant challenge for employee communicators.

326 CHAPTER FOURTEEN   EMPLOYEES

Consequently, internal communications has become a "hot ticket" in public relations, particularly as organizations face the harsh competitive realities that will mark the twenty-first century. With fewer employees expected to do more work, staff members are calling for empowerment—for more of a voice in decision making. Although some managements are willing, others evidently are not. Resultant relations between employer and employee these days are not particularly good. Just about every researcher who keeps tabs on employee opinion finds evidence of the trust gap that exists between management and rank-and-file workers.

Evidence of this trust gap was among the findings of a nearly 300-organization employee opinion study conducted by the International Association of Business Communicators in conjunction with employee benefits consultant Towers, Perrin, Foster and Crosby. Among other findings were these:

- The majority of employees want face-to-face information from first-line supervisors as the preferred source of communication.

- First-line supervisors aren't communicating satisfactorily. Senior management remains invisible and out of touch.

- Even in a day of online communications, the companywide publication still scores high marks from employees in many respects, yet it rates low as a preferred source of information. Although employees are more satisfied with the information they're getting, communications efforts are still not meeting their needs.

- Employees are intensely critical of management's unwillingness to listen to them or to act on their ideas.[3]

There is no such thing today as a single "employee public." The employee public is made up of numerous subgroups. Indeed, today the staff is generally younger, increasingly female, more ambitious and career-oriented, less complacent, and less loyal to the company than in the past. Today's more hard-nosed employee demands candor in communications. Internal communications, like external messages, must be targeted to reach specific subgroups of the employee public. Communications must be continuous to reinforce a consistent management message.

Subsequent research has dramatically confirmed these findings.

- A "1994 Study of the Changing Workforce," conducted by the Families and Work Institute, found that "open communication" far outranked any other item in a list of "very important" qualities looked for when choosing a job.[4]
- A 1995 survey by Deloitte & Touche found that 81 percent of health care respondents found that "employee morale" was the top human resources issue in hospitals today—compared to 75 percent only one year earlier.

- A 1996 survey of those American Management Association member companies that cut jobs revealed that declining morale was a problem in three out of four of them.[5]

Clearly, organizing effective, believable, and persuasive internal communications in the midst of organizational change is a core critical public relations responsibility as our society moves into the twenty-first century.

COMMUNICATING EFFECTIVELY IN A SEA OF DOUBT

An organization truly concerned about "getting through" to its employees in an era of downsizing, displacement, and dubious communications must reinforce five specific principles.

- **Respect.** Employees must be respected for their worth as individuals and their value as workers. They must be treated with respect and not as interchangeable commodities.
- **Honest feedback.** By talking to workers about their strengths and weaknesses, employees know where they stand. Some managers incorrectly assume that avoiding negative feedback will be helpful. Wrong. Employees need to know where they stand at any given time. Candid communications will help them in this pursuit.
- **Recognition.** Employees feel successful when management recognizes their contributions. It is the duty of the public relations professional to suggest mechanisms by which deserving employees will be honored.
- **A voice.** In the era of talk radio and television talk shows, almost everyone wants their ideas to be heard and to have a voice in decision making. This growing "activist communications" phenomenon must be considered by public relations professionals seeking to win internal goodwill for management.
- **Encouragement.** Study after study reveals that money and benefits motivate employees up to a point, but that "something else" is generally necessary. That something else is encouragement. Workers need to be encouraged. Communications programs that can provide encouragement generally produce results.

What distinguishes the communication effort at a "better place to work"? According to Milton Moskowitz, coauthor of the *100 Best Companies to Work For*, six criteria, in particular, are important:

1. **Willingness to express dissent** Employees, according to Moskowitz, want to be able to "feed back" to management their opinions and even dissent. They want access to management. They want critical letters to appear in internal publications. They want management to pay attention.
2. **Visibility and proximity of upper management** Enlightened companies try to level rank distinctions, eliminating such status reminders as executive cafeterias and executive gymnasiums. They act against hierarchical separation, says Moskowitz. He adds that smart CEOs practice MBWA—"management by walking around."

3. **Priority of internal to external communication** The worst thing to happen to any organization is for employees to learn critical information about the company on the 10 o'clock news. Smart organizations always release pertinent information to employees first and consider internal communication primary.

4. **Attention to clarity** How many employees regularly read benefits booklets? The answer should be "many" because of the importance of benefit programs to the entire staff.

   Because most employees never open such booklets, good companies write them with clarity—to be readable for a general audience rather than for human resources specialists.

5. **Friendly tone** According to Moskowitz, the best companies "give a sense of family" in all that they communicate. One high-tech company, says Moskowitz, makes everyone wear a name tag with the first name in big block letters. These little things are most important, declares Moskowitz.

6. **Sense of humor** Most experts agree that in the 1990s organizational work is very serious. People are worried principally about keeping their jobs. Corporate life for many is grim. Moskowitz says this is disastrous. "It puts people in straitjackets, so they can't wait to get out at the end of the day."[6]

What internal communications comes down to—just like external communications—is the single word *credibility*. The task for management, at a disaffected and disloyal time, is to convince employees that it not only desires to communicate with them, but also wishes to do so in a truthful, frank, and direct manner. That is the overriding challenge that confronts today's internal communicator.

THE REST OF THE STORY

AKA "YOU'RE OUTA' HERE"

Nobody in the latter years of the twentieth century got fired or even laid off. Rather, companies described their attempts to pare the staff in the following more palatable terms:

■ Strengthening global effectiveness—Procter & Gamble

■ Focused reduction—Tandem Computer

■ Career transition program—General Motors

■ Reshaping—National Semiconductor

■ Release of resources—Bank of America

■ Normal payroll adjustment—Wal-Mart

■ Schedule adjustments—Stouffer Foods Corp.

■ Involuntarily separated from the payroll—Bell Labs

CREDIBILITY: THE KEY

The employee public is a savvy one. Employees can't be conned because they live with the organization every day. They generally know what's going on and whether management is being honest with them. That's why management must be truthful.

Evidently being truthful isn't easy for many managements. The days when management could say "Trust us, this is for your own good" are over. Research indicates that if organizations (1) communicated earlier and more frequently, (2) demonstrated trust in employees by sharing bad news as well as good, and (3) involved employees in the process by asking for their ideas and opinions, employees would substantially increase their trust in management.[7] The fact is, employees desperately want to know in what direction an organization is headed and what their own role is in getting it there.

Today, smart companies realize that well-informed employees are the organization's best goodwill ambassadors. Managements have become more candid in their communications with the staff. Gone are the days when all the news coming from the communications department was good. In today's environment, being candid means treating people with dignity and giving them the opportunity to understand the realities of the marketplace.[8]

IBM, for example, gutted its award-winning, four-color magazine, *Think*, with the arrival of new CEO Lou Gerstner in 1993. The new *Think* was smaller and more candid than its predecessor, discussing such formally taboo topics as "avoiding getting swallowed up in bureaucracy" and "working without the warmth of a corporate security blanket." The new *Think* was most successful.

So, too, was the no-holds-barred *The SPARK*, the monthly publication of Arco International (Figure 14–1). *The SPARK* poked fun at the company, encouraged blunt feedback from employees, and generally promoted an environment of candor and openness at Arco.

At AT&T, another frank, hard-hitting magazine, *Focus*, was introduced in 1990. As its editor explained, faith in the company had been "shaken," and an honest, straightforward magazine was designed to help restore that faith.[9] Ironically, in 1993, *Focus* became the focus of an embarrassing scandal involving a cartoon perceived as racially insensitive. AT&T subsequently terminated *Focus*. (See the Case Study in this chapter.)

In any organization, employees must feel that they are appreciated. They want to be treated as important parts of an organization; they should not be taken for granted, nor should they be shielded from the truth. Thus, the most important ingredient of any internal communications program must be credibility.

EMPLOYEE COMMUNICATIONS STRATEGIES

Enhancing credibility, being candid, and winning trust must be the primary employee communications objectives in the new century. Earning employee trust may result in more committed and productive employees. But scraping away the scar tissue of distrust that exists in many organizations requires a strategic approach. Five elements are key in any strategic program:

1. **Survey employees' attitudes regularly.** Ironically, it is organizations that audit their financial resources on a daily basis that regularly fail to take the temperature of their own employees. They "fly blind." Attitude surveys can identify problems before they become crises. Employees who are surveyed about their attitudes,

Figure 14–1 *The SPARK*, from ARCO, was perhaps the most well-known employee publication in America. Its candor and openness were legendary. Few similar publications would have the chutzpah to feature their own employees in a *National Enquirer Lifestyles of the Rich and Famous* motif.

consulted on what the surveys reveal, and then shown action as a result of the survey findings will be much more willing to accept management's policies.

2. **Be consistent.** Management that promises open and honest communications must practice it. An open door must remain open—not just partly open part of the time. Communications must be consistent to be believed. That means conveying both good and bad news on a regular basis.

FACILITATING THE PG&E LAYOFFS

When San Francisco's Pacific Gas and Electric Company (PG&E) decided to fire 3,000 workers in 1993, the cutbacks were the largest in the company's 88-year history. As in other similar companies, the restructuring was difficult because of a traditional corporate culture that stood for job security, generous benefits, and recruitment of relatives for employment.

The typical shock faced by employees given such news was exacerbated by the company's clumsy internal notification program.

"My boss read from a script and told me not to return to my office," griped one veteran employee. "It was incredible." Another complained that he learned about his fate through a posting on a department bulletin board. A PG&E guidebook handed out to managers to execute layoffs was leaked to the *San Francisco Chronicle*. Among its highlights were the following:

- The manual likened the possible reaction of a displaced worker to "the fight-or-flight response typical of animals under siege."
- The manual provided a checklist for terminating employees, including "be supportive, but not compromising," "Don't be apologetic," and "Don't threaten or traumatize."
- "Before terminating someone, determine whether that person could easily overpower you or has a belligerent nature. In that event, ensure that you have a witness."
- "The actual act of termination should occur within the first FIVE minutes of the termination interview. The remainder of this time should be spent allowing the individual to express his or her feelings and questions."
- (*Note*: Use the following according to individual situations.) "Under the new structure, your position has been eliminated as of today."

or

"You have not been selected to fill your current position."

Employees, many of them long-time veterans of PG&E, were generally outraged at the impersonal manner in which the company chose to terminate them.

"At a time when the company needs friends, it has cultivated an army of enemies," groused one worker whose job was eliminated.

Might there have been a better way for PG&E to relay the unfortunate news without risking the loss of goodwill and morale among its workers?

3. **Personalize communications.** One study found that 80 percent of corporate chief executives believed that "personally communicating with employees benefits the bottom line." But only 22 percent of them did it on a regular basis. Workers want personal attention from those for whom they work, particularly their immediate supervisor. Given this, companies like Union Carbide conduct "town meetings" at which senior managers barnstorm around the nation to answer employees' questions.

4. **Be candid.** Employees today are younger, less well-educated, less loyal, and include more women, minorities, and immigrants than workers of the past. These

new, more skeptical, less trusting employees demand honesty in everything management says.

5. **Be innovative.**   New employees in the work force and increased skepticism in the workplace demand new communications solutions. This means resorting to the new technology—voice, video, data transmission on PCs, and so on—to reach workers. Today's work force, weaned on a daily diet of high-resolution, mind-numbing television, demands innovative solutions to counteract the trust gap.[10]

EMPLOYEE COMMUNICATIONS TACTICS

Once objectives are set, a variety of techniques can be adopted to reach the staff. The initial tool again is research. Before any communications program can be implemented, communicators must have a good sense of staff attitudes. Perhaps the most beneficial form of research on which to lay the groundwork for effective employee communications is the internal communications audit. Basically, this consists of old-fashioned personal, in-depth interviews to determine staff attitudes about their jobs, the organization, and its management, coupled with an analysis of existing communications techniques. The findings of such audits are often startling, always informative, and never easily ignored.

Once internal communications research is completed, the public relations practitioner has a clearer idea of the kinds of communications vehicles that make sense for the organization. Several of the more popular vehicles are discussed here.

Online Communication

The age of online communication has ushered in a whole new set of employee communications vehicles—from e-mail to voice mail to tailored organizational intranets. Honeywell, Inc is a typical proponent of the newer, immediate means of internal communications. Every Friday, Honeywell dispatches an electronic publication called "Honeywell Headlines," a roundup of key news and events involving the firm. Honeywell also issues "e-mail on demand" to employees wishing to keep abreast of changing corporate information and developments, for example, by summary reports of management meetings. Honeywell reported 800 internal subscribers to its e-mail on demand service.[11]

Online newsletters have started to become popular as a replacement for or adjunct to print newsletters. Increasingly preferred today is the use of e-mail messages as a communications source. The online newsletter is the next logical step to e-mail, and it is likely that the twenty-first century will see a continued movement toward such online internal communications.

Organizations such as Xerox, Exxon, J.P. Morgan, Ford, and the Mayo Clinic already are relying on intranets to communicate. Intranets are becoming more popular because they allow communicators, management, and employees to exchange information quickly and effectively. According to Forrester Research, 62 percent of all American companies either have an intranet or plan to have one soon. And it is likely that in the first few years of the new century, every major company will have intranet capability.[12]

Print Newsletters

Print is still by far the most heavily used medium to communicate with employees. The long-heralded revolution of pictures and electronics may be the wave of the future, but it has not yet supplanted letters, bulletins, brochures, manuals, and particularly the oldest staple in the employee communications arsenal—the employee newsletter.

Although the format and content of the employee newsletter vary from organization to organization. This broad concept has stood the test of time (Figure 14–2).

A traditional first job for an entry-level public relations professional is working on the employee newsletter. When approaching the writing or editing of an employee newsletter, the professional should ponder the following questions:

1. Who is this paper designed to reach?
2. What kinds of articles should be featured?
3. What is the budget for the newsletter?
4. What is the appropriate format for the newsletter?
5. How frequently should the newsletter be published?
6. What is the desired approval process for the newsletter?

Figure 14–2   In the latter half of the 1990s, when cigarette companies like Philip Morris were besieged from every quarter, they used their employee newsletters to air their rebuttal arguments and rally the troops.

The answers to these questions, of course, vary from one organization to another, but all should be tackled before approaching the assignment. Employee newsletters should appear regularly, on time, and with a consistent format. Employees should expect them and even look forward to them.

The employee newsletter still serves as a first-line communications vehicle from management to explain the company's philosophy and policies. In the next century, it will be even more important that such newsletters provide two-way communications, expressing not only management wishes but staff concerns as well.

A typical employee newsletter editor must consider the following steps in approaching the task:

1. **Assigning stories.** Article assignments must focus on organizational strategies and management objectives. Job information—organizational changes, mergers, reasons behind decisions, and so on—should be stressed. Articles must reflect the diversity of the organization: different locations and departments as well as the different kinds of people the organization employs. The editor must review with each writer the desired "thesis" to be conveyed by the article.

2. **Enforcing deadlines.** Employees respect a newsletter that comes out at a specific time—whether weekly, bimonthly, or monthly. An editor, therefore, must assign and enforce rigid copy deadlines. Deadline slippage can't be tolerated if the newsletter is to be respected.

3. **Assigning photos.** Many newsletters include photographs. Because internal publications compete with glossy, high-tech newspapers and magazines, organizational photos can't be dull. Editors must take pains to "think visually" by assigning visually arresting photos—the more provocative, the better (Figure 14–3).

4. **Editing copy.** An editor must be just that: a critic of sloppy writing, a student of forceful prose, a motivator to improve copy style. Employees must want to read about what's going on in the organization. Riveting writing must be the goal of a good newsletter.

5. **Formatting copy.** An editor must also make the final decisions on the format of the newsletter: how long articles should run, where to put photos, how to crop artwork, what headlines should say, and so on. As desktop publishing becomes more pervasive, the task of formatting becomes more important for an editor.

6. **Ensuring on-time publication.** An editor's job doesn't stop when the newsletter is sent to the printer. It is the editor's responsibility to ensure that no last-minute glitches interfere with the on-time publication of the finished product.

7. **Critiquing.** After the publication hits the stands, the editor's job must continue. He or she must scrupulously review copy, photos, placement, content, philosophy, and all the other elements of the current product. The goal in critiquing, stated simply, is to make certain that the next edition will be even better. It is this challenge, in particular, that makes the task of a newsletter editor among the most rewarding in public relations work.

One organization devoted originally to internal communications, the International Association of Business Communicators, has in a relatively short time come to rival the much older Public Relations Society of America. With more than 12,000 members

Figure 14–3   People love to look at other people. Accordingly, when Days Inns of America wanted to celebrate National Tourism Awareness Day, the company assembled 300 corporate employees in the shape of the Days Inns' sunburst logo to provide this visually arresting photo.

throughout the United States and in 40 countries, this association helps set journalistic standards for communicators.[13]

In 1997, after the *Wall Street Journal* noted without evidence that "Newsletters are fast becoming obsolete," public relations professionals leapt to the newsletter's defense.[14] Nonetheless, as online communications continues to increase in popularity, the challenges facing newsletter editors to produce a candid, current, and content-driven publication will increase.

Management Publications

Managerial employees must also know what's going on in the organization. The company needs their support. Continual, reliable communication is one way to ensure it. Many firms publish frequent bulletins for management with updates on personnel changes, office relocations, new telephone numbers, and revised company policies. Occasionally, special bulletins concerning new-product developments, breaking company news, or other matters of urgent interest are circulated.

More formal publications, such as management magazines, are often more technical and more confidential than related employee newspapers. For example, a firm may publicize its corporate mission to all employees through the employee newspaper but may reveal its business profitability objectives only in the management magazine. This element of confidentiality is always a sensitive one. Employees occasionally object that internal publications don't reveal enough pertinent details about corporate decisions and policy. One common complaint is that outside newspaper reporters "know more than we do about our own firm's activities." Although limitations may be necessary for certain issues, those who run the organization must try to be as candid as possible, in particular with fellow managers.

Because of the personal, vested interest of a manager in the organization, management publications are generally among the best read internal communications. Their ability to build confidence, enhance credibility, and promote team spirit shouldn't be underestimated.

Employee Annual Reports

It often makes sense to print a separate annual report just for employees. Frequently, the lure of this report—published in addition to the regular corporate shareholder annual report—is that it is written for, about, and by the employees.

Most employees do care about how their organization functions and what its management is thinking. The annual report to the staff is a good place to discuss such issues informally, yet candidly. The report can be both factual, explaining the performance of the organization during the year, and informational, reviewing organizational changes and significant milestones during the year. It can also be motivational in its implicit appeal to team spirit and pride. Southwest Airlines does perhaps the best job in America in keeping its staff loose and making it feel special through a constant barrage of innovative and fun communications (Figure 14–4).

Staff reports observe few hard-and-fast rules about concept and format. Staff annuals can be as complex as the shareholder annual report itself or as simple as a brief outline of the company's highlights of the year. Typical features of the employee annual report include the following:

1. **Chief executive's letter** A special report to the staff that reviews the performance and highlights of the year and thanks employees for their help.
2. **Use-of-funds statement** Often a graphic chart that describes how the organization used each dollar it took in.
3. **Financial condition** Frequently a chart that describes the assets and liabilities of the corporation and the stockholders' equity.
4. **Description of the company** Simple, graphic explanation of what the organization is and where its facilities are located.
5. **Social responsibility highlights** Discussion of the organization's role in aiding society through monetary assistance and employee participation during the year.
6. **Staff financial highlights** General description, usually in chart form, of salaries, benefits, and other staff-related expense items.
7. **Organizational policy** Discussion of current issues about which management feels strongly and for which it seeks employee support.
8. **Emphasis on people** One general theme throughout the report is the importance of the people who make up the organization: in-depth profiles of people on the job, comments from people about their jobs, and/or pictorial essays on people at work.

Employees appreciate recognition. The special annual report is a measure of recognition that does not go unnoticed—or unread—by a firm's workers.

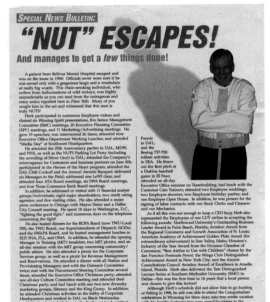

Figure 14–4 Southwest Airlines is "another" kind of company. Its irrepressible founder and chairman, Herb Kelleher, has created a climate of creativity and productivity through spirited communications that encourage airline employees to adopt a "happy family" attitude. Southwest's success suggests the approach pays bottom-line dividends.

DESKTOP PUBLISHING EMERGES

In the 1990s, desktop publishing, by which a professional can produce a newsletter at his or her own desk, promised to revolutionize employee communications.

Introduced in 1985, desktop publishing allows an editor to write, lay out, and typeset a piece of copy. However, the term desktop publishing is a misnomer. Desktop layout or desktop page layout is more accurate. Desktop publishing requires a personal computer, a laser printer, and software for word processing, charts, and drawings, if desired, and publishing applications such as layout. Experts say that anything less than a $10,000 investment for a desktop publishing workstation and software may not be worth the aggravation.

Desktop publishing allows a user to control the typesetting process in-house, provides faster turnaround for clients, and saves money on outside design. The near-term future for desktop publishing includes scanning photos and drawings, incorporating those images into page layouts, using the computer to assign color in design elements, and, instead of printing camera-ready pages, producing entire color-separated pages of film from which a printer can create plates for printing.

To be sure, desktop publishing is still in its infancy for internal communicators. Most who have switched to desktop publishing to gain control and curb the costs of their printed materials combine the new high technology with more conventional editing methods. Some who have tried desktop publishing complain that it takes the human part of writing and editing out of newsletter production.

Nonetheless, with desktop video already being hailed as the next generation of desktop publishing, the continued improvement of the new technology will surely change the way public relations writers and editors approach employee communications.

Bulletin Boards

Bulletin boards are making a comeback in corporations, hospitals, and other organizations. For years they were considered second-string information channels, generally relegated to the display of federally required information and policy data for such activities as fire drills and emergency procedures. Most employees rarely consulted them. But the bulletin board has experienced a renaissance and is now being used to improve productivity, cut waste, and reduce accidents on the job. Best of all, employees are taking notice.

How come? For one thing, yesterday's bulletin board has become today's news center. It has been repackaged into a more lively visual and graphically arresting medium. Using enlarged news pictures and texts, motivational messages, and other company announcements—all illustrated with a flair—the bulletin board has become an important news source of employee communications (Figure 14–5). Hospitals, in particular, have found that a strategically situated bulletin board outside a cafeteria is a good way to promote employee understanding and cooperation.

One key to stimulating readership is to keep boards current. One person in the public relations unit should be assigned to this weekly task.

ETHICS
QUESTIONS OR CONCERNS

For help...

STEP 1

Contact your supervisor. If necessary, take it up the chain of command at your location.

STEP 2

Contact your Company Ethics Officer in person, by phone, or by mail.

LMASC Ethics Director:	Tom Salvaggio
Location:	B-2, 2nd Floor, Col. 28
Phone:	Helpline Coordinator, (770) 494-3999
Mailing Address:	LMASC Ethics Office
	P O Box 1771
	Marietta, GA 30061

STEP 3

If the first two steps do not resolve the matter, contact the Corporate Office of Ethics and Business Conduct for confidential assistance:

Helpline:	800 LM ETHIC (800 563-8442)
Fax:	(818) 876-2082
Or Write:	Corporate Office of Ethics and Business Conduct
	Lockheed Martin Corporation
	P O Box 34143
	Bethesda, MD 20827-0143

STEP 4

Contact the Department of Defense Hotline to report fraud, waste and abuse, and/or security violations.

Hotline:	800 424-9098
Or Write:	Defense Hotline
	The Pentagon
	Washington, DC 20301-1900

IDENTITIES OF WRITERS AND CALLERS ARE FULLY PROTECTED.

LOCKHEED MARTIN

Figure 14–5   Among important announcements included on organizational bulletin boards are updates on key corporate issues such as ethical questions and concerns.

Internal Video

Just as increasing numbers of people are receiving their external news from TV—television, more specifically, videotape—is becoming an internal medium of preference for many organizations. Faced with the fact that almost 90 percent of the public gets most of its news from television and more than half gets all of its news from television, major companies have headed to the tube to compete for their employees' attention.

Internal television can be demonstrably effective. A 10-minute videotape of an executive announcing a new corporate policy imparts hundreds of times more information than an audiotape of that same message, which, in turn, contains hundreds of times more information than a printed text of the same message.

In the 1990s, internal video, like desktop publishing, appears ready to take off.

- Burger King in Miami produces video in an in-house studio and sound stage to train workers in its 5,000 restaurants.
- Miller Brewing Company produces a 20-minute video magazine, distributed every three months to all company locations. It features new company commercials, brand promotions, happenings at Miller plants, and employee human interest stories.
- The Ford Motor Company has taken the unprecedented step of stopping work on assembly lines to show videotapes to workers. In one celebrated incident, Ford showed a quality-improvement videotape at 35 plants employing 100,000 workers.
- Wal-Mart stores began in the late 1980s to turn founder Sam Walton's store visits into simultaneous video meetings with thousands of stores. Using the technology of very small aperture terminals (VSATs), Wal-Mart remains a frequent user of business television.[15]
- Perhaps the most unique internal video ever produced was the legendary "Southwest Shuffle," in which the employees of Southwest Airlines—from maintenance crew to pilots—chimed in on a rap video extolling the virtues of their innovative carrier. Deejay for the rap extravaganza was—who else?—Southwest CEO Herb Kelleher!

Notwithstanding its power, internal video is a medium that must be approached with caution. Specifically, a public relations professional must raise at least a dozen questions before embarking on an internal video excursion:

1. Why are we doing this video?
2. Whom are we trying to reach with this video?
3. What's the point of the video?
4. What do we want viewers to do after seeing the video?
5. How good is our video script?
6. How sophisticated is the quality of our broadcast?
7. How innovative and creative is the broadcast? Does it measure up to regular television?
8. How competent is our talent?
9. How proficient is our crew?
10. Where will our viewers screen the video?
11. With what communications vehicles will we supplement the video?
12. How much money can we spend?

The keys to any internal video production are, first, to examine internal needs; then to plan thoughtfully before using the medium; and, finally, to reach target publics through the highest-quality programming possible. Broadcast quality is a tough standard to meet. If an organization can't afford high-quality video, it shouldn't get involved.

Supervisory Communications

First and foremost, employees want information from their supervisors. Supervisors, in fact, are the preferred source for 90 percent of employees, making them the top choice by far. In 1980, about two-thirds of employees surveyed said that their supervisors discussed job performance at least once a year. Today that proportion has jumped to almost 90 percent.[16]

That's the good news.

The bad news is that whereas 55 percent of employees in 1980 said their supervisor was a good source of information, that percentage has steadily declined since the wave of 1990s downsizing. Although employees today are somewhat more likely to think that their supervisors are being kept informed by higher management, they are not reaping the benefits any more than they did in the 1980s. Thus, even though most employees vastly prefer information from their supervisor over what they learn through rumors, many still rely on the grapevine as a primary source of information.

What can public relations departments do to combat this trend?

Some departments formalize the meeting process by mixing management and staff in a variety of formats, from gripe sessions to marketing/planning meetings. Many organizations embrace the concept of skip-level meetings, in which top-level managers meet periodically with employees at levels several notches below them in the organizational hierarchy. As with any other form of communication, the value of meetings lies in their substance, their regularity, and the candor managers bring to face-to-face sessions. In any event, one key to improved internal communications clearly is increased face-to-face communications between supervisor and subordinate.[17]

DEALING WITH THE GRAPEVINE

In many organizations, it isn't the Internet or cyberspace that dominates communications but rather the company grapevine. The rumor mill can be devastating. As one employee publication described the grapevine:

> It's faster than a public address announcement and more powerful than a general instruction. It's able to leap from L.A. to San Francisco in a single bound. And its credibility is almost beyond Walter Cronkite's.

THE REST OF THE STORY

MAGNA'S CHARTER

Magna International, one of the world's fastest-growing auto-part supply companies, is a model of employee communications for the new century. The Magna culture is an example of the fruits of openness and trust. Here are highlights of its charter:

- Magna's "Corporate Constitution" is posted all over the corridors of every Magna site.
- The Constitution dictates that 10 percent of pretax profits be given to employees in the form of cash bonuses and stock shares.
- The Employee Charter tells employees that "if your total compensation is found not to be competitive, then your wages will be adjusted."
- Managers are required to meet with workers at least once a month, and employees can call a confidential "hot line" to air grievances.
- Workers with perfect attendance can bank two hours a month in time off.
- The company's plant features a baseball diamond, a soccer field, and tennis courts for employees.
- Tea and coffee are always free, and the subsidized cafeteria is open 24 hours a day.

Rumors, once they pick up steam, are difficult to stop. And because employees tend to distort future events to conform to a rumor; an organization must work to correct rumors as soon as possible.

Identifying the source of a rumor is often difficult, if not impossible, and it's usually not worth the time. However, dispelling the rumor quickly and frankly is another story. Often a bad-news rumor—about layoffs, closings, and so on—can be dealt with most effectively through forthright communication. Generally, an organization makes a difficult decision after a thorough review of many alternatives. The final decision is often a compromise, reflecting the needs of the firm and its various publics, including, importantly, the work force. However, in presenting a final decision to employees, management often overlooks the value of explaining how it reached its decision. By comparing alternative solutions so that employees can understand more clearly the rationale behind management decisions, an organization may make bad news more palatable.

As demonic as the grapevine can become, it shouldn't necessarily be treated as the enemy in effective communications with employees. A company grapevine can be as much a communications vehicle as internal publications or employee meetings. It may even be more valuable because it is believed, and everyone seems to tap into it.

SUMMARY

The best defense against damaging grapevine rumors is a strong and candid communications system. Employee communications may be the most neglected strategic opportunity in corporate America. Organizations build massive marketing plans to sell products but often fail to apply that same knowledge and energy to communicating with their own employees.

In the twenty-first century, organizations will have no choice but to build rapport with and morale among employees. The shattering of morale that accompanied the massive downsizings of the 1990s will take time to repair. Building back internal credibility is a long-term process that depends on openness and honesty on the part of senior management. Public relations professionals must seize this initiative to foster the open climate that employees want and the two-way communications that organizations need. To ensure meaningful and effective communication with employees, it will be even more critical than ever for public relations professionals to suggest appropriate vehicles.

DISCUSSION STARTERS

1. According to recent research, are employees satisfied with the level and content of the communications they receive from management?
2. What one element is key to organizational communication?
3. What characteristics constitute the best employee communicators?
4. What method of employee communications is making a comeback in many organizations?
5. What is the status of online internal communications?
6. What are the primary tasks of an employee newsletter's editor?
7. What questions should be raised before communicating through internal video?

8. What is the preferred channel of communications among most employees?
9. What is the best way to combat the grapevine?
10. Why haven't most organizations convinced their employees of top management's sincerity?

NOTES

1. "The Dream in Danger," *The Public Relations Strategist* (Spring 1995): 43.
2. David Rockefeller, "America After Downsizing: Maximizing Society's Profits," address delivered September 12, 1996, before the Economic Club of New York.
3. Julie Foehrenbach and Steve Goldfarb, "Employee Communications in the 90s: Greater Expectations," *IABC Communication World* (May–June 1990): 101.
4. Bob Nelson, "Dump the Cash, Load on the Praise," *Personnel Journal* (July 1996): 66.
5. Bryan W. Armentrout, "The Five Best Gifts to Give Your Employees," *HR Focus* (December 1995): 3.
6. "An Employee's-Eye View of Business," *Ragan Report* (November 25, 1991): 1, 2.
7. "On Communicating with the 'Free Agent Employee,' " *Ragan Report* (January 10, 1994): 3.
8. Fraser P. Seitel, "Internal PR is Thankless but Vital Job in Age of Cutbacks," *O'Dwyer's PR Services Report* (July 1994): 28
9. "Focus' Strives for Credibility Through Candor," *Ragan Report* (October 1, 1990): 3.
10. Fraser P. Seitel, "Leaping the 'Trust Gap,' " *U.S. Banker* (November 1990): 61.
11. Karen Bachman, "Does Anybody Do It Better?" *Across the Board* (January 1997): 55.
12. Scott Rodrick, "Use Intranets" to Connect Employee Owners," *Interactive Investor Relations* (January 1997): 3.
13. For further information about the International Association of Business Communicators, write to IABC, One Hallidie Plaza, Suite 600, San Francisco, CA 94102.
14. "Let's Not Kill the Newsletter Before We Try to Revive It," *Ragan Report* (April 28, 1997): 4.
15. Chuck Wheat, "Video Demand or Supply: Which Came First, the Chicken or the Egg?" *IABC Communication World* (March 1994): 31.
16. Foehrenbach and Goldfarb, op. cit., 104.
17. Wilma K. Mathews, "What the CEO Can Do About It," *The Public Relations Strategist* (Spring 1995): 49.

SUGGESTED READINGS

Cohen, Allan. *Effective Behavior in Organizations*. Burr Ridge, IL: Irwin Professional Publishing, 1995.

Flannery, Thomas P. *People, Performance and Pay: Dynamic Compensation for Changing Organizations*. New York: The Free Press, 1995. Traditional methods of compensation may simply not cut it in an era of employee skepticism and quest for empowerment.

Hammer, Michael and Steven Stanton. *The Reengineering Revolution*. New York: Harper Business, 1995. Reengineering gurus explain why work and workers will differ materially in the twenty-first century.

TOP OF THE SHELF

STANLEY ARONOWITZ AND WILLIAM DIFAZIO

THE JOBLESS FUTURE: SCI-TECH AND THE DOGMA OF WORK

MINNEAPOLIS, MN: UNIVERSITY OF MINNESOTA PRESS, 1994

Wanna read something that will make your hair stand up? Here it is.

These two professors portray a chilling future portrait of work and workers in the twenty-first century. The authors portend a future where jobs are eliminated, not created, by technology. From the worker's perspective, they claim, computerization is "merely a wrinkle in the long process of disempowerment." Technology alienates workers by taking over their skills and finally the workers themselves.

The authors raise questions about the new work(less) environment. How will people define themselves? What will it mean to be human if work is out of the picture? Will the definition of self be shattered when work disappears?

The authors' predictions are grounded in a vast number of theories, from sociology and philosophy to labor relations and Marxism. Optimistic these two ain't. But they certainly are provocative. And if you doubt the difficult challenges ahead for internal communicators, read this book.

Hartley, Jean F. and Geoffrey M. Stephenson. *Employment Relations: The Psychology of Influence and Control at Work*. Colchester, VT: Blackwell Business, 1992.

Kreitner, Robert and Angelo Kinicki. *Organizational Behavior*, 3rd ed.
Burr Ridge, IL: Irwin Professional Publishing, 1995. How to manage change in a learning culture.

Marchington, Mick. *Managing the Team: A Guide to Successful Employee Involvement*. Colchester, VT: Blackwell Business, 1992.

Penzias, Arno. *Harmony: Business Technology and Life After Paperwork*. New York: Harper Business, 1995. Deals with the uncertainty resulting from technology replacing people and the challenges of the technical work force.

Ritvo, Anne H. *Managing in the Age of Change: Essential Skills to Manage Today's Diverse Workforce*. Burr Ridge, IL: Irwin Professional Publishing, 1995.

Sack, Steven Mitchell. *From Hiring to Firing: The Legal Survival Guide for Employers in the 90s*. New York: Legal Strategies Inc., 1995. The first, best defense for a public relations professional: Know the law.

Smith, Alvie L. *Innovative Employee Communication*. Upper Saddle River, NJ: Prentice Hall, 1991. An experienced employee communicator provides a complete guide to internal communications. He counsels communicators to use a variety of media—publications, video, face-to-face meetings—to provide workers with meaningful information consistent with management's objectives.

Williams, Patrick. *How to Create Winning Employee Publications*. Chicago, IL: Joe Williams Communications, Inc., 1990.

CASE STUDY

MONKEYGATE

For three years, AT&Ts full-color monthly publication, *Focus*, was as good as internal communications gets. It was candid and straightforward and allowed employees to be heard. Focus was the envy of the internal communications profession.

All the admiration, however, came to a crashing halt in September 1993 when *Focus* published a cartoon on its "Fun 'N Games" page depicting people around the globe using telephones, except in Africa, where the phone-using individual depicted was a gorilla.

First, AT&T officials handled the incident as an internal matter, but at least some of the 315,000 AT&T employees worldwide who received *Focus* were angered by the illustration. Evidently one offended staffer provided a tip to an Associated Press reporter in Raleigh, North Carolina, that the September issue contained an offensive illustration.

The AP story was carried in several newspapers across the country, and AT&T sprang into action.

First, AT&T communicators tried to defuse the controversy by telling reporters that a staff member had made a proofing error. The staffer, it was argued, approved the illustration using a "fax of a fax," making it difficult to see the sketch, which allowed it to go by unnoticed. AT&T also notified the media that the artist, a freelancer, had been told he could no longer do any work for AT&T.

Local 1058 of the Communications Workers of America, which represented 4,000 AT&T employees and criticized AT&T's failure to catch the illustration, used the incident to attack AT&T's use of nonunion outside contractors.

Formal apologies to the staff trailed the illustration by several days. AT&T's senior vice president for public relations expressed her regrets to all employees in a letter in mid-September. "The offensive cartoon . . . was the result of a serious breakdown in editorial procedures. There is no excuse for it, and we have sincerely apologized for publishing such insulting material," she wrote in part. AT&T's CEO, Robert E. Allen, also took the lead in a letter that acknowledged "the hurt people feel" and promised a redoubling of efforts to drive any vestiges of racism from the company.

The Rev. Jesse Jackson entered the fray by leading a protest in front of AT&T's New York headquarters. And Joseph Lowery, president of the Southern Christian Leadership Conference (SCLC), held a similar protest rally on the steps of AT&T's regional headquarters in Atlanta.

CEO Allen and AT&T, whose domestic work force was almost 15 percent African-American—far higher than that of the 10 percent national workplace average—now had a real problem.

Allen immediately met with several groups, including African-American engineers and managers at AT&T, the Congressional Black Caucus, the SCLC, and the National Association for the Advancement of Colored People (NAACP).

After the meetings, the African-American leaders appeared mollified. For example, after a meeting with the NAACP's executive director, Benjamin F. Chavis, AT&T agreed to work together on minority recruitment, scholarships for African-American students, promotion goals, use of black financial institutions, and senior executive programs. Allen also appointed five senior corporate executives to lead a new "diversity" team of culturally diverse employees to recommend internal communications changes.

A day after the appointment of the diversity team, AT&T's public relations director announced that the two senior editors for *Focus* had been reassigned and the design firm responsible for the magazine terminated. She also announced AT&T's decision to eliminate *Focus* magazine.

To its credit, AT&T, its CEO, communications director, and communications staff remained accessible throughout the crisis. No one could accuse the company of ducking the Monkeygate controversy.

In the aftermath of the *Focus* shutdown, AT&T initiated a "Don't Hate—Communicate" public relations campaign. In early 1994, the company recruited black TV talk show host Montel Williams to moderate a public forum on racial intolerance. Forums were scheduled in Atlanta, Chicago, Dallas, Detroit, and New York.

In the spring of 1994, AT&T announced that three new employee publications would be adopted to replace *Focus*.

Summarized a sadder but wiser public relations chief, "Our employee publications—especially *Focus*—have always reflected an openness and a level of candor unique in industry. I believe they contributed to the development of a more responsive, customer-focused culture at AT&T. I will always be proud of them and of the people who introduced them."

QUESTIONS

1. How well do you think AT&T handled Monkeygate?
2. Should the company have killed *Focus*?
3. How do you feel about the company's decision to reassign or replace those responsible for *Focus*?
4. Was it a good idea to impanel a task force of culturally diverse employees to recommend internal communications changes?
5. How should AT&T restore its credibility with its employees?

For further information on Monkeygate, see Duane Stoltzfus, "Wake Up Call at AT&T," *The Sunday Record* (September 7, 1993): B1, B3; Jerry Walker, "AT&T Introduces New Employee Publications," *Jack O'Dwyer's Newsletter* (March 23, 1994): 3; and Jerry Walker, "AT&T Repairs Damage Caused by Cartoon," *O'Dwyer's PR Services Report* (November 1993): 16, 17.

VOICE OF EXPERIENCE

NANCY IRWIN

Nancy Irwin is internal communications manager of Duke Power Corporation in Charlotte, NC. She and her company have made a concerted effort to persuade managers that communications is an integral part of the internal leadership challenge.

WHAT ARE THE MOST IMPORTANT PRINCIPLES IN DEALING WITH EMPLOYEES?

The fundamentals are based on relationships. Employees trust who they know. What leaders say and do, and the policies and practices they put in place, speak volumes more than a company newsletter. At Duke, we put more energy into teaching leadership to communicate on things important to the business, like company direction and employee performance. Also, as a former Duke Energy chairman said, "Strong, open, forthright communications is the lubricant that makes our machine go." So building relationships and openness and honesty are our fundamental communications principles.

HOW CAN EMPLOYEE COMMUNICATIONS INFLUENCE MORALE?

Good communications can help combat low morale and contribute to good morale, but communications alone is not the driver of morale. Morale is built on trust in leadership, a sense that one's job is relatively secure and a fundamental belief that the future will be better than the past.

SHOULD CERTAIN INFORMATION—LAYOFFS, LOSSES, LAWSUITS, ETC.—BE KEPT FROM EMPLOYEES?

Nothing makes employees more upset than reading something in the local media before they've heard it from the company. So a key criterion is anticipating news coverage about an issue. At Duke, we work hard to report the bad news with the good as quickly as we can. Our main goal is to either "tie" with the media or beat them. Most company grapevines are alive and well and highly accurate. At Duke, we don't just have a grapevine, we have a vineyard! Now I can't say management likes to report bad news—it doesn't. But we counsel our executives that this buys them huge credibility, and our leadership has always been supportive of reporting the bad with the good.

WHAT ARE THE MOST EFFECTIVE WAYS TO COMMUNICATE TO EMPLOYEES?

Ask your employees. We've found the best communications are tailored to the style, culture and preference of the receivers. One size does not fit all. At Duke, our practice is to offer the same information in a wide variety of ways and to segment our audiences and prepare information for them in a style they prefer. Some preach that face-to-face communication is the "best" way to communicate in all cases. I don't agree. We use face-to-face for what we define as "vital" communications, but we rely on cheaper methods (electronic) for other things.

IS THE EMPLOYEE NEWSLETTER DEAD?

Yes, if you develop it in the very traditional "top down" approach; as a "mouthpiece" for what management wants to "send out" to the organization. But no, if you report the company "news" from the perspective of employees. We always put the employee in the article. It's either told from the perspective of the employee in the trenches or how employees contribute to the business. Senior management is the "client" of the newsletter, the payer of the bills. Employees are consumers of the newsletter. They're the ones you're trying to influence. So we always choose subjects based on the company's strategies but tell the story from the eyes of the employees. It seems a formula that works very well.

HOW IMPORTANT IS THE INTRANET IN EMPLOYEE COMMUNICATIONS?

It will be important. I don't think it's a silver bullet. But it's going to enable us to do things quickly and cheaply that we couldn't do before. But it is only a tool. It will not replace thoughtful editorial judgment, excellent communications planning, excellent tactical delivery, good writing, and good audience analysis. Used poorly, it's just a big pipe dumping things on your desk that you didn't want and can't use.

WHAT DISTINGUISHES GOOD EMPLOYEE COMMUNICATORS FROM MEDIOCRE ONES?

The good ones are closely aligned with and support their company's business strategy. They do everything they can, use everything in their toolbox, to advance the company's success. And they are both strategic and tactical in their approach. They are creative. They care passionately about the craft of communications. They are persistent. And they are adamant about what communications can contribute to the overall business success. They identify issues. They partner with anybody and everybody to get the job done. They care about business results more than their own personal measures of success. They fight mediocrity at every turn—especially mediocre writing!

HOW IMPORTANT IS TOP MANAGEMENT INVOLVEMENT IN EMPLOYEE COMMUNICATIONS?

It can be a boon and a curse. Top management support is important, but not completely necessary in all cases. One always hopes for senior level sponsorship for open, honest, rapid employee communications. And most executives will agree to that, even though they may not know why they agree. The really good ones understand that communications is as powerful a business system as compensation, budget, or benefits. And they use it to the advantage of the company. But I would counsel that a communicator not wait for the executive nod. Do good stuff that you know needs to be done. Sooner or later, your management team and senior executives will figure out that this is good.

IS WINNING THE "TRUST" OF EMPLOYEES STILL POSSIBLE TODAY?

Yes, trust of a certain sort. I trust my manager to deal with me as fairly as possible. I trust him or her to let me know how I'm doing and how our department is doing. And I trust the company to be honest with me about whether I have a job. I trust the company to offer me an environment where I can develop myself. I trust in my own abilities to have a job either inside Duke Power or outside of it.

What I don't trust is that things will be predictable. I don't believe in lifetime employment or security anywhere. I don't trust that past success will be a predictor of future success without continuous growth and change on my part. I don't trust that any career moves in a line straight upward. I don't trust or believe that it's highly likely for me to retire having worked at just one company. This is pragmatic trust, and it reflects that the compact with employees has changed a great deal.

CHAPTER FIFTEEN

Multicultural Communities

CULTURAL HERITAGE IS NOTHING TO BE TRIFLED WITH. People are proud of who they are, and don't take well to others demeaning or denigrating that heritage. Consider these examples from 1997 alone.

- New Jersey Nets basketball coach John Calipari was called on the carpet and apologized profusely after calling a newspaper reporter, "a (bleeping) Mexican idiot."[1]
- Golfer Fuzzy Zoeller suggested that Masters Tournament winner Tiger Woods might order "fried chicken and collard greens" at the ceremonial dinner. Zoeller begged the newly crowned Tiger for forgiveness, after the media had branded him a "racist."
- Woods himself was chastised for comments that he made to *Gentlemen's Quarterly* magazine that poked fun at African-Americans and lesbians, among others.

In today's society, multiculturalism is no laughing matter.

America has always been a melting pot, attracting freedom-seeking immigrants from countries throughout the world. Never has this been more true than today, as America's face continues to change. Consider the following:

- In 1990, the U.S. population was 76 percent Anglo, 12 percent African-American, 9 percent Latino, and 3 percent Asian. By the year 2050, the breakdown is projected to be 52 percent Anglo, 16 percent African-American, 22 percent Latino, and 10 percent Asian. Today ethnic minorities spend $600 billion a year out of a total U.S. consumer economy of $4.4 trillion. This amount is certain to increase substantially.[2]
- In 1940, 70 percent of U.S. immigrants came from Europe. In 1992, 15 percent of immigrants came from Europe, 37 percent from Asia, and 44 percent from Latin America and the Caribbean.
- In 1976, there were 67 Spanish-language radio stations in the United States. Today there are 311, plus 3 Spanish-language TV networks and 350 Spanish-language newspapers.

- In New York City alone, 12 percent of the population under 18 is foreign-born, and that percentage continues to increase.

Such is the multicultural diversity enjoyed today by America and the world. The implications for organizations are profound. Almost two-thirds of the new entrants into the work force now are women. People of color make up nearly 30 percent of these new entrants. For the first time since World War I, immigrants will represent the largest share of the increase in the population and the work force.[3]

In light of the increasing diversity of U.S. society, both profit and nonprofit organizations must themselves become more diverse and learn to deal and communicate with those who differ in work background, education, age, gender, race, ethnic origin, physical abilities, religious beliefs, sexual orientation, and other perceived differences.

Those organizations that waver in responding to the new multicultural communities do so at their own peril. To wit:

- Texaco devoted $176 million to settle a 1996 antidiscrimination suit, after incriminating tapes, in which executives disparaged minorities, were made public. (See chapter 1 case study.)
- In 1994, Denny's restaurant chain agreed to pay more than $54 million to settle lawsuits filed by thousands of black customers who had been refused service, forced to wait longer, or pay more than white customers. (See case study at the end of this chapter.)
- The chief of the Los Angeles Police Department was forced to step down, and police officers were jailed, after an African-American motorist, Rodney King, was beaten after a high-speed chase in 1992. The King beating triggered a massive riot and focused attention on the department's problems in dealing with minorities (Figure 15–1).

As the arbiters of communications in their organizations, public relations people must be sensitive to society's new multicultural realities. Society and the workplace are increasingly multicultural. This, in turn, has led to increased "tension" between the majority and minority, and through more open lines of communication public relations professionals can play a meaningful role in reducing that tension. Dealing in an enlightened manner with multicultural diversity and being sensitive to nuances in language and differences in style are logical extensions of the social responsibility that has been an accepted part of American organizational life since the 1960s.

SOCIAL RESPONSIBILITY IN THE COMMUNITY

More and more, companies and other organizations acknowledge their responsibilities to the community: helping to maintain clean air and water, providing jobs for minorities, and, in general, enhancing everyone's quality of life. This concept of social responsibility

THE RIOTS OF '92

CRISIS BRINGS OUT EDISON'S BEST

When civil disturbances erupted in the south-central metropolitan area last Wednesday evening, April 29, no one could guess the material and emotional devastation that would result.

Throughout the next two long, fiery days and an uneasy weekend, Edison employees responded with courage, dedication and a sense of community.

This special issue of SCE NEWS is a salute to Edison's 18,000 employees who worked together to handle problems as they arose and who are continuing to work to heal the wounds and build a community of pride.

Stories on last week's civil disturbances were researched and written by Lynda Baker, Charles Beal, Sandy Doubleday and Ken Perry. Photos are by Mitch Kaufman and Greg O'Loughlin.

EDISON LOSSES
TOTAL $150,000

Damage to Edison facilities from civil unrest after the Rodney King trial totaled $150,000. No Edison employees were injured.

At press time, most of the damage had occurred in the Southern Region, Edison officials said, with nine circuit interruptions affecting 10,500 customers. Eight of the circuits were in the Compton district.

Disturbances delayed repairs, with some outages lasting up to 35 hours. Multiple local outages affecting service to 1,500 customers were the result of secondary conductors destroyed by structure fires. Eight poles, three transformers and 130 services were removed in the Region.

Often escorted by police, Southern Region crews conducted

ON OUR COVER
Edison crews braved fires and looters to restore power to affected areas.

repairs during daylight hours over the weekend. A regional command center was established at the Compton Service Center to coordinate repairs. In Long Beach, an unused Edison building was damaged by fire.

In other regions, the Perris Service Center reopened Monday after being vacated the previous Thursday. Normal field activities in remaining regions resumed and all local offices were open Monday morning.

Above, smoke from unused Edison building blackens Long Beach sky Friday. Left, the fire left only a shell of the building.

Figure 15–1   Los Angeles was sorely tested in the spring of 1992, when the Rodney King beating led to riots. Southern California Edison published a special issue of its *SCE News* to report on the company's response to the disturbances and to salute employees who worked through the crisis. The issue was called "Time to Heal."

has become widely accepted among enlightened organizations. For example, most companies today donate a percentage of their profits to nonprofit organizations—schools, hospitals, social welfare institutions, and the like. Employee volunteer programs to assist local charitable groups are also common. Social responsibility is no longer the exception but the rule among organizations.

This enlightened self-interest among executives has taken time to develop. The social and political upheavals of the 1960s forced organizations to confront the real or perceived injustices inflicted on certain social groups. The 1970s brought a partial resolution of those problems as government and the courts moved together to compensate for past inequities, to outlaw current abuses, and to prevent future injustice.

In the 1980s, the conflict between organizations and society became one of setting priorities—of deciding which community group deserved to be the beneficiary of corporate involvement. Today most organizations accept their role as an agent for social change in the community. For an organization to coexist peacefully in its community requires three skills in particular: (1) determining what the community knows and thinks about the organization, (2) informing the community of the organization's point of view, and (3) negotiating or mediating between the organization and the community and its constituents, should there be a significant discrepancy.

A QUESTION OF ETHICS

AVIS FIGHTS BACK

Organizations faced with accusations of racial discrimination don't always follow the model set by Texaco in settling its 1997 suit. A few categorically reject the charges and fight back.

Such was the case with the Avis rental car company in the spring of 1997.

Avis was sued after outlets in North and South Carolina reportedly refused to rent cars to blacks. Shortly thereafter, the company was accused by two former employees of rejecting corporate accounts in Tulsa, Oklahoma, for people who appeared to be Jewish, especially Hassidic Jews. Employees said that supervisors enforced what they described as this "yeshiva policy" after the office was "stiffed" by several Hassidic customers.

News of the Avis discrimination charges triggered predictable negative publicity and complaints from civil rights groups.

But rather than shrinking from the controversy, CEO Henry R. Silberman of HFS, Inc., which owns Avis, categorically denied the accusations. "We did not discriminate against blacks, against Jews, or against any other majorities or minorities," Silberman told *The New York Times* in a front page business interview.

CEO Silberman candidly admitted that some Avis franchise owners, acting independently, "might have shown bias." Avis, he said, had even tried several times unsuccessfully to remove these owners from the company. He went on to acknowledge that the company abhorred such comments and treatment, but that these were exceptions. Avis, he said, was a company that practiced no institutional bias.

And he didn't stop there.

CEO Silberman then blitzed the airwaves, appearing on CNN, morning shows, and any national venue that would have him. His message? "This is a new way that lawyers for plaintiffs try to extract money from corporations . . . . to manipulate the media and embarrass companies."

And Silberman and Avis held their ground. Unlike Texaco, Avis refused to enter into a huge cash settlement with attorneys representing aggrieved parties. Said Mr. Silberman in describing the goal of the litigants, "I'm trying to use a nicer word than 'extortion.' "

Basically, every organization wants to foster positive reactions in its community. This becomes increasingly difficult in the face of protests from and disagreements with community activists. Community relations, therefore—to analyze the community, help understand its makeup and expectations, and communicate the organization's story in an understandable and uninterrupted way—will prove critical in the next century.

COMMUNITY RELATIONS EXPECTATIONS

The community of an organization can vary widely, depending on the size and nature of the business. The mom-and-pop grocery store may have a community of only a few city blocks; the community of a Buick assembly plant may be the city where the plant is located; and the community of a multinational corporation may embrace much of the world.

What the Community Expects

Communities expect from resident organizations such tangible commodities as wages, employment, and taxes. But communities have come to expect intangible contributions, too.

- **Appearance**   The community hopes that the firm will contribute positively to life in the area. It expects facilities to be attractive, with care spent on the grounds and the plant. Increasingly, community neighbors object to plants that belch smoke and pollute water and air. Occasionally, neighbors organize to oppose the entrance of factories, coal mines, oil wells, drug treatment centers, and other facilities suspected of being harmful to the community's environment. Government, too, is acting more vigorously to punish offenders and to make sure that organizations comply with zoning, environmental, and safety regulations.

- **Participation**   As a citizen of the community, an organization is expected to participate responsibly in community affairs, such as civic functions, park and recreational activities, education, welfare, and support of religious institutions (Figure 15–2). Organizations generally cannot shirk such participation by blaming headquarters' policy.

- **Stability**   A business that fluctuates sharply in volume of business, number of employees, and taxes paid can adversely affect the community through its impact on municipal services, school loads, public facilities, and tax revenues. Communities prefer stable organizations that will grow with the area. Conversely, they want to keep out short-term operations that could create temporary boom conditions and leave ghost towns in their wake.

- **Pride**   Any organization that can help put the community on the map simply by being there is usually a valuable addition. Communities want firms that are proud to be residents. For instance, to most Americans, Battle Creek, Michigan, means cereal; Hershey, Pennsylvania, means chocolate; and Armonk, New York, means IBM. Organizations that help make the town usually become symbols of pride.

What the Organization Expects

Organizations expect to be provided with adequate municipal services, fair taxation, good living conditions for employees, a good labor supply, and a reasonable degree of support for the business and its products. When some of these requirements are missing, organizations may move to communities where such benefits are more readily available.

New York City, for example, experienced a substantial exodus of corporations during the 1970s, when firms fled to neighboring Connecticut and New Jersey, as well as to the Sun Belt states of the Southeast and Southwest. These became commercial centers because of tax moratoriums, lower labor costs, and business incentives. New York's state and city legislators responded to the challenge by working more closely with business residents on such issues as corporate taxation. By the end of the century, not only had the corporate flight to the Sun Belt been arrested, but some firms decided that they agreed with the "I Love New York" ad campaign and returned to the now more business-friendly city and state.

The issue for most urban areas faced with steadily eroding tax bases is to find a formula that meets the concerns of business corporations while accommodating the needs of other members of the community.

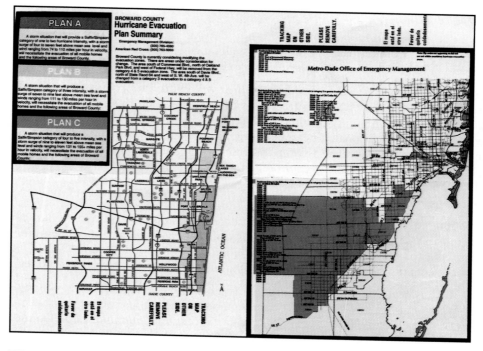

Figure 15–2 A good example of positive community citizenship was this "Hurricane Alert Program," initiated by Florida International University's Public Relations Student Society of America, in conjunction with Amoco and other sponsors.

COMMUNITY RELATIONS OBJECTIVES

Research into community relations indicates that winning community support for an organization is no easy matter. Studies indicate difficulty in achieving rapport with community neighbors, who expect support from the company but object to any dominance on its part in community affairs. One device that is helpful is a written community relations policy. A community relations policy must clearly define the philosophy of management as it views its obligation to the community. Employees, in particular, must understand and exemplify their firm's community relations policy; to many in the community, the workers are the company.

Typical community relations objectives may include the following:

1. To tell the community about the operations of the firm: its products, number of employees, size of the payroll, tax payments, employee benefits, growth, and support of community projects.
2. To correct misunderstandings, reply to criticism, and remove any disaffection that may exist among community neighbors.
3. To gain the favorable opinion of the community, particularly during strikes and periods of labor unrest, by stating the company's position on the issues involved.
4. To inform employees and their families about company activities and developments, so that they can tell their friends and neighbors about the company and favorably influence opinions of the organization.
5. To inform people in local government about the firm's contributions to community welfare and to obtain support for legislation that will favorably affect the business climate of the community.
6. To find out what residents think about the company, why they like or dislike its policies and practices, and how much they know of its policy, operations, and problems.
7. To establish a personal relationship between management and community leaders by inviting leaders to visit the plant and offices, meet management, and see employees at work.
8. To support health programs through contributions of both funds and employee services to local campaigns.
9. To contribute to culture by providing funds for art exhibits, concerts, and drama festivals and by promoting attendance at such affairs.
10. To aid youth and adult education by cooperating with administrators and teachers in providing student vocational guidance, plant tours, speakers, films, and teaching aids and by giving financial and other support to schools.
11. To encourage sports and recreational activities by providing athletic fields, swimming pools, golf courses, and/or tennis courts for use by community residents and by sponsoring teams and sports events.
12. To promote better local and county government by encouraging employees to run for public office or to volunteer to serve on administrative boards; by lending company executives to community agencies or to local government to give specialized advice and assistance on municipal problems; and by making company facilities and equipment available to the community in times of emergency.
13. To assist the economy of the community by purchasing operating supplies and equipment from local merchants and manufacturers whenever possible.

14. To operate a profitable business in order to provide jobs and to pay competitive wages that increase the community's purchasing power and strengthen its economy.

15. To cooperate with other local businesses in advancing economic and social welfare through joint community relations programs financed and directed by the participating organizations.

SERVING DIVERSE COMMUNITIES

What were once referred to as minorities are rapidly becoming the majority.

A revision of the U.S. Census Bureau's long-term population projections, announced at the end of 1992, estimated that by the year 2050 Asians, Latinos, and African-Americans will represent as much as 47 percent of the total population of the United States compared to less than 25 percent today.

According to the Census Bureau, Latinos will overtake African-Americans as the largest minority group early in the next century, but the fastest-growing segment of that population will be Asians and Pacific Islanders, whose numbers will increase five-fold.[4]

For many years, women were considered a minority by public relations professionals. This is no longer the case; women now dominate not only the public relations field but also many service industries. Women, African-Americans, Latinos, Asians, gays, and a variety of other groups have become not only important members of the labor force but also important sources of discretionary income. Public relations professionals must be sensitive to the demands of all for equal pay, promotional opportunities, equal rights in the workplace, and so on.

Communicating effectively in light of the multicultural diversity of society has become an important public relations challenge.

Women

Amid all the breakthroughs and backlashes, "Mommy tracks" and "Mommy wars," glass ceilings and pink-collar ghettos, the fact remains that women were big economic winners in the 1990s. And their gains are likely to keep coming into the twenty-first century.[5] Whereas the median annual salary for men slid 8 percent after inflation between 1979 and 1990—to $28,843 from $31,315—the comparable salary for women rose 10 percent to $20,656 from $18,683.

So, although it's still true that women, by and large, earn less than men, the gap has narrowed dramatically: For each dollar of men's earnings, women's earnings rose to a record 72 cents in 1990.

Things look even better for young women aged 24 to 35. They now earn 80 cents for every dollar earned by men of the same age, up from 69 cents in 1980.

In public relations, where women clearly rank as a majority, the glass ceiling is still a hurdle.[6] Although many more women have graduated into middle-management public relations positions, relatively few are included in department or agency top management. Nonetheless, with increasing numbers of women entering the public relations field and others slowly but surely graduating into the higher reaches of government, and profit and nonprofit organizations, it is only a matter of time before women assume their rightful place in the executive leadership of the public relations profession.

African-Americans

Today, 25 of the nation's largest cities—including Chicago, Detroit, and Los Angeles—have a majority population of African-Americans, Latinos, and Asians. The socioeconomic status of African-Americans also has improved markedly over the past decade.[7] African-Americans have increased their disposable income fivefold over the past decade. Indeed, as one publication put it:

> A new breed of Black American has emerged who is impacting upon decisions and implementing policies at every level of American life. They are more willing to contribute economically to our future in America, more apt to reject the status quo, more assertive and aggressive, ready to seize every opportunity available, and willing to create opportunities where none exist.

Despite their continuing evolution in the white-dominated workplace, African-Americans can still be reached effectively through special media. Magazines such as *Ebony*, *Jet*, *Black Enterprise*, and *Essence* are natural vehicles. *Ebony*, the largest African-American-oriented publication in the world, has a circulation of 1.3 million. Newspapers such as the *Amsterdam News* in New York City and the *Daily Defender* in Chicago also are targeted to African-Americans. Such newspapers are controlled by active owners whose personal viewpoints dominate editorial policy. All should be included in the normal media relations functions of any organization.

Companies in recent years have made a concerted push to reach African-Americans. Occasionally, these attempts have been controversial. In 1990, for example, R. J. Reynolds Tobacco Company announced a promotional campaign to target its "Uptown" cigarette toward African-Americans. Reminiscent of the protests against Aunt Jemima in an earlier era, African-Americans outspokenly opposed the campaign. Reynolds was forced to drop its product after spending $10 million to develop it.[8] African-American leaders, including U.S. Secretary of Health and Human Services Louis Sullivan, condemned the proliferation of advertisements for cigarettes and alcohol in African-American neighborhoods. Other leaders, like civil rights activist Benjamin Hooks, condemned the condemnation as a form of paternalism. "Buried in this line of thinking," he said, "is the rationale that blacks are not capable of making their own free choices."[9] At the root of Hooks' comments was the realization that tobacco companies donated huge sums to support African-American causes, ranging from jazz festivals to the United Negro College Fund.

In recent years, companies have made a concerted effort to understand the family structure, traditions, and social mores of the black community, through sponsorship of programs targeted to pressing community needs (Figure 15–3).

The practice of public relations also has come in for criticism with respect to African-American practitioners. In recent years, the field has been frustrated in its efforts to recruit African-Americans. Surveys indicate that minorities represent a little more than 7 percent of all practitioners, with African-Americans reflecting just a small fraction of that percentage.[10] Public relations leaders agree that minority professionals are not adequately represented in the public relations industry, and that one challenge that confronts the industry is to recruit more minorities, especially African-Americans.

Figure 15–3 Pharmaceutical giant Pharmacia & Upjohn, Inc. was typical of companies that sponsored health care programs for minority communities. In this case, the company recruited former U.S. Surgeon General Joycelyn Elders to lead a roundtable on contraceptive issues.

Latinos

Latinos, like African-Americans, make up a growing proportion of the labor and consumer markets in major American cities. There are 20 million Latinos in the United States, with a median family income of more than $16,000. More than 70 percent of all U.S. Latinos reside in California, Texas, New York, and Florida. New York City has the largest Latin population with 1.8 million Hispanic residents. Los Angeles is the second city with more than one million Hispanics.[11] The majority of U.S. Latinos—62 percent—are of Mexican origin. About 13 percent are of Puerto Rican origin, and 5 percent are of Cuban origin. In Los Angeles, Latino kindergarten enrollment is 66 percent and rising. The Anglo enrollment is 15 percent and falling.

Because 75 percent of Latinos communicate primarily in Spanish, smart organizations can readily identify and target this public—and increase their retail sales—simply by communicating in the Spanish language (Figure 15–4). In an attempt to reach Latinos, advertisers spent $550 million in 1988, with the overwhelming percentage going to television.[12] In addition, radio stations and newspapers that communicate in Spanish, such as New York City's *El Diario* and *La Prensa*, are prominent voices in reaching this increasingly important community.

Beyond Latinos, other ethnic groups—particularly Asians—have increased their importance in the American marketplace. Japanese, Chinese, Koreans, Vietnamese, and others have gained new prominence as consumers and constituents. The 1992 formation of the Asian American Advertising and Public Relations Alliance in California underscored the increasing prominence of Asian Americans in the public relations profession.

Gays, Seniors, and Others

The last years of the twentieth century have introduced a diverse assortment of special communities into the mainstream of American commerce. One such group is the gay market (Figure 15–5). Although "homosexuality may remain a legitimate target of political opprobrium" for many, it also has become big business.[13] The gay market—20 million people, average age 36, household income six times higher than the national average, three times more likely to be college graduates than the national average, with more discretionary income than the average, 86 percent of whom say they would purchase products specifically marketed to them—has become extremely attractive to all kinds of marketers.

THE REST OF THE STORY

"LATINO," NOT "HISPANIC"

One problem in dealing with society's new multicultural diversity is mastering the lingo. Specifically, the preferred identity of a particular minority is often unclear.

The following is excerpted from a memo from the Mexican Empowerment Committee:

TO: News Media, Government, Business, and "Hispanic Organizations"

This is to notify you that the term "Hispanic" is unacceptable when referring to the 18-million-plus Mexican and Mexican-American population in the United States. Hispanic refers to the people, language, and culture of Spain.

It is insulting to include us, Mexicans, and Mexican-Americans, when you use this term that denies us our native Mexican (non-European) roots. We are over 92% of the so-called Hispanics in the Southwest and over 70% in the United States.

We, the activists and proud Mexican and Mexican-Americans, are launching a campaign to defend our identity, culture, history and honor.

When referring to the general Spanish-speaking population and those of Mexican descent, who are over 90 percent of the so-called "Hispanics" in California, please use the following terms: "Mexican/Latino population"; "Mexicans and other Latinos of California"; "Mexican and Latino population of the U.S."; or "Latino" if you must.

But please—NEVER HISPANIC!

poye a **United Way**, y usted, como el resto del mundo, verá que bien se siente.

Puede ser que la gente lo notará: una sonrisa un poco más grande. Una pizca mas de buen humor. Ese aire de satisfacción. Cuando usted da de sí mismo a nuestro United Way — se nota. Porque usted sabe que sus dólares están trabajando en nuestra comunidad. Ayudando a agencias no lucrativas y a voluntarios a proveer alimento y albergue, ayuda en caso de desastre, cuidado diurno de niños y ancianos, y ayuda a quien de veras lo necesite. Así que, como parte de este esfuerzo, no es raro que usted esté luciendo esa brillante sonrisa. La generosidad hace resaltar lo bello en todos nosotros.

REACHING THOSE WHO NEED HELP. TOUCHING US ALL.™

uándo fué la última vez que hizo una inversión con rendimiento garantizado?

Niños más saludables. Ciudadanos mayores más productivos. Jovenes ayudando a jovenes, y hombres y mujeres extraordinarios otorgando tiempo y talento sólo por interés sincero. Estos son los rendimientos que sus dólares brindan cuando usted invierte en nuestro United Way local. Dólares que regresan a nuestra comunidad — ayudando a voluntarios y a agencias no lucrativas a proveer lo necesario, desde alimento y albergue, a ayuda en caso de desastre y cuidado de niños. Y al hacer esa comunidad, todos compartimos de un mejor y seguro lugar para vivir.

REACHING THOSE WHO NEED HELP. TOUCHING US ALL.™

¿Cuándo fué la última vez que hizo una inversión con rendimiento garantizado?

Niños más saludables. Ciudadanos mayores más productivos. Jovenes ayudando a jovenes, y hombres y mujeres extraordinarios otorgando tiempo y talento sólo por interés sincero.

Estos son los rendimientos que sus dólares brindan cuando usted invierte en nuestro United Way local. Dólares que regresan a nuestra comunidad — ayudando a voluntarios y a agencias no lucrativas a proveer lo necesario, desde alimento y albergue, a ayuda en caso de desastre y ciudado de niños. Y al hacer esa comunidad, todos compartimos de un mejor y seguro lugar para vivir.

REACHING THOSE WHO NEED HELP. TOUCHING US ALL.™

Apoye a **United Way**, y usted, como el resto del mundo, verá que bien se siente

Puede ser que la gente lo notará: una sonrisa un poco más grande. Una pizca mas de buen humor. Ese aire de satisfacción.

Cuando usted da de sí mismo a nuestro United Way — se nota. Porque usted sabe que sus dólares están trabajando en nuestra comunidad. Ayudando a agencias no lucrativas y a voluntaria a proveer alimento y albergue, ayuda en caso de desastre, cuidado diurno de niños y ancianos, y ayuda a quien de veras lo necesite. Así que, como parte de este esfuerzo, no es raro que usted esté luciendo esa brillante sonrisa. La generosidad hace resaltar lo bello en todos nosotros.

ALCANZANDO A TODOS LOS QUE NECESITAN ATADA. TOCANDONOS A TODOS.™

Figure 15–4 Latinos have become an increasingly important constituent public, not only as consumers of goods but also as donors of funds. As this United Way ad suggests, "much depends" on the Latino community.

- In 1994, the First National Gay and Lesbian Business Expo in New Jersey drew companies from Perrier to Xerox to AT&T.
- In 1994, Wainwright Bank and Trust Company of Boston launched a special credit card for gay men and women.
- That same year, the annual Gay Games held in New York City attracted athletes—and sponsors—from around the world.

In addition to gay men and women, senior citizens also have become an important community for public relations professionals and the organizations they represent. The baby-boomer generation has hit 50 years of age. Together, the over 50 crowd controls more than 50 percent of America's discretionary income. Soon 13 percent of the population will be older than 65.[14] As the American population grows older, the importance of senior citizens will increase. Public relations professionals must be sensitive to that reality and to the fact that other special communities in the society will increasingly demand specialized treatment and targeted communications. Nowhere was this fact more apparent than when actor Christopher Reeve was paralyzed in 1996 after falling off a horse. Reeve, who once played "Superman," became an effective and outspoken instant advocate for the disabled, calling for an additional $40 million a year in Congressional funding.[15]

Mr. President...

"I believe patriotic Americans should have the right to serve the country as a member of the armed forces, without regard to sexual or affectional orientation."

February, 1992

"I want to make this very clear. This is a very narrow issue. It is whether a person, in the absence of any other disqualifying conduct, can simply say that he or she is homosexual and stay in the military."

January, 1993

Your words. Our lives.

CAMPAIGN FUND
Tim McFeeley, Executive Director
P.O. Box 1396, Washington, DC 20077

Figure 15–5 When President Bill Clinton wavered on his campaign pledge to allow acknowledged homosexuals to remain in the armed forces, he attracted an outpouring of outrage from a well-organized gay community.

NONPROFIT PUBLIC RELATIONS

Among the most important champions of multiculturalism in any community are nonprofit organizations. Nonprofit organizations serve the social, educational, religious, and cultural needs of the community around them. So important is the role of public relations in nonprofit organizations that this sector is a primary source of employment for public relations graduates.

The nonprofit sector is characterized by a panoply of institutions: hospitals, schools, social welfare agencies, religious institutions, cultural organizations, and the like. The general goals of nonprofit agencies are not dissimilar to those of corporations. Nonprofits seek to win public support of their mission and programs through active and open communications. Unlike corporations though, nonprofits also seek to broaden volunteer participation in their efforts.

Because America is a nation of joiners and belongers, nonprofit organizations in our society are encouraged to proliferate. As the number of nonprofit agencies has grown, it has become increasingly difficult to find funding sources. Most nonprofits depend on a combination of government funding and private support. In 1989, total corporate giving to all causes rose to an estimated $6.5 billion, a little over 2 percent of pretax corporate profits. The largest portion of that money—about $2.8 billion—went to educational institutions. Today, as resources have become more scarce and organizations have merged and downsized, the competition among nonprofits to attract funding has become more intense. One Conference Board study showed a 2.5-percent decline in charitable giving among leading corporate donors, with half of the major contributors—those donating more than $10 million annually—cutting back to 78 percent.[16]

All of this suggests that public relations professionals at nonprofits, in addition to writing speeches, dealing with the media, communicating with employees, and counseling managements, must be prepared to devote increased efforts to one activity that corporate communicators ordinarily aren't involved in—fund-raising.

FUND-RAISING

Fund-raising—the need to raise money to support operations—lies at the heart of every nonprofit institution (Figure 15–6). Schools, hospitals, churches, and organizations—from the mighty United Way to the smallest block association—can't exist without a constant source of private funds. Frequently, the fund-raising assignment becomes the province of public relations professionals. Like other aspects of public relations work, fund-raising must be accomplished in a planned and programmatic way.

A successful fund-raising campaign should include the following basic steps:

1. **Identify campaign plans and objectives.**   Broad financial targets should be set. A goal should be announced. Specific sectors of the community, from which funds might be extracted, should be targeted in advance.

2. **Organize fact finding.**   Relevant trends that might affect giving should be noted. Relations with various elements of the community should be defined. The national and local economies should be considered as should current attitudes toward charitable contributions.

You have the power

to help families, kids, those in need,

right in your neighborhood.

The power of U

United Way

1 - 8 0 0 - 4 1 1 - U W A Y

Figure 15–6 The granddaddy of all fund-raisers is the United Way, which uses provocative advertising like this to raise the enormous sums necessary to fund thousands of community nonprofits.

3. **Recruit leaders.** The best fund-raising campaigns are ones with strong leadership. A hallmark of local United Way campaigns, for example, is the recruitment of strong business leaders to spearhead contribution efforts. Leaders should be designated to coordinate the various targets of opportunity defined in the fund-raising program. United Way designates leaders in each industry group to tap potential funding sources.

4. **Plan and implement strong communications activities.** The best fund-raising campaigns are also the most visible. Publicity and promotion must be stressed. Special events should be organized, particularly featuring national and local celebrities to support the drive. Updates on fund-raising progress should be communicated, particularly to volunteers and contributors. Unique communications vehicles—from direct mail to raffles to bazaars to

THE REST OF THE STORY

HEEDING RELIGIOUS MESSAGES

Religious organizations have become a nonprofit source of employment for public relations professionals. One challenge for such practitioners is to edit those church bulletins or risk the following real excerpts:

■ Don't let worry kill you—let the church help.

■ Thursday night—potluck supper. Prayer and medication to follow.

■ Remember in prayer the many who are sick of our church and community.

■ The sermon topic this evening will be, "What is Hell?" Come early and listen to our choir practice.

■ The eighth graders will present Shakespeare's *Hamlet* in the church basement Friday. The congregation is invited to attend this tragedy.

the sale of stamps and seals—should be considered. All help get out the word and increase campaign coffers.

5. **Periodically review and evaluate.** Review the fund-raising program as it progresses. Make mid-course corrections when activities succeed or fail beyond expectations. Evaluate program achievements against program targets. Revise strategies constantly as the goal becomes nearer.

Because many public relations graduates enter the nonprofit realm, a knowledge of fund-raising strategies and techniques is especially important. Beginning practitioners, once hired in the public relations office of a college, hospital, religious group, charitable organization, or other nonprofit organization, are soon confronted with questions about how public relations can help raise money for the organization.

SUMMARY

The increasing cultural diversity of society as we move into the twenty-first century has spawned a wave of "political correctness," particularly in the United States. Predictably, many have questioned whether sensitivity to women, people of color, the physically challenged, seniors, and other groups has gone too far. One thing, however, is certain. The makeup of society—of consumers, employees, political constituents, and so on—has been altered inexorably. The number of discrete communities with which organizations must be concerned will continue to increase as the new century approaches.

Intelligent organizations in our society must be responsive to the needs and desires of their communities. Positive community relations in the new century must begin with a clear understanding of community concerns, an open door for community leaders, an open and honest flow of information from the organization, and an ongoing sense of continuous involvement and interaction with community publics.

Community relations is only as effective as the support it receives from top management. Once that support is clear, it becomes the responsibility of the public relations professional to ensure that the relationship between the organization and all of its multicultural communities is one of mutual trust, understanding, and support.

DISCUSSION STARTERS

1. How is the atmosphere for community relations different today than it was in the 1960s?
2. What is meant by the term *multicultural diversity*?
3. In general terms, what does a community expect from a resident organization?
4. What are typical community relations objectives for an organization?
5. How important is aiming messages at women? African-Americans? Latinos?
6. What are the key steps in mounting a sound fund-raising program?
7. What is the significance of dealing with the gay community?
8. What communications vehicles should be used in appealing to Latinos?
9. What is meant by the term *corporate social responsibility*?
10. What internal factor does community relations most depend on?

NOTES

1. Fred Kerber, "Furor Over Cal Remark," *New York Post* (March 24, 1997): 74.
2. Bob Weinstein, "Ethnic Marketing: The New Numbers Game," *Profiles* (May 1994): 51–52.
3. Paul Holmes, "Viva la Difference," *Inside PR* (March 1994): 13–14.
4. "The First Black Face I Ever Saw in Public Relations was in the Mirror," *Inside PR* (March 1993): 25.
5. Sylvia Nassar, "Women's Progress Stalled? Just Not So," *The New York Times* (October 18, 1992): D1.
6. Elizabeth L. Toth, "Confronting the Reality of the Gender Gap," *The Public Relations Strategist* (Fall 1996): 51.
7. Marilyn Kern-Foxworth, "Status and Roles of Minority Public Relations Practitioners," *Public Relations Review* (Fall 1989): 39.
8. Marilyn Kern-Foxworth, "Plantation Kitchen to American Icon: Aunt Jemima," *Public Relations Review* (Fall 1990): 64.
9. Michael Quinn, "Don't Aim That Pack at Us," *Time* (January 29, 1990): 60.
10. *Employment and Earnings* (Washington, DC: U.S. Department of Labor, Bureau of Statistics): 1991.
11. Ignasi B. Vendrell, "What is Hispanic Public Relations and Where is it Going?" *Public Relations Quarterly* (Winter 1994–95): 33.
12. Anna Veciana-Suarez, "Hispanic Media: Impact and Influence," (Washington, DC: The Media Institute, 1990): 15.
13. "Gay Market Gaining Acceptance," *Inside PR* (September 1992): 6.
14. Peter Kreysa, "You Can Improve Your Bank's Service to Older Customers," *Hoosier Banker* (November 1990): 48.

15. Kendall Hamilton, "Fighting to Fund an 'Absolute Necessity,' " *Newsweek* (July 1, 1996): 56.

16. "Corporate Giving to Rise 5% in 1990, Survey Says," *The Wall Street Journal* (August 8, 1990): A2.

SUGGESTED READINGS

Brion, Denis J. *Essential Industry and the NIMBY Phenomenon*. Westport, CT: Quorum, 1991.

Dines, Gail and Jean M. Humez. *Gender, Race and Class in Media*. Thousand Oaks, CA: Sage Publications, 1995.

D'Souza, Dinesh. *The End of Racism: Principles for a Multicultural Society*. New York: The Free Press, 1995. Challenges the notion that racism is the main obstacle facing black Americans.

Godfrey, Joline. *No More Frogs to Kiss*. New York: HarperBusiness, 1995. Offers a guide to empowering women economically and avoiding economic dependence on men.

Kalbfleisch, Pamela J. and Michael J. Cody. *Gender Power and Communications in Human Relationships*. Hillsdale, NJ: Lawrence Erlbaum Associates, 1995. Focuses on understanding differences in uses of communication by males and females.

TOP OF THE SHELF

SAUL D. ALINSKY

RULES FOR RADICALS

NEW YORK: VINTAGE BOOKS, 1971

As ancient as it is, Alinsky's *Rules for Radicals* is still the classic handbook for those bent on organizing communities, rattling the status quo, and effecting social and political change as well as for those who wish to learn from a legendary master.

Alinsky, a veteran community activist who fought on behalf of the poor from New York to California, provides strategies for building coalitions and for using communication, conflict, and confrontation advantageously. In "Of Means and Ends," Alinsky lists 11 rules of ethics that define the uses of radical power. His discussion of tactics suggests 13 ways to help organizers defeat their foes. Rule Three, for instance, tells activists to go outside the experience of their enemy to "cause confusion, fear, and retreat."

Alinsky supports his principles with numerous examples, the most colorful of which occurred when he wanted to draw attention to a particular cause in Rochester, New York. To do so, Alinsky and his group attended a Rochester Symphony performance—after a meal of nothing but beans. The results were hilarious.

Alinsky died in 1972, but his lessons endure in this offbeat guide to seizing power. Whether your goal is to fluster the establishment or defend it, *Rules for Radicals* is must reading. So read it!

Lukenbill, Grant. *Untold Millions: Positioning Your Business for the Gay and Lesbian Consumer Revolution.* New York: HarperBusiness, 1995. Uncovers truths and debunks myths behind the gay and lesbian consumer patterns and lifestyles.

National Conference of State Legislatures. *Building Communities That Work: Community Economic Development.* Denver, CO: NCSL, 1991.

Newsom, Doug A. and Bob J. Carrell. *Silent Voices.* Lanham, MD: University Press of America, 1995. A collection of articles examining issues concerning the status of women worldwide.

Reardon, Kathleen Kelley. *They Don't Get It, Do They? Communication in the Work Place—Closing the Gap Between Men and Women.* New York: Little Brown, 1995. The message for women in the workplace: Take a stand.

Tingley, Judith C. *Genderflex: Men and Women Speaking Each Other's Language at Work.* New York: AMACOM, 1995. Author refers to the phenomenon of adapting to the language gap between men and women as "genderflexing."

Valdivia, Angharad L. *Feminism, Multiculturalism and the Media.* Thousand Oaks, CA: Sage Publications, 1995.

Whilock, Rita Kirk and David Slayden. *Hate Speech.* Thousand Oaks, CA: Sage Publications, 1995. Examines how hate is manifested and expressed by quoting different authors.

Williams, Joe. *The 1992 Community Relations Idea Book.* Bartlesville, OK: Joe Williams Communications, 1992.

Wilson, Clint C. II. *Race, Multiculturalism and the Media: From Mass to Class Communication.* Thousand Oaks, CA: Sage Publications, 1995. Examines the historical relationship between the four largest racial groups and the mainstream media in the United States.

CASE STUDY

DENNY'S AND EDDIE CONFRONT RACISM

Few allegations are more damaging to a company's reputation than charges of racism.

When systemic racism is revealed in the ranks, strong—and often momentarily painful—remedial action must be taken. This is precisely what Denny's restaurants did—to the tune of $54 million—in the spring of 1994.

But when an isolated incident occurs and an organization is targeted—falsely, in its view—as a symbol of rampant racism, what then? Does it roll over and acquiesce to a multi-million dollar lawsuit? Or does it correct the abhorrent behavior, yet stand its ground and insist on a more moderate course?

This is what clothier Eddie Bauer Co. confronted—to the tune of $85 million—in the winter of 1995.

Painful Breakfast at Denny's

With more than 1,500 company and franchise restaurants located throughout the United States, Denny's is the nation's largest full-service family restaurant chain. On April Fool's Day 1993, 21 members of the Secret Service, preparing for a Naval Academy visit by President Clinton, stopped for breakfast at a Denny's outside Annapolis, Maryland.

Fifteen of the officers were served quickly, but one table of six uniformed men—all black—weren't served at all. As it turned out, although their food was ready for a full 20 minutes, neither the waitress nor her manager felt compelled to serve the black agents, until they got around to it.

The officers' subsequent discrimination suit unleashed a tidal wave of damning national publicity and legal actions against the 43-year-old company. Dan Rather summarized the situation on the CBS News, that these agents "put their lives on the line every day, but they can't get served at Denny's."

Denny's paid $54 million to settle all suits and adopted a far-reaching affirmative action program to hire minority managers, recruit minority franchise owners, and roust out racists in its ranks (Figure 15–7).

"All of us at Denny's regret any mistakes made in the past," said C. Ronald Petty, president and chief executive officer, when Denny's announced its settlement.

"Our company policy is clear and simple: If employees discriminate, they will be fired. If franchisees discriminate, they will lose their franchises," the Denny's CEO said.

After the flare-up, Denny's worked at becoming "a model in the industry." It recruited an African-American woman to join its parent company board of directors. It promoted minorities to supervisory positions, and it introduced a "Fast Track" program to help prepare minority candidates for restaurant ownership. In 1993, there was only one Denny's restaurant owned by an African-American. By 1995, the number had risen to 26, with plans to reach 65 within two years.

Said Karen Randall, public relations director of Denny's parent Flagstar Corporation, "We decided to look inside the organization and focus on 'substance' and change our makeup and management philosophy and the way we serve our customer base. In just a few years, this effort has changed the company," Randall said.

Eddie Bauer's Limited Response

Eddie Bauer, by contrast, refused to adopt any such sweeping response to its racial problem.

In late 1995, right around the time Denny's was announcing its settlement, the *Washington Post* reported that some weeks before, a black teenager was stripped of his shirt while shopping at an Eddie Bauer warehouse outlet in a DC suburb. Two white security guards (off-duty police and not Eddie Bauer employees) suspected the teenager of stealing the shirt and only released him when he retrieved a receipt to prove he had purchased the garment.

Eddie Bauer's immediate response to the *Post* was tentative. A spokesperson labeled the confrontation a "minor incident," and store personnel shuffled reporters over to the police. This was all outside activists needed to go after Eddie Bauer.

A few days later, however, the company got the message and reacted swiftly and decisively to right its wrong. The company issued an apology to the teenager, insisted the incident was not representative of its philosophy or its people, and flew its president to Washington to meet with community leaders who had expressed concern.

"In 75 years of business, this is the first time an incident of this nature has occurred at Eddie Bauer," said Debbie Cooperman, Eddie Bauer corporate public and investor relations executive. "Once management became aware of the situation, it was appalled and sought to respond immediately to the young man and the community, as well as refine internal procedures to ensure that this kind of thing won't happen again," Cooperman said.

Eddie Bauer's tardy but earnest mea culpa wasn't sufficient to placate its critics.

- One local NAACP leader alleged of Eddie Bauer, "a practice of harassment has been exposed that has been going on for years."
- The harassed teenager sued the clothing company and the security guards for false imprisonment, slander, assault, intentional infliction of emotional distress, negligent hiring and supervision, and racial discrimination—seeking $85 million to heal the wounds.

STATEMENT BY C. RONALD PETTY
DENNY'S PRESIDENT AND CHIEF EXECUTIVE OFFICER

As the settlement payout process is completed, Denny's, our managers and our employees will be able to look ahead. We will be able to focus our attention on providing all our restaurant guests with quality, value and excellent service.

All of us at Denny's regret any mistakes made in the past. But I want to emphasize that Denny's does not tolerate racial discrimination. Our company policy is clear and simple: If employees discriminate, they will be fired. If franchisees discriminate, they will lose their franchises.

I am proud to say Denny's and our parent company, Flagstar, have already made important strides in recent years. In fact, Denny's is becoming a model in our industry.

Let me be specific:

Dr. Vera King Farris, an African-American, president of Richard Stockton College in Pomona, N.J., joined the Flagstar board of directors two years ago. Mr. Michael Chu, a Hispanic and Asian-American, has been a board member since 1992. Minorities hold 27 percent of Flagstar restaurant and multi-restaurant supervisory positions. Almost half of Flagstar's 94,000 employees are minorities.

Figure 15-7 Denny's confronted charges of blatant racism at its restaurants with a comprehensive and well-publicized program to cleanse the company.

- And when the company asked Hill & Knowlton to assist it in its crisis, a *Post* headline screamed, "Taking on a high octane public relations firm is prima facie evidence of guilt."

Eddie Bauer—convinced it made a mistake, admitted and regretted it, and having taken proper corrective action—resisted capitulating to finger pointers who would have it appoint an "advisory council" to deal with a problem the company claimed doesn't exist.

"The company sees this issue as an aberration," said Hud Englehart of Hill & Knowlton, which, contrary to the *Post* columnist's charges, had worked for years for Eddie Bauer.

"People, correctly, are concerned about a serious problem like racism," Englehart added. "Eddie Bauer's primary concern was to get to the source of the problem and correct it."

QUESTIONS

1. Should Denny's have capitulated so quickly to charges of racism in its restaurants?
2. How would you assess the company's response to the accusations?
3. Was Eddie Bauer wrong in not adopting a Denny's-like response to its problem?
4. How damaging was Eddie Bauer's original indecision?
5. How would you assess Eddie Bauer's ultimate response?
6. Which company adopted the more appropriate response?

VOICE OF EXPERIENCE

TERRIE M. WILLIAMS

Terrie M. Williams is president of The Terrie Williams Agency, called by New York magazine "the most powerful black [owned] public relations firm in the country." Williams graduated from social worker to adviser to the stars when she landed her first client, Eddie Murphy, in 1988. She has been featured in many national magazines, is a sought-after lecturer on self-development topics, and is author of *The Personal Touch: What You Really Need to Succeed in Today's Fast-Paced Business World.*

HOW DID YOU GET STARTED IN PUBLIC RELATIONS?

I am a strong believer in destiny. I was a practicing medical social worker at New York Hospital and was very deeply affected by my inability to really change a lot of people's circumstances. It was just very, very depressing. I saw an advertisement in the *Amsterdam News*, New York's largest black-owned newspaper, and there was a one-paragraph article about a public relations course being taught at the Y on Lexington and 51st. And the idea of it just seemed intriguing. I didn't know anyone in the field, but it sounded like something I should check out. I did. And that was really it.

HOW WOULD YOU CHARACTERIZE ENTERTAINMENT PUBLIC RELATIONS?

Extremely grueling. You have to put in a full day's work, which, of course, does not end at five. And then you have a movie premiere or a benefit dinner or a concert. And oftentimes, you don't get home till very late, 12 or 1 in the morning. And then you have to be ahead of the game the next morning, to see what's in the papers, to get items in the papers, and to have to function as if you've had a good night's rest when, in fact, you're running on empty. So, I would say that it's not nearly as glamorous and as exciting as it's cracked up to be.

WHAT'S BEEN YOUR MOST DIFFICULT CHALLENGE?

Running a business. It's one thing to be good at what you do and quite another to run a business. It's also hard to find good, strong, talented, intelligent, creative people who have a strong, strong work ethic and integrity. That, I think, is very challenging.

HOW DOES A COLLEGE GRADUATE GET STARTED IN ENTERTAINMENT PUBLIC RELATIONS?

Be adventurous, creative, not afraid to introduce yourself to people and ask for what you want. If you're not able to get a job immediately in the PR business, reach out to people and volunteer, do an internship. Be two steps ahead of people you want to do business with. Keep an eye on all of the trade publications, all the general consumer interest magazines. Get a good, solid feel for who is being written about, who's doing what with whom, what the trend stories are, who's writing what kinds of pieces. All of that information is key.

WHAT IS THE FUTURE OF PUBLIC RELATIONS PRACTICE FOR MINORITIES?

We have a long way to go. But we're making progress. People need to understand the importance of stretching themselves, to do business and interact with people with whom you're not most comfortable. That's probably the single biggest reason why our numbers are not great. It really blows me away when I hear mainstream PR firms and executives say, "There are not qualified minorities out there." I receive two or three resumes a day and an equal number of phone calls, which range from experienced practitioners to entry-level candidates. Many mainstream firms overlook the fact that minority PR professionals bring a much more well-rounded perspective to the table. As a member of an ethnic group, the ability to operate effectively with both majority and minority publics is second nature. Majority practitioners often are without the benefit of being exposed to an ethnically diverse population. We, on the other hand, have to know how to make it, how to be conversant and survive in our own world and the world of the majority. We've got to be culturally aware and sensitive. It's a matter of necessity. And if the numbers are low now—and they are—it's really because nobody has made a real effort to reach out to this segment of PR professionals. And we make it a priority here at our agency that anybody who wants to get into it, or wants to change careers or whatever, has an opportunity to work with us. They hang out with us for a day or assist us in the evening on an event. That's the only way that we are going to increase our numbers in this business.

WHAT'S THE SECRET OF INDIVIDUAL SUCCESS IN PUBLIC RELATIONS?

I don't believe in using race or sex or anything of any kind as an obstacle or a barrier to being able to accomplish great things. If you perfect your craft, treat people correctly, have a strong work ethic, believe in passing it on and giving it back to the community, if you're detail oriented, do the things you say you're going to do, there's no way you can lose. You will, in fact, excel.

VOICE OF EXPERIENCE

RAY DURAZO

Ray Durazo is president of Los Angeles-based Durazo Communications and a nationally recognized authority on Latino public relations. Before forming his own firm, Durazo was a partner in the Latino public relations firm of Moya, Villanueva & Durazo. Earlier, he headed the Los Angeles office of Ketchum Public Relations. Before returning to his native Southern California, Durazo headed Ketchum's Washington, DC, office.

HOW IMPORTANT IS THE ETHNIC MARKET IN THE UNITED STATES?

The United States receives two-thirds of the world's immigrants. Two-thirds of those immigrants will settle in California and Texas. Soon "minorities" will be the "majority" in Los Angeles, Dallas, Denver, Houston, and 23 other major U.S. cities. In Los Angeles, the Latino kindergarten enrollment is 66 percent and rising; Anglo enrollment is 15 percent and falling. Latino, Asians, and African-Americans constitute more than half the population of Los Angeles County. In short, the U.S. ethnic market has become too large to ignore.

WHAT ABOUT COMMUNICATING WITH LATINOS AND ASIANS?

Within these two major categories, there are differences, much of it having to do with the length of time the person has been in the United States and has become "acculturated" or to use a nonscientific term, "Americanized."

- Among Latinos, for instance, there are demographic and psychographic differences between a second-generation Mexican-American and a recently arrived immigrant from, say, Guatemala. The first was educated in the United States, speaks fluent English, and has adopted a mainstream American lifestyle. The new immigrant speaks mostly Spanish, may not have progressed beyond an elementary school education, and maintains a lifestyle very similar to the one he or she practiced in Guatemala.

- Among Asians, the equation may be even more complex. Many Koreans, for example, arrive in this country with extensive education and experience as business people. They tend to be entrepreneurial, aggressive, and ambitious. In contrast, many newly arrived immigrants from war-torn countries such as Vietnam, Cambodia, Thailand, and others are relatively uneducated and sometimes illiterate even in their own languages.

WHY DEAL SPECIALLY WITH ETHNIC MARKETS?

Addressing ethnic audiences is simply another form of market segmentation, a recognition that the lifestyles, the life experiences, and the attitudes and outlooks of ethnic persons may influence their receptivity to certain messages, to the way in which products and ideas are presented to them. As to why it's worth doing, all you have to do is look at the numbers, the buying power, the proportion of the population made up by ethnics, and you conclude that it's worth the effort.

WHAT SHOULD A PRACTITIONER DO TO BECOME CONVERSANT WITH THE ETHNIC MARKET?

The market isn't going to come to you. You have to go out and find it, experience it, learn it. And it isn't hard. Next time there's a Cinco de Mayo festival, or a Chinese New Year celebration, or an African-American heritage celebration, or any other ethnic event in your community, get out of your home or office, get in your car, drive over there, and participate!

WHAT IS THE FUTURE OF MINORITY-ORIENTED PUBLIC RELATIONS?

The world is becoming a more competitive place every day. Recent history has shown that only the strong, the smart, the courageous, will survive in this new international arena. If you are too timid even to venture into your own backyard to reach important new audiences, I hate to think what will happen to you in the future! Aggressive, progressive companies have already concluded that the U.S. ethnic audience is too big to ignore. It isn't about being politically correct. It isn't about being touchy-feeley. It's about the bottom line, about profits, about market share, about winning.

Wake up and smell el cafe!

CHAPTER SIXTEEN

Consumers

IN THE SPRING OF 1997, THE *Wall Street Journal's* lead story proclaimed, "Old-Fashioned PR Gives General Mills Advertising Bargains." The story chronicled how the venerable General Mills, Inc. had hearkened back to tried and true public relations techniques—Betty Crocker Cook Offs, newspaper Q&A food columns, pancake breakfasts for Presidential candidates, etc.—to win recognition. One expert quoted in the story concluded that "a third-party endorsement is almost always more effective than a paid commercial."[1]

With, as Bruce Springsteen has put it, "500 channels and nothing on," all offering commercial after commercial—it has become increasingly difficult for consumers to penetrate the clutter to identify winning products and services. As a consequence, many companies will enter the twenty-first century with a new respect for consumer-oriented public relations.

- In 1995, Microsoft launched its Windows 95 software with a monstrous publicity campaign that included an opening party for more than 2,500 "invited guests," a Q&A session hosted by late-night host Jay Leno, and a marketing theme song performed by the Rolling Stones.[2]
- In 1996, Tyco Toys Inc. used a strategic public relations campaign to introduce its Tickle Me Elmo doll, which worked so well, it created a corporate crisis in not being able to fill orders.[3]
- In 1997, IBM scored the publicity coup of the century by pitting its super computer, Deep Blue, against chess grand master Garry Kasparov in a "battle for the ages." Kasparov eventually gave up in frustration. The machine was just too smart for him. And IBM made every front page in the nation and many around the world.[4]

Such was the new-found clout of public relations techniques in an era overwrought with advertising "noise."

At the same time as the world moves into the new century, con-

TYCO TICKLED WITH TICKLE ME MOMENTUM

Parents who vowed to pay anything to secure a Tickle Me Elmo doll in the winter of 1996 wouldn't believe it—but Tyco Toys Inc., the manufacturer of the hottest toy of the year was originally concerned with Elmo's potential popularity (Figure 16–1).

Figure 16–1 He's cute. He's cuddly. He's the hottest toy in Sesame Street history.

So, together with Freeman Public Relations, Tyco devised a carefully planned campaign that ultimately had difficulty coping with its own success.

The strategy called for getting the $28 red and furry creature into the hands of key members of the print and TV media. Elmo's launch began with a Toy Fair breakfast for 15 toy trade publication editors. One of the guests was so impressed with Elmo that he brought it with him to the *Today Show*, where jolly weather man Al Roker played with it on the air.

Next was a special activity day for the media at Sesame Place, a kids amusement and theme park in Pennsylvania. Editors were invited with their children, and Tickle Me Elmo was the star of the day.

Then came the biggest breakthrough. The company sent a doll to talk show host Rosie O'Donnell, who promptly awarded it to her young son. Alas, the boy dropped the doll down the toilet, and O'Donnell announced on the show one day that she desperately needed another.

Tyco obliged with an offer to supply enough Elmos for the whole O'Donnell audience. O'Donnell's producers responded with a "secret word" contest. If one of O'Donnell's guests mentioned the "secret word," known only to the audience, hundreds of Tickle Me Elmos would cascade from the rafters, one for each audience member. On cue, the last guest of the morning mentioned the word. A sea of Elmos came streaming down into the hands of the wildly cheering audience. And the rest, as they say, is toy history.

Demand for the doll overwhelmed the supply. Tyco had to scramble to produce enough Elmos, eventually pulling its advertising when skirmishes erupted among customers fighting for the last doll in stock. With 15,000 media mentions of the doll and sales exceeding projections by 500 percent, Tickle Me Elmo had ridden its publicity to become one of the most sought-after and talked-about toys ever produced.

sumers simply won't tolerate defective merchandise, misleading advertising, packaging and labeling abuses, quality and safety failures, inadequate service and repair, diffident corporate complaint handlers, incomprehensible or inadequate guarantees and warranties, or slow settlements when products don't live up to advance claims.[5]

Whether or not today's "consumer" is king, he or she demands quality service.

Organizations, locked in an increasingly competitive battle for consumer loyalty, must be responsive to consumer demands. Thus, the practice of consumer relations has increased in importance among business organizations.

GROWTH OF THE CONSUMER MOVEMENT

Although consumerism is considered to be a relatively recent concept, legislation to protect consumers first emerged in the United States in 1872, when Congress enacted the Criminal Fraud Statute to protect consumers against corporate abuses. In 1887, Congress established the Interstate Commerce Commission to curb freewheeling railroad tycoons.

However, the first real consumer movement came right after the turn of the century when journalistic muckrakers encouraged legislation to protect the consumer. Upton Sinclair's novel *The Jungle* revealed scandalous conditions in the meat-packing industry and helped usher in federal meat inspection standards as Congress passed the Food and Drug Act and the Trade Commission Act. In the second wave of the movement, from 1927 to 1938, consumers were safeguarded from the abuses of manufacturers, advertisers, and retailers of well-known brands of commercial products. During this time, Congress passed the Food, Drug, and Cosmetic Act.

By the early 1960s, the movement had become stronger and more unified. President John F. Kennedy, in fact, proposed that consumers have their own Bill of Rights, containing four basic principles:

1. The right to safety—to be protected against the marketing of goods hazardous to health or life.

2. The right to be informed—to be protected against fraudulent, deceitful, or grossly misleading information, advertising, labeling, or other practices and to be given the facts needed to make an informed choice.
3. The right to choose—to be assured access, whenever possible, to a variety of products and services at competitive prices.
4. The right to be heard—to be assured that consumer interests will receive full and sympathetic consideration in the formulation of government policy.

Subsequent American presidents have continued to emphasize consumer rights and protection. Labeling, packaging, product safety, and a variety of other issues continue to concern government overseers of consumer interests.

FEDERAL CONSUMER AGENCIES

Today a massive government bureaucracy attempts to protect the consumer against abuse: upwards of 900 different programs, administered by more than 400 federal entities. Key agencies include the Justice Department, Federal Trade Commission, Food and Drug Administration, Consumer Product Safety Commission, and Office of Consumer Affairs.

- **Justice Department** The Justice Department has had a consumer affairs section in its antitrust division since 1970. Its responsibilities include the enforcement of such consumer protection measures as the Truth in Lending Act and the Product Safety Act.
- **Federal Trade Commission** The FTC, perhaps more than any other agency, has vigorously enforced consumer protection. Its national advertising division covers television and radio advertising, with special emphasis on foods, drugs, and cosmetics. Its general litigation division covers areas not included by national advertising, such as magazine subscription agencies, door-to-door sales, and income tax services. Its consumer credit and special programs division deals with such areas as fair credit reporting and truth in packaging.
- **Food and Drug Administration** The FDA is responsible for protecting consumers from hazardous items: foods, drugs, cosmetics, therapeutic and radiological devices, food additives, and serums and vaccines.
- **Consumer Product Safety Commission** This bureau is responsible for overseeing product safety and standards.
- **Office of Consumer Affairs** This agency, the central point of consumer activities in the government, publishes literature to inform the public of recent developments in consumer affairs.

Under President Clinton, federal regulators continue to occupy positions of great importance to most industry groups. For example, in recent years, the FDA, whether attacking the cigarette companies for the perils of smoking or the pharmaceutical firms for exorbitant prices, has been extremely aggressive. Perhaps most vigilant in this regard was Dr. David Kessler, who retired as head of the FDA after moving vigorously in areas from food labeling to cigarette advertising to breast implants to the regulation of the olestra fat substitute.[6] As the nation moves into the new century the reality is that public companies—from utilities to banks to consumer products firms to cable TV purveyors—must communicate directly and frequently with their regulators in Washington. Often the best policy is to keep regulators advised of corporate developments and to work at winning their understanding and support.

CONSUMER ACTIVISTS

The consumerist movement has attracted a host of activists in recent years. Private testing organizations, which evaluate products and inform consumers about potential dangers, have proliferated. Perhaps the best known, Consumers Union, was formed in 1936 to test products across a wide spectrum of industries. It publishes the results in a monthly magazine, *Consumer Reports*, which reaches about 3.5 million readers. Often an evaluation in *Consumer Reports*, either pro or con, greatly affects how customers view particular products. Consumers Union also produces books, a travel newsletter, a column for 450 newspapers, and monthly features for network television. It has an annual budget of $70 million.

Consumers also have begun taking a more active role in their own affairs. The Consumer Federation of America was formed in 1967 to unify lobbying efforts for pro consumer legislation. Today the federation consists of 200 national, state, and local consumer groups, labor unions, electric cooperatives, and other organizations with consumer interests.

Although companies often find activists' criticism annoying, the emergence of the consumer watchdog movement has generally been a positive development for consumers. Ralph Nader, perhaps the dean of twentieth-century consumer activists, and others have forced organizations to consider, even more than usual, the downside of the products and services they offer. Smart companies have come to take seriously the pronouncements of consumer activists.

BUSINESS GETS THE MESSAGE

Obviously, few organizations can afford to shirk their responsibilities to consumers. Consumer relations divisions have sprung up, either as separate entities or as part of public relations departments. The title of vice president for consumer relations is showing up with more frequency on corporate organization charts.

In many companies, consumer relations began strictly as a way to handle complaints, an area to which all unanswerable complaints were sent. Such units have frequently provided an alert to management. In recent years, some companies have broadened the consumer relations function to encompass such activities as developing guidelines to evaluate services and products for management, developing consumer programs that meet consumer needs and increase sales, developing field-training programs, evaluating service approaches, and evaluating company effectiveness in demonstrating concern for customers.

The investment in consumer service apparently pays off. Marketers of consumer products say that most customer criticism can be mollified with a prompt, personalized reply—and a couple of free samples. Failing to answer a question, satisfy a complaint, or solve a problem, however, can result in a blitz of bad word-of-mouth advertising.[7] More typical of the increased concern shown today by most business organizations are the following:

- When Alamo Rent-A-Car experienced a shortage of vehicles in a busy vacation season at certain locations, it eagerly reimbursed customers for the difference between their reserved Alamo rate and the one they were forced to pay.
- When the Swingline Company received numerous complaints about its Tot Stapler, it reconstituted the product and sent new models, free of charge, to people who complained.

- When Newman's Own Microwave Popcorn received complaints that its bags were leaking, it hired a technical consulting organization to reevaluate the bag sealing system. It also refunded the cost of the purchase.
- In 1994, when mutual funds were criticized for failing to explain their risks to the public, Fidelity Investments, the largest U.S. mutual funds company, became the first investment house to produce its own half-hour infomercial to explain the risks and rewards of mutual fund investing. Three years later, when the company's flagship Magellan Fund underperformed the market, Fidelity dispatched the fund managers on "road shows" around the country, to explain current investment strategy.

In adopting a more activist consumerist philosophy, firms like these have found that consumer relations need not take a defensive posture. Consumer relations people can't afford to be simple complaint handlers. Rather, they must be activists in the very best sense to make certain that consumers understand the benefits and realities of using their products.

CONSUMERIST PHILOSOPHY

Most companies begin with the premise that customers, if they are to remain customers, deserve to be treated fairly and honestly. Historically, the companies that initiated their own activist consumer affairs units have been those to escape the wrath of outside activists.

The Grand Union Company, the second oldest food chain in the nation, began a consumer affairs department two decades ago and drew up its own Consumer Bill of Rights. Its example has been followed by numerous companies in a variety of industries. Typical is Chrysler Motors "Car Buyer's Bill of Rights":

1. Every American has the right to quality.
2. Every American has the right to long-term protection.
3. Every American has the right to friendly treatment, honest service, and competent repairs.
4. Every American has the right to a safe vehicle.
5. Every American has the right to address grievances.
6. Every American has the right to satisfaction.

Chrysler, like other companies, backed up its Bill of Rights with a customer arbitration board to deal with warranty-related problems and commissioned a research organization to survey car owners periodically on customer satisfaction.

Such an enlightened approach to customer relations is typical of businesses in the latter stages of the twentieth century.

CONSUMERIST OBJECTIVES

Building sales is the primary consumer relations objective. A satisfied customer may return; an unhappy customer may not. Here are some typical goals:

- **Keeping old customers** Most sales are made to established customers. Consumer relations efforts should be made to keep these customers happy. Pains should be taken to respond to customers' concerns. For example, telephone companies will typically suspend normal charges in areas of natural disasters to make calls to loved ones.

THE REST OF THE STORY

Figure 16–2   Cabbage Patch Kids in happier times.

PULLING THE CABBAGE PATCH PIRANHA

One of the great success stories in American consumerism has been the lovable Cabbage Patch Doll (Figure 16–2). For years, the Cabbage Patch has been a tried-and-true staple of the Mattel Toy Company. In 1992 and again in 1996, in fact, Cabbage Patch Kids were named the first and only official mascot the U.S. Olympic Team.

But at Christmastime 1996, Mattel introduced the latest doll in the Cabbage Patch line, Cabbage Patch Snack Time Kids, which munched on French fries and carrots with its little mechanical mouth. The problem was, the little muncher also chomped on anything else that got in its vicinity—including the hair and fingers of little girls who received the doll as a gift.

Reports of finger-chomping dolls raged across the national airwaves. In Indiana, a 7-year-old girl reported that a doll munched her hair up to her scalp and would not let go. In New York, one tabloid labeled the new plaything, "Scary, very scary." Mattel tried vanely to contain the problem. At first, the company announced that its dolls would begin carrying a label warning parents of the wandering munching mouth. But as incidents and reports of extracurricular chomping increased, Mattel pulled the plug.

The company announced in January of 1997 that it would remove the Snacktime Cabbage Patch Kids from toy store shelves, agreeing to "eat" a loss of $8 million.

- **Attracting new customers**   Every business must work constantly to develop new customers. In many industries, the prices and quality of competing products are similar. In choosing among brands, customers may base decisions on how they have been treated.

- **Marketing new items or services**   Customer relations techniques can influence the sale of new products. Thousands of new products flood the market each year, and the vast array of information about these products can confuse the consumer. When General Electric's research revealed that consumers want personalized service and more information on new products, it established the GE Answer Center, a national toll-free, 24-hour service that informed consumers about new GE products and services. Building such company and product loyalty lies at the heart of a solid consumer relations effort.

- **Expediting complaint handling**   Few companies are free of complaints. Customers protest when appliances don't work, errors are made in billing, or deliveries aren't made on time. Many large firms have established response procedures. Often a company ombudsman can salvage a customer relationship with a speedy and satisfactory answer to a complaint.

- **Reducing costs** To most companies, an educated consumer is the best consumer. Uninformed buyers cost a company time and money—when goods are returned, service calls are made, and instructions are misunderstood. Many firms have adopted programs to educate customers about many topics—what to look for in choosing fruits and vegetables, how to shop for durable goods, and how to use credit wisely.

A QUESTION OF ETHICS

CALVIN TESTS THE BOUNDS OF KIDDIE PORN

Calvin Klein—dirty old man or cynical businessman cashing in on America's appetite for sexual titillation? That is the question.

Klein, whose fashion empire has made a fortune by testing the bounds of "taste" with provocative "on the edge" commercials, clearly descended over the edge with a series of 1995 ads.

The Calvin Klein jeans commercials focused on teenagers posing suggestively in a wood-paneled, purple shag carpet setting, while being questioned by a leering, off-camera, dirty-old-man-nish moderator. A sample of the dialogue:

> Off-camera voice: You got a real nice look. How old are you?
> Model: Twenty-one.
> OCV: What's your name?
> Model: August.
> OCV: Why don't you stand up . . . are you strong?
> Model: I'd like to think so.
> OCV: You think you could rip that shirt off ya?
> (Model rips off T-shirt)
> OCV: That's a nice body . . . Do you work out?
> Model: Uh huh.
> OCV: Yeah, I can tell.

Not exactly Pulitzer Prize material. In fact, some accused the jeans maker of bordering on child pornography with the offensive commercials.

Klein stood his ground as commentators of every stripe weighed in on the acceptability or lack thereof of the advertising.

Finally, after milking the publicity for all it was worth, the designer announced with great fanfare that he had decided to withdraw the jeans ads, because the message of the advertising "has been misunderstood by some." The announcement was followed by a syrupy full-page ad that talked of "conveying the idea that glamour is an inner quality that can be found in regular people in the most ordinary setting." The ad explained that because Calvin Klein has "a special responsibility to young people," the campaign would stop "as soon as possible."

These last four words proved important, since it was revealed that virtually the entire $6 million TV, print and outdoor advertising campaign had run its course. Calvin, it seemed, was concerned about its "responsibility," but evidently equally concerned about getting its money's worth from the advertising—not to mention the accompanying free publicity.

OFFICE OF THE OMBUDS OFFICER

Research indicates that only a handful of dissatisfied customers—4 percent—will ever complain. But that means that there are 24 or so with the same complaint who never say anything. And the vast majority of dissatisfied customers won't repurchase from the offending company.

In the old days, a frequent response to complaint letters was to dust off the so-called bed bug letter. This stemmed from occasional letters to the railroads complaining about bed bugs in the sleeper cars. To save time, railroad consumer relations personnel simply dispatched a prewritten bed bug letter in response. Today, with the volume of mail and e-mail and faxes at a mountainous level, an occasional bed bug letter still appears from time to time (Figure 16–3).

At many companies the most immediate response to complaints has been the establishment of ombudsman offices. The term *ombudsman* originally described a government official—in Sweden and New Zealand, for example—appointed to investigate complaints against abuses made by public officials. In most firms, the office of the ombuds officer investigates complaints made against the company and its managers. Such an office generally provides a central location that customers can call to seek redress of grievances.

12 King Place
Closter, New Jersey
07624
June 2, 1993

President Clinton
The White House
Washington, D.C. 205000

Dear President Clinton:

    My name is David Seitel, and I am a sixth grader. I'm writing about a very important topic. This topic is SMOKING. Our tobacco companies in the U.S. are setting a bad example for us kids today. They are going to other countries, and encouraging people in their teens especial my age, to smoke.
    Please, won't you try to help stop American tobacco companies from addicting the world's children. Thank you.

Sincerely,
David Seitel

Thank you for writing to me. I enjoy hearing from young people because you are the future of our country. I am honored to be your President.

Bill Clinton

Figure 16–3   Even in these days of direct–mail sophistication, a young consumer still risks the disappointment of his sincere missive being answered with a cursory bed bug letter.

CHRYSLER • PLYMOUTH • JEEP • EAGLE

95 County Road, Tenafly, NJ 07670 • 201-871-9400 • Fax: 201-871-0544

Fraser Seitel
12 King Place
Closter, NJ 07624

December 28, 1996

Mr. Seitel,

We were reviewing our records for our year end close and we discovered
that you overpaid us on the delivery of your new car back in July!

The COD on your Grand Cherokee was $1499.00, which you paid at delivery,
but you had also left us an original deposit of $500. Making the total
monies we recieved from you $1999.00. We know that it is rare to
recieve a refund this long after your delivery, please accept our check
for $500.00.

In the future if you need anything please feel free to count on us.

Sincerely,

Sara Langford
Sales Manager

35 Years of Service Excellence

Figure 16–4   Happy consumers eager to repurchase from beneficent suppliers are born of letters like this.

A five-year study of consumer complaint handling commissioned by the U.S. Office of Consumer Affairs suggested two important caveats for suppliers of consumer goods and services:

1. Consumers who do not complain when they are dissatisfied are often unhappy enough to switch product brands, companies, or both.
2. Because marketing costs are extremely high, it may be less expensive to resolve the complaints of existing customers than to win new ones.

   Typically, the ombuds officer monitors the difficulties customers are having with products. Often, he or she can anticipate product or performance deficiencies. Ombuds officers are in business to inspire customer confidence and to influence an organization's behavior toward improved service. They accomplish this by responding, more often than not, in the following manner:[8]

   - "We'll take care of that for you."
   - "We'll take full responsibility for that defect."
   - "We want your business."
   - "Thank you for thinking of us."
   - "Consider it done."

Such "magic words" should be heard more often in many organizations. Courteous, knowledgeable, and skilled complaint-handling ombuds officers—cheerful, positive, and genuinely concerned with solving a customer's problems—can keep clients happy and loyal for many years (Figure 16–4).

SUMMARY

Despite periodic legislative setbacks and shifting consumerist leadership, the cause of consumerism seems destined to remain strong. The increasing use of seat belts and air bags, increased environmental concerns about packaging and pollution, rising outrage about secondhand smoke and all smoking in general, and numerous other causes indicate that the push for product safety and quality will likely increase in the years ahead.

Business will not sit idly by. Indeed, the consumer affairs function continues to grow in stature. In 1987, the Society of Consumer Affairs Professionals had 600 companies among its members. By 1990, the society boasted 1,400 members.

With the re-election of a Democratic president, public interest groups see a greater opportunity to help set the nation's agenda into the twenty-first century.

The likely reemergence of activism in the new century means that businesses must respond with an even greater sense of consumerism.

- In 1990, when Star Kist Tuna received thousands of letters from schoolchildren protesting the killing of dolphins in the hunt for tuna, the company changed its tuna-fishing policy. As a result of Star Kist's action to refit boats and retrain fishermen, fewer dolphin died and the company was hailed as a hero.[9]
- In 1996, PepsiCo dropped a program to give away 500,000 beepers to teenagers as part of a summer marketing push for Mountain Dew. The company bowed to

pressure from educators, who pointed out that schools have banned beepers because they are disruptive or associated with drug dealing.[10]

- In 1997, when Reebok introduced a new woman's athletic shoe, the *Incubus,* the company was barraged by women's groups complaining that *Incubus* is considered an evil spirit believed to have sexually preyed on women during medieval times. Reebok apologized and dropped the name.[11]

Similarly, any organization interested in muffling activist protests and ensuring a reputation for integrity must meet the consumerist challenge by establishing safety, performance, and service standards that demonstrate good faith and public interest. In the long run, the firm that lives by a pro consumer philosophy will prosper. The firm that ignores the irresistible push of consumerism risks not only growth but survival.

BETWEEN THE LINES

A DAY IN THE LIFE OF THE OMBUDS OFFICER

So you want to handle consumer complaints? Here is a random selection of complaints received by the consumer affairs division of a local bank. How would you have handled them?

1. A businessman carrying an attaché case made a deposit at a midtown branch before going to his office. Inadvertently, he left his case on the main banking floor. By the time he discovered that it was missing, the police bomb squad had smashed the innocent case and cordoned off the area. The owner asked the bank for a replacement. Would you have given it to him?

2. After making a deposit and leaving the bank, a woman reported that a huge icicle fell from the bank's roof and nearly hit her. She complained bitterly to consumer affairs. How would you appease her?

3. A young installment loan customer claimed that his car had been removed for reclamation because of delinquent loan payments. He claimed that he had paid the loan on time and objected to the illegal seizure. On checking, it was determined that several loan payments were, in fact, delinquent. Nevertheless, the car was returned, but in a very damaged condition. The young man sought reimbursement for repairs. What would you recommend?

4. A customer complained that she had received no response to her numerous letters and memos concerning the hostile treatment accorded her at the local branch. After investigation, it was learned that the woman was a nuisance to branch officers, yet kept a very healthy balance in her savings account. Furthermore, all the correspondence to which she referred was written on the backs of checks she submitted in loan payments. How would you handle this problem?

5. The executor of an estate complained that his deceased client, who had been a bank customer, had received a card reading "Best wishes in your new residence." What remedial action would you recommend?

DISCUSSION STARTERS

1. What did President Kennedy contribute to the consumerist movement?
2. What key federal agencies are involved in consumerism?
3. What is Consumers Union?
4. How do companies typically handle the challenge of consumerism?
5. What is a consumer bill of rights?
6. What are typical consumerist objectives?
7. What is the office of the ombuds officer?
8. What is a bed bug letter?
9. Why must firms fear too many dissatisfied customers?
10. What can be learned from the Star Kist, Pepsi, and Reebok experiences in confronting increased consumer activism?

NOTES

1. Kevin Helliker, "Old-Fashioned PR Gives General Mills Advertising Bargains," *The Wall Street Journal* (March 20, 1997): 1.
2. "Microsoft Bash Ushers in Windows 95 Era," *O'Dwyer's PR Services Report* (November 1995): 25.
3. Michelle Healy, "Elmo Doll, 'Space Jam' Toys Top Wish Lists," *USA Today* (October 15, 1996): A1.
4. Bart Ziegler, "Checkmate! Deep Blue is IBM Publicity Coup," *The Wall Street Journal* (May 9, 1997): B1.
5. Paul Burnham Finney, "Everyone Is Shouting the Q Word," Special Digest Advertising Section, *Newsweek* (December 10, 1990): 12.
6. Doug Levy and Nanci Hellmich, "FDA's Tobacco Regulations Final Triumph for Departing Chief Kessler," *USA Today* (February 2, 1997): 4D.
7. Kathleen Deveny, "For Marketers, No Peeve Is Too Petty," *The Wall Street Journal* (November 14, 1990): B1.
8. John R. Graham, "Words to Inspire Confidence," *Communication Briefings* (November 1988): 8.
9. "Star Kist Explains How Consumer Advocacy Inspired Its Decision for Policy Change," *Public Relations Reporter* (May 14, 1990): 4.
10. "PepsiCo Readies Promotion Giving Beepers to Teens," *The Wall Street Journal* (May 13, 1996).
11. "Public Perception Puts Some Cos. in Driver's Seat, Others in Hot Seat," *PR News* (March 3, 1997): 1.

SUGGESTED READINGS

Crego, Edwin T., Jr., and Peter D. Schriffin. *Customer-Centered Reengineering Remapping for Total Customer Value*. Burr Ridge, IL: Irwin Professional Publishing, 1995. Focuses on the failures of many reengineering efforts to make effective long-range change.

AL RIES AND JACK TROUT

THE 22 IMMUTABLE LAWS OF MARKETING

NEW YORK: HARPERBUSINESS, 1993

Public relations professionals interested in the field of consumer relations owe it to themselves to consider *The 22 Immutable Laws of Marketing*, which turns conventional marketing wisdom on its head.

Al Ries and Jack Trout, iconoclastic marketers who have counseled hundreds of leading corporations, lay it on the line in a most untraditional way.

"Billions of dollars have been wasted on marketing," say the authors. "Many managers assume that a well-designed, well-executed, well-financed marketing program will work. It's not necessarily so. And you don't have to look further than IBM, General Motors, and Sears Roebuck to find examples."

Rather, say Ries and Trout, marketers should play straight with the consumer. Herewith, three "immutable laws":

1. **The law of candor**   Tell consumers your problem, point out the negatives, and be honest with them if you want to look better in their eyes.

2. **The law of attributes**   Too often companies attempt to emulate the leader. They must know what works, goes the rationale, so let's do something similar. Not good thinking.

3. **The law of success**   Ego is the enemy of successful marketing. Objectivity is what's needed. When people become successful, they tend to be less objective. They often substitute their own judgment for what the consumer wants.

Public relations aspirants who wish to learn about perfecting their own consumer relations could gain much by reading this book.

Dickman, Steven. "Catching Customers on the Web," *Inc.* (Summer 1995): 56–61. How to turn browsers into customers.

Donnelly, James H., Jr. *Close to the Customer: Management Tips from the Other Side of the Counter.* Homewood, IL: Business One Irwin, 1991.

Fierman, Jaclyn. "Americans Can't Get No Satisfaction," *Fortune* (December 4, 1995): 186–192. Argues how companies, like FedEx, try harder to keep customers happy.

Gibson, Dirk C. "Public Relations Considerations of Consumer Recall," *Public Relations Review* (Fall 1995): 225–241.

Hanan, Mack, and Peter Karp. *Customer Satisfaction.* New York: AMACOM, 1991.

Johnston, Jo-Ann. "Who's Really the Villain?" *Business Ethics* (March–April 1995): 16–19. Relates the futility of community opposition to opening Wal-Mart stores in their area.

Lewis, Jordan D. *The Connected Corporation: How Leading Companies Win Through Customer-Supplier Alliances.* New York: The Free Press, 1995. Finds customers and suppliers forming alliances for their mutual benefit instead of engaging in adversarial wrangling.

Pertschuk, Michael. "Progressive Media Advocacy," *The Public Relations Strategist* (Winter 1995): 52–55. Former head of the Federal Trade Commission calls for consumer groups to use the media more readily in forwarding their cause.

Rice, Faye. "Making Generational Marketing Come of Age," *Fortune* (June 26, 1995): 110–114. Marketers are beginning to segment markets in terms of six discrete generations.

Speer, Tibbett. "How to be a Friend to Your Customers," *American Demographics* (March 1995): 14–16.

Stewart, Thomas A. "After All We've Done For You, Why Are You Still Not Happy?" *Fortune* (December 4, 1995): 178–181. Reports study that shows customer satisfaction down, despite rising expectations.

CASE STUDY

TOBACCO WARS

As the world moves into the twenty-first century, the manufacturers of cigarettes are engaged in nothing short of war.

In the last years of this century, cigarette companies have seen their products and advertising restricted, their executives denigrated before national panels, and their reputations tarnished with accusations of lying and worse.

The enemies of smoking have recast the pastime as nothing short of sin. Today smokers can no longer light up on airplanes, in restaurants, or in offices and stadiums. They have been branded as outcasts, forced to vacate the premises if they wish to light up.

As recently as the 1980s, Congressional and business deals were still made in smoke-filled rooms. Even the first Americans, Christopher Columbus wrote, carried a "fire brand in the hand, and herbs to drink the smoke thereof, as they are accustomed."

Smoking had always been politically sacrosanct, like guns. Tobacco companies produced jobs for workers and profits for shareholders and, not coincidentally, also financed political campaigns. Tobacco was untouchable, right up until 1994.

And then the roof caved in.

Permanent Political Shift

As more activist politicians spoke out against the dangers of smoking, particularly to young people, the political landscape began to shift. Some believe, the shift is irreversible.

- President Clinton proposed steep excise taxes on cigarettes as part of health care reform efforts.
- The Environmental Protection Agency classified secondhand smoke as a serious health risk. The House approved legislation barring smoking from most public places. The Department of Defense prohibited smoking in its workplaces worldwide.
- FDA Commissioner David A. Kessler, considered public enemy number one by tobacco companies, proposed treating tobacco products as drugs, based on "accumulating evidence" that the industry was using unnecessarily high levels of nicotine to create and maintain smokers' addiction.

- Lawsuits began to be filed around the country, including one by Mississippi's attorney general, seeking reimbursement for the estimated tens of millions of dollars that the state spent on medical care for tobacco-related illness. Other states, like Florida, initiated similar efforts.

Pressure on the major manufacturers of tobacco products increasingly found themselves under the spotlight.

Fatal Congressional Testimony

In February of 1994, tobacco makers appeared before Congress, denying that nicotine is addictive and that cigarettes have been proved to cause disease and more than 400,000 deaths a year. It was the first of many bitter confrontations (Figure 16–5).

As part of the hearing process, internal company documents were made public that shed light on the approach of cigarette companies in selling their product.

Among the documents was one detailing minutes of a meeting of Brown & Williamson executives held just before tobacco advertising was banned from radio and television in 1971. Code-named "Project Truth," the text of the presentation made at the meeting read in part:

> Doubt is our product, since it is the best means of competing with the "body of fact" that exists in the minds of the general public. With the general public, the consensus is that cigarettes are in some way harmful to their health.
>
> Unfortunately, we cannot take a position directly opposing the anti-cigarette forces and say that cigarettes are a contributor to good health. No information that we have supports this claim.

The objective of Project Truth was to "lift the cigarette from the cancer identification as quickly as possible and restore it to its proper place of dignity and acceptance in the minds of men and women in the marketplace of American free enterprise."

By the mid-1980s, according to the documents revealed at the hearing, the companies had forsaken attempts to exonerate smoking as a health hazard and seemed to shift to a legal concern "about what would happen if the years of studies on biological hazards of cigarettes were to become available to plaintiffs in court cases."

In later testimony, Kessler revealed information that Brown & Williamson developed a genetically engineered tobacco that would more than double the amount of nicotine delivered in some cigarettes. The company responded by calling Kessler's testimony "exaggerated."

Public Perception Grows Negative

The confusion and disputes resulting from the companies' testimony began to pile up publicly on cigarette manufacturers.

The American Heart Association, American Cancer Society, American Lung Association, and American Medical Association began to work together to win smoking bans.

Activists began to get access to caches of internal tobacco industry documents through lawsuits, such as the one filed by the family of Rose Cipollone, who died in 1984 at age 58. Her family won initially but dropped its suit in 1992 after 10 years of costly litigation. The cigarette companies refused to acquiesce.

Perhaps the most damning report was the EPA document on secondhand smoke, which said that environmental tobacco smoke causes 3,000 lung cancer deaths each year. When incoming Clinton Administration EPA Administrator Carol Browner was apprised

AN OPEN LETTER
TO THE AMERICAN PUBLIC

Tobacco Deals – Will They Protect Our Children?
Or is it About Money?

Big Tobacco can no longer be allowed to lie and deceive the American public about tobacco-related death and disease. In typical fashion, they are attempting to deal.

We are in a health crisis due to tobacco. The tobacco industry must be held accountable for the damage they've consciously caused and will continue to cause. The real issue here is how to preserve the health and lives of our citizens.

Americans should not ignore the issues that can give us the control we need to protect our kids:

- Nicotine, the drug in tobacco, is **addictive** and must be fully regulated by the US Food and Drug Administration.

- Big Tobacco can no longer be allowed to target our kids as new customers.

- We need to fund educational campaigns that tell the truth about tobacco addiction – with budgets that can effectively correct the lies Big Tobacco has planted over the last several decades.

- Big Tobacco and its allies push for federal laws that prevent state and local governments from protecting their citizens with tougher ordinances. This two-faced tactic must be stopped.

- We must protect the rights of present and future victims of tobacco-related disease to seek their own day in court.

All Americans should carefully scrutinize the details of any action or negotiation by Big Tobacco.

Don't let the tobacco industry walk away the winner. FDA authority over nicotine is mandatory. Congress should not get involved.

George Dessart
Chairman, National Board of Directors

Myles P. Cunningham, MD
President

John R. Seffrin, PhD
Chief Executive Officer

Figure 16–5   For years, the tobacco industry was an "untouchable" in Congress. Today, the tide has changed.

of the findings, she said, "Let that thing rip," and she began promoting the report heavily.

In the latter years of the decade, manufacturers faced a steadily declining public position.

- In February 1997, the FDA implemented regulations that forbade merchants from selling tobacco to minors.
- Cigarette advertising was the next to be attacked, with critics vowing to rid such advertising from the airwaves, where minors are exposed to it. Primary target was R.J. Reynolds' Joe Camel advertising campaign. Joe Camel, it was charged, represented a seductive appeal to young people. Although the FTC earlier decided not to pursue a complaint against Joe Camel, activists vowed to do whatever it took to get rid of Joe Camel (Figure 16–6).
- Cigarette package labeling became more restrictive. U.S. legislators looked toward Great Britain, where cigarette advertising is more tightly regulated and packs labeled with dire warnings (Figure 16–7).

Figure 16–6 Perhaps the most visible symbol of tobacco's influence on young people was the ubiquitous Joe Camel.

Figure 16–7   Warnings posted on cigarettes sold in Great Britain leave nothing to the imagination in terms of relative danger.

- In the most damaging blow yet for manufacturers, in 1997 the Liggett Group tobacco company agreed that its tests had indicated that cigarette smoking was in fact harmful to health and agreed to label its products accordingly. Liggett also acknowledged that it had consciously marketed its products for children.

Companies Dig In

For their part, the cigarette companies themselves remained adamant in their fight. Said the Philip Morris public affairs director, "There are risk factors in smoking. But 50 million adults have chosen to smoke and they have the right to make that decision."

In the wake of the Liggett bombshell, the industry's biggest companies, Philip Morris and R.J. Reynolds were reportedly on the verge of offering a $300 billion "global settlement" to "buy" immunity from tobacco litigation. Part of the settlement plan, reportedly, was RJR's willingness to drop Joe Camel from its advertising. Sure enough, as the summer of 1997 approached, the Federal Trade Commission announced it would go after Joe Camel to prevent its "insidious influence on under age smokers." By July 1997, RJR announced that Joe Camel was "dead."

By the end of the century, the cigarette companies stood in their most tenuous position in history. Summarized the communications director of the Tobacco Institute, "Our credibility with the general public has never been terribly high, and I don't think there's a great deal we can do about that."

Ironically, four decades earlier, the leaders of the tobacco industry met in New York with John W. Hill, founder of the world's largest public relations firm at the time, Hill & Knowlton. The subject was the "image of tobacco." A month after that meeting, the attendees ran an ad in more than 400 newspapers and magazines. The ad expressed concern about studies linking smoking to lung cancer in humans and promised that the industry would examine them. It also said, "Although conducted by doctors of professional standing, these experiments are not regarded as conclusive in the field of cancer research."

QUESTIONS

1. How would you assess the credibility of the cigarette industry today?
2. If you were hired as public relations counsel to the tobacco industry, what would you advise it to do?

For further information on the Tobacco Wars see Scott Cutlip, "The Tobacco War: A Matter of Public Relations Ethics," *Journal of Corporate Public Relations* (1992–1993): 26; Stuart Elliott, "When the Smoke Clears, It's Still Reynolds," *The New York Times* (September 13, 1995): D1; Philip J. Hilts, "Cigarette Makers Debated the Risks They Denied," *The New York Times* (June 16, 1994): A1; Youssef M. Ibrahim, "Cigarette Makers Cope with British Ad Restrictions," *The*

New York Times (April 18, 1997): D5; Mary Kuntz and Joseph Weber, "The New Hucksterism," *Business Week* (July 1, 1996); Warren E. Leary, "Cigarette Company Developed Tobacco With Stronger Nicotine," *The New York Times* (June 22, 1994): A1; Tara Parker-Pope, "Danger: Warning Labels May Backfire," *The Wall Street Journal* (April 28, 1997): B1; Eben Shapiro, "RJR Nabisco's Tobacco Unit Escapes Fight with FTC Over Joe Camel Ads," *The Wall Street Journal* (June 2, 1994); John Schwartz, "Double Blow for Tobacco Industry: Waxman Assails Research Council, Justice Dept. Probe Sought," *Washington Post* (May 27, 1994): A1.

VOICE OF EXPERIENCE

DIANE PERLMUTTER

Diane Perlmutter is managing director of Human Resources Worldwide of Burson-Marsteller, the world's largest public relations agency. Previously she was chairman of the U.S. Marketing Practice. She has created and managed multimillion dollar programs in virtually every marketing discipline, including advertising, sales promotion, merchandising, incentives, and employee motivation. Before joining Burson-Marsteller, Perlmutter was vice president of advertising and campaign marketing at Avon Products. Perlmutter also teaches public relations and is a frequent lecturer on public relations topics.

HOW SMART ARE CONSUMERS TODAY?

Today's consumers are very smart, a combination of "street smart" and "educated." Street smart because they are exposed to an incredible array of products in stores, catalogs, and on television. Consumers have a strong sense of value; they know what is good. Educated because they can access a wide range of information from manufacturers, independent evaluators, and stores (e.g., unit pricing).

HOW ENLIGHTENED ARE COMPANIES TODAY?

Companies that are the most successful are the most enlightened. They range from giants like Johnson & Johnson and Xerox to smaller firms like Snapple and Ben & Jerry's.

WHAT'S THE GENERAL STATE OF CONSUMER RELATIONS IN THE UNITED STATES TODAY?

Consumer relations are at an all-time high. And they keep improving every year as more companies make 800 numbers and other fast-response options available to their customers.

WHICH ARE THE MOST RESPONSIVE COMPANIES IN DEALING WITH CONSUMERS?

It's hard to single out the most responsive, but companies like GE, Gerber, and Cadillac are all doing an outstanding job.

WHAT ARE THE KEYS TO ORGANIZING A SUCCESSFUL CONSUMER RELATIONS PROGRAM?

The most successful are the most consumer friendly. Their attributes can be summed up with the acronym FRIEND: *F*lexible, *R*esponsive, *I*mmediate, *E*ducational, *N*eed-driven, and *D*edicated.

HOW POWERFUL IS THE CONSUMER MOVEMENT TODAY?

The consumer movement is so powerful that it's really no longer a movement. It's a way of life.

HOW SHOULD A COMPANY REACT TO CRITICISM OF ITS PRODUCTS BY CONSUMER ADVOCATES OR THE MEDIA?

Although all companies dislike having their products criticized, they should base their reaction on three key elements: (1) source of criticism, (2) reason for criticism, (3) validity of criticism. There's no silver bullet; each scenario requires a different response.

WHAT SHOULD A COMPANY DO IF ITS PRODUCTS ARE CONTAMINATED OR SABOTAGED?

A company has a responsibility to ensure that its products do not create a health and safety risk for the consumer. The company's response should always be based on this.

WHAT ROLE IS PUBLIC RELATIONS LIKELY TO CONTINUE TO PLAY WITH CONSUMER PRODUCT COMPANIES?

Public relations will become an increasingly important communications tool in consumer products companies. In a world that is growing increasingly complex, public relations is the best communications vehicle to give consumers complicated information in a meaningful and understandable way.

CHAPTER SEVENTEEN

Government

IN THE SPRING OF 1997, THE *New York Times* unloaded a page one bombshell, accusing the Clinton White House of securing suspicious Asian consulting work for an Arkansas friend, Whitewater confidante, and soon-to-be-jailed former Justice Department official Webster Hubbell. It was a story that, in the old days, would have put the White House on "red alert."

But in the spring of 1997, with the power of the media omnipresent, politicians handled things differently.

That afternoon, First Lady Hillary Clinton, appearing on a radio talk show, dismissed the latest Whitewater revelation as a "never-ending fictional conspiracy that honest-to-goodness reminds me of some people's obsession with U.F.O.'s and the Hale-Bopp comet some days." When "informed" of his wife's comments, President Clinton howled. The whole episode, duly reported on the same front page of the next day's *New York Times*, helped torpedo interest in the prior day's revelations.[1]

Such was the primary use of the media and the importance of public relations techniques in the arsenal of political forces in the latter days of the twentieth century.

Many argue that the government's ultimate power is the "power of persuasion," and once a politician loses sight of that, the results can be disastrous.

Indeed, a few months after Hillary's public relations coup in defusing the Hubbell story, Congressional Republicans demonstrated how negative public relations can harm a public office holder—or a political party. After horrendous floods devastated areas of North Dakota, in the summer of 1997 Congressional Republicans held a flood relief bill hostage to two meaningless and irrelevant amendments—despite the pleas of flood victims. Finally, after weeks of wrangling and bad press, the Republican leadership backed off and permitted the flood relief bill to pass—taking responsibility for a duly reported "public relations fiasco."[2]

Accordingly, as the twenty-first century approached, government officials had to be particularly mindful of the influence of the media, in particular, in the court of public opinion.

President John F. Kennedy was probably the first American president to recognize this. Kennedy went after the presidency "out of turn and essentially destroyed the old system of electing presidents." The only way he could get the job was by creating a new system in which the press was more important than old-fashioned politics.[3]

Nowhere was the immense power of communications in government more amply demonstrated than in the presidential campaign of 1996. Both parties shelved the traditional political conventions and instead held "prime time TV shows," in which events were controlled, choreographed and scripted down to the last second.

The Wall Street Journal labeled the practice, "the Oprahfication of American politics," where "image is everything, ideas are inconsequential, politicians are from Venus and reporters are from Mars."[4]

President Clinton, in the best communications traditions of Ronald Reagan before him, is a master communicator, who specializes in personalizing his messages and empathizing with his audiences. Indeed Clinton's walloping of Republican Bob Dole was interpreted by many as testimony to the former's formidable communications skills and the latter's valiant but unsuccessful attempt to shed his "darker image".

PUBLIC RELATIONS IN GOVERNMENT

The growth of public relations work both with the government and in the government has exploded in recent years. Although it is difficult to categorize exactly how many public relations professionals are employed at the federal level, it's safe to assume that thousands of public relations–related jobs exist in the federal government and countless others in government at state and local levels. Thus, the field of government relations is a fertile one for public relations graduates.

Since 1970 some 20 new federal regulatory agencies have sprung up, ranging from the Environmental Protection Agency to the Consumer Product Safety Commission to the Department of Energy to the Department of Education to the Drug Enforcement Agency. Moreover, according to the Government Accounting Office (GAO), some 116 government agencies and programs now regulate business.

Little wonder that today, American business spends more time calling on, talking with and lobbying government representatives on such generic issues as trade, interest rates, taxes, budget deficits, and all the other issues that concern individual industries and companies. Also, little wonder why political interest groups of every stripe—from Wall Street bankers to Asian influence seekers to friends of the earth—contribute more to political coffers than ever before. Thus, today's organizations continue to emphasize and expand their own government relations functions.

Beyond this, the nation's defense establishment offers some 3,000 public relations jobs in military and civilian positions. Indeed, with military service now purely voluntary, the nation's defense machine must rely on its public information, education, and recruiting efforts to maintain a sufficient military force. Thus, public relations opportunities in this realm of government work should continue to expand.

Ironically, the public relations function has traditionally been something of a stepchild in the government. In 1913, Congress enacted the Gillett amendment, which almost barred the practice of public relations in government. The amendment stemmed from efforts by President Theodore Roosevelt to win public support for his programs through the use of a network of publicity experts. Congress, worried about the potential of this unlimited presidential persuasive power, passed an amendment stating: "Appropriated funds may not be used to pay a publicity expert unless specifically appropriated for that purpose."

Several years later, still leery of the president's power to influence legislation through communication, Congress passed the gag law, which prohibited "using any part of an appropriation for services, messages, or publications designed to influence any member of Congress in his attitude toward legislation or appropriations." Even today, no government worker may be employed in the practice of public relations. However, the government is flooded with public affairs experts, information officers, press secretaries, and communications specialists.

GOVERNMENT PRACTITIONERS

Most practitioners in government communicate the activities of the various agencies, commissions, and bureaus to the public. As consumer activist Ralph Nader has said, "In this nation, where the ultimate power is said to rest with the people, it is clear that a free and prompt flow of information from government to the people is essential."

It wasn't always as essential to form informational links between government officials and the public. In 1888, when there were 39 states in the Union and 330 members in the House of Representatives, the entire official Washington press corps consisted of 127 reporters. Today there are close to 4,000 full-time journalists covering the capital.

In 1990, the U.S. Office of Personnel Management reported nearly 15,000 public relations–related jobs in government. These consisted of nearly 4,000 in public affairs; 2,000 in writing and editing; 1,700 in technical writing and editing; 2,000 in visual information; 3,300 in foreign information; and 2,000 in editorial assistance.[5]

In 1986, the GAO responded to an inquiry by former Senator William Proxmire, the last great government critic of federal waste, requesting "how much federal executive agencies spend on public relations." The GAO reported that the 13 cabinet departments and 18 independent agencies spent about $337 million for public affairs activities during fiscal 1985, with almost 5,600 full-time employees assigned to public affairs duties. In addition, about $100 million was spent for congressional affairs activities, with almost 2,000 full-time employees assigned. Also, about $1.9 billion—that's $1.9 billion—was spent, primarily in the Department of Defense, "for certain public affairs–related activities not classified as public affairs." These included more than $65 million for military bands, $13 million for aerial teams, $11 million for military museums, and more than $1 billion for advertising and printing regarding recruitment.

United States Information Agency

The most far-reaching of the federal government's public relations arms is the United States Information Agency (USIA), an independent foreign affairs agency within the executive branch. The USIA maintains 190 posts in 141 countries, where it is known as the U.S. Information Service (USIS). The agency employs 8,500, most of whom are Americans working in Washington, DC, and overseas and almost 4,000 foreign nationals hired locally in countries abroad.

Under law, the purpose of the USIA is to disseminate information abroad about the United States, its people, culture, and policies (Smith-Mundt Act of 1948) and to conduct educational and cultural exchanges between the United States and other countries (Fulbright-Hays Act of 1961). The director of the USIA reports to the president and receives policy guidance from the secretary of state.

The USIA employs 7,032 people, of whom 740 are foreign service personnel assigned overseas, assisted by 2,936 foreign service nationals. There are 3,356 employees based in the United States, of whom 2,093 are engaged in international broadcasting. The USIA's fiscal 1997 appropriation was a healthy $1.059 billion—slightly down from the days when America battled communism in the world of ideas.

In the latter stages of the twentieth century, with democracy spreading throughout the globe, the USIA's mission—"to support the national interest by conveying an understanding abroad of what the United States stands for"—has been modified to include five new challenges:

1. Build the intellectual and institutional foundations of democracy in societies throughout the world
2. Support the War on Drugs in producer and consumer countries
3. Develop worldwide information programs to address environmental challenges
4. Bring the truth to any society that fails to exercise free and open communication
5. Advise the president on foreign public opinion considerations[6]

Under the direction of such well-known media personalities as Edward R. Murrow, Carl Rowan, and Frank Shakespeare, the agency prospered. However, under the Reagan administration's director, Charles Z. Wick, the USIA became an unsurpassed force in communicating America's message. One of Wick's innovations was WORLDNET, a 30-country satellite television network, dubbed the "jewel in the crown" of the USIA's communication techniques. Other USIA vehicles include the following:

1. **Radio** Voice of America broadcasts 660 hours of programming weekly in 52 languages, including English, to an international audience. In addition to Voice of America, the USIA in 1985 began Radio Marti, in honor of José Marti, father of Cuban independence. Radio Marti's purpose is to broadcast 24-hours-a-day to Cuba in Spanish and "tell the truth to the Cuban people." TV Marti telecasts four and a half hours daily.
2. **Film and television** The USIA annually produces and acquires an extensive number of films and videocassettes for distribution in 125 countries.

3. **Media**   About 25,000 words a day are radiotele-typed to 214 overseas posts for placement in the media.
4. **Publications**   Overseas regional service centers publish 16 magazines in 18 languages and distribute pamphlets, leaflets, and posters to more than 100 countries.
5. **Exhibitions**   The USIA designs and manages about 35 major exhibits each year throughout the world, including Eastern European countries and the former Soviet Union.
6. **Libraries and books**   The USIA maintains or supports libraries in over 200 information centers and binational centers in more than 90 countries and assists publishers in distributing books overseas.
7. **Education**   The USIA is also active overseas in sponsoring educational programs through 111 binational centers where English is taught and in 11 language centers. Classes draw about 350,000 students annually.
8. **Electronic information**   USIA's electronic journals were created to communicate with audiences overseas on economic issues, political security and values, democracy and human rights, terrorism, the environment, and transnational information flow. The journals are transmitted in English, French, and Spanish to the USIS overseas. They are also transmitted on USIA's domestic World Wide Web site: *http:/www.usia.gov.*[7]

In 1993, President Clinton nominated Joseph D. Duffey, former president of American University, to head the USIA. His appointment was confirmed by the Senate in May 1993.

Government Agencies

Nowhere has government public relations activity become more aggressive than in federal departments and regulatory agencies. Many agencies, in fact, have found that the quickest way to gain recognition is to increase their public relations aggressiveness.

The Federal Trade Commission (FTC), which columnist Jack Anderson once called a "sepulcher of official secrets," opened up in the late 1970s to become one of the most active government communicators. In an earlier heyday, a former FTC director of public information described the agency's attitude, "The basic premise underlying the commission's public information program is the public's inherent right to know what the FTC is doing."[8] When the FTC found a company's products wanting in standards of safety or quality, it often announced its complaint through a press conference. Although corporate critics branded this process "trial by press release," it helped transform the agency from a meek, mild-mannered bureau into an office with real teeth.

The late nineties successor to the FTC was the Food and Drug Administration, particularly under President Clinton appointee Dr. David Kessler. Kessler, as noted, was an unbridled critic of products from fat substitutes to cigarettes to silicone breast implants. When Kessler stepped down in 1997, consumer advocates groaned while business groups cheered.

Other government departments also have stepped up their public relations efforts. The Department of Defense has more than 1,000 people assigned to public relations–related work. The Air Force alone answers about 35,000 letters annually from schoolchildren inquiring about this military branch. The Department of Health and Human

A QUESTION OF ETHICS

BAD CARMA FOR THE SECRETARY

Few individuals in authority—whether business, government or labor—relish being reported on. But in late 1995, Energy Secretary Hazel O'Leary may have gotten just a tad too paranoid (Figure 17–1).

Figure 17–1   Embattled Energy Secretary Hazel O'Leary.

According to a front page story in *The Wall Street Journal*, Secretary O'Leary "spent thousands of dollars in government money for a consulting firm, Carma International, to monitor the reporters who covered her department and rank them in terms of how favorable they were."

Carma evaluated articles about the department and ranked them on a scale of 1 to 100 in terms of "favorability." From this list, the firm ranked the 25 most favorable and 25 least favorable reporters, with the man from the Associated Press ranked lowest and the man from *The New York Times* ranked next lowest. The Carma analysis evaluated reporting on subjects as diverse as cleaning up nuclear waste to perceptions of the Secretary's own image.

The *Journal* story triggered a storm of protest, including from the White House, where the president's press secretary labeled the behavior "unacceptable." One senator demanded that Mrs. O'Leary herself reimburse the Treasury Department for spending $46,500 on Carma's monitoring. Said Nevada Democrat Richard H. Bryan, "Spending tax dollars to investigate and evaluate reporters and media coverage, complete with charts, is completely inappropriate. As Energy Secretary, she should be concerned with energy policy and not her image."

Carma officials and others in the public relations profession were quick to defend the research. Said Carma's senior vice president, "All we're trying to do is analyze the news coverage and let our clients know what's being said about them and then to put it in a context for them with regard to other reporters."

Another public relations professional, quoting the philosopher Socrates, who never had the benefit of computer analyses or electronic databases, said, "The way to gain a good reputation is to endeavor to be what you desire to appear."

In any event, the Energy Secretary herself, mightily embarrassed by the media blowup, nonetheless defended the practice as well. Carma, she said, "absolutely were not, as *The Wall Street Journal* inaccurately alleged, 'poking around in the lives of reporters who have been poking around the DOE.'" Nonetheless, after the flap died down, the Energy Department deepsixed the research, while questions lingered about the ethical propriety of evaluating reporters' coverage.

About the only ones pleased about the whole mess were the man from the Associated Press and the man from *The New York Times*.*

---

*For further information about Secretary O'Leary and Carma see, Neil A. Lewis, "Energy Secretary Used Fund to Monitor Reporters," *The New York Times* (November 10, 1995): 1; Paul Maccabee, "Ranting Over Ratings," *Public Relations Tactics* (January 1996): 1; and Joseph T. Nolan, "Track Performance Not Reporters," *The Public Relations Strategist* (Spring 1996): 14.

Services has a public affairs staff of 700 people. The departments of Agriculture, State, and Treasury each have communications staffs in excess of 400 people, and each spends more than $20 million per year in public relations–related activities. Even the U.S. Central Intelligence Agency has three spokesmen. Out of how many CIA public relations people? Sorry, that's classified.

The President

Despite early congressional efforts to limit the persuasive power of the nation's chief executive, the president today wields unprecedented public relations clout. Almost anything the president does or says makes news. The broadcast networks, daily newspapers, and national magazines follow his every move. His press secretary provides the White House press corps (a group of national reporters assigned to cover the president) with a constant flow of announcements supplemented by daily press briefings. Unlike many organizational press releases that seldom make it into print, many White House releases achieve national exposure.

Ronald Reagan was perhaps the most masterful presidential communicator in history. Reagan gained experience in the movies and on television, and even his most ardent critics agreed that he possessed a compelling stage presence. As America's president, he was truly the Great Communicator. Reagan and his communications advisors followed seven principles in helping to "manage the news":

1. Plan ahead.
2. Stay on the offensive.
3. Control the flow of information.
4. Limit reporters' access to the president.
5. Talk about the issues you want to talk about.
6. Speak in one voice.
7. Repeat the same message many times.[9]

So coordinated was Reagan's effort to "get the right story out" that even in his greatest public relations test—the accusation at the end of his presidency that he and his aides shipped arms to Iran and funneled the payments to support Contra rebels in Nicaragua, in defiance of the Congress—the president's "Teflon" image remained largely intact. The smears simply washed away.

George Bush was not as masterful as his predecessor in communicating with the American public. Indeed, Bush met his communications match in 1992, when Bill Clinton beat him soundly in the presidential race.

Clinton, learning from the disastrous presidential campaign of Democrat Michael Dukakis before him, organized a "media swat team" to beat back Republican allegations during the campaign. As soon as the Bush forces issued a charge against the Democrats, the Clinton "truth squad" rebutted the accusation.[10]

President Clinton, like Reagan before him, is a skilled communicator—particularly on a personal level. Using a technique mastered during the campaign, Clinton, in his first term, sought to escape the confines of the "Washington Beltway" by staging "town meetings" throughout America to help promote health care and other programs. Clinton has also brought presidential politics into the satellite era by appearing on CNN's *Larry King Live* program and conducting presidential satellite media tours similar to the ones staged in the campaign.[11] President Clinton's accessibility to the media and his common sense approach to dealing with media is greatly responsible for his popularity, despite a series of embarrassing scandals afflicting his administration during both terms of his presidency.

The President's Press Secretary

Some have called the job of presidential press secretary the second most difficult position in any administration. The press secretary is the chief public relations spokesperson for the administration. Like practitioners in private industry, the press secretary must communicate the policies and practices of the management (the president) to the public. Often, it is an impossible job.

In 1974, Gerald terHorst, President Ford's press secretary, quit after disagreeing with the pardon of former President Richard Nixon. Said terHorst, "A spokesman should feel in his heart and mind that the chief's decision is the right one, so that he can speak with a persuasiveness that stems from conviction."[12] A contrasting view of the press secretary's role was expressed by terHorst's replacement in the job, former NBC reporter Ron Nessen. Said Nessen, "A press secretary does not always have to agree with the president. His first loyalty is to the public, and he should not knowingly lie or mislead the press."[13] A third view of the proper role of the press secretary was offered by a former public relations professional and Nixon speechwriter who became a *New York Times* political columnist, William Safire:

> A good press secretary speaks up for the press to the president and speaks out for the president to the press. He makes his home in the pitted no-man's-land of an adversary relationship and is primarily an advocate, interpreter, and amplifier. He must be more the president's man than the press's. But he can be his own man as well.[14]

In recent years, the position of press secretary to the president has taken on increased responsibility and has attained a higher public profile. Jimmy Carter's press secretary, Jody Powell, for example, was among Carter's closest confidants and frequently advised the president on policy matters. After Powell left the government, he went on to found his own Washington public relations agency. Powell's successor as press secretary, James Brady, was seriously wounded in 1981 by a bullet aimed at President Reagan as they both departed from a Washington, DC, hotel. Although Brady was permanently paralyzed, he retained his title as presidential press secretary and returned for limited work at the White House. Later, the "Brady Bill," establishing new procedures for licensing handguns, was passed by the Congress, ironically due largely to Democratic support.

Brady was then replaced by Larry Speakes, a former Hill & Knowlton executive, who was universally hailed by the media for his professionalism. During Reagan's second term, Speakes apparently was purposely kept in the dark by Reagan's military advisors planning an invasion of the island of Grenada. An upset Speakes later apologized to reporters for misleading them on the Grenada invasion.

Speakes was replaced by a low-key, trusted, and respected lifetime government public relations professional, Marlin Fitzwater. Fitzwater distinguished himself in the last two years of the Reagan presidency and in the subsequent administration of President Bush. Fitzwater, in turn, was replaced by another career political public relations professional, Dee Dee Myers. Myers was equally respected by the media and brought a refreshing perspective to her role as President Clinton's press secretary. She later went on to become a cable talk show host and magazine editor.

The trend toward retaining experienced communications people continued in the second Clinton White House, with the president retaining experienced political hand Mike McCurry (see interview chapter 1) and the First Lady retaining Congressional staff veteran Marsha Berry (see interview this chapter) to head their respective communications operations.

Over the years, the number of reporters hounding the presidential press secretary—dubbed by some an imperial press corps—has grown from fewer than 300 reporters during President Kennedy's term to around 3,000 today. Salaries approaching six figures, rare in most media offices in prior years, are today common in Washington bureaus. And TV network White House correspondents command higher incomes, with each major network assigning two or three correspondents to cover the White House simultaneously. Dealing with such a host of characters is no easy task. Perhaps Lyndon Johnson, the first chief executive to be labeled an imperial president by the Washington press corps, said it best when asked by a TV reporter what force or influence he thought had done the most to shape the nature of Washington policy. "You bastards," Johnson snapped.[15]

```
       THE REST OF THE STORY
```

THE RAGIN' CAJUN AND THE SULTANS OF SPIN

One of the more unfortunate outgrowths of the Clinton years was the proliferation of "spin patrols" that followed every presidential appearance, debate or speech to influence the media to report a certain way.

So successful was the Clinton truth squad that batted back George Bush campaign accusations in 1992 that the president and his team kept the practice going throughout his presidency.

Undisputed leader of the Clinton "spinners" was James Carville, a no-holds-barred, out of the bayou political consultant, who parlayed his Clinton advice into lucrative book, movie, and lecture deals. No matter how controversial the issue, Carville took it on in defense of the president. In 1996, when special prosecutor Kenneth W. Starr focused his Whitewater investigation on Bill and Hillary Rodham Clinton, the president's "perception ambassador without portfolio" attacked Starr and his motives at every turn. Carville, in fact, conducted a one-man, preemptive public relations strike force against Starr.[16]

In attacking Starr publicly, even the president's supporters wondered whether Carville had gone too far, perhaps even influencing potential witnesses and grand jurors chosen to sit in judgment of the Clintons in their real estate dealings in Arkansas. Carville himself, oblivious to criticism, waved off the complaints. "Anybody that knows me knows that the last realm that I'm dealing in is a grand jury. I'm dealing in the realm of public perception."

Gradually, when even his Clinton allies began to keep their distance from the ranting Cajun, Carville's attacks on Starr's credibility simmered down. Nonetheless, the advisor's guerrilla public relations tactics were typical of the hard-nosed spin control that both parties, despite their disclaimers to the contrary, will likely continue to use into the twenty-first century.

Indeed, the Republican Party included its own Carville-like guerrilla spinner, Mary Matalan, chief party public hatchet wielder for the ill-fated Bush campaign. Ms. Matalan's married name? What else—Mrs. James Carville.

LOBBYING THE GOVERNMENT

The business community, foundations, and philanthropic and quasi-public organizations have a common problem: dealing with government, particularly the mammoth federal bureaucracy. Because government has become so pervasive in organizational and individual life, the number of corporations and trade associations with government relations units has grown steadily in recent years.

Government relations people are primarily concerned with weighing the impact of impending legislation on the company, industry group, or client organization. Generally, a head office government relations staff complements staff members who represent the organization in Washington, DC, and state capitals. These representatives have several objectives:

1. To improve communications with government personnel and agencies.
2. To monitor legislators and regulatory agencies in areas affecting constituent operations.
3. To encourage constituent participation at all levels of government.
4. To influence legislation affecting the economy of the constituent's area, as well as its operations.

5. To advance awareness and understanding among lawmakers of the activities and operations of constituent organizations.

Carrying out these objectives requires knowing your way around the federal government and acquiring connections. A full-time Washington representative is often employed for these tasks.

To the uninitiated, Washington (or almost any state capital) can seem an incomprehensible maze. Consequently, organizations with an interest in government relations usually employ a professional representative, who may or may not be a registered lobbyist, whose responsibility, among other things, is to influence legislation. Lobbyists are required to comply with the federal Lobbying Act of 1946, which imposed certain reporting requirements on individuals or organizations that spend a significant amount of time or money attempting to influence members of Congress on legislation.

In 1996, the Lobbying Disclosure Act took effect, reforming the earlier law. The new act broadened the activities that constitute "lobbying" and mandate government registration of lobbyists. Under the new law, a "lobbyist" is an individual who is paid by a third party to make more than one "lobbying contact," defined as an oral or written communication to a vast range of specific individuals in the executive and legislative branches of the federal government. In addition, lobbyists are prohibited from paying for meals for members of Congress or their aides. The law also broadened the definition of "lobbying activities," to include research and other background work prepared for a lobbying purpose.[17]

In fact, one need not register as a lobbyist in order to speak to a senator, congressional representative, or staff member about legislation. But a good lobbyist can earn the respect and trust of a legislator. Because of the need to analyze legislative proposals and to deal with members of Congress, many lobbyists are lawyers with a strong Washington background. Lobbying ranks are loaded with former administration officials and congressional members, who often turn immediately to lobbying when they move out of office.

Although lobbyists, at times, have been labeled everything from influence peddlers to fixers, such epithets are generally inaccurate and unfair. Today's lobbyist is more likely to be well informed in his or her field, furnishing Congress with facts and information. Indeed, the lobbyist's function is rooted in the First Amendment right of all citizens to petition government.

What Do Lobbyists Do?

The number of lobbyists registered with the U.S. Senate has increased from just over 3,000 in 1976 to upwards of 40,000 today. With the cost of lobbying efforts in the neighborhood of $100 million per year, lobbying has become big business.

But what exactly do lobbyists do?

In the spring of 1994, the Treasury Department issued a 30-page definition of lobbying that confounded most readers.[18] Among other decisions, the department ruled that anyone employed to "follow" federal or even state issues—say, by reading newspapers or magazines—is not engaged in lobbying. However, if the articles are clipped and filed as part of research intended to influence legislation, that, the department ruled, is lobbying.

The fact of the matter is, the essence of a lobbyist's job is to inform and persuade.

The contacts of lobbyists are important, but they must also have the right information available for the right legislator. The time to plant ideas with legislators is well before a bill is drawn up, and skillful lobbyists recognize that timing is critical in influencing legislation. The specific activities performed by individual lobbyists vary with the nature of the industry or group represented. Most take part in these activities:

1. **Fact finding** The government is an incredible storehouse of facts, statistics, economic data, opinions, and decisions that generally are available for the asking.

2. **Interpretation of government actions** A key function of the lobbyist is to interpret for management the significance of government events and the potential implications of pending legislation. Often a lobbyist predicts what can be expected to happen legislatively and recommends actions to deal with the expected outcome.

3. **Interpretation of company actions** Through almost daily contact with congressional members and staff assistants, a lobbyist conveys how a specific group feels about legislation. The lobbyist must be completely versed in the business of the client and the attitude of the organization toward governmental actions.

4. **Advocacy of a position** Beyond the presentation of facts, a lobbyist advocates positions on behalf of clients, both pro and con. Often, hitting a congressional representative early with a stand on pending legislation can mean getting a fair hearing for the client's position. Indeed, few congressional representatives have the time to study—or even read—every piece of legislation on which they are asked to vote. Therefore, they depend on lobbyists for information, especially on how the proposed legislation may affect their constituents.

5. **Publicity springboard** More news comes out of Washington than any other city in the world. It is the base for thousands of press, TV, radio, and magazine correspondents. This multiplicity of media makes it the ideal springboard for launching organizational publicity. The same holds true, to a lesser degree, in state capitals.

6. **Support of company sales** The government is one of the nation's largest purchasers of products. Lobbyists often serve as conduits through which sales are made. A lobbyist who is friendly with government personnel can serve as a valuable link for leads to company business.

In recent years, there has been no shortage of controversy surrounding former lobbyists entering the government and then allegedly assisting former clients. In 1997, as noted, President Clinton's closest advisors were called to task for allegedly recommending as a quasi-lobbyist, disgraced Justice Department official and former Hillary Clinton law partner Webster Hubbell to wealthy Indonesian business executives. In 1994, Secretary of Commerce Ron Brown was accused of interceding on behalf of a Vietnamese businessman. Secretary Brown managed to dodge the bullet and two years later was tragically killed in a Bosnian air crash. Later in the Clinton presidency, White House adviser Howard Paster left to become chairman of the Hill & Knowlton public relations firm. Although Paster did nothing wrong by accepting his new job, the furor over his appointment underscored the dilemma in the relationship of professional lobbyists to those being lobbied.

Grass-Roots Lobbying

Particularly effective in recent years has been the use of indirect, or grass-roots, lobbying (as opposed to conventional lobbying by paid agents). The main thrust of such lobbying is to mobilize local constituents of congressional members, together with the general public, to write, telephone, fax, or buttonhole members of Congress on legislation.

Grass-roots lobbying is a tactic that has been used most effectively by everyone from consumer advocates, such as Ralph Nader's organization and Common Cause, to the plaintiffs' bar in behalf of class action lawsuits to Presidents Bush and Clinton. In the early 1980s, a resurgence of citizens' activism, not seen since the 1960s, began to appear. Coalitions formed on both national and local levels on issues from arms to economics. Locally, tenants' organizations, neighborhood associations, and various other groups won significant concessions from government and corporate bodies.

The success of such grass-roots campaigns was not lost on big business. Business learned that grass-roots lobbying in the 1990s—applying pressure in the 50 states and the 435 congressional districts, from corporate headquarters to plant communities—lies at the heart of moving the powers in Washington. In one of the most successful campaigns in history, a massive grass-roots coalition beat back President's Clinton's energy tax in 1993. Constituents from all over the country—representing farmers, coal miners, aluminum manufacturers, the natural gas industry, home owners concerned about heating oil costs, and so on—wrote their congressional representatives and state legislators to pressure the White House. When the dust settled, the White House gave up on enacting a tax on the heat content of fuels.[19] A similar grassroots offensive torpedoed the Clinton health care initiative, to forward the cause of managed care.

Whatever the objectives, grass-roots lobbying and lobbying in general are very much in vogue as the nation heads into the twenty-first century (Figure 17–2). Rare is the group not represented in Washington. The popcorn industry has its Popcorn Institute. The International Llama Association has its own lobbyists. Hunters have Safari Club International. Those against hunting have the Fund for Animals. Those opposed to increased packaging requirements have United We Resist Additional Packaging (UN-WRAP). And all believe their lobbying efforts are most worthwhile.

POLITICAL ACTION COMMITTEES

The rise of political action committees (PACs) has been among the most controversial political developments in recent years. PACs grew in number from about 600 in 1974 to about 4,172 registered with the Federal Election Commission at the end of 1990. They contributed $159.3 million to candidates for the Senate and House of Representatives. Their influence on the political process is enormous.[20]

The increased influence of such groups on candidates is one reason why many people—including some legislators themselves—would like to see PACs severely curtailed or even banned. Indeed, in 1994, Congress severely limited what its members could accept in the form of trips and other niceties from the sponsors of PACs.

With just under 2,000 corporations, 750 associations, and 346 labor organizations sponsoring PACs, concern continues about the influence wielded by these committees. The evidence thus far is inconclusive. Although the number and size of PACs have increased, evidence of PAC-inspired indiscretions or illegalities has been minimal. Nonetheless, the furor over the heightened role of PACs in funding elections is bound to continue until campaign reform becomes reality.

HEALING HEALTH CARE THROUGH COOPERATION NOT CONFRONTATION

An open letter to Government leaders and all Americans concerned about health-care reform:

As a physician, I am deeply concerned about the state of our nation's health-care system. It is sick — not terminally ill by any means — but under great stress from costs that have gone up too fast and from inadequate care for 37 million Americans who lack insurance.

Like any serious illness, leaving this one unattended would be irresponsible and self-destructive. It would threaten our people's physical health and our nation's economic strength.

But the problem is very complex, reflecting the diversity of our society. And in our eagerness to fix it, the worst thing would be to look for a quick fix. In this case, we need a search for truth, not for scapegoats.

Unfortunately, the truth has been lost twice in recent searches for scapegoats: last week when America's immunization crisis was blamed on the rising price of vaccines; and earlier, when the Senate Special Committee on Aging reported that we at Merck broke our pledge not to raise prices faster than inflation. In both of these cases, information that was essential to understanding the whole truth was left out.

The truth is: vaccine distribution, not cost, stands between our children and full immunization. It is misleading to ignore the Government's own findings of why so many children aren't being vaccinated. A 1991 report by the National Vaccine Advisory Committee cited 13 barriers to immunization, *none of which was the cost of vaccines.*

A separate study by the Centers for Disease Control said the Government's delivery system was missing many children in rural areas and inner cities — children whose shots are already provided free by the public health clinics.

Comparing today's price for complete immunization to that of 10 years ago misses the mark for other reasons too:
1) In 1988, the Federal Government added an excise tax onto the price of all pediatric vaccines to fund The Childhood Vaccine Injury Compensation Act.
2) As a benefit of new research, children are now being immunized with two additional vaccines to provide protection against two serious infections: Hib meningitis and hepatitis B.

Fully 80% of the increase in cost to vaccinate children was due to these two factors. Only 20% was due to price increases.

Merck is a world leader in children's vaccines, and, for the last two years, our price to the Federal Government for our M-M-R®II vaccine (Measles, Mumps, Rubella) has been unchanged. I think our vaccine that protects children from three potentially debilitating diseases provides outstanding value for the $10.89 per dose it costs the Federal Government. As the President has noted, every dollar invested in immunization saves $10 in avoidable health-care costs.

I would also like to address the Senate Committee's report that said Merck broke its pledge not to raise prices faster than inflation. We take this charge very seriously, because it questions Merck's most valuable asset — our integrity and corporate reputation.

> "We need a search for truth, not for scapegoats."

> "Merck is committed to helping cure America's health-care ills."

The truth is: Merck kept its promise, and we will continue to do so.

Three years ago, we were the first pharmaceutical company to pledge not to raise our prices faster than inflation, calculated on a *weighted average* basis across our entire product line. We defined inflation as measured by the Consumer Price Index. And we have most definitely kept our pledge.

In 1992, for example, we didn't even recover inflation, because the end result of all our pricing actions — increases, rebates and discounts — was only a 2.7% increase. For the full three years, inflation in the United States averaged 4.0%, and our three-year price increases averaged 3.6%.

That's a far cry from how Merck was portrayed in the Senate Committee report. Unfortunately, the report focused on only 10 products rather than the entire 76 products in our line. This was misleading and unfair.

Like the Clinton Administration, Merck is sincere about improving health care — but the search for solutions must be honest and complete. Prescription drugs account for less than 7 cents of every health-care dollar. And good medicines save more money than they cost by keeping people out of hospitals, out of operating rooms, and out of nursing homes.

I strongly encourage Government officials to work *with* companies like Merck — companies striving to solve our problems. We are participants in the health-care system. We have insights that we'd like to contribute to any discussion of health-care reform. What's more, we're eager to work with Government leaders and health-care providers to bring about meaningful changes that improve the lives of all Americans.

We are dedicated to improving health care. That's why Merck plowed back over $1.1 billion into research and development in 1992 in a tireless effort to conquer AIDS, cancer, Alzheimer's and other devastating diseases.

I want our leaders and all Americans to know that Merck is true to its word. We weren't being "America's Most Admired Corporation"* seven years in a row based on deceit and broken promises. We stand by our pledge, and we stand by the record.

Merck is committed to helping cure America's health-care ills. But to do so, we need unwavering cooperation from every American, both inside and outside of Government. Above all, we need dedication to the truth — the whole truth.

Roy Vagelos

P. Roy Vagelos, M.D.
Chairman & Chief Executive Officer
Merck & Co., Inc.

 MERCK

Fortune magazine's annual Survey of Corporate Reputations

Figure 17–2 One way to reach government officials is to go over their heads to the ultimate authority: The American people. That's what Merck & Company did in 1994 on the burning national issue of health care.

▲▲▲▲▲

THE REST OF THE STORY

THE "BE" LIST OF GETTING THROUGH TO LEGISLATORS

Pat Choate, a veteran government relations professional at TRW Corporation, offered the following "be" list for anyone wishing to get through to legislators:

- **Be independent.** Policymakers value an independent view.
- **Be informed.** Government thrives on information. Timely facts, a deep knowledge of the subject, and specific examples are invaluable.
- **Be bipartisan.** Matters are more likely to be addressed on merit if approached in a bipartisan manner. Although it is necessary to be sensitive to political nuances, politics is best left to the politicians.
- **Be published.** Clear and cogent thinking, in articles and op-ed pieces, is noticed in Washington and at the statehouse.
- **Be broad-minded.** Don't peddle petty self-interest. Address the broader interests, and your counsel will be sought.
- **Be persistent.** A long-term, persistent commitment of time is mandatory in dealing with legislators.
- **Be practical.** Politicians value practical recommendations they can defend to their constituents.
- **Be honest.** Politicians and the press are skilled at spotting phonies. Honesty is the best policy. It works.

Source: Cindy Skrzycki, "Possible Leaders Abound in Business Community," *The Washington Post* (January 24, 1988): D-2.

DEALING WITH LOCAL GOVERNMENT

In 1980, Ronald Reagan rode to power on a platform of New Federalism, calling for a shift of political debate and public policy decisions to state and local levels. Presidents Bush and Clinton picked up the same initiative when they assumed power. Thus, it became more important for public relations people to deal with local, state, and regional governments.

Dealing with such local entities, of course, differs considerably from dealing with the federal government. For example, opinion leaders in communities (those constituents with whom an organization might want to affiliate to influence public policy decisions) might include such sectors as local labor unions, teachers, civil service workers, and the like. Building a consensus among such diverse constituents is pure grass-roots public relations. The very nature of state and local issues makes it impossible to give one, all-encompassing blueprint for successful government relations strategies.

Although the federal government's role—in wielding power and employing public relations professionals—is significant, state and local governments also are extremely important. Indeed, one viable route for entry-level public relations practitioners is through the local offices of city, county, regional, and state government officials.

In local government offices themselves, the need for public relations assistance is equally important. Local agencies deal directly—much more so than their counterparts in Washington—with individuals. State, county, and local officials must make themselves available for local media interviews, community forums and debates, and even door-to-door campaigning. In recent years, local and state officials have found that direct contact with constituents—often through call-in radio programs—is invaluable, not only in projecting an image, but also in keeping in touch with the voters.

Such officials, assigned to ensure the quality of local schools, the efficiency of local agencies, and the reliability of local fire and police departments, increasingly require smart and experienced public relations counsel. State and local information officer positions, therefore, have become valued and important posts for public relations graduates.

SUMMARY

The pervasive growth of government at all levels of society may not be welcome news for many people. However, government's growth has stimulated the need for increased public relations support and counsel.

The massive federal government bureaucracy, organized through individual agencies that seek to communicate with the public, is a vast repository for public relations jobs. The most powerful position in the land—that of president of the United States—has come to rely on public relations counsel to help maintain a positive public opinion of the office and the incumbent's handling of it.

On state and local levels, public relations expertise also has become a valued commodity. Local officials, too, attempt to describe their programs in the most effective manner. In profit-making and nonprofit organizations alike, the need to communicate with various layers of government also is imperative. Government relations positions in industry, associations, labor unions, and nonprofit organizations have multiplied.

Like it or not, the growth of government in our society appears unstoppable. As a result, the need for public relations support in government relations will clearly continue to grow into the next century.

DISCUSSION STARTERS

1. Why is the public relations function regarded as something of a stepchild in government?
2. What is the primary function of the USIA?
3. What is meant by "trial by press release"?
4. Why was Ronald Reagan called the Great Communicator?
5. What is the function of the White House press secretary?
6. What are the objectives of government relations officers?
7. What are the primary functions of lobbyists?
8. What is meant by "grass-roots lobbying"?
9. What are the pros and cons of PACs?
10. What is President Clinton's strength as a communicator?

NOTES

1. James Bennet, "First Lady Denies a Scheme on Hubbell and Whitewater," *The New York Times* (April 11, 1997): 1.
2. Jerry Gray, "Flood Relief Bill Passes as G.O.P., in Turmoil, Yields," *The New York Times* (June 13, 1997): 1.
3. Richard Reeves, "The Exterminator," *CJR* (November/December 1996): 67.
4. "Bathos and Credibility," *The Wall Street Journal* (August 20, 1996): A8.
5. Interview with Office of Communications, U.S. Office of Personnel Management, December 10, 1990.
6. "A Critical Article About Bruce Gelb," *Public Relations News* (June 25, 1990): 1.
7. "Fact Sheet," United States Information Agency, 301 4th Street, S.W., Room 602, Washington, DC 20647, November 1996.
8. David H. Buswell, "Trial by Press Release?" *NAM Reports* (January 17, 1972): 9–11.
9. Mark Hertsgaard, "Journalists Played Dead for Reagan—Will They Roll Over Again for Bush?" *Washington Journalism Review* (January–February 1989): 31.
10. Douglas Jehl and Thomas B. Rosenstiel, "Clinton Camp Orchestrates Effort at Message Control," *Los Angeles Times* (August 18, 1992): A1, A12.
11. Richard L. Berke, "Satellite Technology Allows Campaigns to Deliver Their Messages Unfiltered," *The New York Times* (October 22, 1992): A16.
12. Robert U. Brown, "Role of Press Secretary," *Editor & Publisher* (October 19, 1974): 40.
13. I. William Hill, "Nessen Lists Ways He Has Improved Press Relations," *Editor & Publisher* (April 10, 1975): 40.
14. William Safire, "One of Our Own," *The New York Times* (September 19, 1974): 43.
15. Michael J. Bennett, "The 'Imperial' Press Corps," *Public Relations Journal* (June 1982): 13.
16. Katharine Q. Seelye, "Carville's Theatrics Jolt Holiday Calm," *The New York Times* (December 17, 1996): 21.
17. "PR Is Lobbying? Read the New Law," *Next*, Number 2 1996, Edelman Public Relations Worldwide, 1500 Broadway, New York, NY 10036.
18. Robert D. Hershey, Jr., "In Very Fine Print the Treasury Defines a Lobbyist," *The New York Times* (May 11, 1994): A16.
19. Michael Wines, "Taxes' Demise Illustrate First Rule of Lobbying: Work, Work, Work," *The New York Times* (June 14, 1993): A1, A14.
20. Edward Zuckerman, *Almanac of Federal PACs: 1992* (Washington, DC: Amward Publications, 1992): IX.

SUGGESTED READINGS

Bogart, Leo. *Cool Words, Cold War*. Lanham, MD: University Press of America, 1995. Examines principles and beliefs that have guided American propaganda operations.

Byrnes, Mark E. *Politics and Space: Image Making by NASA*. Westport, CT: Praeger, 1994. The National Aeronautics and Space Administration has had a provocative public relations history. Its performance in the ill-fated Challenger tragedy was, itself, tragic. But beyond that, NASA is one of the most effective government agencies in communicating its messages. This book looks comprehensively at NASA's communications history.

DICK MORRIS

BEHIND THE OVAL OFFICE: WINNING THE PRESIDENCY IN THE NINETIES

NEW YORK: RANDOM HOUSE, 1997

JOHN BRADY

BAD BOY: THE LIFE AND POLITICS OF LEE ATWATER

NEW YORK: ADDISON WESLEY, 1997

Disgraced Clinton advisor Dick Morris and the late Bush advisor Lee Atwater had much in common. Both were brash, egotistical, and never in doubt. They also were arguably the brightest of a new wave of political consultants, who go for the jugular first and ask questions later.

In his memoir (which was written without the knowledge of his employers), Morris reveals a president eager for strong advice from a media-savvy consultant. Morris claims to have given Clinton the key advice that led to his triumph in 1996 over Senator Robert Dole. While attacking Dole in ads that ran outside the media capitals of New York and Washington (and thus were imperceptible to nosy reporters), Morris claims to have advised Clinton to run on his record and not stoop to *ad hominem* attacks.

Although Morris' self-congratulatory tone tests one's patience ("Nobody ever talks to a president as I had," is one understated comment.), Bill Clinton did get elected listening to the consultant's advice.

So, too, did George Bush listening to Lee Atwater. Atwater, who died of brain cancer, was every bit as potent in the Bush White House as Morris was in Clinton's. This book describes Atwater's blood and guts tactics and the strategies that underpinned them.

To learn what political consultants do and the power they exert on candidates, these two books are eminently worthwhile.

Dennis, Lloyd. *Practical Public Affairs in an Era of Change.* New York: The Public Relations Society of America, 1995. A comprehensive guide to contemporary public affairs practice, offering the latest thinking and action programs impacting government and public policy.

Eggers, William D., and John O'Leary. *Revolution at the Roots: America's Quest for Smaller, Better Government.* New York: The Free Press, 1995. Maintains that a revolution is sweeping across America to return power and influence to states and municipalities.

Elster, Jon, ed. *Local Justice in America.* New York: Russell Sage Foundation, 1995. Justice plays a central role in public relations practice, and this book examines aspects of justice, including government relations principles.

Fisher, Louis. *Presidential War Power.* Lawrence: University Press of Kansas, 1995. Few command the public relations prominence and power as the president of the United States, particularly during war time. This book examines this unique phenomenon.

Fitzwater, Marlin. *Call the Briefing! Reagan and Bush, Sam and Helen: A Decade with Presidents and the Press.* New York: Times Books, 1995. The trials and tribulations of a longtime political press secretary, done occasionally humorously but also with deadly seriousness in other spots.

Greenberg, Mike. *The Poetics of Cities: Designing Neighborhoods that Work.* Columbus: Ohio State University Press, 1995. Examines the politics of municipalities, including communications aspects on the local level.

Grossman, Lawrence K. *The Electronic Republic: Reshaping Democracy in the Information Age.* New York: Viking, 1995. A discussion of government relations in a democracy rooted in information technology. How times will change.

Howard, Philip K. *The Death of Common Sense: How Law is Suffocating America.* New York: Random House, 1995. Posits the view that regulation at all levels is breeding contempt for the governmental system of the United States.

Manheim, Jarol B. *All of the People, All of the Time: Strategic Communications and American Politics.* Armonk, NY.: M. E. Sharpe, 1991.

Pratkanis, Anthony, and Elliot Aronson. *Age of Propaganda: The Everyday Use and Abuse of Persuasion.* New York: W. H. Freeman and Company, 1996. This book focuses on the peculiar persuasion proclivities of politicians in the midst of running for office.

Public Affairs Council. *Leveraging State–Government Relations.* Washington, DC.: Public Affairs Council, 1990.

Smucker, Bob. *The Nonprofit Lobbying Guide.* San Francisco: Jossey-Bass, 1991.

Susskind, Lawrence, and Patrick Field. *Dealing with an Angry Public: The Mutual Gains Approach to Resolving Disputes.* New York: The Free Press, 1996. Outlines the six key elements of the "mutual gains approach" to help business and government get along.

Walsh, Kenneth T. *Feeding the Beast: The White House Versus the Press.* New York: Random House, 1996. The press that covers the executive branch of government is characterized by a surly, snarling bunch of pit bulls. And those are the pleasant ones! Or at least that's what Kenneth Walsh argues in this book. A former senior correspondent for *U.S. News and World Report*, he knows whereof he speaks.

Wittenberg, Ernest, and Elizabeth Wittenberg. *How to Win in Washington.* Cambridge, MA.: Basil Blackwell, 1990.

Yinger, John. *Closed Doors, Opportunities Lost: The Continuing Costs of Housing Discrimination.* New York: Russell Sage Foundation, 1995. Another aspect of government relations—dealing with the important issue of housing and the lack thereof among certain groups in society.

CASE STUDY

WHITEWATER

> "Whitewater is not about cover-ups, it's about screw-ups."—David Gergen, White House Adviser

On April 22, 1994, more than two years after the name "Whitewater" first appeared in the public press, Hillary Clinton conducted a press conference to clear the air. Sitting in a simple chair in front of a White House portrait of Abraham Lincoln, the First Lady gave a masterful performance, answering an hour's worth of reporters' questions about the ill-fated land deal known as Whitewater.

As effective as the First Lady's performance was, it also underscored the serious public relations crisis that the president and his associates had let Whitewater become. For a while Clintonian defenders, ranging from former U.S. Senator George McGovern to former Watergate lawyer Samuel Dash to humorist Garrison Keillor, bristled at what they claimed were "trumped-up charges that Whitewater was Bill Clinton's Watergate," the crisis was as serious as any impacting the Clinton presidency.

As proof, shortly before the First Lady's press conference, an emergency panel of public relations heavyweights—including Anne Wexler of the Wexler Group, Jody Powell of Powell/Tate, and Paul Costello of Edelman, Inc.—hurriedly formed the Back to Business Committee to defend the Clintons from Whitewater attacks. "This was a political, not an ethical, situation," Costello said. "We wanted to provide perspective."

The background of the president's Whitewater investment and subsequent connection to a failed savings and loan institution was an intricate and complicated story. The story broke originally on the front page of *The New York Times* in March 1992 and was promptly ignored by the world.

The story may well have remained ignored had not one unfortunate incident befallen the Clinton administration (Figure 17–3).

Figure 17–3 Although President Clinton put up a good front during the Whitewater mess, including this effort in behalf of National Youth Service Day, he couldn't run away from the crisis.

Vince Foster, trusted Clinton confidante and personal attorney on such matters as Whitewater, shot himself in the head and was found dead in a Washington park near the Potomac River.

Thus were the floodgates of Whitewater unleashed for a critical press and a curious public. Although all the facts surrounding Whitewater may never be known, what is known is that at several key junctures, the Clinton public relations machinery fell asleep at the switch. Consider the following:

As early as 1990, when then Governor Clinton faced stiff opposition in Arkansas, he released his tax returns for the previous 10 years. Curiously, he drew the line at 1980 even though he'd been governor in 1978–1979. Tax returns for 1978–1979 were conveniently not shared.

In 1992, during the presidential campaign, *The New York Times* asked how the Clintons could afford a $60,000 down payment on a house in 1980 when they'd both been earning much smaller salaries.

The answer, according to Mrs. Clinton, was that the money came from "savings and a gift from our parents." The Clinton campaign, meanwhile refused to release the 1978–1979 returns, causing media mavens to wonder what they were hiding.

Later on, in 1994, when Whitewater reemerged as a national issue after the Foster suicide, Clinton officials still refused to disclose pertinent data.

- White House Counsel Bernard Nussbaum removed Whitewater files from Foster's office after his death; people wondered what was being withheld.
- The White House initially refused to reveal how much of her own money Mrs. Clinton had used to make a miraculous $100,000 profit in the cattle futures market. People wondered what was being covered up.
- When Republicans called for a special investigator, the president first refused and then agreed to appoint a special counsel to investigate Whitewater. People wondered what he was shielding.

Meanwhile, Mrs. Clinton fared even worse.

Up to the time of Whitewater, the transformation of Hillary Clinton from obedient campaign spouse to White House policy dynamo was unprecedented in American political history.

In the first year of the Clinton presidency, no administration figure was more powerful and revered than the First Lady. Even Capitol Hill Republicans agreed that Hillary's health care testimony was pointed, poignant, and persuasive.

But when Whitewater struck, Hillary clammed up.

She ducked. She was unavailable. When she appeared in public at hospitals and schools, reporters were kept out of conversational range. When her good friends, Nussbaum, and Justice Department attorney Webster Hubbell, were forced to depart Washington, she uttered no public word.

Opined *New York Times* columnist Frank Rich, "Since she has the political capital, the firsthand knowledge, the poise and brains to answer many of the growing list of Whitewater questions, why not do so?"

Why not, indeed?

And then there were the president's spokespeople. Almost from the beginning, Whitewater was a study in spokesperson futility.

- George Stephanopoulos, the president's senior advisor, returned to Washington fresh from a New Year's 1994 ski holiday and declared on national television, "All of the pertinent papers in the Whitewater matter have been turned over to the Justice Department."

Wrong. In fact, no papers had been delivered.

It was left to Dee Dee Myers, the valiant White House press secretary, to correct Stephanopoulos's ill-timed remarks. The president's adviser, Myers suggested, had, in a phrase reminiscent of Nixonian Washington, "misspoken himself."

- Later on, the president's attorney, David Kendall, finally released the long-sought 1978–1979 tax returns in what he called "a spirit of full cooperation and openness."

Well, sort of.

The returns reported Mrs. Clinton's windfall cattle futures profits, all right, but failed to include supporting records. The media screamed.

- Finally, in what may have been the most unfortunate example of "misspeaking oneself," Paul Begala, a longtime Clinton spokesman, purred to a *Larry King* national television audience, "Both Clintons, they just missed the 1980s. These people are just not motivated by money."

Shortly thereafter, Mrs. Clinton's $100,000 cattle futures return on a $1,000 "investment" was revealed.

Perhaps the most unfortunate victim of Whitewater was public relations veteran David Gergen. Until Whitewater occurred, David Gergen was the unquestioned savior of the presidential image. The former Nixon-Ford-Reagan loyalist was recruited by President Clinton to turn around a reeling reputation. Over the ensuing months, as the president's popularity ascended, Gergen became the most prominent administration strategist and most visible presidential booster.

Then came Whitewater.

And counselor Gergen disappeared from the radar screen. He remained inexplicably invisible for weeks until the day *The New York Times* rousted him out for a front-page roasting.

"With Boss Besieged, Gergen Finds Himself," clucked the *Times* headline.

Several weeks later, it was reported that adviser Gergen was on his way out of the administration and back to college (to teach at Duke). Yet another impeccable reputation had been drenched by Whitewater.

Whitewater refused to go away in the second Clinton administration. With independent prosecutor Kenneth Starr firmly on the case, the president and his wife just couldn't seem to shake the lingering charges and counter charges. When the president's former Whitewater business partners, James and Susan McDougall were thrown in jail, suspicions lingered that the imprisoned pair would eventually "rat out" their former partners. Meanwhile, the press—particularly *The New York Times*—which broke the Whitewater story years earlier, would not relent in its hounding of the first couple on Whitewater, continuing to report on the controversy well into 1997.

In the aftermath of the Whitewater saga, it was left to Leonard Garment, a close advisor to President Nixon during his Watergate trauma, to put the whole thing in perspective: "In Watergate, there were two guys trying to get the Pulitzer, and in Whitewater there are roughly 50,000. Therefore, there has been an intensification by a very large factor of the pressure for disclosure . . . the creation of a mood of suspicion . . . and a generalized sense of outrage in Congress and the press at any attempts to withhold information."

In Whitewater, as in Watergate—and as in countless other crises afflicting countless other organizations—the best public relations remedy remained the oldest public relations bromide: "Whenever possible, tell the truth."

QUESTIONS

1. How would you characterize the Clintons' approach to disclosure with respect to Whitewater?
2. What was wrong with Mrs. Clinton's initial silence on Whitewater?
3. How would you assess Mr. Clinton's press conference in April 1994?
4. What lessons can be drawn from the missteps of the president's spokespeople?
5. What lessons can be drawn from the experiences of David Gergen?
6. What would you advise the president to do now to put Whitewater behind him?

For further information on Whitewater, see Richard L. Berke, "With Boss Besieged, Gergen Finds Himself," *The New York Times* (March 10, 1994): A1, A20; George J. Church and Michael Kramer, "Into the Line of Fire," *Time* (April 4, 1994): 20–26; Nancy Gibbs, "The Trials of Hillary," *Time* (March 21, 1994): 28–37; Frank Rich, "The Silent Partner," *The New York Times* (March 10, 1994): A23; William Safire, "The Whitewater Pulse," *The New York Times* (April 11, 1994): A24; and "Whitewater, Watergate," The *Wall Street Journal* (March 11, 1994): A12.

VOICE OF EXPERIENCE

MARSHA BERRY

Marsha Berry was named Director of Communications for the First Lady in June of 1996. Berry spent more than 16 years working in the U.S. Senate for Senator Patrick Leahy (D-VT) and Senator Robert Byrd (D-WV). During that time, she worked her way up through the ranks to become the press secretary for Senator Byrd and the Senate Appropriations Committee. Berry is a 1975 graduate of the University of Vermont.

WHAT DO YOU CONSIDER YOUR PRIMARY MISSION?

I view my job as having two primary goals. My first duty is to see that the public gets to know the First Lady and her interests and goals. I also have responsibility to assist the media who cover Mrs. Clinton to help assure their stories are as accurate and fair as possible and that the coverage of this is meaningful and lasting.

WHAT IS YOUR DAILY ACCESS TO THE FIRST LADY?

I meet regularly with Mrs. Clinton, although this can vary depending on the circumstances of a given day.

HOW WOULD YOU CHARACTERIZE YOUR RELATIONSHIP WITH THE FIRST LADY?

I have a relationship with Mrs. Clinton that is professional but also caring and respectful.

HOW DOES YOUR JOB DIFFER FROM THAT OF YOUR COUNTERPART ON THE PRESIDENT'S STAFF?

The President's press secretary is responsible for a broad range of issues effecting the nation both domestically and internationally. As a result, his press secretary is really in the "hot seat" on a daily basis. Needless to say, our focus is much narrower and thus my dealings with the press are less frenetic.

WHAT SHOULD BE THE PROPER RELATIONSHIP BETWEEN THE WHITE HOUSE AND THE MEDIA?

I believe the key to the relationship between the White House and the media that cover the White House is mutual respect. Quite frankly, the press has an important and necessary role in our democracy. I think that although there can be disagreements about specific stories, I value reporters who produce stories that are fair and balanced.

WHAT ARE THE MOST IMPORTANT ATTRIBUTES IN YOUR JOB?

I think the most important attributes are to maintain the respect and confidence of both the First Lady and the press. This often requires persistence, flexibility, patience, and good humor.

WHAT HAS BEEN YOUR TOUGHEST ASSIGNMENT IN THIS ROLE?

The toughest part of my job was to gain the confidence of those I work with and for.

HOW DOES THE FIRST LADY FEEL ABOUT THE MEDIA?

She understands the incredible power and influence the media have in our system of government. I think she wishes they would spend more time focusing on what is positive and working in our country.

WHAT IS THE MOST REWARDING PART OF YOUR JOB?

I find it very satisfying to be part of actions and events that affect and change public policy and sometimes history.

HOW DOES ONE BECOME COMMUNICATIONS DIRECTOR FOR THE FIRST LADY?

In my case, I worked for over two decades in Washington including 16 years on Capitol Hill. Quite honestly though, a dose of good timing and luck always helps.

CHAPTER EIGHTEEN

Public Relations and the Law

THERE CAN BE LITTLE DOUBT THAT AS the nation rolls into the twenty-first century, public relations practice has become a priority for lawyers in the midst of pleading their cases.

- In perhaps the most celebrated legal case of this century, charging sports icon O. J. Simpson with the brutal killings of his wife and her friend, the Heisman Trophy winner's high-priced lawyers studiously worked the media and, despite overwhelming evidence against their client, managed to evoke a "not guilty" verdict from a Los Angeles jury.
- When celebrated Air Force bomber pilot Lieutenant Kelly Flinn was charged with adultery, violating a direct order and lying to her superiors, she and her advisors seized an unprecedented strategy on the way to her court-martial trial: They went public. After tearful appearances with her family on *60 Minutes* and interviews with all the major media, Lt. Flinn convinced Air Force Secretary Sheila Widnall to grant her a general discharge, thus staving off a tidal wave of negative publicity for the military.[1]
- And when the Supreme Court ruled against President Clinton in his attempt to delay the Paula Jones sexual harassment suit against him, the President's lead attorney Robert Bennett told interviewer Ted Koppel that if the case proceeded, he would have no choice but to disclose Jones' past sexual history. Later, after backing down from this threat, the President's and Jones' lawyers appeared on competing Sunday morning television talk shows, each launching "trial balloons" to seek an out-of-court settlement.

Today, publicity and public relations have become so important, particularly in high profile legal cases, that many times such activities became more critical than events in the courtroom—in the rare instances when such cases actually reached the courtroom.

Despite increasing use by lawyers of public relations strategies and methods, the job of a lawyer differs markedly from that of a public relations counselor.

A lawyer, the old saw goes, tells you what you must do. A public relations professional, on the other hand, tells you what you should do. Therein lies the difference and the tension between the two functions.

A lawyer, correctly, must counsel the client on how best to perform in a court of law. A public relations professional must counsel a client on how to perform most effectively in another court—the court of public opinion.

There is a huge difference.

"Conclusions to be reached in a case will be induced only by evidence and argument in open court and not by outside influence, whether private talk or public print," proclaimed U.S. Supreme Court Justice Oliver Wendell Holmes in 1907. The esteemed justice obviously had no idea that approximately 90 years later, advances in technology would allow potential jurors throughout the community, as well as worldwide, to view an incident on video dozens of times and to listen to hundreds of commentators offer their opinions on a case before ever being invited to enter a courtroom.[2]

In recent years, defendants ranging from sports stars Frank Gifford and Mike Tyson to broadcaster Marv Albert to the president of the United States have found themselves judged guilty before ever entering a courtroom. So pervasive and powerful is communication in our society that public relations professionals have come to play an increasingly pivotal role in influencing public opinion, winning contested settlements, and, in general, affecting the outcome of legal issues.

PUBLIC RELATIONS AND THE LAW: AN UNEASY ALLIANCE

The legal and public relations professions have historically shared an uneasy alliance. Public relations practitioners must always understand the legal implications of any issue with which they become involved, and a firm's legal position must always be the first consideration.

From a legal point of view, normally the less an organization says prior to its day in court, the better. That way, the opposition can't gain any new ammunition that will become part of the public record. A lawyer, the saying goes, tells you to say two things: "Say nothing, and say it slowly!" From a public relations standpoint, though, it may often make sense to go public early on, especially if the organization's integrity or credibility is being called into public question. In the summer of 1997, for example, when respected broadcaster Marv Albert was charged with abusing a woman friend, Albert immediately held a press conference denying the charges, and his advisors followed with questions about the woman's veracity. (Later, he pleaded guilty to a lesser charge.)

The point is that legal advice and public relations advice may indeed be different. In an organization, a smart manager will carefully weigh both legal and public relations counsel before making a decision.

It also should be noted that law and ethics are interrelated. The PRSA Code of Professional Standards (Appendix A) notes that many activities that are unethical are also illegal. However, there are instances where something is perfectly legal but unethical, and other instances in which things might be illegal but otherwise ethical. Thus, when a public relations professional reflects on what course to take in a particular situation, he or she must analyze not only the legal ramifications but also the ethical considerations.[3]

This chapter will examine the relationship between the law and public relations and the more prominent role the law plays in public relations practice and vice versa. The discussion will not be all-encompassing. Rather, it will introduce the legal concerns of public relations professionals today: First Amendment considerations, insider trading, disclosure law, ethics law, privacy law, copyright law, and the laws concerning censorship of the Internet—concerns that have become primary for public relations in these latter stages of the twentieth century.

PUBLIC RELATIONS AND THE FIRST AMENDMENT

Any discussion of law and public relations should start with the First Amendment, which states: "Congress shall make no law . . . abridging the freedom of speech or the press." The First Amendment is the cornerstone of free speech in our society: this is what distinguishes America from many other nations.

The 1990s have seen a blizzard of First Amendment challenges.

- In the summer of 1990, North Carolina Senator Jesse Helms introduced an amendment to restrict the National Endowment for the Arts from funding "obscene" or "indecent" materials, defined as a host of antisocial acts (Figure 18–1).
- That same summer, the rap group 2 Live Crew was arrested in Hollywood, Florida, when they sang tunes from their album "As Nasty as They Want To Be," whose sexual explicitness a federal judge ruled was obscene.
- In 1993, the Federal Communications Commission decided to delay deals totaling $170 million by the Infiniti Broadcasting Corporation because it employed foul-mouthed radio personality Howard Stern. As a result of Stern's scatological humor, Infiniti was fined well over $1 million by the FCC.[4]
- That same year, the Supreme Court reaffirmed its view that advertising is a form of speech protected by the First Amendment. The Court ruled that a city may not automatically exclude advertising brochures from the newspaper vending machines that it licenses for use on public property. The Court's ruling reaffirmed the First Amendment protection of commercial speech.[5] Such a privilege was established in a landmark 1978 case, First National Bank of Boston v. Belloti, in which the Supreme Court struck down a Massachusetts law that permitted a business corporation to speak only on those issues "that materially affect its business, property or assets."[6]
- In the summer of 1996, Reebok International was chastised for reaching a tentative agreement with the University of Wisconsin on a sports product contract that included a clause that prohibited the university from criticizing the company. The resulting free speech furor caused Reebok to drop the clause.

Figure 18–1 The arts community was chilled in 1990s by the attempts of Senator Jesse Helms and others in Congress to restrict federal funding from anything considered "indecent or obscene."

- In the spring of 1997, the publisher of *The Wall Street Journal*, Dow Jones & Company, was stunned when a Texas court awarded a brokerage firm $222.7 million in damages for an article that the company claimed put it out of business.[7]
- In the summer of 1997, a Delaware judge dismissed a lawyer for a teenager charged with murdering her newborn son, because the girl's attorney made comments about the impending case on ABC's *20/20* show, including an assertion that his client was innocent. The judge claimed the lawyer's statements had a "substantial likelihood of materially prejudicing" potential jurors.[8]

THE REST OF THE STORY

PROMOTING O. J.

Figure 18–2   Fallen—but not convicted—hero, O. J. Simpson.

Perhaps never has a legal trial gripped the entire nation so pervasively as the murder charges against Orenthal J. Simpson in the killings of Nicole Brown Simpson and Ron Goldman in 1994. O. J. Simpson was a revered football player, broadcaster, and actor who seemed to be leading a charmed life, when the nation was stunned one summer evening as he led it—via national live TV—on a low-speed car chase through the highways and byways of Brentwood, California (Figure 18–2).

The Simpson trial shocked the nation, but the real drama lay in how Simpson's high-powered attorney team of Johnnie Cochran, F. Lee Bailey, and Robert Shapiro used publicity to forward their cause and wallop the hapless Los Angeles District Attorney's Office.

Here's how one of O. J.'s lawyers, Robert Shapiro, described the winning public relations approach.

- **Lawyer as public relations person**   "When we are retained for those high-profile cases, we are instantly thrust into the role of a public relations person—a role for which the majority of us have no education, experience, or training. The lawyer's role as spokesperson may be [as] equally important to the outcome of a case as the skills of an advocate in the courtroom."

- **Power of the media**   "The importance and power of the media cannot be overemphasized. The first impression the public gets is usually the one that is most important."

- **"No comment"**   "No comment is the least appropriate and least productive response. Coming at the end of a lengthy story, it adds absolutely nothing and leaves the public with a negative impression."

- **Lying to the media**   "It is never a good idea to lie to the press. To simply make up facts in the hope that they will later prove correct is too big a risk."

- **Media relationships**   "Initial relationships with legitimate members of the press are very important. Many times a lawyer will feel it is an intrusion to be constantly beset by seemingly meaningless questions that take up a tremendous amount of time. But the initial headlines of the arrest often make the sacred presumption of innocence a myth. In reality, we have the presumption of guilt. This is why dealing with the media is so important.

- **Responding to the press**   "The wire services depend on immediate updates. Therefore, all calls should be returned as quickly as possible. Wire service reporters can also provide a valuable source of information to you."

- **Framing answers**   "Just as you would do in trial, anticipate the questions a reporter will pose. Think out your answers carefully. My personal preference is to initially talk to a reporter off the record and get an idea what questions the reporter is interested in and where the story is going. I then respond to the questions that are appropriate. Use great care in choosing your words. Keep your statements simple and concise. Pick and choose the questions you want to answer. You do not have to be concerned with whether the answer precisely addresses the question, since only the answer will be aired."

- **The tabloids**   "My experience is that cooperating with tabloid reporters only gives them a legitimate source of information which can be misquoted or taken out of context and does little good for your client. My personal approach is not to cooperate with tabloid reporters."

- **Dealing with TV hordes**   "The television media, either consciously or unconsciously, create an atmosphere of chaos. Immediately upon arriving at the courthouse, you are surrounded by television crews. We have all seen people coming to court and trying to rush through the press with their heads down or covering them with newspapers or coats. Nothing looks worse. I always instruct my clients upon arrival at the courthouse to get out in a normal manner, to walk next to me in a slow and deliberate way, to have a look of confidence and acknowledge with a nod those who are familiar and supportive."[9]

As these recent skirmishes suggest, interpreting the First Amendment is no simple matter. One person's definition of obscenity may be another's definition of art. Interestingly, the verdict in the Dow Jones case was later reduced; the case against 2 Live Crew ultimately was dismissed; as was the case against Infiniti; as was a celebrated case against the Cincinnati Contemporary Arts Center, which had exhibited a graphic retrospective on the effects of AIDS. Despite continuing challenges to the First Amendment, Americans continue to enjoy broad freedom of speech and expression. Because the First Amendment lies at the heart of the communications business, defending it is a front-line responsibility of the public relations profession.

PUBLIC RELATIONS AND INSIDER TRADING

Every public relations professional should know the laws that govern an organization. A practitioner in a hospital should have an understanding of managed care and its ramifications. A practitioner working for a nonprofit organization should understand the laws that govern donors and recipients. A practitioner who works in a particular industry—chemicals, computers, sports—should understand the laws germane to that particular area.

Nowhere in public relations practice is an understanding of the law more important than in the area of financial disclosure. Every public company has an obligation to deal frankly, comprehensively, and immediately with any information that is considered material in a decision to buy, sell, or even hold the organization's securities. The Securities and Exchange Commission (SEC)—through a series of court cases, consent decrees, complaints, and comments over the years—has painted a general portrait of disclosure requirements for practitioners (see Appendix F), with which all practitioners in public companies should be familiar. The SEC's mandate stems from the Securities Act of 1933 and the Securities Exchange Act of 1934, which attempted to protect the public from abuses in the issuance and sale of securities.

The SEC's overriding concern is that all investors have an opportunity to learn about material information as promptly as possible. Through its general antifraud statute, Rule 10b-5 of the Securities and Exchange Act, the SEC strictly prohibits the dissemination of false or misleading information to investors. It also prohibits insider trading of securities on the basis of material information not disclosed to the public.

In the early part of the nineties, the public was shocked by a series of celebrated cases involving the use of insider information to amass illegal securities gains. The two most celebrated insider trading cases were those of Ivan Boesky and Michael Milken, Wall Street legends who were both slapped with nine-figure fines and jail terms. A host of their associates, equally guilty of insider trading violations, also were dispatched to the slammer.

Nor have journalists escaped the ignominy of insider trading convictions. The most famous case involved a *Wall Street Journal* reporter, R. Foster Winans Jr., who was convicted in the summer of 1985 of illegally using his newspaper column in a get-rich-quick stock-trading scheme. Basically, Winans gave favorable opinions about companies in which a couple of his stockbroker friends had already invested heavily. The stocks then generally went up, the brokers and their clients profited handsomely, and Winans was sentenced to prison. In 1996, *Money* magazine columnist Dan Dorfman was similarly accused of running stock tips from which his sources profited. He, too, was not renewed.

The Supreme Court, in 1987, upheld Winans's conviction for securities fraud by the narrowest of votes. In so doing, the Court reasoned that by "misappropriating information belonging to the *Journal*," Winans had violated the newspaper's intangible property rights. According to legal experts, this ruling has widespread implications for anyone with access to business information, including public relations professionals.

What the Supreme Court ruling means, in effect, is that an employer can adopt work rules or a code of ethics that can carry a criminal penalty. This may create problems for those, like public relations people, who share information with journalists; for whistle blowers, who could be threatened with prosecution for unauthorized disclosure of confidential information; or for anyone involved in the dissemination of sensitive company data.

PUBLIC RELATIONS AND DISCLOSURE LAW

Besides cracking down on insider trading, the SEC has challenged public relations firms on the accuracy of information they disseminate for clients. In 1982, the SEC issued a 95-page release, "Adoption of Integrated Disclosure System," which attempted to bring some order to the chaotic SEC requirements. Essentially, the document tried to make more uniform the instructions governing corporate disclosure of information. Today, in an environment of mergers, takeovers, consolidations, and the incessant rumors that circulate around them, a knowledge of disclosure law, a sensitivity to disclosure requirements, and a bias toward disclosing rather than withholding material information is an important attribute of public relations officials.

The burgeoning practice of investor relations, which transcends the scope of this book, has emerged as an important element of public relations that focuses on proper disclosure to investors.

PUBLIC RELATIONS AND ETHICS LAW

The laws on ethical misconduct in society have gotten quite a workout in recent years. Regrettably, public relations practitioners have, in several well-known cases, been at the center of the storm. In 1988, Lyn Nofziger, former White House political director and communications counselor, was sentenced to 90 days in prison and fined $30,000 for violating the Federal Ethics in Government Act, which forbids lobbying former contacts within one year of leaving the government. Also in 1988, former White House Deputy Chief of Staff Michael K. Deaver, another well-known public relations professional, was found guilty of perjury about his lobbying activities. He also faced a lengthy jail sentence and a serious fine. In response, Deaver railed against the "outrageousness of congressmen saying that I violated the public trust, when they go out and make all the money they want on speaking fees" paid for by special-interest groups. A decade later, public relations counselor John Scanlon faced a grand jury subpoena, stemming from his efforts to discredit a critic of cigarette client Brown & Williamson.[10]

The problems of Nofziger, Deaver, and Scanlon called into question the role of lobbyists in government. In the late nineties, eyebrows were raised when President Clinton's White House congressional liaison Howard Paster was named CEO of the Hill & Knowlton public relations firm. As explained in chapter 17, the activities of lobbyists have been closely watched by Congress since the imposition of the Lobbying Act of 1947. Inrecent years, however, the practice of lobbying has expanded greatly.

Complicating the lobbyist issue still further, foreign governments are particularly eager to retain savvy Washington insiders to guide them through the bureaucratic and congressional maze and to polish their images in the United States. This was the problem late Commerce Secretary Ron Brown confronted when he reportedly was approached by Asian business operatives. Indeed, in 1997, after Brown's death in a plane crash, he was charged by a former business partner of taking money from foreign business executives. That same year, the Clinton Administration faced a scandal involving Asian campaign contributions. Public relations counselors are strictly mandated by law to register the foreign entities they represent. However, in recent years, a number of representatives of foreign clients have, themselves, been the subject of scandals and legal investigations.

The increasing number of government officials who resign to become play-for-pay lobbyists may indicate that those who govern and those who attempt to influence them will in the future be scrutinized more closely for how ethically they do business and how scrupulously they follow the law.

PUBLIC RELATIONS AND PRIVACY LAW

The laws that govern a person's privacy also have implications for the public relations profession. Privacy laws, particularly those that touch on libel and slander by the media, are curious indeed. When such alleged defamation involves a public figure, the laws get

DESERVING OF COUNSEL?

Every individual in a free society is entitled to the best legal defense in a court of law. You are "innocent until proven guilty."

But no such similar representation is guaranteed of public relations counselors. In the "court of public opinion," it is up to the individual public relations counselor to decide whether an entity is "worthy" of representation.

This was the backdrop in late 1996 when Kekst & Co., a New York firm long associated with Jewish causes, was drafted to represent the Swiss Bank Association against attacks that Swiss banks made it impossible for Jews to get back the assets they, themselves, or their relatives turned over during the Holocaust.

The controversy erupted when it was revealed that Swiss banks had been used by thousands of Jews to shield assets from the Nazis. After the war, the banks in Basel and Munich that had willingly

Figure 18–3   Kekst & Co.'s representation of the Swiss Bank Association drew criticism in the Israeli press.

accepted the Jewish deposits were decidedly less anxious to release the funds. They insisted on precise documentation, including certificates of death. The problem, of course, was that the death Cadre of Auschwitz and Dachau didn't issue death certificates to the families of their six million victims.

And in 1996, 50 years after the Nazi catastrophe, few of the world's citizens had much tolerance for a banking system that stood on such ceremony, with the exception, evidently, of Kekst & Co.

Kekst, whose founder and chairman was also chairman of the Jewish Theological Seminary, readily accepted the Swiss bank account. Said a Kekst & Co. partner in defense of his firm's role, "We are playing a constructive role in helping resolve a very sensitive manner." In support, the national director of the Anti-Defamation League, concluded, "We would rather have someone represent them who is sensitive to our issues and our history."

But other Jews were not as sanguine. An article in the Jewish *Daily Forward* newspaper said Kekst's involvement "illuminates how some seek to exploit the firm's credentials."

An Israeli public relations counselor labeled the firm's representation "comforting the bankers." He urged Kekst & Co. to withdraw from the account.

But Kekst held its ground.

In March of 1997, the Swiss government announced a $5 billion fund to aid victims of the Holocaust. Jewish groups and others were ecstatic, although the Israeli public relations counselor who earlier blasted Kekst & Co. described the fund as "nebulous" and with ill-defined purposes.

For its part, Kekst & Co. was hopeful the new fund would defuse the controversy. "When the hysteria over this issue is concluded, we hope the world will look at the Swiss and say they did the right thing," said a Kekst partner.

And there the debate remains, as does the question: "Is any entity, regardless of what they've done, entitled to public relations representation?"

Specifically, in this case should Kekst & Co. have defended the Swiss Bank Association? (see Figure 18–3.)

For further information, see Charley J. Levine, "Danke but No Danke," *The Public Relations Strategist* (Spring 1997): 43–44; "Jewish PR Firm Defends Banks," *Daily Forward* (December 13, 1996): 1; "Israeli Publicist Attacks Kekst," *Jack O'Dwyer's Newsletter* (January 22, 1997): 1; "Kekst & Co. Handles Swiss Bank Group," *PR Services Report* (February 1997): 1.

even more curious. Generally, the privacy of an ordinary citizen is protected under the law. A citizen in the limelight, however, has a more difficult problem, especially in proving defamation of character.

To prove such a charge, a public figure must show that the media acted with actual malice in its reporting. "Actual malice" in a public figure slander case means that statements have been published with the knowledge that they were false or with reckless disregard for whether the statements were false. In a landmark case in 1964, *New York Times v. Sullivan*, the Supreme Court nullified a libel award of $500,000 to an Alabama police official, holding that no damages could be awarded "in actions brought by public officials against critics of their official conduct" unless there was proof of "actual malice." And proving actual malice is difficult.

Several libel cases were particularly prominent.

- In 1992, *The Wall Street Journal* and its award-winning reporter Bryan Burrough were served with a $50 million libel suit by Harry L. Freeman, former executive vice president of American Express. The suit stemmed from the way Freeman was characterized in Burrough's book, *Vendetta: America Express and the Smearing of Edmund Safra.*[11]

- In 1993, writer Janet Malcolm was sued by Dr. Jeffrey M. Masson over charges that Malcolm fabricated quotations in her *New Yorker* magazine article, which defamed Dr. Masson. Jurors agreed that in several instances Malcolm acted with "reckless disregard" for the accuracy of the quotations and that Masson had indeed been damaged.[12]
- A decade earlier, in a landmark case, *The Washington Post* initially lost a $2 million suit after a federal jury decided that the newspaper had libeled William P. Tavoulareas when it alleged that he had used his position as president of Mobil Oil to further his son's career in a shipping business. The next year, a federal judge overturned the verdict against the *Post* because the article in question didn't contain "knowing lies or statements made in reckless disregard of the truth."

Later, a federal appeals court reinstated the $2 million libel verdict against the *Post*. But later that year, the U.S. Court of Appeals of the District of Columbia agreed to reconsider the reinstatement. Finally, almost six years after the initial verdict, the Supreme Court ruled in favor of the *Post* by throwing out the Tavoulareas suit for lack of merit. A contrary ruling would have restricted the limits of investigative journalism and broadened the interpretation of defamation of character. Reporters breathed a sigh of relief at the decision.

- In another celebrated case in 1985, Israeli General Ariel Sharon brought a $50 million libel suit against *Time* magazine. It, too, ended without a libel verdict. However, once again, the jury criticized *Time* for negligent journalism in reporting Sharon's role in a massacre in a Palestinian refugee camp.
- In 1988, the Supreme Court threw out a suit brought by conservative televangelist/preacher Jerry Falwell against *Hustler* magazine and publisher Larry Flynt, accusing the sex-oriented periodical with defaming his character in a fictitious liquor advertisement about his mother. Despite the grossness of the ad, the Supreme Court ruled that what was written was clearly a spoof of a public figure and that Falwell, therefore, didn't have a case. In 1996, filmmaker Oliver Stone glorified the smarmy publisher in *The People vs. Larry Flynt*.
- In perhaps the most celebrated recent case, in 1996, Atlanta security guard Richard A. Jewell sued both *NBC News* and the *Atlanta Journal-Constitution* for reporting that he was the lead suspect in the Atlanta Olympic bombing, which led to two deaths. The reports caused a media feeding frenzy, which disrupted Jewell's life and tarnished his name (Figure 18–4). Late in the year, Jewell was cleared of any involvement in the bombing and reached a settlement with his media accusers, averting a libel lawsuit and presumably compensating him handsomely for the undeserved humiliation.[13]
- In 1997, *The Wall Street Journal* lost its $227 million libel verdict in Texas when it was found to have inaccurately reported on the troubles of MMAR Group, a mortgage-backed securities firm in Houston, which ultimately went out of business after the *Journal* story.[14] Later that year, hedge fund manager Julian Robertson commenced an action against *Business Week* magazine for $1 billion, after a critical cover story on his firm.

What all these cases illustrate is a growing trend in society to challenge the media over their invasion of personal privacy. Although cases like these tend to confirm the rights of the media to report on public figures, in other cases—particularly those involving gossip-oriented tabloids—the courts have awarded settlements to celebrities who have been wronged.

Figure 18–4   Litigious victim of the media, Atlanta security guard Richard A. Jewell.

PUBLIC RELATIONS AND COPYRIGHT LAW

One body of law that is particularly relevant to public relations professionals is copyright law and the protections it offers writers. Copyright law provides basic, automatic protection for writers, whether a manuscript is registered with the Copyright Office or even published. Under the Copyright Act of 1976, an "original work of authorship" has copyright protection from the moment the work is in fixed form. As soon as an article, short story, or book is put on paper or a computer disk or is spoken into a tape recorder, it is protected by copyright law. You created it, and you own it. What you sell to an editor isn't the article itself but the right to use the material.

Copyright protection exists for broad categories of works: literary works; musical works, including any accompanying words; dramatic works, including any accompanying music; pantomimes and choreographic works; pictorial, graphic, and sculptural works; motion pictures and other audiovisual works; and sound recordings. Copyright law gives the owner of the copyright the exclusive right to reproduce and authorize others to reproduce the work, prepare derivative works based on the copyrighted material, and perform and/or display the work publicly. That's why Michael Jackson had to pay $47.5 million for the rights to the Beatles' compositions to the duly sworn representatives and heirs of John, Paul, George, and Ringo.

WHAT'S IN A SQUIGGLE?

People are curious about the tiny squiggles that appear above the names of certain company products or slogans.

They're trademarks.

A trademark is a kind of copyright that protects intellectual property. It gives one exclusive use of a particular word, name, symbol, or slogan—Kleenex®, Xerox®, and Coke®, for example. The squiggle ® indicates the mark you have registered with the U.S. Office of Patents and Trademarks.

A similar squiggle is called a service mark. This applies to an organization selling a service rather than a product—American Airlines' slogan, "Something Special in the Air,"SM or the U.S. Army Reserve's slogan we used to chant, "Be All That You Can Be."SM

A similar squiggle,™, is the trademark symbol. (TM also stands for transcendental meditation, but that's another story completely.)

In 1989, the Supreme Court strengthened the copyright status of freelance artists and writers when it ruled that such professionals retain the right to copyright what they create "as long as they were not in a conventional employment relationship with the organization that commissioned their work." The Court's revision of the copyright law set the stage for a wholesale reassessment of the ownership of billions of dollars in reproduction rights for computer programs, fiction and nonfiction writing, advertising copy, drawings, photographs, and so on. As a result of the modification, public relations professionals must carefully document the authorization that has been secured for using freelance material. In other words, when engaging a freelance professional, public relations people must know the law.

Several categories of material are not eligible for copyright protection, such as titles and short slogans; works consisting entirely of information from common sources and public documents, such as calendars, lists, and tables; and speeches and performances that have not been fixed on paper or recorded. Work in the public domain—material that was never covered by copyright or for which the copyright has lapsed, material that lacks sufficient originality, and basic themes and plots—can't be protected by copyright.

Ideas cannot be protected either. This means that an old idea newly packaged is absolutely permissible, legal, and even recommended. Indeed, there are few truly new ideas in the world, only old ideas put together in new and different ways. So a public relations practitioner shouldn't be overly concerned with violating copyright laws when devising a campaign, program, or manuscript in support of a client's activity.

PUBLIC RELATIONS AND INTERNET LAW

The Internet has introduced a new dimension to the law affecting free speech.

The premise in American law is that "not all speech is created equal."[15] Rather there is a hierarchy of speech, under Supreme Court precedents dating back many decades that calibrate the degree of First Amendment protection with the particular medium of expression. For example, speech that would be perfectly acceptable if uttered in a public park could constitutionally be banned when broadcast from a sound truck.

As the twenty-first century approached, dealing with the Internet introduced new ramifications to this legal principal.

In 1996, the Congress passed the Communications Decency Act (CDA) as an amendment to a far-reaching telecommunications bill. The CDA introduced criminal penalties, including fines of as much as $250,000 and prison terms up to two years for making "indecent" speech available to "a person under 18 years of age." A Philadelphia court a few months later struck down the law, contending that such censorship would chill all discourse on the Net.[16]

Then, in the summer of 1997, the Supreme Court, in a sweeping endorsement of free speech, declared the CDA unconstitutional. The decision, unanimous in most respects, marked the highest court's first effort to extend the principles of the First Amendment into cyberspace and to confront the nature and the law of this new, powerful medium. In summarizing the court's finding, Justice John Paul Stevens said the court considered the "goal of protecting children from indecent material as legitimate and important," but concluded that "the wholly unprecedented breadth of the law threatened to suppress far too much speech "among adults and even between parents and children."[17] The issue, like all free speech law, is extraordinarily complex.

On the one hand are those who argue that the Internet is the most democratic of democratic institutions, allowing all access to all manner of speech. As such, this argument goes, adults should have every right to exercise their constitutional right to free speech. On the other side are those who contend that the Internet threatens to give children a "free pass into an adult bookstore."[18] Further complicating the issue, of course, is the fact that the Net is changing every day. A law that applies today may be irrelevant or outdated tomorrow.

This, in essence, is the conundrum that confronts lawmakers as they attempt to construct laws to govern the Internet.

PUBLIC RELATIONS AND THE LEGAL PROFESSION

What has always been an uneasy alliance between lawyers and public relations professionals has today evolved into a relationship of grudging mutual respect. Lawyers, in fact, are making more use of public relations strategies than ever before.

By 1990, it was estimated that 75 percent of all major law firms used public relations consultants.[19] Lawyers and legal consultants attributed the increased use of public relations firms to heightened competition within the top tier of the legal profession. Many law firms have grown rapidly in the last decade and have to fight harder for clients and for top law school graduates. As a result, public relations has emerged as an important tool to get these firms' names circulated among clients, potential clients, and possible hires.

In 1984, the Supreme Court eased the ban on self-advertisement by lawyers. And although some lawyers are still reluctant to trumpet their capabilities, others are not. The leader of this ilk is Jacoby & Meyers, which, because of its pervasive national advertising, was derided by some as a "fast-food law firm."[20] But there was nothing funny about Jacoby & Meyers's client roster of 175,000 people and its $42 million business in 1989. For Jacoby & Meyers, advertising and publicity have paid off very well indeed.

Other law firms, like Searcy Denney Scarola Barnhart & Shipley of West Palm Beach, use community relations techniques to enhance their image in the local area.

Searcy Denney, for example, contributes significantly to community causes, provides volunteers for community events, and sponsors public service announcements to promote the good works of particular local charities. The firm's slogan in such endeavors is, "Taking Time to Care."

For their part, public relations counselors have become more open to lawyers and have relaxed the tensions that have existed between the two professions. One public relations practitioner offers this advice for working with lawyers:

1. **Become an equal partner with legal counsel.** At all times, maintain an overview of the legal cases that are before your organization or industry. Take the initiative with legal counsel to discuss those that you believe may have major public relations implications.
2. **Combat the legal no-comment syndrome.** Research cases in which an organization has publicly discussed issues without damage.
3. **Take the initiative in making announcements.** This will help manage the public perception of the issue. If an indictment is pending, consult the legal staff on the advisability of making statements—before you become a target.
4. **Research the background of the jury.** Past lists of jurors in a particular jurisdiction indicate occupations and other important demographic information.
5. **Winning may not be everything.** Outside law firms, trained in an adversarial mode and charging fees that depend on the size of the award, always want to "win." For legal counsel the stakes may also include a winning reputation, which helps to secure future cases. Public relations must bring a long-term perspective to strategic decisions.
6. **Beware of leaving a paper trail.** Any piece of paper that you create may end up in court. That includes desk calendars and notes to yourself. So be careful.[21]

Litigation Public Relations

The most critical use of public relations strategies and techniques for lawyers arrives prior to, during, or after litigation. In the latter years of the twentieth century, court cases at every level involving every manner of defendant—from celebrities like O. J. Simpson, Marv Albert, and Bill Clinton to lesser known individuals on the local level—have used public relations assistance to complement legal litigation techniques.

Although court proceedings have certain rules and protocol, dealing in the public arena with a matter of litigation has no such strictures. Lawyers often are unprepared for the spontaneity and unpredictability of dealing with the media. That's why public relations counsel is so important in a public legal battle.

According to one counselor who works exclusively with litigation, there are seven keys to litigation visibility.

1. **Learn the process.** All involved should be aware of the road map for the case and the milestones ahead, which may lend themselves to publicity.
2. **Develop a message strategy.** Think about what should be said at each stage of a trial to keep the press and public focused on the key messages of the client.
3. **Settle fast.** Settlement is probably the most potent litigation visibility management tool. The faster the settlement, the less litigation visibility there is likely to be. This is often a positive development.

> ### THE REST OF THE STORY
>
> ## LADIIEEEEES AND GENTLEMEN, LET'S GET READY TO SUE
>
> America at the end of this century is the world's most litigious society. Nowhere is this more true than in the world of celebritydom, where stars of every description have taken to the courts to protect their identity, their looks, their acts, their mannerisms, their voice, and, in one case, their five-word signature slogan.
>
> The latter distinction belonged to one, Michael Buffer, former model and journeyman announcer, who all of a sudden struck it rich with a call to arms, developed for the World Wrestling Federation. "Let's get ready to rumble!"
>
> Buffer parlayed his clarion call into high-paid appearances in championship fights, NFL football broadcasts, NBA playoff games, movies, concerts and even on the supreme honorary platform, an appearance as himself on *The Simpsons*.
>
> No wonder Buffer sued Sony's Columbia Pictures for appropriating his "rumble" call in promotional ads for the epic movie, *Booty Call*. When the Disney company wanted to use the call in its 1997 release, *Hercules*, Buffer was paid a license fee. Buffer made it clear to one and all—including former colonel turned talk show host Oliver North, who used the call without permission—that he would sue to protect his trademark.
>
> Buffer was typical of suing celebrities from game show hostess Vanna White, who sued a videocassette recorder company for its "Vanna the Robot," to warbler Bette Midler, who sued an ad agency for using a soundalike in a Ford car ad.

4. **Anticipate high-profile variables.** Often in public cases, everybody gets into the act—judges, commentators, jury selection experts, psychologists, etc. Always anticipate all that could be said, conjectured, argued about the case. Always try to be prepared for every inevitability.

5. **Keep the focus positive.** Ultimately, it's a positive, productive attitude that leads to effective negotiations with the other side. So the less combative you can be—especially near settlement—the better.

6. **Try settling again.** Again, this ought to be the primary litigation visibility strategy—to end the agony and get it out of the papers.

7. **Fight nicely.** Wars are messy, expensive, and prone to produce casualties. It is much better to be positive. This will give both sides a greater chance of eventually settling.[22]

SUMMARY

As our society becomes more contentious, fractious, and litigious, public relations must become more concerned with the law. Indeed, public relations has already become involved with the law in many areas of communications beyond those already cited in this chapter.

BATTLE OF THE EGOTISTS: THE ULTIMATE LEGAL FIGHT

With all the lawsuits over free speech and First Amendment and celebrity rights and the like flying across the landscape, it was probably inevitable that a judge would fight back.

That's precisely what happened in the summer of 1997, when no-nonsense, high-profile New York Supreme Court Justice Harold Rothwax sued radio personality Don Imus, for comments the irrepressible, equally high-profile talk show host made after his wife was called for jury duty in Judge Rothwax's court.

Among other things, Imus called the judge a "drunk" and wondered if he was "senile." Rothwax, it seemed, gave Imus's wife a hard time when she asked to be excused from jury duty. Adding to Imus's pique was the fact his network, MSNBC, eagerly handed over without a fight, tapes of the offensive broadcasts in question.

Despite Imus's later apology, Justice Rothwax wasn't budging. And the battle of two super egos was joined. It probably didn't help matters much that Imus had a book of his Southwest photographs on the best-seller list, while Rothwax's book chronicling his experiences on the bench sunk with a thud after it was published.

The battle ended when Judge Rothwax died later that year, and Imus agreed to donate $50,000 to charity in the Judge's memory.

- The Federal Communications Commission (FCC) ruled in 1987 that the Fairness Doctrine, the subject of years of debate among broadcasters and others, unconstitutionally restricted the First Amendment rights of broadcasters. The FCC said that broadcasters were no longer obligated to provide equal time for dissenting views. Congressional efforts to turn the doctrine into law were vetoed by President Reagan, but the debate may not be finished.
- The right of publicity has been challenged by the estates of deceased celebrities like Charlie Chaplin, W. C. Fields, Mae West, and the Marx brothers, whose likenesses have been portrayed in product advertisements without the permission of their heirs.
- In 1993, the Supreme Court ruled that the rap group 2 Live Crew could release a vulgar rewrite of the old Roy Orbison hit "Pretty Woman," even though those who copyrighted the original material had refused permission. The Court ruled that the raunchy rappers were entitled to "fair use" of the material for the purpose of parody. But in 1997, Texas became the first state in the nation to prohibit its agencies from investing in companies that produce or distribute music with lyrics that are sexually explicit or extol violence, aka "gangsta rap."[23]
- Also in 1997, in a landmark agreement with a group of state attorneys generals, the tobacco industry agreed to a $368 billion agreement that ultimately would over time impose strict limits on tobacco marketing and advertising, including a ban on vending machines and outdoor billboards.[24]

In addition to all of these legal areas, the public relations business itself increasingly is based on legal contracts: between agencies and clients, between employers and employees, between purchasers and vendors. All contracts—both written and oral—must be binding and enforceable.

In recent years, controversy in the field has erupted over "non compete clauses," in which former employees are prohibited, within certain time parameters, from working for a competitor or pitching a former account. Legal issues also have arisen over the postal laws that govern public relations people who disseminate materials through the mails. Add to these the blurring of the lines between public relations advice on the one hand and legal advice on the other, and it becomes clear that the connection between public relations and the law will intensify dramatically in the next century.

DISCUSSION STARTERS

1. What is the difference between a public relations professional's responsibility and a lawyer's responsibility?
2. What have been recent challenges to the First Amendment?
3. What is meant by the term *insider trading*?
4. What was the essence of the Foster Winans *Wall Street Journal* case?
5. What kinds of information must public companies disclose immediately?
6. What is meant by the legal term *actual malice* with respect to privacy law?
7. Whom does copyright law protect?
8. What are the issues in legislating the Internet?
9. What is the attitude of law firms toward public relations counsel?
10. What general advice should a public relations professional consider in working with lawyers?

NOTES

1. Steven Komarow and Patrick O'Driscoll, "Case Forces the Military to Take a Look at Itself," *USA Today* (May 21, 1997): 1.
2. "Guilty Until Proven Innocent?" *Inside PR* (August 1993): 41.
3. Gerhart L. Klein, *Public Relations Law: The Basics* (Mt. Laurel, NJ: Anne Klein and Associates, Inc., 1990): 1–2.
4. Edmund L. Andrews, "F.C.C. Delays Radio Deals by Howard Stern's Employer," *The New York Times* (December 31, 1993): A1, D2.
5. Linda Greenhouse, "Rights of Commercial Speech Affirmed," *The New York Times* (March 25, 1993): A7.
6. Stephen Wermiel, "U.S. State Officials Win Wider Leeway to Restrict Free Speech of Corporations," *The Wall Street Journal* (June 30, 1989): B6.
7. Iver Peterson, "Firm Awarded $222.7 Million in a Libel Suit vs. Dow Jones," *The New York Times* (March 21, 1997): D1.
8. Robert Hanley, "Judge Ousts Lawyer for Teen-Ager Charged in Baby's Death," *The New York Times* (July 4, 1997): B4.
9. Robert Shapiro, "Secrets of a Celebrity Lawyer," *Columbia Journalism Review* (September/October 1994): 25–29.
10. Alix M. Freedman and Suein L. Hwang, "Brown & Williamson Faces Inquiry," *The Wall Street Journal* (February 6, 1996): A1.
11. Thomas K. Grose, "$50 Million Lawsuit Against WSJ and Burrough May Make Some Authors-to-Be Think Twice," *TFJR Report* (April 1992): 3.

12. Jane Gross, "Impasse Over Damages Over *New Yorker* Libel Case," *The New York Times* (June 4, 1993): A1.
13. "Media Briefs," *Jack O'Dwyer's Newsletter* (December 18, 1996): 3.
14. Larry Reibstein, "One Heck of a Whupping," *Newsweek* (March 31, 1997): 54.
15. Linda Greenhouse, "What Level of Protection for Internet Speech?" *The New York Times* (March 24, 1997): D5.
16. Steven Levy, "U.S. v. the Internet," *Newsweek* (March 31, 1997): 77.
17. Linda Greenhouse, "Decency Act Fails," *The New York Times* (June 27, 1997): 1.
18. Levy, op. cit.
19. Ellen Joan Pollock, "Lawyers Are Cautiously Embracing PR Firms," *The Wall Street Journal* (March 14, 1990): B1.
20. Robyn Kelley, "Legal Beagles," *Spy* (August 1990): 74.
21. Lloyd Newman, "Litigation Public Relations: How to Work with Lawyers," *PR Reporter Tips and Tactics* (November 23, 1987): 2.
22. James E. Lukaszewski, "Managing Litigation Visibility: How To Avoid Lousy Trial Publicity," *Public Relations Quarterly* (Spring 1995): 18–24.
23. "Elsewhere," *San Jose Mercury News* (June 21, 1997): 11A.
24. John M. Broder, "Cigarette Makers in a $368 Billion Accord to Curb Lawsuits and Curtail Marketing," *The New York Times* (June 21, 1997): A1.

SUGGESTED READINGS

Klein, Gerhart L. *Public Relations Law: The Basics*. Mt. Laurel, NJ:Anne Klein and Associates, Inc., 1990. Presents the legal issues practitioners need to check before performing their duties, including the First Amendment, restrictions on free speech, copyright and trademark law, and financial disclosure.

Nally, Margaret. *International Public Relations in Practice: Firsthand Experience of 14 Professionals*. Cambridge, MA: Kogan Page Limited, 1991.

The SEC, the Securities Market and Your Financial Communications. New York: Hill & Knowlton, 1991.

Trademark Basics. New York: International Tradmark Association, 1995. Defines trademarks, how they differ from patents and copyrights, and spells out the rights and protection of trademark owners.

What Non-U.S. Companies Need to Know About Financial Disclosure in the United States. New York: Hill & Knowlton, 1990.

Wouters, Joyce. *International Public Relations: How to Establish Your Company's Product*. New York: Amacom, 1991.

CASE STUDY

BURNED BY THE MEDIA: GENERAL MOTORS EXTINGUISHES NBC

It is difficult now to believe that a proposal to send a camera crew to Indiana to tape an old car being pushed along a narrow road beside a corn field into an old truck fitted with igniters would be taken seriously.

TOP OF THE SHELF

SUSANNE A. ROSCHWALB AND RICHARD A. STACK

LITIGATION PUBLIC RELATIONS: COURTING PUBLIC OPINION

LITTLETON, CO: FRED B. ROTHMAN & CO., 1995

This is as good a treatise on legal public relations as currently exists. The authors explore the importance of communications in helping prevail in court.

The book is divided into three sections: "Relating to the Media," "Relating to the Courtroom," and "Relating to Special Publics." Included in each section are essays by various authorities.

With the media attention and television coverage of high profile O. J. Simpson-like court cases and Clarence Thomas-like Congressional hearings, litigation public relations has become increasingly important. Fourteen authors, including judges, journalists, and public relations professionals, give their overview of the various aspects of this developing part of the practice.

Many of the cases discussed here are landmark ones in the use of public relations techniques, such as pretrial publicity, servicing the media covering a trial or communications methods pending appeals.

Because more and more public relations people need to be conversant in the law, this book has particular relevance to students of the field.

Report of Inquiry Into Crash Demonstrations Broadcast on *Dateline* NBC November 17, 1992, NBC Internal Report, Issued March 21, 1993

The estimated 17 million viewers of the November 17, 1992, *Dateline* NBC program couldn't help but be horrified as they observed a General Motors full-size pickup truck burst into flames after being hit broadside by a remote control-operated car. The clear conclusion for any viewer watching the debacle was that GM trucks were dangerous and ought to be taken off the road—immediately!

There was only one slight problem.

The NBC crash demonstration was a sham. The test was rigged. The segment was flawed from start to finish. And the reporting of *NBC News* was flatly fraudulent.

NBC News would have gotten away with its trickery had not GM struck back with a public relations vengeance unprecedented in American corporate history.

Immediately after the damaging NBC broadcast, GM embarked on a painstaking mission to research the facts of the NBC demonstration and expose the network's falsified report. But that effort would never have been seen had it not been for a lucky break—a call from a newsman who had discovered witnesses to the rigged demonstration on a rural road near Indianapolis.

Pete Pesterre, editor of *Popular Hot Rodding Magazine*, wrote an editorial criticizing the *Dateline NBC* story. Soon afterward, a reader of the magazine turned up a firefighter who had witnessed the filming of the crash and had filmed his own video of the incident.

Soon thereafter, GM obtained the firefighter's video. This proved to be the turning point in GM's efforts. The video clearly showed that the test was rigged. GM investigators located the trucks used in the staged crash. The investigators found the trucks at a salvage yard in Indiana and purchased them. In one of the pickups, a used model rocket engine was found.

Between the time the show aired in November of 1992 and January of 1993, four letters were sent to NBC by GM. They received no adequate response. GM then threatened suit. NBC continued to state that the story, according to NBC News President Michael Gartner, "was entirely accurate." In February of 1993, GM filed a lawsuit against the National Broadcasting Company, charging that *Dateline NBC* had rigged the crash. GM also immediately went into crisis mode.

GM's crisis communications program was managed by two members of its recently reorganized communications staff—William J. O'Neill, then director of communications for GM's North American Operations (NAO), and Edward S. Lechtzin, director of legal and safety issues for the NAO communications staff. O'Neill, in fact, had agreed that GM would participate in the original *Dateline NBC* program but hadn't been told during the interview session about NBC's taped test. O'Neill and Lechtzin spearheaded a unique public relations team that also included three GM attorneys and two engineers.

The public relations professionals, attorneys, and engineers together provided a nucleus that could make key decisions quickly and authoritatively.

Lechtzin's boss, GM General Counsel Harry J. Pearce, was selected to face off with the media. At the center of the group's public relations offensive would be a press conference, conducted by Pearce, to lay bare the NBC deception. Further, the GM crisis communications team made a conscious decision to target television as the key medium to deliver GM's strongest message that it had been wronged and wasn't going to take it.

Going to War with NBC

Given the old adage "Don't pick a fight with the guy who buys ink by the barrel," a large number of "crisis communications consultants" wondered aloud during the days before the Pearce press conference if GM was doing the right thing.

At GM, there was never any doubt that the NBC deception should be publicized—as widely as possible. Briefed during an inaugural event for President Clinton, GM President Jack Smith told his public relations executives, "Don't overplay it, but do what's right."

During the three-week period between the tip and the press conference, the group pulling together the case against NBC was asked only two questions: (1) Do we have enough information? and (2) Are we doing the right thing? No presentations. No briefing books. No background meetings. No groups of 15 to 20 people in a room trying to decide what was right. It was left to the small crisis task force to select the right strategy.

Harry Pearce was scheduled to take the stage in the GM showroom at 1 P.M. on February 8, 1993. Only one question remained: How would the media react?

The Pearce Press Conference

From the moment Harry Pearce strode on stage until the time he concluded more than two hours later, the assembled media personnel—numbering nearly 150 journalists and 25 camera crews—were mesmerized.

"What I'm about to share with you should shock the conscience of every member of your profession and mine, and I believe the American people as well," Pearce began, speaking to an uncommonly quiet media audience. "I will not allow the good men and women of General Motors and the thousands of independent businesses who sell our products and whose livelihood depends upon our products to suffer the consequences of NBC's irresponsible conduct transmitted via the airwaves throughout this great nation in the November *Dateline* program. GM has been irreparably damaged and we are going to defend ourselves."[1]

For the next two hours, speaking without notes, Pearce systematically shredded any vestiges of defense that NBC might have had. The media audience was transfixed. There was no rushing to phones to call in the story, no shuffling of papers or sighs of boredom. The only sound that interrupted Pearce's devastating dissection of NBC was the intermittent click of camera shutters. Pearce was a skilled trial lawyer weaving a two-hour summation.

The GM attorney concluded by reading a brief statement issued earlier in the day by NBC in which the network said, "We feel that our use of those demonstrations was accurate and responsible." His reply was a challenge of the kind that a good lawyer gives to a jury—in this case, the assembled reporters and thousands of others watching the broadcast. "Well, you decide that one," Pearce said. "And that's going to prove your mettle within your own profession. It's sometimes most difficult to police abuse in one's own profession."

The Crash Demonstration

At the heart of the Pearce press conference was a repeat of NBC's 55-second crash demonstration within a 16-minute broadcast segment. Using videotape, Pearce demonstrated that the segment was flawed from start to finish. It loaded the evidence to prove that GM's full-size C/K pickup trucks, equipped with so-called side-saddle fuel tanks, had a fatal flaw that in a high-speed side impact collision caused them to rupture and spew burning gasoline. The clear implication was that the trucks were unsafe.

However, no source—not even the internal report generated by NBC after the affair—fully explained what the crashes of two aged Citations being pushed into the sides of two Chevy pickups were supposed to prove. They certainly didn't prove the trucks were dangerous. If anything, the performance of the two old trucks—hit at speeds of 39 and 48 miles per hour, respectively—was superb. The only fire generated, as Pearce showed the reporters, was a 15-second grass fire caused by gasoline spewing from an overfilled filler tube after an ill-fitting gas cap came off on impact.

Careful editing from three views left the impression of a conflagration. As NBC's own investigative report indicated:

> We believe that the combined effect of the shot from the bullet car and the slow motion film creates an impression that the flames are about to consume the cabin of the truck. These images in the edited tape convey an impression quite different from what people saw at the scene. The fire was small, it did not consume the cabin of the truck, and it did not last long.[2]

Although the subsequent filmed truck crash resulted in no holocaust, the program, coupled with a well-orchestrated campaign by the plaintiff's attorneys, helped build public pressure that led the National Highway Traffic Safety Administration (NHTSA) to open an investigation into the safety of GM's trucks just one month later.

The NBC Retraction

GM's historic news conference literally brought *NBC News* to its knees.

On the day following Pearce's performance, NBC initiated a negotiating session with the company that lasted for 12 hours. GM would accept nothing less from NBC than a full public retraction of its prior broadcast.

And on February 9, 1993, a day after the news conference, that is precisely what NBC did. *Dateline* NBC coanchors Jane Pauley and Stone Phillips read a four-minute, on-air retraction that put the blame for the bogus broadcast squarely at NBC's door and apologized to GM.

In the aftermath, three *Dateline* producers were fired, the on-air reporter was demoted and reassigned, and ultimately, NBC News President Gartner resigned in humiliation. NBC agreed to reimburse GM the roughly $2 million it had spent in a three-week period investigating the false report. In exchange, GM agreed to drop the defamation suit it had filed against NBC.

For its part, GM was spared years of costly litigation over its suit. The company also was quickly able to put to rest what could have been a nightmarish visual every time GM trucks were mentioned on the evening news.

The cloak-and-dagger story on how GM put its case together remains tantalizingly vague. Nonetheless, what is clear was that in a single day, with a single press conference, GM successfully transformed the pickup truck story from a sensationalized and slanted media feeding frenzy into a serious question of journalistic ethics and integrity.

GM Communications Director O'Neill was blunt in his assessment: "I quite honestly wanted this to happen and I was glad it did happen, because I think these people purposely lied and misrepresented the facts and knew they were doing it. I do not think there is any room for that in this business."[3]

The Aftermath

After NBC's stunning mea culpa, GM increased its public relations offensive to counter concerns about the safety of its trucks.

It sought to show that the plaintiff's bar—the trial lawyers—had a vested financial interest in nurturing the idea that the trucks were dangerous. Another group was the so-called safety experts, cited by NBC and others, who either were financed by the plaintiff's attorneys or served as expert witnesses in mounting legal action against the company.

In the same scrupulous way it had dissected NBC's case, GM systematically discredited the credentials and objectivity of the so-called safety experts.

Apparently galvanized by the publicity, the NHTSA demanded—even before it had completed its own investigation—that GM voluntarily recall its pickup trucks. The company refused. In April of 1993, GM sponsored two two-hour shirtsleeve briefings by Pearce with key members of the media, explaining why the company wouldn't recall its trucks and why NHTSA's conclusions were flawed. Interestingly, television representatives were not invited to these sessions because it was felt that the medium could only "enflame the situation further."

In subsequent months, the GM-NBC News controversy received lengthy coverage in newspapers and magazines. In most, NBC fared poorly. Summarized one journalist:

> An investigation of past network auto-safety coverage reveals that both CBS and ABC have run the same sorts of material facts about the tests and relied on the same dubious experts with the same ties to plaintiff's bar.[4]

The Executive Summary of NBC's internal report concluded, "The story of this ill-fated crash demonstration and its aftermath is rather a story of lapsed judgment—serious lapses—by persons generally well-intentioned and well-qualified. And it is a story of a breakdown in the system for correction and compliance that every organization, including a news organization and network, needs."[5]

One could add that it is also a story that may never have been told had it not been for a gutsy, unyielding public relations initiative by an organization that refused to be dealt with unfairly.

QUESTIONS

1. What other options did GM have in addition to going public in the wake of the *Dateline* NBC report?
2. What was the downside risk for GM of being so public in its response?
3. Do you agree with GM's strategy on sending its general counsel to confront the media?
4. Do you agree with GM's decision not to invite television to its media briefings after the initial Pearce press conference?
5. In terms of reputation/credibility, what do you think its response to the *Dateline NBC* broadcast meant to GM?

1. General Motors press conference transcript, Detroit, February 8, 1993.
2. "NBC Internal Report of Inquiry Into Crash Demonstrations Broadcast on *Dateline NBC*, November 17, 1992," issued March 21, 1993.
3. Catherine Gates, "NBC Learns a Lesson," *Public Relations Quarterly* (Winter 1993–1994): 42.
4. "It Didn't Start with *Dateline NBC*," *National Review* (June 21, 1993): 41.
5. "Report of Inquiry Into Crash Demonstrations Broadcast on *Dateline NBC*, November 17, 1992," Issued March 21, 1993, p. 8.

VOICE OF EXPERIENCE

HARRY J. PEARCE

Harry Pearce, an executive vice president in charge of all corporate staffs at General Motors, was the automaker's general counsel at the time of the *Dateline NBC* affair in 1992 and 1993. He also is responsible for GM Hughes Electronic Corporation and Electronic Data Systems Corporation.

He also is a member of GM's President's Council. Pearce's extensive legal background prior to joining GM included service as staff judge advocate in the Air Force and service as a municipal judge and police commissioner in Bismarck, North Dakota. Pearce served as GM's chief spokesman in the *Dateline NBC* crisis.

WHAT WERE THE RELATIVE CONTRIBUTIONS OF PUBLIC RELATIONS AND LAW TO GM'S HANDLING OF THE DATELINE NBC ISSUE?

GM's handling of the *Dateline NBC* issue was unique because the traditional distinctions between the purely legal and public relations lines got blurred. Dedicating key disciplines to a single team allowed each member the ability to focus on the same goal, and the individual contributions of the members became irrelevant.

Because of the litigation aspect of the pickup truck issue, there were some technical issues that only an attorney could address. However, in the larger challenge presented by NBC and the likely media coverage of the dispute, the common goal eliminated a lot of the traditional boundaries between lawyers, engineers, and public relations experts.

What Was Your Objective in Going After NBC?

The common goal was at once simple and critical. GM needed to create an environment where facts—not shrill and rhetorical sound bites or sensational video footage—would prevail. In simple terms, we had to neutralize the rhetoric with hard facts, and we needed to shock the media so that it would listen to our message. We knew that we had solid evidence that the *Dateline NBC* segment had crossed the ethical boundaries. And we knew that we had the right facts about the safety of our pickup trucks. We needed to create a climate where that became more, rather than less, important.

Once the facts about NBC's irresponsible conduct were clear to us, the question was really quite easy to answer. The lawsuit was necessary to preserve our legal rights. We then had to ask: "How do we best communicate the truth about the inaccuracies and deception NBC perpetrated against GM and the American people?" It would have been wrong to let the *Dateline NBC* segment go unchallenged. It was obviously a high-stakes decision to go as public as we did, but when you operate on the principle that you are going to do what's right, it really isn't difficult to understand what needs to be done once you have the facts.

How Would You Characterize the Journalistic Ethics in the Dateline Case?

In retrospect, NBC was probably shell-shocked because, as gross as we revealed the segment to be, I'd bet there are dozens of other examples of TV news programs that exhibited a similar bias. The difference in this case was that we were able to obtain the hard physical evidence of the deception—and it was one that we felt the American public would understand. Frankly, the work their so-called experts did was so sloppy, and the technical advice they got was so incompetent, that it made our job easy once we knew where to look.

The "ethics" of what *Dateline* did, and failed to do, are manifest throughout the 16-minute segment itself. Though some at the network once would have liked to hide behind a facade that the show was fair except for the "rigged rocket" segment, the fact is that it was biased from start to finish. It was evident that Dateline had already decided the trucks were unsafe before even starting to film the segment and relied heavily on plaintiff attorneys and a family ready to go to trial for much of its input. There was never an attempt to present an objective look at the issue—just to provide sensational footage and grieving parents to gain rating points.

How Important is the Practice of Public Relations for a Company Like GM?

Public relations is a critical function, but we need to be clear how we at GM view this role. These folks aren't just mouthpieces.

We will ultimately succeed or fail in any endeavor based on the quality of our products and services. That's as it should be. The role for PR at GM is to help communicate the facts effectively on any given situation. It sounds simple, but when you commit yourself as a company to being straightforward with employees, the public, and the media, you eliminate a lot of unnecessary complication.

WHAT SHOULD BE THE RELATIONSHIP BETWEEN PUBLIC RELATIONS AND LAW?

We live in an age when instant communications and sound bites are a way of life, so the link between the law and public relations is both obvious and unavoidable. However, corporations don't often try to win their cases in the media, as do plaintiff attorneys and industry critics. We simply try to neutralize the bombastic rhetoric and distortions to create an environment where the facts can become the focus of the discussion. That's all we ever wanted, and we believe GM was able to achieve that environment in the truck issue.

However, given the media's love of sensationalism and the willingness of members of the legal profession to exploit it, there is a temptation on the part of some on our side of the fence to engage in the same tactics. It's a temptation that both the public relations and legal staffs have to resist.

HOW WOULD YOU COMPARE THE ETHICAL PRINCIPLES OF A LAWYER TO THOSE OF A PUBLIC RELATIONS PROFESSIONAL?

In general, the legal duties of a lawyer to a client and to the profession are much higher than the legal or ethical duty of a public relations person. Although there is no Code of Professional Responsibility, with the associated legal consequences, for a member of the public relations profession who fails to follow specific ethical guidelines, PR professionals do have a Code of Ethics administered by the Public Relations Society of America. It is strict and brings with it consequences for inappropriate actions.

In practical terms, all GM PR professionals must conduct themselves by the highest ethical standards. We will not compromise integrity at GM, and our PR staff is the public face of credibility.

HOW WOULD YOU CHARACTERIZE THE SHIFT IN GM'S PUBLIC RELATIONS STRATEGY IN RECENT YEARS?

It's probably a fair criticism of GM that we've tended to hold back and avoid taking very aggressive public positions when we were unfairly attacked in the press. Maybe it's a function of our history of being the biggest target for such abuse.

However, it makes no sense to us to let false reports and inaccurate statements about our products go unchallenged. We don't seek an unfair advantage with the media, but we fervently believe that GM is entitled to fair treatment. If that means we must be aggressive to get the facts out, so be it.

CHAPTER NINETEEN

Crisis Management

THE MOST RESPECTED AND HIGHEST PAID PEOPLE in public relations have achieved this status through their efforts in attempting to "manage" crises.

In a world of instantaneous communications, tabloid news journalism, and exploding communications challenges, the number and depth of crises affecting business, government, labor, nonprofits and even private individuals have expanded exponentially.

- The World Trade Center in New York City is bombed, and the Federal Building in Oklahoma City is blown up.
- A six-year-old beauty queen is found brutally murdered in Boulder, Colorado and her parents and immediate family are among the chief suspects.
- The Prudential Insurance Company of America, the largest life insurer in North America, agrees to pay a record $35 million in fines and reimburse customers for what regulators call "widespread abuses by the company in the sale of life insurance."[1]
- Disney Corporation hires and then fires CEO Michael Eisner's friend and hot shot talent agent Michael Ovitz, paying him $96 million in severance pay after barely a year on the job.
- Mitsubishi Motor Manufacturing of America Inc. is rocked by a major class action suit by the Equal Employment Opportunity Commission for sexual harassment of 29 women.[2] Similar allegations are charged at W. R. Grace, CNA Insurance, Smith Barney, and a host of other firms.
- Airlines from USAir to TWA to ValuJet suffer horrendous crashes, killing passengers and threatening their very viability.
- President Clinton, Vice President Gore, sportscasters Marv Albert and Frank Gifford, and even golf legend-in-the-making Tiger Woods are accused in embarrassing scandals.

And these are but the tip of the iceberg—a very few of the hundreds of small and large crises that afflict elements of society today in ever-expanding magnitude (Figure 19–1).

Figure 19–1   In a day of managed care and more competitive hospitals, health care institutions have accelerated communications appeals to the public to deal with individual crises.

No wonder when public relations professionals are asked what subject they want covered in mid-career seminars, "crisis communications" invariably heads the list. Helping to manage crisis is the ultimate assignment for a public relations professional. Smart managements value public relations advice in developing an organization's response not only to crises but to public issues in general. Hundreds of American companies, in fact, have created executive posts for "issues managers," whose task is to help the organization define and deal with the political, economic, and social issues that affect it.

The list of such issues—and of the crises they often evoke—is unending.

In the latter years of the twentieth century, society is flooded with front-burner issues that affect individuals and organizations. From abortion to AIDS, from discrimination to downsizing, from environmentalism to energy conservation, the domain of issues management has become increasingly important for public relations professionals.

ISSUES MANAGEMENT

The process of issues management has been around for two decades. The term was coined in 1976 by public relations counselor W. Howard Chase, who defined it this way:

> Issues management is the capacity to understand, mobilize, coordinate, and direct all strategic and policy planning functions, and all public affairs/public relations skills, toward achievement of one objective: meaningful participation in creation of public policy that affects personal and institutional destiny.[3]

Issues management is a five-step process that (1) identifies issues with which the organization must be concerned, (2) analyzes and delimits each issue with respect to its impact on constituent publics, (3) displays the various strategic options available to the organization, (4) implements an action program to communicate the organization's views and to influence perception on the issue, and (5) evaluates its program in terms of reaching organizational goals.

Many suggest that the term *issues management* is another way of saying that the most important public relations skill is "counseling management." Others suggest that issues management is another way of saying "reputation management"—orchestrating the process whose goal is to help preserve markets, reduce risk, create opportunities, and manage image as an organizational asset for the benefit of both an organization and its primary shareholders.[4]

In specific terms, issues management encompasses the following elements:

- **Anticipate emerging issues.** Normally, the issues management process anticipates issues 18 months to 3 years away. Therefore, it is neither crisis planning nor post-crisis planning, but rather pre-crisis planning. In other words, issues management deals with an issue that will hit the organization a year later, thus distinguishing the practice from the normal crisis planning aspects of public relations.

DEATH OF A TINY BEAUTY QUEEN

The horrible killing of JonBenet Ramsey, six-year-old daughter of a wealthy Boulder, Colorado couple, on Christmas Day 1996, stunned the nation.

Boulder police reported no signs of forced entry and concluded that the murderer was either someone known to the family or perhaps even a family member (Figure 19–2).

Almost immediately, JonBenet's image was flashed, non-stop across the country on TV news and tabloid programs. The Ramseys had encouraged JonBenet to become a child beauty queen, complete with makeup, teased hair, and fashion model clothing. The media jumped on this bizarre aspect of the case with a vengeance. And predictably, the girl's parents became prime suspects in her murder.

The Ramsey's response to the national outcry was equally bizarre. They embarked on a public relations campaign to proclaim their innocence.

Figure 19–2 The late JonBenet Ramsey.

- First, they hired two teams of high-powered criminal attorneys—one for Mr. Ramsey, the other for his wife, to assist in the investigation.

- Second, they secured a Washington, DC, crisis management firm, led by a former Ronald Reagan public relations professional, to handle the hundreds of reporters covering the story.

- Third, both parents appeared on national TV a week after the killing to deny they had killed their little girl. "We are a Christian, God-fearing family," a teary Patsy Ramsey told CNN. "We love our children."[5]

- Finally, JonBenet's parents began their own web site to explain their innocence in vivid detail: "They left for the airport at approximately 6:45 A.M. EST on Dec. 26, 1996, and departed for Atlanta at approximately 8:36 A.M. on Delta flight 954," the site reported about JonBenet's stepbrother and sister. It went on to detail flight tickets, the names of witnesses and various sworn statements from witnesses.

Not surprisingly, other web sites sprang up, including, *www.execpc.com/kopolzin/jbramsey.html*, which included newspaper clippings, TV transcripts, and photos about the unusual case.

While the Boulder police continued to struggle with the investigation into the winter of 1997, some wondered why the little girl's parents seemed more concerned about proving their own innocence with an elaborate public relations offensive, than they were with finding their daughter's killer.

- **Identify issues selectively.** An organization can influence only a few issues at a time. Therefore, a good issues management process will select several—perhaps 5 to 10—specific priority issues with which to deal. In this way, issues management can focus on the most important issues affecting the organization.
- **Deal with opportunities and vulnerabilities.** Most issues, anticipated well in advance, offer both opportunities and vulnerabilities for organizations. For example, in assessing promised federal budget cuts, an insurance company might anticipate that less money will mean fewer people driving and therefore fewer accident claims. This would mark an opportunity. On the other hand, those cuts might mean that more people are unable to pay their premiums. This, clearly, is a vulnerability that a sharp company should anticipate well in advance.
- **Plan from the outside in.** The external environment—not internal strategies—dictates the selection of priority issues. This differs from the normal strategic planning approach, which, to a large degree, is driven by internal strengths and objectives. Issues management is very much driven by external factors.
- **Profit-line orientation.** Although many people tend to look at issues management as anticipating crises, its real purpose should be to defend the organization in light of external factors as well as to enhance the firm's business by seizing imminent opportunities.
- **Action timetable.** Just as the issues management process must identify emerging issues and set them in order, it must propose policy, programs, and an implementation timetable to deal with those issues. Action is the key to an effective issues management process.
- **Dealing from the top.** Just as a public relations department is powerless without the confidence and respect of top management, the issues management process must operate with the support of the chief executive. The chief executive's personal sanction is critical to the acceptance and conduct of issues management within a firm.

Implementing Issues Management

In a typical organization, the tactical implementation of issues management tends to consist of four specific job tasks:

1. **Identifying issues and trends** Issue identification can be accomplished through traditional research techniques as well as through more informal methods. Organizations are most concerned about issues that affect their own residential area. For example, in 1990, when Southern California's sunny skies were steadily threatened by increasingly significant doses of smog, the Unocal Corporation, a Los Angeles–based oil company, seized the initiative. Unocal announced an innovative program, called SCRAP, in which it promised to spend more than $5 million to eliminate six million pounds of air pollution by paying for and scrapping 7,000 old cars. Thanks to SCRAP, in four months California rid its highways of 8,376 gas-guzzling pollution machines. And Unocal won millions of dollars in goodwill (Figure 19–3).

   One way to keep informed about what is being said about a company, industry, or issue is to subscribe to issues-oriented publications of every political persuasion-from *Mother Jones* and *The Village Voice* on the far left to the *Liberty Lobby's Spotlight* on the far right and everything else in between.

Unocal Corporation
1201 West 5th Street, P.O. Box 7600
Los Angeles, California 90051

UNOCAL 76

News Release

Contact: Barry Lane   213/977-7601
         Jim Bray   213/977-5390
         Jeff Callender 213/977-7208

FOR IMMEDIATE RELEASE

Los Angeles, May 10 -- The end of the road is already in sight for more than 2,500 of the 7,000 model year 1970 or older cars Unocal has promised to junk through its SCRAP project.

As part of its South Coast Recycled Auto Program announced last month to fight air pollution in the Los Angeles basin, Unocal has pledged to remove 7,000 1970 or older cars from Southern California freeways. Beginning June 1, the company will pay $700 for each vehicle.

Since the program was announced April 26, Unocal has made appointments to accept autos from more than 2,500 prospective sellers. The cars, which pollute 15 to 30 times more than new models, will be crushed and shredded, and the metal recycled.

The response by sellers to a toll-free telephone number (800-866-2251) was so heavy it prompted telephone company intervention and required the installation of numerous additional lines, according to Richard J. Stegemeier, chairman, president and chief executive officer.

MORE...

-2-

"We were swamped with calls," Stegemeier said. "We couldn't answer the phones fast enough. We're well on our way to reaching the 7,000-car mark and taking millions of pounds of pollutants out of our air permanently."

The 7,000 vehicles Unocal will scrap are estimated to emit 6 million pounds of carbon monoxide, reactive organic gases and nitrogen oxides annually, according to Stegemeier. Among automobiles, 1970 or older cars are the worst polluters on the road.

Other companies also think the program is a good idea. T. J. Rodgers, president and chief executive officer of Cypress Semiconductor, San Jose, Calif., sent Stegemeier a note and a check for $700.

"What a great idea!" Rodgers wrote. "The employees of Cypress Semiconductor and I would like you to buy and bury one for us, too."

The program is part of a three-point Unocal offensive against vehicle emissions. They cause at least 60 percent of the basin's smog, according to the California Air Resources Board.

Besides SCRAP, the other programs are Smog-Fighter, which offers free smog checks and low-emission tune-ups to owners of 1974 and older vehicles, and Protech Patrol, in which emergency vehicles will offer free service to motorists stranded on freeways.

-30-

May 10, 1990

Figure 19–3 Unocal's campaign in the spring of 1990 to rid the Los Angeles Basin of millions of pounds of air pollution was an outstanding example of managing a public relations opportunity.

2. **Evaluating issue impact and setting priorities**   Evaluation and analysis may be handled by issues committees within an organization. Committees can set priorities for issues management action. At the Upjohn Company, for example, a senior policy committee—composed of managers in each of the firm's major divisions, as well as public affairs and legal staff members— meets quarterly to set issues priorities.

3. **Establishing a company position**   Establishing a position can be a formal process. After the Upjohn senior policy committee has met and decided on issues, Upjohn's public affairs staff prepares policy statements on each topic. At PPG Industries, individual issues managers prepare position papers for executive review on topics of direct concern.

4. **Designing company action and response to achieve results**   The best-organized companies for issues management orchestrate integrated responses to achieve results. Typically, organizations may coordinate their Washington offices, state lobbying operations, management speeches, advertising messages, and employee communications to their point of view (Figure 19–4).

Figure 19–4 As a complement to its national religious broadcasts, the group Focus on the Family sponsored this ad in response to such developments as the public school distribution of condoms. This ad was placed in more than 1,300 newspapers across the country and was translated into six languages in eight foreign countries.

Growth of Risk Communication

The 1990s saw the emergence of "risk communication" as an outgrowth of issues management. Risk communication is basically the process of taking scientific data related to health and environmental hazards and presenting them to a lay audience in a manner that is both understandable and meaningful.[6]

Models of risk communication have been developed based on the position that "perception is reality"—a concept that has been part of public relations for years. Indeed, the disciplines of risk communication and public relations have much in common. Risk communication deals with a high level of emotion. Fear, confusion, frustration, and anger are common feelings in dealing with environmental issues. For example, when the tobacco industry was charged with withholding scientific data linking cigarette smoking to cancer, the public was outraged (Figure 19–5), and by 1997, the industry was paying severely for its deception.

Occasionally—even often—intense emotion flows from a lack of knowledge and understanding about the science that underlies societal risk. Therefore, frequent and forceful communication is necessary to inform, educate, and even dampen emotion. The first rule in responding to a perceived public risk is to take the matter seriously. After this, according to risk management expert William Adams, seven steps are helpful in planning a risk communication program:

1. Recognize risk communication as part of a larger risk management program and understand that the whole program is based on politics, power, and controversial issues.
2. Encourage management to join the "communications loop" and help train them to deal effectively with the news media.
3. Develop credible outside experts to act as news sources for journalists.
4. Become an in-house expert, in your own area of risk to enhance your credibility with journalists.
5. Approach the news media with solid facts and figures before they approach you. Verify the veracity of your data.
6. Research perceptions of your organization by the media and other publics to gauge credibility and help determine if your messages will be believable.
7. Understand your target audiences and how the news media can help you communicate effectively.[7]

Like any other area of public relations, risk communication depends basically on an organization's actions. In the long run, deeds, not words, are what count in communicating risk.

MANAGING IN A CRISIS

The most significant test for any organization comes when it is hit by a major accident or disaster. How it handles itself in the midst of a crisis may influence how it is perceived for years to come. Poor handling of events with the magnitude of Pepsi-Cola's syringe scare, Dow Corning's silicone breast implant controversy, NASA's shuttle disaster, Tylenol's capsule poisoning, or ValuJet's Everglades airline crash not only can cripple an organization's reputation but also can cause it enormous monetary loss. It is essential, therefore, that such emergencies be managed intelligently and forthrightly with the news media, employees, and the community at large.

Tobacco is an addictive drug — as addictive as heroin.*
Tobacco addiction is America's leading cause of preventable death.*

How do they
live with themselves?

Si Newhouse

He could voluntarily refuse to push tobacco in his magazines, as many major magazines do. But he hasn't. His magazines probably do more to make smoking seem attractive and sophisticated — what every young person wants to be — than any others. *Fortune* puts his net worth at $5 billion.

Rupert Murdoch

Tobacco advertising is banned on TV, so tobacco companies go after kids in Murdoch's *TV Guide.* He could say no. He's worth $3 billion.

Larry Tisch

As the man who controls Lorillard Tobacco, he could ask Congress to halt all tobacco advertising and promotion. The tobacco companies would save $4 billion a year. That's $4 billion more annual profit for their shareholders — in the short run. In the long run, fewer kids would be enticed to replace smokers who die or quit. But is that bad? *Fortune* says Tisch is a billionaire.

Henry Kravis

Since his company, RJR, began using a cartoon character to push Camels, Camel's share of the teen and pre-teen market has jumped from 1% to 32%. He could become a health hero by joining with Tisch in asking Congress to ban all tobacco promotion — and boost the industry bottom line by $4 billion. Judging from the *Forbes* 400 list, he can afford this risk. He's worth half a billion.

Michael Miles

Miles runs Philip Morris. Who'd have more reason to want a total ad ban than the shareholders of Philip Morris? Marlboro smokers wouldn't quit buying Marlboros just because the advertising stopped; yet Philip Morris could quit spending all those billions trying to defend its market share. Miles — who himself quit smoking long ago — made $5 million last year.

> Like most people who profit from the sale of addictive, unhealthy substances, these men have the good sense not to use those substances themselves. Not one of them smokes cigarettes.

Si, Rupert, Larry, Henry, Mike: If you'll agree it's crazy for a society to *promote* its leading cause of preventable death, and stop doing it, we'll take out an ad **twice as big** honoring you and saying thanks. There's no greater contribution you could make to America's health.

*U.S. Surgeon General

STAT *Stop Teenage Addiction to Tobacco*
NATIONAL OFFICE 511 East Columbus Avenue, Springfield, MA 01105 (413) 732-STAT

For a free book, KIDS SAY DON'T SMOKE, send four 29-cent stamps. If you can help us pay for more ads like this, we'd appreciate it!

Figure 19–5 Led by the Clinton Administration, the tobacco industry was besieged in the late 1990s. So, too, was anyone even remotely related to the industry.

As any organization unfortunate enough to experience a crisis recognizes, when the crisis strikes, seven instant warning signs invariably appear:

1. **Surprise** When a crisis breaks out, it's usually unexpected. Often, it's a natural disaster—a tornado or hurricane. Sometimes, it's a human-made disaster— robbery, embezzlement, or large loss. Frequently, the first a public relations professional learns of such an event is when the media call and demand to know what immediate action will be taken.

2. **Insufficient information**   Many things happen at once. Rumors fly. Wire services want to know why the company's stock is falling. It's difficult to get a grip on everything that's happening.

3. **Escalating events**   The crisis expands. The Stock Exchange wants to know what's going on. Will the organization issue a statement? Are the rumors true? While rumors run rampant, truthful information is difficult to obtain. You want to respond in an orderly manner, but events are unfolding too quickly. This is what Johnson & Johnson experienced as the reports of deaths from Tylenol kept rising.

4. **Loss of control**   The unfortunate natural outgrowth of escalating events is that too many things are happening simultaneously. Erroneous stories hit the wires, then the newsstands, and then the airwaves. As in the case of the Coors mouse in the can, rampant rumors can't easily be controlled.

5. **Increased outside scrutiny**   The media, stockbrokers, talk-show hosts, and the public in general feed on rumors. "Helpful" politicians and observers of all stripes comment on what's going on. The media want responses. Investors demand answers. Customers must know what's going on.

6. **Siege mentality**   The organization, understandably, feels surrounded. Lawyers counsel, "Anything we say will be held against us." The easiest thing to do is to say nothing. But does that make sense?

7. **Panic**   With the walls caving in and with leaks too numerous to plug, a sense of panic pervades. In such an environment, it is difficult to convince management to take immediate action and to communicate what's going on.[8]

PLANNING IN A CRISIS

One irrefutable key in crisis management is being prepared. If there is one certainty in dealing with crisis, it is that all manner of accidents or disruptions make for spectacular headlines and sensational reporting. Reporters, as noted, march to a different drummer. They consider themselves the "guardians of the public trust" and therefore may be quick to point fingers and ascribe blame in a crisis.

Thus, heightened preparedness is always in order.

In terms of dealing with the media, four planning issues are paramount.

- First, for each potentially impacted audience, define the risk.
  "The poison in the pill will make you sick." "The plant shutdown will keep you out of work." "The recall will cost the stockholders $100 million." The risk must be understood—or at least contemplated—before framing crisis communications.
- Second, for each risk defined describe the actions that mitigate the risk.
  "Don't take the pill." "We are recalling the product." "We are studying the possibility of closing the plant." If you do a credible job in defining the risk, the public will more closely believe in your solutions.
- Third, identify the cause of the risk.
  If the public believes you know what went wrong, they are more likely to accept that you will quickly remedy the problem. That's why people get back on airplanes after crashes. Moreover, if the organization helps identify the cause of the problem, the coverage of the crisis is likely to be more balanced.
- Fourth, demonstrate responsible management action.[10]

THE REST OF THE STORY

THE SAD SAGA OF SUSAN SMITH

On October 25, 1994, at 9:15 P.M., America was about to be catapulted again into a media frenzy that would, at least briefly, kick the O. J. Simpson murder case off the front page. In rural South Carolina, Susan Smith, a young mother in her twenties, frantically told police that a black man had carjacked her vehicle and driven off with her two small sons (Figure 19–6).

BOLO

1990 MAZDA PROTEGE', Burgandy Color
South Carolina Tag
GBK 167

Above vehicle taken in a carjacking and abduction occuring on 10/25/94 at approximately 0900 pm. The subject sought is a Black Male appx. 30 years old, wearing a plaid shirt, blue jeans and stocking cap. Subject is considered armed and dangerous. In the victims vehicle are her 14 month old white male and 3 year old white male.

Anyone with information please contact the Union County Sheriff's Department at (803)429-1611, or SLED Headquarters at (803)737-9000.

Figure 19–6   Sheriff's report of the supposedly carjacked Susan Smith vehicle and the "suspect" she described.

For nine days, the country was spellbound as federal, state, and local law enforcement scoured the countryside, looking for the two children. The huge cadre of news media that descended on tiny Union, South Carolina, transported the Smith case from a routine child-knapping to an international event in less than 48 hours.

In reality, the story was a huge deception, fabricated by one person—Susan Smith.

In the end, the South Carolina Law Enforcement Division (SLED) used the media to help crack the case.

■ Immediately upon learning of the "carjacking," SLED officials notified local television in an effort to keep the suspect within a general geographic area.

■ The next day, a decision was made to expand media exposure nationwide, SLED fearing the suspect had eluded the two-state dragnet.

■ SLED made its chief executive, Sheriff Howard Wells, available for constant updates of the situation. With two-a-day news briefings, SLED was able to "control" the speculation.

■ SLED issued interactive recorded announcements to provide updates for radio around the nation. Radio talk shows, in particular, were used heavily to keep the crisis alive and the suspect at bay.

■ Meanwhile, Susan Smith was convinced to appear on network TV and at news conferences to constantly explain what happened and to increase the pressure on her.[9]

Then the case broke. After constant behind-the-scenes prodding from SLED officials while publicly prodding the young mother to appear in public, Susan Smith admitted the crime. On November 9, she was arrested for locking her children in her car, pushing the car into a lake and murdering them. In the end, thanks to savvy police work and a helpful media, Susan Smith received a sentence of life in prison.

Essential to the planning phase is to appear to be in control of the situation. Certainly early on in a crisis, control is lost. But the best firms are those who seize command early and don't acquiesce it to outside, so-called experts. Letting people know that the organization has a plan and is implementing it—helps convince them that you are in control.

Simple but appropriate watchwords for any crisis plan are the following:

● Be prepared.
● Be available.
● Be credible.

All of this implies that you must be willing to communicate in a crisis.

COMMUNICATING IN A CRISIS

The key communications principle in dealing with a crisis is not to clam up when disaster strikes. Lawyers invariably advise clients to (1) say nothing, (2) say as little as possible and release it as quietly as possible, (3) say as little as possible, citing privacy laws, company policy or sensitivity, (4) deny guilt and/or act indignant that such charges could possibly have been made, or (5) shift, or, if necessary, share the blame with others.[11]

Public relations advice, by contrast, takes a different tack. The most effective crisis communicators are those who provide prompt, frank, and full information to the media in the eye of the storm. Invariably, the first inclination of executives is to say, "Let's wait until all the facts are in." But as President Carter's press secretary, Jody Powell, used to say, "Bad news is a lot like fish. It doesn't get better with age." In saying nothing, an organization is perceived as already having made a decision. That angers the media and compounds the problem. On the other hand, inexperienced spokespersons, speculating nervously or using emotionally charged language, are even worse.

Most public relations professionals consider the cardinal rule for communications during a crisis to be

TELL IT ALL AND TELL IT FAST!

As a general rule, when information gets out quickly, rumors are stopped and nerves are calmed. There is nothing complicated about the goals of crisis management. They are (1) terminate the crisis quickly; (2) limit the damage; and (3) restore credibility.[12]

When crisis hits, the organization must assess its communications—particularly in evaluating media requests—by answering the following questions:

1. **What do we gain by participating?** If you have absolutely nothing to gain from an interview, then don't give one. Period.
2. **What are the risks?** The answer is based on your level of comfort with the medium, who the interviewer is, the amount of preparation time available to you, legal liability, and how much the organization loses if the story is told without the interview.
3. **Can we get our message across?** Will this particular medium allow us to deliver our message clearly to the public?
4. **Is this audience worth it?** Often, a particular television program or newspaper may not be germane to the specific audience the organization needs to reach.
5. **How will management react?** An important variable in assessing whether to appear is the potential reaction of top management. In the final analysis, you have to explain your recommendation or action to them.
6. **Does your legal liability outweigh the public interest?** This is seldom the case, although company lawyers often disagree.
7. **Is there a better way?** This is a key question. If an uncontrolled media interview can be avoided, do so. However, reaching pertinent publics through the press is often the best way to communicate in a crisis.

A shorthand approach to communicating in crisis would include the following 10 general principles:

1. Speak first and often.
2. Don't speculate.
3. Go off the record at your own peril.
4. Stay with the facts.
5. Be open, concerned, not defensive.
6. Make your point and repeat it.
7. Don't war with the media.
8. Establish yourself as the most authoritative source.
9. Stay calm, be truthful and cooperative.
10. Never lie.

In the final analysis, communicating in a crisis depends on a rigorous analysis of the risks versus the benefits of going public. Communicating effectively also depends on the judgment and experience of the public relations professional. Every call is a close one, and there is no guarantee that the organization will benefit, no matter what course is chosen. One thing is clear: Helping to navigate the organization through the shoals of a crisis is the ultimate test of a public relations professional.

THE REST OF THE STORY

THE LESSONS OF VALDEZ

Remember the Exxon Valdez case discussed in chapter 2? Because you've probably already dissected it thoroughly, it won't matter if we divulge here, courtesy of crisis expert Tim Wallace, how Exxon should have handled the situation.

1. **Develop a clear, straightforward position.** In a crisis, you can't appear to waffle. You must remain flexible enough to respond to changing developments, but you must also stick to your underlying position. Exxon's seemed to waver.

2. **Involve top management.** Management must not only be involved, it must also appear to be involved. In Exxon's case, from all reports, Chairman Lawrence Rawl was involved with the Gulf of Valdez solutions every step of the way. But that's not how it appeared in public. Rather, he was perceived as distant from the crisis. And Exxon suffered.

3. **Activate third-party support.** This support may come from Wall Street analysts, independent engineers, technology experts, or legal authorities. Any objective party with credentials can help your case.

4. **Establish an on-site presence.** The chairman of Union Carbide flew to Bhopal, India, in 1984, when a Carbide plant explosion killed thousands. His trip at least showed corporate concern. When Chairman Rawl explained that he "had better things to do" than fly to Valdez, Exxon effectively lost the public relations battle.

5. **Centralize communications.** In any crisis, a communications point person should be appointed and a support team established. It is the point person's job—and his or hers alone—to state the organization's position.

6. **Cooperate with the media.** In a crisis, journalists are repugnant; they're obnoxious; they'll stoop to any level to get the story. But don't take it personally. Treat the media as friendly adversaries and explain your side of the crisis. Making them enemies will only exacerbate tensions.

7. **Don't ignore employees.** Keeping employees informed helps ensure that the organization's business proceeds as normally as possible. Employees are your greatest ally. Don't keep them in the dark.

8. **Keep the crisis in perspective.** Often management underreacts at the start of a crisis and overreacts when it builds. The prevailing wisdom seems to be "Just because we're paranoid doesn't mean they're not out to get us!" Avoid hunkering down. Exxon made this mistake, and it cost them dearly.

9. **Begin positioning the organization for the time when the crisis is over.** Concentrate on communicating the steps that the organization will take to deal with the crisis. Admit blame if it's due. But then quickly focus on what you are doing now rather than on what went wrong.

10. **Continuously monitor and evaluate the process.** Survey, survey, survey. Take the pulse of your employees, customers, suppliers, distributors, investors, and, if appropriate, the general public. Determine whether your messages are getting through. Constantly check to see which aspects of the program are working and which are not. Adjust accordingly.

SUMMARY

Although prevention remains the best insurance for any organization, crisis management has become one of the most revered skills in the practice of public relations. Organizations of every variety are faced, sooner or later, with a crisis. The issues that confront society—from energy and the environment, to health and nutrition, to corporate social responsibility and minority rights—will not soon abate. Indeed, issues such as AIDS have gripped society to such a degree that no organization can be silent on the topic (Figure 19–7).

All of this suggests that experienced and knowledgeable crisis managers, who can skillfully navigate and effectively communicate, turning crisis into opportunity, will be valuable resources for organizations in the twenty-first century. In the years ahead, few challenges will be more significant for public relations professionals than helping to manage crisis.

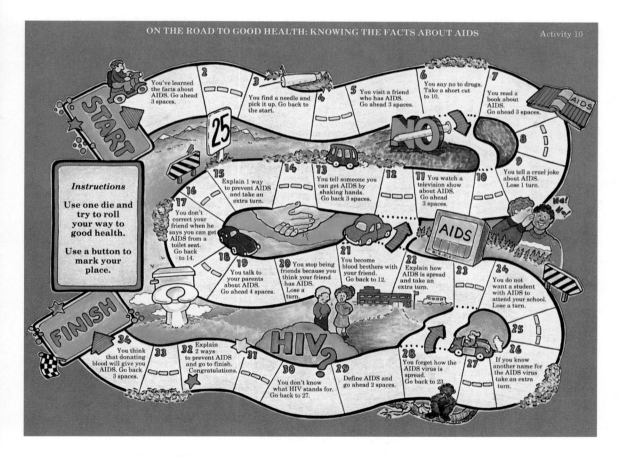

Figure 19–7   Canadian Life and Health Insurance companies teamed up with the Canadian Public Health Association to produce Canada's first AIDS teaching resource for fifth- and sixth-grade students. The package included a student booklet, teacher's guide, word games, and quizzes about the deadly disease.

THE REST OF THE STORY

THE "GATES" OF SCANDAL

Government crisis has dogged every recent American administration. And most of the time, the crisis is conveniently dubbed "gate" of one form or another. Here, alphabetically listed, are some of the most well known presidential "gates."

- **Billygate**—President Carter's brother represented terrorist Libya.
- **Bimbogate**—Collective reference to charges that President Clinton has a roving eye.
- **Coffeegate**—President Clinton hosted White House "coffees" to raise funds for Democrats.
- **Filegate**—Low-level operatives in the Clinton Administration obtained hundreds of classified FBI files.
- **Irangate** (aka Olliegate or Contragate)—Operatives in President Reagan's administration traded arms for U.S. hostages and use the cash to finance Nicaraguan rebels.
- **Iraqgate**—President Bush's administration encouraged massive shipments of arms to Saddam Hussein in his fight against Iran.
- **Lancegate**—President Carter's budget director Bert Lance entangled himself in dubious banking deals.
- **Lippogate**—President Clinton was accused of currying favor with an Indonesian industrial family that gave massive campaign contributions.
- **Nannygate**—President Clinton's attorney general appointees were defeated because of federal tax infractions regarding child-care workers.
- **Passportgate**—President Bush's State Department searched for rival Clinton's passport records to prove he dodged the draft.
- **Travelgate**—President Clinton's White House travel staff was dismissed for apparent political motives.
- **Watergate**—President Nixon's undoing that started it all.

DISCUSSION STARTERS

1. What is meant by the term *issues management*?
2. How can an organization influence the development of an issue in society?
3. What are the general steps in implementing an issues management program?
4. What are the usual stages that an organization experiences in a crisis?
5. What are the principles in planning for crisis?
6. What is the cardinal rule for communicating in a crisis?
7. What are the keys to successful crisis communication?
8. What is the meaning of the term *reputation management*?
9. Why were people suspicious of the parents of JonBenet Ramsey?
10. What are likely to be the flashpoint crisis issues in the the new century?

NOTES

1. Kenneth N. Gilpin, "Prudential Agrees to Pay $35.3 Million in State Fines," *The New York Times* (July 10, 1996): D-1.
2. Rochelle Sharpe, "Mitsubishi U.S. Unit Hasn't Contacted Government of Sexual Harassment Cases," *The Wall Street Journal* (April 26, 1996): B2.
3. "Issues Management Conference—A Special Report," *Corporate Public Issues* 7, no. 23 (December 1, 1982): 1–2.
4. Kerry Tucker and Glen Broom, "Managing Issues Acts as Bridge to Strategic Planning," *Public Relations Journal* (November 1993): 38.
5. Marc Peyser and Sherry Keene-Osborn, "Body in the Basement," *Newsweek* (January 13, 1997): 38.
6. Jeffrey P. Julin, "Is 'PR' a Risk to Effective Risk Communication?" *IABC Communication World* (October 1993): 14–15.
7. William C. Adams, "Strategic Advice in Handling Risk," presented during the Business, Environmental Issues and Risk Conference, Washington, DC, November 12, 1992.
8. Fraser P. Seitel, "Communicating in Crisis," *U.S. Banker* (December 1990): 49.
9. Hugh Smith, "Learning from Crisis: The Sad Saga of Susan Smith," *The Public Relations Strategist* (Summer 1996): 41–43.
10. Sam Ostrow, "Managing Terrorist Acts in the Age of Sound Byte Journalism," *Reputation Management* (November/December 1996): 75–76.
11. Kathy R. Fitzpatrick and Maureen Shubow Rubin, "Public Relations vs. Legal Strategies in Organizational Crisis Decisions," *Public Relations Review* (Spring 1995): 22.
12. Tim Wallace, "Crisis Management: Practical Tips on Restoring Trust," *The Journal of Private Sector Policy* (November 1991): 14.

SUGGESTED READINGS

Center, Allen H., and Patrick Jackson. *Public Relations Practices, Managerial Case Studies & Problems*, 5th ed. Upper Saddle River, NJ: Prentice Hall, 1995.

Cheney, Lynne V. *Telling the Truth: Why Our Culture and Our Country Have Stopped Making Sense and What We Can Do About It*. New York: Simon & Schuster, 1995. The former head of The National Endowment for the Humanities presents an impassioned defense of truth and standards in our society.

Davidson, D. Kirk. *Selling Sin: The Marketing of Socially Unacceptable Products*. Westport, CT: Quorum Books, 1996. Discusses the way crisis-oriented products, such as cigarettes, alcohol, gambling, and firearms are marketed and the problems they present.

Dennis, Everette E., ed. "Covering the Environment." *Gannett Center Journal*, vol. 4, no. 3 (Summer 1990).

Fallows, James. *Breaking the News: How the Media Undermine American Democracy*. New York: Pantheon, 1996. *U.S. News and World Report's* editor-in-chief goes at the journalistic jugular vein, exposing the media as a collection of pompous pretenders who delight in creating crisis out of any insignificant issue. (And that's the good part!)

JACK A. GOTTSCHALK, EDITOR

CRISIS RESPONSE: INSIDE STORIES ON MANAGING IMAGE UNDER SIEGE

DETROIT: VISIBLE PRESS, 1993

This unique volume contains 25 firsthand accounts of crises recounted by those involved in the situations.

Crises are divided into three broad areas: business calamities, consumer troubles, and human tragedies. All contain invaluable lessons about managing in a crisis.

As contributing editor Kurt Stocker says, "The right response to a crisis for one organization may be the exact opposite of the right response for another." Indeed, there is never one right anwser in dealing with a crisis. Each response is as unique as the organization involved.

The crises included in this book—from environmental mishaps, such as the "Meltdown on Three Mile Island" and "The Exxon Valdez Paradox," to great human tragedies, such as "Disaster at Lockerbie" and "Massacre at My Lai"—offer many valuable insights. This book takes a sophisticated look at both capturing the reality and the cost of crises without attempting to provide simplistic solutions. Reading about what others did when placed in the catbird seat of crisis will add greatly to the crisis management expertise of students and practitioners. It is worth the voyage.

Fearn-Banks, Kathleen. *Crisis Communications: A Casebook Approach*. Mahwah, NJ: Lawrence Erlbaum Associates, 1996. Recommends a plan for preventing and dealing with crises based on communication theories.

Ferguson, Mary Ann, Joann M. Valenti, and G. Melwani. "Communicating with Risk Takers: A Public Relations Perspective." *Public Relations Research Annual*, vol. 3. Hillsdale, NJ: Lawrence Erlbaum Associates, 1993.

Gantz, Stanton A., John Slade, Lisa A. Bero, Peter Hanauer, and Deborah E. Barnes. *The Cigarette Papers*. Berkeley: University of California Press, 1996. The authors analyze some 10,000 pages of documents from Brown and Williamson Tobacco Corporation on the company's research into the addictive aspects of cigarettes and smoking. A fascinating dissection.

Gjelten, Tom. *Sarajevo Daily: A City and Its Newspaper Under Siege*. New York: HarperCollins Publishers, 1995. A story from the heart of the Bosnian crisis, written by the National Public Radio correspondent in the region during the vicious Bosnian war.

Hendrix, Jerry A. *Public Relations Cases*, 3rd ed. Belmont, CA: Wadsworth, 1995.

Holmes, Paul A., ed. "Risk Communication: Outrage Causes Misperception." *Inside PR New York* (September 1992): 2.

Lerbinger, Otto. *The Crisis Manager*. Mahwah, NJ: Lawrence Erlbaum Associates, 1997. Focuses on organizations that have no choice but to accept crises as the price of doing business.

O'Dwyer, Jack, ed. *Jack O'Dwyer's Newsletter*. Weekly newsletter. (271 Madison Ave., New York, NY 10016).

Pocket Guide to Preventing Sexual Harassment. Madison, CT: Business & Legal Reports, Inc., 1996. Thorough analysis of what constitutes sexual harassment and what to do about it.

Prato, Lou. *Covering the Environmental Beat.* Washington, DC: RTNDA/Media Institute, Environmental Reporting Forum, 1991.

PR Reporter. Weekly newsletter. (Box 600, Exeter, NH 03833).

Public Relations Review. Quarterly. (Available from the Foundation for Public Relations Research and Education, University of Maryland College of Journalism, College Park, MD 20742.)

Sandman, Peter M. *Addressing Skepticism About Responsible Care.* Washington, DC: Chemical Manufacturers Association, March 1991.

Sandman, Peter M. Risk *Hazard 1 Outrage: A Formula for Effective Risk Communication.* Akron, OH: American Industrial Hygiene Association, 1991.

Shrader-Frechette, K. S. *Risk and Rationality: Philosophical Foundations for Populist Reforms.* Berkeley: University of California Press, 1991.

Simon, Raymond, and Frank W. Wylie. *Cases in Public Relations Management.* Lincolnwood, IL: NTC Publishing Group, 1994. Two eminent professionals discuss some of the most famous crisis management cases, including Hill & Knowlton and Kuwait and P&G and news leaks.

Suskind, Lawrence E. *Dealing with an Angry Public.* New York: The Free Press, 1996. Recommends strategies for dealing with crises, issues, and major public policies.

Young, Davis. *Building Your Company's Good Name: How to Create the Reputation Your Organization Wants & Deserves.* New York: AMACOM, 1996. A how-to book on reputation for business managers in organizations of all types.

CASE STUDY

REBOUNDING FROM THE ULTIMATE CRISIS

The worst tragedy that can befall any company is to see people die as a result of using your product.

When people died after contracting botulism from eating Bon Vivant soup, the company couldn't contain the media onslaught and quickly went out of business. By contrast, in history's greatest example of an effective public relations response, when individuals lost their lives after ingesting tainted Tylenol capsules, Johnson & Johnson and its clear-thinking CEO James Burke immediately stripped the product from store shelves—not once, but twice—to preserve the company's reputation and integrity.

And on Saturday, May 11, 1996, after a ValuJet flight went down in the alligator-infested waters of Florida's Everglades, the company added its name to the growing number of organizations opting for candor and honesty and human concern in the face of unspeakable horror, in this case the deaths of all 110 on board.

The Crash

When CEO Lewis Jordan got the call he was heading a group of ValuJet employees as they built a Habitat for Humanity home that ValuJet Airlines was donating to a needy family. The program called for construction to be done on Saturday May 11th, with Sunday May 12th off and six days of work after that with a dedication the following Saturday. This was the first day.

The communications director's pager registered "911," which signified an emergency. Jordan knew instinctively that the news wasn't good.

He jumped in his car and drove quickly to ValuJet's headquarters, near the Atlanta airport. When he reached the building and met with operational staff members, he knew the worst had happened. ValuJet had lost an airplane with 110 passengers and a crew of five—including a captain Jordan had personally hired.

The Press Conference

Although he didn't have a great deal of information, approximately two hours later, Jordan removed his work shirt, put on a blue ValuJet pullover shirt, and proceeded to lead a hastily organized press conference. He decided immediately to communicate whatever information he had as quickly as possible.

Jordan understood the pitfalls that were possible in going public early, talking openly to the press, and in dealing with the toughest questions. He decided not to screen out any questions nor to refuse to take any questions and not to cut anybody short. "To the contrary, I decided to take more time and if it meant answering the same question 10 times to do so. I've been in the airline industry long enough that I certainly had an appreciation that legal liability is a concern. I had an appreciation that there were financial implications and insurance issues and all kinds of issues. But I can tell you that beyond any of those thoughts—far and above any of the other concerns—the human side of this issue was the most important. And it was my honest belief that in setting the tone for what kind of a company ValuJet Airlines is in the face of a crisis—it was a certainty to me to put human compassion above everything else."

Crisis Priorities

Jordan also decided not to fly to the Everglades crash scene immediately. Rather, he decided to prioritize those things that needed to be done, that would have the most realistic and genuine probability of effectively handling the situation. At 2 A.M. Sunday he was on a flight to Miami for a morning media briefing, and to attend a family meeting.

The number one concern was for the family members who lost loved ones on the airplane. The ValuJet president said, "I also had a responsibility for leadership to the people of ValuJet Airlines. I had a responsibility to the community where this airline is based to answer any questions. As the news began to unfold, we still had another 50 airplanes out there in operation and part of my responsibility was to stand up and talk openly to the public about everything we knew and the things that we didn't know. I considered it not particularly wise in light of all this to depart Atlanta until later after first conducting a press briefing."

Jordan also chose not to subordinate the role of chief spokesperson to the press. "I really never thought that was an option," he said. He felt that with 30 plus years in the airline business, his background as an aerospace engineer and experience in running maintenance and operations dictated that he was the one best suited to stand up there.

Added Jordan, "We knew there was speculation about whether the age of the airplane was a problem, and we didn't think that that was something that would be appropriate for others to be faced with answering. That was not a public relations issue. This was a real issue for our company, our customers, our employees, our shareholders."

The Coverage

Immediately after the crash, Lewis Jordan went on a one-man offensive to save his company. Although the government suspended ValuJet in the aftermath of the crash, the company's president continued to publicly assert that ValuJet would survive and "be back stronger than ever."

What Jordan particularly resented about the coverage was what he called the "rush to judgment." He urged the press to withhold their thoughts on what might have caused the accident. Nonetheless, in the first 48 hours reports aired all over the United States speculating on what may have caused the accident. Some reported, "These are 26-year-old airplanes; this must be an aging aircraft issue." Others said, "Everybody knows that ValuJet requires it's pilots to pay for their own training." Some questioned the Pratt & Whitney engine, which had had failures in other airplanes. Jordan viewed all of this as "unfair, especially to family members who deserved to have facts." In the end, mismarked flammable containers placed in the cargo hold were found to have caused the tragedy.

Despite problems with coverage, ValuJet and Jordan maintained a totally open posture with the media. Assessing the coverage, Jordan said that he: "found some really class people who showed a tremendous amount of dignity and poise and compassion. They understood what we were going through, and many would come up after the interview and shake hands and say, 'We're pulling for you and hang in there and you're doing a great job.' But we had others trying to win some sort of 'jerk of the year award.' Frankly, there were some isolated cases of people who just seemed to want to be nasty and provoke me. We were on a battlefield, where we were going to take hits. And we began to understand that certain publications and certain producers weren't going to tell our side in the world of sound bites and quick quotes; they would get something negative and put it out there."

The Employees, The Critics, The Aftermath

Through the crisis, ValuJet "embraced" its employees as surrogates in the company's fight for survival. The company began to immediately share all the information that it had with key managers. ValuJet put out internal bulletins, internal faxes, and regular updates through its voice mail system. At least once a week, Jordan would conduct a systemwide voice mail update for all employees.

Critics, like former government aviation watchdog Mary Schiavo, and various similarly disposed reporters, took ValuJet to task for inferior operations. The airline took the criticism stoically, choosing not to respond frontally but rather to point out how speculative the allegations were.

Although the airline faced difficult odds, it made a commitment not to give up. Jordan pointed to the support of his 4,000 employees that kept the organization going. By the summer of 1997, ValuJet was back up to about half the size of the airline when the crash occurred; with about 2,000 employees operating 31 airplanes and serving 24 cities. Even the harshest industry critics commended ValuJet and Jordan for facing up without hesitation to the enormity of the situation and the barrage of questions and accusations that could have spelled the demise of ValuJet itself.

Through it all, ValuJet's Jordan continually expressed a sincere concern for the families touched by the tragedy and a steadfast resolve that ValuJet, as an airline, would overcome its awful adversity. And, despite significant odds against it, ValuJet returned to the skies and slowly but steadily, increased its routes and regained customer confidence. In 1997, the airline merged with Airtrans Airways and—probably wisely—changed its name to Airtran.

Figure 19–8   ValuJet and its CEO persevered with a policy of openness and candor in the face of tragedy.

As now Chairman Jordan put it when he was asked what advice he would give to fellow CEOs faced with similar crisis, he replied, "All I did was be myself. I was raised by parents who taught me to stand up and do the right thing" (see Figure 19–8).

BONUS CASE

THE FALL OF TWA

Two months after the ValuJet crash, tragedy struck the airline industry again. TWA Flight 800, shortly after taking off from Long Island's Kennedy Airport, blew up in a ghastly fireball over Long Island on July 12, 1996.

As opposed to the generally positive reviews that ValuJet received in its handling of its crash, TWA was assessed much more harshly.

Within hours of the initial reports of the crash, a frazzled TWA vice president of airport operations reluctantly faced the cameras and microphones. He was jacketless, his TWA employee badge draped around his neck, and way over his head.

As the questions poured in—"Was it terrorism?" ... "Are there survivors?" ... "Was it a new crew?"—it became obvious that the TWA spokesman had few answers. Mercifully, after 15 minutes of non-answers, the operations manager excused himself and went home to sleep.

Meanwhile, TWA CEO Jeffrey Erickson was stranded in London, desperately trying to get to the Long Island crash. TWA's public relations spokespersons were stuck in corporate headquarters in St. Louis, also desperately trying to get to New York.

Alas, they arrived barely in time to pick up the pieces.

By the day after the crash, New York City Mayor Rudy Giuliani, other government officials, and even the families of those who died on board all blamed TWA management for "callousness and indifference." By the end of the tumultuous first week of the crash, President Clinton promised to "look into TWA's handling of the tragedy."

Later, TWA became more focused on its public relations response, and CEO Erickson appeared on network TV—most of the time in tandem with the head of the TWA flight attendants union. In fairness, TWA was hampered by an FBI and National Transportation Safety Board investigation that suspected terrorism and probably didn't want to say too much too soon. How much this hampered the TWA response is unclear. What is clear is that the airline's credibility was severely damaged by its non-response response to its most devastating crash.

Three months later, in October, Erickson, a CEO widely credited with reviving the financial fortunes of the airline, abruptly resigned as president of TWA. By the winter of 1997, the cause of what brought down Flight 800 was still not proven.

QUESTIONS

1. How would you characterize ValuJet's response to its crisis?
2. How would you describe Lewis Jordan's approach to public relations?
3. Was it wise for ValuJet not to delegate the role of chief spokesperson?
4. How would you contrast ValuJet's response to that of TWA in its crash?
5. How would you contrast the image of ValuJet's Jordan to TWA's Erickson?
6. Assuming the FBI limited TWA's response in its crash, what could the airline have done or said to bolster its credibility?

For further information about the ValuJet and TWA cases, see John Elasser, "TWA's Long, Hot Summer," *Public Relations Tactics* (September 1996): 1; Chris Francescani and Kyle Smith, "Horror in the Sky: Downs 747 Off L.I.," *New York Post* (July 18, 1996): 3; Kenneth N. Gilpin, "TWA Chief Quits After Report of Loss," *The New York Times* (October 25, 1996): D1; Michael J. Major, "After the Crash: Will ValuJet Fly High Again?" *Public Relations Tactics* (August 1996): 1; "Nothing Can Prepare You for This," *Reputation Management* (September/October 1996): 69; Carl Quintanilla, "TWA's Response to Crash is Viewed as Lesson in How Not to Handle Crisis," *The Wall Street Journal* (July 19, 1996): Fraser Seitel, "TWA: Tragically Wrong Approach," *Ragan Report* (July 29, 1996): 2.; "ValuJet Rebounding from Tragedy," *The Public Relations Strategist* (Summer 1997): 6.

VOICE OF EXPERIENCE

ROBIN COHN

Robin Cohn is president of Robin Cohn and Company, a New York City–based public relations counseling firm. Ever since her handling of the Air Florida crash in Washington, DC, in 1982, Cohn has become a recognized authority on crisis management and corporate communications. Prior to forming her own company in 1989, she served as head of public and investor relations for financier Ronald O. Perelman's holding companies MacAndrews and Forbes Group and Revlon Group.

WHAT SHOULD BE ONE'S MOST IMPORTANT CONCERNS IN RESPONDING TO CRISIS?

With today's lightning speed of news delivery, it's essential for a company to respond swiftly to limit damage. That being said, the underlying principles of a response include focusing on the victims as well as the cause. A company has to show the public that it believes people come before dollar signs. While it has to explain the problem and correct it, the company also has to be visually accountable to the victims.

WHAT ROLE CAN EFFECTIVE PUBLIC RELATIONS PLAY IN CRISIS?

Public relations is the gas that makes the race car run. The car is not going anywhere without fuel, regardless of its power. Unless a company communicates rapidly and responsibly, the public will assume the worst no matter how well the organization responds internally.

WHAT ARE THE KEY STEPS IN RESPONDING TO CRISIS?

A company should act, not react, in crisis. If an organization has planned for a crisis, it can take control from the beginning by acting quickly and cohesively. This is accomplished through the internal meshing of key players, policies, and procedures:

1. **Take responsibility.** Find out what went wrong and explain how you intend to fix it. Do not indulge in finger-pointing.

2. **Communicate.** Begin communicating with the public as soon as the problem occurs. If there is no accurate information, explain why and provide it when it becomes available. (During the early stages, there will likely be little information.) Communicate to the media, employees, shareholders, local officials, and other key stakeholders at the same time. Get bad news out fast. By trying to bury it, a company risks dragging the story on longer and loses credibility.

3. **Show compassion.** Victims and their families are a top priority. Be prepared to meet their needs.

4. **The buck stops at the CEO.** The CEO is ultimately responsible for the situation. His or her reputation is on the line as well as the company's.

5. **Remember Legal considerations.** Legal advice is a component of crisis management decisions but should not be the driving force. Legal protection does no good if a company has lost its customers and/or credibility. In today's litigious society, people are going to sue no matter what the company says or does.

WHAT IS THE PRIMARY ROLE OF THE CEO?

During the early stages of a crisis, it's crucial that the CEO express the company's feeling for those affected. The CEO is also the one who should explain what's gone wrong and what the company is doing to correct the problem. If the CEO is not immediately accessible, another top ranking official should step in. (TWA, for example, was severely criticized during the early stages of the 800 disaster when there was no response from any top TWA executive.) However, a designated spokesperson should be responsible for disseminating information throughout the crisis. All top executives and spokespeople need to be media trained.

WHAT CONSTITUTES POOR CRISIS MANAGEMENT?

Crises have been poorly managed by companies who weren't accessible to the media, blamed others instead of taking responsibility, and/or didn't tell the truth.

The result is always prolonged media focus; angry customers, shareholders and other stakeholders; law suits; government investigations; attention from public interest groups; and a drop in share price and earnings. The longer a negative story is covered, the bigger the hit to the firm's reputation and bottom line.

WHAT WAS THE MOST DIFFICULT CRISIS YOU'VE HAD TO DEAL WITH?

The Air Florida crash in the Potomac River in 1982. In addition to my personal sorrow for the loss of lives and injuries, I was managing a Murphy's Law crisis. The plane crash was the first to be covered live, complete with dramatic rescue attempts; it occurred in the nation's capital, one of the largest media centers in the world; and the recovery effort to find bodies went on for a week. Most damaging, the jet's tail section with its jaunty logo was stuck in the ice of the Potomac for a full week—a dramatic ongoing visual reminder that made a lasting impression in the public's mind.

WHAT'S THE BEST WAY TO "CONTAIN" A CRISIS?

The only way to contain a crisis and remain credible is by getting the truth out fast. Once it is out, how long can the media keep covering it? It soon becomes old news. A company denial becomes a challenge to reporters, thus prolonging coverage. Bad news can't stay hidden, due to such "sources" as disgruntled employees, incensed customers, or competitors. In the end, when the facts come out, a company looks even worse than if it had been honest in the beginning.

CHAPTER TWENTY

The Future

IN 1996, THE BIGGEST PUBLIC RELATIONS AGENCY in the world, Burson-Marstteller, reported net fees of more than $230 million. The top 50 public relations firms, in fact, recorded net fees in excess of $1.5 billion—the most successful year ever (Figure 20–1). And by the year 2000, the practice of public relations will be even more successful.

As the world moves into the next century, effective public relations has become a commodity that no organization or individual can either take lightly or for granted.

- Early in 1997, *The Wall Street Journal's* lead story, "Old Fashioned PR Gives General Mills Advertising Bargains," spoke glowingly about the return of the revered food maker to tried-and-true public relations techniques, such as Betty Crocker bake offs and sports star tie-ins on Wheaties boxes, to regain its lost luster and sales.[1]
- In the spring of 1997, one of the world's largest shoe companies, Reebok, had to backpedal after attracting a public outcry over the name of its new *Incubus* running shoe. After it was reported that the name *Incubus* meant "an evil spirit believed to descend upon and have sex with women while they sleep"—a horrified Reebok dropped the name.[2]
- In the summer of 1997, an even larger shoe company, Nike, dispatched Andrew Young, former Atlanta mayor and United Nations representative, to look into its overseas labor practices for worker mistreatment. The Young report seemed to satisfy critics.[3]
- That same summer, the world's largest hamburger chain, McDonald's was caught in an embarrassing public relations debacle, when it spent $16 million suing two protesters in Great Britain, who charged Mickey D's with unfair labor practices, animal cruelty, and environmental degradation. The company was shocked when a British judge expressed some agreement with the defendants.[4]
- Even later in 1997, a chagrined—but public relations savvier—boxer Mike Tyson immediately and publicly apologized to the world for biting the ear of heavyweight champion Evander Holyfield.

Why did PR firms have their best year ever?

(A) means ad agency related		1996 Net Fees	Employees	% Fee Change from 1995
1.	Burson-Marsteller (A)	$233,344,022	1,863	+10.1
2.	Shandwick	190,700,000	1,969	+11.4
3.	Hill and Knowlton (A)	160,800,000	1,320	+13.9
4.	Porter Novelli International (A)	121,178,280	1,175	+25.0
5.	Edelman Public Relations Worldwide	111,680,350	1,151	+24.8
6.	Fleishman-Hillard	107,494,000	935	+20.0
7.	Ketchum Public Relations (A)	74,836,000	614	+16.3
8.	GCI Group including GTFH PR (A)	52,293,330	445	+17.4
9.	Ogilvy Adams & Rinehart (A)	48,544,000	410	+17.7
10.	Manning, Selvage & Lee (A)	47,925,000	370	+25.7
11.	Bozell Sawyer Miller Group (A)	43,900,000	276	+8.0
12.	Ruder Finn	41,870,165	366	+26.8
13.	Cohn & Wolfe (A)	25,034,552	198	+35.9
14.	Financial Relations Board	20,224,882	209	+23.7
15.	Morgen-Walke Assocs.	16,504,604	126	+30.9
16.	Cunningham Communication	15,661,623	109	+38.8
17.	The Weber Group (A)	14,595,156	156	+18.6
18.	Powell Tate	14,324,343	70	+15.0
19.	The Kamber Group	11,250,000	95	+28.1
20.	Technology Solutions	10,795,000	121	+44.5
21.	MWW/Strategic Communications	10,479,000	92	+24.0
22.	Gibbs & Soell	9,605,000	97	+5.4
23.	Stoorza, Ziegaus & Metzger	8,884,417	71	-4.6
24.	Dewe Rogerson	8,725,427	69	+21.0
25.	Pacific/West Communications Group	7,969,000	55	+4.0
26.	Dan Klores Assocs.	7,428,839	46	+48.0
27.	Interscience (A)	7,341,458	40	+29.0
28.	SCIENS Worldwide PR (formerly NCI PR)(A)	7,066,779	50	+52.0
29.	EvansGroup PR (A)	7,013,993	64	+17.0
30.	Dix & Eaton	6,787,312	51	+24.7
31.	Makovsky & Co.	6,504,000	58	+24.6
32.	Noonan/Russo Communications	6,400,000	34	+25.0
33.	Padilla Speer Beardsley	5,920,220	59	+24.2
34.	Earle Palmer Brown Cos. (A)	5,824,196	50	-16.9
35.	KCSA Public Relations	5,720,350	58	+14.63
36.	Nelson Communications Group	5,624,940	45	-0.04
37.	Wilson McHenry Co.	5,394,026	40	+31.8
38.	Cramer-Krasselt Public Relations (A)	5,130,000	47	+21.0
39.	Blanc & Otus	5,079,647	44	+4.7
40.	Karakas, VanSickle, Ouellette (A)	4,933,132	45	+45.0
41.	Morgan & Myers	4,849,673	56	+33.6
42.	The Tierney Group	4,836,786	33	+15.2
43.	Bender, Goldman & Helper	4,743,368	52	+6.2
44.	Dennis Davidson Assocs.	4,605,175	61	+19.0
45.	Dye, Van Mol & Lawrence	4,571,156	69	+11.3
46.	Ryan-McGinn	4,549,521	23	+66.3
47.	Public Communications	4,386,601	46	+15.4
48.	Edward Howard & Co.	4,255,626	40	+6.1
49.	MCC	4,235,324	41	+75.0
50.	William Silverman and Co.	4,223,378	31	+21.7
	Totals:	**1.547 billion**	**13,395**	**average +20.0%**

Because PR works.

1996 fee income of firms reporting to O'Dwyer's Directory of PR Firms

O'Dwyer's Directory of PR Firms tells you how to hire a PR firm and gives you 1,800 firms in the U.S. and 500 worldwide. $145 from the O'Dwyer Co. Call **212/679.2471** to place order. Fax is **212/683.2750**. MasterCard and Visa accepted.

Figure 20–1 The latter years of this century have proven to be a "golden age" for public relations.

The point of these examples is that public relations—whether people like it or not—is here to stay and can only expand its impact on society as communications in the twenty-first century becomes even more omnipresent.[5]

On the other hand, in its "Report and Recommendations," the Second Task Force on the Stature and Role of Public Relations, released by the Public Relations Society of America, concluded:

Public relations will either become recognized as an indispensable key to all organizations' viability or it will be relegated to merely carrying out a range of useful techniques.

There is evidence that since 1980, while the field has grown greatly in number of practitioners, the majority of additions have been at the tactical level.[6]

Therein lies the difficulty in which public relations finds itself as we approach the millennium. On the one hand, the ability of individuals and organizations to communicate has never been more critical. On the other hand, the mergers, consolidations, takeovers, and downsizings that have ravaged America and the world have taken a heavy toll on the ranks of public relations professionals.[7]

The challenge, then, for all who practice public relations in the years ahead is to seize the tremendous opportunities that accompany the emerging issues of the day.

Public relations is faced with all of the challenges associated with an increasingly popular field. The practice is "hot," and many want to enter it. Indeed, according to *Fortune* magazine, public relations jobs will rank just behind such popular areas as computer software, home health care, and motion picture production in terms of attracting applicants in the new century.[8] However, as noted, with the recession and cutbacks of the 1990s, public relations positions have become increasingly competitive in terms of applicants.

In addition, as management becomes more aware of the role of public relations, its performance expectations of the practice become higher. Thus, the standards to which public relations professionals are held will also increase. Finally, because access to top management is a coveted role and public relations is generally granted that access, key public relations positions will be sought eagerly by managers outside the public relations discipline. This is yet another key challenge that will confront public relations professionals in the next century.

ISSUES OF THE MILLENNIUM

Undeniably, the people who practice public relations today must be better than those who came before them. Institutions today operate in a pressure-cooker environment and must keep several steps ahead of the rapid pace of social, economic, and political change. The environment is being shaped by many factors.

- **Economic globalization.** This is affecting all organizations, even nonmultinational companies. The world is getting smaller. Communism is dead or dying. Democracy and free enterprise reign supreme. Competition will intensify, and so will communications, making it easier to communicate around the world but much more difficult to be heard. Public relations has become a growth industry around the world.
- **Shifting public opinion.** Sudden shifts in public opinion are being ignited by instantaneous communications, challenging the ability of communicators to respond to fast-moving events. Interest groups of every stripe are jockeying for position on the public stage.

▲▲▲▲▲▲▲

THE REST OF THE STORY

RAPPING IN THE MILLENNIUM

One of the communications challenges of the new century is understanding the current language, as spoken by the "leaders" of our society—from Beck to Mariah Carey to the Wu-Tang Clan. Toward that end, here is the updated lexicon of rap—which may or may not be obsolete by the time you read this!

- No diggity: That's the truth.
- Props: Kudos, respect.
- Peeps: Friends.
- Butter: Smooth, nice.
- Shorty: Girlfriend.
- Playa hater: A person jealous of another's success.
- Floss: Bragging and boasting.
- Mad: Great.
- Flava: Style.
- Sweat: Harass.
- Cronkite: News.

- **Aging of society.** Baby boomers have turned 50 and dominate society. Households headed by people over 55 are the fastest-growing segment of the consumer market in America, and this group controls an increasing percentage of all personal income.
- **Downsizing.** The new reality of employment is that "nothing lasts forever." Lifetime employment is no longer possible in most organizations. With downsizing, companies are continuing to pare overhead and trim staff to become more competitive. The effect on business and employee morale is profound, and the need for good internal communications is critical.
- **Corporate responsibility.** This buzzword of the 1960s and 1970s, which all but disappeared in the 1980s and resurfaced in the 1990s, will become even more critical in the 2000s. This is especially true as organizations eliminate jobs and as legal and ethical questions arise on issues from smoking to sexual harassment to AIDS to corporate democracy to proper treatment of the environment.
- **Technology.** The emerging "information highway" that will link television, telephones, and databases is a potential gold mine for public relations professionals, who can help consumers navigate their way through the many electronic offerings.[9] Indeed, already public relations professionals have become masters of the web and organizational home pages. Public relations agencies, which specialize in communicating in cyberspace have sprouted. In addition, the emergence of on-line data sources, facts on demand, computer software programs, and CD-ROM disks are revolutionizing the way public relations practitioners target their messages (Figure 20–2).

Coupled with these factors is a society that seems incapable of curbing its voracious appetite for costly litigation. No product or service area is immune from potential suit.

Figure 20–2   Maximizing the potential of CD-ROMs is one of the significant challenges that confronts the public relations profession as society approaches the year 2000.

Bigness is back in vogue, with mergers not only among huge industrial corporations, but also among hospitals, banks, media companies, and others. Yet, at the same time, a growing body of opinion sees big business as a threat, especially because it has become more active politically. Once the delivery of the Sears Roebuck catalog was an "event" in rural America. But today that time and goodwill is long gone from our culture.[10] Consumers are demanding greater accountability from all institutions, as well as higher standards of ethical conduct.

In the face of all these changes, it is understandable that management today is giving greater attention than ever before to the public's opinions of its organization and to public relations professionals who can help deal with these opinions.

PUBLIC RELATIONS CHALLENGES IN THE MILLENNIUM

As the significance of the practice of public relations intensifies, so will the challenges confronting the public relations profession. The challenges will be worldwide, just as the field itself has become worldwide. The power of communication, especially global communication, will no longer be an American domain. Among the significant challenges confronting public relations professionals are the following:

- **Need for tailored approaches**   Demographic changes will affect the way professionals communicate. Public relations practitioners will have to target messages across cultural lines to special groups within the population. This will involve narrowcasting, as opposed to broadcasting. With the mass media, as noted, playing a less important role, more emphasis will be required on personalized, tailored approaches.
- **Development of new medias**   As technology continues to advance, new and exotic forms of information dissemination will evolve. These media will capture public attention in the most creative ways—interactive video, talking billboards, blimps, in-flight headsets, and myriad others. Public relations will have to be equally creative to keep up with the new media and harness them for persuasive purposes.
- **Increased specialization**   Public relations professionals will have to be much more than a conduit between an organization and the public. They will have to be much more fully informed about company policy and activities. They will have to be specialists—experts in dealing with, for example, the media, consumers, and investors—possessing the sophisticated writing ability that management demands. At the same time, public relations will have to avoid what some have called the "balkanization" of the practice into discrete functions and away from management counseling.[11]
- **Results orientation**   The growth of research to measure and evaluate public relations results will continue. Public relations professionals must find ways to improve their measurement capability and justify their performance—that is, the results of their actions—to management.
- **Creativity**   Innovation in the new century will be at a premium. Management will expect public relations people to provide creative approaches to organizational problems, thoughtful programs for overcoming or avoiding trouble, and novel ideas for getting attention. This will be particularly true in the increased need for marketing support by public relations professionals. The public relations department must be the storehouse of creativity in the organization.
- **Decreased sexism**   Women are becoming more dominant in public relations and in fact outnumber men in the practice. Their numbers are increasing, and the salary gap with men, although not yet acceptable to many, is nonetheless narrowing. According to a 1995 study of the Public Relations Society of America, women practitioners were paid less than men, even when other factors—age, years of experience, education—were considered.[12] This is another challenge for the field in the new century.
- **Increased globalization**   The globalization of public relations will accelerate for three reasons in the 2000s. First, U.S. and international companies will increasingly recognize the potential of overseas expansion. Second, media globalization will mandate that stories be told worldwide and not be kept within national borders. Third, more countries will realize the benefits of professional public relations assistance.
- **Technology**   Public relations professionals, as noted, will be blessed with an expanding array of technological tools to cope with the speed and impact of rapid, more global communications. Professionals must be aware of and master the new technology described in chapter 10 if the field is to continue to develop.[13]

PUBLIC RELATIONS GOES GLOBAL

In the twenty-first century, no emerging trend will be more important for the field than that of globalization. According to one leader in the field: "Clearly, there are great challenges for us ahead in public relations to tell the true story of global competition and our new world economic order. And that story must be told accurately, objectively, clinically, if we are to stave off a return to trade barriers and to regionalized economic wars."[14]

Major political shifts toward democracy throughout the world, coupled with the rapidity of worldwide communications and the move to form trading alliances of regional nations, have focused new attention on public relations. The collapse of communism, the coming together of European economies, and the outbreak of democracy everywhere from Eastern Europe to South Africa have brought the global role of public relations into a new spotlight.

Canada

Canadian public relations is the rival of American practice in terms of its level of acceptance, respect, sophistication, and maturity. The Canadian Public Relations Society, formed in 1948, is extremely active. Canada differs from the United States in the aggressiveness of its public relations practice. Although most communications programs, activities, and theories appear, on the surface, to be the same as in the United States, Canadian communications—particularly internal communications—is still some years behind those of its southern neighbor.[15]

Latin America

In Latin America the scene is more chaotic. The field is most highly developed in Mexico, where public relations practice began in the 1930s. Mexican corporations all have communications and public relations departments, and many employ local or U.S. public relations agencies. Mexican schools of higher learning also teach public relations. The passage of the North American Free Trade Agreement (NAFTA) in 1993 means increasing opportunities for U.S.–Mexican trade and therefore for public relations growth. In the other countries of Latin America, public relations is less well-developed. However, the expanding economies of Argentina, Brazil, Venezuela, and Chile, in particular, indicate clearly that Latin American public relations will grow in the years ahead. Chile, with its booming economy and approach to capitalism is a particularly prominent candidate for increased public relations activity in the initial years of the new century.

The New Europe

Like Canada, public relations developed more or less simultaneously in Europe and the United States during the nineteenth century.[16] In Germany, in particular, public relations writings appeared in the early 1900s.

In the latter years of the 1990s, privatization and the synthesis of the European Community into a more unified bloc have spurred increased public relations action in many European countries. For example, public relations has experienced tremendous growth in Great Britain. The largest U.K.-based public relations operation is one of the world's largest independent agencies, the Shandwick Group, with more than $190 million in net fees in 1996.

THE REST OF THE STORY

A "TOO AMERICAN" PUBLIC RELATIONS APPROACH?

Volkswagen AG, the huge German car maker, hired Klaus Kocks in 1996 to bring some sanity to a standoffish, no-comment public relations posture that wasn't serving the company well on the world stage. Volkswagen sought to be more disclosure-oriented and looked to Kocks for guidance. Kocks was one of Germany's premier public relations professionals and eminently knowledgeable about U.S. public relations techniques, having taught for a while in Minneapolis. Volkswagen looked to him to be its spokesman.

The company got a bit more than it bargained for.

At first Kocks was a breath of fresh air at the tight-lipped company, repairing relations with leading media and being available for comment at any time. But then in rapid order, Kocks:

- In an interview, called his boss's lawyers and public relations advisors "idiots."
- Hired disgraced former Clinton adviser Dick Morris to speak to VW's public relations staff during the Paris Auto Show and also to "help clean up VW's image."
- Told a packed press conference that a book tying the VW Beetle to the Nazi regime might encourage General Motors to play the "Jewish card" in its continuing battle with Volkswagen.
- Was quoted by the *Los Angeles Times* as saying, "Here I am, sitting in Germany, a Kraut . . . facing a civil suit in the U.S. . . . with an Austrian CEO who happens to look like Hitler when he smiles. We have all the luck."

Through it all, Kocks remained resolute that his shoot-from-the-lip approach was helping his employer. "In the past, VW failed to explain what it really meant," he said. "We're now very outspoken and understandable."

With that, there could be no argument.

The Institute of Public Relations, headquartered in London, is the largest professional organization in Europe for public relations practitioners. It encompasses 13 regional groups located throughout Britain. It maintains close relations with another group, the European Confederation of Public Relations Associations, with branches in 19 European countries.

Recent surveys indicate that the public relations issues germane to the United States also are prominent in Europe. Among them, global competition, government regulation, environmental issues, and new technology head the list.[17] As European organizations pay increased attention to their reputations and how they are perceived, public relations is certain to be at the forefront of European commercial concern in the years ahead.

Asia

Although public relations has evolved slowly in Asia, in the 1990s Asian public relations has experienced sharp growth.[18]

In Japan, the public relations profession was established after World War II. Although the Japanese take a low-key approach to public relations work—especially self-advocacy—the field is growing, particularly as the media—six major national newspapers and four national networks—become more aggressive in investigating a proliferation of national scandals. Japanese public relations differs markedly from that of the West. For example, Keiretsu business associations—which bring together individual firms—operate with enormous influence as intermediaries in arranging press events. In the 1990s, television in general and talk shows in particular have become increasingly popular in Japan.

Elsewhere in Asia, public relations also has begun to take root. Korea has an active public relations community, as do Indonesia, Taiwan, and Singapore. In Singapore, for example, public relations is dominated by new companies raising funds through a booming stock market and active economy. Technology, financial services, and real estate development also are burgeoning areas of public relations growth.[19]

China, after a number of false starts, holds great potential for public relations expansion. By 2020, some predict that 70 percent of the world will name Mandarin as their principal language. China is the world's fastest growing economy, second only to the United States, which it should pass soon. As the nation with the largest consumer population, China ranks eleventh in world trade and holds magnificent promise. Even with government control, some 150,000 Chinese log onto the Internet every day.[20] The opening of McDonald's outlets in Beijing and Guangzhou, as well as a growing number of American corporate fixtures portend that China will be a growing hub for public relations activity as the new century unfolds.

Opportunities for public relations work also will emerge in Vietnam, as it rejoins the world community. Indeed, a major U.S. business and trade mission to Hanoi in 1993 and the return of a U.S. ambassador to the country in 1997 suggest the public relations potential of a newly rediscovered Vietnam.

Eastern Europe

There are 370 million consumers in recently democratized Eastern Europe. The prospects for public relations expansion are enticing.

- More than 80 percent of all Eastern Europeans watch television daily. Nearly 100 percent watch several times a week.
- In Hungary, about 20 percent of the population have TV sets connected to satellite dishes.
- In Poland, 13 percent of the population report owning VCRs.
- In Hungary, Serbia, and Croatia, about two-thirds of the population read newspapers daily.[21]

A newly-capitalist Russia also comprises burgeoning public relations work place. AT&T, Intel, Coca-Cola, and many other companies are already ensconced there. Large American public relations firms have also set up bases. PR Newswire, in combination with the news agency TASS, distributes news releases from U.S. companies to locations in the Commonwealth of Independent States. Releases are translated into Russian and reach 40 newspapers in Moscow alone.

Australia

The 1988 International Public Relations Association Conference in Melbourne was indicative of the rapid advance of the public relations practice "down under." The Public Relations Institute of Australia is an extremely active organization and the practice is widespread, particularly in the country's two commercial centers, Melbourne and Sydney.

Middle East

Although the public relations profession is less active in the Middle East, the power of public relations is well known and understood. Indeed, during the 1990 invasion of Kuwait, Iraq's leader Saddam Hussein was quick to harness the world's communications apparatus to spread his views. The Kuwaitis, as noted, responded by hiring Hill & Knowlton to represent the country in an appeal for American support. Even in countries as traditional as Saudi Arabia, public relations work has begun to carry increased significance.[22] One positive sign in the growth of the field in the Middle East was the admission of 20 women students into the public relations major program at the United Arab Emirates University in Al-Ain in 1995.[23]

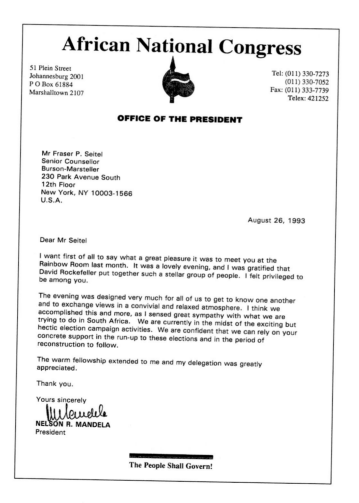

Figure 20–3   A worldwide communications campaign for sympathy and support fueled the dramatic sea change in South Africa when Nelson R. Mandela became the first democratically elected president of that nation in the spring of 1994.

Africa

In Africa, too, the practice of public relations is growing. In 1990, the largest public relations meeting in the history of the continent was held in Abuja, Nigeria, with 1,000 attendees from 25 countries. In 1994, as a result of an extensive worldwide communications and public relations campaign, Nelson R. Mandela was elected the first democratically elected president of the nation of South Africa (Figure 20–3). Africa, too, has discovered the power of public relations.

A QUESTION OF ETHICS

BRUSHING AWAY A DARK BLOT

Colgate-Palmolive is one of the most savvy international conglomerates. Colgate's toothpaste, shampoo, detergent, and other household and hygiene products account for more than $6 billion in worldwide sales.

However, when Colgate purchased 50 percent of the Hawley & Hazel Company in Hong Kong in 1985, it had no idea of the international controversy the union would spark. Hawley & Hazel marketed "Darkie," the best-selling toothpaste brand in several Asian countries. Darkie toothpaste was identifiable in Asia by the picture of a minstrel in black face on the package. The minstrel became part of the product's package design in the 1920s, after the then CEO of Hawley & Hazel saw American singer Al Jolson and thought his wide, white, toothy smile would make an excellent logo.

And for many years, it did—until the union with Colgate-Palmolive brought intense criticism from religious groups and others, not only for the depiction of the minstrel, but also for using the name Darkie.

In 1986, three Roman Catholic groups filed a shareholder petition demanding that Colgate-Palmolive change the Darkie name and logotype.

Michigan Congressman John Conyers joined the fracas when he learned about Darkie while traveling in Taiwan in 1988.

Colgate responded by conducting extensive consumer studies and considering hundreds of alternatives. Because Darkie accounted for nearly all of Hawley & Hazel's business, with a market share ranging from 20 to 70 percent in Hong Kong, Malaysia, Singapore, Taiwan, and Thailand, the company feared a false step.

Finally, in 1989, Colgate Chairman Ruben Mark announced the toothpaste would be renamed Darlie, and the logotype would become a portrait of a man of ambiguous race wearing a silk top hat, tuxedo, and bow tie. Said Mark, "It's just plain wrong. It's just offensive. The morally right thing dictated that we must change. What we have to do is find a way to change that is least damaging to the economic interests of four partners."

Under the agreement, Colgate-Palmolive agreed to pay for all redesign and repackaging costs and for the added advertising costs involved in the changeover. It also said it would reimburse Hawley & Hazel for any loss in profits caused by customer confusion over the change to Darlie.

How do you think Colgate-Palmolive handled this controversy?

COUNSELING TOP MANAGEMENT

No challenge for public relations professionals in the future is more important than counseling senior management. Top managers in companies, hospitals, associations, governments, educational institutions, and most other organizations need counsel. Most CEOs think in terms of "tangibles"—revenue, income, costs per thousands, etc. Public relations professionals think in terms of "intangibles"—attitudes, opinions, motivation, tomorrow morning's headline and the like. Top management needs advice in these areas, and public relations practitioners must provide it.

Public relations people in the years ahead must be willing and eager to provide a counseling role to management. Accomplishing such a task will depend on the following 10 characteristics:

1. **Intimate knowledge of the institution** A public relations professional may be an excellent communicator, but without knowledge of the industry or institution represented, his or her ultimate value will be limited.

2. **Access to and respect for management** The public relations professional who acquires the respect of top management is a powerful force in an organization. Respect comes only from exposure. Thus, it is essential that the public relations professional have ready access to the most senior managers in an organization.

3. **Access to an intelligence network** Public relations professionals need their own intelligence network to give them the unvarnished truth about programs and projects. If the executive vice president is an idiot, if the employee incentive program isn't working, or if the chairman's speech was terrible, the public relations professional must be able to tap a team of candid employees who will tell the truth so that the practitioner can tell the unvarnished truth to top management—unexpurgated, uncensored, between the eyes.

4. **Familiarity with the reporter on the beat** A public relations professional, no matter how high up in an organization, should keep in touch with the reporters and analysts who follow the organization. Valuable information can be gleaned from such observers and can be most helpful to top management.

5. **Solid skills base** The most competent public relations counselors don't just give orders, they demonstrate skills. They are generally good writers who don't mind pitching in to complete a job competently. In public relations, communications competence is a prerequisite for counseling competence.

6. **Propensity toward action** In working for top management, results and performance are all that count. Certainly, planning and setting strategies are critical aspects of public relations. But practitioners, especially those who counsel management, must be inclined toward action. They must be doers. That's what management demands.

7. **Knowledge of the law** Public relations work today confronts legal issues: privacy, copyright, lobbying, securities laws, broadcasting regulations, and so on. Although public relations professionals need not be trained lawyers, they must at least be conversant in the general concepts of the law in order to counsel management effectively and to deal with legal counselors.

8. **Knowledge of technological change** The Internet, the World Wide Web, cyberspace—all must be part of the purview of the savvy public relations counselor. Harnessing the new technology is imperative for communications in the twenty-first century. Therefore, public relations people must master the technology.

9. **Strong sense of integrity and confidence**   As noted throughout these pages, public relations professionals must be the ethical conscience of organizations. Their motives and methods must be above reproach. It's also important that public relations counselors demonstrate confidence in their own positions and abilities. They must surround themselves with the highest-caliber performers to enhance the status of the public relations function within the organization.

10. **Contentment with anonymity**   Public relations counselors must understand that they are exactly that—counselors to top management. It is the chief who delivers the speeches, charts the strategies, and makes the decisions. It is the chief, too, who derives the credit. Public relations counselors must remain in the background and should try to stay anonymous. Today, with newspapers demanding the names of spokespersons, with some public relations practitioners attaining national celebrity status, and with the field itself becoming more and more prominent, the challenge of anonymity becomes increasingly more difficult.[24]

THE REST OF THE STORY

THINK MULTILINGUAL—OR ELSE

According to America's foremost "nameologist," Steve Rivkin, organizations dealing overseas better think multilingual—or else.

Or else what? Or else this:

■ A food company named its giant burrito a "Burrada." Big mistake. The colloquial meaning of that word in Spanish is "big mistake."

■ Estee Lauder was set to export its "Country Mist" makeup when German managers pointed out that "mist" is German slang for "manure." (The name became "Country Moist" in Germany.)

■ General Motors introduced the Chevrolet "Nova" in South America and was shocked to learn that "no va" is Spanish for "does not go." After GM realized it wouldn't sell many of the "go-less" cars, it renamed the vehicle "Caribe" in Spanish markets.

■ Ford had a similar problem in Brazil when it introduced the "Pinto." The name it turned out was Brazilian slang for "tiny male genitals." Red faced Ford pried off all the nameplates and renamed the car "Corcel", which means horse.

■ Colgate introduced a toothpaste in France called "Cue," the name of a notorious French porno magazine.

■ The name "Coca-Cola" in China was first rendered as "ke-kou-ke-la." Unfortunately, Coke did not discover until after thousands of signs had been printed that the phrase means "bite the wax tadpole." Coke then researched 40,000 Chinese characters and found a close phonetic equivalent, "ko-kou-ko-le," which loosely translates as "happiness in the mouth." Much better.

■ A leading brand of car deicer in Finland will never make it to America. The brand's name: "Super Piss."

■ Ditto for Japan's leading brand of coffee creamer. Its name: "Creap."*

*Courtesy of Rivkin & Associates, 233 Rock Road, Glen Rock, NJ 07452

EMERGING ISSUES IN PUBLIC RELATIONS

The issues that concern public relations professionals vary from organization to organization and from industry to industry. Nonetheless, several issues concern all practitioners, especially as the field continues to become increasingly respected and to improve its credibility.

Public Relations Education

For public relations to continue to prosper, a solid educational foundation for public relations students must be in place. Today's practitioner has two key stakes in public relations education: future employees and the profession itself.

Over the last few years, the Public Relations Society of America (PRSA) and other organizations have focused on the formal education of public relations students. Among the highlights of a design for undergraduate public relations education, authored by the Public Relations Division of the Association for Education in Journalism and Mass Communication, the Educator's Section of PRSA, and PRSA itself, were the following recommendations:

- Two subjects tied for the highest ratings by practitioners and educators: English (within general education) and an internship/practicum/work-study program (within public relations education).
- It is recommended that public relations students, especially those planning to enter the corporate or agency world, give strong consideration to business as their secondary area of study.
- The traditional arts and sciences remain the solid basis for the undergraduate education of public relations students, essential to their professional functioning in a complex society.[25]

The report indicated strong agreement between practitioners and educators on the ideal content of undergraduate public relations education. Basically, strong emphasis was placed on communications studies, public relations principles and practices, and ethics. The report further concluded that the growing cooperation and relationships between professionals in the practice of public relations and in education should be nurtured and strengthened to benefit today's students in the field. Indeed, most practitioners agree that internships in the field are crucial to nurturing the next generation of public relations professionals.[26]

Women in Public Relations

Another issue of concern in the field is the aforementioned impact of the increasing percentage of women in public relations and business communications. In 1980, women accounted for only 10 percent of the public relations population. Today that number is well over 50 percent.[27] Many practitioners express concern that public relations could become a "velvet ghetto," populated almost entirely by women. The expansion of women in public relations is not surprising. Women account for up to 65 percent of all journalism graduates in the United States.

One of the most comprehensive studies of this issue was launched in 1986 by the International Association of Business Communicators. Its results indicated that women are increasingly filling the ranks of communications technicians rather than managers. As a result, women are being paid less than men, with gender being the strongest predictor of salary. Among its conclusions, the report found that the situation does not appear to be improving. Instead, men are turning to other professions or are positioning themselves in the most highly paid areas within the field, such as communications management.

Despite this, changes should arrive soon—perhaps by the end of this decade. Clearly, more women will enter top management jobs, not only in public relations but in many other fields. Some predict that the 1990s will be the "Decade of Women in Leadership Positions." Two who do are John Naisbitt and Patricia Aburdene, coauthors of *Megatrends 2000*, who point to the following:

- Women already hold 39 percent of the 14 million U.S. executive, administrative, and management jobs, according to the Bureau of Labor Statistics—nearly double the figure of two decades ago.
- More than half of all officers, managers, and professionals in the nation's 50 largest commercial banks are women.
- More than one-third of Procter & Gamble's marketing executives are women. At the Gannett Company, almost 40 percent of the managers, professionals, technicians, and sales force are women. At Apple Computer, the numbers are similar.
- Of today's MBA degree recipients, 33 percent are women. Women now earn 13 times more engineering degrees than they did 15 years ago.
- In 1966, fewer than 7 percent of M.D. degrees were granted to women. Today the number is 33 percent. In 1966, women were awarded 3 percent of all law degrees. Today, 40 percent of all law degrees are granted to women.
- Women are starting their own businesses at twice the rate of men.[28]

The fact is that women are moving toward parity in salary and position in the practice of public relations. These trends indicate that an increasing number of women will join the ranks of public relations leadership in the twenty-first century.

External Challenges

Inevitably, as public relations has enhanced its role in society and increased its respect within organizations, the field itself has attracted others—lawyers, accountants, personnel managers, and general managers of varying backgrounds. Because the public relations executive of an organization is usually close to top management and because access is power in an organization, the role occupied by public relations has become a coveted one.

Incursions into public relations by others in an organization have intensified. Public relations practitioners must use their special expertise and unique experience to reinforce their prominent positions in the organizational hierarchy.

One antidote for the incursion into the field by others is for public relations professionals to become well-versed in the multiplying array of issues that concern organizations and the public. The issues that capture public attention are diverse and rapidly changing. This suggests that the truly successful practitioner in the years ahead must stay abreast of the changing issues that dominate public discourse (Figures 20–4 and 20–5).

Public relations professionals today also must be sensitive to public criticism. Twenty years ago, public relations people were anonymous. They operated as faceless spokespersons and behind-the-scenes operatives. Today, however, with the ascension of the practice of public relations, practitioners have had to forsake their anonymity. Newspapers and

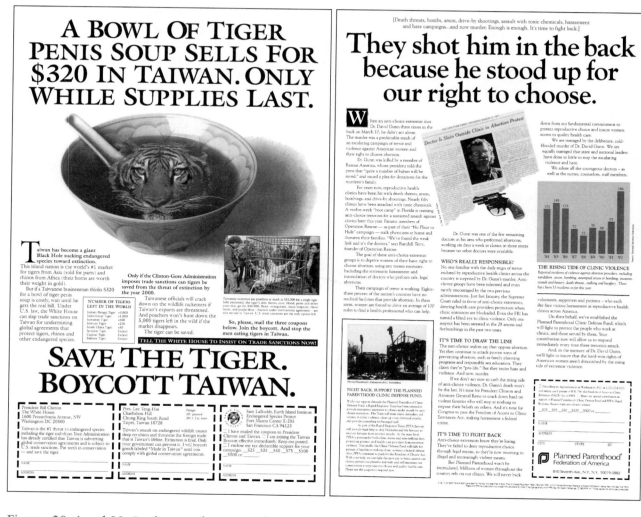

Figures 20–4 and 20–5   Among the most influential—and controversial—public issues advocates in the 1990s is the Public Media Center, a nonprofit ad agency based in San Francisco. The Public Media Center is responsible for some of the most riveting issues ads of the day.

magazines insist on quoting public relations people by name and assume that they speak as policymakers. In recent years, this has forced public relations practitioners into the spotlight, often embarrassingly, when they are targeted in unethical or questionable dealings.

Implications for Beginners

The reality of a more respected and, therefore, more competitive public relations profession has numerous implications for people just starting out in the field. Although competition for public relations positions is stiff, experience is the great equalizer, and smart beginners can optimize their potential for employment by getting a jump on the competition through early experience. How?

- By becoming involved with and active in student public relations organizations
- By securing—through faculty or others—part-time employment that uses the skills important in public relations work
- By attending professional meetings in the community, learning about public relations activities, and meeting public relations practitioners who might prove to be valuable contacts later on

THE REST OF THE STORY

ALL IS NOT WON . . .

*"Ethnic cleansing. It's got a nice ring to it.
Let's find out who's doing their P.R."*

Figure 20–6 Even in the latter stages of the 1990s, public relations still suffers an image problem. To wit, this cynical view in response to the 1994 Serbian attack on Muslims in Croatia.

THE REST OF THE STORY

...BUT ALL IS NOT LOST

Anybody who doubts the power of public relations in the new technological society evidently never heard of Deep Blue (Figure 20–7).

Figure 20–7   Deep Blue, the world chess—and publicity—champion.

Deep Blue was IBM's 6-foot 5-inch, 1.4-ton super computer, which took on 5-foot 10-inch, 176-pound world chess champion Garry Kasparov. Deep Blue's chess playing program was designed by a special IBM team, which included research scientists, engineers, and one chess grand master. By joining special purpose hardware and software with general purpose parallel computing, the team developed a system with a brute force computing speed capable of examining 200 million moves per second—or 50 billion positions in the three minutes allocated for a single move in a chess game.

More than 250 journalists from around the world flocked to New York City in May of 1997 to view the historic showdown between "man and machine." After a bitter struggle, Kasparov threw in the towel, surrendering to the stoic IBM computer. In a blaze of worldwide, front page publicity, Deep Blue had vanquished arch rival Kasparov (Figure 20–8).

The event constituted one of the most extensive publicity barrages in history. More than two billion media impressions were generated by the match—most of the publicity prominently played in worldwide media.

Figure 20–8   The crowd is hushed as Garry Kasparov contemplates his next move, as IBM Deep Blue team member, F. H. Hsu, looks on.

After the match, IBM dedicated the system to solve other complex problems, such as pharmaceutical drug design, financial analysis and decision support. But a deeply disappointed Kasparov insisted on a rematch with another IBM chess computer. One had to believe that IBM would oblige the defeated champ, especially in light of all that positive publicity.

And if it was any consolation to Kasparov, he probably didn't feel half as badly as the people at Microsoft and Dell and Intel and Compaq, who also could have produced, but didn't, the internationally renowned super computer.

- By seizing every opportunity from informal internships to voluntary work for non-profit associations or political candidates to service on the school newspaper to merchandising in-class projects to local merchants

The key to finding and securing a job in public relations is experience. So, rather than bemoan the catch 22 reality of a field in which you must have worked first in order to land a job, full-time students should use their college days to begin to acquire working knowledge in public relations. That way, when they look for that first job, they already have experience.

SUMMARY

Most professions undergo constant change, but few experience more critical or frequent change than public relations. In the latter years of the 1990s, practitioners have been introduced to a tidal wave of primary concerns: consumerism, environmentalism, government relations, and public policy forecasting. Areas of public relations opportunity have shifted from marketing publicity to financial relations to employee communications to public issues management. Steadily, the field has expanded its horizons and increased its influence.

As the millennium approaches, public relations stands at the threshold of its golden age. To get there, however, public relations professionals must exhibit certain qualities. Among them are the following:

- **Professionalism** Practitioners must recognize that every time someone in public relations is accused of bending the truth, all in the practice suffer. The cardinal rule must always be: "Tell the truth."

  Being professional also means standing for something. At base, public relations people are professional communicators. Communications standards therefore must remain high, and practitioners must take pride in the communications products for which they are responsible.

- **Generalized specialization** The old notion that people in public relations must be generalists rather than specialists simply won't wash in the new century. As noted, the competition today is ferocious. Public relations people must have an edge to differentiate themselves from others. Clearly, a solid general base of communications knowledge is still obligatory for public relations work. But at the same time, it has become more urgent today to master a specialty—to become conversant in and knowledgeable about a specific aspect of public relations work—investor relations, government relations, or speechwriting, for example—or about a particular industry—such as computers, health care, sports, insurance, banking, or the arts. Public relations people must become generalized specialists.

- **Guts** Public relations people also must be willing to stand up for what they stand for. Too often, public relations managers are posturers rather than practitioners, politicians rather than professionals, corporate lap dogs rather than leaders. Such faint-hearted communications counsel won't be sufficient in the twenty-first century. As top management gets better, public relations must also improve its standing.

- **Ethics** The public relations professional must be the most ethical individual in the organization. Public relations must be the conscience of the corporation, the standard bearer for honor and ethics and integrity. Public relations people therefore should never compromise their values. The first question the public relations professional must ask is, "Are we doing the right thing?" Few others in the organization will ever pose this question.

- **Leadership** Finally, public relations professionals must be leaders. To accomplish this, they must have the vision, courage, and character to lead themselves, their organizations, and their profession into the next golden century.

This is the challenge that awaits the new and future leaders entering the expanding and changing practice of public relations.

THE LAST WORD

COMMENTARY FROM JACK O'DWYER

For three decades, Jack O'Dwyer has been observing, critiquing, and tweaking the practice of public relations. A former business reporter for the late *New York Journal American* and advertising reporter for the *Chicago Tribune*, O'Dwyer is publisher and editor of *O'Dwyer's Newsletter*, the weekly "bible" of what's happening in public relations (Figure 20–9). He also publishes, among other periodicals, the field's foremost directories of agency and corporate public relations.

As a "parting shot," O'Dwyer offers his own unique commentary on the contemporary and future practice of public relations.

Specialist Versus Generalist

Public relations, like other professions, is becoming more and more specialized. Clients are looking for PR firms with expertise in high tech, health care, financial, foods/beverages, beauty/fashion, and travel, to mention a few of these areas. Public relations people like to position themselves as communicators of "anything." But savvy users of public relations are not buying this. If you hired a lawyer or doctor, you would go to a specialist if you had anything more than a routine ailment.

Figure 20–9   Jack O'Dwyer.

Hottest Areas

The three fastest-growing areas of public relations, according to the statistics we collect annually from more than 150 public relations firms, including all but three or four of the 50 largest firms, are high-tech, financial, and health care. Public relations people need lots of specialized knowledge in each area to succeed. The National Investor Relations Institute is the fastest-growing national public relations association. It has doubled to 3,500 members in the past 10 years and has been able to raise dues 55 percent to $425 annually. The Public Relations Society of America, with 18,000 members, and the International Association of Business Communicators, with 12,500 members, haven't been able to raise dues for nearly 10 years. Public relations people will be respected by clients and the press to the extent they have specialized market knowledge.

Interface with Advertising/Marketing

They should be interfacing with reporters and analysts and stay away from marketing and advertising people, who mostly deal in positive facts and news about companies and products. Public relations people must be able to handle negative developments with the same zeal they bring to positive developments. The investor relations pros do this, and their practice has thrived.

Advertising and public relations can work well together but in tandem, rather than at the same time. Advertising is like the bombing that precedes a landing by soldiers. Advertising softens up the prospect and glamorizes a product, but public relations does the actual work of the sale. Few people buy anything any more just based on what they see in ads. They ask friends, get specialized publications, check the Internet, etc.

The Internet/Employee Communications

Product knowledge and good debating skills are needed by anyone using the Internet. It's the public forum. Public relations people in recent years have been stressing employee communications. What works with employees will often be savaged in the public arena. Public relations and employee relations are two completely different things.

Agency Versus Corporate

The trend is for most public relations to be in the agencies. Corporate public relations units have been downsizing for many years. Information trading with the press is simply too dangerous an activity for corporate public relations people. When a crisis comes up, a public relations firm is called in. If the wrong advice is given, it is the firm that is fired, not the internal public relations director.

The advertising business went external many years ago. Companies used to have big advertising departments. But advertising is 99 percent in the agencies these days.

What Clients/Employers Want

Clients want public relations firms that are knowledgeable about their practice areas. Intelligence gathering is one of the main functions of public relations, but one that is rarely mentioned. Both corporate and agency public relations people should spend most of their time in the field talking to reporters, analysts, the public, and other information sources so that their advice will have relevance.

There's too much emphasis these days on putting out a "message" rather than finding out what's going on.

DISCUSSION STARTERS

1. What evidence can you point to that indicates the increased stature of public relations practice?
2. What factors are shaping the new environment?
3. What are the primary challenges for public relations into the next century?
4. What are the skills requisite for counseling management?
5. How should a public relations professional regard anonymity?
6. What are the pressing issues in public relations education?
7. What is the outlook for women in public relations?
8. How important is technological knowledge for public relations practitioners?
9. What is the key challenge for entry-level public relations professionals in the 1990s?
10. What is the outlook for public relations practice?

NOTES

1. Kevin Helliker, "A New Mix: Old-Fashioned PR Gives General Mills Advertising Bargains," *The Wall Street Journal* (March 20, 1997): 1.
2. "Reebok Trips on its Laces with the 'Incubus' Shoe," *The Naming Newsletter* (2Q 1997), Rivkin & Associates, 233 Rock Road, Glen Rock, NJ 07452.
3. Dana Canedy, "Nike's Asian Factories Pass Young's Muster," *The New York Times* (June 25, 1997): D2.
4. "McLibel Case is Worth $98,000," *The Jersey Journal* (June 20, 1997).
5. Art Stevens, "Public Relations in the Year 2000," *Public Relations Quarterly* (Summer 1996): 19–22.
6. "Report and Recommendations of the Second Task Force on Stature and Role of Public Relations," Public Relations Society of America, November 1991, released by the PRSA board of directors in August 1993.
7. Remarks by Fraser P. Seitel at Sixth Annual Harold Burson Distinguished Lecturer, Raymond Simon Institute for Public Relations, Utica College–Syracuse University, April 1, 1992.
8. James Aley, "Where the Jobs Are," *Fortune* (September 18, 1995): 53–56.
9. "PR to Help Map Trip Down the 'Information Highway,' " *O'Dwyer's PR Services Report* (January 1994): 1.
10. Howard Paster, "The New Public Relations Manifesto," *The Public Relations Strategist* (Spring 1995): 14.
11. Philip Lesly, "The Balkanizing of Public Relations," *The Public Relations Strategist* (Fall 1996): 41.
12. Elizabeth L. Toth, "Confronting the Reality of the Gender Gap," *The Public Relations Strategist* (Fall 1996): 51–53.
13. Dirk C. Gibson, "Future Trends in Public Relations," *Social Science Monitor* (February 1990): 1–3.
14. "H&K Chief Cites Six Trends That Will Change the Face of PR," *PR News* (May 4, 1992): 1.

15. Roger Feather, "Internal Communications in Canada," *IABC Communications World* (December 1990): 37.
16. Karl Nessmann, "Public Relations in Europe: A Comparison with the United States," *Public Relations Review* (Summer 1995): 151.
17. Susan Fry Bovet, "Trends in the 'New' Europe," *Public Relations Journal* (September 1993): 19.
18. Monique El Faizy, "It's No Occident PR Firms Fill Asian Void," *Crain's New York Business* (April 12, 1993): 13.
19. "Gavin Anderson Moves into Growing Singapore Market," *PR News* (February 10, 1997): 1.
20. Steven L. Lubetkin, "China's Growth Makes Understanding of Media Crucial," *Public Relations Tactics* (December 1996): 18.
21. Ray Hiebert, "Special Report: Communication in Eastern Europe," *Social Science Monitor* (November 1990): 1.
22. Abdulrahman H. Al-Enad, "Values of Public Relations Conduct in Saudi Arabia," *Public Relations Review* (Summer 1992): 213.
23. Pamela J. Creedon, Mai Abdul Wahed Al-Khaja, and Dean Kruckeberg, "Women and Public Relations Education and Practice in the United Arab Emirates," *Public Relations Review* (Spring 1995): 59.
24. Fraser P. Seitel, "Relevance: The Key to Success in Public Relations." Address before ISDP: Communications Management Program, Syracuse University, August 20, 1995.
25. "The Design for Undergraduate Public Relations Education." Study cosponsored by the Public Relations Division of the Association for Education in Journalism and Mass Communications, the Public Relations Society of America, and the Educators Section of PRSA (1987): 1.
26. William C. Adams, "Nurturing Neophytes: The Key to Our Future," *The Public Relations Strategist* (Fall 1996): 35–38.
27. David M. Dozier, and Glen M. Broom, "Evolution of the Managerial Role in Public Relations." Paper presented at the Association for Education in Journalism and Mass Communications Convention, August 1993.
28. John Naisbitt and Patricia Aburdene, *Megatrends 2000* (New York: William Morrow, 1990): 224–225.

SUGGESTED READINGS

Basye, Dale. "Why Is PR a Dumping Ground?" *Across the Board* (September 1994): 48–49.

Brody, E. W. *Communication Tomorrow: New Audiences, New Technologies.* Westport, CT: Praeger, 1990.

Brody, E. W., ed. *New Technology and Public Relations: On to the Future.* Sarasota, FL: Institute for Public Relations and Education, 1992.

Careers in Public Relations. (Available from the Public Relations Society of America, 33 Irving Place, New York, NY 10003.)

Cavusgil, Tamer, and Michael R. Czinkota. *International Perspective on Trade Promotion and Assistance.* Westport, CT: Greenwood Press, 1990.

Design for Public Relations Education. (Available from the Public Relations Society of America, 33 Irving Place, New York, NY 10003.)

TOP OF THE SHELF

PHILIP SEIB AND KATHY FITZPATRICK

PUBLIC RELATIONS ETHICS

FORT WORTH, TX: HARCOURT BRACE COLLEGE PUBLISHERS, 1995

The key to the practice of public relations is ethics. That one characteristic distinguishes the public relations field from other professions.

This book, the authors explain, "exists primarily to raise ethical consciousness—to make ethics more comprehensible to both students and practitioners of public relations."

The authors cover a spectrum of ethical questions from the ethics of truth and the dangers of lying and deception to the ethical consciousness and behavior to which practitioners of public relations must adhere. The authors also explore a number of hypothetical cases that stimulate thought and discussion of ethical conundrums.

There is no subject more important to the practice of public relations than ethics. Books like this one, therefore, should be required background reading.

Drucker, Peter F. *Managing for the Future: The 1990s and Beyond*. New York: Nal-Dutton, 1992.

European Public Affairs Directory, 1992. Bristol, PA: International Publications Services, 1992.

Futurist. (Available from World Future Society, 4916 St. Elmo Ave., Washington, DC 20014.) This bimonthly journal includes forecasts, trends, and ideas about the future on all topics.

Gates, Bill. *The Road Ahead*. New York: Viking, 1996. The guru of cyberspace gurus describes his vision of the future in which all of us will live (if we make it).

Hart, Norman A. ed. *Strategic Public Relations*. London: Macmillan Press LTD, 1994. Explains the role of public relations as a strategic management function in organizations.

International Directory of Business Information Sources. Chicago: Probus, 1991.

Mintu-Wimsatt, Alma, and Hector R. Lozada, eds. *Green Marketing in a Unified Europe*. Binghamton, NY: The Haworth Press, 1996. This book gives public relations professionals insights into the opportunities for positioning in an environmentally aware Europe.

Naisbitt, John, and Patricia Aburdene. *Megatrends 2000*. New York: William Morrow, 1990.

Pincus, J. David, and Nicholas DeBonis. New York: McGraw-Hill, 1994. Part novel, part business how-to, this book combines fact and fiction to emphasize the importance of communications and leadership skills.

Taylor, Jim, and Watts Wacker. *The 500-Year Delta*. New York: HarperBusiness, 1996. The language of the millennium, say the authors, will begin with "re"—reengineering, reclamation, reintermediation, etc., rather than the "dis" that characterized the 1990s.

CASE STUDY

THE TYLENOL MURDERS

Arguably, the single most important cases in the history of the practice of public relations occurred within four years of each other to the same company and product.

For close to 100 years, Johnson & Johnson Company (J&J) of New Brunswick, NJ, was the epitome of a well-managed, highly profitable, and tight-lipped consumer products manufacturer.

Round I

That image changed on the morning of September 30, 1982, when J&J faced as devastating a public relations problem as had confronted any company in history. That morning, J&J's management learned that its premier product, extra-strength Tylenol, had been used as a murder weapon to kill three people. In the days that followed, another three people died from swallowing Tylenol capsules loaded with cyanide. And although all the cyanide deaths occurred in Chicago, reports from other parts of the country also implicated extra-strength Tylenol capsules in illnesses of various sorts. These latter reports were later proved to be unfounded, but J&J and its Tylenol-producing subsidiary, McNeil Consumer Products Company, found themselves at the center of a public relations trauma the likes of which few companies had ever experienced.

Tylenol had been an astoundingly profitable product for J&J. At the time of the Tylenol murders, the product held 35 percent of the $1 billion analgesic market. It contributed an estimated 7 percent to J&J's worldwide sales and almost 20 percent to its profits. Throughout the years, J&J had not been—and hadn't needed to be—a particularly high-profile company. Its chairman, James E. Burke, who had been with the company for almost 30 years, had never appeared on television and had rarely participated in print interviews.

J&J's management, understandably, was caught totally by surprise when the news hit. Initially, J&J had no facts and, indeed, got much of its information from the media calls that inundated the firm from the beginning. The company recognized that it needed the media to get out as much information to the public as quickly as possible to prevent a panic. Therefore, almost immediately, J&J made a key decision: to open its doors to the media.

On the second day of the crisis, J&J discovered that an earlier statement that no cyanide was used on its premises was wrong. The company didn't hesitate. Its public relations department quickly announced that the earlier information had been false. Even though the reversal embarrassed the company briefly, J&J's openness was hailed and made up for any damage to its credibility.

Early on in the crisis, the company was largely convinced that the poisonings had not occurred at any of its plants. Nonetheless, J&J recalled an entire lot of 93,000 bottles of extra-strength Tylenol associated with the reported murders. In the process, it telegrammed warnings to doctors, hospitals, and distributors, at a cost of half a million dollars. McNeil also suspended all Tylenol advertising to reduce attention to the product.

By the second day, the company was convinced that the tampering had taken place during the product's Chicago distribution and not in the manufacturing process.

Therefore, a total Tylenol recall did not seem obligatory. Chairman Burke himself leaned toward immediately recalling all extra-strength Tylenol capsules, but after consulting with the Federal Bureau of Investigation, he decided not to do so. The FBI was worried that a precipitous recall would encourage copycat poisoning attempts. Nonetheless, five days later, when a copycat strychnine poisoning occurred in California, J&J did recall all extra-strength Tylenol capsules—31 million bottles—at a cost of over $100 million.

Although the company knew it had done nothing wrong, J&J resisted the temptation to disclaim any possible connection between its product and the murders. Rather, while moving quickly to trace the lot numbers of the poisoned packages, it also posted a $100,000 reward for the killer. Through advertisements promising to exchange capsules for tablets, through thousands of letters to the trade, and through statements to the media, the company hoped to put the incident into proper perspective.

At the same time, J&J commissioned a nationwide opinion survey to assess the consumer implications of the Tylenol poisonings. The good news was that 87 percent of

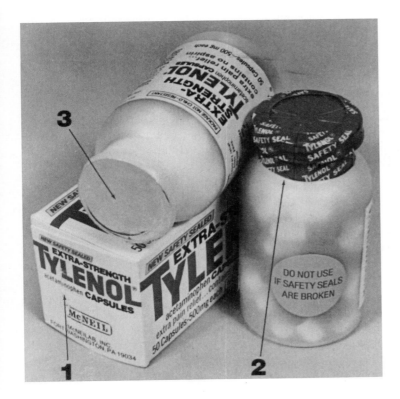

Figure 20–10 The triple-safety-sealed, tamper-resistant package for Tylenol capsules had (1) glued flaps on the outer box, (2) a tight plastic neck seal, and (3) a strong inner foil seal over the mouth of the bottle. A bright yellow label on the bottle was imprinted with a red warning: "Do not use if safety seals are broken." As it turned out, all these precautions didn't work.

Tylenol users surveyed said they realized that the maker of Tylenol was not responsible for the deaths. The bad news was that although a high percentage didn't blame Tylenol, 61 percent still said they were not likely to buy extra-strength Tylenol capsules in the future. In other words, even though most consumers knew the deaths weren't Tylenol's fault, they still feared using the product.

But Chairman Burke and J&J weren't about to knuckle under to the deranged saboteur or saboteurs who had poisoned their product. Despite predictions of the imminent demise of extra-strength Tylenol, J&J decided to relaunch the product in a new triple-safety-sealed, tamper-resistant package (Figure 20–10). Many on Wall Street and in the marketing community were stunned by J&J's bold decision.

So confident was J&J's management that it launched an all-out media blitz to make sure that people understood its commitment. Chairman Burke appeared on the widely watched Phil Donahue network television program and skillfully handled 60 minutes of intense public questioning. The investigative news program *60 Minutes*—the scourge of corporate America—was invited by J&J to film its executive strategy sessions to prepare for the new launch. When the program was aired, reporter Mike Wallace concluded that although Wall Street had been ready at first to write off the company, it was now "hedging its bets because of J&J's stunning campaign of facts, money, the media, and truth."

Finally, on November 11, 1982, less than two months after the murders, J&J's management held an elaborate video press conference in New York City, beamed to additional locations around the country, to introduce the new extra-strength Tylenol package. Said J&J's chairman to the media:

> It is our job at Johnson & Johnson to ensure the survival of Tylenol, and we are pledged to do this. While we consider this crime an assault on society, we are nevertheless ready to fulfill our responsibility, which includes paying the price of this heinous crime. But I urge you not to make Tylenol the scapegoat.

In the days and months that followed Burke's news conference, it became clear that Tylenol would not become a scapegoat. In fact, by the beginning of 1983, Tylenol had recaptured an astounding 95 percent of its prior market share. Morale at the company, according to its chairman, was "higher than in years" (Figure 20–11). The euphoria lasted until February of 1986, when, unbelievably, tragedy struck again.

Round II

Late in the evening of February 10, 1986, news reports began to circulate that a woman had died in Yonkers, New York, after taking poisoned capsules of extra-strength Tylenol.

The nightmare for J&J began anew.

Once again, the company sprang into action. Chairman Burke addressed reporters at a news conference a day after the incident. A phone survey found that the public didn't blame the company. However, with the discovery of other poisoned Tylenol capsules two days later, the nightmare intensified. The company recorded 15,000 toll-free calls at its Tylenol hotline. And, once again, production of Tylenol capsules was halted. "I'm heartsick," Burke told the press. "We didn't believe it could happen again, and nobody else did either."

This time, although Tylenol earned some 13 percent of the company's net profits, the firm decided once and for all to cease production of its over-the-counter medica-

---

OUR CREDO

We believe our first responsibility is to the doctors, nurses and patients,
to mothers and fathers and all others who use our products and services.
In meeting their needs everything we do must be of high quality.
We must constantly strive to reduce our costs
in order to maintain reasonable prices.
Customers' orders must be serviced promptly and accurately.
Our suppliers and distributors must have an opportunity
to make a fair profit.

We are responsible to our employees,
the men and women who work with us throughout the world.
Everyone must be considered as an individual.
We must respect their dignity and recognize their merit.
They must have a sense of security in their jobs.
Compensation must be fair and adequate,
and working conditions clean, orderly and safe.
We must be mindful of ways to help our employees fulfill
their family responsibilities.
Employees must feel free to make suggestions and complaints.
There must be equal opportunity for employment, development
and advancement for those qualified.
We must provide competent management,
and their actions must be just and ethical.

We are responsible to the communities in which we live and work
and to the world community as well.
We must be good citizens — support good works and charities
and bear our fair share of taxes.
We must encourage civic improvements and better health and education.
We must maintain in good order
the property we are privileged to use,
protecting the environment and natural resources.

Our final responsibility is to our stockholders.
Business must make a sound profit.
We must experiment with new ideas.
Research must be carried on, innovative programs developed
and mistakes paid for.
New equipment must be purchased, new facilities provided
and new products launched.
Reserves must be created to provide for adverse times.
When we operate according to these principles,
the stockholders should realize a fair return.

Johnson & Johnson

Figure 20–11

tions in capsule form. It offered to replace all unused Tylenol capsules with new Tylenol caplets, a solid form of medication that was less tamper-prone (Figure 20–12). This time the withdrawal of its capsules cost J&J upward of $150 million after taxes.

And, once again, in the face of tragedy, the company and its chairman received high marks. As President Reagan said at a White House reception two weeks after the crisis hit, "Jim Burke of Johnson & Johnson, you have our deepest appreciation for living up to the highest ideals of corporate responsibility and grace under pressure."*

A special message from the makers of TYLENOL products.

If you have TYLENOL capsules, we'll replace them with TYLENOL caplets.

And we'll do it at our expense.

As you know, there has been a tragic event. A small number of Extra-Strength TYLENOL Capsules in one isolated area in New York have been criminally tampered with.

This was an outrageous act which damages all of us.

Both federal and local authorities have established that it was only capsules that were tampered with.

In order to prevent any further capsule tampering, we have removed all our capsules from your retailers' shelves. This includes Regular and Extra-Strength TYLENOL capsules, CO-TYLENOL capsules, Maximum-Strength TYLENOL Sinus Medication capsules, Extra-Strength SINE-AID capsules, and DIMENSYN Menstrual Relief capsules.

And Johnson & Johnson's McNeil Consumer Products Company has decided to cease the manufacture, sale, and distribution of **all** capsule forms of over-the-counter medicines.

If you're a regular capsule user, you may be wondering what to use instead. That's why we'd like you to try TYLENOL caplets.

The caplet is a solid form of TYLENOL pain reliever, which research has proven is the form most preferred by consumers. Unlike tablets, it is specially shaped and coated for easy, comfortable swallowing.

And the caplet delivers a full extra-strength dose quickly and effectively.

So, if you have any TYLENOL Capsules in your home, do one of the following:

1. Return the bottles with the unused portion to us, together with your name and address on the form below. And we'll replace your TYLENOL capsules with TYLENOL Caplets (or tablets, if you prefer). We'll also refund your postage. Or...

2. If you prefer, you can receive a cash refund for the unused capsules by sending the bottle to us along with a letter requesting the refund.

We are taking this step because, for the past 25 years, over 100 million Americans have made TYLENOL products a trusted part of their health care.

We're continuing to do everything we can to keep your trust.

> *Send to:*
> **TYLENOL Capsule Exchange**
> **P.O. Box 2000**
> **Maple Plain, MN 55348**
>
> Please send my coupon for free replacement caplets or tablets to:
> *Please print*
> Name _____
> Address _____
> City _____
> State _____ Zip _____
> Offer expires May 1, 1986

(Courtesy of Johnson & Johnson)

Figure 20–12
(Courtesy of Johnson & Johnson)

QUESTIONS

1. What might have been the consequences if J&J had decided to "tough out" the first reports of Tylenol-related deaths and not recall the product?

2. What other public relations options did J&J have in responding to the first round of Tylenol murders?

3. Do you think the company made a wise decision by reintroducing extra-strength Tylenol?

4. In light of the response of other companies not to move precipitously when faced with a crisis, do you think J&J should have acted so quickly to remove the Tylenol product when the second round of Tylenol murders occurred in 1986?

5. What specific lessons can be derived from the way in which J&J handled the public relations aspects of these tragedies?

*For further information on the first round of Tylenol murders, see Jerry Knight, "Tylenol's Maker Shows How to Respond to Crisis," *The Washington Post* (October 11, 1982): 1; Thomas Moore, "The Fight to Save Tylenol," *Fortune* (November 29, 1982): 48; Michael Waldholz, "Tylenol Regains Most of No. 1 Market Share, Amazing Doomsayers," *The Wall Street Journal* (December 24, 1982): 1, 19; and *60 Minutes*, CBS-TV, December 19, 1982.

For further information on the second round of Tylenol murders, see Irvin Molotsky, "Tylenol Maker Hopeful on Solving Poisoning Case," *The New York Times* (February 20, 1986); Steven Prokesch, "A Leader in a Crisis," *The New York Times* (February 19, 1986): B4; Michael Waldholz, "For Tylenol's Manufacturer, the Dilemma Is to Be Aggressive—But Not Appear Pushy," *The Wall Street Journal* (February 20, 1986): 27; and "Tylenol II: How a Company Responds to a Calamity," *U.S. News & World Report* (February 24, 1986): 49.

◆◆◆◆◆◆◆
VOICE OF EXPERIENCE

DEBRA A. MILLER

Debra A. Miller was elected president of the Public Relations Society of America in 1996. An associate professor in the Department of Advertising and Public Relations at Florida International University, Miller was formerly the assistant dean of Florida International University's School of Journalism and Mass Communication. She has authored numerous articles in professional publications and is author of *Multicultural Communications: An Annotated Bibliography.*

HOW WOULD YOU CHARACTERIZE THE STATUS OF THE PUBLIC RELATIONS PROFESSION TODAY?

It is in a much better state than we were even five years ago. We have experienced consistent growth, despite the downsizings, layoffs, and mergers. Salaries are higher, but jobs are rather scarce in some parts of the country and in certain areas of public relations. We are more accepted today than ever before.

WHAT ARE THE MAJOR CHALLENGES FOR THE FIELD?

We still have a few problems that will undoubtedly hinder our rise in stature if we do not deal with them strategically and soon. Among them: how we view ourselves; a continued lack of respect and loss of credibility in the workplace and marketplace; a lack of leadership among public relations professionals; continued concern about the abundance of women in the field as well as a continued gap in salary among men and women in public relations; the obvious lack of people of color in the field; heightened competition from other disciplines; failure to embrace the concept of lifelong learning and continuing professional development; and a general lack of understanding of what public relations is for senior management and society as a whole, why it's needed and what its value is for society.

WHAT IS THE STATUS OF WOMEN IN THE FIELD?

That depends on whether you are a man or a woman who looks at the glass as half-full or half-empty. A man might say women have made great strides and have entered the profession in great numbers. A woman might say that men still receive higher compensation in most markets and that sexism still exists in this profession. Frankly, I'm fed up and and I'm sure many of my female colleagues feel the same way. As we enter the twenty-first century, organizations who fail to integrate women into their upper echelons, who pay them less than their male counterparts, or who fail to recognize and deal with sexual discrimination and the mistreatment of women in the workplace are destined to lose their competitive edge in the marketplace. Their damaged reputations will force them to see it our way.

WHAT IS THE STATUS OF MINORITIES IN PUBLIC RELATIONS?

It is the best of times and the worst of times. As more and more people of color enter the profession, there do not appear to be enough jobs or clients to go around. Tensions still exist. Practitioners of color report outright hiring discrimination, but at the same time we encourage students of color to consider public relations as a career. Things have changed over the past 10 years, but the progress has been unusually slow. Organizations such as the Black Public Relations Society, the Hispanic Public Relations Association, and the Asian American Advertising and Public Relations Alliance keep an active membership list and directories. There are a few enlightened agencies and corporations who recognize the value of having a diverse public relations staff. However, those are few and far between. The issue of the status of people of color in the public relations profession will be discussed long into the next century.

WHERE ARE THE OPPORTUNITIES FOR YOUNG PEOPLE IN THE FIELD?

There are opportunities everywhere. You need to be prepared when opportunity knocks. And you need to approach your job search the same way you would conduct a public relations campaign, for example, research, action/planning, communications, and evaluation. The promising areas for entry-level public relations into the next decade include:

- Public relations firms
- Health care organizations
- Real estate development companies
- Hospitality management (conventions and tourism)

- Service industries
- Professional service firms (accounting, legal, management)
- Athletic and sportswear companies
- Associations
- Entertainment
- State and municipal government agencies

ARE YOU OPTIMISTIC ABOUT THE FUTURE OF THE PRACTICE OF PUBLIC RELATIONS?

I am cautiously optimistic. As the field matures and as public relations practitioners engage more and more in reputation management, I see us finally becoming a welcomed addition to the senior management team. To ensure our future, we have to make sure that the general public and other specific publics finally understand what we do, how we do it, and the invaluable contribution we make to society. If we do this successfully, the public relations profession will survive and thrive in the next decade and beyond.

Appendix A

CODE OF PROFESSIONAL STANDARDS FOR THE PRACTICE OF PUBLIC RELATIONS

PUBLIC RELATIONS SOCIETY OF AMERICA

This code was adopted by the Assembly of the Public Relations Society of America (PRSA) in 1988. It replaces a Code of Ethics in force since 1950 and revised in 1954, 1959, 1963, 1977, and 1983.

On November 12, 1988, PRSA's Assembly approved a revision of the Society's code for the following reasons:

1. To make the language clearer and more understandable—hence easier to apply and to follow.

     As Elias "Buck" Buchwald, APR, chairman of the Board of Ethics and Professional Standards, explained to the Assembly, the revision introduced no substantive changes to the code; it merely clarified and strengthened the language.

2. To help advance the unification of the public relations profession—part of PRSA's mission.

     The PRSA code's revision was based on the Code of the North American Public Relations Council, an organization of 13-member groups, including PRSA. Eight of the 13 have now revised their own codes in accordance with the NAPRC code—an important step toward unification.

     Code interpretations, as published on pages 17–20 of the 1988–1989 Register, remain in effect. However, the Board of Ethics and Professional Standards is in the process of revising and updating them.

DECLARATION OF PRINCIPLES

Members of the Public Relations Society of America base their professional principles on the fundamental value and dignity of the individual, holding that the free exercise of human rights, especially freedom of speech, freedom of assembly, and freedom of the press, is essential to the practice of public relations.

In serving the interests of clients and employers, we dedicate ourselves to the goals of better communication, understanding, and cooperation among the diverse individuals, groups, and institutions of society, and of equal opportunity of employment in the public relations profession.

We pledge:

To conduct ourselves professionally, with truth, accuracy, fairness, and responsibility to the public;

To improve our individual competence and advance the knowledge and proficiency of the profession through continuing research and education;

And to adhere to the articles of the Code of Professional Standards for the Practice of Public Relations as adopted by the governing Assembly of the Society.

CODE OF PROFESSIONAL STANDARDS FOR THE PRACTICE OF PUBLIC RELATIONS

These articles have been adopted by the Public Relations Society of America to promote and maintain high standards of public service and ethical conduct among its members.

1. A member shall conduct his or her professional life in accord with the **public interest**.
2. A member shall exemplify high standards of **honesty and integrity** while carrying out dual obligations to a client or employer and to the democratic process.
3. A member shall **deal fairly** with the public, with past or present clients or employers, and with fellow practitioners, giving due respect to the ideal of free inquiry and to the opinions of others.
4. A member shall adhere to the highest standards of **accuracy and truth**, avoiding extravagant claims or unfair comparisons and giving credit for ideas and words borrowed from others.
5. A member shall not knowingly disseminate **false or misleading information** and shall act promptly to correct erroneous communications for which he or she is responsible.
6. A member shall not engage in any practice which has the purpose of **corrupting** the integrity of channels of communications or the processes of government.
7. A member shall be prepared to **identify publicly** the name of the client or employer on whose behalf any public communication is made.
8. A member shall not use any individual or organization professing to serve or represent an announced cause, or professing to be independent or unbiased, but actually serving another or **undisclosed interest**.
9. A member shall not **guarantee the achievement** of specified results beyond the member's direct control.
10. A member shall **not represent conflicting** or competing interests without the express consent of those concerned, given after a full disclosure of the facts.
11. A member shall not place himself or herself in a position where the member's **personal interest is or may be in conflict** with an obligation to an employer or client, or others, without full disclosure of such interests to all involved.
12. A member shall **not accept fees, commissions, gifts, or any other consideration** from anyone except clients or employers for whom services are performed without their express consent, given after full disclosure of the facts.
13. A member shall scrupulously **safeguard** the **confidences and privacy rights** of present, former, and prospective clients or employers.
14. A member shall not intentionally **damage the professional reputation** or practice of another practitioner.
15. If a member has evidence that another member has been guilty of unethical, illegal, or unfair practices, including those in violation of this Code, the member is obligated to present the information promptly to the proper authorities of the Society for action in accordance with the procedure set forth in Article XII of the Bylaws.
16. A member called as a witness in a proceeding for enforcement of this Code is obligated to appear, unless excused for sufficient reason by the judicial panel.
17. A member shall, as soon as possible, sever relations with any organization or individual if such relationship requires conduct contrary to the articles of this Code.

INTERNATIONAL CODE OF ETHICS
Code of Athens

English Version
adopted by IPRA General Assembly at Athens on 12 May 1965
and modified at Tehran on 17 April 1968

CONSIDERING that all Member countries of the United Nations Organization have agreed to abide by its Charter which reaffirms "its faith in fundamental human rights, in the dignity and worth of the human person" and that having regard to the very nature of their profession, Public Relations practitioners in these countries should undertake to ascertain and observe the principles set out in this Charter;

CONSIDERING that, apart from "rights", human beings have not only physical or material needs but also intellectual, moral and social needs, and that their rights are of real benefit to them only in so far as these needs are essentially met;

CONSIDERING that, in the course of their professional duties and depending on how these duties are performed, Public Relations practitioners can substantially help to meet these intellectual, moral and social needs;

And lastly, CONSIDERING that the use of techniques enabling them to come simultaneously into contact with millions of people gives Public Relations practitioners a power that has to be restrained by the observance of a strict moral code.

On all these grounds, the undersigned Public Relations Associations hereby declare that they accept as their moral charter the principles of the following Code of Ethics, and that if, in the light of evidence submitted to the Council, a member of these associations should be found to have infringed this Code in the course of his professional duties, he will be deemed to be guilty of serious misconduct calling for an appropriate penalty.

Accordingly, each Member of these Associations:

SHALL ENDEAVOUR

1. To contribute to the achievement of the moral and cultural conditions enabling human beings to reach their full stature and enjoy the indefeasible rights to which they are entitled under the "Universal Declaration of Human Rights";

2. To establish communication patterns and channels which, by fostering the free flow of essential information, will make each member of the society in which he lives feel that he is being kept informed, and also give him an awareness of his own personal involvement and responsibility, and of his solidarity with other members;

3. To bear in mind that, because of the relationship between his profession and the public, his conduct—even in private—will have an impact on the way in which the profession as a whole is appraised;

4. To respect, in the course of his professional duties, the moral principles and rules of the "Universal Declaration of Human Rights";

5. To pay due regard to, and uphold, human dignity, and to recognise the right of each individual to judge for himself;

6. To encourage the moral, psychological and intellectual conditions for dialogue in its true sense, and to recognise the right of the parties involved to state their case and express their views;

SHALL UNDERTAKE

7. To conduct himself always and in all circumstances in such a manner as to deserve and secure the confidence of those with whom he comes into contact;

8. To act, in all circumstances, in such a manner as to take account of the respective interests of the parties involved; both the interests of the organisation which he serves and the interests of the publics concerned;

9. To carry out his duties with integrity, avoiding language likely to lead to ambiguity or misunderstanding, and to maintain loyalty to his clients or employers, whether past or present.

SHALL REFRAIN FROM

10. Subordinating the truth to other requirements;

11. Circulating information which is not based on established and ascertainable facts;

12. Taking part in any venture or undertaking which is unethical or dishonest or capable of impairing human dignity and integrity;

13. Using any "manipulative" methods or techniques designed to create subconscious motivations which the individual cannot control of his own free will and so cannot be held accountable for the action taken on them.

Appendix B

ADVERTISING EFFECTIVENESS TRACKING STUDY

Contemporary Marketing Research Inc.
1270 Broadway
New York, NY 10001

6-1-107
February 1999

ADVERTISING EFFECTIVENESS TRACKING STUDY
MAIN QUESTIONNAIRE

CARD 1
(11-17Z)

RESPONDENT'S NAME: —————————————————

1a. Today I am interested in obtaining your opinions of financial institutions. To begin with, I'd like you to tell me the names of all the financial institutions you have heard of. (DO <u>NOT</u> READ LIST. RECORD FIRST INSTITUTION MENTIONED SEPARATELY FROM ALL OTHERS UNDER "FIRST MENTION.") (PROBE:) Any others? (RECORD BELOW UNDER "OTHERS.")

1b. Now, thinking only of <u>banks</u> in the New York area, what (other) banks have you heard of (RECORD BELOW UNDER "OTHERS.")

2. And what financial institutions, including banks, have you seen or heard advertised within the past 3 months? (DO <u>NOT</u> READ LIST. RECORD BELOW UNDER Q.2.)

3. <u>FOR EACH ASTERISKED INSTITUTION LISTED BELOW AND NOT MEN-TIONED IN Q.1a/1b OR Q.2, ASK:</u>

Have you ever heard of (<u>NAME</u>)? (RECORD BELOW UNDER Q.3.)

4. FOR EACH ASTERISKED INSTITUTION CIRCLED IN Q.1a/1b OR Q.3 AND NOT CIRCLED IN Q.2, ASK:

Have you seen or heard advertising for (NAME) within the past 3 months? (RECORD BELOW UNDER Q.4.)

| | Q. 1a/1b | | Q.2 | Q.3 | Q.4 |
	AWARE OF FIRST MENTION (18)	AWARE OTHERS (21)	OF ADVTG. (24)	AWARE ADVTG. (AIDED)	AWARE (AIDED)
Anchor Savings Bank	1	1	1		
Apple Savings Bank	2	2	2		
Astoria Federal Savings	3	3	3		
Bank of Commerce	4	4	4		
Bank of New York	5	5	5		
Bankers Trust	6	6	6		
Barclays Bank	7	7	7		
Bowery Savings Bank	8	8	8		
*Chase Manhattan Bank	9	9	9	9 (27)	9 (29)
*Chemical Bank	0	0	0	0	0
*Citibank	X	X	X	X	X
Crossland Savings Bank	Y	Y	Y		
*Dean Witter	1 (19)	1 (22)	1 (25)	1 (28)	1 (30)
Dime Savings Bank	2	2	2		
Dollar Dry Dock Savings Bank	3	3	3		
*Dreyfus	4	4	4	4	4
Emigrant Savings Bank	5	5	5		
European American Bank	6	6	6		
Fidelity	7	7	7		
Goldome Savings Bank	8	8	8		
*Manufacturer's Hanover Trust	9	9	9	9	9
*Marine Midland Bank	0	0	0	0	0
*Merrill Lynch	X	X	X	X	X
*National Westminster Bank	Y	Y	Y	Y	Y
Prudential Bache	1 (20)	1 (23)	1 (26)		
Shearson-Lehman	2	2	2		
Other (SPECIFY):					
————————	X	X	X		

REFER BACK TO Q.2 AND 4. IF RESPONDENT IS AWARE OF ADVERTISING FOR CHASE MANHATTAN BANK IN Q.2 OR Q.4, ASK Q.5a. OTHERWISE, SKIP TO Q.6.

5a. Today we are asking different people about different banks. In your case, we'd like to talk about Chase Manhattan Bank. You just mentioned that you remember seeing or hearing advertising for Chase Manhattan Bank. Please tell me everything you remember seeing or hearing in the advertising. (PROBE FOR SPECIFICS) What else?

_____ (31) _____

_____ (32) _____

_____ (33) _____

_____ (34) _____

_____ (35) _____

5b. And where did you see or hear advertising for Chase Manhattan Bank? (Do <u>NOT</u> READ LIST) (MORE THAN ONE ANSWER MAY BE GIVEN)

	(36)
Television	1
Radio	2
Newspaper	3
Magazine	4
Billboard	5
Other (SPECIFY): _____	X

6. Different banks use different slogans. (START WITH THE X'D QUESTION BELOW AND CONTINUE UNTIL ALL FOUR QUESTIONS (Q.6a-6d) HAVE BEEN ASKED.)

<u>START</u>:

(√) **6a.** What slogan or statement do you associate with Chase Manhattan Bank? (DO <u>NOT</u> READ LIST)

	(37)
Chase. The Experience Shows	1
You Have a Friend at Chase	2
Ideas You Can Bank On	3
The Chase Is On	4
Other (SPECIFY) _____	X

( ) 6b.What slogan does Chemical Bank use? (DO <u>NOT</u> READ LIST)

	(38)
The Chemistry's Just Right at Chemical	1
Other (SPECIFY) _____X	

(√) 6c .What slogan or statement do you associate with Citibank? (DO <u>NOT</u> READ LIST)

	(39)
It's Your Citi	1
The Citi Never Sleeps	2
Other (SPECIFY)_____X	

_____

( ) 6d. What slogan does Manufacturer's Hanover Trust use? (DO <u>NOT</u> READ LIST)

	(40)
The Financial Source. Worldwide	1
We Realize Your Potential	2
Other (SPECIFY)_____	X

_____

7. Now, I'd like to know how likely you yourself are to consider banking at several different banks in the future. For each bank I read, please tell me whether you would definitely consider banking there, probably consider banking there, might or might not consider banking there, probably not consider banking there, or definitely not consider banking there in the future. Now, how likely are you to consider banking at (READ X'D BANK) in the future? (REPEAT SCALE IF NECESSARY. OBTAIN A RATING FOR EACH BANK.)

	START: ( ) CHASE MAN-HATTAN BANK	( ) CHEMICAL BANK	( ) CITIBANK	(√) MANU-FACTURER'S HANOVER TRUST
Definitely Consider Banking There	5 (41)	5 (42)	5 (43)	5 (44)
Probably Consider Banking There	4	4	4	4
Might Or Might Not Consider Banking There	3	3	3	3
Probably Not Consider Banking There	2	2	2	2
Definitely Not Consider Banking There	1	1	1	1
(DO <u>NOT</u> READ) → (Currently Bank There)	X	X	X	X

(45-1)

8a. Now, I'd like you to rate one bank on a series of statements—<u>Chase Manhattan Bank</u>. If you have never banked there, please base your answers on what you know about this bank and your perceptions of it. After I read each statement, please tell me whether you agree completely, agree somewhat, neither agree nor disagree, disagree somewhat, or disagree completely that this statement describes <u>Chase Manhattan Bank</u>. (START WITH X'D STATEMENT AND CONTINUE UNTIL ALL ARE RATED.)

START HERE:	AGREE COM-PLETELY	AGREE SOME-WHAT	NEITHER AGREE NOR DIS-AGREE	DIS-AGREE SOME-WHAT	DIS-AGREE COM-PLETELY
[ ] Is Responsive to Your Needs	5	4	3	2	1 (46)
[ ] Offers High Quality Accounts and Services	5	4	3	2	1 (47)
[ ] Deals With Its Customers on a Personalized Level	5	4	3	2	1 (48)
[ ] Helps Make Banking Easier	5	4	3	2	1 (49)
[ ] Has Bank Personnel That Are Concerned About You	5	4	3	2	1 (50)
[ ] Designs Accounts to Meet Your Special Needs	5	4	3	2	1 (51)
[ ] Is Responsive to Community Needs	5	4	3	2	1 (52)
[ ] Makes It Easy to Open an IRA Account	5	4	3	2	1 (53)
[ ] Has a Full Range of Banking and Investment Services	5	4	3	2	1 (54)
[ ] Is a Bank Where You Want to Have Most of Your Accounts	5	4	3	2	1 (55)

START HERE:	AGREE COM-PLETELY	AGREE SOME-WHAT	NEITHER AGREE NOR DIS-AGREE	DIS-AGREE SOME-WHAT	DIS-AGREE COM-PLETELY
[ ] Has Bank Personnel That Are Experienced	5	4	3	2	1 (56)
[ ] Has Innovative Accounts and Services	5	4	3	2	1 (57)
[ ] Understands Your Banking Needs	5	4	3	2	1 (58)
[ ] Has Branches That Are Pleasant to Bank In	5	4	3	2	1 (59)
[ ] Has Accounts to Help People Just Starting Out	5	4	3	2	1 (60)
[ ] Continuously Develops Services to Meet Your Needs	5	4	3	2	1 (61)
[ ] Has Bank Personnel That Are Friendly and Courteous	5	4	3	2	1 (62)
[ ] Has Accounts and Services That Are Right for You	5	4	3	2	1 (63)
[√] Puts Customers' Needs First	5	4	3	2	1 (64)
[ ] Is a Modern, Up-to-Date Bank	5	4	3	2	1 (65)

END CARD 1

Appendix C

DEFINITIONS OF SELECTED TERMS USED IN PUBLIC RELATIONS EVALUATION

Advertising Equivalency—A means of converting editorial space in the media into advertising costs, by measuring the amount of editorial coverage and then calculating what it would have cost to buy that space, if it had been advertising. Most reputable researchers contend that advertising equivalency computations are of questionable validity, since in many cases the opportunity to "buy" advertising in space that has been specifically allocated to editorial coverage simply does not exist.

Attitude Research—Consists of measuring and interpreting the full range of views, sentiments, feelings, opinions, and beliefs that segments of the public may hold toward given people, products, organizations and/or issues. More specifically, attitude research measures what people say (their verbal expressions), what they know and think (their mental or cognitive predispositions), what they feel (their emotions), and how they're inclined to act (their motivational or drive tendencies).

Bivariate Analysis—Examination of the relationship between two variables.

Causal Relationship—A theoretical notion that

change in one variable forces, produces, or brings about a change in another.

Circulation—Refers to the number of copies sold of a given edition of a publication, at a given time, or as averaged over a period of time.

Communications Audit—A systematic review and analysis—using accepted research techniques and methodologies—of how well an organization communicates with all of its major internal and external target audience groups.

Confidence Interval—In a survey based on a random sample, the range of values within which a population parameter is estimated to fall. For example, in a survey in which a representative sample of 1,000 individuals is interviewed, if 55% express a preference for a given item, we might say that in the population as a whole, in 95 out of 100 cases, the true proportion expressing such a preference probably would fall between 52% and 58%. The plus or minus 3% range is called the *confidence interval*. The fact that we are using 95 out of 100 cases as our guide (or 95%) is our *confidence level*.

Content Analysis—The process of studying and tracking what has been written and broadcast and translating this qualitative material into quantitative form through some type of counting approach that involves coding and classifying of specific messages.

Correlation—Any association or relationship between two variables.

Correlation Coefficient—A measure of association (symbolized as r) that describes the direction and strength of a linear relationship between two variables, measured at the interval or ratio level (e.g. Pearson's Correlation Coefficient).

Cost Per Thousand (CPM)—The cost of advertising for each 1,000 homes reached by radio or television, for each 1,000 copies of a publication, or for each 1,000 potential viewers of an outdoor advertisement.

Cross-Sectional Study—A study based on observation representing a single point in time.

Demographic Analysis—Consists of looking at the population in terms of special social, political, economic, and geographic subgroups, such as a person's age, sex, income-level race, education-level, place of residence, or occupation.

Ethnographic Research—Relies on the tools and techniques of cultural anthropologists and sociologists to obtain a better understanding of how individuals and groups function in their natural settings. Usually, this type of research is carried out by a team of impartial, trained researchers who "immerse" themselves into the daily routine of a neighborhood or community, using a mix of observation, participation, and role-playing techniques, in an effort to try to assess what is really happening from a "cultural" perspective.

Evaluation Research—Determines the relative effectiveness of a public relations program or strategy, measuring outputs and outcomes against a predetermined set of objectives.

Experiment:—Any controlled arrangement and manipulation of conditions to systematically observe specific occurrences, with the intention of defining those criteria that might possibly be affecting those occurrences. An experimental, or quasi-experimental, research design usually involves two groups—a "test" group which is exposed to given criteria, and a "control" group, which is not exposed. Comparisons are then made to determine what effect, if any, exposures to the criteria have had on those in the "test" group.

Factor Analysis—A complex algebraic procedure that seeks to group or combine items or variables in a questionnaire based on how they naturally relate to each other, or "hang together," as general descriptors (or "factors").

Focus Group—An exploratory technique in which a group of somewhere between 8 and 12 individuals—under the guidance of a trained moderator—are encouraged, as a group, to discuss freely any and all of their feelings, concerns, problems, and frustrations relating to specific topics under discussion. Focus groups are ideal for brainstorming, idea-gathering, and concept testing.

Frequency—The number of advertisements, broadcasts, or exposures of given programming or messaging during a particular period of time.

Gross Rating Point—A unit of measurement of broadcast or outdoor advertising audience size, equal to 1% of the total potential audience universe; used to measure the exposure of one or more programs or commercials, without regard to multiple exposure of the same advertising to individuals. A GRP is the product of media reach times exposure frequency. A *gross-rating-point buy* is the number of advertisements necessary to obtain the desired percentage of exposure of the message. In outdoor advertising, GRPs, often used as a synonym for showing, generally refer to the daily effective circulation generated by poster panels, divided by market population. The *cost per gross rating point* (CPGRP) is a measure of broadcast media exposure comparable to the *cost per thousand* (CPM) measure of print media.

Hypothesis—An expectation about the nature of things derived from theory.

Hypothesis-Testing—Determining whether the expectations that a hypothesis represents are, indeed, found in the real world.

Impressions—The number of those who might have had the opportunity to be exposed to a story that has appeared in the media. Sometimes referred to as "opportunity to see." An "impression" usually refers to the total audited circulation of a publication or the audience reach of a broadcast vehicle.

Incidence—The frequency with which a condition or event occurs within a given time and population.

Inquiry Study—A systematic review and analysis, using content analysis or sometimes telephone and mail interviewing techniques, to study the range and types of unsolicited inquires that an organization may receive from customers, prospective customers or other target audience groups.

Judgmental Sample—A type of nonprobability sample in which individuals are deliberately selected for inclusion in the sample by the researcher because they have special knowledge, position, characteristics or represent other relevant dimensions of the population that are deemed important to study. Also known as a "purposive" sample.

Likert Scale—Developed by Rensis Likert, this is a composite measure in which respondents are asked to choose from an ordered series of five responses to indicate their reactions to a sequence of statements (e.g., strongly agree . . . somewhat agree . . . neither agree nor disagree . . . somewhat disagree . . . strongly disagree).

Longitudinal Study—A research design involving the collection of data at different points in time.

Mall Intercept—A special type of in-person interview, in which potential respondents are approached as they stroll through shopping centers or malls. Most mall intercept interviews are based on nonprobability sampling.

Market Research—Any systematic study of buying and selling behavior.

Mean—A measure of central tendency that is the arithmetic average of the scores.

Median—A measure of central tendency indicating the midpoint in a series of scores, the point above and below which 50% of the values fall.

Mode—A measure of central tendency that is the most frequently occurring, the most typical, value in a series.

Multivariate Analysis—Examination of the relationship among three or more variables.

Omnibus Survey—An "all-purpose" national consumer poll usually conducted on a regular schedule—once a week or every other week—by major market research firms. Organizations are encouraged to "buy" one or several proprietary questions and have them "added" to the basic questionnaire. Those adding questions are usually charged on a per-question basis. Also, sometimes referred to as "piggyback" or "shared-cost" surveys.

Panel Study—(1) A type of longitudinal study in which the same individuals are interviewed more than once over a period of time to investigate the processes of response change, usually in reference to the same topic or issue. (2) Also, a type of study in which a group of individuals are deliberately recruited by a research firm, because of their special demographic characteristics, for the express purpose of being interviewed more than once over a period of time for various clients on a broad array of different topics or subjects.

Probability Sample—A process of random selection in which each unit in a population has an equal chance of being included in the sample.

Psychographic Analysis—Consists of looking at the population in terms of people's nondemographic traits and characteristics, such as a person's personality type, life style, social roles, values and beliefs.

Q-Sort—A personality inventory introduced in the 1950s in which respondents are asked to sort opinion statements along a "most-like-me" to "most-unlike-me" continuum. Q-Sorting allows researchers to construct models of individual respondents' belief systems.

Qualitative Research—Usually refers to studies that are somewhat subjective, but nevertheless in-depth, using a probing, open-end, free-response format.

Quantitative Research—Usually refers to studies that are highly objective and projectable, using closed-end, forced-choice questionnaires. These studies tend to rely heavily on statistics and numerical measures.

Quota Sample—A type of nonprobability sample in which individuals are selected on the basis of prespecified characteristics, so that the total sample will have the same general distribution of characteristics as are assumed to exist in the population being studied.

Range—A measure of variability that is computed by subtracting the lowest score in a distribution from the highest score.

Reach—Refers to the range or scope of influence or effect that a given communications vehicle has on targeted audience groups. In broadcasting, it is the net unduplicated radio or TV audience—the number of different individuals or households—for programs or commercials as measured for a specific time period in quarter-hour units over a period of 1 to 4 weeks.

Regression Analysis—A statistical technique for studying relationships among variables, measured at the interval or ratio level.

Reliability—The extent to which the results would be consistent, or replicable, if the research were conducted a number of times.

Screener Question—One or several questions usually asked in the beginning of an interview to determine if the potential respondent is eligible to participate in the study.

Secondary Analysis—A technique for extracting from previously conducted studies new knowledge on topics other than those that were the focus of the original studies. It does this through a systematic re-analysis of a vast array of already-existing research data.

Situation Analysis—An impartial, often third-party assessment of the public relations and/or public affairs problems, or opportunities, that an organization may be facing at a given point in time.

Standard Deviation—An index of variability of a distribution. More precisely, it is the range from the mean within which approximately 34% of the cases fall, provided the values are distributed in a normal curve.

Statistical Significance—Refers to the unlikeliness that relationships observed in a sample could be attributed to sampling error alone.

Survey—Any systematic collection of data that uses a questionnaire and a recognized sampling method. There are three basic types of surveys: those conducted *face-to-face* (in-person) . . . those conducted by *telephone* . . . and those that are *self-administered* (usually distributed by mail, e-mail, or fax.)

Univariate Analysis—The examination of only one variable at a time.

Validity—The extent to which a research project measures what it is intended, or purports, to measure.

Variance—A measure of the extent to which individual scores in a set differ from each other. More precisely, it is the sum of the squared deviations from the mean divided by the frequencies.

Appendix D

Audiovisual Supports

Material	Advantages	Limitations
Slide series A form of projected audiovisual materials easy to prepare with any 35-mm camera	1. Prepared with any 35-mm camera for most uses 2. Requires only filming, with processing and mounting by film laboratory 3. Colorful, realistic reproductions of original subjects 4. Easily revised, updated, handled, stored, and rearranged 5. Can be combined with taped narration for greater effectiveness 6. May be played through remote control presentation	1. Requires some skill in photography 2. Requires special equipment for close-up photography and copying 3. Prone to get out of sequence and be projected incorrectly
Filmstrips Closely related to slides, but instead of being mounted as separate pictures, remain uncut as a continuous strip	1. Compact, easily handled, and always in proper sequence 2. Can be supplemented with captions or recordings	1. Relatively difficult to prepare locally 2. Requires film laboratory service to convert slides to filmstrip form

Material	Advantages	Limitations
	3. Inexpensive when quantity reproduction is required 4. Projected with simple, lightweight equipment 5. Projection rate controlled by presenter	3. In permanent sequence and therefore cannot be rearranged or revised
Overhead transparencies A popular form of locally prepared materials, requiring an overhead projector for presentation	1. Can present information in systematic, developmental sequences 2. Simple-to-operate projector with presentation rate controlled by presenter 3. Requires limited planning 4. Can be prepared by a variety of simple, inexpensive methods	1. Requires special equipment facilities, and skills for more advanced preparation methods 2. May be cumbersome and lack finesse of more remote processes

Appendix E

DEFINING KEY CYBERSPACE TERMS

Understanding the Following Words and Phrases Is Essential to Surviving in Cyberspace

Access—The means of getting into an online system. Different systems require different types of access. For instance, CompuServe access requires an account, a CompuServe access telephone number, a password, and (optionally) special software designed just for CompuServe; however, any old phone line and modem will do. Conversely, a direct Internet connection that provides you with access to the graphical version of the World Wide Web requires a special configuration for your computer called a TCP/IP stack in addition to an Internet access account.

Address—Where somebody can send mail or files to you at an online site. Depending on the type of service you use, the look of an address can vary a great deal. For example, my CompuServe address is ⟨76346,627⟩; my America Online address is ⟨She1H⟩, and my Internet address is ⟨shel@ccnet.com⟩.

ASCII—The American Standard Code for Information Exchange. These are the characters that you type on a computer keyboard. "Low" ASCII refers to those characters available on your keyboard only—Aa through Zz, 0–9, and several symbols: ~'@#$%^&*()_+|\{}[]:;"'⟨⟩,.?/. In UNIX applications, including "shell" Internet accounts, Lower ASCII is all there is. Upper ASCII refers to characters available through a combination of keystrokes on higher-level systems and applications, such as ®, ©, and õ.

Baud (or bauds per second or bps)— Refers to the rate of speed at which information travels from computer to computer and is related to the type of communication device you have. A 2400-bps modem sends and receives information at 2400 bauds per second, while a 28,800-bps modem works at more than ten times that speed. Other nonmodem connections (such as ISDN and T1) are much faster.

BBS—Bulletin Board System, an electronic version of the old bulletin boards on which people attached notices with thumb tacks. Generally includes a public message area, a section for the storage of files, live chat, e-mail (either limited to the system's boundaries or connected to some larger e-mail system, including the Internet), and other features.

Browser—Software designed to allow you to "parse"—or view—documents created specifically for the Internet's World Wide Web. More recent browsers also allow you to access other Internet services, including gopher and FTP. The most popular browsers currently are Netscape and Mosaic.

Chat—Real-time online conversation conducted when two or more people type to one another. Services like America Online provide chat "rooms," while Internet Relay Chat (IRC) is the most notorious chat venue.

Client—A software application used to do something online. A piece of software that allows you to retrieve documents from an FTP site, for example, is an FTP client; one that allows you to search gopher sites is a gopher client.

Commercial Online Service—An online bulletin boardlike service that provides an array of services for a fee. Local dial-ups (a phone number in your area) is another feature of the commercial online services, which include CompuServe, America Online, Prodigy, eWorld, Transom, and Delphi.

Cyberspace—A term that refers to the unreal world in which information passes between computers. Originally coined by cyberpunk novelist William Gibson in his groundbreaking novel, *Neuromancer*, the term has become widely accepted as the geographical name for the place where online conversations, e-mail exchanges, flame wars, spam attacks, and information transfers occur.

Distributed—Computing that exceeds the bounds of a restricted hierarchy. The Internet is a "distributed" network because a message can be sent to any location (or number of locations) on the Internet, generally without limitation. It is its internationally distributed nature that makes the Internet a bit of an anarchy, difficult (make that impossible) to control or regulate.

Download—Move files from a remote computer to your own.

Electronic Newsletter—A newsletter distributed digitally from one computer to many other computers.

E-mail—Short for electronic mail. A message passed from one person to one or more other people via computer, generally using an e-mail program of one kind or another. These programs can reside on the user's computer, or on a "host" computer.

Extension—The last part of an IBM PC-compatible file name. In the file name ⟨program.exe⟩, ⟨exe⟩ is the extension.

FAQ—Frequently Asked Questions, lists of questions about a particular Usenet newsgroup and the newsgroup's particular topic. An FAQ from sci.agriculture.beekeeping would include information about the newsgroup, but also the fundamentals of beekeeping.

File—A single archive of information recognized as an information unit by a computer. A file may store a text document, a graphic image, an executable program that launches an application, a sound, a video, or some indecipherable collection of characters that only the computer understands but requires to execute some function. Most computer programs are comprised of many files.

Flame—An angry response to a posting, usually in a newsgroup.

Flame War—A flurry of flames generated from a single source, usually drawing in several newsgroup participants.

Forum—A gathering place based on a theme, specifically in CompuServe. There are professional forums, special interest forums (including the Public Relations and Marketing Forum), and hobby-oriented forums, where people can leave messages on a public notice area, contribute and download files, and chat.

FTP—File Transfer Protocol, one of the principal means by which you retrieve files from the Internet.

Gopher—A means of finding information on the Internet. Gopher was developed at the University of Minnesota (home of the Minnesota Golden Gophers). Computer systems store information in gopherspace so that people using Gopher software can easily find the information stored there.

Information Retrieval Service—Online services that search databases of information and return references to that information based on user queries. These services include Lexis-Nexis, Dialog, IQuest, and Dow Jones.

Internet—A vast system of computer networks connected together, allowing computers in one part of the world to instantly access computers in another. Used to send e-mail across various systems, to find information stored on various systems, and to engage in person-to-person and many-to-many exchanges.

LAN—Local Area Network, a small system of computers that are linked together by a "server." On a LAN, you can use an application (such as a word processor) that is resident on your own computer to read files that reside on the server, or you can actually run applications that reside on the server. Particularly handy for organizations that desire employees to share information.

Listserv—A program that allows you to maintain an e-mail-based mailing list.

Mailing List—Participants who subscribe to mailing lists receive all posts that are sent to the list. Say you subscribe to a list about people who hate the Los Angeles Rams. You might send a message to the list that asks, "Does anybody actually remember the name of any Rams quarterback?" Even though you only sent your message to one address—the list address—every subscriber would receive the message. If somebody responded, "Come to think of it, I can't think of a single one," everybody on the list would receive *that*, too. Simple commands allow you to cancel subscriptions and, in some cases, to take advantage of other list services, such as accessing files stored in the list archives.

Majordomo—A program that allows you to maintain an e-mail-based mailing list.

Network—Two or more computers linked together comprise a network.

Newsgroup—An area where people can discuss common topics by leaving postings, as on a bulletin board, that others can read when they log on. "Newsgroups" generally refer to discussions on Usenet, which most people access via the Internet. There are over 10,000 newsgroups with topics from journalism and media to mysticism, bondage, holocaust revisionism, gun control, cartoons, photography, horses—if people have an interest in it, there's probably a newsgroup where they get online to discuss it.

Online—Any situation when two computers are talking to each other.

Provider—An entity (university, association, corporation, or private business) that provides you with Internet access.

Service Provider—An organization or institution that provides access to the Internet for people like you.

UNIX—The original language developed by Bell Labs that allows computers of differing platforms to communicate with one another. UNIX is the infrastructure of the Internet. If you have a shell account, you will end up learning some very fundamental UNIX commands in order to get around.

Upload—To send a file from your computer to a remote system, such as a commercial online service, an Internet FTP site, or a BBS file storage area.

URL—Uniform Resource Locator, an address where stuff on the Internet is located.

Usenet—An international meeting place where people gather (but not in real time) to meet their friends, discuss events, keep up with trends, discuss politics or other issues, seek information, or just talk. Over 10,000 newsgroups exist on Usenet, which resides primarily on the Internet. You'll find discussions on engineering, environmental issues, television shows, college classes, O.J. Simpson, and any other subject about which more than one or two people have a passing interest.

YOUR GUIDE TO FINDING PR ON THE WEB

ADI Press Track—http://www.presstrac.com Information about its news and media content analysis; company directory, a search mechanism and links.

Admark Corp—http://www.admarkcorp.com Information on Admark Corp.'s software packages.

Agenda Online—http://www.agendaonline.com Information about event planning including finding hotel rooms, best caterer, locating photographer.

American Association Of Advertising Agencies—http://www.commercepark.com/AAAA/ Information on membership benefits, legislative news, roster of members.

American College Media Directory—http://www.webcom.com/shambhu/acmd/welcome.html Describes the college media directory listing approximately 3,000 college newspapers, radio stations, and TV stations.

Association for Education in Journalism and Mass Communication—http://www.aejmc.sc.edu/online/home.html

Business Wire—http://www.hnt.com/bizwire Information about purchasing a location on site for distribution of releases, corporate profile, quarterly reports; create a virtual media kit.

Canadian Public Relations Society—http://www.cprs.ca Provides information about new services and upcoming events.

Cato Communications—http://www.sidcato.com Site is by publisher of monthly newsletter *Sid Cato's Newsletter on Annual Reports*.

Center for Corporate Community Relations at Boston College—http://www.bc.edu/bc_org/avp/acavp/cccr.

Direct Marketing Association—http://www.the-dma.org. Areas include Business Affairs, Newsstand, Research Observatory.

Delahaye Group—http://www.delahaye.com Devoted to communications measurement; offers case studies, tips, techniques for communications professionals.

Dryden Brown—http://www.dryden.co.uk This marcom firm helps organizations worldwide pinpoint suitable press event locations in major cities in UK and Ireland.

DWJ Television—http://www.dwjtv.com This broadcast PR firm provides a "clip of the week", daybook, client pages, news section as well as a digital media and broadcast report.

Editor & Publisher—http://www.mediainfo.com/edpub E&P provides online newspapers, lists of conferences centers, research, classifieds and a Web edition of the magazine.

Edgar Online—http://www.edgar-online.com Features up-to-the-minute listings of SEC EDGAR corporate filings.

Feature Photo—http://www.featurephoto.com Distributes color and black and white photos to the media, nationwide. Media can download images.

Institute For Crisis Management—http://www.crisis-mgmt.com Information about the center, events and publications.

Institute For Public Relations Research & Education—http://www.jou.ufl.edu/iprre/home-page.htm Information on the latest news, research projects, academic papers, a newsletter, seminars, awards, and competitions.

International Association of Business Communicators—http://www.iabc.com Information about the association, conferences, services, publications, products.

Investor Relations Network Services—http://www.irnetserv.com PR execs can put their company's annual report on this site; educational resources to PR professionals for investor relations.

Journalism Forum—http://www.jforum.org Online resource for journalists to discuss topics about news issues. PR execs also can post news releases on the site.

Luce Press Clippings—http://www.lucepress.com The first national clipping service on Web, has information about print, broadcast coverage, clipping analysis.

Market Place Media—http://www.marketmedia.com. Includes the Media Analysis Tool with access to 3,000-plus publications in four market segments (college, military, minorities, seniors)

Medialink—http://www.medialinkworldwide .com Medialink established a unique classroom on the web that provides video, video production, television station relations, ethical guidelines, and links to useful sites.

MediaMap—http://www.mediamap.com Database of media addresses, editorial opps.

Mediasource—http://www.mediasource.com Source for journalists, information on hundreds of subscriber companies. For a company will develop and promote homepage for you.

NAPS-NET—http://www.napsnet.com Features and graphics from more than 750 companies, associations, PR firms, and government information offices.

National Investor Relations Institute—http:// www.niri.org Lists membership information, conferences, and other NIRI resources.

North American Network—http://www.radiospace.com/welcome.html Information on how to use sound files and scripts as well as lists of radio networks, stations, interviews, and news.

PiMS—http://www.pimsinc.com Information about distribution of press kits, media list development, broadcast faxing, and word processing as well as an e-mail book and news and notes.

PR Cybermall—http://www.prgenius.com An open market Web site with a forum section, ideas, publications, products, and research.

PR Newswire—http://www.prnewswire.com/ cnoc.html Lets users read news from members, get financial insight from leading commentators.

ProfNet—http://www.vyne.com/profnet Site describes ProfNet, an e-mail, phone, and fax service linking journalists with experts; includes list of sources.

PR Watch—http://users.aol.com/srampton/center/html Information on abuses in public affairs, grass-roots programs. Resource for counter-PR research services.

Public Relations Society of America—http:// www.prsa.org The world's largest organization for public relations professionals provides information about membership, chapters, accreditation, seminars, and publications.

Southwest Newswire—http://www.swenewswire .com Information about its corporate profile, newsletter, wire services, news releases, headlines, Internet services, and listings.

U.S. Newswire—http://access.digex.net/~usnwire. Lists information about national newswire; including headlines from previous day's evening newscast.

Weick PhotodataBase—http://www.wieckphoto .com View photos in three databases: auto, corporate, and travel; links to various news wires and breaking business news images.

West Glen Communications—http://www.westglen.com Video news release production and distribution company.

Appendix F

On-Line Databases

Particularly important for public relations research are on-line databases, which store vast quantities of information on current and historical subjects. Some of the major service information vendors available to public relations practitioners are described here.

CD Plus Technologies
333 Seventh Avenue
4th Floor
New York, NY 10001

For over a decade, this service has supplied a large number of databases, with primary emphasis on medical, engineering, educational, and business-oriented information. Price structure varies according to the type of service selected. The Open Access Plan has an annual password fee of $80, a per connect-hour charge of between $10 and $139, depending on the service, and a telecommunications charge of about $12.

DIALCOM Services, Inc.
2560 N. First Street
P.O. Box 49019
San Jose, CA 95161-9019
800-872-7654

DIALCOM, begun in 1970, was purchased by MCI. It offers gateways to databases such as UPI, the Official Airline Guide, and the Bureau of National Affairs. It also offers gateway services to other on-line vendors, which enable customers to access databases offered on Dow Jones News/Retrieval Service, BRS, and DIALOG. The fee structure is based on the number of hours used, not the databases accessed. Costs for accessing the gateway services are based on the rates charged by other vendors. The service operates 24 hours a day, 7 days a week.

DIALOG Information Services, Inc.
Lockheed Corporation
3460 Hillview Avenue
Palo Alto, CA 94304
800-334-2564

DIALOG was started as a commercial venture in 1972 by the Lockheed Corporation. It is one of the largest on-line services, offering nearly 400 databases that range from business and economics to science and technology. DIALOG charges a $295 initiation fee, $100 of which can be applied to future use, and has a wide variation in connect-hour cost. Each database has a set hourly cost, ranging from $30 to $300. DIALOG is available 24 hours a day, 7 days a week.

Dow Jones News/Retrieval
P.O. Box 300
Princeton, NJ 08543
800-522-3567

This is part of Dow Jones and Company, publisher of *The Wall Street Journal*. More than 60 databases are offered, primarily relating to business and economics, financial and investment services, and general news and information. *The Wall Street Journal* is available in summary form as well as in its entirety. The fee structure for companies is complex. For individuals, costs start with a $29.95 sign-up fee and an $18 annual service fee that kicks in after the first year. Then fees range from $.50 to $2.85 per minute for prime time and from $0.08 to $0.60 per minute for nonprime time. The service is available 24 hours a day.

Facts on File
460 Park Avenue South
New York, NY 10016
212-683-2244

Facts on File summarizes information daily from leading U.S. and foreign periodicals, the publications of Commerce Clearing House, *Congressional Quarterly*, *Congressional Record*, *State Department Bulletin*, presidential documents, and official press releases. Subject areas are as diverse as the news of the day. The annual subscription fee is $680.

Find/SVP
625 Avenue of the Americas
New York, NY 10011
212-645-4500

Find/SVP provides quick consulting and research services by telephone for decision makers as a primary information resource to small and medium-sized companies and as a supplemental service to larger corporations that maintain in-house research and information centers. It has access to more than 3,000 online databases, 2,000 periodical subscriptions, tens of thousands of subject company and company files, hundreds of directories and reference works, dozens of cabinets of microfiche, and extensive CD-ROM sources. Its activities

are organized into 10 consultant teams: (1) business/financial, (2) consumer products, (3) technical/industrial, (4) human resources/-employee benefits, (5) document services, (6) accounting/tax, (7) legal, (8) health care, (9) society and media, and (10) PC help. Hourly rates range from $40 to $175, depending on the complexity of the request. Retainers of $500 to $1,500, plus out-of-pocket expenses, entitle unlimited use. Find/SVP promises that "in most cases, you'll have your answer in less than 48 hours from the time you call."

LEXIS and NEXIS
Mead Data Central
9443 Springboro Pike
P.O. Box 933
Dayton, OH 45401
800-227-4908

LEXIS and NEXIS are two of the information services provided by this division of Mead Corporation. LEXIS is a legal information database containing the full text of case law from state, federal, and international courts; state and federal regulations; and other legal records. NEXIS is a full-text database containing 750 major newspapers, magazines, and newsletters. In 1988, a group of media in the NEXIS databank was organized as the Advertising and Public Relations Library, including news wires and communications-oriented publications. The fee structure is complex, but the range of costs varies from $6 to $50 for the search and $35 per hour for connect charges. Both services are available 24 hours a day on weekdays and all weekend, except from 2 A.M. to 10 A.M. Sunday.

NewsNet, Inc.
945 Haverford Road
Bryn Mawr, PA 19010
800-345-1301

NewsNet was started in 1982 by Independent Publications. It offers primarily newsletters and wire services. There are more than 400 specialized business newsletters and wire services covering more than 35 industries, including telecommunications, publishing, broadcasting, electronics and computers, energy, investment, accounting, and taxation. Prices range from $24 to more than $100 an hour, depending on the newsletter being accessed. There is also a monthly minimum charge of $15. NewsNet is available 24 hours a day.

Appendix G

LEADING MEDIA DIRECTORIES

When public relations professionals are asked which media directories they use most often, their answers are as varied as the tasks their firms perform. Publishers have carved such precise market niches for their wares that direct comparison of one directory to another is usually inappropriate. A comprehensive list of media directories begins on this page. Directories are listed by category and then alphabetically. Another list provides complete names and addresses of the publishers cited.

DIRECTORIES

Newspapers

E&P International Yearbook. Annual list of U.S. and Canadian daily newspaper personnel and other data. $60. **Editor & Publisher.**

Family Page Directory. $60 for two editions printed at six-month intervals. Contains information about home, cooking, and family interest sections of newspapers. **Public Relations Plus.**

Media Alerts. Data on 200 major dailies as well as 1,900 magazines. $155. **Bacon's.**

National Directory of Community Newspapers. Listings on newspapers serving smaller communities. $35. **American Newspaper Representatives.**

Publicity Checker, Volume 2: Newspapers. $155 when purchased with Volume 1 on magazines. Two volumes list over 7,500 publications. **Bacon's.**

Working Press of the Nation, Volume I: Newspapers. Part of a $260 five-volume set with 25,000 publicity outlets. **National Research Bureau.**

1988 News Bureaus in the U.S. $133. **Larimi.**

Magazines

Media Alerts. Data on 1,900 magazines and 200 major daily newspapers. $155. **Bacon's.**

National Directory of Magazines. Lists basic information on 1,300 magazines in the United States and Canada. $125. **Oxbridge.**

Publicity Checker, Volume 1. Part of a two-volume set (for magazines and newspapers) with over 7,500 listings. $155 for both volumes. **Bacon's.**

Standard Periodical Directory. Has 60,000 titles with 50 fields of data per title, divided into 250 subject areas. $295. **Oxbridge.**

Working Press of the Nation, Volume 2: Magazines. Part of a $260 five-volume set with data on 25,000 publicity outlets. **National Research Bureau.**

Television

Cable Contacts Yearbook. Lists all cable systems. $184. **Larimi.**

Radio-TV Directory. Over 1,300 TV stations and 9,000 radio stations. $155. **Bacon's.**

Talk Show Selects. Identifies talk show contacts nationwide for both TV and radio. Emphasizes network and syndication programs. $185. **Broadcast Interview.**

Television Contacts. Updated extensive listings. $233. **Larimi.**

TV News. Guide to news directors and assignment editors. $172. **Larimi.**

TV Publicity Outlets. Two editions are printed at six-month intervals. $159.50. **Public Relations Plus.**

Working Press of the Nation, Volume 3: TV and Radio. Part of a $260 five-volume set with 25,000 publicity outlets. **National Research Bureau.**

Radio

National Radio Publicity Outlets. Two editions are printed at six-month intervals. $159.50 for both. **Public Relations Plus.**

Radio Contacts. Extensive, updated listings. $239. **Larimi.**

Radio-TV Directory. Over 9,000 radio and 1,300 TV stations. $155. **Bacon's.**

Talk Show Selects. Identifies both radio and TV talk show contacts nationwide. Emphasis is on syndicated and network programs. $185. **Broadcast Interview.**

Working Press of the Nation, Volume 3. Includes both radio and TV. Part of a five-volume $260 set that contains data on 25,000 publicity outlets. **National Research Bureau.**

Newsletters

Directory of Newsletters. Has 13,500 newsletters in the United States and Canada. Publications are divided into 168 categories. $125. **Oxbridge.**

The Newsletter Yearbook Directory. Lists worldwide newsletters available by subscription. $60. **Newsletter Clearinghouse.**

Newsletters Directory. Guide to more than 8,000 subscription, membership and free newsletters. $140. **Gale Research.**

1988 Investment Newsletters. Lists over 1,000 newsletters. $160. **Larimi.**

Regional

Burrelle's Media Directories. Regional directories for New York State ($85), New Jersey ($70), Pennsylvania ($38), New England ($95), Connecticut ($32), Maine ($25), New Hampshire ($25), Massachusetts ($44), Rhode Island ($25), Vermont ($25), and Greater Boston ($29). **Burrelle's.**

Metro California Media. Detailed listing of California media. $89.50 includes semiannual revised edition. **Public Relations Plus.**

Minnesota Non-Metro Media Directory. Guide to the media in the Twin Cities region. $90. **Publicity Central.**

New York Publicity Outlets. Media within a 50-mile radius of New York City. $89.50 includes the semiannual revised edition. **Public Relations Plus.**

New York TV Directory. Lists producers, directors, and others active in the New York market. Published annually. $15. **National Academy.**

Vermont Media Directory. TV, radio, newspaper, and magazine listings. $99. **Kelliher.**

Washington News Media. Detailed listings of wire services, newspapers, magazines, radio-TV, and foreign correspondents. $99. **Hudson's.**

1988 Media Guide and Membership Directory. Chicago media outlets. $75. **Publicity Club of Chicago.**

International

International Literary Market Place. $85. **R. R. Bowker.**

International Media Guide. Publishers of *Newspapers Worldwide* and *Consumer Magazines Worldwide.* A four-volume set covers business and professional publications for Asia/Pacific; Middle East and Africa; Latin America; and Europe. Each volume sells for $100. **International Media Guide.**

International Publicity Checker. Lists 10,000 Western European business, trade, and technical magazines and 1,000 national and regional newspapers. $165. **Bacon's.**

Ulrich's International Periodicals Directory. Lists 70,730 periodicals in 542 subject areas in two volumes. Over 40,000 entries from the previous edition have been updated. $159.95. **Ulrich's.**

United Kingdom

Benn's Media Directory. Available in two books, one for the United Kingdom and the other for international listings. Each is $95; both are $160. Published by Benn Business Information Services. **Nichols.**

Bowdens Media Directory. Updated three times annually, with complete media listings. **Bowdens.**

Editors Media Directories. Series of directories covering journalists, features, and profiles. **Editors.**

Hollis Press and Public Relations Annual. Over 18,000 organizations in the public relations industry, with a full range of media. $36. **Hollis.**

PIMS United Kingdom Financial Directory. Detailed listings. $300 annually or $90 for a single copy. **PIMS U.S.A.**

PIMS United Kingdom Media Directory. Provides detailed access to the total range of U.K. media. $390 annually, $220 quarterly, or $90 for a single issue. **PIMS U.S.A.**

Willing's Press Guide. Extensive U.K. media listings. $105 plus $5 shipping. Published by Thomas Skinner Directories. **Business Press International.**

Canada

Matthews List. Contains 3,600 media throughout Canada. Updated three times annually. $130 per year. **Publicorp.**

Australia

Margaret Gee's Media Guide. Lists 2,400 Australian media. Updated three times annually. $100. **Margaret Gee.**

Japan

Publishers in English in Japan. Media selection for English-speaking readers. Published by Japan Publications Guide Service. **Pacific Subscription Service.**

Africa

African Book World and Press. Lists over 4,000 publishers. The latest edition is 1983. $78. **K. G. Saur.**

Specialists

Business and Financial News Media. Print, electronic, syndicated columns, and individual writers. $85. **Larriston.**

Business and Technical Media. Available on paper and floppy disk, at $200 total for both. **Ron Gold.**

Computer Industry Almanac. Extensive industry data, as well as a publications directory. $49.50 hardcover; $29.95 softcover. **Computer Industry Almanac.**

Directory of the College Student Press in America. Has 5,000 student newspapers and magazines on 3,600 campuses. $75. **Oxbridge.**

Encyclopedia of Association Periodicals. Three-volume directory sells for $150; individual volumes sell for $60. Vol. I: business and finance. Vol. II: science and medicine. Vol. III: social sciences and education. **Gale Research.**

Medical and Science News Media. Specialized listings with major news contacts. $85. Larriston.

Medical Press List. Available on paper and floppy disk at a combination price of $125. **Ron Gold.**

Nelson's Directory of Investment Research. Contact information and areas of specialization for over 3,000 security analysts. $259. **W. R. Nelson.**

TIA International Travel News Directory. Comprehensive travel media listings. $35. **Travel Industry Association.**

Travel, Leisure and Entertainment News Media. Major nationwide contacts. $85. **Larriston.**

1988 College/Alumni/Military Publications. Over 1,150 publications in these three fields. $87. **Larimi.**

Working Press of the Nation, Volume 5. Internal Publications Directory. Describes house organs published primarily for distribution inside companies. Part of a five-volume library selling for $250. **National Research Bureau.**

Ethnic

Black Media in America. $50. **Hall Co.**

Burrelle's Special Directories. Directories of Black, Latino, and women's media are covered in three volumes at $50 each. **Burrelle's.**

Hispanic Media, U.S.A. Provides a narrative description of Spanish-language media. Includes newspapers, radio, and TV stations. $75 plus $1.50 handling. **The Media Institute.**

General

Business Publications Rates and Data. Monthly directory of magazines and newspapers categorized by field. $398 for 12 monthly issues, or $194 for one copy. **Standard Rate and Data Service.**

Directory of Directories. More than 10,000 entries in two volumes. $195. **Gale Research.**

Gale Directory of Publications. Annual directory to newspapers, magazines, journals, and related publications. $135. **Gale Research.**

Gebbie All-In-One Directory. Comprehensive listings of all media. $79.25. **Gebbie Press.**

Market Guide. Has data on population, income, households, and retail sales for markets around the nation. $70. **E&P.**

Print Media Editorial Calendars. Lists 12-month editorial calendars for 4,200 trades, 1,700 newspapers, 1,500 consumer magazines, and 400 farm publications. $195. **Standard Rate and Data Service.**

Experts and Writers

Directory of Experts, Authorities and Spokespersons. Access to over 3,569 experts. $19.95 plus $3.50 shipping. Can be ordered on Rolodex cards for $165. **Broadcast Interview.**

1988 Syndicated Columnists. Over 1,400 columnists listed. $157. **Larimi.**

Syndicate Directory. Lists syndicated features by classification and by-lines, as well as how material is furnished. $6. **E&P.**

Working Press of the Nation, Volume 4: Feature Writer and Photographer Directory. Part of a five-volume set selling for $260. **National Research Bureau.**

Directory of Publishers

Publishers of media directories are presented in alphabetical order in the list that follows.

American Newspaper Representatives
12 South Sixth St., Ste. 520
Minneapolis, MN 55402
612/332-8686
National Directory of Community Newspapers

Bacon's PR and Media Information Systems
332 S. Michigan Ave.
Chicago, IL 60604
800/621-0561
International Publicity Checker
Media Alerts
Publicity Checker
Radio-TV Directory

Bowden's Information Services
624 King Street West
Toronto ON M5V 2X9, Canada
416/860-0794
Bowden's Media Directory

Broadcast Interview Source
2500 Wisconsin Ave., NW
Suite 930
Washington, DC 20007
202/333-4904
Directory of Experts
Talk Show Selects

Burrelle's Press Clipping Service
75 East Northfield Ave.
Livingston, NJ 07039
201/992-6600
Regional Media Directories

Computer Industry Almanac
8111 LBJ Freeway, 13th floor
Dallas, TX 75251-1313
214/231-8735
Computer Industry Almanac

Editor and Publisher
11 West 19th St.
New York, NY 10011
212/675-4380
E&P International Yearbook
Market Guide
Syndicate Directory

Editors Media Directories
9/10 Great Sutton St.
London EC1 VOBX England
Editors Media Directories

Gale Research
Book Tower
Detroit, MI 48226
313/961-2242
Directory of Directories
Directory of Publications
Encyclopedia of Association Periodicals
Newsletters Directory

Gebbie Press
Box 1000
New Paltz, NY 12561
914/255-7560
Gebbie All-In-One Directory

Hollis Directories
Contact House
Sunbury-on-Thames
Middlesex TW16 5HG, England
Hollis Press and Public Relations Annual

International Media Guide Enterprises
22 Elizabeth St.
South Norwalk, CT 06856
203/853-7880
International Media Guide

Kelliher/Samets
130 South Willard St.
Burlington, VT 05401
802/862-8261
Vermont Media Directory

Larimi Communications Associates
5 West 37th St.
New York, NY 10018
800/634-4020
212/819-9310
Cable Contacts Yearbook
1988 News Bureaus in the U.S.
Radio Contacts
Television Contacts
TV News

Larriston Communications
P. O. Box 20229
New York, NY 10025
212/864-0150
Business and Financial News Media
Medical and Science News Media Travel,
Leisure and Entertainment News Media

Margaret Gee Media Group
384 Flinders Lane
Melbourne, Victoria 3000 Australia
Information Australia
Margaret Gee's Media Guide

The Media Institute
3017 M Street
Washington, DC 20007
202/298-7512
Hispanic Media, U.S.A.

National Academy of Television
Arts and Sciences
New York Chapter
110 West 57th St.
New York, NY 10019
212/765-2450
New York TV Directory

National Research Bureau
310 S. Michigan Ave.
Chicago, IL 60604
312/663-5580
Working Press of the Nation

W. R. Nelson Co.
1 Gateway Plaza
Port Chester, NY 10573
914/937-8400
Nelson's Directory of Investment
Research

Newsletter Clearinghouse
44 W. Market St.
P. O. Box 311
Rhinebeck, NY 12572
914/876-2081
Hudson's Washington News
Media Newsletter Yearbook
Directory

Nichols Publishing
P. O. Box 96
New York, NY 10024
212/580-8079
Benn's Media Directory

Oxbridge Communications
150 Fifth Ave.
New York, NY 10011
212/741-0231
National Directory of Magazines
Standard Periodical Directory

Pacific Subscription Service
P. O. Box 811
FDR Station
New York, NY 10150
212/929-1629
Publishers in English in Japan

PIMS U.S.A.
1133 Broadway
New York, NY 10010
212/645-5112
United Kingdom Financial Directory
United Kingdom Media Directory

Public Relations Plus
P. O. Drawer 1197
New Milford, CT 06776
203/354-9361
All TV Publicity Outlets
Metro California Media
National Radio Publicity Outlets
New York Publicity Outlets
The Family Page Directory

Publicity Club of Chicago
1441 Shermer Rd. (#110)
Northbrook, IL 60062
1988 Media Guide
Publicity Club of Chicago Membership Directory

Publicorp Communications
Box 1029
Pointe Claire PQ
W9S 4H9 Canada
Matthews List

Reed Business Publishing
205 E. 42nd St., Ste. 1705
New York, NY 10017
212/867-2080
Willing's Press Guide

Ron Gold, N.A.
1341 Ocean Ave. (#366)
Santa Monica, CA 90401
213/399-7938
Business and Technical Media
Medical Press List

R. R. Bowker
245 West 17th St.
New York, NY 10011
212/645-9700
Ulrich's International Periodicals Directory

Appendix H

CORPORATE REPORTING REQUIREMENTS

Periodically, the Hill & Knowlton public relations firm updates this compilation of "Disclosure and Filing Requirements for Public Companies." It details the specific requirements of the various exchanges as well as the Securities
and Exchange Commission.

DISCLOSURE REQUIREMENTS

Reporting Required for:	Securities and Exchange Commission	New York Stock Exchange	American Stock Exchange	National Association of Securities Dealers	Generally Recommended Publicity Practice, All Companies
Accounting: Change in Auditors	Form 8-K; if principal accountant (or accountants for a subsidiary) resigns, declines to be reelected, or is dismissed or if another is engaged. Disclose date of resignation, details of disagreement (any adverse opinions, disclaimers of opinion, or qualifications of opinion occurring during the audits of the two most recent fiscal (years), comment let-	Prompt notice to Exchange, 8-K when filed.	Prompt notification of Listing Representative, prior to filing of 8-K, *and* must state reason for change (Listing Form SD-1, Item 1a).	Prompt notification concurrently with press disclosure (company must file 8-K with SEC, and information may be material enough to warrant trading halt, See NASD Schedule D). Contact NASD's Market Surveillance Section at (202) 728-8187, preferably before public release and when in doubt about "material information."(NASD Schedule D.)	Press release desirable at time of filing 8-K if differences are major. Consider clear statement in annual report or elsewhere on independence of auditors, including their reporting relationship to Board's audit committee; state company policy on rotation/nonrotation of auditors periodically.

Reporting Required for:	Securities and Exchange Commission	New York Stock Exchange	American Stock Exchange	National Association of Securities Dealers	Generally Recommended Publicity Practice, All Companies
	ters to SEC for former accountant on whether he agrees with the company's statements in the 8-K. See also Regulations S-K, Item 304.			Promptly confirm in writing all oral communications to NASD. If public release made after 5:30 p.m. Eastern Standard Time, notify NASD by 9:30 a.m. the following trading day. (NASD Schedule D).	
Annual (or Special) Meeting of Stockholders	10-Q following meeting, including date of meeting, name of each director elected, summary of other matters voted on.	Five copies of all proxy material sent to shareholders filed with Exchange not later than date material sent to any shareholder. Ten days' advance notice of record date or closing transfer books to Exchange. The notice should state the purpose(s) for which the record date has been fixed. Preferably, notice should be given by TWX (TWX No. 710-581-2801); or, if by telephone, promptly confirmed by TWX, telegram, or letter.	Six copies of all material sent to shareholders should be sent to the Securities Division as soon as mailed to shareholders (Listing Form SD-1, Item 13). Other requirements same as for NYSE (Listing Form SD-1. Item 1H for notice regarding record date).	File 10-Q concurrently with SEC filing.	Press release at time of meeting. Competition for news space minimizes public coverage except on actively contested issues. Check NYSE schedules for competing meetings. Recommended wide distribution of post-meeting report to shareholders.
Annual Report to Shareholders: Contents	Requirements listed under Rule 14a-3 of the 1934 Act. They include audited balance sheets for two most recent fiscal years; audited income statements and changes in financial position for each of three most recent fiscal years; management's discussion and analysis of financial condition and results of financial operations; brief description of general nature and scope of the business; industry segment information;	Include in annual report principal office's address; directors' and officers' names; audit committee and other committee members; trustees, transfer agents, and registrars; numbers of employees and shareholders (*NYSE Company Manual* Section 203.01). Also include the number of shares of stock issuable under outstanding options at the beginning of the	Annual report must contain: balance sheets, income statements, and statements of changes in financial position. Financial statements should be prepared in accordance with generally accepted accounting principles, and SEC Regulation S-X.	No specific requirements, but NASD receives 10-K.	Check printed annual report and appropriate news release to ensure that they conform to information reported on Form 10-K. News releases necessary if annual report contains previously undisclosed material information. Trend is to consider report a marketing tool.

Reporting Required for:	Securities and Exchange Commission	New York Stock Exchange	American Stock Exchange	National Association of Securities Dealers	Generally Recommended Publicity Practice, All Companies
	company directors and officers; stock price and dividends. SEC encourages "freedom of management expression."	year; separate totals of changes in the number of shares of its stock under option resulting from issuance. exercise, expiration, or cancellation of options; and the number of shares issuable under outstanding options at the close of the year, the number of unoptioned shares available at the beginning and at the close of the year for the granting of options under an option plan, and any changes in the price of outstanding options, through cancellation and reissuance or otherwise, except price changes resulting from the normal operation of antidilution provisions of the options (NYSE Listing Agreement, Section 901.01).			
Annual Report to Shareholders: Time and Distribution	Annual report to shareholderes must precede or accompany delivery of proxy material. State law notice requirements govern the timing of proxy material mailing prior to annual meeting. Form 10-K must be filed within 90 days of close of year.	Published and submitted to shareholders at least 15 days before annual meeting but no later than three months after close of fiscal year. Four copies to Exchange together with advice as to the date of mailing to shareholders. PROMPTEST POSSIBLE ISSUANCE URGED. Recommended release of audited figures as soon as available.	Published and submitted to shareholders at least 15 days before annual meeting but no later than four months after close of fiscal year. PROMPTEST POSSIBLE ISSUANCE URGED. Recommend release of audited figures as soon as available. Six copies of the report to be filed with the Securities division of the Exchange (Listing Form SD-1, Item 17).	File 10-K concurrently with SEC filing.	Financial information should be released as soon as available; second release at time printed report is issued if report contains other material information. NYSE and AMEX urge broad distribution of report—including distribution to statistical services—so that company information is available for "ready public reference."

Reporting Required for:	Securities and Exchange Commission	New York Stock Exchange	American Stock Exchange	National Association of Securities Dealers	Generally Recommended Publicity Practice, All Companies
Annual Report: Form 10-K	Required by Section 13 or 15(d) of Securities Exchange Act of 1934 on Form 10-K. To be filed with SEC no later than 90 days after close of fiscal year. (Some schedules may be filed 120 days thereafter.) Extensive incorporation by reference from annual report to shareholders and from proxy statement now make integration of Form 10-K and report to shareholders more practical (see general instructions G and H of Form 10-K).	Four copies must be filed with Exchange concurrently with SEC filing; also provide notice to Exchange as to date mailed to shareholders. (*NYSE Company Manual* Sections 203.01 and 204.04).	Three copies must be filed with Exchange concurrently with SEC filing. (See *Company Guide*, pp. 12–2.)	File 10-K concurrently with SEC filing.	Publicity usually not necessary unless 10-K contains previously unreported material information.
Cash Dividends (see Stock Split)	All issuers of publicly traded securities are required to give notice of dividend declarations pursuant to Rule 10B-17. Over-the-counter companies must provide the NASD with advance notice of record date for subsequent dissemination to investors, extending comparable stock exchange requirements to OT market. Failure to comply places issuer in violation of Section 10(b) of the Securities Exchange Act of 1934.	Prompt notice to Exchange and immediate publicity required for *any* action related to dividend, including omission or postponement of dividend at customary time. The NYSE prefers that it be given notice by TWX (TWX No. 710-581-2801) or by telephone promptly confirmed by TWX. telegram, or letter. Ten days' advance notice of record date. NYSE manual implies announcement of management intention prior to formal board action may be required in case of a "leak" or rumor. *Notice regarding declaration of a cash dividend should include* declaration date; record date(s) for closing or reopening transfer	Same as NYSE. Notification to Exchange by telephone or telegram, with confirmation by letter (Listing Form SD-1, Item 1g).	Prompt notification 10 days before record date. File one copy of 10b-17 Report (included in "Reporting Requirements for NASDAQ Companies") with officer's signature.	Prepare publicity in advance and release immediately by a designated officer on word of declaration. Publicity especially important when dividend rate changes. Statement of dividend policy now common in annual reports. Statements of "intention" to take dividend policy now common in annual reports. Statements of "intention" to take dividend action also becoming common.

Reporting Required for:	Securities and Exchange Commission	New York Stock Exchange	American Stock Exchange	National Association of Securities Dealers	Generally Recommended Publicity Practice, All Companies
		books (or any other meaningful dates); per share amount of tax to be withheld with respect to the dividend, description of tax, net after-tax fee share dividend; any conditions upon which payment of dividend hinges.			
Earnings	Form 10-Q required within 45 days of close of each of first three fiscal quarters. Include information outlined in 10-Q plus a narrative management analysis in form outlined in Form S-K, Item 303. Summary of quarterly results for two years in "unaudited" annual report footnote. Form 10-K required to report full year's earnings.	Quarterly. Publicity required. No fourth quarter statement is required, though items of unusual or nonrecurring nature should be reflected in the company's interim earnings statements.	Quarterly. Should be published within 45 days after end of the first, second, and third fiscal quarters. (No statement is required for the fourth quarter, since that period is covered by the annual report.) Five copies of release should be sent to the Exchange. Press release must be sent to one or more New York City newspapers regularly publishing financial news and to one or more of the national newswires.	Prompt notification and press disclosure if earnings are unusual. File 10-Q and 10-K concurrently with SEC filings.	Immediate publicity; do not hold data until printed quarterly report is published and mailed. Release no later than 10-Q filing; annual results as soon as available. Information in news release must be consistent with 10-Q. Breakout of current quarter results together with year-to-date totals desirable in second, third, and fourth quarter releases.
Legal Proceedings	Form 10-Q at start or termination of proceedings and in any quarter when material development occurs (generally damage claims in excess of 10% of current assets); also any suit against company by an officer, director, or major stockholder. See Regulation S-K, Item 103. See also appendix entry entitled "environmental matters."	No notice to NYSE required unless proceeding bears on ownership, dividends, interest, or principal of listed securities, or start of receivership bankruptcy, or reorganization proceedings.	"Significant litigation." Public disclosure if material. Prompt notice to Exchange.	Prompt notification and public disclosure if material or if company must file report with SEC.	Public disclosure recommended if outcome of legal proceeding could have material effect on company and news of proceeding has not already become public. Court filings now commonly distributed to key business media with or without press release.
Merger: Acquisition or Disposition of Assets	Form 8-K if company acquires or disposes of a significant (10% of total assets or whole subsidiary)	Form 8-K filed (where assets acquired). Immediate public disclosure. Prompt notice	Form 8-K if filed, for acquisition or disposition of assets. Immediate public disclosure.	Prompt notification and public disclosure (8-K filed with SEC).	Exchange policy requires immediate announcement as soon as confidential

Reporting Required for:	Securities and Exchange Commission	New York Stock Exchange	American Stock Exchange	National Association of Securities Dealers	Generally Recommended Publicity Practice, All Companies
	amount of assets or business other than in normal course of business. Proxy soliciting material or registration statement may also be required. Check application of Rule 145 (b) of Securities Act of 1933, to any such transaction involving exchange of stock (see also Tender Offers).	to Exchange where assets disposed of.			disclosures relating to such important matters are made to "outsiders" (i.e. other than "top management" and their individual confidential "advisers"). Immediate publicity, especially when assets consist of an entire product line. division, operating unit, or a "substantial" part of the business.
Merger: Commenting on Unusual Market Activity	After SEC ruling in *In re Carnation*, and appeals court decision in *Levinson, et al., v. Basic Industries*, company can state "no comment" about merger discussions when stock shows unusual market activity. However, if company comments in response to Exchange or regulatory inquiry, it must do so truthfully and acknowledge that merger discussions are taking place.	Prepare to make immediate public announcement concerning unusual market activity from merger negotiations. Immediate, candid public statement concerning state of negotiations or development of corporate plans, if rumors are correct or there are developments. Make statements as soon as disclosure made to outsiders (from business appraisals, financing arrangements, market surveys, etc.). Public statements should be definite regarding price, ratio, timing, and any other pertinent information necessary to evaluation. Should include disclosures made to outsiders (*NYSECompany Manual*, Sections 202.01 and .03).	Promptly and publicly disseminate previously undisclosed information contained in any "leak" that resulted in market action. If company unable to determine cause of market action. Exchange may suggests that company issue "no news" release stating that there have been no undisclosed recent developments affecting the company that would account for unusual market activity. Company need not issue public announcement at each state of merger negotiations, but may await agreement in principle on specific terms or point at which negotiations stabilize. However, publicly release announcement setting forth facts to clarify rumor or report material information. (See *Company Guide*, p. 4-7 to 4-8.)	Prompt notification and public disclosure if material or if company must file report with SEC	Either issue "no comment" statement or explain reason for market activity known to company. Comment asserting that company is "unaware of any reason" to explain market activity is a comment. If company knows the reason for market activity but denies its awareness, it has made a false comment and is probably liable.

Reporting Required for:	Securities and Exchange Commission	New York Stock Exchange	American Stock Exchange	National Association of Securities Dealers	Generally Recommended Publicity Practice, All Companies
Projection: Forecast or Estimate of Earnings	See Reg. S-K General Policy (b). SEC policy encourages use of projections of future economic performance that have "a reasonable basis" and are presented in an appropriate format. Obligation to correct promptly when facts change. Should not discontinue or resume projections without clear explanation of action.	Immediate public disclosure when news goes beyond insiders and their confidential advisers.	Exchange warns against "unwarranted promotional disclosure," including premature announcements of products, and interviews with analysts and financial writers that would unduly influence market activity.	Prompt notification and public disclosure if material (NASD Schedule D).	Projections should be either avoided altogether or widely circulated, with all assumptions stated. Projections by others may require correction by company if wrong but widely believed. Once having made projection, issuer has obligation to update it promptly if assumptions prove wrong. Press releases and other communications should include all information necessary to an understanding of the projection. Legal counsel should be consulted.
Stock Split, Stock Dividend, or Other Change in Capitalization	10-Q required for increase or decrease if exceeds 5% of amount of securities of the class previously outstanding. Notice to NASD or exchange 10 days before record date under Securities Exchange Act's antifraud provisions.	Exchange suggests preliminary discussion, Immediate public disclosure and Exchange notification. Issuance of new shares requires prior listing approval. Either "telephone alert" procedure should be followed or, preferably, wire by TWX. Separate confirmation letter to Exchange. Company's notice to Exchange should indicate brokers' and nominees' requirements and date by which they must notify disbursing agent of full and fractional share requirements. Exchange will publicize this in its *Weekly Bulletin* or special circulars. *Notice regarding stock dividend, split, or distribution should include:* ratio	Immediate public disclosure and Exchange notification. Issuance of new shares requires prior listing approval. Treatment of fractional shares must be announced.	Prompt notification and public disclosure 10 days before record date. File one copy of 10b-17 Report (included in "Reporting Requirements for NASDAQ Companies") with officer's signature. File 10-Q concurrently with SEC filing.	Immediate publicity as soon as proposal becomes known to outsiders, whether formally voted or not. Discuss early whether to describe transaction as a split, dividend, or both and use terminology consistently.

Reporting Required for:	Securities and Exchange Commission	New York Stock Exchange	American Stock Exchange	National Association of Securities Dealers	Generally Recommended Publicity Practice, All Companies
		of stock dividend or split; record date for holders entitled to receive distribution; conditions upon which transaction hinges; date for mailing of certificates for additional shares.			
Tender Offer	Conduct and published remarks of all parties governed by Sections 13(d), 13(e), 14(d), 14(e) of the 1934 Act and regulations thereunder. Schedule 14D-1 disclosure required of raider. Target required to file Schedule 14D-9 for any solicitation or recommendations to security holders. (See also *Hart-Scott-Rodino* requirements.)	Consult Exchange Stock List Department in advance. Immediate publicity and notice to Exchange. Deliver offering material to Exchange no later than distribution date to shareholders. Consult Exchange when terms of tender are at variance with Exchange principles regarding tender offers.	Consult Exchange Securities Division in advance. Immediate publicity and notice to Exchange.	Prompt notification and public disclosure (NASD Schedule D).	Massive publicity effort required: should not be attempted without thorough familiarity with current rules and constant consultation with counsel. Neither raider nor target should comment publicly until necessary SEC filings have been made. "Stop, look, listen" letter permitted under Rule 14D-9(e).

Appendix I

ANNUAL MEETING CHECKLIST

By Frank Widder
The following annual shareholder's meeting checklist can be adapted to serve as a "preflight" plan for almost any major meeting.

I. Meeting announcement
   A. Shareholder's proxy statement and general notice
   B. Investment houses', major brokers', and institutional investors' notice and invitation
   C. Financial media invitations
   D. Employee notice of meeting
   E. Guests

   Follow-up (by phone or in person)
   A. Investor relations contacts with major shareholders to determine participation, major areas of interest, potential problems
   B. Major investment houses involved with company
   C. Local financial press
   D. Guest relations

II. Management announcement
   A. Notify all key management personnel to make sure they will be there and arrange alternates for those who cannot make it
   B. Notify all members of the board to determine their ability to make the meeting
   C. Arrange flight times and book hotel in advance; guarantee arrival if necessary

III. Management coaching
   A. Draft basic list of shareholders' problems and questions

    B. Arrange meeting with CEO and chairman to prepare answers, with key staff and legal department to run down answers, and practice those answers

    C. Review and practice management speeches

IV. Presentation materials

    A. Review orders for graphs and slides, compare with financial review speech

    B. Screen any films

    C. Review displays

V. Agenda: order of presentations with approximate running times (in minutes)

    A. Introduction—chairman calls meeting to order and introduces board and management (4:00)

    B. Opening comments by chairman and review of overall activities of company (6:00)

    C. President's message (with visuals) (15:00)

    D. Financial report by vice president, finance (with slide highlights) (5:00)

    E. Film (20:00)

    F. Present proposals in proxy (limit each shareholder to one statement per issue; hand out ballots to shareholders at beginning) (20:00)

    G. Voting, collect ballots (3:00)

    H. General discussion (limit shareholders to one question each) (30:00)

    I. Announce voting results (3:00)

    J. Present company awards of appreciation (2:00)

    K. Adjournment (1:00)—total: 1 hour, 49 minutes

    Agenda allows 20 additional minutes for discussion or for more questions during presentation of proposals. Final agenda will be printed and passed out by ushers at meeting.

VI. Site preparation

    A. Staff

        1. Electrician, lighting, and sound equipment specialists on hand from 8 A.M. to 5 P.M.

        2. Supervisor of custodial, security, and equipment staffs

        3. Walkie-talkie communications network with equipment staff

        4. Waiters for lounge

        5. Caterers for lounge

    B. Parking

        1. Traffic direction displays at parking lot entrances

        2. Parking attendants directing traffic to proper area

        3. Signs pointing to meeting entrance in parking lot

    C. Entrance/reception

        1. Reception tables with pencils and guest roster

        2. Receptionists to staff tables and answer questions about facilities (need to be briefed beforehand)

        3. Well-marked rest areas and signs indicating meeting area

        4. Unarmed security guards to control crowd and provide protection

        5. Armed security guards located in discrete areas of meeting room

        6. Name tags for all representatives of company

    D. Display area

        1. Displays set up along walls, to avoid impeding foot traffic, and checked for operation 24 hours in advance

        2. Representatives to staff each booth and be prepared for questions about display

        3. Tables to display necessary financial information—annual report, 10-K, proxy statement, quarterlies

E. Lounge area
   1. Adequate seating for participants and guests
   2. Breakfast/luncheon tables
F. Meeting areas
   1. Sound, lighting, and video checks
   2. Sound mikes for all stage participants
   3. Additional speakers for amplification
   4. Alternate hookup in case of failures—sound, lighting, and video; alternate film in case of breakage
   5. Large screen for slide and film
   6. Slide and film projectors for presentation
   7. Audio and lighting mixers
   8. Portable, remote mikes with long cords for audience questions
   9. Tape-recorder hookup to record proceedings
G. Construction
   1. Podium constructed high enough for everyone to have direct view of all participants
   2. Area blocked off for board and management to view film
   3. Area blocked off for lighting and sound equipment
   4. Exits properly marked
   5. Access to podium and all chairs necessary for seating board and management
   6. Logo prominently displayed and lighted above podium
H. Staff
   1. Ushers with flashlights at all entrances for seating
   2. Security at far corners of room
   3. Backstage technicians for sound emergencies
   4. Remote mike monitors on both aisles or in front and back of room
   5. Photographer to shoot proceedings, displays, and key presentations
I. Stage seating arrangements
   1. Podium in middle, chairs to either side
   2. Arrange board members in tenure order
   3. Management in hierarchy order
   4. Chairman sits on board side
   5. President on management side
   6. Nameplates for all participants on podium
   7. Glasses, water, and ashtrays
J. Shareholder seating
   1. First-come basis
   2. Areas roped off for invited shareholders and guests
   3. Areas roped off for film viewing by participants
   4. Special area for members not represented on stage—public accountants, special staff, and guests

VII. Final run-through
   A. Day prior to meeting, complete mock session of annual report, with key principals and timing of presentation—including possible questions and responses.
   B. Review slide show and cues four hours before meeting.
   C. Check screening room communications to begin film; make sure time is allowed to clear stage.
   D. Make sure award is ready for presentation.
   E. Hand out scripts to key participants and technical people.

VIII. Day of meeting
   A. Review with supervisor to ensure that all technical checks are okay.
   B. See that all displays are up and working.
   C. Contact board and management people to check for emergencies in transportation; arrange backup accommodations if necessary.
   D. Sit-down breakfast with key participants to go over agenda and cover any last-minute questions.
   E. Go to convention center, check in with supervisor, security head, parking attendant; ensure that copies of scripts are placed at podium.
   F. Greet participants and guide to lounge.
   G. Wait for shareholders and investors, media; be available for questions and arrange interviews.
   H. Sit down and wait.
   I. Guide participants and guests to luncheon in lounge; make sure bar is set up.
   J. Have a drink—and good night.

Credits

Index